Love Beads for VideoHound's Groovy Movies

"*VideoHound's Groovy Movies* is a bazaar of bizarre movies you may have forgotten, or forgot to see in the first place. The ringmaster of this terrific collection, Irv Slifkin, swings us through the best and blightest of 1965–1975—an amusing, revealing *wheee* of a ride through previews of past attractions. Slifkin knows his stuff, and he and his cohorts have packed the pages with zestful, festful enjoyment. Close the door, turn off the phone, turn up this volume, and have a wonderful time. (Rated 'R' for 'Right on!')"

—Gene Shalit, *Today,* NBC-TV

"A fascinating look into a vibrant era of filmmaking that provides hours of fun reading for those who want to revisit the '60s—or who missed them the first time around. . . . Fun-filled, fact-filled, and a riveting read!"

—Paula Parisi, the *Hollywood Reporter*

"Usedta be if you weren't around during one of the most turbulent periods in America, the '60s and early '70s, you were (bummer!) just shit outta luck, but now one of the most fascinating periods in movie history lives again for those who were there and those who missed out, thru VideoHound's unprecedented survey of the cool, the crazy, and the just plain freaky. Why didn't somebody think of doing this before??"

—Joe Dante, director of *Gremlins, Matinee,* and *Innerspace*

"Irv Slifkin has done a remarkable job of mining the gems from the boom days of America's proudest, most provocative, and most productive era."

—Jack Mathews, film critic, *New York Daily News*

"Compulsively readable. An insightful, enlightening, and very entertaining book about the most colorful and vital period in film history. Slifkin and company bring an accomplished movie lover's perspective to the subject, underlining the wide array of films of the New Wave of the 1960s and '70s. Each analysis is impressively balanced and provides great clarity on the importance of the 'psychedelic era.' I love this book."

—Joe Baltake, film critic, McClatchy Newspapers/
Scripps Howard News Service

"They say if you can remember the '60s then you weren't really there. But these wonderful films can help even the most hardened acid casualty retrieve it all—in vivid sound and color. A one-of-a-kind guide to an indispensible time."

—Shawn Levy, author of *Ready, Steady, Go!*
The Smashing Rise and Giddy Fall of Swinging London

VideoHound's GROOVY MOVIES

FAR-OUT FILMS OF THE PSYCHEDELIC ERA

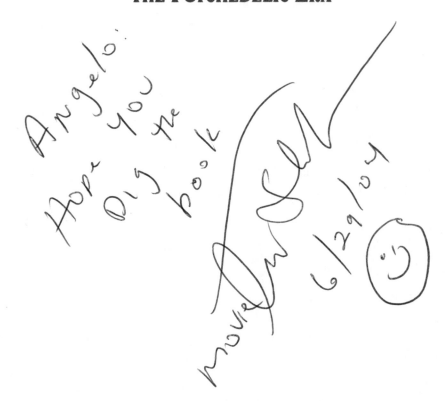

Angelo:
Hope you
Dig the
book

movie[signature]
6/29/04
☺

To my incredible wife, Margie,

and my amazing daughters, Sarah and Rose—

the three grooviest chicks I know

VideoHound's GROOVY MOVIES

FAR-OUT FILMS OF THE PSYCHEDELIC ERA

IRV SLIFKIN

VISIBLE INK PRESS

Detroit

FAR-OUT FILMS OF
THE PSYCHEDELIC ERA

Visible Ink Press®
43311 Joy Rd. #414
Canton, MI 48187-2075

Visible Ink Press and A Cunning Canine Production are registered trademarks of Visible Ink Press LLC.

VideoHound and the VideoHound logo are registered trademarks.

Most Visible Ink Press books are available at special quantity discounts when purchased in bulk by corporations, organizations, or groups. Customized printings, special imprints, messages, and excerpts can be produced to meet your needs. For more information, contact Special Markets Director, Visible Ink Press, at www.visibleink.com or (734) 667-3211.

Art Direction: Mary Claire Krzewinski
Typesetting: Graphix Group

Cover photos: *Barbarella* (Paramount / The Kobal Collection); *Austin Powers: International Man of Mystery* (New Line / The Kobal Collection); *Easy Rider* (Columbia / The Kobal Collection); *Beyond the Valley of the Dolls* (20th Century Fox / The Kobal Collection). Back cover: *The Graduate* (Embassy / The Kobal Collection). Spine: *What's New, Pussycat?* (United Artists / The Kobal Collection).

Chapter-opener photos not credited elsewhere in the book: Chapter 7, *A Clockwork Orange* (Warner Bros. / The Kobal Collection); Chapter 10, *Easy Rider* (Columbia / The Kobal Collection); Chapter 13, *Pink Flamingos* (Dreamland Productions / The Kobal Collection); Chapter 14, *The Producers* (Embassy Pictures / The Kobal Collection); Chapter 17, *Tommy* (Rbt Stigwood Prods / Hemdale / The Kobal Collection); Chapter 19, *Ocean's 11* (Warner Bros. / The Kobal Collection); Chapter 20, *Get Carter* (MGM / The Kobal Collection).

Author photo, p. xxiv: Courtesy of Scott Soffen.

Cataloging-in-Publication Data is on file with the Library of Congress.
ISBN 1-57859-155-4

10 9 8 7 6 5 4 3 2 1

A Cunning Canine Production™

Contents

5. BLACK LIKE US

6. SHOCKS TO THE SYSTEM

7. FAR OUT, MAN

8. DON'T BOGART THAT TRIP

9. MILITARY MADNESS

10. ROAD RULES

Contents

Foreword

by Roger Corman

The '60s were a time of turbulence and triumphs for me. With each film, I attempted to entertain, excite, and, ultimately, be profitable. But in the 1960s, I also wanted to touch on some of the controversial topics that interested American moviegoing audiences, whether it be drugs, rebellion, race relations, crime, gun control, or the threat of war. I really wanted audiences to come out of theaters with something to think about.

In the early part of the decade, I directed a film called *The Intruder,* starring William Shatner in a tale of racial intolerance that was influenced by my feelings toward the problems of school desegregation in the South. While making the movie on location, community groups and the Ku Klux Klan tried to put a stop to production. Ultimately, the film received very good reviews and won awards, but because of its controversial nature, it didn't play in many theaters or for very long. Although *The Intruder* turned out to be one of the few films I made that didn't show a profit, it remains among the films I am most proud of today.

Working with Samuel Z. Arkoff and James Nicholson at American International Pictures (AIP), I began a series of horror films based on Edgar Allan Poe stories in the early 1960s. The ball started rolling in 1960, when AIP wanted me to make two B&W pictures—to be shot in ten days—for a double bill. I convinced them to let me instead make one color film, based on a Poe story I had read in high school. The result was *House of Usher,* which I shot in fifteen days for $200,000, a relatively high budget for us at the time. I recruited Vincent Price to star, and he later appeared in my Poe adaptations of *The Pit and the Pendulum, The Tomb of Ligeia, The Raven,* and *The Masque of the Red Death.* None of them was very expensive to produce, and each was shot very quickly. They were all successful, looked great, and have remained popular throughout the years.

By the early 1960s, I felt that young people, an increasingly large part of the market, weren't getting what they wanted at their local movie houses or drive-in theaters. Motorcycle clubs were becoming more popular and more notorious at that time. To me, they seemed like an interesting subject for a movie. I decided to depict the biker world with *The Wild Angels* in 1965. To be as accurate as possible, I hung out with Hell's Angels, the most famous of all motorcycle gangs. I learned how to ride a chopper and even picked up the bill for some of their parties.

For authenticity, I based the film on stories they told me and shot it on location. Some Hell's Angels members even appeared in the film, along with stars Peter Fonda, Nancy Sinatra, and Bruce Dern. To me the rebellious motorcycle gang subculture was the precursor to the counterculture that became prevalent in the late 1960s. In many ways, I saw the bikers as modern-day cowboys who rode motorcycles instead of horses.

The film must have struck a nerve with audiences. It won acclaim at the Venice Film Festival and became a big hit, leading to over fifty similar pictures about motorcycle gangs.

The Hell's Angels, widely feared well before the release of *The Wild Angels,* asserted they had been misrepresented in this picture. They attempted to make some extra money off of me, suing me for $2 million for defamation of character. They claimed they were portrayed in the film as an outlaw motorcycle gang, but that, in reality, they were a social organization spreading technical information about motorcycles. Things got ugly when the leader of Hell's Angels threatened to kill me. We later settled for $2,000, and I happily remained alive.

The next year, I decided to look at another aspect of youth culture with *The Trip.* The film focused on the burgeoning drug scene. It was written by Jack Nicholson, who was a good friend and an AIP regular I had worked with in such pictures as *Little Shop of Horrors* and *The Terror.* Also cast in the film were Dennis Hopper and Peter Fonda. Bruce Dern was the only principal cast member not interested in experimenting with LSD at the time.

As with *The Wild Angels,* realism was important to me. I decided to read Timothy Leary's book on LSD. Eventually, I even took the drug to find out what everyone was talking about and to give my film some perspective. I decided to take LSD after meeting some friends at Big Sur, one of the most beautiful places in the world. But "a few friends" turned into a caravan of people, so we worked out a schedule with some people designated for tripping while other people served as guides. It turned out I had a wonderful experience.

The Trip won some awards and did extremely well at the box office, though AIP made some changes I wasn't thrilled with. The studio put a disclaimer at the beginning of the film, telling the audience that LSD was not good. They also changed the ending from ambiguous to antidrug in nature. Their efforts led me to ultimately become frustrated with the way the project was handled.

A project I was happy about, however, was 1968's *Targets,* which was Peter Bogdanovich's first feature film. Peter was a film scholar and critic who wanted to make movies. He worked with me on *The Trip* and other projects. I had Boris Karloff available to me for three days, and I offered Peter the opportunity to make a film if he could use Karloff in the picture.

He conceived *Targets* as two parallel stories that eventually came together—one about a mentally unbalanced sniper and the other with Karloff as a horror-movie star named Byron Orlock, who was making a special appearance at a drive-in theater. The film was so impressive that Paramount Pictures decided to distribute it. I believe it resonated with audiences and critics, who related its subject to such assassins as Lee Harvey Oswald and Charles Whitman, who had murdered his wife, his mother, and sixteen other people in Texas. The terrific reception of *Targets* led to Peter's next project, the Oscar-winning *The Last Picture Show.*

My final movie for American International Pictures, the company I had been involved with throughout the '60s, was *Gas-s-s-s,* in 1969. The premise of this surreal comedy was that, as a result of the accidental leak of a nerve gas developed by the military, everyone over the age of twenty-five died, leaving young people to take over the world. The different factions of surviving young people tried to relate to each other and to their different philosophies. Eventually, they tried to gather together to find a new utopia.

I had a bright young cast that included Robert Corff, Talia Shire, Cindy Williams, Bud Cort, and Ben Vereen. Unfortunately, AIP believed the film would be too controversial, so they re-edited it.

To me, this was the last straw. I believed AIP's interference damaged the picture, so I decided to start the 1970s in a fresh way. After directing the World War II movie *Von Richthofen and Brown* in Ireland for United Artists, I began my own company, New World Pictures, in 1970.

At New World, I produced such pictures as *Piranha, Caged Heat, Death Race 2000, Rock and Roll High School,* and *Eat My Dust.* As I had done in the 1960s with such young, talented filmmakers as Monte Hellman, Jack Hill, Martin Scorsese, Peter Bogdanovich, Dennis Hopper, and Francis Ford Coppola, I was able, through New World, to give filmmaking opportunities to Joe Dante, Jonathan Demme, Paul Bartel, Ron Howard, John Sayles, and James Cameron, among others. I also turned my attention to importing foreign films from directors like François Truffaut, Federico Fellini, and Ingmar Bergman.

Since 1985 I have been president of Concorde/New Horizons, a company I started after selling New World. With this company, I continue to give young filmmakers a chance to make movies. My goal is to make good pictures, entertain audiences, and, of course, make a profit.

But if we can touch on some of the topics that strike a chord with contemporary audiences, so much the better. That's a lesson I learned from the 1960s.

Roger Corman has produced more than three hundred movies, directed fifty-four films, and acted in twenty-seven other efforts. The website for his company, Concorde/New Horizons, is www.newconcorde.com.

Introduction

by Irv Slifkin

"This is my happening and it freaks me out!"
—Ronnie "Z-Man" Barzell (John LaZar),
Beyond the Valley of the Dolls
—Austin Powers (Mike Myers),
Austin Powers: International Man of Mystery

'll never forget that elderly cashier with the rhinestone glasses and flaming red lipstick who wouldn't let me into the theater to see *Wild in the Streets*. I had seen the trailer the previous week, and I was willing to pay her the full adult admission price of $1.25. But, damn, she refused to budge because it was an "R"-rated movie and I was just eleven years old. "I'll show her," I thought.

Well, it's taken me thirty-six years, but I hope with this book, I finally have shown her. Not only have I since seen *Wild in the Streets* and hundreds of other movies from that era ("R" rated and otherwise), I've now written a book about them in the hope of turning others on to the joys, laughs, and weirdness of those films.

That experience with the cashier at the movies pretty much represents how the 1960s were for me: I missed out on a lot of the excitement because I was just too young. In "For What It's Worth," Buffalo Springfield's classic anthem of the times, they sing, "There's something happening here / What it is ain't exactly clear." And that's how I felt. I knew stuff was going on—a whole lot of stuff, both good and bad—but it wasn't exactly clear to me what I was missing; I was just a shade too inexperienced to take it all in.

I sure tried to act like I was in on the '60s. My relatively strait-laced Mom had no problem with me wearing tie-dyes, army jackets with peace symbols, and medallions around my neck. I wore granny glasses and strung love beads at overnight camp. A poster of Bob Dylan was stapled to the shade in my room. Once, when I arrived at a friend's house, his older brother announced, "Hey, Jack, it's the hippie-dippy!" I smiled, taking the description as a compliment, though I'm not sure it was meant as such.

At the movies, I was exposed primarily to mainstream Hollywood. My grandparents made sure I got a steady diet of what they enjoyed, usually musicals like *The Unsinkable Molly Brown* or romantic comedies like *Move Over, Darling*. I cheered on John Wayne in *The Green Berets*, unaware of his or the film's politics at the time. After the movie, I ran out and bought the 45-rpm single of Sergeant Barry Sadler's "The Ballad of the Green Berets." I also managed to see *2001: A Space Odyssey* when it was released the first time. It sure was something to look at, but except for me, my friends, and a few others, everybody in the theater appeared to be on some type of unknown substance, their mouths agape, drool count high during the psychedelic light-show sequence. Of course, I had no clue what the apes had to do with the spaceships or the baby at the end.

So I saw a lot of movies during the 1960s, but I sensed there was something more going on that I wasn't privy to. Later, in the 1970s, at Philly-area repertory theaters like the TLA and the New World, I played catch-up, watching films that the cashier with the rhinestone glasses wouldn't have let me see the first time around. Double features abounded: *The Graduate* and *Carnal Knowledge, Bonnie and Clyde* and *Cool Hand Luke, M*A*S*H* and *The French Connection, King of Hearts* and *Harold and Maude.*

You may wonder: apart from my obsession with the films, what made me want to write this book, which took almost five years from concept to completion? Well, to paraphrase another fab 1960s song by Thunderclap Newman, there was something in the air. A few years ago, I recognized that the '60s and '70s were happening again.

Austin Powers was a smash, quoting and referencing such '60s icons, fictional and otherwise, as James Bond, Derek Flint, Harry Palmer, Modesty Blaise, and Burt Bacharach.

Cable stations like American Movie Classics were running a steady stream of films from the era—sometimes with elaborate "making of" documentaries to accompany their showings.

Contemporary rock performers like Beck, Phish, Jet, Lenny Kravitz, and Prince have been saluting the psychedelic sound in their music with great regularity.

Sixties pop and folk icons—such as a reunited Crosby, Stills, Nash & Young and Simon & Garfunkel, as well as Santana and Bob Dylan—continue playing to crowds as large as ever. And the Grateful Dead are still hugely popular, even after leader Jerry Garcia went to that big opium den in the sky. As for the Beatles, they may have wanted us to "let it be," breaking up decades ago, but they are always around, one way or another.

Fashions from the '60s have seen a major resurgence, with people once again wearing tie-dye, bell bottoms, miniskirts, high leather boots, and sideburns.

The advent of DVD spurred video companies to continually excavate long-lost '60s and '70s wonders like *Two-Lane Blacktop, I'll Never Forget What's 'isname,* and *The Hired Hand.*

Meanwhile, Hollywood has pumped out a steady stream of not-so-classic remakes of gems like *Point Blank* (remade as *Payback*), *Get Carter, Ocean's 11,* and *The Italian Job,* with more promised on the way.

Peter Biskind's 1998 book *Easy Riders, Raging Bulls: How the Sex-Drugs-and-Rock 'n' Roll Generation Saved Hollywood* turned into a best-seller, inspiring a documentary, and it was followed by the film *A Decade Under the Influence,* a similar examination of the films and filmmakers who came to the fore in the '60s and '70s. Although the book and subsequent films were stimulating, I felt there were things being left out, movies that were significant but may not have had the impact of, say, *Easy Rider, M*A*S*H, Barbarella,* or *Goldfinger.* Some of the films overlooked by other surveys of the era are great efforts that few people know about, while others are awful but eminently watchable flops, often funny in unexpected ways. Good, bad, or ugly, they all convey important aspects of their times, whether through their style, their viewpoint, or the way in which their characters are portrayed. I felt that fans of psychedelic-era cinema had to know what *The Day the Fish Came Out, Skidoo,* and *F.T.A.* were really all about.

Hence, *VideoHound's Groovy Movies: Far-out Films of the Psychedelic Era.*

This doesn't mean, of course, that I've ignored the popular films of the era that roughly stretches from 1965 to 1975. The important, trendsetting groovy movies are here too, and the contributors and I have tried to add some new perspective to them in our reviews. Along with these reviews are "Groovy Extras"—essays and short histories on specific types of films popular during the era, as well as interviews with and profiles of some of the actors and filmmakers involved in the featured entries. We've also dug up some boss illustrations, more than one hundred in all: scene stills, lobby cards, posters. And we've packed the pages with memorably outrageous quotes and movie taglines that were designed to turn on the kids then—and will manage to connect with the inner flower child or secret agent in you now.

You'll notice that some of the films featured in *VideoHound's Groovy Movies* are of more recent vintage. Why? Because I feel that they were conceived in the mold or spirit of movies from thirty to forty years ago. That's why the book's subtitle is "Far-out Films *of* the Psychedelic Era" rather than "Far-out Films *from* the Psychedelic Era." These contemporary works, some of which are remakes, intentionally channel the 1960s or 1970s. For example, Steven Soderbergh's *The Limey,* released in 1999, pits '60s icons Peter Fonda and Terence Stamp against each other in a revenge thriller similar to 1967's *Point Blank* and 1971's *Get Carter.* Soderbergh's film comes complete with music by the Who, Steppenwolf, and the Byrds, as well as film clips of a young Stamp in 1967's *Poor Cow.* Talk about déjà vu! And what are the enjoyable *Spy Kids* pictures but witty, CGI-fueled reconfigurations of James Bond adventures (more '70s Moore than '60s Connery or recent Brosnan) for kids?

Of course, it would be impossible to cover every one of the hundreds of films released during that ten-year period, so *Groovy Movies* offers a cross-section of the different genres, styles, filmmakers, and performers of the time, concentrating on those "magical" films that best capture the essence of the era.

You may wonder where you can find the titles showcased in *Groovy Movies.* First, at the end of every review, the available format is noted, whether it's VHS, DVD, or both. The writers and I have managed to locate each and every one of the titles featured in these pages, either at video stores, through mail-order outlets, or via collectors' websites. But not all of the titles have been issued by their respective studios, for one reason or another. If you can't find these movies through the regular channels, try typing the title and the preferred format into your favorite Internet search engine. This will generally lead you in the right direction. If not, you can try any one of a number of collectors' sites (www.robertsvideo.com, www.revengeismydestiny.com, and www.5minutestolive.com are very helpful). Satellite channels and cable networks are also a good place to look for movies you can't find at your regular stops.

If you were hip to the '60s scene, or if you just feel like you were there after having heard colorful stories from older relatives—aunts and uncles, parents, or, dare I say, grandparents—let *VideoHound's Groovy*

Movies: Far-out Films of the Psychedelic Era take you back to the Age of Aquarius. Particularly if you have an interest in the films of the era, I hope you'll find some light shed on them by reading this book.

VideoHound's Groovy Movies

xix

Acknowledgments

Groovy Movies: *Far-out Films of the Psychedelic Era* began as a collaboration with another writer (he knows who he is), but things didn't work out as planned. Then I figured, "Great! I can do this on my own!" I soon realized, however, that a project of this magnitude could only work as a collaborative effort. If I hadn't had help, I'd probably still be writing, and the publishers would be very unhappy. So I sought assistance, lots of it, from some great sources and terrific, talented people—fellow writers and editors, personal friends, business associates, and family members.

Books in my home library, many of which I hadn't looked at for years (see, I told you not to throw them out, hon) came in handy. I'd suggest these essential tomes to readers interested in learning more about the groovy movies and people showcased in this book: *Easy Riders, Raging Bulls: How the Sex-Drugs-and-Rock 'n' Roll Generation Saved Hollywood,* by Peter Biskind; *Cult Movies, Cult Movies 2,* and *Cult Movies 3,* by Danny Peary; *Midnight Movies,* by J. Hoberman and Jonathan Rosenbaum; *Sex, Drugs, Violence, Rock 'n' Roll: Hollywood Films of the Seventies,* by Seth Cagin and Philip Dray; *Rock on Film,* by David Ehrenstein and Bill Reed; *Hollywood Rock,* edited by Marshall Crenshaw (with major contributions from my pal, Jay Schwartz); *The Films of the Sixties,* by Douglas Brode; *The Films of the Seventies,* by Robert Bookbinder; *Fast and Furious: The Story of American International Pictures,* by Mark Thomas McGee; *The Film Encyclopedia,* by Ephraim Katz; *Slimetime: A Guide to Sleazy, Mindless Movies,* by Steve Pulchaski; *A Clean Breast,* by Russ Meyer; *How I Made a Hundred Movies in Hollywood and Never Lost a Dime,* by Roger Corman with Jim Jerome; *The Movie World of Roger Corman,* by J. Philip Difranco; *Getting Away with It; Or: The Further Adventures of the Luckiest Bastard You Ever Saw,* by Steven Soderbergh with

Richard Lester; *Videoscope: The Ultimate Guide to the Latest, Greatest and Weirdest Genre Videos,* by the Phantom of the Movies; *Ready, Steady, Go: The Smashing Rise and Giddy Fall of Swinging London,* by Shawn Levy; *Leonard Maltin's Video and Film Guide,* by Leonard Maltin; *Kings of the Bs: Working within the Hollywood System,* by Todd McCarthy and Charles Flynn; *The Psychotronic Guide to Film,* by Michael Weldon; and the *Variety Movie Guide,* edited by Derek Elley.

There are also numerous websites devoted to various aspects of films from the '60s and '70s and movies in general. The following highly selective list of sites covers all sorts of groovy-related topics:

All Movie Guide (www.allmovie.com)
All Music Guide (www.allmusic.com)
Bad Movie Planet (www.badmovieplanet.com)
Blaxploitation.com (www.blaxploitation.com)
Bright Lights Film Journal (www.brightlightsfilm.com)
British Movies (www.britmovie.co.uk)
The Complete Rod Taylor Site (www.rodtaylorsite.com)
Cool French Comics (www.coolfrenchcomics.com)
Cult Sirens (www.cultsirens.com)
The Films of Doris Day (www.dorisday.net)
Firesign Theatre (www.firesigntheatre.com)
Glamour Girls of the Silver Screen (www.glamourgirlsofthesilver-
    screen.com)
The Greatest Films (www.filmsite.org)
Internet Encyclopedia of Cinematographers
    (www.beer1.freeler.nl/doph.htm)
The Internet Movie Database (www.imdb.com)
Mr. Kiss Kiss Bang Bang: The Premier James Bond Website
    (www.ianfleming.org)
Modculture.com (www.modculture.co.uk)
The Movies of Russ Meyer (www.rmfilms.com)
Pimpadelic Wonderland: The Weird World of '70s Cinema (www.pim-
    padelicwonderland.com)
Robert Forster (www.robertforster.com)
Senses of Cinema (www.sensesofcinema.com)
Sixties City (www.sixtiescity.com)
Sixties Pop (www.sixtiespop.com)
Sky-High Picture Show (www.skyhighpictureshow.com)
Swingin' Chicks of the '60s (www.swinginchicks.com)
The Thrilling Detective (www.thrillingdetective.com)
The Unknown Movies (www.unknownmovies.com)
The Unofficial Quiller Website (www.quiller.net)

The World of James Bond Webzine (http://target007ezine.tripod. com/target007/index.html)

On the people front, I want to thank the following good Samaritans who got into the groove from the get-go, generously supplying essential information and offering me and my contributors an opportunity to screen the movies needed for this book: Woody Wise, Haskell Wexler, Mike Mayo, Richard Fuller, Joe Santagata (my man in Canada), Jessica Villines, Pete Hurd of Warner Home Video, Patrick McHugh of Allied Advertising, Andy Preiss, Ray Murray, Dave Bleiler, Jay Medley, and Adrian Hickman, all of TLA Video (www.tlavideo.com), Johnny Schulze of Incredibly Strange Film-works (www.incrediblystrangefilm.com), Marc McClellen from Homevision (www.homevision.com), Marc Walkow from the Criterion Collection (www.criterionco.com), Mike Vraney and Lisa Petrucci of Something Weird Video (www.somethingweird.com), Sue Procko of Anchor Bay Video/Sue Procko Public Relations (www.anchorbayentertainment.com), Kelly Har-graves from First Run Features (www.firstrunfeatures.com), Marina Pervak from New Concorde Pictures (www.newconcorde.com), Andy Kemp from MPI Home Video (www.mpihomevideo.com), and Spencer Savage of Image Entertainment (www.image-entertainment.com).

These people and their fine companies generously came through with titles I couldn't find anywhere: Glenn and Janet Gasser (www.video-discounters.com), Robert Ligtermoet of Robert's Hard to Find Videos (www.robertsvideos.com), Sam McAbee and Lynora Good of 5 Minutes to Live (www.5minutestolive.com), and Mark Johnston of Shocking Videos (www.revengeismydestiny.com).

I also want to thank Tony Malczon, Ed Weiss, Jerry Frebowitz, Joe McLaughlin, Mike Wunsch, Joe Ditella, Steve Blum, Brian Burkhardt, John Tartaglia, Andrea Seitchik, and the rest of the folks at Movies Unlimited (www.moviesunlimited.com) for their good karma and under-standing. Also, a major "solid" to Steve Rusk for his support.

At WIP Radio, Angelo Cataldi, Joe Weachter, Al Morganti, Anthony Gargano, hockey legend Keith Jones, and "Clothing" Scott Soffen offered encouragement along with laughs.

My agents from the Sheree Bykofsky Agency showed enthusiasm for *Groovy Movies* from the earliest stages of this project: my gratitude goes to Sheree B., Megan Buckley, and especially Janet Rosen, the fun-niest author's rep in the business.

Lovingly recalling the good ol' days of the '60s were family mem-bers Selma Chopinsky, Rick Slifkin, and Ellen Segal, and psychedelic-era friends Mitch Neiburg, David Beck, Jack Blank, and Marc Scheffler.

Acknowledgments

Here in spirit were Seymour Slifkin, Rose Slifkin, and Ed Chopinsky, all of whom affectionately helped me cultivate a love for movies.

The book was bolstered big-time by the work of two talented, indefatigable editors, Jeff Hermann and Judy Galens, who did a far-out job pulling everything together in the stretch. Thanks also go to indexer Jeff Muhr, proofreader Gerry Anders, image digitizer Robert Huffman, and typesetter Marco Di Vita. Christa Brelin Gainor of Visible Ink Press offered astute management and guidance. The Kobal Collection provided terrific photos and gave assistance whenever needed.

And finally, kudos to designer Mary Claire Krzewinski for making everything look good and to Marty Connors and Roger Jänecke of Visible Ink for their patience, support, and willingness to take a chance.

To all: peace and thanks!

Contributors

Author

As a writer and editor of the *Movies Unlimited Video Catalog* and website (www.moviesunlimited.com), **Irv Slifkin** has written more than his fair share about film over the years. Listeners to the popular morning radio program on Philadelphia's WIP-AM know him as "Movie Irv," weekly reviewer of films and videos. He has written for the *Los Angeles Times*, the *Chicago Tribune*, *Entertainment Weekly*, the *Philadelphia Inquirer*, the *Hollywood Reporter*, *TV Guide*, *VideoHound's Cult Flicks and Trash Pics*, and *Delaware Valley Magazine*, where he served as film critic. Slifkin has also discussed films and video on National Public Radio, ABC-TV, and the Comcast Cable Network, and he has lectured on film at Rutgers University and at Temple University, his alma mater. He once spent some time sleeping in director Russ Meyer's pool house. He resides with his wife and two daughters in New Jersey, not far from buildings that were once the Castor, the Benner, and the Tyson, Philadelphia movie theaters he frequented during the 1960s and 1970s. His website address is www.movieirv.com.

Contributing Writers

Steven Austin is a Los Angeles–based independent filmmaker. His most recent movie won six awards and garnered the praise of author Harlan Ellison, who said that *Moment of Silence* "is sharp, funny, and beautifully executed."

Lewis Beale has written for several publications, including the *New York Times* and the *Los Angeles Times.*

In the late 1960s, **Gary Cahall** was a Delaware grade-school student who watched way too much TV and whose interests included comic books, monster movies, dinosaurs, and hoping his beloved Boston Red Sox would win a World Series. Four decades later, he coauthors and edits the catalog for a Philadelphia-based video mail-order company and writes freelance articles on film. He was thrilled to become a piece of TV trivia by winning $250,000 on *Who Wants to Be a Millionaire?* and has a wide range of interests, including comic books, monster movies, dinosaurs, and hoping his beloved Boston Red Sox will win a World Series.

Jon Caroulis is director of media relations at La Salle University in Philadephia. Growing up in the 1960s, his favorite movies were *The Guns of Navarone* and *It's a Mad Mad Mad Mad World.*

Charles A. Cassady Jr. was too young to be cognizant of much of the 1960s, but he later experienced the decade via a vintage stash of *Life, Look, Newsweek,* the *Saturday Evening Post,* and *Mad* magazines in his grandparents' attic in suburban Cleveland, Ohio. Still plaintively wondering when the revolution is going to go down, Cassady writes on cinema and the arts for the *Cleveland Free Times, Westlife News,* the *Morning Journal of Lorain,* and VideoHound publications.

Alan Cylinder is a former print and broadcast critic and cofounder of the National Society of Film Historians. He currently works in film restoration and owns a company that distributes motion pictures to private collections and archives throughout the world.

Chuck Darrow has been an entertainment columnist/critic for thirty years. For the past twenty, he has covered a variety of show business beats for the *Courier-Post* of Cherry Hill, New Jersey. When not on the job, he can usually be found playing bass guitar in various South Jersey bars or at a Texas Hold 'Em table in Atlantic City.

Lou Gaul, who has a master's degree in cinema studies from New York University, has served as film critic for Calkins Media in New Jersey, Pennsylvania, and Florida since 1973. In addition, he has written for *Rolling Stone, Fighting Stars,* and *Video Business* magazine, and he has served as critic for Philadelphia radio stations WDVT-AM and WWDB-FM. In 1996 he was named the New Jersey Library Association's first "Library Champion" for his donations of film-related material to libraries and his volunteer efforts on behalf of library systems. He is the author of *The Fist That Shook the World: The Cinema of Bruce Lee*

(Midnight Marquee Press), a political, critical, and social examination of the films of the late martial-arts superstar.

Lowell Goldman has written for the *Psychotronic Film Guide*, *Boxoffice*, *Starlog*, *Cinefantastique*, *Film Journal*, *HorrorFan*, and *Prevue*, as well as the men's magazines *Gallery*, *Genesis*, and *Knave*.

Ed Grant edited three volumes of the comprehensive library reference volume *The Motion Picture Guide*. He previously served as a staff writer for *TV Guide* and as managing editor of *Movies on TV*. He has proudly produced and hosted *Media Funhouse*, Manhattan cable viewers' premier guide to high and low culture, for over a decade.

Barry Gutman, who is based in the Philadelphia area, was editor and video music columnist for the home video industry trade publication *Video Insider* from 1984 to 1992. He is a longtime freelance music and video journalist whose reviews and interviews have appeared in Tower Records/Video's *PULSE!*, *Video Business*, *Philadelphia Weekly*, *Entertainment Weekly*, *Billboard*, *The Philadelphia Inquirer*, and *The Aquarian Weekly*, among other publications. He is also an active freelance publicity and marketing writer.

Dr. **Bruce H. Klauber** is an author, film producer, jazz educator, multi-instrumentalist, and editor. He is the biographer of jazz great Gene Krupa (*World of Gene Krupa*, Pathfinder Publishing of California), creator/producer of the Warner Bros. and Hudson Music *Jazz Legends* multimedia series, and a lecturer in music journalism at the University of the Arts in Philadelphia. His website address is www.jazzlegends.com.

Laurence Lerman is the programs review editor at *Video Business* and has written for *Playboy*, *Gallery*, *Variety*, and other publications.

Margaret Lloyd doesn't remember much from the '60s, not because she was stoned but because she was a toddler. She believes she would have made a great hippie but instead lives her life as a suburban New Jersey wife and mother of two, working in corporate America for "the Man."

Amy Longsdorf's articles on film appear in many publications. Her movie reviews run regularly in Allentown, Pennsylvania's *Morning-Call* and in the *Courier Post* of Cherry Hill, New Jersey.

Mike Mayo has written three books for the VideoHound: *Video Premieres*, *Horror Show*, and *War Movies*. He has contributed to *VideoHound's Cult Flicks and Trash Pics* and to *VideoHound's Sci-Fi Experience*. He also edited three volumes of *VideoHound's DVD Guide*. He's the host of the nationally syndicated *Movie Show on Radio* (www.movieshow.com).

When not performing online marketing and website care and maintenance for the film buff's best friend, www.moviesunlimited.com, **Jay Steinberg** spends a chunk of his idle time writing features and DVD reviews for www.turnerclassicmovies.com. His work appears here because Irv Slifkin asked him politely.

Brian Thomas is the author of the massive and wildly successful *VideoHound's Dragon: Asian Action & Cult Flicks.* He was also a major contributor to three other VideoHound guides: *Cult Flicks & Trash Pics, DVD Guide,* and *Sci-Fi Experience.* He is a founding member of the Psychotronic Film Society (www.psychotronic.info), for which he still participates as house critic and Propaganda Minister of the Sinister. As a writer and columnist, he has contributed to many print and online film journals, including *Video Watchdog* and *Cinescape* (www.cinescape.com), home of his weekly "DVD Shopping List" column. He currently resides in his hometown, Chicago, Illinois, unless he's been crushed under a fallen pile of DVDs.

Andy Wickstrom is a lifelong film enthusiast and former editor of several home video magazines. From 1983 to 1996 he wrote a weekly column on home video for the Knight-Ridder News Service. On the whole, he thinks they don't make 'em like they used to, which makes this book valuable.

Alphabetization

Within each chapter of *Groovy Movies,* the film reviews are arranged in alphabetical order on a word-by-word basis, ignoring punctuation marks such as colons and commas. Leading articles ("a," "an," "the") are ignored in English-language titles. The equivalent foreign articles are not ignored (because so many people—not you, of course—don't recognize them as articles). Acronyms appear alphabetically as regular words; for example, *F.T.A.* is alphabetized as "FTA," and *M*A*S*H* as "MASH." Common abbreviations in titles file as if they were spelled out, so *Dr. Goldfoot and the Bikini Machine* will be alphabetized as "Doctor Goldfoot." Movie titles with numbers, such as *2001: A Space Odyssey,* are alphabetized as if the number were spelled out, so the title of this Stanley Kubrick classic is alphabetized as if it were "Two Thousand One: A Space Odyssey." For reviews that cover multiple films, only the first title is considered in the alphabetical order.

Bone Ratings

Movies are rated by the Hound's patented bone rating system. In this book, "good" movies are either 1) good, or 2) so bad they're good, or 3) cult classics; lower-rated movies are so bad they're just bad, without any redeeming camp value.

🦴🦴🦴🦴	The best of the best, as well as the best of the beasts
🦴🦴🦴	Worthy efforts, high in artistic merit and *demerit*
🦴🦴	More mundane mongrel movies
🦴	Dime-a-dozen trash flicks
WOOF!	Not worth *anyone*'s time

Country of Origin Codes

The country of origin codes indicate the country or countries in which a film was produced or financed. Please note that we have used the geopolitical designation that was in place at the time the film was made; for example, "West Germany" is used instead of "Germany."

FR	France
GR	Greece
IT	Italy
LG	Luxembourg
MX	Mexico
PO	Poland
SP	Spain
SW	Sweden
UK	United Kingdom
US	United States
WG	West Germany
YG	Yugoslavia

Sample Review

Each review contains up to twelve tidbits of information, as enumerated below. Please realize that we faked a bit of info in this review for demonstration purposes. For example, we invented a rating for this film, and we listed the country of origin (US) even though in the book, U.S. is not listed as a country of origin unless the film was made in multiple countries, including the United States. In other words, if no country of origin is listed, it's safe to assume that the film was made in the United States.

1. Title
2. Critical rating of the movie (🦴 to 🦴🦴🦴🦴, or **WOOF!**, with 🦴🦴🦴🦴 being the ultimate praise)
3. Synopsis/review
4. Year movie was released
5. MPAA rating (if any)
6. Length in minutes
7. Black and white (B) or Color (C)
8. Country of origin; see above
9. Credits, including cast, voice cast (V), narrator (N), director (D), screenwriter (W), cinematographer (C), and music composer/lyricist (M)
10. Video formats (VHS and/or DVD)
11. Alternate titles; an alphabetical list of all such titles can be found in the Alternate Title Index, located at the back of the book.
12. Byline of reviewer (if no byline is listed, the review was written by the book's author)

① Faster, Pussycat! Kill! Kill! ② 🎵🎵🎵🎵

③ **F**or bodacious superbabes, overwrought psychodrama, and hardboiled mid-'60s sleaze, it just doesn't get any better than this Russ Meyer classic. Meyer had recently completed a biker picture called *Motor Psycho* in an attempt to switch from sexploitation to straight action. After finding that project's final results unsatisfying, he came up with a brilliant idea. Why not make the brutal biker villains statuesque and equally violent women?

Three tough go-go dancers—savage karate expert Varla (Tura Satana), vicious lesbian Rosie (Haji), and girl-next-door-gone-bad Billie (Lori Williams)—get their after-work kicks by hot-rodding their "bombs" across the California desert. They soon find themselves enveloped in murder, kidnapping, lust, and robbery after an impromptu desert race gets out of hand. Psychotic Varla, always on the lookout for someone or something to dominate, challenges clean-cut car-club president Tommy (Ray Barlow) to a race. When she discovers that nearly wrecking his car isn't enough to incite him, she openly attacks him. Before anyone can stop her, she snaps the teen's back like a twig. The girls keep Tommy's girlfriend, Linda (Sue Bernard, *Playboy*'s Miss December 1966), on sleeping pills until they can think of a way to dispose of her. The answer to their problem comes from an expository gas station attendant (Meyer regular Michael Finn). He tells them of a hateful old man in a wheelchair (Stuart Lancaster, another Russ fave) who lives on a desert ranch with his two grown sons. The old lecher is rumored to be hiding a fortune somewhere on the property, and Varla sees in their virginal captive a chance to finagle their way into the old man's house. Before long, the trio is engineering various wiles in an effort to remove all obstacles between them and the loot. Of course, everything goes violently wrong —for everybody.

Faster, Pussycat! Kill! Kill! is an exploitation masterpiece that takes the Bad Girl persona and raises it to operatic proportions. The three leads, all well-known exotic dancers when they weren't appearing in films, gnaw on their insane roles with gusto. Williams perfectly embodies the self-destructive child of privilege willing to go to any length in her pursuit of kicks. At the other end of the spectrum is Haji's vaguely Italian cauldron of hatred. At the apex of this triangle stands Tura Satana, an instant exploitation icon in low-cut black outfits and a Bettie Page hairdo. As narrator John Furlong intones at the very beginning, "Welcome to Violence!" Whether you love the film for its obvious cheap-thrills value or as an underappreciated piece of camp noir, you have to admit, *Pussycat* is a classic.

④ **1965** ⑤ **(R)** ⑥ **83m** ⑦ **B** ⑧ *US* ⑨ Tura Satana, Haji, Lori Williams, Sue Bernard, Stuart Lancaster, Paul Trinka, Dennis Busch, Ray Barlow, Michael Finn. *D:* Russ Meyer. *W:* Russ Meyer, Jack Moran. *C:* Walter Schenk, Russ Meyer. *M:* Paul Sawtell, Bert Shefter. ⑩ *VHS*
⑪ *AKA: Leather Girls; Pussycat; Mankillers*

⑫ —Brian Thomas

Chapter 1

Bond and Beyond

T hanks to the efforts of James Bond of Her Majesty's Secret Service, the spy craze hit full tilt in the 1960s. And like a pinball, it spun from post to post, sometimes racking up a big score, other times barely registering at all.

It was, of course, 007's initial feature appearance in 1962's *Dr. No* that got the secret agent machine rolling. Other players immediately lined up to put their quarters into the slots, hoping they'd get an action-packed ride—or at least a hit movie. Even Bond's own coproducer, Harry Saltzman, closed a deal for a new secret agent series, this one featuring Len Deighton's intellectual, working-class operative Harry Palmer, to be played by cockney newcomer Michael Caine. Three Palmer pictures were eventually produced—*The Ipcress File, Funeral in Berlin,* and *The Billion Dollar Brain*—but the solemn series eventually ran its course. Bond, meanwhile, continued to trot ahead of the pack, pulling in gargantuan worldwide grosses with the fourth, fifth, and sixth entries in the series.

Aside from the in-house competition from Palmer, another British series tried to form its own fan club. "Bulldog" Drummond, a character popularized in hair-raising adventures during the 1920s and 1930s, was resurrected as a suave new-school secret agent for 1966's *Deadlier Than the Male* and 1969's *Some Girls Do.* Playing the Bulldog was theatrically trained actor Richard Johnson, once a leading contender for the Bond role. The films adopted the 007 formula, making Drummond a man's man, filling out the female parts with such bikini-clad lookers as Elke Sommer and Sylva Koscina, and offering some tight jams against despicable villains. It was a nice imitation, but no Bond.

Many other secret agents came and went. Of the more noteworthy, David Niven's doctor-spy, pulled into Middle Eastern intrigue in 1965's *Where the Spies Are,* worked well, but Niven moved on to play Sir James himself shortly thereafter in the all-star *Casino Royale* fiasco. Then there was Rod Taylor, who brought his sturdy, macho manner to the half-joking *The Liquidator* in 1965; George Segal, surprisingly effective as an agent enmeshed in European espionage in 1966's *The Quiller Memorandum;* Gregory Peck, playing a college professor battling Middle Eastern troublemakers and bedding Sophia Loren in 1966's *Arabesque;* and George Peppard, an American agent searching for a mole in London in 1970's underrated *The Executioner.*

As long as the Cold War continued to stay hot, there would be no shortage of spy outings. After all, who could trust those Commies? Bond pursued Cold War intrigue in *From Russia with Love,* his second cinematic adventure, and the subject became the focus of two of the '60s' less Bondian espionage entries.

The Manchurian Candidate, released in 1962, the same year as *Dr. No,* was written by Richard Condon as a satire, but director John Frankenheimer and screenwriter George Axelrod's daring cinematic treatment was nothing less than chilling in its depiction of brainwashing, paranoia, political conspiracies, and the games spies and governments play.

In 1965 Martin Ritt brought John Le Carré's double-cross-filled *The Spy Who Came in from the Cold* to the big screen. Richard Burton plays the soon-to-retire British agent who gets more than he bargained for when sent behind the Iron Curtain to track his troublesome counterpart in East Berlin. As viewed in this low-key but intense and intelligent film, the world of spies does not always involve hanging out with gorgeous women in resorts, playing baccarat at casinos, driving fast sports cars, and saving the world in the coolest way imaginable.

As the song says, nobody does it better than James Bond. But some sure do it more convincingly.

Arabesque ♫♫♫♩

As with *Charade,* which he directed three years earlier, Stanley Donen brought a Hitchcockian sensibility and a sophisticated '60s style to *Arabesque,* a complex and highly enjoyable thriller packed with double crosses, duplicitous characters, and, of course, spies.

Following a colorful, abstract title sequence created by Maurice Binder and set to Henry Mancini's tingly, urgent theme, we're introduced to Gregory Peck as David Pollock, an American hieroglyphics expert lecturing in England. Pollock is urged to decipher a piece of Hittite writing for associates of Bashraavi (Alan Badel), a Middle Eastern shipping tycoon. Having trouble making ends meet, Pollock agrees to the job and the $30,000 fee. But he's soon contacted by Mohammed Lufti (Harold Kasket), a diplomat and peace negotiator. Lufti, whom Pollock admires, warns the professor that Bashraavi is probably up to no good, but, to avoid suspicion, he should complete the assignment anyway.

Pollock begins the work, but his attention is soon disrupted by the appearance of Yasmin Azir (Sophia Loren), a fetching foreigner who is also Bashraavi's lover. Azir seems intently interested in Pollock's work for reasons that are not entirely clear.

As Bashraavi, Azir, and other factions vie for the translation and for Pollock, the professor is tossed into a whirlwind of danger, trying to sort out the good guys from the bad.

Arabesque is not among the most original suspensers of its time, but it holds up remarkably well all these decades after its release. Of course, the casting of Peck and Loren helps. Peck's stoicism is spiked with a nice twist of sarcasm, and we get a real kick watching the egghead prof wiggle out of a series of dire situations using his wits and athleticism, both of which seem to surprise everyone—including himself.

Loren is, of course, dazzling, and dons everything from leopard skin to lingerie, wide-brimmed hats to turban headdresses. Her character shifts alliances as often as she changes clothing, and every man she comes into contact with seems to be willing to do handstands to be close to her.

> **"I have a vivid imagination, but I must say . . . I never saw myself unpacking a prime minister!"**
>
> —David Pollock (Gregory Peck), in *Arabesque*

Also scoring points in this cast are Badel as the treacherous Bashraavi, getting his kicks threatening enemies and underlings with his pet falcon and not-so-subtly dabbling in foot fetishism with Loren, and Kieron Moore as an oily associate of Loren who uses lingo like "daddy-o" in a comically condescending fashion.

Director Donen, the former MGM musical wizard behind *Singin' in the Rain* and *On the Town* (both of which starred Gene Kelly), as well as *Charade* and, later, *Bedazzled,* brings a touch of class and a high suspense quotient to the picture, giving us some well-choreographed Hitchcock-style chase pieces involving (separately) threshing machines, the London zoo, and helicopters and horses. There's also a dandy extended sequence involving a stop at Buckingham Palace where Peck and Loren try to track down a message hidden in a piece of candy.

Donen gets the most out of the double entendre–stuffed interplay between Peck and Loren. And, this being the '60s, the director delivers a great freak-out scene: drugged with "truth serum," Peck is kicked out of a van into oncoming traffic. He hallucinates that he is rushed by wild animals, and he begins playing matador to the speeding cars, which soon pile up in heaps. The sequence is scary, intense, and funny at the same time. Like the rest of *Arabesque,* Hitch would have given it his shrug of approval.

1966 107m/C Gregory Peck, Sophia Loren, Alan Badel, Kieron Moore, Carl Duering, John Merivale, Harold Kasket. **D:** Stanley Donen. **W:** Julian Mitchell, Stanley Price, Peter Stone. **M:** Henry Mancini. *VHS*

Deadlier Than the Male 🦴🦴🦴

Some Girls Do 🦴🦴

It's easy to see why Richard Johnson was once considered a leading candidate for the role of James Bond. The graduate of the Royal Shakespeare Company possessed some of the physical prowess of Sean Connery, the model looks of George Lazenby, the unpredictable edginess of Timothy Dalton, and a nice way with a sarcastic quip à la Pierce Brosnan. But Johnson was a "serious actor," cutting his teeth on the London stage with such greats as John Gielgud, and he didn't want to get hampered by a serious commitment, especially after making a strong impression next to Frank Sinatra in the World War II tale *Never So Few* in 1959 and as a paranormal expert in 1963's classic ghost story *The Haunting.*

With secret agents all the rage throughout the 1960s, Johnson finally answered his calling when leading British producers recruited him to play Hugh "Bulldog" Drummond in *Deadlier Than the Male* and *Some Girls Do.* Drummond was already a well-known figure populating mystery novels and movies. The character was introduced after World War I in a series of books

Gregory Peck and Sophia Loren find trouble and romance in *Arabesque.* UNIVERSAL / THE KOBAL COLLECTION

TV SPIES: THE MEN AND WOMEN FROM THE TUBE

by Gary Cahall

Robert Vaughn, *The Man from U.N.C.L.E.* MGM-TV / THE KOBAL COLLECTION

In the early 1960s, as the Saturday matinee cowboys of the cinema were heading into their last roundups and their TV counterparts were similarly waning in popularity, the hot new breed of action hero to make the jump from big screen to small was the secret agent. Certainly, there had been spies on the tube pretty much from its inception: Richard Carlson portrayed real-life undercover Commie-catcher Herbert Philbrick in the McCarthy era–flavored *I Led Three Lives,* and before he donned white greasepaint to play a *Batman* villain, Cesar Romero was a dashing diplomatic courier in *Passport to Danger.* There was even a short-lived NBC anthology series in 1963 entitled *Espionage,* which featured an appearance by James Bond creator Ian Fleming.

The boom in TV cloak-and-dagger drama, however, didn't start until 1964, just as America was launching headlong into 007 mania with the release that year of the third Bond film, *Goldfinger.* NBC beat the moviemakers to the punch with the fall debut of *The Man from U.N.C.L.E.* Suave superagent Napoleon Solo (Robert Vaughn) was just as quick with a gun and as fast with the ladies as his big-screen inspiration, and, in an interesting bit of détente in those Cold War days, Solo's partner was a Russian, Illya Kuryakin (David McCallum). The duo didn't work for any one country; they were operatives of the United Network Command for Law Enforcement, a top-secret international troubleshooting agency headquartered in New York. Veteran character actor Leo G. Carroll played Mr. Waverly, the head of U.N.C.L.E., who regularly sent the pair around the world on missions of great global consequence and increasingly wilder plots. Their most frequent foes were not any particular government but rather one of those Bondian criminal cabals bent on world domination, T.H.R.U.S.H.—which, as you all know, stood for the Technological Hierarchy for the Removal of Undesirables and the Subjugation of Humanity. It was all very stylish and often silly, and for three and a half years adults and kids alike were ready to say "Uncle" to the original series, a few feature films cobbled together from episodes, and its short-lived 1966–67 spin-off, *The Girl from U.N.C.L.E.,* with Stefanie Powers as agent April Dancer.

The 1965–66 season saw increasing numbers of clandestine crimefighters join the ranks. Robert Culp and Bill Cosby made TV history as the first interracial costars of a prime-time drama series, mixing action and laughs as globetrotting government agents posing as a pro tennis player and his trainer in the Sheldon Leonard series *I Spy.* Gene Barry's two-year-old private-eye series *Burke's Law* was transformed into *Amos Burke—Secret Agent,* with Barry's millionaire sleuth now working for Uncle Sam. Introduced in a *Burke's Law* episode was Honey West, a sexy female private eye played by Anne Francis, who got her own one-year series that year. West wasn't a spy per se, but she possessed such gimmicks as a mastery of judo and a pet ocelot named Bruce, which alone merit her inclusion. Meanwhile, Patrick McGoohan lived a life of danger as British operative John Drake in the classy overseas import *Secret Agent,* best known for the hit Johnny Rivers theme song and its cult favorite 1968 follow-up that mixed psychedelics and Kafka, *The Prisoner.* Secret agents even populated the American frontier of the 1870s: Robert Conrad and Ross Martin played two-fisted government agent Jim West and his quick-change cohort, Artemis Gordon, in the genre-blending *The Wild Wild West.* For four seasons on CBS, the twosome used the latest steam-era technology to battle twisted villains and keep the country safe for President Grant. The most offbeat entry of the year, though, was the sidesplitting spy spoof *Get Smart,* created by Mel Brooks and Buck Henry. Don Adams was forever typecast as bumbling Agent 86, Maxwell Smart, with Ed Platt as his boss, the Chief, and Barbara Feldon as Max's fellow sleuth and love interest, Agent 99. They all worked for CONTROL, which apparently didn't stand for anything. Smart's less-than-awe-inspiring arsenal included a shoe phone, the always-malfunctioning Cone of Silence, and a string of catchphrases ("Sorry about that, Chief" and "Would you believe . . . ?" among them).

The 1966–67 season saw such short-lived entries as the intriguing World War II espionage series *Jericho,* with Robert Loggia playing a former acrobat involved in dangerous missions as the agile burglar "T.H.E. Cat" and with Robert Lansing as a millionaire playboy who assumes the identity of a spy who was his exact double in the TV series *The Man Who Never Was.* ABC scored a hit with another transatlantic transplant, *The Avengers,* boasting Patrick Macnee as bowler-hatted sophisticate John Steed and the lovely Diana Rigg as his leather-clad compatriot, Mrs. Emma Peel. The pair's lighthearted adventures against mad scientists, female killer robots, and the like were at times more Batman than Bond, but English wit and pluck prevailed on-screen and off.

The real big news that season, however, was the debut of *Mission: Impossible.* First Steven Hill, then Peter Graves, would receive self-immolating messages that charged the members of the Impossible Missions Force with assignments ranging from retrieving a defecting scientist from behind the Iron Curtain to toppling a seemingly endless series of Latin American dictators. Martin Landau, Barbara Bain, Greg Morris, Peter Lupus, and Leonard Nimoy were some of the better-known IMF agents in the series, which became famous for its elaborate plots, rapid editing, classic Lalo Schifrin theme song, and cinematic filming style before self-destructing for good in 1973 (not counting an '80s revival series and the ongoing Tom Cruise films, of course).

By the fall of 1968, the genre had pretty much run its course, with the only new entry even close to the category being Robert Wagner's *It Takes a Thief,* in which cat burglar Alexander Mundy (Wagner) is recruited into pulling off capers for the government. The networks would continue to bring out new series over the years—the secret agent now a full-fledged member of that job pantheon that includes cops, lawyers, doctors, cowboys, and even the occasional blind, wheelchair-bound, or otherwise infirm private detective—but for the golden era of small-screen spies, it was "case closed."

by Herman Cyril McNeile under the pen name Sapper. On-screen, the crafty war veteran–turned-adventurer and detective was played by the likes of Ronald Colman, John Howard, and Ray Milland.

Could a character created in 1919 be revamped for the sexy, swinging '60s? Well, yes and no.

Deadlier Than the Male, released in 1967, found Johnson's Drummond working for Lloyd's of London, investigating the deaths of a Texas oilman and a former friend. Seems that Irma and Penelope (Elke Sommer and Sylva Koscina, the latter of *Hercules* fame) were the culprits, but they were far from acting alone: enter the power-mad millionaire (sans a respectable-sounding power-mad-millionaire name), Carl Petersen (Nigel Green).

After fighting off thugs and narrowly averting death via exploding cigar, Drummond drops in to see Petersen and soon learns of his radical new business strategy: knock off all CEOs who get in his way, then grab their companies. And you thought the board at Enron was ruthless!

Irma and Penelope
(Elke Sommer and
Sylva Koscina) are
Deadlier Than the Male.

UNIVERSAL / THE KOBAL
COLLECTION

The Drummond character is cool—smoking European cigarettes, drinking Bullshot, driving a convertible, and inflicting karate on his enemies. Of course, this makes him popular with the chicks—even drawing the attention of those hired to keep him in check. In fact, it's not long before the partners-in-grime, jealous Irma and Penelope, have hissy fits as they jostle for his affections.

Deadlier Than the Male, which was directed by Ralph Thomas, veteran of the series of *Doctor* comedies, and written by Hammer Studios regular Jimmy Sangster (*Dracula: Prince of Darkness*), offers many of the Bond conventions of the era, but with an added spike of nastiness. When Drummond turns the tables on a group of parking-lot thugs, he makes them sweat by ramming the front of his car into their legs, threatening to break their appendages. And when facing off against Petersen in a surreal confrontation amidst life-size chess pieces on a giant computerized board, he delights in inflicting maximum suffering on his nemesis.

But Drummond isn't the only one with a mean streak here. Irma and Penelope, with their cleavage squeezed into microbikinis and a talent for han-

dling harpoon guns, could be poster girls for T&A director Andy Sidaris. Macho, sexy, and not always in the best of taste, *Deadlier Than the Male* is the blue-collar version of a Bond outing.

Unfortunately, the sequel *Some Girls Do* doesn't fare as well. Archvillain Petersen is back, but Nigel Green is replaced by James Villiers. And like Dick Sargent replacing Dick York in *Bewitched,* the substitution just doesn't cut it: Villiers lacks the dastardly "oomph" of his predecessor.

In this outing, Petersen and an army of female robots (take note, *Austin Powers* fans!) are out to snuff an experimental jetliner. Drummond gets into the action, but the pace is lethargic for the most part, in spite of a few interesting appearances: the always watchable Daliah Lavi, Robert Morley camping it up as cooking expert "Miss Mary," and a brief role in the film's opening scene by *Absolutely Fabulous* star Joanna Lumley as a lethal stewardess.

Despite Johnson's best efforts, *Some Girls Do* didn't do much at the box office, and the Bulldog Drummond revival faded into oblivion. Perhaps some clever producer will take a shot at resurrecting the old Bulldog at some point. He has life left in him yet.

Richard Johnson, as Hugh "Bulldog" Drummond, surrounds himself with the girls of *Some Girls Do.*

RANK / UNITED ARTISTS / THE KOBAL COLLECTION

Deadlier Than the Male
1967 90m/C *UK* Richard Johnson, Elke Sommer, Sylva Koscina, Nigel Green, Suzanna Leigh, Steve Carlson, Virginia North. **D:** Ralph Nelson. **W:** Jimmy Sangster. **C:** Ernest Steward. **M:** Malcolm Lockyer. *VHS, DVD*

Some Girls Do
1969 88m/C *UK* Richard Johnson, Daliah Lavi, James Villiers, Robert Morley, Sydney Rome, Beba Loncar, Vanessa Howard, Joanna Lumley. **D:** Ralph Nelson. **W:** Liz Charles-Williams, David D. Osborn. **C:** Ernest Steward. **M:** Don Black, Charles Blackwell. *VHS*

Goldfinger ♫♫♫♫

Nobody did it better then, and to this day, *nobody* does it better than 007. Sure, there have been spoofs, imitators, quick-buck artists, and competitors—even some from Bond's own creators. Michael Caine's Harry Palmer pictures were, after all, produced by Harry Saltzman of Bond fame. But through thick and thin, James Bond could almost always be called on to deliver the goods in terms of charm, charisma, fearlessness, smarts, physical agility, and, of course, unsurpassed attractiveness to the gals. (Notable exceptions do exist—times when 007 was his own worst enemy, embarrassing himself in cartoon style when the creative well ran dry. Have you watched *A View to a Kill* or *Moonraker* lately?) In the end, he is and always will be *the* secret agent man for all seasons.

Everybody has a favorite Bond film. Some rank *Dr. No,* 007's 1962 screen introduction, at the top for its freshness and the template it established for the series. (Of course, Ursula Andress nearly naked on a beach didn't hurt either.)

Fans of purer spy stories seem to prefer *From Russia with Love* (1963), the second 007 outing, which takes a more serious approach, accenting the espionage angle. Still others argue that *On Her Majesty's Secret Service* is superior, citing the strengths of Diana Rigg's Bond girl, Telly Savalas's memorably evil Blofeld, and some spectacular stunt work. Champions of the film claim these pluses more than compensate for model George Lazenby's one-time (mis)casting after Sean stepped aside.

Then there are the staunch Ian Fleming followers who believe Timothy Dalton is truer to the author's conception of James than are the others, or the new generation of Pierce Brosnan devotees who know Sean Connery only as that old, balding guy starring with Catherine Zeta-Jones in *Entrapment.*

Poll the die-hard James Bond fans—people who have followed the secret-agent character over the forty-plus years of his screen existence—and you'd surely discover that *Goldfinger* ranks as the leading favorite of all James Bond movies. In terms of thrills and entertainment value, *Goldfinger* is, well, pure gold—maybe one of the best adventure/thriller films ever made. Few films have as many classic scenes and memorable characters.

In the film, Sean Connery's Bond comes up against Auric Goldfinger (Gert Frobe), a British megalomaniac who, as the wonderfully bombastic theme song tells us over the sexy, silhouetted credit sequence, loves only gold, only gold. Goldfinger lives a high, globe-trotting life, pulling off shady smuggling deals involving his much-beloved element. But it's simply not enough. He wants more, more, more! His grand diabolical plan involves breaking into Fort Knox and spraying the U.S. gold supply with radiation, an act that will shake up the world economy and make his own supply of gold ten times more valuable.

Of course, 007 is the only one who can stop him. To do so, Bond must get close to Goldfinger to find out what he's up to. Not an easy task considering the bad guy has a seemingly indestructible golf caddy/bodyguard named Oddjob (Harold Sakata) who wields a flesh-slicing, boomerang-like derby.

Leading up to the final, airborne showdown, Bond faces a variety of memorable run-ins with Auric and associates. First, in Miami, Bond disrupts Goldfinger's rigged card game by busting into the room of Jill Masterson (Shirley Eaton), an associate who is calling cards to her boss. The incident and subsequent tête-à-tête between the secret agent and the comely Masterson lead to her bizarre death by skin asphyxiation after Goldfinger has her body covered in gold paint. Another notable scene involves Bond luring Goldfinger into a game of golf and, after pointing out his cheating ways, teasing him with a bar of gold bullion.

Goldfinger poster

Then, just in time, the action and intensity increase: a wild car chase gives 007 the chance to drive his new, gadget-filled Aston Martin; we're introduced to Pussy Galore (Honor Blackman), Goldfinger's kinky pilot and ally; a disgruntled mobster's association with Goldfinger ends in a compact and crushing way; and 007 battles Oddjob in the Fort Knox vaults—you know, the old Secret-Agent-Man-vs.-Maniacal-Asian-with-a-Steel-Hat routine.

Just sampling the precredit sequence of the film will demonstrate why *Goldfinger* cemented James Bond's no-nonsense international nickname of Mr. Kiss-Kiss Bang-Bang. In a matter of minutes, Bond blows a warehouse sky-high, doffs his scuba outfit to reveal a tuxedo, makes out with a nightclub dancer, and electrocutes a would-be assassin in the bathtub. Shirley Bassey's wonderful reading of the theme song over Maurice Binder's artsy, erotic montage follows, introducing a bigger-than-life motif the film (and, from here on, the series) adopts. *Goldfinger* is a turning point for the James Bond series. *From Russia with Love,* the previous Bond film, was more down to earth, more

FLEMING IS FOREVER: AN IAN FLEMING DOSSIER
by Charles A. Cassady Jr.

Some biographers of British spy novelist extraordinaire Ian Fleming don't hesitate to compare him to his most famous invention, James Bond. Others liken Fleming to his sadistic, hedonistic villains. What that means, basically, is that there was plenty of Fleming to go around, as a womanizer, globe-trotter, gambler, bibliophile, soldier, car fancier, rogue, alcoholic, reporter, and international chap of intrigue.

Ian Lancaster Fleming was born on May 28, 1908, into a prosperous banking family. Fleming, whose father was killed in World War I, would later describe his upbringing throughout Europe as "overprivileged." While at school in Eton he enjoyed his first taste of literature with a self-produced student magazine called *The Wyvern*. Soon after, he brought out a self-published volume of poetry, *The Black Daffodil*, the content of which so embarrassed Fleming later that he destroyed every copy he could find (an understandable but uncharacteristic gesture from a man who eventually built up a priceless collection of rare first editions). Meanwhile, his older brother Peter had significant success as a writer, dedicating one of his books to Ian.

During that rosy period "between the wars" so cherished in U.K. nostalgia, a number of Fleming's mentors, at school and at a brokerage firm where he spent much of the 1930s, had been involved in espionage, and a three-year stint as a European-affairs reporter for the Reuters news service influenced the creator of 007. By that time, Fleming had learned to speak French, German, and a little Russian. Such worldly qualities led to Fleming's recruitment by British Naval Intelligence, with an honorary rank of lieutenant, at the dawn of World War II. "I couldn't have possibly had a more exciting or interesting war," Fleming said in one of his last interviews (for *Playboy* magazine). "Of course, it's my experience in Naval Intelligence, and what I learned of secret operations of one form or another, that finally led me to write about them . . . with James Bond as a central figure."

Fleming's six years of clandestine ops, replete with secret weapons, propaganda feints, high-stakes gambles (the cloak-and-dagger kind and the casino variety), and impromptu love affairs, took him at one point to the island of Jamaica. The climate made such a positive impression on him that he bought fifteen acres of beachside property there in 1946, after landing a comfy job with the *Sunday Times*. Fleming began a routine of spending ten months of the year in London and two in Jamaica, where he built a seaside villa he called Goldeneye—a name chosen in part because he was reading Carson McCullers's *Reflections in a Golden Eye* at the time, and in part because of an "Operation Golden Eye" Fleming had helped concoct to thwart a theoretical fascist attack on British-held Gibraltar during World War II. At Goldeneye, Fleming—"Commander" to the household staff—hosted adventurers, authors, media moguls, entertainers, aristocrats, military officers, and, of course, ladies. At one point, on board the *Queen Mary* in the Atlantic, Ian Fleming had the opportunity to meet Winston Churchill, a family friend. The prime minister was disappointed that it was only Ian—Churchill would rather have rubbed shoulders with Fleming's brother Peter.

Ian Fleming himself helped spread the questionable lore that he spun the first James Bond yarn, *Casino Royale* (1952) to calm his nerves over his impending wedding to Anne Rothermere, a longtime flame (whose first marriage to a London newspaperman had been no serious obstacle to frequent liaisons with Ian). It is absolutely true, however, that Fleming took Bond's name from an esteemed ornithologist who wrote the book *Field Guide to Birds of the West Indies.* In typical self-deprecating fashion, the Commander invited the real James Bond to name any particularly unpleasant bird "Ian Fleming." Distilling Fleming's experiences in wartime, at card tables, in the bedroom, and around the world, *Casino Royale* (once published in pulp paperback form in the United States as *You Asked for It*) was swiftly followed by *Live and Let Die, Moonraker, Diamonds Are Forever,* and thirteen other Bond novels and short-story collections. These books were not well received by everyone. "Rather passé," snorted the *Cleveland Plain Dealer* book critic. "A symbol of capitalist imperialism," charged the Soviets. "Disgusting drivel," clamored one British weekly. Fleming never counted himself among the literary greats he most admired, like Graham Greene and Georges Simenon. But the creator of 007 saw his books published profitably around the world.

The prose Bond differs significantly from the swashbuckling spy the moviegoing public came to embrace; Fleming's 007 is a heavy drinker, world-weary, cold, and moody. Early unromantic descriptions of Bond as a government tool and contract killer who was heroic only in comparison to his grotesque foes brought the author (who, on the side, wrote high-profile newspaper pieces, assorted nonfiction, and even a children's fantasy, *Chitty Chitty Bang Bang*) frequent charges that he actively disliked James Bond. Indeed, Fleming toyed with killing the character off for good in a couple of tales (even writing a Bond obituary, *Sunday Times* style), but he never carried out the deed.

Bond-mania escalated in the early 1960s with reports that Ian Fleming was President John F. Kennedy's favorite adventure storyteller. Fleming indeed met with JFK; commentators have ruminated on the extent to which the Commander advised the young commander-in-chief on policy matters, and there is a bizarre allegation that both Kennedy and Lee Harvey Oswald were reading Ian Fleming on that fateful day in Dallas. The Bond mystique reached even further heights with the release of *Dr. No* and other movie blockbusters based on Fleming's writings.

At this point, as the author cultivated a public image as an urbane gentleman of leisure, his health began to fail. His chain-smoking, his drinking, an inherited heart defect, and the breakneck pace of life as a jet-setting celebrity writer all took their toll. He had suffered a cardiac arrest in 1961; in 1964, on his son's twelfth birthday, Ian Fleming died in London, a victim of pleurisy and hemorrhaging of the heart. That same year the movie version of *Goldfinger* came out, soon followed by *Thunderball*. Other authors, like John Gardner and Kingsley Amis, took over writing the Bond adventures. The life of Ian Fleming continued to intrigue his fans long after his death, as evidenced by such projects as the somewhat fictionalized account of Ian Fleming's life called *Spymaker: The Secret Life of Ian Fleming*. Made for British TV and available from Turner Home Entertainment, the movie cannily cast Jason Connery, actor-son of Sean Connery, as Ian Fleming.

In 1965 Fleming's Bond books sold twenty-seven million copies in eighteen different languages, and Agent James Bond 007 merchandise included everything from jigsaw puzzles to a line of clothing to deodorant. Even after the author's death, the world was not enough.

serious about characters and spying. From the get-go, *Goldfinger* picks you up by the lapels and roughs you up, something Bond has continued to do, decade after decade.

1964 (PG) 112m/C *UK* Sean Connery, Honor Blackman, Gert Frobe, Harold Sakata, Shirley Eaton, Tania Mallet, Bernard Lee, Martin Benson, Cec Linder, Lois Maxwell. *D:* Guy Hamilton. *W:* Richard Maibaum, Paul Dehn. *C:* Ted Moore. *M:* John Barry. *VHS, DVD*

The Ipcress File ♫♫♫♩

Funeral in Berlin ♫♫♩

The Billion Dollar Brain ♫♫♩

Michael Caine's Harry Palmer looks like the egghead version of James Bond. He's got those oversized black glasses and slightly unruly hair, and he wears dark, cheap suits and black ties. He looks like he'd be more at home figuring out a physics problem or selling insurance than getting entangled in international espionage.

Despite his outward appearance, Caine's Palmer is anything but the professorial type. As we discover in his first big-screen outing, Palmer is a former crook whose hobbies include cooking and wooing the ladies. In fact, it's because of his criminal activities that he's been recruited into the spy world.

Based on the first Harry Palmer novel, written by Len Deighton, *The Ipcress File* sets up the working-class spy's backstory. Turns out Palmer got into trouble while based in Germany with the British military. In lieu of a prison sentence, he makes a deal with the government that has him pitching in to crack a case in which scientists are being kidnapped and having their brains scrambled by an Albanian madman and his bald sidekick. With two browbeating superiors—Dalby (Nigel Green) and Ross (Guy Doleman)—breathing down his neck, Harry, who's labeled "insolent, perhaps with criminal tendencies," risks his sanity to solve the mystery and uncover a double agent in his midst.

The Harry Palmer films are more rooted in classic espionage than are the escapist fantasies of James Bond. The production is more realistic and fairly drab: Harry lives in a lower-middle-class London flat and there's little eye-catching gadgetry offered to him by the employment agency that doubles as spy headquarters. Even his romantic interest, coworker Jean Courtney (Sue Lloyd), is on the glum side.

Interestingly, *The Ipcress File* and two subsequent Palmer thrillers were produced by Harry Saltzman, the man who, along with partner "Cubby" Broccoli, served up the Bond adventures. Flying solo with Palmer, Saltzman

PIERCE BROSNAN: THE MAN WHO WOULD BE BOND
by Amy Longsdorf

Pierce Brosnan believes he was fated to play James Bond. He was born in 1953, the same year *Casino Royale* was published. The first movie he saw in his native Ireland was *Goldfinger*. And his late wife, Cassandra Harris, was a Bond girl opposite Roger Moore in *For Your Eyes Only*.

Bond might have been Brosnan's destiny, but first he had to play the waiting game. In 1986, after Brosnan's NBC-TV series *Remington Steele* was placed on hiatus, he was asked to play Bond in *The Living Daylights,* the sixteenth installment of the profitable series. He got as far as wardrobe fittings before the network forced the actor back for what wound up being a mere six episodes of *Steele.* Unwilling to see their hero on the small screen, the Bond producers cast Timothy Dalton instead.

It wasn't until *Goldeneye* that Brosnan was able to prove that he was, indeed, the right man to shake the martini.

Q: Do you remember your first impression of *Goldfinger*?

A: It was a staggering experience for an eleven-year-old boy. There was a naked lady all painted gold and a guy with a hat that decapitated people. Then there was this really cool guy who could have any girl he wanted and could knock the hell out of anyone who got in his way. It left an impression on me, let's just say.

Q: For a Bond fan, what was it like visiting your wife on the set of *For Your Eyes Only*?

A: It was the first time I met [Bond producer] Cubby Broccoli. And, as a matter of fact, I used the money Cassandra made on the movie to get us to Hollywood so I could audition for other roles. So that was thanks to James Bond, too.

delivers an anti-Bond, a *veddy* British conception that won favor because of its less campy take on the spy racket. To jazz up the intricate storyline, Saltzman hired director Sidney J. Furie. The Canadian-born filmmaker, who would go on to helm such varied works as *Lady Sings the Blues, The Boys in Company C, Iron Eagle,* and a host of straight-to-video features, uses every arty trick in the book, including bizarre camera angles, distorted lenses, and oddball framing techniques. Surprisingly, his efforts pay off, as his approach, along with a tingly score by 007 composer John Barry, brings a heightened sense of paranoia to the proceedings.

Caine returned as Harry Palmer in *Funeral in Berlin,* a suspenser that finds our deadpan spy heading to East Berlin to ensure that Colonel Stok (Oskar Homolka), a Russian, defects to the West. Harry's scheme is to stage a phony funeral for Stok, but when the wrong body turns up in the coffin,

Q: How disappointing was it to be cast in *The Living Daylights* and then be forced to drop out because of your TV commitment to *Remington Steele*?

A: Very disappointing. No one knows how close I came to the role before. My late wife and I had already decided we were going to move back to Europe. We'd put the kids in school. We were gearing our lives toward me doing Bond.

Q: So, how did you find out they wanted you again for *Goldeneye*?

A: I picked up the phone and it was my agent. He said, "Congratulations, Mr. Bond." I'm still flabbergasted Bond is back in my life. In a way, I'm glad I had to wait ten years to do *Goldeneye*. I was older. There's a bit more age on the face, and certainly more scars on my soul.

Q: Do you ever worry about Bond being politically incorrect?

A: Bond is a sexist and that's what turned people on thirty-two years ago when Sean Connery did it, and that's what turns people on now. I think there's a fantasy in some women's heads that they would like to have a man who just makes the decisions and takes command sexually.

Q: Any thoughts on Halle Berry's orange *Die Another Day* bikini?

A: Halle is at the top of her game; she's beautiful, gorgeous, and right on the money. When she wore the bikini, they had me doing her toenails in that scene. That makes sense because they ain't going to be looking at me.

things go awry. Soon enough, Harry encounters operatives with bogus identities and a beautiful woman (Eva Renzi) who may or may not be working for the Israeli secret service.

Funeral in Berlin is a more complicated affair than *The Ipcress File,* and while one can get lost amid its dizzying array of side-switching characters, it's not without its pleasures. Guy Hamilton (*Goldfinger, Diamonds Are Forever*) directs this time out, and, while he doesn't have Furie's flashy touch, he does have the good sense to keep things moving at a rapid, European-location-hopping clip. While Renzi is gorgeous as the femme fatale with questionable motives and Homolka is charismatic as the larger-than-life Soviet military man, it's Caine who is terrific, raising Palmer's droll impudence up a notch and engaging in smart, sarcastic banter with his superior, Ross (again played by Doleman).

Ross comes back—though in smaller doses—to cause Harry more headaches in 1967's *The Billion Dollar Brain,* the last in the Harry Palmer feature-film cycle. This time, Caine's Harry is out of intelligence and into private investigation, until Ross tries to entices him back into the spy world with the offer of a three-hundred-pound-a-year raise. Despite his initial reservations, the impoverished Palmer takes the plunge and is soon sent to Helsinki to deliver virus-infected eggs to General Stok (again played by Homolka). His Scandinavian trip becomes more complicated when he runs into an old ally, Leo Newbigen (Karl Malden). Leo is a middle-aged operative enjoying the good life after dumping wife and family for naked adventures with young, doe-eyed European babe Anya (Françoise Dorléac). Harry learns that Newbigen is working for powerful Texas billionaire General Midwinter (Ed Begley), who has plans to destroy Communism in Eastern Europe and eventually Russia by financing a revolution in Latvia. Does Harry, with his exceptional intelligence contacts, want in with Newbigen and Midwinter with the promise of lots of cash in return?

The underrated and little-seen *Billion Dollar Brain* is the wild card of the three Palmer flicks. Not surprising, considering it was helmed by the up-and-coming master of flamboyant filmmaking, Ken Russell. The first half of the film is a fairly terse spy thriller, made creepy by the robotic voice giving Harry his orders by telephone. We learn later that the disembodied voice is actually the title character, a monstrous, Texas-based computer calling the shots of the Latvian invasion. Once Palmer lands in the Lone Star State to meet the not-so-good General Midwinter, the movie heads in a much broader direction. Begley's Midwinter is a sweaty, cartoonish mix of Joseph McCarthy, Jerry Falwell, and George C. Scott's General Buck Turgidson from *Dr. Strangelove,* spouting his love of country, hatred of Commies, and the will of God, usually in the same sentence. Russell clearly digs this larger-than-life louse who, if it were not for the politics, could have been the heel in a James Bond movie, circa late Roger Moore. The director also jolts us with a frenetic staging of the Latvian invasion, complete with bombastic music and Eisensteinian montage.

Unfortunately, Russell's off-kilter approach took Harry Palmer to no-return territory when all was said and done. *Billion Dollar Brain,* which as of this writing has not been officially released on video in the United States, failed to score at the box office like the previous Palmers, clipping the wings of the potentially long-running series. Saltzman, who probably could have rejuvenated things, decided to spend his spare time between 007 adventures with Caine in such war projects as *Play Dirty* and *The Battle of Britain.*

Harry Palmer did return years later in two enjoyable cable films, *Bullet to Beijing* and *Midnight in St. Petersburg,* which, oddly enough, costarred Jason Connery, Sean's son. But the initial Harry Palmer trilogy is really where it's at, especially for spy fans who like their secret agents stirred, not shaken.

The Ipcress File
1965 109m/C *UK* Michael Caine, Nigel Green, Guy Doleman, Sue Lloyd, Gordon Jackson, Aubrey Richards, Frank Ratliff. **D:** Sidney J. Furie. **W:** Bill Canaway, James Doran. **C:** Otto Heller. **M:** John Barry. *VHS, DVD*

Funeral in Berlin
1967 102m/C *UK* Michael Caine, Oskar Homolka, Eva Renzi, Guy Doleman, Paul Hubschmid, Hugh Burden. *D:* Guy Hamilton. *W:* Evan Jones. *C:* Otto Heller. *M:* Konrad Elfers. *VHS, DVD*

The Billion Dollar Brain
1967 111m/C *UK* Michael Caine, Karl Malden, Oskar Homolka, Françoise Dorléac, Guy Doleman, Vladek Sheybal. *D:* Ken Russell. *W:* John McGrath. *C:* David Harcourt, Billy Williams. *M:* Richard Rodney Bennett. *VHS*

The Liquidator ♫♫♪

Part spoof and part thriller, *The Liquidator* is a handsomely mounted spy story based on the book and featuring the character created by John Gardner, the man who succeeded Ian Fleming as author of the James Bond novels.

The strapping, immediately likable Rod Taylor plays the title character, Boysie Oaks, a World War II vet whose restaurant business is about to shutter. Oaks is approached by Colonel Mostyn (Trevor Howard) to work for a branch of the British Secret Service following a series of embarrassing espionage mishaps. Oaks, who years earlier saved Mostyn's life during a bizarre incident on V-E Day in Paris, is enlisted as an assassin, targeting international troublemakers who dare threaten the British Empire.

While Mostyn believes his new hire could be the perfect cold-blooded killer, Oaks is more Cowardly Lion than Richard the Lionhearted. On top of that, Oaks has a fear of flying, which prevents him from carrying out jobs far from home. But Oaks is in after the Colonel offers him a slick apartment (complete with "automatic" bar), a comfy salary, a chance to meet beautiful women, and (just in case he wasn't sold) a jail term on a trumped-up treason charge if he turns down the offer.

So how will the flight-averse pacifist oblige his superior and his country? Secretly hire a professional killer to do the dirty work, of course. So, while Oaks gets ample time to snuggle up to Mostyn's voluptuous secretary ('60s überbabe Jill St. John with a British accent), the freelance assassin is out poisoning bad guys, pushing nefarious enemy agents off train platforms, and setting booby-traps.

The Liquidator starts like gangbusters, and the film's first half is a crafty and engaging lampoon of the spy genre. Taylor is letter-perfect as the naive, ever-resourceful fellow who thinks nothing of lying to his superiors and having opponents cold-heartedly offed as long as he gets a chance to live the good life. Other strong points of the film include an effective B&W prologue depicting the beginning of Oaks and Mostyn's relationship, an eye-catching title sequence by animator Richard Williams (*Who Framed Roger Rabbit*), a theme song belted out by *Goldfinger* songstress Shirley Bassey, and a flute-flavored bossa nova score by Lalo Schifrin.

Meet the Secret Service's secret weapon. His lips are on fire! His gun is not for hire! He fills girls with desire! What a man!

Tagline for *The Liquidator*

ON HER MAJESTY'S ENDLESS LAWSUIT
by Charles A. Cassady Jr.

From the outset, the James Bond movies were envisioned as part of the scheme for 007 world domination, and it is a sad irony of author Ian Fleming's life that he died before seeing his ultimate spy-hero series become the most popular cinematic franchise ever. Some say it was a lawsuit over Bond films that hastened Fleming's demise, a suit that has left a question mark to this day over who owns legal rights to the on-screen 007.

The plaintiff with the golden gun, as it were, is Kevin McClory, an up-and-coming producer-director from Ireland when he met Fleming in 1958, during production of McClory's feature debut, a whimsical outing called *The Boy and the Bridge*. McClory, screenwriter Jack Whittingham, and Fleming brainstormed ten treatments, including one for a Bond adventure that took place largely underwater, in the Bahamas. Either McClory, Fleming, Whittingham, or some combination of the three (this became of critical importance later in court) also concocted a new nemesis (instead of the usual Soviets): apolitical international baddies S.P.E.C.T.R.E., or Special Executive for Counterintelligence, Terrorism, Revenge, and Extortion.

Add hijacked A-bombs, scuba gear, and a heroine named Domino, and the results will be recognizable to 007 fans as *Thunderball*. But what percentage of the story was legally McClory's, under his authority as a potential Bond film producer? By 1961, as the novel went to print, Fleming had soured on the movie collaboration with McClory (poor box-office returns for *The Boy and the Bridge,* which never had a U.S. release, were part of it) and saw better prospects in London-based Canadian producer Harry Saltzman and Hollywood agent-turned-financier Albert Broccoli.

McClory and Whittingham sued Fleming—who days later was stricken with a heart attack—asking for an injunction against all copies of *Thunderball*. After exhaustive legal wrangling (compelling Saltzman and Broccoli to select *Dr. No* as the first Bond yarn to reach cinema screens instead of *Thunderball*), McClory and Whittingham got story credit in the *Thunderball* novel, and McClory won his case in court. But just what had he won?

Director (and Oscar-winning cinematographer) Jack Cardiff, who also teamed with Taylor on *Young Cassidy* and *Dark of the Sun* and helmed *Girl on a Motorcycle,* seems to have everything cooking perfectly. That is, until Oaks heads for Monte Carlo for a secret liaison with St. John. Upon discovering Oaks's verboten affair, Mostyn calls on associates in the field to stop his supposed lethal executioner—and the film takes a wrong turn. Extraneous spies, not-so-surprising double-crosses, and overlong action sequences send the second half of the film into generic thriller territory—a shame, given the good-natured ribbing of *The Liquidator*'s beginnings.

In the decades since, Kevin McClory has claimed the right to produce James Bond thrillers in which Agent 007 fights S.P.E.C.T.R.E. He succeeded in seeing two such films to fruition. Although actor Sean Connery was still under contract to Saltzman and Broccoli, a profit- and credit-sharing agreement allowed *Thunderball* to materialize in 1965, a year after Fleming's death. As part of the deal, McClory could not make another Bond picture for ten years. It took eighteen, in fact, for McClory and a new producer to sign Connery (who had filed a lawsuit of his own, feeling he wasn't paid fairly for past Bond-age) on to a remake of *Thunderball*, 1983's *Never Say Never Again.* In theaters it went head-to-head against Broccoli's "official" Bond offering, *Octopussy,* starring Roger Moore, which outgrossed it considerably (though reviews were lukewarm on both).

From time to time McClory would announce another Bond epic. Titles floated included Ian Fleming's *James Bond of the Secret Service, Warhead, Warhead 8,* and *Warhead 2000 A.D.,* with potential castings of Connery, Trevor Howard (as M), and Orson Welles (as Blofeld) and with spy novelist Len Deighton as scriptwriter. But these efforts mainly spawned further lawsuits from long-time Bond partners MGM and Danjaq (the latter is the company created by the late Broccoli and inherited by his children) to prevent further Thunderballing.

In 1998 the rights became the object of an exceptionally high-profile court case between MGM and Sony, which had taken over a then-slumping Columbia Pictures and which hoped to issue its own Bonds via McClory's piece of 007. Complete with accusations of corporate espionage (a movie executive supposedly switched sides with a dossier of 007 long-range movie plans) and e-mail threats against McClory, the copyright case began with a U.S. District Court ordering Columbia to halt their preproduction on the film adaptation of one of the *Warhead* books.

MGM and Sony settled privately in 1999, but McClory refused what he claims was a substantial payoff in exchange for his proper portion of the Bond legacy. He charged that "startling new evidence came to light in the Danjaq/MGM vs. Sony infringement counterclaim in the U.S District Court, California." Such evidence purportedly proves that cloak-and-dagger elements dreamt up by Whittingham and McClory were deliberately "borrowed" many decades earlier, having shown up in *Dr. No, From Russia with Love,* and *The Spy Who Loved Me.* So 007's longest battle continues.

McClory has taken his case to the Internet. You can check out the details and latest developments (complete with transcripts) at http://www.spectreorganization.com.

The Liquidator may not live up to its potential, but its abundant charms and strong cast outweigh the cookie-cutter elements that eventually derail it from being something special.

1966 104m/C *UK* Rod Taylor, Trevor Howard, Jill St. John, Wilfrid Hyde-White, David Tomlinson, Eric Sykes, Akim Tamiroff, Suzy Kendell. *D:* Jack Cardiff. *W:* Peter Yeldham. *C:* Ted Scaife. *M:* Lalo Schifrin. *VHS*

The Million Eyes of Su-Muru 🦴🦴

Future Women 🦴🦴

Shirley Eaton, best known as the woman who was painted gold in *Goldfinger,* goes black in *The Million Eyes of Su-Muru.* That's black as in black leather jumpsuit, which Eaton wears throughout this adaptation of the 1951 book by *Fu Manchu* writer Sax Rohmer.

Eaton, as Su-Muru, is one mean mama, a man-hating harpy who likes to whip members of the opposite sex into a frenzy when she's not busy commanding her minions of miniskirted femmes fatale to kill, kill, kill! Her home: an island off the coast of Hong Kong. Her accessories: a cigarette holder and a kimono. Her goal: destroy the male species. And just to keep things interesting, she employs a nifty gun against the men she keeps imprisoned in her torture chamber that turns them to stone. Her main target is Boong (Klaus Kinski), the wild-eyed president of nearby Sunasia, who likes to have his way with women (though there's more than a hint that Boong is gay—perhaps this is what ticks Su-Muru off to no end).

Some "Sax"-y S&M, a twist of deranged feminist allegory, and loads of good-looking babes in revealing outfits and heavy eye makeup—sounds like we're headed in the direction of camp classic here. But faster than you can say *Pussycat! Kill! Kill!,* Su-Muru's eyes grow cataracts. Blame some of it on chintzy production values (which is curious as it was filmed in the Shaw Brothers' Hong Kong studios, site of many a lavish kung fu epic). Blame most of it, however, on the lame dialogue and the cockamamie idea of having the two male leads overdoing the rancid humor throughout the picture. American agents Nick West and Tommy Carter wisecrack their way through the proceedings like a ninth-rate Hope and Crosby. West is abducted by Su-Muru, taken to her little island, and blackmailed into killing President Boong. Meanwhile, Carter sort of hangs around the airport until he meets Helga (Maria Rohm), a Su-Muru slave with a lousy dye job and a desire to fly the coop.

West, the supposed playboy, is essayed by George Nader, a journeyman actor best known for some cheap European thrillers. He's also the acknowledged former lover of Rock Hudson and the author of a gay sci-fi novel called *Chrome.* His macho shtick just doesn't make it here. And his well-documented private life gives a new meaning to a line like "I vote we blow." Frankie Avalon, meanwhile, attempts to change his beach-party persona with his part as Carter. But what was cool with Annette and Erich Von Zipper doesn't cut the mustard against a group of female gladiators who could eat Russell Crowe for breakfast. And when Frankie wonders aloud "if this is the part when I'm supposed to sing," we're almost willing to pay an extra three bucks to hear a verse of "Venus" or "Beach Blanket Bingo."

Two years after *Eyes,* Shirley Eaton went back to black again, playing Su-Muru one more time in *Future Women,* an even more mind-boggling production than was the first. Here, the antimale protagonist has started her own country, called Feminina, which is headquartered in an abandoned South American airport. There her minions of scantily-clad gal gladiators train and traumatize wealthy men by practically teasing them to death. After his daughter is swiped by Su-Muru and taken to Feminina, crime lord Sir Masius, who also enjoys torturing people (doubling his pleasure during such acts by reading Popeye comics at the same time), dispatches special-agent-with-plaid-sport-jacket Jeff Sutton (Richard Wyler) to retrieve her. But Sir Masius has additional plans: all-out war against Su-Muru with Sutton blackmailed to act as his general.

Cultists will be pleased to know that *Future Women* was directed by Jesus Franco, the incredibly prolific Spaniard whose credits and aliases outnumber those of most of his peers, and produced by Harry Alan Towers, whose name appears on nearly one hundred low-budget film and TV productions dating back to the 1950s. But this dynamic duo's experience didn't figure into *Future Women*. Despite Eaton's heavy eye makeup and her man-bashing brigade's Wonder-Woman-as-dominatrix get-ups, the film is exceedingly ugly and often downright incompetent. When the camera isn't zooming in or out, it appears to be searching for dirty airport windows to focus on. Cut! Print! Squeegee!

The Million Eyes of Su-Muru
1967 95m/C *UK* Frankie Avalon, George Nader, Shirley Eaton, Wilfrid Hyde-White, Klaus Kinski, Patti Chandler, Salli Sachse, Maria Rohm. *D:* Lindsay Shonteff. *W:* Kevin Kavanaugh. *C:* John Kotze. *M:* John Scott. *VHS*
AKA: The 1000 Eyes of Sumaru; The Slaves of Sumaru

Future Women
1969 90m/C *WG/SP/US* Shirley Eaton, Richard Wyler, George Sanders, Maria Rohm, Walter Rilia, Marta Reves. *D:* Jesus Franco. *W:* Franz Eichhorn, Karl Leder, Harry Alan Towers. *C:* Manuel Merino. *M:* Daniel White. *VHS, DVD*
AKA: Future Woman; The Seven Secrets of Sumuru; Rio 70; That Girl from Rio

The Quiller Memorandum ♪♪♪♪

B ased on the first of nineteen *Quiller* novels by Adam Hall (a nom de plume for *The Flight of the Phoenix* writer Eleston Trevor), *The Quiller Memorandum* is a tightly woven espionage yarn showcasing George Segal as an American spy employed by a British intelligence agency. Segal is known only as Quiller and works the Europe and Middle Eastern route, troubleshooting and digging up important information on government foes.

Two British operatives—one a friend of Quiller—are killed in Berlin, and our spy is enlisted to investigate the incident and figure out what role a group of neo-Nazis played in the murders and other treachery. After being briefed on his assignment in Berlin's massive Olympic Stadium by Pol (Alec Guinness), a no-nonsense superior, Quiller immediately gets to work trying to

Bond and Beyond

PETER HUNT: JAMES BOND MVP by Lowell Goldman

Peter Hunt recalled the night in London like it was yesterday. He was the film editor on a B&W war comedy called *Operation Snafu,* which featured an ambitious young Scottish actor named Sean Connery.

"The producer of *Snafu* (Ben Fisz) was a good friend of Harry Saltzman," related Hunt during a 1988 interview. "Anyway, we were all having dinner when Harry said somewhere during the conversation that he was looking for an actor to play James Bond in the Ian Fleming stories. I think that I might have suggested Sean and Harry asked to have a look at him. So we sent over a reel of *Snafu* for Harry and Cubby Broccoli to see at their office. They must have liked what they saw since out of it came . . . well, you know . . . out of it came Sean Connery as James Bond 007."

Hunt, who died in 2002, was quick to add that the casting of Connery was probably just a matter of luck and timing. "I can't really say that I was the one who did it. I can't take the credit for his casting. But I guess it did come out of that dinner meeting. I was just in the right place at the right time."

Dr. No director Terence Young also had a hunch about Connery. He knew the rising actor from a 1957 adventure flick he helmed entitled *Action of the Tiger.*

"The character of James Bond was originally patterned a great deal after Terence," revealed Hunt. "But the character of Bond was really based on Fleming himself. He imagined himself as that character. Yet, I must add that Terence was very instrumental in putting his personal stamp on Bond."

Hunt had also been Young's editor on a few films. His editing technique on *Dr. No* was quite innovative for the time. It's probably the first major film to cut in the middle of panning and tracking shots. "*Dr. No* was a particular style of editing," explained Hunt. "For the early '60s, it was a very advanced style. I just tried to move the movie along at a faster tempo. I also wanted to keep the scenes short. I must tell you that a lot of encouragement came from Terence. And it worked out really well."

The worldwide success of *Dr. No* was a pleasant surprise to all concerned. "It was a matter of luck and timing," exclaimed Hunt. "You see, the Bond film was made at a time when we had a lot of kitchen-sink dramas in England. It was the era of the turgid realistic sort of film. Then came along this piece of illusion. *Dr. No* was really pure entertainment and escapism."

After directing the first two Bond films (*Dr. No* and *From Russia with Love*), Terence Young departed the series to pursue other projects. Guy Hamilton was selected by the producers to direct *Goldfinger*. Hunt was the film's editor and did some second-unit work. Meanwhile, Hunt wasn't sure if Hamilton was the right man for the job. "Guy to me is a little heavy-handed. He hasn't got the personality of Terence. He hasn't got his light touch. You just have to look at the first two Bonds with Roger Moore to see what I mean."

Hunt continued his editing on *Thunderball,* for which Terence Young returned to the helm, his final 007 assignment. "*Thunderball* was a very involved story to transfer into a film. But, I honestly think it turned out to be a very fine film that still holds up quite well."

Thunderball was noted for its exciting, ultrarealistic underwater footage featuring killer sharks. Hunt recalled, "Well, you know we were very surprised to find those sharks swimming around down there. The art department had submerged the plane and then the sharks came out. Of course, we got some great shots. That's just another example that proves you need luck when you do a film."

Hunt then served as second-unit director for new Bond director Lewis Gilbert on *You Only Live Twice.* "That film was the last of the really extravagant, big-budget Bonds [at that time]," lamented Hunt. "No expense was spared on *You Only Live Twice.* We must have spent at least six months on location in Japan. They also built the largest indoor set for any movie at Pinewood Studios. It was really something special."

With all this invaluable experience under his belt, Hunt was now ready to handle the directing job himself for *On Her Majesty's Secret Service.* But instead of concentrating on the mechanics of filmmaking, Hunt suddenly became a casting director when Sean Connery vowed he wouldn't return to play 007.

"I think it was generally agreed by United Artists and the producers that we should start looking for another Connery. But, believe me, it was an extremely difficult task. We must have seen literally hundreds of applicants. We actually spent some months doing just that.

"United Artists didn't make a decision about a new Bond until we were about three weeks away from shooting," revealed Hunt, who also directed such action films as *Gold* and *Shout at the Devil.* "Then Cubby found this fellow that he thought might make a good Bond. I believe he actually saw him in a magazine ad while he was sitting in his barbershop of all places."

George Lazenby was now the screen's new James Bond. But he was not an accomplished actor—he was a male model from Australia who had only done some TV commercials.

"I think he did extremely well considering the pressure of the situation," said Hunt. "During the actual shooting of the movie, I never had any real trouble with George. I think most of his problems came about after the film was completed. For one thing, he was very badly advised about the business side of the film industry."

Hunt was also keenly aware of the film's cult status. "The movie was highly acclaimed in most circles," he stated proudly. "You know, they said that if Sean Connery had been in the part, it would have been the best of the Bond films. And even though it didn't have Connery, I still think that it was the best Bond film."

locate the neo-Nazis' headquarters before they can find where his agency has secretly set up shop.

His investigation takes him to several interesting locations, including a bowling alley, a health spa swimming facility, and an elementary school where one of the Nazis recently taught. It's at the school that Quiller meets a beautiful teacher named Inge (Senta Berger). To get information from Inge, Quiller poses as a Philadelphia newspaper reporter working on a story about the rise of Nazism in Berlin. It isn't long, however, before Quiller complicates matters by getting romantically involved.

Although *The Quiller Memorandum* might never have been produced if it were not for the James Bond phenomenon, the film follows a more old-school, Harry Palmer tradition. Code phrases, uncertain allegiances, high paranoia, and a believably creepy chief villain (Max von Sydow as Oktober) keep things more grounded than in the usual 007 adventures.

There are other, more specific similarities to the Palmer films as well. Segal's Quiller, like Michael Caine's Palmer, is a world-weary spy entrusted with dangerous and dirty work. But while stopping the rise of fascism may be professionally satisfying, Quiller is suffering personally—his heart is broken over his involvement with Inge. Production-wise, the *Quiller* filmmakers use actual European locations in the same manner as the Palmer pictures. And the composer John Barry, who provided a memorable soundtrack for *The Ipcress File* (as well as many of the Bond efforts), supplies a terrifically tense *Quiller* score.

On paper, Segal doesn't seem like he'd make a good lead in a spy film, but the actor, soon to be a star in such '70s comedies as *Where's Poppa, The Owl and the Pussycat,* and *A Touch of Class,* does a bang-up job. He's got an edgy sarcasm that underscores the more serious elements of the story and, though younger than the mid-forties character envisioned in Hall's books (Segal was thirty-two when he made the film), he displays a certain cragginess that fits the part nicely.

The supporting cast is uniformly excellent, with European knockout Berger (a soon-to-be Matt Helm girl in *The Ambushers*), von Sydow (very disturbing in the interrogation scenes), and Guinness (with a chip on his shoulder) as standouts. Director Michael Anderson, more accustomed to larger productions like *Around the World in 80 Days,* does some of his tightest work here, abetted by Harold Pinter's witty and intelligent screenplay that keeps you on the edge of your seat until the very end.

It seemed Quiller could have easily returned to the big screen if Segal was willing, but a sequel was not to be. A short-lived TV series, however, starring Michael Jayston as Quiller, was broadcast in Britain in 1975, and occasionally there are rumblings about *Quiller Solitaire,* a feature that, at one point, was to have starred John Travolta.

1966 105m/C *UK* George Segal, Alec Guinness, Max von Sydow, Senta Berger, George Sanders, Robert Helpmann, Robert Flemyng. *D:* Michael Anderson. *W:* Harold Pinter. *C:* Erwin Hillier. *M:* John Barry. *VHS*

Where the Spies Are 🦴🦴🦴

Two years before creating *Casino Royale,* star David Niven, director Val Guest, and writer Wolf Mankowitz tuned up for their silly Bond hijinks with this serio-comic offering. While the action and spoofing aren't in the same spirit as James Coburn's kitschy Flint films, it does manage to success-fully mix the dramatic with the satiric in an intelligent, sophisticated style.

David Niven, ever the debonair Englishman, plays Dr. Jason Love, a physician about to go on a well-deserved three-week holiday in France when he's interrupted by MacGillivray (John Le Mesurier), a leading British secret service operative. Mac, an acquaintance of Love's from World War II, recruits his old pal to fly to Beirut and attend a conference on malaria. His real mis-sion, however, is to investigate the disappearance of fellow agent Rosser (Cyril Cusack). With Mac's promise of a '36 Cord convertible to replace his current car, Love agrees to take the assignment.

After being briefed and given some helpful spying instruments (includ-ing a dental cap that can make nearby mechanical devices go haywire), Love heads to Beirut. But during a layover in Italy, he meets and immediately falls for Vikki (Françoise Dorléac), a stunning model/British intelligence agent. From there, Love narrowly escapes a harrowing plane bombing (a disturbing scene in the post-9/11 world), thwarts an assassination attempt on a Middle

Eastern leader, dodges Russian agents, and befriends Parkington (Nigel Davenport), a bibulous fellow Brit agent.

Like *Arabesque,* in which college professor Gregory Peck consistently surprises himself and the audience with his survival skills, part of the fun of *Where the Spies Are* is watching a distinguished, somewhat demure doctor reluctantly but successfully rise to the physical demands of the secret-agent life. It's no surprise that Niven delivers a spry, winning turn, but *Where the Spies Are* also scores surprisingly well in the espionage area. Director Guest shows us, with a nimble but serious touch, how the Soviets intervene politically in Middle Eastern affairs, while colorful double agents and assassination plots abound.

The film is also sparked by a strong supporting cast, especially Davenport as a hard-living operative out to show Niven the ropes, and Dorléac, who proves more complex than the knockout, one-dimensional model Niven originally thinks her to be. And there's Mario Nascimbene's self-consciously hip score—punctuated by organs and bongos—which sounds like Billy Preston with percussion backing playing for the roller-skating crowd.

1965 113m/C *UK* David Niven, Françoise Dorléac, John Le Mesurier, Cyril Cusack, Eric Pohlman, Richard Marner, Noel Harrison, Paul Stassino, Nigel Davenport. *D:* Val Guest. *W:* Wolf Mankowitz. *C:* Arthur Grant. *M:* Mario Nascimbene. *VHS*

Chapter 2

Silly Secret Agents

Once *Dr. No,* the first James Bond outing, became an international sensation in 1962, secret agents started coming out of the woodwork and onto movie screens. Throughout the rest of the 1960s, there was certainly no shortage of serious secret agents—Harry Palmer, "Bulldog" Drummond, and Quiller among them—but many of the super-spy knockoffs took the Bond template of espionage mixed with sly humor to a sillier, sometimes more satiric, level.

Actually, the trend of making light of the dangerous world of espionage could be traced to earlier efforts, such as Bob Hope in 1950's *My Favorite Spy* and Alec Guinness in 1960's *Our Man in Havana.* But Bond opened the floodgates for the likes of James Coburn's Derek Flint, Dean Martin's Matt Helm, Raquel Welch as Fathom, and Fred Flintstone as . . . Fred Flintstone.

Almost all of the spy comedies issued in the 1960s shake, rather than stir, the Bond formula with ample doses of exaggeration and, often, idiocy. The best of the batch don't go too far astray of 007's rules. For example, *Our Man Flint* and *In Like Flint* boast newfangled gadgets, international beauties, nefarious villains plotting to control the world, and a he-man hero well versed in everything from martial arts to talking to dolphins. But the *Flints,* while frolics, are snappily written and intelligently realized, and Coburn's secret agent has a mean streak that isn't tempered by the spoofing that goes on around him.

While based on serious source novels by Donald Hamilton, Dean Martin's four Matt Helm movies—*The Silencers, Murderers' Row, The Ambushers,* and *The Wrecking Crew*—take a tongue-in-cheek approach to the spy game. Spat out in rapid succession over a three-year period, the Helm movies offer the ever-smooth Rat Packer Dino drinking, smoking, shooting, getting laid, drinking, brawling, smoking, drinking, smoking, getting laid . . . and did we mention drinking?

With Bond making big bucks around the world and Flint and Helm holding their own at the box office, who could blame the copycats for the mad rush to get into the silly secret agent act? Doris Day, attempting to capture a new, younger audience, starred in two espionage-oriented comedies, *The Glass Bottom Boat* and *Caprice.* Raquel Welch tried to parlay her skimpy loincloth of *One Million Years B.C.* into a tight skydiving suit in *Fathom.* Monica Vitti, best known for serious roles in brooding Italian dramas from Michelangelo Antonioni, gave French comic-book favorite *Modesty Blaise* a psychedelic whirl. Even the animated Fred Flintstone was recruited for big-screen secret-agent duty in the family-friendly *A Man Called Flintstone.* Foreign filmmakers got into the act as well, with Yves Robert and Philippe de Broca delivering *The Tall Blond Man with One Black Shoe* and *La Magnifique,* respectively.

Meanwhile, the best spy satire of the era also took on politics, suburbia, war, and corporate America: 1967's *The President's Analyst* features James Coburn as a shrink who becomes more and more paranoid when asked to serve as analyst for the troubled U.S. leader.

Just because James Bond or Sean Connery appeared to be exclusive to series producers Harry Saltzman and Albert Broccoli didn't mean others couldn't tweak the hand that fed them. *Casino Royale,* the 007 story that got away from the official producers, offered multiple James Bonds, played by Peter Sellers, David Niven, Woody Allen, and trained seals, in a mod, mod, mod mess of a movie. And Neil Connery tried to cash in on his sibling's popular role in *Operation Kid Brother,* an Italian production from 1967 in which a bunch of Bond series veterans join him for some bottom-of-the-barrel spyjinks. Neil plays Dr. Neil Connery, a plastic surgeon enlisted into the world of espionage when a famous secret agent is unavailable for the mission. Talk about your odd jobs.

The Assassination Bureau

The Assassination Bureau is a queer duck, part period quasi-spy film, part swashbuckler, and part darkly comic social satire. It's an oddball amalgam that only the late 1960s could have given us, and, while not totally successful because of its strange genre blend, it is certainly enjoyably daffy for most of its running time.

After an intro of faux newsreels depicting assassinations throughout history, we're told of an actual company, called the Assassination Bureau, Ltd., that specializes in murdering people for a fee. They're selective with who they'll whack, only offing those who really deserve it and those who pose a threat to society.

Sitting on the company's board are diplomats and businessmen from across Europe, and acting as the company's president is Ivan Dragomiloff (Oliver Reed), whose ancestors started the enterprise decades ago. Sonya Winter (Diana Rigg), a pretty British feminist, has discovered this secret organization and is appalled by its existence. She plans to put it out of commission by offering Dragomiloff £20,000 for his own murder. Backing her is Lord Bostwick (Telly Savalas), a newspaper owner, who enlists Winter to write about her experiences for his London paper.

Surprisingly, Dragomiloff accepts Winter's offer and, at a board meeting, explains to the Bureau that because he has taken up the offer, the members must kill him . . . before he kills them. So the cat and mouse game is on, with Dragomiloff traveling across Europe in various disguises, trying to knock off his associates before they murder him, while Winter tags along, providing dispatches to Bostwick back in London. Some of the stops include a Paris bordello, a bank in Switzerland, and a restaurant in Vienna where sausages have a tendency to explode. Through it all, Winter doesn't realize that Bostwick is actually a member of the Bureau himself who wants Dragomiloff knocked off so he can take control and turn the group into a less discriminating murder-for-hire service, providing higher profits and greater power.

Handsomely mounted by director Basil Dearden (*Victim, Khartoum*) with elaborate production design by the film's screenwriter, Michael Relph,

Zeppelins. Bombs. Bordellos. Burials. You name it. We have it.

—Tagline for *The Assassination Bureau*

and sumptuous cinematography by the great Geoffrey Unsworth (*2001: A Space Odyssey, The Magic Christian*), *The Assassination Bureau* is a treat to watch even when it veers off in ill-advised directions.

Reed seems to be enjoying the opportunity to ham it up. He dons several costumes and makeup and takes part in a number of scenes that showcase his expert athletic abilities and comedic timing skills, including a hair-raising finale on a zeppelin. Call this a tune-up for his work in the Richard Lester *Musketeer* movies a few years later. Then there's Rigg, just two years after her sassy stint as Emma Peel in *The Avengers* and just before her Bond experience in *On Her Majesty's Secret Service*. She is fetching, even as a buttoned-up rights activist. But the filmmakers did "Rigg" the film, allowing the actress a scene in which she gets down to her petticoats. The rest of the cast is equally game and first-rate, including superior character actors Philippe Noiret, Curd Jürgens, Warren Mitchell, and Clive Revill.

The story behind the story that inspired *The Assassination Bureau* is about as oddball as the film itself. Legend has it that Sinclair Lewis sold the idea for *The Assassination Bureau* to Jack London, who started to turn it into a novel but never finished, claiming he didn't know where to go with the story. Decades later, historian Robert L. Fish discovered the work and completed it himself, adding fifty pages in the process. It was finally published in 1963, more than fifty years after London finished his end of it.

1968 105m/C Oliver Reed, Diana Rigg, Telly Savalas, Curd Jürgens, Philippe Noiret, Warren Mitchell, Beryl Reid, Clive Revill, Kenneth Griffith. **D:** Basil Dearden. **W:** Michael Relph. **C:** Geoffrey Unsworth. **M:** Ron Grainer. *VHS*

Casino Royale

Casino Royale, the 1967 James Bond spoof, sure lives down to its reputation. There's no denying that it is the bloated, barely coherent, all-star mish-mash of a movie it's always been accused of being. Yet there remains something fascinating about this mess that makes it irresistible.

The Ian Fleming story was one producers Harry Saltzman and Cubby Broccoli didn't snag for Sean Connery because it was sold before Bond became a big deal. And it had already served as the basis for a 1954 episode of the TV series *Climax!* (which featured Barry Nelson as the secret agent, Peter Lorre as the gambling-addicted villain Le Chiffre, and Linda Christian as the gal stuck between them). The property was picked up by agent-turned-producer Charles K. Feldman (*What's New, Pussycat?*) and Columbia Pictures, who sunk $12 million into the project and set out to assault the senses of Connery fans.

As an assault, *Casino* succeeds. The film's major gimmick was more, more, more! of everything, including multiple James Bonds. Here the "real" Bond is actually Sir James Bond (David Niven), the famed British agent who has retired to a stately English countryside mansion, where he spends his days listening to Debussy and standing on his head. His former boss, M (John

Huston, affecting a bizarre Irish brogue), and a group of other head operatives from the U.S. (William Holden), Russia (Kurt Kasznar), and France (Charles Boyer) visit Sir James, hoping to entice him back into service in order to stop a world domination plot cooked up by an organization known as SMERSH. Of course, the aging superagent is reticent. But the situation changes after M is blown to bits in an explosion (except for his toupee, the "family hair-loom," it's explained). Following James's stop at his late boss's Scottish estate to pay his respects to the man's widow (Deborah Kerr) and six comely daughters, and after some bizarre Scottish rituals that seem to have some link to Austin Powers's Fat Bastard character, Sir James is back in action.

Figuring that the best way to smash SMERSH is to confuse them, James hires impersonators, who soon do indeed confuse all involved, including the film's audience. A lineup of Bonds is trotted out: the fetching Mata Bond (Joanna Pettet), Sir James's abandoned daughter, a "great dancer but lousy spy"; Jimmy Bond (Woody Allen), James's neurotic nephew, last seen facing a firing squad in South America; and, not so finally, Evelyn Tremble (Peter Sellers), a baccarat expert who is given the James Bond moniker after being seduced and recruited by millionaire Vesper Lynd (Ursula Andress). His mission is to face off against SMERSH operative Le Chiffre (Orson Welles) in a high-stakes baccarat match at the Casino Royale, a French gambling hall.

The characters and situations are enough to keep anyone on their toes. But put these elements under the guidance of five different directors and nearly

Woody Allen and Daliah Lavi star in the 1967 Bond spoof *Casino Royale.*

twenty screenwriters (including the uncredited Billy Wilder and Ben Hecht), and add some nasty in-fighting among the cast (Sellers hated Welles so much he quit during production), and it's no surprise that *Casino Royale* is such a jumble.

But what a jumble! As much as there is to loathe—rotten jokes, incomprehensible plotting, and little regard for continuity—there are things to admire and even love about the picture. One can sense the sheer desire of the filmmakers to top themselves scene after scene until everything explodes (literally) at the casino showdown where all the Bonds, SMERSH agents, cowboys, Indians, seals, the French Foreign Legion, and probably a kitchen sink are thrown together. And then there's the cast. All involved seem to have accepted the fact that they're in it just for a nice paycheck and a good time in Europe—they breeze through the proceedings with tongue firmly planted in cheek and wallet. And let's not forget the incredible array of women, a veritable who's who of swinging '60s chicks of all nationalities, usually dressed in lingerie or other undergarments.

Casino Royale's most memorable aspect, however, may be its tremendously lively score by Burt Bacharach, with performance assistance from Herb Alpert and the Tijuana Brass. What's odd is that these artists may have been (and maybe still are) hip in a middle-of-the-road way, but they were enlisted to score what producer Feldman envisioned as an all-out psychedelic movie. It's Bacharach's catchy, hummable melodies and Alpert's spry horn playing that hold this smorgasbord together until the bombastic, bitter end.

1967 131m/C Peter Sellers, Ursula Andress, David Niven, Orson Welles, Joanna Pettet, Daliah Lavi, Woody Allen, Deborah Kerr, William Holden, Charles Boyer, John Huston, Kurt Kasznar, George Raft, Jean-Paul Belmondo, Terence Cooper, Peter O'Toole, Tracey Crisp, Jacqueline Bisset. **D:** John Huston, Ken Hughes, Robert Parrish, Val Guest, Joseph McGrath. **W:** Wolf Mankowitz, John Law, Michael Sayers, Billy Wilder, Val Guest, Ben Hecht, Joseph Heller, Terry Southern. **C:** Jack Hildyard. **M:** Burt Bacharach. *DVD, VHS*

Dr. Goldfoot and the Bikini Machine 🦴🦴

Dr. Goldfoot and the Girl Bombs 🦴

With *Goldfinger* still fresh in the minds of the public, American International Pictures—always on the lookout to cash in on a trend for a quick buck—decided to ape the popular James Bond title and deliver *Dr. Goldfoot and the Bikini Machine,* a kooky concoction of spy spoof, horror opus, and beach party bonanza.

The studio enlisted Vincent Price, for years their Most Valuable Performer in the popular Edgar Allan Poe films, to play the title character. No, not the Bikini Machine—Price is Dr. Goldfoot, a mad scientist with a henchman named Igor (Jack Mullaney), a San Francisco–based laboratory, and a devious

plan: snag the savings of the world's richest men by having sexy bikini-clad robots seduce them, marry them, and make them sign over all their assets, which are then acquired by Goldfoot.

Craig Gamble (AIP's other MVP, *Beach Party* partner Frankie Avalon) is an inept secret agent working for Secret Intelligence Command (SIC) who meets one of the mechanical gals, Diane (Susan Hart), by accident. It seems that Diane, AKA Number 11, has made a mistake, confusing Gamble for her real target, the rich Todd Armstrong (Dwayne Hickman, TV's Dobie Gillis). But Gamble's brief encounter has him smitten, so he tries to track her down. Meanwhile, Diane has found and wooed Armstrong, bilking him out of his holdings. So, the secret agent and the hoodwinked rich kid team up to investigate Diane. This, of course, leads them to Dr. Goldfoot's headquarters.

You can't expect something like *Dr. Goldfoot and the Bikini Machine* to be on the same comedic level with, say, Oscar Wilde's *The Importance of Being Earnest,* so an *Ernest Goes to Camp* level will just have to suffice. Under the direction of veteran Norman Taurog, who handled lots of Martin and Lewis and Elvis movies, the film's a parade of head bumping, pratfalls, and fainting—especially when robot-babe Diane's disembodied hand turns up. A running gag has Avalon trying to please his SIC superior, who just happens to be his uncle (played by cantankerous character actor Fred Clark). Avalon is Agent 00½ and is told that only when he gets a digit instead of a fraction will he be allowed to carry a gun. The other secret agent stuff is pretty superfluous and

Dr. Goldfoot (Vincent Price) encounters Diane (Susan Hart) and Igor (Jack Mullaney) in the lab in *Dr. Goldfoot and the Bikini Machine.*

includes such gadgets as a lipstick that emits an explosive ray and a diabolical and all-knowing computer. As expected, smarmy double entendres abound, as do the impressive bikini bods, including *Playboy* Playmates Deanna Lund (best known later for *Land of the Giants* and for dating Larry King) and China Lee, wife of comic Mort Sahl.

Thankfully, AIP script regular Robert Kaufman gives Vincent Price an opportunity to spoof his AIP persona. Dr. Goldfoot's screaming room is a virtual "best of" collection of inside jokes, containing photos of Price as various Poe villains, the instrument of torture from *The Pit and the Pendulum,* and appearances from studio faves Annette Funicello, Harvey Lembeck, and others. And the film has some other things going for it: an opening stop-motion credit sequence by Art "Gumby" Clokey; a truly zany car, motorcycle, and cable-car chase through the hilly streets of San Francisco that predates Steve McQueen's *Bullitt;* and a theme song by the Supremes, on loan from Motown.

Dr. Goldfoot and the Bikini Machine may not have been a gold mine for AIP, but despite racking up the low-budget studio's record-high $1 million budget, it did turn a tidy profit, especially at drive-ins, where it was the featured attraction with other AIP offerings.

In fact, *Dr. Goldfoot* brought in enough cash to justify a sequel, *Dr. Goldfoot and the Girl Bombs,* a year later. Price was recruited to replay the doctor, while Philly-born teen idol Frankie Avalon was replaced by another Philly-born teen star, Fabian.

In this film, Dr. Goldfoot assembles a group of scantily clad superhuman babes who have the ability to make men who come close to them blow up real good. Tracking down the gorgeous fembots in Italy are SIC secret agent Dexter (Fabian) and Italian comics Franco and Ciccio, bumbling hotel workers who aspire to become secret agents.

The shift to an Italian locale was predicated by a deal between AIP and a producer named Fulvio Lucisano. Both parties wanted sequels, AIP for the original *Goldfoot* and Lucisano for the Franco and Ciccio hit *Two Mafia Guys vs. Goldfinger.* The idea was to market the picture differently to each of the markets, American and Italian, editing the footage to suit each producer's needs. Hired to handle the directing chores was Mario Bava, the Italian macabre specialist behind the classics *Black Sunday, Black Sabbath,* and the soon-to-come *Danger: Diabolik.*

The results are nothing less than a cross-cultural calamity. The slapstick antics of Franco (the spitting image of film critic Michael Medved) and Ciccio (a Dick Shawn look-alike) are jaw-droppingly awful; Fabian seems to be wandering around Rome in search of a cheesesteak; and the film's action sequences—including an elaborate balloon chase—make Benny Hill's work look like William Friedkin's. On the plus side, Les Baxter's score at times plays like an affectionate salute to Burt Bacharach's *Casino Royale* work; a young Laura Antonelli offers us a peek at a sexpot-in-the-making; and Price is, as usual, priceless.

Dr. Goldfoot and the Bikini Machine
1965 88m/C Vincent Price, Frankie Avalon, Dwayne Hickman, Susan Hart, Jack Mullaney, Fred Clark, Alberta Nelson, Milton Frome. *D:* Norman Taurog. *W:* Elwood Ullman, Robert Kaufman. *C:* Sam Leavitt. *M:* Les Baxter. *VHS, DVD*

Dr. Goldfoot and the Girl Bombs

1966 90m/C *IT* Vincent Price, Fabian, Franco Franchi, Ciccio Ingrassia, Francesco Mulé, Laura Antonelli. *D:* Mario Bava. *W:* Louis Hayward, Robert Kaufman. *C:* Antonio Rinaldi. *M:* Les Baxter. *VHS, DVD*
AKA: Dr. Goldfoot and the "S" Bomb; Dr. Goldfoot and the Love Bombs; Dr. Goldfoot and the Sex Bombs

Fathom 🦴🦴

It didn't hurt that the promotional posters for *Fathom* featured Raquel Welch in a bikini. Hell, Raquel Welch in a bikini could pretty much sell anything in 1967. Even phony dinosaurs didn't stop people from going to see her perform in a loincloth in *One Million Years, B.C.*

This time out, the folks at 20th Century Fox decided to give her a movie with an actual plot—perhaps too much plot. As Fathom Harvill, Raquel is probably the world's first skydiving dental hygienist spy—or at least the world's first skydiving dental hygienist spy with the measurements of 39-22-33.

Fathom is an American engaged in a skydiving tour of Spain when she's recruited by operatives from an organization called HADES to save the world. Her mission: parachute into the area near the home of two agents working for the Red Chinese (played by Anthony Franciosa and Greta Chi) and try to retrieve "Fire Dragon," a contraption that can detonate an atomic bomb. As she completes her mission, Raquel jiggles from one action scene to another in skimpy swimsuits and micro-minis and runs into a host of threatening characters including a shifty Soviet antiques dealer (Clive Revill) and an imposing skin diver (Tom Adams).

Fathom offers a seductive title sequence, designed by Bond regular Maurice Binder, in which Fathom gets her skydiving gear in erotic order. The film has gorgeous Spanish locales and unpredictable, potentially colorful characters, including Franciosa in a bleached-blond Terence Stamp–like 'do. Despite the numerous Raquel-in-peril diving sequences, there's little energy to the proceedings, which is surprising since director Leslie Martinson and screenwriter Lorenzo Semple Jr. (*Pretty Poison, Flash Gordon*) were fresh off the highly entertaining big-screen version of the *Batman* TV show.

Ultimately, the film's fortunes lie on the bosom of its star. But here, Welch, despite the killer bod and dynamite looks, has zero personality: she seems little more than a cardboard cutout of a risk-taking heroine. Sure, she's nice to watch, but once she opens her mouth, we can't buy her as a real person. In the acting department, she's flat. Ironic, isn't it?

1967 104m/C Raquel Welch, Anthony Franciosa, Ronald Fraser, Greta Chi, Tom Adams, Clive Revill, Richard Briers. *D:* Leslie Martinson. *W:* Lorenzo Semple Jr. *C:* Douglas Slocombe. *M:* John Dankworth. *VHS, DVD*

The Glass Bottom Boat 🦴🦴🦴

Caprice 🦴🦴

The Glass Bottom Boat is a spy movie your whole family can watch. In fact, I can recall seeing the film with my grandmother when I was nine years old. I don't know if she really expected a movie about spies, but she knew that with Doris Day's name on the picture, whatever adult material was on the screen would be clean enough for her movie-savvy grandson.

Doris Day, year after year one of Hollywood's box-office champs, had to get hip to the times and appeal to a younger audience, and it's no surprise that she went the spy route so popular in 1966. And, as sort of a farewell to that virginal Doris everyone had come to know and love, The Glass Bottom Boat begins with Doris losing her fins in order to make new fans.

Let me explain: Jennifer Nelson (Day) is a mermaid in father Arthur Godfrey's Florida sea show, where he runs a glass-bottomed boat cruise and plays the ukulele. One day her costume comes off after a mishap involving the fishing rod of Bruce Templeton (Rod Taylor), a scientist working at a local think tank. But this was still a family movie, and the people on the glass-bottomed boat didn't get a good glimpse of the finless Day. Jennifer's other job (the mermaid gig probably doesn't keep her in kelp) is at Templeton's think tank. At this point, though, Jennifer doesn't realize that he's the same guy who de-finned her.

Templeton is an inventor whose newest discovery is a thingamajig called GISMO, used to prevent weightlessness in space. It's obvious early on that mistaken identity will play a part in the secret-agent goings-on; in fact, most of the comedy in the film hinges on it. When Jennifer's phone calls to her dog Vladimir are misconstrued as contact with the Russians, she's mistaken for a Soviet spy out to snag Templeton's device. Templeton, meanwhile, is smitten with Jennifer, and he hires her to write his biography. Jennifer starts to like him right back. But soon the FBI, General Wallace (Edward Andrews), and Bruce's coworker, Zack (Dick Martin), are misreading Jennifer as well.

Even though the plot seems routine, The Glass Bottom Boat is fairly successful at spoofing the spy genre. Day is game and sexy as the gal innocently caught up in the internecine thrills. What's weird about her character is that every time she comes close to Taylor or kisses him, she seems to be on the verge of collapse. Can she really be that needy for human contact, or is he so much of a stud that women lose muscle control when they get anywhere near him?

Along with the always dependable Taylor, the film sports a notable cast of '60s comedians that includes a frighteningly thin and hairy Dom DeLuise (as a real Soviet spy), a pre–Laugh-In Martin, and Paul Lynde as a suspicious security guard who gets to dress in drag for a lengthy party scene. In that same scene is a nifty cameo by Robert Vaughn as Napoleon Solo, the character from TV's The Man from U.N.C.L.E., which was running at the time on NBC. (Both Glass Bottom Boat and U.N.C.L.E. were produced by MGM.)

Director Frank Tashlin, the onetime Warner Bros. cartoon maestro who also helmed some of Jerry Lewis's better efforts as well as *The Girl Can't Help It,* shows he's an old pro at slapstick and character juggling.

The Glass Bottom Boat proved successful at the box office, and Day and her production company, headed by then-husband Martin Melcher, must have assumed that winning over the new, young audience without alienating her aging fans was a breeze. So, the actress tried to take things higher, '60s style, with *Caprice,* a year later.

Doris is Patricia Fowler, the daughter of an Interpol agent who was murdered by drug smugglers. She's hired by Femina, a cosmetics company, to swipe formulas from rival firm May Fortune, which has introduced such "miracle drugs" as a water repellent hairspray, developed by former Femina employee Stuart Clancy (Ray Walston). Soon, Fowler finds herself in a web of silly suspense involving the different cosmetics companies, secret agents, drug dealing, and her romantic interest, Christopher White (Richard Harris), a spy working for both Femina and May Fortune.

For the most part, *Caprice*'s plot is a jumble. One can sense Tashlin, who was recruited to call the shots after the success of *The Glass Bottom Boat,* huffing and puffing to keep the spies, action sequences, jokes, and expected Doris Day–type elements afloat. Meanwhile, Day is given a genuine '60s wardrobe, filled with polka-dot miniskirts, checkerboard-style trench coats, and mod hats. Her appearance must have elicited open-mouthed amazement among her middle-aged fans—among the few that showed up, anyway.

Caprice marked the beginning and the end of Day's calculated attempt to win over the children of her typical fans. And it may have marked the beginning of the end of her illustrious career: after two more movies—the more conventional *Ballad of Josie* and *With Six You Get Egg Roll*—Day retired. Que sera sera.

The Glass Bottom Boat
1966 110m/C Doris Day, Rod Taylor, Arthur Godfrey, John McGiver, Paul Lynde, Edward Andrews, Eric Fleming, Dom DeLuise, Dick Martin. *D:* Frank Tashlin. *W:* Everett Freeman. *C:* Leon Shamroy. *M:* Frank De Vol. *VHS*

Caprice
1967 95m/C Doris Day, Richard Harris, Ray Walston, Jack Kruschen, Edward Mulhare, Lilia Skala. *D:* Frank Tashlin. *W:* Jay Jayson, Frank Tashlin, Martin Hale. *C:* Leon Shamroy. *M:* Frank De Vol. *VHS*

The Last of the Secret Agents? ♫♫

As Bondmania swept into the '60s following the mega box-office returns of Sean Connery's debut as 007 in 1962's *Dr. No,* every Hollywood studio was looking to capitalize on the secret agent's success. Some of them went the comedy route: Columbia gave Dean Martin a handgun to go with his martini and created a Matt Helm cycle that started with *The Silencers.*

And 20th Century Fox spoofed Bond with the ingenious *Flint* films featuring super-suave James Coburn as the dick named Derek. MGM even enticed Doris Day to go undercover with 1966's *The Glass Bottom Boat.* Paramount's jump into the spy fray, 1966's *The Last of the Secret Agents?,* gave them the chance to replace their highly profitable but now defunct comedy team of Martin and Lewis. This largely misguided spoof features Marty Allen and Steve Rossi as Americans slumming it in Cannes. They are enlisted by a top-secret British organization to track down a hairless fiend named Zoltan Schubach (Theodore Marcuse), who has been stealing the world's greatest art treasures.

At the time, Allen and Rossi were a popular act in nightclubs and regulars on *The Ed Sullivan Show.* Rossi's handsome crooner played straight man to pop-eyed, fuzzyheaded Allen's "Hello dere!" shtick. In the film, the twosome stumble about while unknowingly thwarting Zultan, finally foiling his attempt to swipe the *Venus de Milo* from a museum in England. But Allen and Rossi were middle-of-the-road entertainers who had more appeal on the Vegas Strip than with moviegoing kids, and the movie's fish-out-of-water experiment turns into a fish fry.

Writer-director Norman Abbott (*The Munsters, Get Smart*) mounts this production with a clichéd grooviness that doesn't jibe with the personalities of its leading duo. His attempts at hip include a swinging title sequence (chirped by costar Nancy Sinatra and featuring lots of scantily clad people in Ray-Bans), a topless restaurant, a bevy of babes (like Sinatra, Mariana Hill, and Phyllis Davis), and high-tech gadgets that wouldn't make it into Q's junk pile. Particularly puzzling is an Ed Sullivan cameo and a sequence that comes from way out in left field where Allen and Rossi get caught up in the filming of a war movie in which Harvey Korman plays a Nazi commandant.

The Last of the Secret Agents? was Allen and Rossi's first attempt to bring their act to the big screen. It was also, appropriately, pretty much the last we ever heard of the comedy team's big-screen career. Goodbye, dere!

1966 92m/C Marty Allen, Steve Rossi, John Williams, Nancy Sinatra, Lou Jacobi, Carmen, Theodore Marcuse, Connie Sawyer, Harvey Korman. **D:** Mel Tolkin. **W:** Mel Tolkin, Norman Abbott. **C:** Harold E. Stine. **M:** Lee Hazlewood, Neal Hefti, Pete King. *VHS*

The Man Called Flintstone ♫♫♫

In 1966 the spy craze was heating up as the run of the animated TV show *The Flintstones* was winding down. So producers William Hanna and Joseph Barbera decided to arm Fred and Barney and company with a secret-agent story and set them loose on the big screen. The result is a surprisingly engaging cartoon adventure that, while no great shakes in the plot department, manages to get some laughs and elicit thrills from those accustomed to seeing the first family of Bedrock in short form on their TV screens.

The Man Called Flintstone concerns a secret agent named Rock Slag, a Fred Flintstone look-alike who is out to stop the ominous Green Goose and foil his plans for world domination. After being chased by Green Goose henchmen Ali and Boo-Boo, Slag winds up in the hospital on the mend. Chief Boulder, seeing the spitting image of Slag in Fred, entices Flintstone, with cash and first-class tickets to Eurock, to track down the Green Goose. A joint Flintstone/Rubble family vacation is put on hold and soon, after a crowded bird-plane ride, the families land in Paris. Before long, Ali and Boo-Boo are on Fred's trail. Chief Boulder then sends Fred and family (Rubbles in tow, of course) to Rome, where Fred is to join forces with Triple X, a foreign operative and master of disguise, to locate the Green Goose's base of operation.

Bond and his secret agent progeny are saluted throughout *The Man Called Flintstone* with some genuine wit: there's a catchy theme song over a montage of shadowy images; Fred becomes hot with the ladies when he's mistaken for the real Rock Slag; Ali and Boo-Boo are the sort of inept sidekicks Bond often finds himself up against; and the Green Goose's world domination plot involves the firing of a missile from a missile-shaped amusement ride. There's also Tanya, the femme fatale with a cigarette holder and Russian accent who bears more than a slight resemblance to Natasha of *Rocky and Bullwinkle* fame. And no wonder: the voice behind the cartoon face belongs to June Foray, AKA Natasha (and many other cartoon voices of the past four decades).

Fun as it is, *The Man Called Flintstone* does have problems: too many musical numbers (though one in which Pebbles and Bam-Bam imagine they're in an interstellar amusement park is downright trippy) and, in a waste of his thespian talent, Barney barely gets involved in the action. Still, if you're a fan of TV's *The Flintstones* and the spy flicks of the era, you'll likely get at least a few yabba-dabba-doos out of the experience.

1966 90m/C V: Alan Reed, Mel Blanc, Jean Vander Pyl, Gerry Johnson, Don Messic, Janet Waldo, June Foray, Paul Frees, Harvey Korman. **D:** Joseph Barbera, William Hanna. **W:** Harvey Bullock, R. S. Allen. **C:** Charles Flekal. **M:** Marty Paich, Ted Nichols. *VHS*

Modesty Blaise

> **Nothing can faze Modesty Blaise, the world's deadliest and most dazzlingly female agent!**
>
> —Tagline for *Modesty Blaise*

I f movies were graded on accessories, *Modesty Blaise* would be on a par with *Citizen Kane*.

This incomprehensible botch of good source material—Peter O'Donnell's 1960s comic books and subsequent novels—is misconceived on almost every level, from casting on down. Italian sexpot and Michelangelo Antonioni favorite Monica Vitti (*L'Eclisse*) is the title character, a special agent called out of retirement by a British intelligence agency to get in the middle of a deal involving a 50,000-pound diamond shipment. At first, Modesty—sporting a scorpion tattoo on her thigh, gun umbrella, and lots of tough 'tude—remains reticent about getting back into the espionage game, vowing she'll take the diamonds from the British stiff-upper-lips who hired her if she's double-crossed. But it doesn't take her long to get gung-ho about her return. It helps that her onetime partner, Willie Garven (Terence Stamp), a swinging spy who can seduce and kill with the best of them, is joining her on the assignment.

The primary bad guy in *Modesty Blaise* is the outrageously rich, more-than-slightly effeminate creep Gabriel, who actually announces at some point

Monica Vitti, with help from Terence Stamp (left) and Dirk Bogarde, takes *Modesty Blaise* to hallucinogenic excess.

20TH CENTURY FOX / THE KOBAL COLLECTION

that "I'm the villain of the piece." Gabriel's ornate island compound serves as his headquarters for dastardly maneuvers, the latest of which involves the deal with the diamonds. Dirk Bogarde has such a gay old time playing the flamboyant Gabriel that the entire role seems like the then-closeted Bogarde's coming-out party.

The source material and premise provide more than enough on which to hang a solid Bond spoof or serious thriller. But director Joseph Losey, an American exiled in Europe since the 1950s because of Communist ties, was apparently obsessed with being outré and overly eager to burst out of the constraints of the sophisticated, dialogue-driven dramas (like *The Servant* and *Accident*) that had won him so much praise. This desire to be so "with it," so trendsetting, is perhaps the best explanation for *Modesty Blaise*'s very 1960s excesses. After all, who cares if the English language—corrupting Vitti is terribly miscast as long as we have plenty of costume changes (gold lamé is big), a wide array of hair styles and colors, and production touches that include Escher-inspired wallpaper designs and real goldfish in martini glasses? Add to this a tendency for Oscar-winning cinematographer Jack Hildyard (*The Bridge on the River Kwai*) to go gaga with his zoom lens and you've got one big, fat hallucinogenic headache.

While the film's critical and box-office failure killed the chance of a proposed film series, the Modesty Blaise character wasn't completely KO'd. A short-lived 1982 TV series posited ex-model (and former wife of Richard Harris)

Anne Turkel as Modesty, though it left airwaves in a blaze. As of this writing, a major Quentin Tarantino–produced project with Uma Thurman returning Modesty to her not-so-modest beginnings has been downshifted to a streamlined direct-to-video feature from Miramax's low-budget Dimension Pictures offshoot. Sounds like a "been there, done that, got a gold lamé T-shirt" type of project.

To be fair, *Modesty Blaise* does have its fans, most of whom claim that it takes four or five viewings to get into the film's frame of mind and appreciate it on its own extravagant terms. Others think the film suffers from a case of being all dressed up with nowhere to go, whether you've watched *Modesty Blaise* two or twenty-two times.

1966 (NR) 119m/C Monica Vitti, Terence Stamp, Dirk Bogarde, Harry Andrews, Michael Craig, Clive Revill, Alexander Knox, Rossella Falk. **D:** Joseph Losey. **W:** Evan Jones. **C:** Jack Hildyard. **M:** John Dankworth. *VHS, DVD*

Operation Kid Brother

Blazing a trail that would later be traveled by Don Swayze, Jim Hanks, Joey Travolta, and Pamela Springsteen, Neil Connery tries to sponge off of the name his talented sibling made famous. But this Italian production is more than just a cash-in vehicle for the junior Connery: *Operation Kid Brother* is also probably the most blatant rip-off in cinema history. For not only does Neil appear in a Bond-like spy movie at the height of 007 mania, but the producers also managed to call his character Connery, make mention of the role his brother plays, and contract several faces familiar from the Bond series to take part in this production, including regulars Bernard Lee (M) and Lois Maxwell (Miss Moneypenny).

While Neil is not challenged in the hairline department like Sean, he does come up short when it comes to emoting, adding zero charisma to his character, a hypnotist from Columbia University who has arrived in Monte Carlo to demonstrate his groundbreaking work in the field of facial surgery and hypnosis. Although the link between the two is muddy at best, we learn that Dr. Connery has used the power of suggestion to help his patients' horrible scars to heal at an amazingly rapid rate. The problem arrives in the form of a woman with a dark secret planted in her subconscious, making her the target of a group of creeps who want to use her to control the world and get rich in the process. The solution? Dr. Connery is recruited by an intelligence agency to track down the patient and foil the plan before it's too late.

Adolfo Celi plays the chief bad guy, and as in every other film he made after his memorably villainous turn as Largo in *Thunderball,* he seems to be riffing on that character. Here he wears a monocle in lieu of Largo's eyepatch, smokes extremely long, thin cigars, and gets horny watching his treacherous moves projected onto the naked backs of his yacht's female crewmates. Hey, it's a living.

In addition to the aforementioned Lee and Maxwell (who merely go through the motions here), other Bond refugees on hand are Daniela Bianchi,

OPERATION KID BROTHER Is Too Much for One Mother!

—Tagline for *Operation Kid Brother*

Tatiana Romanova (both of *From Russia with Love* fame), and Anthony Dawson (*From Russia with Love* and *Dr. No*).

As shameless and embarrassing as *Operation Kid Brother* is at times, it is not unwatchable, and it's even worth recommending to anyone who has a fascination for films that are truly one of a kind. Such viewers will stare in open-mouthed amazement and wonder how the producers got away with this folly, from the bombastic, 007-ish title tune to the swiping of John Barry and Monty Norman's classic Bond score (the great Ennio Morricone and Bruno Nicolai are the culprits).

Some demerits must be given to Italian director Alberto De Martino, who trots out the Bond trappings like a kid at show-and-tell and does so with little style and even less wit. De Martino later honed his craft of knocking off box-office bonanzas by cashing in on *The Exorcist* with his *The Tempter* and on *The Omen* with his *Holocaust 2000* (AKA *The Chosen*).

At the center of it all, however, is Neil Connery. You'd think pulling in some cash from under his brother's nose with *Operation Kid Brother* would have been enough, but no, it wasn't. In 1984 Neil did the James Bond thing again in the Hong Kong caper film *Aces Go Places 3* (AKA *Mad Mission 3*), which also featured *Goldfinger*'s Harold Sakata, reprising his Oddjob character, and Richard Kiel, AKA Jaws.

Wouldn't you like to be a fly on the wall at a Connery family dinner?

1967 104m/C Neil Connery, Daniela Bianchi, Adolfo Celi, Agata Flori, Bernard Lee, Lois Maxwell, Guido Lollobrigida. *D:* Alberto De Martino. *W:* Paolo Levi, Frank Walker, Stanley Wright, Stefano Canzio, Vincenzo Mannino. *C:* Alejandro Ulloa, Gianni Bergamimi. *M:* Ennio Morricone, Bruno Nicolai. *VHS*
AKA: OK Connery; Secret Agent 00; Operation Double 007

> ## "Repeat after me: I am not a pleasure unit."
>
> —Derek Flint (James Coburn), in *Our Man Flint*

Our Man Flint 🦴🦴🦴

In Like Flint 🦴🦴🦴

Ask Mike Myers and he'll fess up: there would be no *Austin Powers* if it weren't for the two James Coburn *Flint* films of the 1960s. The inspiration is plain as day—the women, the gadgets, the villains, the "fembots," the attitude, the production design, even the sound of the phone ring.

The two Flint films were, in fact, 20th Century Fox's attempt to carve out a piece of the secret-agent pie that United Artists so successfully baked. And while the first outing—1966's *Our Man Flint*—was a fairly successful movie, Derek Flint has, in many ways, lived in the shadow of 007. So we can at least thank Mike Myers for shining a spotlight on the special agent and his two movies, which are usually overlooked by the young crowd who idolize the *Austin Powers* movies.

Derek Flint is a cool, calculating superspy with an overactive libido to match his outsized self-assurance. Played by James Coburn, himself a bastion of '60s cool (taking martial arts lessons from Bruce Lee, participating in LSD experimentation with Ken Kesey), Flint is also an easygoing operative, a genuine eccentric with an unpredictable rebellious streak, making him trouble for both the criminal masterminds he confronts and the secret service types who hire him.

In *Our Man Flint,* Flint is summoned by Cramden (Lee J. Cobb), a top dog at ZOWIE (Zonal Organization of World Intelligence and Espionage), to stop a nefarious group called Galaxy from controlling the world's weather. Flint lives in a posh Manhattan apartment, which is guarded by German shepherds and populated by a quartet of international beauties who cater to the agent's every desire, from sex to massages.

When it's time for Flint to go to work, however, he's all business, using his intellect and masterful karate moves to destroy Malcolm Rodney (Edward Mulhare), Galaxy's reigning megalomaniac; his sexy sidekick, Gila (Gila Golan, Miss Israel 1961); and assorted henchmen and scientists (recruited to make inactive volcanoes erupt and icebergs crash into the Mediterranean).

There's no denying that Bond is the satirical target here, but Coburn, director Daniel Mann (*Willard*), and screenwriter Hal Fimberg (who penned some Marx Brothers and Abbott and Costello films) get points for creating a fresh and original character. Beyond the gals, the guns, and the gadgets

JAMES COBURN: OUR MAN JIM by Lowell Goldman

James Coburn

"**T**he producer, Saul David [*Fantastic Voyage*], was really responsible for the success of the Flint films," declared the late James Coburn in a 1991 interview. "He deserves all the credit."

David cast Coburn, who died in 2002, as the title character of *Our Man Flint*. "What I liked about the character was that he was his own man," Coburn stated. "He even trained himself in the martial arts.

"The challenge in the first film was the idea of the individual versus the Establishment," continued Coburn. "We wanted to make it the antithesis of [James] Bond. After all, Bond was really in bondage to the British government. We tried to work from that theme."

Coburn revealed that the cast and crew often improvised scenes. "In one scene in the first film, Flint was attacked in the men's room. When I jumped up and kicked the poor guy, the toilet paper flew up in the air and slowly floated down. It was just an accident. But, it worked on screen and got a few laughs."

As *Our Man Flint* was a surprise box-office hit, the studio (Fox) quickly ordered a sequel. "If you recall, the women were trying to take over the world in the second Flint," stated Coburn. "It was very topical. But the studio really didn't support us with that concept. They just wanted to make the film and get it out."

According to Coburn, the script for *In Like Flint* wasn't ready when they began shooting. "We actually started the picture without an ending. The script wasn't finished in time. Then they made

(including a multitasking cigarette lighter), there's a real edge to Flint because of his unpredictability.

Galaxy's ultimate plan is to stop nuclear arms and wipe out wars. In order to do so, they want to distribute an aphrodisiac to the world's population and release sex-seeking female zombie "pleasure units" (or fembots, as Mike Myers might call them).

One would think that Flint, given his hedonistic lifestyle and keen interest in international politics, would be on board with such a plan. But as he's about to squash Galaxy for good, our secret agent informs his rivals, "Now it won't be a perfect world." Why? "Because it was your idea, not mine!" he says. A suave but surly secret agent hung up on his own good-guy heroics is the kind of complex character that makes *Our Man Flint* so interesting decades after its release.

Unfortunately, *In Like Flint,* the 1967 follow-up, is less so. Cramden once again calls Flint into the world of espionage when three minutes in the up an end for the film while Saul [David] was working on a different ending."

Although vet helmer Gordon Douglas (*The Detective*) received credit on screen, Coburn revealed that he wasn't the only director. "My stunt double [Buzz Henry] and the cinematographer [William H. Daniels] really directed most of the film. And I'd include myself," added Coburn. "You see, Gordon Douglas was ill for most of the shoot. He had a heart problem or something. We had to work fast. We also shot a lot of the film in Jamaica. But that was the fun of it. We really had a great group of team players."

In Like Flint also featured a bevy of scantily clad young women. "Most of them were girlfriends of the men working at the studio. It was playtime for those guys," recalled Coburn with his distinctive laugh.

The sequel also did brisk business at the box office. "The studio wanted more Flint films. But it just didn't work out. The studio just didn't seem to care about quality anymore. And they eventually lost interest in the series."

After the first Flint film, Coburn was in demand as a leading man. He starred in *Dead Heat on a Merry-Go-Round* (1966) and *The President's Analyst* (1967), both satires that have risen to the status of cult films over the years.

Candy (1968) was loosely based on Terry Southern's sexy novel. Coburn, who played an eccentric brain surgeon, was joined by Marlon Brando, Richard Burton, Ringo Starr, Walter Matthau, and Charles Aznavour in the all-star cast. "That film could have been much better and a lot more amusing," lamented Coburn. "We had a French director [Christian Marquand]. And the director's timing was of a European nature. The jokes were always a beat behind. They were often a beat off. When you do a comedy like *Candy,* you've got to be fast."

The flick *Duffy* (1968) was a cool crime caper with Coburn as the title character, a hippie living in Europe who takes part in swindling the wealthy father of two half-brothers. "You know, Duffy was one of my favorite characters," noted the actor. "At least that cat had something to say."

life of U.S. President Trent (Andrew Duggan) can't be accounted for. Something's fishy, all right: unbeknownst to Cramden or the rest of the world, during those three minutes, the president was kidnapped and replaced with an actor.

Behind the kidnapping is a group of women led by Lisa (Jean Hale, in a role intended for Catherine Deneuve). The group is working out of an exclusive health spa in the Caribbean and aims to run the world by brainwashing other women through beauty parlor hairdryers. They also have an interest in two female cosmonauts involved in a Russian space program called Project Damocles. Flint's investigation takes him to Moscow (where he has a liaison with a Russian ballerina played by Yvonne "Batgirl" Craig) and to Cuba, via a hijacked airplane, where he poses as Fidel Castro.

If *In Like Flint* sounds like it's all over the place, that's because it is, moving from country to country and world-threatening predicament to world-threatening predicament without the greatest of ease. And though director Gordon Douglas (the Rat Pack's fave filmmaker) gets Coburn to maintain his unflappable persona, Flint is simply less interesting here, tackling a group of diabolical feminists he basically pooh-poohs as being no match for him—or any man for that manner. The anti–women's lib dialogue delivered by Flint and Cramden is so insensitive and misogynistic that you end up rooting for these evil gals.

Our Man Flint
1966 (NR) 107m/C James Coburn, Lee J. Cobb, Gila Golan, Edward Mulhare, Benson Fong, Shelby Grant, Sigrid Valdis, Gianna Serra, James Brolin. *D:* Daniel Mann. *W:* Hal Fimberg, Ben Starr. *C:* Daniel Fapp. *M:* Jerry Goldsmith. *VHS, DVD*

In Like Flint
1967 (NR) 104m/C James Coburn, Lee J. Cobb, Jean Hale, Andrew Duggan, Anna Lee, Hannah Landy, Steve Ihnat. *D:* Gordon Douglas. *W:* Hal Fimberg. *C:* William H. Daniels. *M:* Jerry Goldsmith. *VHS, DVD*

The President's Analyst ♫♫♫♩

O ne of the most absorbing and darkly humorous films of the 1960s, *The President's Analyst* is a gonzo satire that tackles a wide variety of subjects ranging from international politics to racism, from gun control to undercover intelligence, and from the free love movement to the phone company. The phone company? More on that later.

James Coburn is the title character, a successful New York psychiatrist named Sidney Schaefer who is invited by patient Don Masters (Godfrey Cambridge) to work as the personal shrink to the president of the United States. Masters is, in fact, a government agent who has been investigating Schaefer between psychiatry sessions (which encompass some disturbing, racially oriented dreams), particularly looking into his work assassinating Albanian agents in the garment district of Manhattan.

Coburn takes the gig and moves to a nifty government-appointed home in Georgetown, the trendy D.C. neighborhood. He is joined by his commitment-weary girlfriend Nan (Joan Delaney).

At first, Schaefer seems happy with the situation, serving as a sounding board for the most powerful man in the free world. But because of his erratic schedule, the president can have no set appointments, leaving Schaefer on call at all times. Soon after their first session, Schaefer gets another call. And another. And another. The commander-in-chief needs lots of help, and Schaefer grows frustrated with the frequency and timing of the calls. Sensing his irritability, two federal agents decide that the secrets being told to Schaefer are so delicate that Nan must move into a hotel rather than risk hearing classified information if Schaefer talks in his sleep.

Dr. Schaefer begins having delusions, and soon nightmares and paranoia set in. He believes enemy agents, Nan among them, are after him and that he's constantly being watched and bugged. As quitting the job is out of

Does your mother still think Folk-Rock is a landmark in New England? Your daughter's boyfriend have longer hair than she has? Is your football helmet crushing the flowers in your hair?

—Tagline for *The President's Analyst*

James Coburn—playing Sidney Schaefer, head-shrinker to the commander-in-chief—and Joan Delaney star in the dark satire *The President's Analyst*. PARAMOUNT / THE KOBAL COLLECTION

the question, he seeks advice from his own analyst and mentor (Will Geer), but the doctor is nowhere to be found.

The President's Analyst is a fairly straightforward satire until Schaefer begins to wig out. Watching the ultracool Coburn become unhinged is downright unsettling. As the character slides into paranoia and loses control of his tightly controlled life, the film seems to be losing control as well. It becomes more episodic and more absurd but also more daring: the line between what Schaefer is imagining and what is really happening to him becomes blurred.

The film tackles an abundance of subjects, and writer/director Theodore Flicker, a veteran TV director who would later work regularly on *Barney Miller,* lines up his targets and blows them away in rapid succession and with gusto. Consider:

. . . Schaefer goes AWOL from the White House, joining a family of tourists on a trip back home to Seaside Heights, New Jersey. But this self-professed liberal family—a gun-toting dad (the father from *The Graduate,* William Daniels), a karate-obsessed mother (Joan Darling), and a teenage son whose hobbies include wiretapping—are not textbook "liberals" by any stretch of the imagination. In these sequences, the film sets about decimating the values of middle-class suburbia and liberalism.

. . . Seeking shelter from hit men in New York's Chinatown, Schaefer holes up in an RV populated by a druggie rock group and their groupies. Free love and the flower power movement are given a good satirical thumping here, with Coburn (who, ironically, was an early LSD experimenter) looking hilariously out of place, donning a Beatles-style wig while hiding out with hippies.

. . . The number of spies and assassins out to either kill or kidnap Schaefer grows larger as the film goes on. In one of the film's most memorable sequences, Schaefer makes love to Snow White (Jill Banner), a fetching hippie chick, in a field of flowers. At the same time, he's being spied on by several assassins, each unaware of the others, whose various weapons are eventually used not on Schaefer but on each other. The sequence's punchline is a real kicker, a hilarious but sobering commentary on the futility of espionage.

. . . The Russian agent Kropotkin (Severn Darden), who attempts to convince Schaefer to defect after failing to kill him in the aforementioned scene, is downright sympathetic, eventually confessing some deep-rooted problems to his target/analyst. In 1967, with the Cold War still raging, this is pretty daring stuff. Just say "nyet" to Cold War caricatures!

The ultimate put-down, however, is saved for the "Phone Company," a thinly disguised Bell Telephone, portrayed here as a universally hated, corrupt operation. Run in a secret lair by a robotic man in a three-piece suit (Pat Harrington Jr., AKA Duane Schneider of *One Day at a Time*), the Phone Company uses brainwashing, blackmailing, and bugging as standard operating procedures.

It's no wonder *The President's Analyst* has been causing trouble since Paramount first released it, about the same time as *The Graduate* hit theaters, in 1967. For example, the FBI and CIA, reportedly steamed over being portrayed as murderous AND incompetent, have had their acronyms in the film changed to FBR and CEA, and any mention of them in the film's dialogue appears to have been dubbed over. The funny takeoff on J. Edgar Hoover—a cranky, megalomaniacal little man who sits in a big chair giving out orders—certainly didn't help relations with the feds either. And some copyright problems have forced the studio to change bits of the soundtrack and alter a scene or two.

Will we ever see the complete, unexpurgated version of *The President's Analyst* again? If not, we can only draw one conclusion: it's a conspiracy!

1967 (PG) 103m/C James Coburn, Godfrey Cambridge, Severn Darden, Joan Delaney, Arlington Hewes, Barry Maguire, Jill Banner, Eduard Franz, Walter Burke, Will Geer, William Daniels, Joan Darling, Arte Johnson. *D:* Theodore J. Flicker. *W:* Theodore J. Flicker. *C:* William A. Fraker. *M:* Lalo Schifrin. *VHS, DVD*

The Silencers 𝄢𝄢ᵛ

Murderers' Row 𝄢𝄢

The Ambushers 𝄢𝄢

The Wrecking Crew 𝄢𝄢

In the four Matt Helm movies, star Dean Martin drinks like a fish, smokes like a chimney, and beds down members of the opposite sex like a jackrabbit. For the most part, Dino seems to be having the time of his life, taking *The Dean Martin Show* to the big screen and, for good measure, adding a few stunts here, some secret-agent ingredients there.

The Matt Helm series was Columbia Pictures' response to United Artists' James Bond films. Every Hollywood studio—and many of the independent producers—trotted out their Bond knockoffs in the wake of *Dr. No*'s success, but Columbia's excursion into "Bond-age" was a little more personal: producer Irving Allen was a former business partner of 007 impresario Albert "Cubby" Broccoli. When the two severed ties, Allen wanted to get his own supersleuth franchise off the ground at Columbia. He chose Matt Helm as his subject.

Helm was created by Donald Hamilton, but the writer's concept was worlds away from the movies' version. As introduced in the 1960 novel *Death of a Citizen,* Helm is a World War II vet who gets tangled up in Cold War intrigue, a steely assassin working secret missions for the U.S. government. Amazingly, Hamilton, a writer best known for his work in the western genre before he introduced his secret-agent character, continued to pen Helm books into the 1990s, long after Dino rode Helm into the cinematic sunset.

Martin's Matt Helm made his debut in 1966 with *The Silencers,* a film that took ideas from the book of the same name and from *Death of a Citizen.* The Helm movie staples are introduced promptly, beginning with a groovy title sequence that tips its cowboy hat to Maurice Binder's Bond sequences. But instead of getting arty with silhouettes and chroma-key naked figures, *The Silencers* gets off the ground with a pretty racy striptease. We know immediately what the producers are going for: an all-American steak-and-potatoes approach, no fancy-schmancy Euro-spy stuff.

As Matt Helm, Martin gives us his easygoing Rat Pack persona: a nice guy willing to go along for the ride as long as there's a promise of a belt of booze, a smoke, a chick, and a kick delivered at the end. He's comfy in an apartment that looks like it was designed by Liberace, replete with a circular bed that dumps him into a bubble bath when he needs a wake-up call. Like his print counterpart, Helm doubles as a photojournalist, but Martin seems a lot happier and more comfortable aiming his camera at sizzling sirens than aiming his gun at incredulous creeps.

Helm is semiretired but gets called back into action by his former Intelligence and Counter Espionage (ICE) honcho MacDonald (James Gregory), who wants him to thwart a criminal enterprise called BIGO. BIGO plans to launch Operation Fallout, which involves diverting a government-sponsored underground atomic bomb test in New Mexico, creating a nuclear disaster that will lead to international finger-pointing and, they hope, World War III.

Other 007-inspired elements come fast and furious. There are tricked-out gadgets (a gun that shoots backwards, mini hand-grenades), ridiculous double entendre names (Helm's secretary is Lovey Kravezit, played here and in the other Helms flicks by Beverly Adams), and, yes, a villain of Asian origin à la *Dr. No* (essayed here by the always hammy Victor Buono, King Tut of the *Batman* TV series). We also get soon-to-be-repeated Helm features like Sinatra jokes and offscreen crooning by Dino himself.

The Silencers is moderately enjoyable but not to be taken seriously on any level. Just when you think a line has been drawn on Helm's antics, the producers go one better (come on—a car bar?). Dino gets to ogle the disguised vixen Stella Stevens and the exotic femme fatale Daliah Lavi, but, approaching fifty when the film was made, he comes across not as a swinging bachelor but as a dirty old man trying to keep up with gals half his age.

Handling the directing on *The Silencers* is Phil Karlson, a journeyman B-movie helmer who enjoyed adoration from French critics for his prolific output and edgy thrillers like *Scandal Sheet, Kansas City Confidential,* and *The Phenix City Story.* Karlson, who would go on to make the vigilante smash *Walking Tall,* was afforded the biggest budget of his career and the assistance of legendary cinematographer Burnett Guffey (*Bonnie and Clyde*). But he seems to have been a slave to the burlesque-like proceedings, bringing little flair to the episodic nature of the story.

Of course, audiences hardly noticed, hailing Helm at the box office in such numbers that Columbia Pictures issued *Murderers' Row* later that same year. Karl Malden was enlisted to play Riviera-based villain Julian Wall, who is obsessed with using the sun as a deadly ray-gun to destroy Washington, D.C.

Dean Martin, as super-suave secret agent Matt Helm, finds time for kicks with Ann-Margret in *Murderers' Row.* COLUMBIA / THE KOBAL COLLECTION

Along with kidnapping the scientist who developed the potentially deadly beam, Wall has cream-of-the-crop operatives from around the world knocked off—all of them goners except, of course, for Helm, who escapes being blasted out of his beloved pool and has his own funeral staged (attended by sobbing former female conquests) in order to dupe Wall. Matt then slides into his fashion-magazine photographer guise to get the goods on Wall, while the abducted scientist's daughter (Ann-Margret in improbably short miniskirts) tries to track down Daddy.

Despite such unimaginative gadgetry as a cigarette that shoots darts, forgettable songs by the band Dino, Desi, and Billy (featuring Dean Martin's son), and an extended disco sequence in which Martin really shows his age trying to keep up with the gyrating Ann-Margret in a feathered micro-mini, *Murderers' Row* struck enough of the right chords for fans of *The Silencers* to prove to the studio that they were yet to get ho-hum over Helm.

A year later, in 1968, *Murderers' Row* director Henry Levin (*Genghis Khan*) was asked back to tackle another Helm pic, *The Ambushers*. Here, Martin is called on to investigate the swiping of an experimental government flying saucer by a brutish bad guy named Ortega (Albert Salmi) who wants to use the spacecraft for . . . well, it's never really clear what it would be used for. Helm discovers that his former partner (Janice Rule) piloted the craft and was manhandled by Ortega when he swiped the saucer. Now she's in a near-catatonic state and has suddenly acquired an intense fear of men, but she has to join Helm on his mission because only she can navigate the spacecraft. And besides, everyone knows that "electromagnetic fields are lethal to men," right?

The Ambushers is a messy mix of sci-fi, Cold War espionage, secret-agent hijinks, and beer jokes (Ortega is nefariously involved with a Montezuma Beer distillery). The mish-mash is made even more confusing by Rule's psychosis and Salmi's loutish behavior. And it has not aged as well as the other Helm outings—that Perry Como joke at the film's finale doesn't help matters.

While signs pointed to the Helm franchise winding down, there was room for at least one more entry, and Phil Karlson was brought back behind the camera for *The Wrecking Crew* the following year. The story involves a count (played by ubiquitous '60s creep Nigel Green) whose theft of—cue *Austin Powers*'s Dr. Evil—*one billion dollars* in gold threatens the financial future of the United States and England. Helm is summoned to Copenhagen to catch the culprit.

Alas, Dino was tired of the Helm routine after three movies, and it really shows in *The Wrecking Crew*. The producers tried to compensate for the star's lack of enthusiasm with elaborate production pieces, martial arts sequences (staged by Bruce Lee!), a bouncy pop score by *I Dream of Jeannie* composer Hugo Montenegro, and more va-va-voom vixens (including Elke Sommer, Tina Louise, Nancy Kwan, and the up-and-coming—and ill-fated—Sharon Tate) than could be found in a month of Bob Hope specials.

While the end credits of *The Wrecking Crew* promise another entry in the series, titled *The Ravagers,* Martin's Matt Helm adventure was finished. Dino decided to concentrate on his popular TV show and soon won some of the best notices of his big-screen career for his role in the 1970 smash hit *Airport*.

The character of Matt Helm, however, was resurrected in 1975 with '60s icon Tony Franciosa (*The Swinger, The Sweet Ride*) tackling the title character in the ABC TV series that ran for two years. Franciosa's Helm was a hip ex-operative working as a detective in Los Angeles. And while the show was applauded for its more serious approach to the character, the TV incarnation was still light years away from Donald Hamilton's rugged model.

There have been rumblings of yet another Matt Helm makeover, this time reportedly closer to the character's serious secret-agent origins. But for now, moviegoers are left to raise a glass to Dino, the only cinematic Matt Helm.

The Silencers
1966 103m/C Dean Martin, Stella Stevens, Daliah Lavi, Victor Buono, Arthur O'Connell, Robert Webber, James Gregory, Nancy Kovack, Roger C. Carmel, Cyd Charisse, Beverly Adams, Richard Devon. **D:** Phil Karlson. **W:** Oscar Saul. **C:** Burnett Guffey. **M:** Elmer Bernstein. *VHS, DVD*

Murderers' Row
1966 106m/C Dean Martin, Ann-Margret, Karl Malden, Camilla Sparv, James Gregory, Beverly Adams, Richard Eastham. **D:** Henry Levin. **W:** Herbert Baker. **C:** Sam Leavitt. **M:** Lalo Schifrin. *VHS, DVD*

The Ambushers
1967 109m/C Dean Martin, Senta Berger, Janice Rule, James Gregory, Albert Salmi, Kurt Kasznar, Beverly Adams. **D:** Henry Levin. **W:** Herbert Baker. **C:** Burnett Guffey, Edward Colman. **M:** Hugo Montenegro. *VHS, DVD*

The Wrecking Crew
1969 105m/C Dean Martin, Elke Sommer, Sharon Tate, Nancy Kwan, Nigel Green, Tina Louise, John Larch. **D:** Phil Karlson. **W:** William P. McGivern. **C:** Sam Leavitt. **M:** Frank De Vol, Hugo Montenegro. *VHS, DVD*

What's Up, Tiger Lily? ♪♪♪

What's Up, Tiger Lily? is Woody Allen's first directing credit. From the man who would later go on to emulate Ingmar Bergman and Federico Fellini, his first outing seems sophomoric, crude, and amateurish, but it's also one of the funniest things the actor/writer/director has ever done.

After acquiring a rotten Japanese gangster flick called *Kagi No Kagi* (*Key of Keys*), producer Abe Saperstein paid Woody to spruce it up. Along with some friends, writer Mickey Rose and his wife, actress Louise Lasser, Allen rewrote and redubbed the dialogue. Reportedly against Allen's wishes, incidental rock music and performance sequences by John Sebastian and the Lovin' Spoonful were added by Saperstein to attract a younger audience. It's no surprise that the results are totally off-the-wall and spasmodically hilarious, as Allen and company cook up a poke at the popular secret-agent flicks of the time.

The new, altered story concerns secret agent Phil Moskowitz (Tatsuya Mihashi) and his search for an egg salad recipe "so delicious you could

"**Don't tell me what I can do, or I'll have my mustache eat your beard.**"

—Wing Fat (Susumu Kurobe), in *What's Up, Tiger Lily?*

STELLA STEVENS by Ed Grant

One of the most versatile sex symbols to grace the big screen in the '60s, Stella Stevens was equally adept at conveying smoldering sensuality and comic ditziness. Her range as a performer is reflected by the roster of directors she worked with during this era: John Cassavetes, Vincente Minnelli, Sam Peckinpah, and Jerry Lewis.

A Southern charmer, this native of Yazoo City, Mississippi, had her first speaking role in *Li'l Abner* (1959), but she became internationally known when she became a *Playboy* Playmate in January 1960. She played an introverted beauty contest winner in Minnelli's *The Courtship of Eddie's Father* (1963). Her first "heavy" dramatic role, however, was in Cassavetes's *Too Late Blues* (1962). The movie was Cassavetes's first after his underground triumph *Shadows* (1960), so it was bound to represent either a major step forward or a mercenary sellout. As it stands, the film is an underrated gem, full of bitter moments that seem out of place in a Hollywood love story. Stevens, who starred as Bobby Darin's torch-singer girlfriend, recalled that Cassavetes's brand of filmmaking was what she called "no-directing directing": "I was scared to death. I wanted [John] to give me great *reams* of things to do and think about. 'Be natural' is about all you *can* do to make it good, see. And I learned that from him. I didn't like it at first. Later, as I looked back on it, I wish more directors had done that."

In 1963 Stevens played one of her best-remembered roles, that of level-headed student Stella Purdy in Jerry Lewis's Jekyll-and-Hyde *chef d'oeuvre*, *The Nutty Professor*. The film is filled with distinctly Freudian moments (probably more than Jerry intended); one of the most eye-catching is the sequence where Dr. Julius Kelp (Lewis) envisions his object of desire, Stella, in different sexy outfits (tennis costume, swimsuit, toga). "[That's] the private fantasy of *every* man," Stevens theorized, "wanting a woman that would look good playing tennis or going to a ball or just going as a schoolgirl. All the visions [Kelp] has of her. Wasn't that a wonderful way to show that? A visual thing without any words, and it's one of the most memorable scenes in the picture."

Stella worked with Jerry's old partner Dean Martin in two gleefully sexist comedies, *The Silencers* (1966) and *How to Save a Marriage (and Ruin Your Life)* in 1968. The former is one of her favorites, as director Phil Karlson (*The Phenix City Story, Walking Tall*) told her that she reminded

plotz!" While on his mission, Moskowitz battles Wing Fat (Susumu Kurobe) and Shepherd Wong (Tadao Nakamaru), two archvillains vying for control of the formula. Also figuring into the story are the beautiful Teri Yaki (Mie Hama) and Suki Yaki (Akiko Wakabayashi), sisters who, when not being tied up, are continually forced to remove articles of clothing.

Anything and everything that could draw a laugh has been packed into the film: snappy one-liners that seem to have come from Allen's stand-up act ("The last time I made love on a ship it was on the *Titanic*. Unfortunately, we never finished"); goofy voices slightly out of synch with the characters' him of Carole Lombard. A redheaded Stella plays an inveterate klutz in this Matt Helm adventure, delivering a wonderfully silly performance. Apparently Jerry Lewis was not amused, as Stevens recalled: "Well, when I worked with Dean Martin, Jerry did not speak to me after that for maybe twenty years. *The Nutty Professor* was known as Jerry's masterpiece, and I was his leading lady in that. He and Dean Martin were not speaking at that time, and so he didn't speak to me either." Stevens has noted that Jerry has since forgiven her, and the two are now good friends again (so much for the "brotherly" love that Jerry declares he maintained for his ex-partner).

Stevens made two notable genre movies at the end of the '60s, the David McCallum action opus *Sol Madrid* (1968) and the horror movie *The Mad Room* (1969). These were followed by the movie that allowed her to give her subtlest, most refined performance, Sam Peckinpah's gentle western elegy *The Ballad of Cable Hogue* (1970). Working with Peckinpah was never dull, said Stevens: "It was like working with a wounded rattlesnake. You never knew what he was gonna do. . . . He wore sunglasses with mirrors in the front of them, so you couldn't see his eyes—and he mumbled. He didn't want to give a lot of direction."

Throughout the early '70s, Stella appeared in one-dimensional roles in movies that have become cult favorites, the most famous being what has become the new-age *Rocky Horror Picture Show*, Irwin Allen's stultifyingly melodramatic *The Poseidon Adventure* (1972). On the exploitation front, Stevens had featured roles in *Slaughter* (1972), *Arnold* (1973), and *Las Vegas Lady* (1976), but her most notorious performance during this period was as the villainous ninja-woman in the cartoon-like *Cleopatra Jones and the Casino of Gold* (1975). Stevens relished playing the bad girl: "My favorite thing to do in a film is to have a catfight with a woman, and Cleopatra Jones and I get to fight at the end. Of course, she does kill me, but I *am* the villain."

Stella hasn't stopped working in the past four decades, and she has even found time to direct a comedy starring her son Andrew (*The Ranch*) and a documentary called *The American Heroine*. Most fans relish the sight of her as "Miss Purdy" or as the scantily clad ex-hooker in *Poseidon*, but hardcore movie buffs have seen the best sides of her in the low-key, moody masterworks of Cassavetes and Peckinpah. There are times when a sultry torch singer can be infinitely sexier than a hooker, even if the hooker is wading through deep pools of water in her underwear.

mouths (like the bartender-henchman who sounds like Peter Lorre and even says, "This Peter Lorre impersonation is killing my voice"); and Yiddish terms and references to rabbis coming out of the mouths of Japanese characters. Allen even gets into the act himself, adding commentary in a few inserted segments and, over the end credits, nonchalantly eating an apple while a busty Asian dancer (China Lee, a *Playboy* centerfold and wife to comic Mort Sahl) does a striptease.

Tiger Lily seems innocuous enough today, yet its influence on future comedic projects can't be ignored. *Mystery Science Theater 3000*'s brand of

Title card for Woody Allen's redubbed comic masterpiece *What's Up, Tiger Lily?*

TOHO / BENEDICT / THE KOBAL COLLECTION

offscreen/on-screen ribbing certainly owes a lot to the picture. And the film's anarchistic style supplied at least the spirit for the Zucker-Abrahams-Zucker team's anything-goes shenanigans in *Airplane!* and the *Naked Gun* films. The Firesign Theatre found success with *J-Men Forever,* in which they added new voices, hip dialogue, and lots of drug references to the 1940s serial *Radar Men of the Moon.* Then there's 2002's *Kung Pow: Enter the Fist,* Steve Oedekerk's salute to *Tiger Lily* that took a martial-arts flick and added voices and some new sections.

These days, one's fondness for *What's Up, Tiger Lily?* depends on one's feelings toward Allen himself. Can you overlook the unsavory events of Woody Allen's personal life and still laugh at one of his funniest movies? Or is it impossible to get over the fact that Allen is a "Saracen pig, Spartan dog, or Roman cow," as *Tiger Lily*'s great Phil Moskowitz would put it?

1966 (PG) 80m/C Tatsuya Mihashi, Akiko Wakabayashi, Mie Hama, Susumu Kurobe, Tadao Nakamaru, Woody Allen, John Sebastian. **D:** Woody Allen, Senkichi Taniguchi. **W:** Woody Allen, Julie Bennett, Fran Buxton, Louise Lasser, Len Maxwell, Mickey Rose, Bryan Wilson. **C:** Kazuo Yamada. **M:** Jack Lewis, the Lovin' Spoonful. *VHS, DVD*

Chapter 3

New Spies on the Block

Goofy. Dopey. Happy. Grumpy. Bashful. Flaky. Brawny.

No, they're not some newfangled version of the Seven Dwarfs. Rather those terms describe the type of spies we're getting these days, played by actors ranging from Chevy Chase to Vin Diesel, Leslie Nielsen to Val Kilmer, Matt Damon to a couple of kids nobody ever heard of before.

James Bond, Derek Flint, and Harry Palmer may have inspired them, but the "new spies on the block" have managed to put fresh spins on the tried-and-true secret-agent scene. Sometimes, they're merely accepted as suitable substitutes until 007 brings his latest adventure to theaters; other times, they stand on their own two feet, making us feel like we'd be happy to say "never" again to Bond.

Even if Ian Fleming's superspy had never made it to the silver screen, cinematic spies would still be among us, but who knows how frequently. Lull times between 007 outings usually signal spy time for others, so it's no surprise that 1985's *Spies Like Us* became a hit, issued right around the time that Roger Moore was saying "adios" to Bond and the leaner, meaner Timothy Dalton climbed aboard the 007 juggernaut. While some may argue you couldn't make a spy spoof any funnier than *A View to a Kill,* Moore's Bond bon voyage, *Spies Like Us* provided laughs a-plenty with former *Saturday Night Live* stars Chevy Chase and Dan Aykroyd playing misplaced operatives unwittingly making mincemeat of a secret mission in—of all places—Afghanistan.

Another former *SNL* standout hit paydirt with his secret-agent man. After flopping with *So I Married an Axe Murderer,* Mike Myers turned his fascination with 1960s pop culture into 1997's *Austin Powers: International Man of Mystery.* Mocking Bond, *Blow-Up,* the *Flint* series, and more, Myers's bespectacled, sex-savvy secret agent drew well at the box office but really brought home the bacon when it hit video and cable. Two even bigger sequels followed, skewering similar turf along with blaxploitation flicks, Michael Caine's Harry Palmer movies, and a parade of pop-culture references. Their amazing box-office tallies—collectively, the *Austin Powers* pictures have amassed more than half a billion dollars—pretty much dictate more shagadelic cinema is on the way.

Austin hasn't been the only spy to try to tickle the public's funny bones in recent years. The *Airplane!/Naked Gun* trio of Jerry Zucker, Jim Abrahams, and David Zucker (ZAZ) sent a young Val Kilmer to Germany for some espionage work and guitar playing in 1984's overlooked *Top Secret!,* an affectionate ribbing of Elvis flicks and old-school espionage. And the ZAZ team's MVP, Leslie Nielsen, brought his stoic heroics to *Spy Hard,* a film that starts off with a bang—"Weird Al" Yankovic's ingenious parody of a 007 theme song—and then huffs and puffs to keep the laughs coming. Also on the lighter side of Bonded filler are Arnold Schwarzenegger, now governor of California, dodging evil agents and performing incredible stunts in James Cameron's elaborate *True Lies,* and Rowan Atkinson, "Mr. Bean" himself, making a shambles of everything while trying to save the Crown Jewels in 2003's *Johnny English.*

For kids, Robert Rodriguez's *Spy Kids* series, boasting child stars Daryl Sabara and Alexa Vega as pint-sized private eyes, updated the cool gadgetry found in past secret-agent outings for family consumption. Showcasing many Hispanics in the casts and shot digitally on the cheap, writer-director-producer-editor-cinematographer-composer Rodriguez's trilogy proved that kids and their parents just want to have fun, and they *will* have fun as long as the pacing is quick and the films are set in such cool places as an amusement park or inside a computer game. In the same mold, *Agent Cody Banks* moved the *Spy Kids* demographics up a few years to the early teens, as TV idols Frankie Muniz and Hillary Duff try to stop the production of evil super-robots. *Banks* netted enough dough that a follow-up was ordered.

Not all recent espionage enterprises have explored the funnier or more juvenile side of the shadowy spy business. Even in its serious guise, espionage still draws crowds, proven in several recent films that have prompted sequels. *The Bourne Identity* (2003) retooled Robert Ludlum's thriller, with Matt Damon as the amnesiac operative trying to figure out his identity in Eastern Europe, so effectively that we're going to get *Bourne* again. The *Mission: Impossible* movies may offer a remixed version of the identifiable theme song from the '60s TV favorite, but don't look for any other nostalgia here. Star-producer Tom Cruise surveys international intrigue, explosions, chases, and elaborate stuntwork as Ethan Hunt, a slick superspy unlike any of us. A similar formula was adapted for 2002's *XXX,* boasting musclebound Vin Diesel as Xander Cage, an extreme-sports daredevil turned undercover agent working to make the world safe, especially for its fifteen-to-twenty-five-year-old target demographic.

Austin Powers: International Man of Mystery 🦴🦴🦴

Austin Powers: The Spy Who Shagged Me 🦴🦴

Austin Powers in Goldmember 🦴🦴

Yeah, baby!

Good. Now that that's out of the way, let's talk Austin Powers. He's buck-toothed and has Bond and *Blow-Up* on his British noggin. The carpeting is shag and so is the chest hair. He's got glasses and goes gaga for the girls. Oh, behave.

His success is astonishing for a number of reasons. First, the sheer numbers the series has amassed: more than half a *billion* dollars at the box office, millions of video units sold, plus book and toy and TV spin-offs. And let's not forget the heavy anticipation factor. People just can't wait for the next series entry (and there will be others); these films' releases have become genuine events.

Of course, Austin is Mike Myers's baby. The former *Saturday Night Live* member created, cowrote, and plays multiple characters in the films. Director Jay Roach, who has helmed all three movies, and Michael McCullers, who cowrote the second and third films with Myers, certainly deserve ample credit. But in spite of the abundant talents of these people, the fact remains that Austin Powers, in all his mammoth incisor glory, would not have existed beyond the first film if it weren't for the big AM dial for dollars.

AM is "ancillary markets," the term industry people give to home video and cable sales. If it weren't for the electronic afterlife made possible by AM, *Austin Powers: International Man of Mystery* would have faded into the sunset, somewhere near a CGI-generated Big Ben.

Flashback time: I'm sitting at the United Artists Grant Avenue Theater in northeast Philadelphia on Friday, May 4, 1997. It's the 5:25 showing of the first *Austin Powers* movie. Fifteen people are scattered throughout the theater. I generally enjoy movie spoofs, everything from *The Naked Gun* on down to *Mafia* and *Loaded Weapon 1.* I've enjoyed Myers over the years and I love '60s spy films. So, I'm the prime audience. I look around at the nearly empty

theater and wonder: "Am I one of only a handful?" A last-minute publicity blitz that includes Myers on an MTV special heightens my suspicion that New Line, the film's studio, is a little nervous about this baby.

The movie begins. Myers's shtick is funny. I love Dr. Evil. Elizabeth Hurley isn't tough to look at. The references to *Blow-Up* and mod London and James Bond and Derek Flint and the other cinematic secret agents of ages past are good for some laughs. The audience members, primarily teenagers, chuckle a few times, mostly at the toilet humor. I leave the theater generally pleased. On the hit-and-miss scale usually used to judge movie send-ups, there seem to be more hits than misses, but I think the movie's references are too obscure for the masses. When the film garners $55 million at the box office, I'm amazed. Not bad for a movie with a modest $15 million budget.

The real mania starts when *Austin* hits home video. People buy the hell out of it. They watch it over and over. I'm even invited to an *Austin Powers* party! Do the people throwing the party want me to explain that the ring of the phone sounds just like Derek Flint's phone or that Dr. Evil resembles Donald Pleasence in *You Only Live Twice* or Theo Marcuse in *Last of the Secret Agents*? Do they get all the jokes? I doubt it. Do they care? Boo freakity hoo!

Austin fever continues. The public clamors for a sequel. Two years later, they get it with *Austin Powers: The Spy Who Shagged Me.* With its audience fed a steady Austin Powers diet from video and cable, there's no surprise to the hearty reaction the sequel gets, pulling in a whopping $55 million on its opening weekend alone. The film's story promises something hot—at least to those viewers who were familiar with the mod era: Austin loses his mojo and must find it. And now, Mike Myers is not only playing Austin and the cue-ball-headed villain Dr. Evil, but a bloated, ill-tempered, gaseous Scotsman named Fat Bastard as well. In addition to grotesquely impressive work from makeup master Stan Winston, the introduction of this Bastard brought with it as many poo-poo jokes as you can squeeze into a PG-13 movie. This move seemed a desperate one so early on in a series. The characters were still funny, some of the sight gags and cameos hilarious, and you certainly can't go wrong showcasing Burt Bacharach and Elvis Costello duetting on "Never Fall in Love Again." But come on, Mike and company—do you really have to go down the road of farts and toilet paper?

After skirting the sequel issue for a few years while working on an *SNL* character–inspired Dieter movie that imploded, doing a wonderful voice characterization in *Shrek* (with a hint of the Fat Bastard Scottish accent), and acting in some low-budget and short films, Myers soon went back to *Powers* work.

The result, after some legal wrangling with MGM over the Bond-like title, was *Austin Powers in Goldmember.* The third go-round certainly has its ingenious—even uproarious—moments. Inspired cameos by the likes of Steven Spielberg, Tom Cruise, Britney Spears, John Travolta, Kevin Spacey, and others, are marvelous for the most part. The appearance of Michael Caine as Austin's estranged father is a nifty idea. A spirited music video of "A Hard-Knock Life" with Dr. Evil and Mini-Me is so bizarre it tickles. And some of the sight gags—especially one involving a statue, surveillance cameras, security guards, and Austin—are wonderfully demented.

First, he fought for the Crown. Now he's fighting for the Family Jewels.

—Tagline for *Austin Powers: The Spy Who Shagged Me*

Mike Myers, AKA Austin Powers, makes a swinging entrance in *Austin Powers: International Man of Mystery.* NEW LINE / THE KOBAL COLLECTION

MIKE MYERS: EXPLORING GROOVY POWERS

by Amy Longsdorf

To hear Mike Myers tell it, he was as shocked as anyone when *Austin Powers: International Man of Mystery* became a smash hit in 1997. Almost overnight, Austin's pet phrases like "Oh, behave!" and "Yeah, baby!" became part of the vernacular. Since then, the secret-agent man with the bad overbite, carpet-like body hair, and form-fitting velveteen jacket has kept on going and going. Myers's two sequels—*Austin Powers: The Spy Who Shagged Me* and *Austin Powers in Goldmember*—were even bigger box-office champs than the original, and a fourth installment is inevitable. As Austin would say, it's groovy, baby.

Q: Have you ever lost your mojo?

A: I lost my mojo in 1991 when my father passed away. I lost all interest in doing anything, so I took time off. And that's how I came up with *Austin Powers*.

Q: So Austin is based on your dad?

A: Not exactly, but he'd love Austin. . . . He was a huge fan of James Bond movies. He loved Peter Cook and Dudley Moore, *Monty Python,* and Matt Helm, even though Matt Helm wasn't English.

Q: How is Mike Myers most like Austin Powers?

A: I'm not like Austin Powers at all. I'm a nerd. Basically, I'm a sexless geek. Look at me. I have no chin. I have acne scarring. And I'm five-foot-nothing. It's not exactly a recipe for sexual dynamism.

Q: Why does Austin have better teeth in the sequels than he did in the original?

> **He's still evil . . . he's still deadly . . . and he's still surrounded by frickin' idiots!**
>
> —Tagline for *Austin Powers in Goldmember*

At the same time, however, Caine is given little to do but look like an embalmed Harry Palmer, Beyoncé Knowles as Pam Grier/blaxploitation clone Foxxy Cleopatra is a waste, and Fat Bastard, even with abbreviated screen time, seems like a bad idea that should never have been resurrected.

The aforementioned shortcomings and the general feeling that the third trip to the *Austin Powers* well was coming up dry had little effect on its ever-swelling legion of shagadelic fans. They answered the call in droves, contributing $215 million at the U.S. box office alone. The first weekend, the film took in a record-breaking $73 million, recouping its budget in those two short days. Its returns on video alone were $147 million.

The *Austin Powers* franchise has proven to be Teflon. The core audience—the eighteen-to-thirty-four demographic who have Xboxes and watch MTV—don't care that the plots are incomprehensible, that the jokes that didn't work the first time are repeated, that Myers and company are referencing—hell, copying—ideas from older, better movies and sometimes even from their own. As long as someone just throws them a freakin' bone, they're happy. And so is Mike Myers.

A: For the Trekkies, at the end of the first one, he gets his teeth fixed in the '90s. But when he travels back to the '60s, they go back to the way they were. Okay?

Q: Okay. Why do you think Austin Powers strikes such a chord with moviegoers?

A: I don't have a clue. It's especially bizarre to me that little kids love Austin so much. [Director] Jay Roach's theory is that Austin is like Barney. He's happy. He likes to have fun and dance. And the colors are bright.

Q: Where did you get the idea for Mini-Me?

A: I was watching *The Island of Dr. Moreau* with Marlon Brando. All of a sudden this little Brando appears and I'm screaming, "Oh my God! What the heck is that?" I kept screaming, "It's a mini Marlon Brando! Oh my God, he's playing piano!" That one was covered in chocolate and rolled in nuts. It was a nutbar maneuver. I thought, "Dr. Evil has got to have one! A Mini-Me!"

Q: Does it drive you crazy when people come up to you and impersonate Austin Powers and Dr. Evil?

A: No, most of the time, it's cool. I was taking a pee at Maple Leaf Gardens and some guy went, "Oh, behave!" I just said, "I'm peeing, buddy." C'mon, that's crazy. But just imagine you're me for a second. You're in a room and you come up with some weird idea you think is funny. Cut to three years later, you're at a red light and you look over and there's some guy who's looking back at you, sucking his pinky like Dr. Evil. It's like, bing, bam, boom! What the hell is that? That came from me. It never ceases to amaze me. That came from me, some guy from Toronto.

Austin Powers: International Man of Mystery
1997 (PG-13) 89m/C Mike Myers, Elizabeth Hurley, Michael York, Mimi Rogers, Robert Wagner, Seth Green, Mindy Sterling. *D:* Jay Roach. *W:* Mike Myers. *C:* Peter Deming. *M:* George S. Clinton. *VHS, DVD*

Austin Powers: The Spy Who Shagged Me
1999 (PG-13) 99m/C Mike Myers, Heather Graham, Michael York, Robert Wagner, Rob Lowe, Seth Green, Verne Troyer, Mindy Sterling. *D:* Jay Roach. *W:* Mike Myers, Michael McCullers. *C:* Ueli Steiger. *M:* George S. Clinton. *VHS, DVD*

Austin Powers in Goldmember
2002 (PG-13) 94m/C Mike Myers, Beyoncé Knowles, Michael York, Seth Green, Verne Troyer, Mindy Sterling, Fred Savage, Robert Wagner. *D:* Jay Roach. *W:* Mike Myers, Michael McCullers. *C:* Peter Deming. *M:* George S. Clinton. *VHS, DVD*

Ralph Fiennes is secret agent John Steed in the 1998 film version of *The Avengers.*

The Avengers 🦴

In the incredibly exciting, unpredictable world of movie criticism, only a few things are close to certain. One of them is that if a major studio film is not screened for critics before its opening day, there's trouble ahead.

With *The Avengers,* a big-screen version of the stylish 1960s British cult TV series, Warner Bros. decided to forgo advanced screening for this project that was chock-full of promise. A sizable budget, loads of special effects, big-name stars, and easy-to-adapt source material were in its favor. Still, when the studio decided not to allow critics a sneak peek, the stench of failure was in the air. Sadly, the evidence was on the screen as well.

In what seemed like a good idea at the time, Ralph Fiennes plays John Steed, a dapper English secret agent working for an organization called the Ministry. Steed is called on by Mother (Oscar-winner Jim Broadbent), the group's reclusive but fearless leader, to investigate the recent strange weather. Steed teams with Dr. Emma Peel (Uma Thurman), an alluring expert on atmospheric conditions, to track down the chief suspect, Sir August de Wynter (Sean Connery), a former operative for the Ministry now nastily tampering with science for blackmail purposes.

Evidencing its $50 million budget, *The Avengers* looks great. Lots of attention was obviously paid to production details, from de Wynter's castle-like estate to the impeccable tailoring of Steed's Saville Row suits and Peel's S&M-inspired skintight leather outfits. And there are a host of elaborate CGI effects, including ominous tornadoes and floods and some hyperactive bumblebees featured in a quick-paced chase sequence.

Unfortunately, director Jeremiah Chechik (of the Sharon Stone *Diabolique* remake) and screenwriter Don MacPherson (*Absolute Beginners*) seem to have forgotten that chemistry and energy is what made the original series click so well. In the original, Steed, played by the jaunty Patrick Macnee (who has a small role here), and Peel, played by plucky Diana Rigg, had great rapport and a sexual spark. There's no evidence of that here, as Fiennes takes things a tad too seriously and Thurman remains dour, showcasing little of Rigg's sex a-Peel. Their comradeship seems forced when they are together, downright lethargic when they're apart. Yes, Steed brandishes his trademark umbrella in a fencing duel and Peel offers us a chance to witness her martial arts prowess as she throttles her assailants, but they're just going through the motions. Not helping the situation is Connery, in a strangely truncated villainous role. He brings style to the table but little else. One imagines that if Vincent Price, in his heyday, had played de Wynter, he would have given the role the devilish "oomph" it needed.

To compensate for the shortcomings, the filmmakers lay the accessories on heavily, preferring to draw attention to the film's colorful surroundings and a half-baked cloning subplot. But these trappings can't disguise this edition of *The Avengers* as a solid idea for an update gone sadly awry. The outcome is true to the forecast: gloomy throughout.

1998 (PG-13) 89m/C Ralph Fiennes, Uma Thurman, Sean Connery, Jim Broadbent, Patrick Macnee, Fiona Shaw, Eddie Izzard. *D:* Jeremiah Chechik. *W:* Don MacPherson. *C:* Roger Pratt. *M:* Joel McNeely. *VHS, DVD*

Spies Like Us ♫♫♫

More lively and entertaining than any movie starring Dan Aykroyd and Chevy Chase has a right to be, *Spies Like Us* is an engaging espionage comedy that allows director and cowriter John Landis (*Animal House, Trading Places*) to pay tribute to *three* types of films at once. First, of course, is the spy movie. Second, a tip of the fez is given to desert adventure movies in the mold of *Lawrence of Arabia*. Finally, the easygoing, cameo-laden *Road* pictures of Bob Hope and Bing Crosby are affectionately saluted.

In *Spies Like Us,* doofus Emmett Fitz-Hume (Chase) and expert codebreaker Austin Millbarge (Aykroyd) are government workers caught cheating on their civil service exams. This mistake brings them to the attention of high-ranking intelligence figures who decide they'd be a perfect pair to act as decoys in a secret mission overseas. After some grueling training ("Thanks for the bruises, and you can keep the stool samples," Chase tells his training leader), the duo are sent to Afghanistan.

Once in Afghanistan they encounter Soviet intelligence agents posing as American liaisons; are called upon to halt a Russian missile launch; and

> **"My objective? Well I object to taking a girl out, you know, and buying her dinner and then she won't put out for you."**
>
> —Chevy Chase as Emmett Fitz-Hume, in *Spies Like Us*

discover that a fellow decoy is not a fellow at all, but a beautiful woman (Donna Dixon, AKA Mrs. Aykroyd), whom Fitz-Hume takes a liking to.

Granted, the plot ain't much and it sure is all over the place. But the film works because of the chemistry of its stars, some impressive location work, and an array of nifty sight gags and smart jokes provided by screenwriters Aykroyd, *Second City TV*'s Dave Thomas, Lowell Ganz, and Babaloo Mandel (*Parenthood*). Landis liberally sprinkles in his trademark cameos (by a number of directors *and* Bob Hope himself) and, for the guys, scenes of a bodacious Russian soldier (Vanessa Angel) wearing lingerie that appears to have been ordered from Natasha's Secret.

Spies Like Us may not reach classic status, but it is a reminder that *SNL* cast members are capable of putting out a decent farce with an idea that *didn't* originate on the show. Who would have thought we'd ever say that we miss the good ol' days when Aykroyd and Chase made funny movies?

1985 (PG) 102m/C Dan Aykroyd, Chevy Chase, Steve Forrest, Donna Dixon, Bruce Davison, Bernie Casey, Vanessa Angel. **D:** John Landis. **W:** Dan Aykroyd, Dave Thomas, Lowell Ganz, Babaloo Mandel. **C:** Robert Paynter. **M:** Elmer Bernstein. *VHS, DVD*

Spy Hard 🦴🦴🦴

Leslie Nielsen certainly knows on which side his bread has been buttered since making *The Naked Gun: From the Files of Police Squad* in 1988. Since that surprise hit, a spin-off from the failed TV show, Nielsen has done regular work on the send-up route, spoofing police movies (two sequels to *The Naked Gun*), *The Fugitive* (*Wrongfully Accused*), sci-fi films (*2001: A Space Travesty*), vampire flicks (Mel Brooks's *Dracula: Dead and Loving It*), and, with *Spy Hard*, spy movies.

As with most of the other spoofs (remember the uproarious baseball gags in the original *Naked Gun*?), *Spy Hard* doesn't rely solely on the genre it's based on. The filmmakers find time to tease the likes of *Speed* (Ray Charles is driving the bus, see . . . and he's blind!), *In the Line of Fire, True Lies, Pulp Fiction,* Michael Jackson music videos, and even *Butch Cassidy and the Sundance Kid.* Hey, if Mel Brooks could get away with Nazis, a fey Dom DeLuise choreographing a Hollywood musical, and a brawl at the Warner Bros. commissary at the end of *Blazing Saddles,* why should a little ribbing harm Nielsen's popularity with filmgoers?

The spy spoofery in *Spy Hard* hits its mark 50 percent of the time, a solid grade for this type of film. Nielsen is Dick Steele, AKA Agent WD-40, a retired secret agent called back into action to fight the evil General Rancor (Andy Griffith), an armless Blofeld-type villain Steele thought he had destroyed years ago. Rancor has kidnapped fellow operative Barbara Dahl (Stephanie Romanov), whose mother was once romantically involved with Steele. Rancor has a plan to strap Dahl to a missile that could destroy the world.

While Griffith seems sadly miscast as Rancor (his homespun personality shows through), Nielsen has the time of his life bedding babes half his age

and narrowly escaping sticky situations. He's also aided by a host of oddball cameo guests, including Dr. Joyce Brothers, Mr. T, Roger Clinton, Robert Culp, Pat Morita, Fabio, and Hulk Hogan.

Nicolette Sheridan and Leslie Nielsen work hard to keep straight faces in the secret-agent spoof *Spy Hard.*

The main problem with *Spy Hard* is that its best moments are at the very beginning. An ingenious opening lampoons Maurice Binder's famed silhouetted Bond credit sequences and the classic bombast of 007 title songs. Here, behind the credits, we get the outlines of overweight and cat-fighting women, submerged and sometimes swimming in water, while "Weird Al" Yankovic croons the theme in his best Shirley Bassey style:

> A man of intrigue, he lives for the thrill
> Always has places to go and people to kill
> Danger is the game he plays and he holds every card
> 'Cause if you wanna win, you gotta spy hard

That alone is worth the price of admission.

1996 (PG-13) 81m/C Leslie Nielsen, Nicolette Sheridan, Andy Griffith, Charles Durning, Marcia Gay Harden, Barry Bostwick, Stephanie Romanov. **D:** Rick Friedberg. **W:** Rick Friedberg, Jason Friedberg, Dick Chudnow, Aaron Seltzer. **C:** John R. Leonetti. **M:** Bill Conti. *VHS, DVD*

Spy Kids ♫♫♫

Spy Kids 2: Island of Lost Dreams ♫♫♫

Spy Kids 3-D: Game Over ♫♫♫

For the *Spy Kids* series, filmmaker Robert Rodriguez delved into his childhood, making the coolest movies a teenaged boy could fantasize about, circa 1977. In other words, Rodriguez took James Bond spy material and gadgetry, some *Star Wars*–style CGI special effects, a token hot babe, creatures that would give H. R. Pufnstuf *and* H. R. Giger nightmares and—voilà!—it's hitsville. Who cares if the films' top-heavy elements clash every once in awhile? What kid doesn't want extra whipped cream and a cherry on top of his or her milkshake?

The premise of the first *Spy Kids* finds Gregorio and Ingrid Cortez (Antonio Banderas and Carla Gugino) as former rival secret agents who married nine years ago, then retired to start a family. Their young teen children, Carmen (Alexa Vega) and Juni (Daryl Sabara), are unaware of their parents' adventures in the spying game. They get a rude awakening when, after being called back into action by the Office of Strategic Services (OSS), their parents are snatched away from home, leading the kids into an abrupt indoctrination into the world of espionage. Their mission is to save their parents from Fegan Floop (Alan Cumming), a criminal mastermind who doubles as the host of a highly rated TV show for kids.

In *Spy Kids 2: The Island of Lost Dreams,* Carmen and Juni are hurled back into action, facing enough hairy predicaments to make James Bond dizzy. First, they encounter competition from Gary (Matthew O'Leary) and Gerti Giggles (Emily Osment, Haley Joel's sister), siblings who seek to take the top spot as kid OSS operatives. These two unlikable kiddies are the offspring of Donnagon Giggles (Mike Judge), the newly appointed OSS leader and rival to Carmen and Juni's father.

Of course, there's more to the Donnagon children and their father than meets the eye, and there are more twists and turns in the *Spy Kids* films than in any other releases aimed at young viewers these days. These films are bubbling over with ideas and Rodriguez's sneaky creativity. Consider the amusement park in *Spy Kids 2,* offering such "thrill" rides as the Nerve Wracker and the Vomiter, as well as a batch of freaky stop-motion-style creatures that take the terms "spider monkey" and "horseflies" literally.

Rodriguez tries something even bolder with *Spy Kids 3-D: Game Over.* First, he's gone the tricky 3-D route, something few contemporary filmmakers

try given the expense and potential technical problems. Then, the filmmaker threw Sylvester Stallone a career bone, offering the down-on-his-luck Oscar winner the villainous role of the Toymaker.

Daryl Sabara and Alexa Vega are the titular heroes of Robert Rodriguez's *Spy Kids.*

The result is on par with the other two *Spy Kids* outings—a nice achievement since most series run out of steam by the third go-'round. The story has a retired Juni called back to work in order to enter a high-tech videogame where Carmen is being held captive by the Toymaker, a creep threatening the future of the world by imprisoning its kids. Juni gets his wheelchair-bound grandfather (Ricardo Montalban) some virtual legs, then dodges screen-popping toads and creepy robots in order to stop the Toymaker's deadly game.

Rodriguez's *Spy Kids* efforts have been successful in part because they work on three levels. Kids like them because they're filled with the thrill of invention, because they show them things they haven't seen before, and because they offer likable, pint-sized heroes Carmen and Juni, who depend on their wit and intellect to get out of difficult situations. Adults appreciate the secret-agent and spy elements and the fact that Rodriguez requires viewers to pay close attention to intricate plotting amidst whiz-bang pacing. Film buffs, meanwhile, respond to the homages to stop-motion maestro Ray Harryhausen and to the cool special effects they've read about on the Ain't It Cool News website or in the pages of *Cinefex.*

Rodriguez also shows real respect for family and for his Mexican American heritage, making many of the lead characters Latino and spicing his sup-

Huge New Adventure— Slightly Larger Spies

—Tagline for *Spy Kids 2: Island of Lost Dreams*

ROBERT RODRIGUEZ: THE MASTER OF SPY KIDS
by Lou Gaul

Robert Rodriguez

COLUMBIA / THE KOBAL
COLLECTION / TORRES, RICO

For Robert Rodriguez, being a father means he has to act like an adult, though the filmmaker still thinks like a child.

That youthful mental process led him to create the *Spy Kids* series, wildly colorful tales about a couple of retired spies (Antonio Banderas and Carla Gugino) drafted back into service, while their young daughter (Alexa Vega) and even younger son (Daryl Sabara) are recruited into their perilous vocation.

Rodriguez, whose credits include 1992's *El Mariachi* (made for an astonishing $7,000), 1995's *Desperado*, 1996's *From Dusk Till Dawn*, 1998's *The Faculty,* and 2003's *Once Upon a Time in Mexico* grew tired of taking his children to see stale family films that aroused little excitement and displayed even less creativity. He decided to take matters into his own hands with the first *Spy Kids* film.

"When I was growing up, we had films like *Willy Wonka and the Chocolate Factory* [1971] and *Chitty Chitty Bang Bang* [1968], pictures that people took more seriously and were handled more imaginatively," Rodriguez said. "It's a sad show business fact that studios today will take an old idea, seek corporate sponsors [for merchandising], and then make a movie.

"The executives have been considering the product line first and the movie second, which is totally backward. Being a kid myself, I want to see youngsters who are empowered and active on the screen."

According to Rodriguez, most people have their childlike qualities driven out of them early in life. The talented filmmaker, who was the third oldest of ten children raised by his parents in Texas, believes people should make every effort to retain their sense of wonder and an openness to accept challenges.

porting cast with such performers as Cheech Marin, Danny Trejo, Salma Hayek, and Ricardo Montalban. To this and the *Spy Kids* movies, we say, *Olé!*

Spy Kids
2001 (PG) 88m/C Antonio Banderas, Carla Gugino, Alexa Vega, Daryl Sabara, Alan Cumming, Tony Shalhoub, Teri Hatcher, Cheech Marin, Robert Patrick, Danny Trejo. *D:* Robert Rodriguez. *W:* Robert Rodriguez. *C:* Guillermo Navarro. *M:* Danny Elfman. *VHS, DVD*

Spy Kids 2: The Island of Lost Dreams
2002 (PG) 99m/C Antonio Banderas, Carla Gugino, Alexa Vega, Daryl Sabara, Steve Buscemi, Mike Judge, Danny Trejo, Matthew O'Leary, Emily Osment. *D:* Robert

"For any art, it's important to retain a creative spirit," said Rodriguez, who's married to Elizabeth Avellan, with whom he has three children. They reside in Austin, Texas. "If you want to have fun, ask some young children who [among them] can sing, dance, or write an opera, and all of them will raise their hands.

"Ask that same question twenty years later, and maybe one hand will rise tentatively. There's no self-critic when you're young and you're willing to try things and grow. How do we lose that?"

With the three *Spy Kids* movies, Rodriguez basically takes the two children in the story and turns them into James Bond–like characters, complete with special weapons, colorful enemies, and daring escapes. The special effects–heavy, fast-moving pictures, made with relatively modest budgets, serve as tributes to the filmmaker's hard-working mother and father.

"My parents taught me so well," said Rodriguez. "They had ten children and numerous pressures and always stayed together. I wanted to put that type of family love and loyalty into a picture, because that's what the movie is really about.

"Of course, I disguise those sentiments with 007-like gadgets, but the story is really about the struggle—the impossible mission—to keep a family close together."

While growing up, the Mexican American filmmaker saw people from south of the border portrayed as either bloodthirsty villains needing to be destroyed or weak-willed peasants waiting to be saved in films such as *The Magnificent Seven* and *The Wild Bunch*. He knew the key to changing that unenlightened image was to enjoy a level of success that would guarantee him control of his cinematic work.

"Making the family Latin, which I did in *Spy Kids,* comes down to a decision by the person creating the film," said Rodriguez, who was originally hired to direct Banderas in *The Mask of Zorro* but dropped out when studio executives demanded too much creative control over the expensive adventure tale. "It was important for me to make *Spy Kids* a film which had universal appeal, but I also wanted Latin viewers to identify with the characters, whom I present in an exotic, almost dream-like world that I think members of all families will enjoy."

Rodriguez. *W:* Robert Rodriguez. *C:* Robert Rodriguez. *M:* John Debney, Robert Rodriguez. *VHS, DVD*

Spy Kids 3-D: Game Over
2003 (PG) 84m/C Antonio Banderas, Carla Gugino, Alexa Vega, Daryl Sabara, Ricardo Montalban, Holland Taylor, Sylvester Stallone. *D:* Robert Rodriguez. *W:* Robert Rodriguez. *C:* Robert Rodriguez. *M:* Robert Rodriguez. *VHS, DVD*

Top Secret! ♩♩♩♪

You've got to hand it to Jerry Zucker, Jim Abrahams, and David Zucker, or, as they've been collectively termed, "ZAZ." The directing trio was offered mucho dinero to do a sequel for *Airplane!* after it took off in 1981, but they steadfastly refused, opting instead to delve into more obscure waters. The result is *Top Secret!*—an oddball but affectionate send-up of World War II spy thrillers and Elvis movies, two seemingly incongruous genres. But while the movie's title offered an eerily on-target prediction regarding its fate with the public, *Top Secret!* remains ingeniously realized and fall-down funny throughout.

Before he channeled the spirit of Jim Morrison in *The Doors* and portrayed a caped crusader with pert nipples in *Batman Forever,* a twenty-five-year-old Val Kilmer showed us an easygoing charm and an effortless way with physical buffoonery in *Top Secret!* He plays Nick Rivers, a bleached-blonde surf/pop star whose career is so hot he's the headliner at a Madison Square Garden concert that includes Stevie Wonder, Linda Ronstadt, and Frank Sinatra. Rivers is recruited to serve as the first rock 'n' roller to play in communist East Germany on a goodwill tour. After arriving behind the Iron Curtain, Rivers comes into contact with Hillary (Lucy Gutteridge), a beautiful German woman and Rivers fan, who helps him discover that there's a Nazi uprising afoot. Rivers aims to put a stop to it, working with French resistance fighters with such names as Flick, Latrine, Chocolate Moose, and Déjà Vu.

Top Secret! utilizes all sorts of humor to get its yuks. It dishes out non sequiturs, visual puns, slapstick, general genre send-ups, and specific goofs on such movies as *The Blue Lagoon* and *The Wizard of Oz.* It's also overflowing with bizarre but effective cameos by the likes of Omar Sharif, Peter Cushing, and Michael Gough—and they actually play characters who have something to do with the film's plot. For the most part, ZAZ's lampoon grenades hit their targets dead on.

Carrying the film is Kilmer. It's his first feature, and he proves he's a gifted comic actor, equal to any and all of the filmmakers' tasks. He sings, he dances, he gyrates like Elvis. He shows nice timing with the physical demands of the role. And he does it all with a large degree of charisma, something the actor isn't really noted for.

Those who missed *Top Secret!* in theaters should check it out now. It ranks right up there with *Airplane!* and the first of *The Naked Gun* movies for inspired lunacy. It's "all that ZAZ" and then some.

1984 (PG) 88m/C Val Kilmer, Lucy Gutteridge, Warren Clarke, Omar Sharif, Peter Cushing, Michael Gough, Christopher Villier. *D:* Jim Abrahams, David Zucker, Jerry Zucker. *W:* Jim Abrahams, David Zucker, Jerry Zucker, Martyn Burke. *C:* Christopher Challis. *M:* Maurice Jarre. *VHS, DVD*

Asia Argento and Vin Diesel star in the alterna-spy flick *XXX*.

COLUMBIA / REVOLUTION STUDIOS / THE KOBAL COLLECTION / CLOSE, MURRAY

XXX ♫♫

Vin Diesel is da bomb as the James Bond for Gen Y-ers in *XXX*, a souped-up, dumbed-down spy adventure with a serious case of attention deficit disorder.

Directed in loud, mind-numbing, quickly edited fashion by Rob Cohen, Diesel's *The Fast and the Furious* filmmaker, *XXX* features Diesel as Xander Cage, an extreme-sports enthusiast who lives for danger and the thrill of pulling off high-risk stunts. His latest accomplishment is swiping, then destroying, a conservative senator's prized Corvette, an act that lands him in legal trouble. Cage cuts a deal with Gibbons (Samuel L. Jackson), an official with a government agency called NSA. In lieu of jail time, Cage agrees to go to Prague, where he is to infiltrate Anarchy 99, a group of Russian bio-terrorists, led by Yorgi (Marton Csokas), who are planning to unleash a killer chemical on the world.

Of course, Cage—bald, tattooed, cranky, and bearing a striking resemblance to Sad Sack of Harvey Comics fame—is equal to the task. Cage is sent on practice missions in South America and then heads to Eastern Europe, where he encounters Soviet creeps with names like Kolya and Viktor. He gets romantically entangled with a despondent Eurotrash chick named Yelena (played by despondent Eurotrash actress Asia Argento).

XXX runs on Diesel's fuel—his antiauthority routine and rugged charisma—which carried the film to $142 million in U.S. theaters. It did huge numbers overseas and in DVD sales, too, nearly guaranteeing a sequel. But the actor, who made an impression in more down-to-earth roles in *Boiler Room* and *Saving Private Ryan,* is also the reason *XXX* fails to register as a vehicle for a 007-type hero. Diesel's blunt demeanor and buff physical impressiveness, along with his character's extreme-sports expertise, make Xander Cage look like Tony Hawk crossed with Evel Knievel and Superman. He never appears to be in real danger. No matter how big his enemy's machetes, AK-47s, bazookas, choppers, or biochemical weapons are, Xander Cage can pull off some snowboarding, skiing, or skydiving trick to get himself out of harm's way.

The action sequences and stunt work in *XXX* are mighty impressive, and the film looks great. It globe-trots beautifully from California and the South American jungles to a shadowy Eastern Europe Czechoslovakia with the benefit of photography by Oscar-winner Dean Semler (*Dances with Wolves*), but, oh, what little humanity!

As for Diesel's Cage, a bead of real sweat would be nice every once in a while.

2002 (PG-13) 124m/C Vin Diesel, Asia Argento, Samuel L. Jackson, Marton Csokas, Michael Roof, Richie Muller. ***D:*** Rob Cohen. ***W:*** Rich Wilkes. ***C:*** Dean Semler. ***M:*** Randy Edelman. *VHS, DVD*

Chapter 4

Wild, Wild West

The Duke may have reigned supreme throughout the 1950s, but by the late 1960s John Wayne's brand of heroics was on the way out. Sure, Wayne could still be counted on for larger-than-life old-time oaters like *Chisum* (1970), *Cahill U.S. Marshal* (1973), and even *True Grit* (1969), which won him his first and only Academy Award for Best Actor. But Wayne's following was getting older and film audiences were getting younger. Wayne's old-fashioned style was being supplanted by a new type of lead western character—rebellious, angry, philosophical, sometimes even sensitive. In other words, the antihero.

Clint Eastwood, the former TV star and studio contract character actor, made a big splash worldwide playing the antiheroic "man with no name" character in *A Fistful of Dollars* and *For a Few Dollars More,* two of Italian director Sergio Leone's operatic shot-in-Spain spaghetti westerns, then essayed a similar role in *The Good, the Bad and the Ugly.* Eastwood's character was a loner, a quiet man with a poncho around his shoulders and a cheroot in his mouth. Unlike most of the heroes of yesteryear, he had a bad attitude, looked like he needed a bath and a shave, worked by himself, and was not above playing two sides against each other for fun and profit. In westerns of another era, these character traits would have been found in a villain, not a hero. Leone's vision was both a salute to the past and a call to take a closer look at our heroes. "Here's the good guy," the filmmaker is saying," but he's as unpredictable, ornery, and filthy as the black hats in the film." When Leone couldn't land Eastwood for *Once Upon a Time in the West,* his 1968 masterpiece, he settled on Charles Bronson—an actor best known for his cragginess and scowl even in heroic roles—for the lead, a character who communicates primarily through a harmonica and firearms. And, in an unsettling twist that both acknowledges and spits in the eye of westerns past, Leone cast Henry Fonda—the beacon of American goodness as the titular *Young Mr. Lincoln* and Tom Joad in *The Grapes of Wrath*—as one of the vilest villains in screen history.

All-American icon Henry Fonda as a no-good, lily-livered desert rat? Can't be! But it was, and so all of the myths of westerns and western icons were exploding from the 1960s into the 1970s. Veteran heroes of sagebrush sagas from previous decades, like Kirk Douglas, Burt Lancaster, and Charlton Heston, were now taking on roles portraying imperfect men who were often fighting to maintain their dignity as the sun set on the West they knew.

Sam Peckinpah, a veteran of TV oaters, unleashed his—and the country's—anger in one foul swoop, exploding genre conventions with the balletic, blood-soaked *The Wild Bunch* in 1969. The film sent a message to filmmakers that it was cool to delve into what was *really* happening in the wild, wild West. Now, revisionist efforts like *Little Big Man* and *Soldier Blue* could explore the treatment of Native Americans with candor—and a whole lot of blood. The traditional cowboys-versus-Indians story that John Wayne, director John Ford, and others had brought to the world was quickly fading away.

Although moving counterculture ideals into the western world of loners, misfits, and antiauthority outlaws seems like it may have been a natural fit, the mix of hippies and "Hi-yo, Silver" never really worked. Sex, drug-influenced sequences, and rock 'n' roll were more distractions than anything in *Zachariah,* known as the first electric western. *Greaser's Palace,* helmed by underground auteur Robert Downey, and *Lonesome Cowboys,* the Warhol factory's idea of a western, were frontier failures fueled by the same stuff that shot down *Zachariah.* When the genre got personal with the artier, anti-Establishment moodiness of Robert Altman's *McCabe and Mrs. Miller* and Peter Fonda's *Easy Rider* follow-up, *The Hired Hand,* the results were more challenging and interesting but financially unsuccessful. Filmmakers attempting to merge some of the facets of the western's weather-beaten traditions with modern sensibilities understood that they faced a tricky proposition indeed.

Perhaps the biggest obstacle westerns faced during the psychedelic era, however, came from two of the genre's biggest hits ever made. On the surface, the 1969 blockbuster *Butch Cassidy and the Sundance Kid* may be a western, but such contemporary embellishments as the "Raindrops Are Falling on My Head" bicycle sequence and the smart-alecky interplay between stars Paul Newman and Robert Redford smack more of the 1960s than of the film's 1890s setting. It was a revisionist western designed for people who didn't know or care about the genre, who were perfectly content with just being entertained. Instead of providing the firepower needed from a hit to give westerns a much-needed boost, Butch and Sundance did little for the genre, creating instead a demand for more self-effacing buddy movies in a variety of genres.

Meanwhile, Mel Brooks's *Blazing Saddles,* an uproarious, not-too-subtle skewering of cowboys, Indians, lawmen, land-snatchers, *Destry Rides Again, High Noon,* and so on, became a surprise smash hit. It sure made—and still makes—everyone laugh, western fanatic or not, but it also made people wonder if they could ever take a western seriously again.

Blazing Saddles ♩♩♩♩

Mel Brooks has often told the story about the reaction he got from Warner Bros. executives after the first showing of his western spoof *Blazing Saddles*—not a laugh in the screening room. And not only were the suits unmoved by what they had just witnessed, they were also offended by several things in the movie. Among their requests: remove the flatulence scene where cowboys let loose after eating beans around a campfire; eighty-six the horse-punching sequence with Alex Karras as Mongo; and excise the heavy use of the "n" word. Brooks eventually won out, denying their requests. He had final cut.

Thank heavens. Watching a trimmed version of this lewd, crude sagebrush satire would be the equivalent of watching it on network TV or a cable "family" channel—something we've all done on occasion, just to catch how the censors tinkered with it. Belches are substituted for the wind-breaking. The "n" word is removed or electronically garbled. And an organ sound effect drowns out some of the more imaginative expletives.

Blazing Saddles could never be made today. It's too politically insensitive. Along with the un-PC language, there are racial stereotypes, Nazi sympathizers, hostility toward animals (that horse!), disparaging remarks about many religious and ethnic groups, and drug use. Yet we still laugh and laugh, over and over again. "It's OK," we say to ourselves. "It's *Blazing Saddles.*"

Saddles had a shaky ride to the screen and, once completed, to acceptance by viewers. *Tex Ex* and *Black Bart* were its original titles, nixed by studio honchos. Richard Pryor, one of the film's cowriters, was to play Bart, the lead character, but his reputation as a radical, comedic troublemaker scared Warner Bros., leading to the casting of the easygoing Cleavon Little for the role. Shortly before the film opened—on a fairly limited basis—Warner Bros. contemplated selling it directly to TV. During its first week, it barely drew flies.

Among the few who did go to see it that first week there were some ardent fans who spread the good word near and far. The buzz surrounding this movie grew, and *Saddles* eventually went on to make over $100 million. The

> **"Badges? We don't need no stinkin' badges!"**
>
> —A Mexican bandit, in *Blazing Saddles*

Sheriff Bart (Cleavon Little) and the Waco Kid (Gene Wilder) bond in Mel Brooks's western-spoofing classic, *Blazing Saddles.*

WARNER BROS. / THE KOBAL COLLECTION

film lives on decades later, ranking high on many people's lists of the funniest movies ever made.

Such success is surprising. It's hard to think of a bigger clash of comic sensibilities than what's showcased in *Blazing Saddles.* Essentially, it's a genre parody, poking fun at the clichés we've been served with our westerns since the world's first narrative film, *The Great Train Robbery.* The story, a cop on *Rancho Notorious, Johnny Guitar,* and *Once Upon a Time in the West,* involves an unscrupulous land-snatcher, Hedley Lamarr (Harvey Korman), who wants to destroy the peaceful town of Rock Ridge so he can profit from a railroad being built in the area. Called on to defend the town is Bart (Cleavon Little), the newly appointed black sheriff, who enlists down-and-out gunman the Waco Kid (Gene Wilder) to help outsmart Lamarr and his henchmen.

The film doesn't hold together, but it's so funny, who cares? Consider the diverse participants in the writing and its klutziness makes sense. Brooks brought his Borscht Belt shtick to the proceedings, obvious in the ribald sexual innuendoes, antiquated inside references to the likes of sagebrush icon Randolph Scott and screen siren Hedy Lamarr (who sued him), and his own turn as the Jewish Indian chief who speaks Yiddish when encountering a black family's wagon train. Pryor no doubt had a hand in Bart's encounters with Rock Ridge's racist citizens ("You've got to remember that these are just simple farmers. These are people of the land. You know . . . morons."), the hipper touches like Bart's spiffy sheriff outfit, and much of the jive humor and profanity. And Andrew Bergman (a film scholar who wrote an acclaimed book on movies of the Prohibition era and went on to work on the original incarnation of *The In-Laws* and to write and direct *The Freshman*) probably pitched in with some of the comic nods to *Stagecoach, Destry Rides Again, High Noon, The Treasure of the Sierra Madre* ("Badges? We don't need no stinkin' badges!"), Busby Berkeley musicals, and Roy Rogers's B-movie westerns.

Blazing Saddles ends in shambles, with Brooks literally bringing down the western houses he had built to reveal the modern Warner Bros. studios behind them. He then proceeds to trot out a musical number with Dom DeLuise as a fey choreographer, starts a food fight at the studio commissary, and stages a shoot-out in front of Hollywood's historic Grauman's Chinese Theatre. It's a mess, but then so is most of *Blazing Saddles*—a messy classic comedy from a most unorthodox filmmaker.

1974 (R) 105m/C Cleavon Little, Gene Wilder, Madeline Kahn, Harvey Korman, Slim Pickens, David Huddleston, Mel Brooks, Alex Karras, Claude Ennis Starrett Jr., Dom DeLuise, Count Basie. ***D:*** Mel Brooks. ***W:*** Mel Brooks, Richard Pryor, Andrew Bergman, Norman Steinberg, Alan Ugar. ***C:*** Joseph Biroc. ***M:*** John Morris. *VHS, DVD*

Blue 🦴🦴🦴

To escape his past, he had to destroy it.

—Tagline for *Blue*

This curious British production boasts terrific Utah locations and a spaghetti-western sensibility, but its most interesting aspect is its leads, Terence Stamp and Joanna Pettet, two icons of '60s beauty.

By the time this film was made, Clint Eastwood was finished with his Man with No Name character, and the genre had begun to settle into new-fangled western clichés—empty landscapes and towns, more desolate than majestic; a fetishistic glamorization of weapons; laconic amoral characters; heightened sound effects, particularly evident in gunshots; and stylized graphic violence. All of those elements are in *Blue,* but director Silvio Narizzano (*Georgy Girl*) and legendary second-unit director Yakima Canutt had strong ties to more conventional westerns, and that influence is easy to see. The most obvious sign of that influence involves a shot of Stamp framed in a doorway, clearly evoking John Ford's famous conclusion to *The Searchers. Blue*'s plot is a tip of the hat to Ford's masterpiece, too, and of course Canutt was the great stuntman who worked with Ford and John Wayne on *Stagecoach* and many other films.

In the opening precredit sequence, Blue (Stamp) helps a gang of Mexican outlaw revolutionaries led by Ortega (Ricardo Montalban) ambush a group of *federales.* He then kisses the commanding officer before shooting him, establishing an unusual, ambivalent mood.

Who is this guy? Why does Ortega refer to him as a son when he's so clearly different from everyone else in the gang? And more important, why doesn't he talk (almost fifty minutes of the movie go by before Stamp utters a

word)? Is he taking this whole laconic hero business to the next level, or is there something wrong with him?

Ortega decides to see how things are going north of the Rio Grande. He arranges a raid on a small American settlement on the Fourth of July. The gringos are having a traditional celebration, enjoying a picnic while hanging and burning a "greaser" in effigy. The most prominent citizen in the settlement is Doc Morton (Karl Malden, in a role that echoes the characters he played in *One-Eyed Jacks* and *Nevada Smith*). Meanwhile, his daughter, Joanne (Joanna Pettet), the prettiest girl around, is clearly dissatisfied with her prospects.

She and Blue meet during Ortega's raid, where some adroit plotting keeps them away from the central action. He's wounded; her nostrils flare. It's not difficult to keep up with that side of the story. The other side involves the revealing of Blue's background and his temptation to rejoin Ortega's gang. That aspect of the plot is not particularly engrossing, but it does give Canutt and Narizzano the opportunity to stage some energetic action scenes. One extended chase through a field of reeds is nicely done, and the big finish at the river has moments, too, though it never comes close to the intensity of *The Wild Bunch,* made just one year later.

The real focus is on the young leads; Narizzano certainly did his best to protect and flatter them. They're beautifully photographed and costumed. Although the movies were still a few years away from really good sex scenes, Stamp and Pettet manage to generate considerable heat while keeping their clothes on.

Having Stamp maintain his silence for the first half of the film works well because when he opens his mouth, his dialogue sounds a bit strangled and odd, appropriate to his character. Pettet, another Brit, doesn't fare much better. Let's just say that her American accent is not something that Meryl Streep would have been envious of. But the two stars are not called upon to talk very much. Narizzano sticks with close shots of their finely wrought, elfin faces as they stare soulfully into the middle distance.

In the end, *Blue* is very much a product of its time. If the blatant politics, youthful sexuality, and generational conflicts don't add up to a thoroughly satisfying western, they were at least—to use a then-popular word—relevant. And that's really the main problem, in the long run. Seen today, the film simply seems to take things far too seriously. But, man, they sure did look good.

1968 (R) 113m/C Terence Stamp, Joanna Pettet, Karl Malden, Ricardo Montalban, Stathis Giallelis, Anthony Costello. **D:** Silvio Narizzano. **W:** Ronald M. Cohen, Meade Roberts. **C:** Stanley Cortez. **M:** Manos Hadjidakis. *VHS*

—*Mike Mayo*

Terence Stamp, the title character in Silvio Narizzano's *Blue,* stands framed in a doorway in a shot that pays tribute to John Ford's *The Searchers.* PARAMOUNT / THE KOBAL COLLECTION

SPAGHETTI WESTERNS: FROM LEONE WITH LOVE
by Lewis Beale

It sure sounded like a stupid idea at the time: an Italian director of muscleman epics decided to rip off the plot of a Japanese samurai movie, hire an American TV actor, and go to Spain to shoot a western. But Sergio Leone's *A Fistful of Dollars,* starring a barely known Clint Eastwood and based on Akira Kurosawa's *Yojimbo,* was not only a huge commercial success, it influenced hundreds of other movies. The "spaghetti western" genre was born.

What made these films successful? Let us count the ways.

First, they are shot through with cynicism, which makes the spaghetti western very contemporary and a real antidote to the falsely mythic image of the old West peddled by Hollywood.

Second, they feature gonzo violence, which is often portrayed in highly operatic terms. This approach, in fact, was one of Leone's main contributions to film. He'd shoot gunfights as if they were arias, with swirling camerawork and a pumping Ennio Morricone score on the soundtrack. Puccini's "Nessun Dorma" from *Turandot* is all right, but that final throwdown in *The Good, the Bad and the Ugly* has it beat for pure over-the-top grandiosity.

Third, they are just plain cool. Maybe it's the stripped-down plotlines (lots of revenge dramas) or the "who needs dialogue?" screenplays. Or it's the deliberate pacing (very Euro), grungy clothing, and oh-so-macho attitudes.

Fact is, the best of the spaghetti western genre is a perfect example of cultural cross-pollination. Take American westerns, already mythic, filter them through a European sensibility, then add a dash of up-to-the-minute '60s reaction to all things bourgeois. John Wayne, make way for the Man with No Name!

But there's a significant downside here. Let's be honest—other than the Leone epics (*For a Few Dollars More, A Fistful of Dollars, The Good, the Bad and the Ugly*), most of the genre really sucks. We're talking hundreds of movies, starring their Djangos, Ringos, Trinitys, and nobodies. Like most imitations, they just don't make it. Produced on the cheap, with badly dubbed dialogue, second-rate actors, and third-rate directors, pictures like *A Bullet for Sandoval* and *A Few Dollars for Django* show what happens when inferior talent tries to copy superior ideas. It's like watching a sixth-generation duplication of something that was once good.

Yet even though many of these flicks were never released in this country—have you ever heard of a spaghetti western star named George Hilton? How about Anthony Steffen?—they must have kept a whole generation of Europeans entertained. In the end, however, the spaghetti western movement is all about Sergio Leone's iconoclastic vision. Many have imitated it, none have duplicated it. That remains the genre's primary legacy.

The Hired Hand 🎵🎵🎵

After the amazing success of *Easy Rider,* Dennis Hopper and Peter Fonda, the film's two creators, chose to make western films as their follow-up projects. Hopper's effort was *The Last Movie,* a trippy, pretentious, expensive disaster that remains famous today for being, well, a trippy, pretentious, expensive disaster. *The Hired Hand,* Fonda's directorial debut, languished in obscurity following mixed reviews and lethargic box-office reception. Universal Studios, the company that distributed the picture, thought so little of it that they licensed it to a small, independent video label, and it disappeared from the market almost immediately.

A restoration in 2001, some limited theatrical exposure in England and the United States, and a new DVD release helped *The Hired Hand* gain some of the respect the film and its filmmaker/star deserve. While not in the same league as Robert Altman's morose masterpiece *McCabe and Mrs. Miller* or as earth-shattering as Sam Peckinpah's blood opera *The Wild Bunch, The Hired Hand* does offer elements similar to those two seminal films and proves worthy of being excavated from the prairie dust of the era's forgotten sagebrush sagas.

The Hired Hand begins in striking fashion with a gorgeous survey of three cowboys fishing and swimming in a stream. Different shots of the glistening blue water slowly dissolve into each other, forming near-psychedelic images of natural beauty. The men are Harry (Fonda), Arch (Warren Oates), and Dan (Robert Pratt). We soon learn that Harry and Arch have spent seven years together, drifting along the countryside. Now Arch is seriously considering going to California. But Harry seems afraid to journey to the West Coast for a number of reasons. Two of those reasons turn out to be a wife named Hannah (Verna Bloom) and a young daughter named Janey (Megan Denver), who, he reveals, he left behind and now wants to contact. But is this just an excuse to curtail Arch's plans or does he *really* want to see them?

Arch and Dan decide to accompany Harry home, but first the three stop at a small, dilapidated town. It's here that the men get into trouble, as Dan is shot and killed after being accused of raping the Mexican wife of McVey (Severn Darden), one of the townspeople. Harry and Arch reciprocate in a vengeful act that leaves McVey temporarily crippled, then the two take off to Harry's old home.

Harry is not met with open arms. Hannah, who is ten years older than her husband, feels betrayed by his departure and has told Janey that he's dead. Even the locals address her as "widow." Harry eventually coerces Hannah to take him and Arch in as hired hands in hopes of reconciling. Eventually, an unusual bond grows among Harry, Hannah, and Arch, and important choices about the future must be made.

Like *McCabe and Mrs. Miller, The Hired Hand* features lustrous photography (by Vilmos Zsigmond in both films), a memorably mellow score (by folk legend Bruce Langhorne in *The Hired Hand*), and a tone of quiet desperation shared by its characters. While the film offers only a few scenes of quickly rendered violence, the acts are shown in slow motion, à la *The Wild Bunch*. There are also hip cameo appearances by Larry Hagman and beat poet Michael McClure.

On the surface, *The Hired Hand* looks simple, but complexity lies beneath. Consider Hannah's anger, years later, over Harry's deciding to stay with Arch rather than remain with her. "He's had more of you than I'll ever know," she tells Harry. "He's what you left me for. You didn't know it when you left, but he's what you were looking for."

The ending of *The Hired Hand* offers a sad but sardonic resolution to the conflicts at hand, and the film proves to be an affecting, subtle character piece showing that sometimes, you really can't go home again.

1971 (R) 90m/C Peter Fonda, Warren Oates, Verna Bloom, Robert Pratt, Severn Darden, Rita Roger, Ann Doran. *D:* Peter Fonda. *W:* Alan Sharp. *C:* Vilmos Zsigmond. *M:* Bruce Langhorne. *VHS, DVD*

The Last Movie

As the story goes, the first test screening of Dennis Hopper's *The Last Movie* was held at the University of Iowa. Fresh from the success of *Easy Rider*, Hopper was one of the hottest directors in the business. He'd been given a virtually free hand to go down to Peru—then the cocaine-production capital of the world—and make a sort of experimental western. When, at length, he finished filming and editing, studio executives had no idea what to make of the result.

But then, they hadn't known what to make of *Easy Rider*, either. Thinking that a college crowd would be the perfect audience to tell them what they had, they set out for Iowa. Alas, the event went poorly. Even the long-haired youth didn't respond to Hopper's fractured tale of filmmaking in the Andes. In fact, the question-and-answer session was downright hostile. A studio executive had to hustle Hopper out of the theater.

In the lobby, they were stopped by an exceptionally pretty coed. She flirted with Hopper and asked if he'd made that film. When he said yes, she hauled off and smacked him right in the nose, screaming that he was a sexist pig.

This unnamed young woman established the proper critical response for anyone else who has watched or will watch *The Last Movie*. If you sit through the whole thing, you're entitled to give Dennis Hopper a pop on the schnozz. He created one of those cosmically bad movies that deserves comparison to *Battlefield Earth* and *Freddie Got Fingered*. That's not to say it's not without its moments, particularly if you experience it with a properly altered consciousness. So we hear, anyway.

Apparently, in its first incarnation, the script made sense. It told the story of Kansas (Hopper), a subnormal stuntman who goes down to Peru to work on a movie about Billy the Kid that is being directed by real-life auteur Sam Fuller. Kansas remains after the rest of the crew go home and becomes

involved with villagers who reenact the filmmaker's work as a religious ceremony. While all that's going on, Kansas's screen life mirrors Hopper's real life:
he abuses women, comes up with harebrained schemes, and gets drunk.

All of the most obnoxious excesses of '60s movies are brought together here: romantic sentimentality (the clichéd young lovers frolicking in a field
of wildflowers); incoherence masquerading as intellectual experimentation
(no narrative flow, missing scenes); and really bad, off-key music (memorable
lyric: "Only when it rains does it rain").

On the plus side, the story resembles *The Stuntman* in its infrequent
moments of lucidity, and some of the Peruvian landscapes are spectacular.
On the other hand, many of the night scenes are so dark you can't make out
any of the action, and the hambone acting is roaringly funny.

Viewers expecting a decently made movie will probably be disappointed
by this haphazard collection of half-baked sequences. But if you enjoy witnessing
the downward spiral of self-destruction, Hopper's alternative folly fills the bill.

1971 (R) 104m/C Dennis Hopper, Julie Adams, Stella Garcia, Tomas Milian, Samuel
Fuller, Don Gordon, Sylvia Miles. *D:* Dennis Hopper. *W:* Dennis Hopper, Stewart Stern.
C: Laszlo Kovacs. *M:* Leonard Cohen, Severn Darden, Kris Kristofferson, Chabuca
Granda. *VHS*
AKA: Chinchero

—*Mike Mayo*

Dennis Hopper
directed and starred in
the experimental and
unsuccessful *The Last
Movie,* 1971.

UNIVERSAL / THE KOBAL
COLLECTION

Little Big Man

This film adaptation of Thomas Berger's picaresque masterpiece by director Arthur Penn (*Bonnie and Clyde*) is as much about Vietnam as it is about the West. It's meant to be an "answer" to the many myths propagated about American Indians by the westerns of the 1940s and '50s, but the parallels between the cavalry's attacks and U.S. Army tactics in Vietnam are impossible to ignore.

Director Penn made it clear in his debut, *The Left-Handed Gun*—Gore Vidal's take on the legend of Billy the Kid as played by Paul Newman—that he was not interested in the traditional Hollywood approach to westerns. Where John Ford's cavalrymen are bravely defending the settlement of new territories, Penn's troopers are murderous butchers who slaughter women and children at the command of a lunatic. The noble, humble, reluctant American warriors we had seen before, and who have reappeared since, are nowhere to be found.

The story of *Little Big Man* is told by an aged Jack Crabb (Dustin Hoffman) to an interviewer's tape recorder. He says, in a screeching voice that becomes increasingly irritating as it is used in voice-overs, "I am the sole white survivor of the Battle of Little Bighorn, popularly known as Custer's Last Stand."

Flashback to a small wagon train that has just been attacked and destroyed by Indians. The only members left are a young Jack and his sister Caroline (Carol Androsky). They're rescued by a Cheyenne brave who brings them back to Old Lodge Skins (Chief Dan George). As it happens, the wagon train was attacked by Pawnee, who, we are told, are low-class, treacherous Indians, always sucking up to white people. Cheyenne, on the other hand, are "human beings." They're kind, tolerant, funny, wise, forgiving, and, as depicted in the film, even accepting of gay Indians.

Jack grows up among them but eventually moves back into the white world, where he's taken in by a sadistic preacher (Thayer David) and his sexually voracious wife (Faye Dunaway). Under the tutelage of Mr. Merriwether (Martin Balsam), Jack briefly tries his hand at being a con man. When that doesn't work out, he tries his hand as a gunfighter, calling himself the Soda Pop Kid, and becomes a pal to Wild Bill Hickok (Jeff Corey). A stint as a storekeeper brings Jack into the orbit of General George Armstrong Custer (Richard Mulligan). Although Chief Dan George got a Best Supporting Actor Oscar nomination, it's Mulligan who delivers a beautifully shaded performance that never crosses into caricature. His Custer is a fully believable holy fool surrounded by sycophants.

The violence in the second half is shocking (though at times the battle scenes appear to be thinly populated), and it's astonishing that the film received a PG rating. The most intense moments come close to the brutality of *The Wild Bunch*.

Little Big Man was made around the time when the most appalling facts concerning the government-sanctioned genocide against American

"Well, Jack. Now you know. This is a house of ill fame. And I'm a fallen flower. This life is not only wicked and sinful. It isn't even any fun."

—Louise Pendrake (Faye Dunaway), in *Little Big Man*

Jack Crabb (Dustin Hoffman) stands over Old Lodge Skins (Chief Dan George) in Arthur Penn's 1970 film *Little Big Man*. CINEMA CENTER / THE KOBAL COLLECTION

Indians were coming into wide public knowledge, and trust in established institutions was at a low ebb. The film makes use of all that, but it still has an uneven quality. Some scenes end abruptly while others go on far too long. Some fairly realistic location touches are undermined by haircuts straight from the '70s and off-target casting. Glamour-puss Aimée Eccles as Jack's Cheyenne "wife" is utterly out of place. Hoffman's performance is inconsistent, too. He brings bits of Chaplin and Keaton to some of the comic episodes, but he's never completely comfortable in the role.

The main problem, though, is Chief Dan George. Yes, he's wise and lovable and the movie brightens up every time it comes back to him. But called upon to deliver tiresome sermonettes about the many virtues of the "human beings," he's also the noblest noble savage you've ever seen.

Opinion has always been divided on the "It's a good day to die" conclusion. This reviewer would call it an unsatisfactory finale to an uneven work. At its best, though, *Little Big Man* is a familiar story told in a way never attempted before.

1970 (PG) 135m/C Dustin Hoffman, Faye Dunaway, Chief Dan George, Martin Balsam, Richard Mulligan, Jeff Corey, Aimée Eccles, Carol Androsky. **D:** Arthur Penn. **W:** Calder Willingham. **C:** Harry Stradling Jr. **M:** John Hammond *VHS, DVD*

—*Mike Mayo*

Name Your Poison.

—Tagline for *McCabe and Mrs. Miller*

McCabe and Mrs. Miller ♪♪♪♪

Of all the "revisionist" westerns that were made in the '60s and '70s— *Blue, Little Big Man, Pat Garrett and Billy the Kid*—Robert Altman's take on the genre remains one of the least dated and most interesting. Sure, the anti-Establishment, antiauthoritarian attitude found in those other films (and so many more of the era) is easy to spot here as well, but Altman wasn't interested in a polemic. He had a good story to tell about flawed characters, and he told it through striking, memorable images. In the course of telling that story, he turns every western stereotype inside out.

There are no grand vistas, no Monument Valley or wide open spaces. Instead, the action takes place within a heavily forested valley that's made even more claustrophobic by continuous rain and snow. The characters aren't hearty, straight-shooting pioneers who are going forth bravely to tame the wilderness. They're rough, ignorant, and poor. Physical action is limited. Everything moves slowly—even the horses seem tired—but the pace doesn't drag. Nary a shot is fired nor a punch thrown until the film's last twenty minutes. Finally, instead of a soaring orchestral score, the film makes fine use of Leonard Cohen's dirge-like songs.

McCabe (Warren Beatty) is a gambler who wanders into the hamlet of Presbyterian Church, Washington, still under construction, and realizes that the burg lacks a whorehouse. He brings in three "chippies," who barely meet the absolute minimum requirements for their profession, and manages to be

fairly successful. Enter Mrs. Miller (Julie Christie), who shows McCabe how he could boost his profits by investing a little more, sprucing things up, and importing quality talent. He reluctantly takes her on as a partner and they prosper. They're so successful that a powerful mining company wants to buy them out. That's where their real problems begin.

McCabe is one of those guys who always manages to do exactly the wrong thing. He's dim-witted, greedy, and shortsighted. But by the end, at least he understands these things about himself. (In some ways, the role is similar to the hairdresser Beatty plays in *Shampoo,* and his work here is almost as strong—restrained and believable throughout.) Mrs. Miller is more resourceful and intelligent, but she's got problems of her own and is no help in that final act, which quickly becomes a variation on *High Noon.*

Much of the film's appeal is due to the superb visual work of Altman and cinematographer Vilmos Zsigmond. They use smoke, dim light, and grainy focus to give the whole film a rough texture that's perfectly suited to its subject (and mirrors Mrs. Miller's opium-induced moods). Balanced against the grim autumn and winter settings is a bracing bawdiness. In the end, *McCabe and Mrs. Miller* is one of the best and most original westerns of its time.

Today, *McCabe and Mrs. Miller* enjoys a strong following, as its reputation has grown over the years. When it was first issued in theaters, the reviews were all over the map. Some critics praised its fresh and unusual

Julie Christie and Warren Beatty are ill-fated partners in Robert Altman's *McCabe and Mrs. Miller.*

approach to the genre, while others found it distracting. The box office, however, was less ambiguous: as is the case with many of Altman's post-*M*A*S*H* projects, the returns were dismal.

1971 (R) 121m/C Warren Beatty, Julie Christie, Rene Auberjonois, Keith Carradine, Michael Murphy, William Devane, Shelley Duvall. **D:** Robert Altman. **W:** Robert Altman, Brian McKay. **C:** Vilmos Zsigmond. **M:** Leonard Cohen. *VHS, DVD*

—*Mike Mayo*

Pat Garrett and Billy the Kid ♫♫♫

"You'll just end up like all the other gringos—drinkin' tequila, shittin' out chili peppers, and waitin' fer . . . nothin'."

—Luke (Harry Dean Stanton), in *Pat Garrett and Billy the Kid*

The stories that swirl around Sam Peckinpah's last great western really are the stuff of Hollywood legend.

Throughout the production he fought vicious battles with MGM studio head James Aubrey, who seems to have been determined to undermine the picture. Filming in Mexico was a nightmare, with terrible influenza striking cast and crew. Peckinpah was also battling his own demons, drinking heavily, fighting with family members, and trying to get over a nasty divorce. Even as production began on the film, the script was being rewritten and important equipment was failing.

Despite all that, the filmmakers came up with a brilliant, albeit flawed, masterpiece—one that essentially remained unseen until something like a director's cut was released on home video. Peckinpah's cut of the story runs a little over two hours. After considerable studio infighting, a butchered ninety-minute version was released to theaters in 1973. Critical response was mixed; box office was terrible.

The story revolves around the relationship between Pat Garrett (James Coburn at his understated best), an outlaw turned lawman, and Billy Bonney (Kris Kristofferson), a baby-faced killer who's a sort of surrogate son to the older Garrett. As the New Mexico of 1881 becomes civilized, the powers that be grow fed up with Billy's menacing and murderous ways. They order Garrett to remedy the situation. Billy is given a chance to leave.

The long version of the film begins with a scene set in 1909, years after the events of the rest of the film, linking the deaths of the two men. It's beautifully staged but implies that they're dramatic equals. They're not. This is Garrett's story—Garrett's and Peckinpah's. Both have made too many compromises and are trying to find safe places for themselves in a world where they just don't fit. At least, that's what they *say* they're doing. Both are so self-destructive that it's hard to tell what they really want. That side of the story comes to a wonderfully weird conclusion when Peckinpah shows up for a cameo as a coffin maker who tries to force Garrett to see himself. Unfortunately, whenever the focus shifts to Billy, the film becomes more predictable.

The best thing about the film, though, is the supporting cast. It is perhaps the finest collection of character actors ever brought together for one project. One or more of these guys (and Katy Jurado) had appeared in virtually every important western and hundreds of unimportant ones. The list begins with R. G. Armstrong as Bob, the Bible-thumping deputy who screams at Billy, "Repent, you son of a bitch! . . . I'll take you for a walk across hell on a spiderweb." The other minor legends show up in a loosely connected series of memorable scenes and include Slim Pickens, Chill Wills, Barry Sullivan, Jason Robards, Luke Askew, John Beck, Matt Clark, Jack Elam, Emilio Fernandez (General Mapache from *The Wild Bunch*), Paul Fix, L. Q. Jones, Charles Martin Smith, Harry Dean Stanton, Mike Mikler, Walter Kelley, Elisha Cook Jr., Dub Taylor, and Don Levy.

On the downside, Rudy Wurlitzer's script is overly talky, especially for a film that seems to care little about plot. Bob Dylan's score, including the classic "Knockin' on Heaven's Door," may be superior, but his turn as Alias, a former printer who busts out of jail with Billy, plays like a casting stunt that just didn't work. The music icon appears to have wandered onto the set by mistake and almost never makes eye contact with anyone. His big scene involves reading aloud from canned food labels.

Pat Garrett and Billy the Kid is a slow, meditative examination of failure and disappointment. It's too bad the film was never given its chance in the marketplace. It might have done very well in a year that embraced such unconventional stories as *The Last Detail, The Exorcist, Serpico, Badlands, Don't Look Now,* and *Mean Streets.* It's overdue for a full restoration and reappreciation on DVD.

1973 (R) 122m/C James Coburn, Kris Kristofferson, Jason Robards, Katy Jurado, Richard Jaeckel, Chill Wills, Bob Dylan, Rita Coolidge, R. G. Armstrong, Slim Pickens, Barry Sullivan, Luke Askew, John Beck, Matt Clark, Jack Elam, Emilio Fernandez, Paul Fix, L. Q. Jones, Charles Martin Smith, Harry Dean Stanton, Mike Mikler, Walter Kelley, Elisha Cook Jr., Dub Taylor, Don Levy. **D:** Sam Peckinpah. **W:** Rudy Wurlitzer. **C:** John Coquillon. **M:** Bob Dylan. *VHS, DVD*

—*Mike Mayo*

> **Stained with the blood of the innocent.**
>
> —Tagline for *Soldier Blue*

Soldier Blue 🦴🦴🦴

I n 1968 John Wayne won his only Best Actor Academy Award for his performance in *True Grit.* Two years later, *Soldier Blue* told audiences that everything they had learned from John Wayne movies was a complete, unadulterated lie.

Soldier Blue warns you of its unromantic stance from the get-go. Over the title credits, Buffy Sainte-Marie sings a sad, poetic, ironically patriotic song about America's early days. A screen crawl notes that the film is based on fact and many of the horrific incidents depicted actually occurred.

The story is set in Colorado in the 1860s, where Honus Gent (Peter Strauss), a young cavalry soldier, is caught in the middle of a vicious Indian attack while on a payroll-guarding assignment. As his fellow troop members

SAM PECKINPAH: GUNS OVER HOLLYWOOD

Sam Peckinpah

THE KOBAL COLLECTION

Ernst Lubitsch had his "touch," Alfred Hitchcock his MacGuffin, and Sam Peckinpah his blood.

Slow-mo violence with plasma spewing all over is the legacy of the hard-living Peckinpah, a legacy established by one film, 1969's *The Wild Bunch.* Westerns were on the way out, but Sam stirred the kettle big-time, eliciting shock and occasionally nausea from audiences. This tale of aging outlaws who join leader William Holden on one last, doomed mission polarized critics as well. Judith Crist, then film critic for *New York* magazine, called the film's final showdown "the bloodiest and most sickening display of slaughter I can ever recall in a theatrical film." At the same time, Vincent Canby of the *New York Times* deemed *The Wild Bunch* "the first truly interesting American-made western in years."

Branded as an outlaw himself even before *The Wild Bunch* was released, "Bloody Sam" wrestled with reactions to the film for the rest of his career, sometimes embracing its violence, other times consciously trying to prove he was a kinder, gentler filmmaker (if not a kinder, gentler man).

A former Marine, Peckinpah worked with the great Don Siegel on several low-budget efforts and played a meter man in the classic *Invasion of the Body Snatchers.* He made an early mark helming such TV series as *The Westerner, The Rifleman,* and *Gunsmoke,* then graduated to features with *The Deadly Companions* with Maureen O'Hara and Brian Keith. His sophomore outing, *Ride the High Country,* was a bona fide masterpiece, an elegiac western with genre icons Joel McCrea and Randolph Scott as two men—coping with the loss of the West they have known and conflicted by their past friendship—pitted against each other on one final, dangerous mission—in other words, a foreshadowing of *The Wild Bunch.*

Major Dundee (1965) began the filmmaker's long-running hate affair with the Hollywood Establishment. The Civil War epic, an interesting mess that was re-edited by studio hacks, was marked by many on-set altercations between Peckinpah and star Charlton Heston.

It took Peckinpah four years to get studio backing for another project. The result was *The Wild Bunch,* a savage western, yes, but also a movie reflective of the ongoing Vietnam War and the rebelliousness felt in the United States at the time.

The director responded to critics of the violence in *The Wild Bunch* with *The Ballad of Cable Hogue* the following year, a genial western fable with Jason Robards as an entrepreneur trying to cash in on a water source he finds in the desert and Stella Stevens as the whore he loves.

Cable Hogue tanked at the box office, so Peckinpah returned to his fascination/repulsion ambivalence toward violence with 1971's *Straw Dogs,* boasting Dustin Hoffman as a meek mathematician who takes matters into his own hands when wife Susan George is raped in a small English town. Peckinpah was marked again as a violence-obsessed lunatic by many because of the film's graphic nature. His answer? *Junior Bonner,* an understated look at the uneasy homecoming of a rodeo champ, played by Steve McQueen.

But *Junior* was a bummer with audiences. Peckinpah piggy-backed Bonner that same year with another McQueen vehicle, *The Getaway,* a nasty, high-octane bank robbery thriller based on a Jim Thompson story.

The Getaway was a 1972 hit that fueled Peckinpah's shoot-'em-up slate through the rest of the decade. Also gassed was Sam, who took to the bottle big-time and began popping pills, snorting coke, and getting into trouble off the set.

In succession, Peckinpah delivered:

- *Pat Garrett and Billy the Kid,* which presented a new twist on the Billy the Kid legend and western myths with James Coburn, Kris Kristofferson, and Bob Dylan. MGM, its studio, did some drastic recutting.

- *Bring Me the Head of Alfredo Garcia,* an amazing but poorly reviewed riff on *The Treasure of the Sierra Madre* with Warren Oates as a desperate Peckinpah-like figure in search of the noggin of a young man who impregnated a Mexican crime lord's daughter.

- *The Killer Elite,* a strangely remote thriller with *Godfather* costars James Caan and Robert Duvall as dueling CIA agents, offering before-their-time kung fu fighting sequences.

- *Cross of Iron,* a vivid but sometimes confusing look at German troops on the Eastern Front during World War II, featuring Coburn and Maximilian Schell.

- *Convoy,* a messy road movie inspired by the hit C. W. McCall ballad of the same name, involving renegade trucker Kris Kristofferson, gal pal Ali McGraw, and frustrated smokey Ernest Borgnine.

After *Convoy,* sadly, Sam was out of steam, and his career was shot. He directed one more film, the lethargic Robert Ludlum adaptation *The Osterman Weekend* with Burt Lancaster and Rutger Hauer, and he also helmed some music videos for Julian Lennon.

A year later, in December 1984, at the age of 59, Peckinpah died of heart failure. A surplus of artificial stimulants, tempestuous relationships with women, and Hollywood meddling had gotten the best of cinema's misunderstood wild man.

Donald Pleasence (right) plays the creepy Isaac Q. Cumber opposite Candice Bergen and Peter Strauss in the unconventional *Soldier Blue.*

AVCO EMBASSY / THE KOBAL COLLECTION

are brutally killed, Gent and "Cresta" Lee (Candice Bergen) manage to escape. The two soon take to the wilderness in an attempt to find their way back to Fort Reunion, a military encampment.

Emotionally frazzled by the violent nature of the attack, Gent is dependent upon the very able Cresta. But Gent, nicknamed Soldier Blue by his female companion, has a hunch there's more to Cresta's survival skills and Indian knowledge than she's admitting. Further arousing Gent's suspicions is her anger at the U.S. government for their treatment of Native Americans.

Cresta and Gent's initial uneasiness dissipates, and the two soon become romantically involved. It's not long before Gent discovers Cresta's secrets: she has spent two years with the Cheyenne, and she is engaged to a cavalry officer. After a series of adventures that include an altercation with a group of Kiowa Indians and a run-in with a perverted arms dealer named Isaac Q. Cumber (Donald Pleasence at his creepiest), Cresta and Gent reach Fort Reunion. There, Cresta has an apprehensive meeting with her fiancé and learns that Colonel Iverson (John Anderson) is planning a sneak attack on an encampment of Cheyenne who have reached peaceful terms with the U.S. government. She flees to alert Spotted Wolf (Jorge Rivero), the leader of the tribe (with whom she previously lived), but Gent stays to blindly fulfill his duties as a soldier.

In its unedited form (the U.S. video release has been watered down to a PG version), the final fifteen minutes of *Soldier Blue,* depicting the cavalry's confrontation with the Cheyenne, stand among the most harrowing ever committed to celluloid. As the arrogant Colonel Iverson, looking like a demonic Custer, leads the charge, innocent men are shot, women are raped, tortured, and decapitated, and children are trampled. Somewhere in the middle of all this madness, Gent loses his mind and Cresta gives in to the realization that there is nothing she can do about the chaos that surrounds her.

It appears obvious that director Ralph Nelson (*Charly*) and screenwriter John Gay (*No Way to Treat a Lady*) intended the Cheyenne slaughter to represent the Vietnam War's My Lai massacre of 1968, in which U.S. troops, led by Lieutenant William Calley, killed three hundred innocent South Vietnamese villagers. But as the opening of the film reminds us, there was a similar incident that occurred earlier in American history and on which *Soldier Blue* is based. During what became known as the Sand Creek Massacre of 1864, a peaceful Cheyenne tribe, led by Black Kettle, became the victims of horrible atrocities by the racist Colonel John Chivington and his troops in Colorado.

The echoes of My Lai are not the only contemporary element to *Soldier Blue*. At times, Bergen's Cresta seems like she could have just walked off the beach at Malibu. Wearing a homemade peasant dress, swearing, and reminding Gent that she's down with what's really happening with the Native Americans and the cavalry, she plays the irritating conscience of the film. Still, it's forgivable, as her character is the necessary tie between the film's traditional and modern threads.

Soldier Blue never caught on with American audiences and, after a few weeks, was filling the third bill at drive-ins. In Europe, however, the film was well received and had a longer theatrical life. Over the years, it has developed a healthy following, particularly in England, where it's available on video. In the U.S., though it is much requested, the film is virtually impossible to find, even in its truncated form.

Soldier Blue is an uneasy assemblage of contrasts: modern and traditional; love story and war drama; peace preaching and gratuitous violence. One would imagine John Wayne probably hated the hell out of it.

1970 (R) 115m/C; (PG) 109m/C Candice Bergen, Peter Strauss, Donald Pleasence, John Anderson, Jorge Rivero, Dana Elcar, James Hampton. *D:* Ralph Nelson. *W:* John Gay. *C:* Robert B. Hauser. *M:* Roy Budd. *VHS*

> **Two gunfighters separate and experience surreal visions on their journey through the West.**
>
> —Tagline for *Zachariah*

Zachariah 🦴🦴

Billed as "the first electric western," *Zachariah* is a mind-boggling oddity that shows what happens when the wild, wild West gets dosed on acid.

Filled with flighty philosophical musings, religious symbolism, mostly bad country-rock music, and an out-of-left-field gay subtext, *Zachariah* is a film that surely would have made John Wayne cringe. The problem is that it made pretty much everyone cringe, including its targeted hip, young audience.

PHIL PROCTOR: DADDY OF THE ELECTRIC WESTERN

It's not every day that you see a western with trippy sequences, rock stars as out-laws, and modern musical instruments sharing the screen with pistols and ponies. But not every western is *Zachariah,* cowritten by the Firesign Theatre, the hip, irrever-ent comedy troupe that scored with such popular records and radio projects as *We're All Bozos on This Bus* and *Everything You Know Is Wrong* in the 1960s and 1970s.

Firesign member Phil Proctor remembers the filming of *Zachariah* fondly. "It started with a guy named Joe Massot, a documentary filmmaker who had done a movie with Bob Dylan and wanted Dylan to star in this film," said Proctor. "He came up with the idea of modernizing the western with New Age touches, and he brought us into the project.

"We started working in a little place on Vine [in Hollywood]. We wanted to bring a Zen-like quality to the film, show how an approaching bullet would look slow to a gunslinger, kind of how athletes had an unusual understanding of time."

According to Proctor, Massot had an argument with producer George Englund and then quit the production. Englund took over the directorial reins of the film. "The idea was always to do the Herman Hesse *Siddhartha* story in the Old West, but with comedy and that Zen approach," recalled Proctor. "But when George took over it became less psychedelic and more surreal. Englund just didn't have the same spirit of Massot. We envisioned it like a samurai film with humor, a lot wilder, maybe something in the Mel Brooks style. But the script and ideas were treat-ed more literally."

Proctor believes the film still has some of the elements Massot and fellow Firesign members Peter Bergman, Philip Austin, and David Ossman originally envisioned. "For me, the film is not a failure. It just went in a different direction than we originally wanted it to go. What we have now is a surrealist, homoerotic fantasy that has some flashes of what we wanted it to be."

Proctor says the experience working on *Zachariah* was still a memorable one, especially when he and other Firesigners joined the production in Mexico for location shooting. "The produc-tion designer of *Cleopatra* was hired," Proctor recalled. "He said his secret to making things like the Old West was to bury the clothes, so he buried the clothes all over the place.

"George Englund was married to Cloris Leachman at the time," said Proctor. "I remember that we turned her on to some really good weed out there. We had a great old time. Not long after the movie production was over, she won an Academy Award [for *The Last Picture Show*]. So we felt we had something to do with that."

The hippie '70s meet cowboy criminals when Zachariah (John Rubinstein), a farmer, receives a pistol through the mail. (Luckily, Michael Moore hadn't caught wind of it.) Playing with his new gun, Zachariah exclaims, "Far out," then goes about trying to make a name for himself as an outlaw. Joined by blacksmith pal Matthew (Don Johnson), Zachariah hooks up with an outlaw bunch known as the Crackers (played by rockers Country Joe & the Fish).

After the not-too-crisp Crackers botch some holdups, Zachariah and Matthew ditch the gang and decide to find their own way. They mosey into a saloon populated by hookers dressed in modern garb and a group of surly ruffians (real-life rockers the James Gang with Joe Walsh). Also in the joint is Job Cain (Elvin Jones), an African American gunslinger who, as showcased in an extended drum solo, is also quite the percussionist.

A shoot-out demonstrates Zachariah's rapidly improving ability with firearms, but he's more interested in proving his love—for Matthew! "We're not on the same trip," is Matthew's cool response to Zachariah's profession of affection, and the young guns part ways. Moving on, Zachariah befriends an old codger (William Challee), has sex with Belle Starr (*Alice's Restaurant*'s Pat Quinn), and eventually reunites with a much-changed Matthew.

Zachariah's search for enlightenment and self-discovery was inspired by Herman Hesse's *Siddhartha,* a popular book with the campus crowd at the time. But *Zachariah,* for all of its mixing of Old West motifs with contemporary lingo, music, and conventions, is mostly a slow-moving bummer. The problem starts with the casting. In a role that was reportedly offered to Bob Dylan before director George Englund made the character gay, Rubinstein, though he brings nice wide-eyed innocence to the proceedings, looks like he's ready to take to the disco at any second. (It must be those Leo Sayer–style curly locks.) The ever-enthusiastic Johnson, alarmingly rail-thin and a bit manic, looks like a young Tom Petty with better teeth. And Country Joe & the Fish's supporting turns were eclipsed by their Woodstock performance.

Zachariah has its moments—Dick Van Patten as a shyster horse dealer is nifty—but it's eventually buried by its own heavy-handed approach and a grating, self-conscious attitude that screams, "Hey, ain't I hip?" For the world's first electric western, a power failure may have been just what the sheriff ordered.

1970 (R) 91m/C John Rubinstein, Don Johnson, Pat Quinn, Elvin Jones, William Challee, Country Joe & the Fish, the James Gang, Joe Walsh. **D:** George Englund. **W:** Joe Massot, Philip Austin, Peter Bergman, Philip Proctor, David Ossman. **C:** Jorge Stahl. **M:** Jimmie Haskell. *VHS, DVD*

Chapter 5

Black Like Us

For many decades, with rare exceptions, Hollywood overlooked black audiences. The studios were fully aware that a sizable portion of the ticket-buying public was black, but would they produce movies specifically for African Americans, starring or even directed by African Americans? No way. Unless it was Sidney Poitier, Tinseltown wouldn't touch a black leading actor or actress.

This incredible policy, engendered by shortsightedness and ignorance, changed dramatically in the early 1970s. Melvin Van Peebles, a black American filmmaker who had to go to France to start his writing and directing career, decided to raise money for a new film. He had two features under his belt: *The Story of a Three-Day Pass,* an autobiographical independent film, and *Watermelon Man,* a moderately successful studio-sanctioned satire about a racist who magically turns black one day.

But Van Peebles had a lot to say, and he knew the studios weren't going to give him the resources to say it. He scratched together a few hundred thousand dollars and wrote, directed, edited, composed the music for, and starred in *Sweet Sweetback's Baadasssss Song.* The film immediately angered everyone who was involved with it. The MPAA gave it an "X" rating. Movie theaters initially refused to book it. And even its distributor wanted the film's title altered. Van Peebles persevered, refusing to change the title and accepting the "X" rating, using it to his advantage in his advertising campaign. Curiosity among blacks prompted urban theaters to show it. The angry, borderline avant-garde film about a black man (played by Van Peebles) on the run from white police through a hellish Los Angeles became a sensation, amassing $15 million.

Sweet Sweetback's payoff was sweet for other talented blacks stuck in a rut as well. Savvy independents like American International Pictures and Dimension Pictures followed in this film's footsteps, cranking out black-oriented efforts. Soon, the major studios joined in the parade as well, and black performers suddenly had an unprecedented abundance of roles.

With Afro, mustache, leather jacket, and cool attitude, Richard Roundtree played *Shaft,* a detective who fought crime on the grimy streets of New York to the beat of Isaac Hayes's far-out Oscar-winning theme music. Directing the MGM production was Gordon Parks, a renowned photojournalist who had broken the color line to become the first black filmmaker hired by a major studio when he helmed *The Learning Tree,* an auto-biographical drama, in 1969. *Shaft* proved such a smash it spawned two sequels, a TV series, and a remake almost twenty-five years later.

Although the original *Shaft* was a solid bit of detective work, once the floodgates had opened, a number of shoddy productions aimed at a black audience poured onto the market. Studio backers both large and small viewed black films with a hint of trepidation, allocating small budgets to most of the offerings geared to an African American crowd. Because of the studios' timidity, most of the films were genre-oriented—action (*Hell up in Harlem*), some horror (the *Blacula* films), occasional comedy (*Five on the Black Hand Side*)—and were built squarely on the shoulders of the movies' stars. The plotting was often perfunctory, taking a backseat to the action, violence, or laughs. Stereotypes of both the black and white variety abounded. And recognizable personalities from the sports world, such as Jim Brown (*Gunn*) and Fred Williamson (*The Legend of Nigger Charley*), and from the music business, including Isaac Hayes (*Truck Turner*), were recruited for the silver screen. For the most part, these were exploitation flicks geared squarely to the African American moviegoer, movies that were termed "black exploitation" or "blaxploitation" by trade publications like *Variety* and the *Hollywood Reporter* during the mid-1970s, a few years after their cycle began spinning.

On rare occasions, a 1970s-era black-oriented project would try something more substantial than a typical effort of its time. In several cases, producers remade classic films with black casts, including reworkings of *Get Carter* (*Hit Man*), *Little Caesar* (*Black Caesar*), *Odd Man Out* (*The Lost Man*), *The Informer* (*Up Tight!*), and *The Asphalt Jungle* (*Cool Breeze*).

Unfortunately for the black actors and actresses, once performers were featured in a hit blaxploitatation film, their careers often became ghettoized, and they were subsequently unable to get roles in non-exploitation movies, whether higher-quality black movies or mainstream "white" film projects. But, at least for the women—such as Pam Grier (*Coffy*), Tamara Dobson (*Cleopatra Jones*), Carol Speed (*Abby*), and Gloria Hendry (*Slaughter's Big Rip-Off*)—blaxploitation movies made the difference between working in movies and not, offering otherwise rare opportunities to star in films.

By the end of the 1970s, the blaxploitation films were beginning to lose steam with audiences and studios alike. The stories—many of which feature a white character as the bad guy—were repetitive, and the budgets remained restrictively small despite the successful cost-to-profit ratio these films showed. Black audiences were growing weary of genre pictures, even when the casts featured African American performers.

After a dry spell of several years, films geared expressly to black audiences, made by black filmmakers, began to be produced again starting in the mid-1980s, thanks to the first films of the likes of Spike Lee (*She's Gotta Have It*), Allen and Albert Hughes (*Menace II Society*), Robert Townsend (*Hollywood Shuffle*), Reginald and Warrington Hudlin (*House Party*), and Mario Van Peebles (*New Jack City*), the son of Melvin Van Peebles, the man who, for better or worse, started the blaxploitation cycle in the first place.

Across 110th Street ♪♪♪♪

When independent film companies like American International Pictures hit it big with low-budget blaxploitation films in the early 1970s, the major studios jumped into the fold and quickly cranked out their own knockoffs. One of the most down and dirty of these is *Across 110th Street,* an enterprise that not only foreshadowed elements of the still nascent black exploitation surge, but added an unsavory helping of *Godfather*-era violence into the mix as well.

An over-the-top Anthony Quinn (who also produced) stars in this ultraviolent outing as Captain Mattelli, a corrupt New York detective investigating a bookie joint robbery that turned into a bloodbath. Teamed with his no-nonsense African American partner, Lieutenant Pope (Yaphet Kotto), Mattelli finds himself caught between a trio of bad elements: mafioso Nick D'Salvio (Anthony Franciosa), who regularly greases Mattelli's palms and is on the hunt to find the loot and send a message; his NYPD compadres; and the criminals who, dressed in police uniforms, botched the heist in the first place.

With gritty Harlem locales, boiling racial tensions, expletive-punctuated dialogue, and a throbbing Bobby Womack score (Quentin Tarantino used this film's theme song for the opening and ending of *Jackie Brown*), *Across 110th Street* crosses the boundaries of good taste to deliver a film that's both incendiary and wildly entertaining at the same time. Director Barry Shear (*Wild in the Streets*) lays the tension on thick as Quinn's Mattelli is pinched by all sides and has to cope with an unending parade of potential catastrophes, all of which threaten to bring his long career, and possibly his life, to an end. Franciosa's D'Salvio, too, is in a constant state of duress, which leads him into fits of brutal fury over the potentially deadly ramifications of the botched heist.

Except for the commanding Kotto's upright cop, nobody in the film walks the straight and narrow. Appropriately, the film is populated by a rogues' gallery of '70s character actors who lend able and slimy support.

Best among them is Antonio Fargas, Huggy Bear of *Starsky and Hutch,* who meets his demise in one of the film's, and maybe the era's, most unsettling scenes.

Released during the Christmas season of 1972, *Across 110th Street* pulled in surprisingly solid numbers at the box office, playing well into '73, drawing primarily African American audiences because of its marketing campaign geared toward blaxploitation fans. But talk about inappropriate holiday entertainment! With bloodletting galore, prostitutes, seamy locales, and an entourage of unscrupulous characters, *Across 110th Street* is the kind of movie guaranteed to send Santa back to the fridge for an extra swig of eggnog.

1972 (R) 110m/C Anthony Quinn, Anthony Franciosa, Yaphet Kotto, Paul Benjamin, Ed Bernard, Antonio Fargas. ***D:*** Barry Shear. ***W:*** Luther Davis. ***C:*** Jack Priestley. ***M:*** Bobby Womack, J. J. Johnson. *VHS, DVD*

Anthony Quinn plays a corrupt cop and Yaphet Kotto his honest partner in *Across 110th Street.*

Cotton Comes to Harlem ♫♫♫

Come Back, Charleston Blue ♫♫♩

An adaptation of Chester Himes's novel directed by actor and sometime-director Ossie Davis, *Cotton Comes to Harlem* is one of the earliest and most influential of the blaxploitation cop films. Made a couple of years before *Shaft,* it's a New York story that's shot on some terrific locations.

The opening sequence of a Rolls Royce gliding through the streets of Harlem sets the tone. The confrontations and chase that follow establish a brash mixture of alarming and comic violence that's lost in today's action movies.

The central figure is Reverend Deke O'Malley (Calvin Lockhart), a slick charlatan who has conned $87,000 from people who have signed on for his Back to Africa movement. During a rally, masked thieves of unknown race abscond with the loot and stash it inside a bale of cotton. But police detectives "Gravedigger" Jones (Godfrey Cambridge) and "Coffin" Ed Johnson (Raymond St. Jacques) refuse to tolerate that kind of disturbance on their turf. For director Davis, the resolution of various crimes is much less important than portraying Harlem at a time when race relations were bubbling over with turmoil and flux.

Himes's novels have never received the popularity they deserve. At the center of his story—and the film—are two strong, memorable characters. For my money, Cambridge and St. Jacques get Jones and Johnson absolutely right. They're violent, angry, and evenhanded in their contempt for the predators and fools they deal with every day. As their boss says, "Ed and Digger, they have their own special way of dealing with things up here."

It's worth noting that while most of the film's clothes are horribly, sometimes laughably, dated, Cambridge and St. Jacques still look sharp and smooth. The same can be said of the film itself. Compared to most of its contemporaries—and the cheaper films that would follow—it's a very polished production: well lit, well photographed, and well paced. The music was written by Galt MacDermot, who was also responsible for the musical *Hair.* It's easy to hear echoes of that '60s icon here, and the music simply adds to the enjoyable atmosphere.

Gravedigger Jones and Coffin Ed came back for the sequel, *Come Back, Charleston Blue,* two years later. In this outing, the team take on a sleazy photographer (Peter De Anda) who concocts a story about a ghost returning to Harlem in order to wrest control of the local drug trade from the current kingpin (Maxwell Glanville). The film didn't fare as well as the original at the box office, ending Hollywood's interest in Himes's work until 1991's *A Rage in Harlem.*

With these films' successful mix of action and comedy, and given the popularity of recent productions geared toward urban audiences, don't be

Godfrey Cambridge plays "Gravedigger" Jones and Raymond St. Jacques is "Coffin" Ed Johnson in *Cotton Comes to Harlem.* UNITED ARTISTS / THE KOBAL COLLECTION

surprised if there is renewed interest in Gravedigger and Coffin, or in other Himes characters, in the near future.

Cotton Comes to Harlem

1970 (R) 97m/C Godfrey Cambridge, Raymond St. Jacques, Calvin Lockhart, Judy Pace, Redd Foxx, John Anderson, Emily Lancy, J. D. Cannon. **D:** Ossie Davis. **W:** Arnold Perl. **C:** Gerald Hirschfeld. **M:** Galt McDermot. *VHS, DVD*

Come Back, Charleston Blue

1972 (PG) 100m/C Godfrey Cambridge, Raymond St. Jacques, Peter De Anda, Percy Rodrigues, Jonelle Allen. **D:** Mark Warren. **W:** Peggy Elliott. **C:** Richard C. Kratina. **M:** Donny Hathaway. *VHS, DVD*

—Mike Mayo

Dolemite 🦴🦴🦴

A nightclub comic and recording artist who specialized in "blue" material and profane poetry, Rudy Ray Moore spun some of his savings into producing a movie in 1975. Inspired by a real-life character Moore told stories about in his act, *Dolemite* was made for about $100,000 and was directed by the film's costar, D'Urville Martin, a regular in black-oriented features of the period like *Hell up in Harlem* and *Book of Numbers*.

The beefy Moore plays Dolemite, a club owner who spent time in prison after being set up. Upon his release, Dolemite plans to get even while exposing Willie Green (Martin), the creep who helped put him in the slammer. Willie's been running Dolemite's club and has ties to the town's crooked white leader, Mayor Daley (Hy Pike), so Dolemite's task isn't going to be easy.

Even in freshly transferred DVD and VHS incarnations, *Dolemite* remains a shoddy-looking production, with ugly color, lots of background shadows, scenes obviously shot on soundstages, and even the occasional boom mike. Audiences at the time, however, didn't seem to mind. They were getting off on Moore's expletive-filled dialogue and songs and a plot in which the white mayor and his associates get theirs. Add some truly outrageous flourishes, like a wardrobe of pimp-friendly clothing, a preacher with a sex addiction, a team of kung-fu-kicking mamas, lots of gratuitous nudity, and a scene in which Rudy Ray makes like Sonny Chiba and pulls Willie's heart out of his chest in a fight, and you have enough of a hit to bankroll Moore's next out-of-sight effort.

In fact, Moore's career has resembled the Energizer bunny. While other, more popular blaxploitation stars have a tough time eking out a living these days, Moore keeps going and going. He's had amazing longevity as a movie performer since *Dolemite*'s debut, producing, writing, and starring in several other features. Among them are low-budget but financially successful offerings such as *The Human Tornado* (1976), in which Dolemite returns to battle an evil white mobster who has strong-armed Queen Bee (club comic Lady Reed) and her girls to work for him; 1977's *Petey Wheatstraw* (AKA *The*

Poster advertising Rudy Ray Moore as *Dolemite* THE KOBAL COLLECTION

ENTER THE FU! A MARTIAL ARTS EXPLOSION by Brian Thomas

It's hard to believe now that forty years ago the Asian martial arts were almost completely unknown in America. Sure, we'd seen Peter Lorre as Mr. Moto practicing jujitsu, and both Elvis Presley and Frank Sinatra had had movie karate fights, but Chinese kung fu was as alien as Mr. Spock. That is, until a gentleman named Bruce Lee appeared on television.

Born in China, raised in the United States, Lee was the messiah of both martial arts and modern action movies. Having been a Hong Kong child star while beginning his training in *wing chun* kung fu, the adult Lee was anxious to bring his acting and athletic skills to Hollywood. He was teaching his own style of kung fu he called *jeet kune do* at a school he had started, and this style was shaking up the martial-arts community. He came to the attention of Hollywood producer William Dozier, who was casting for a follow-up to his hit TV series *Batman.* Lee's extremely adaptable style proved perfect for fight choreography, and the fight scenes Lee created for *The Green Hornet* were like nothing anyone had ever seen before. After the series ended, Lee created a series called *Kung Fu,* about a fugitive Shaolin monk in the old American West, but prejudice prevented him from being cast in the series himself, and David Carradine was hired to star.

Bitter, Lee went back to Hong Kong to pursue offers to star in features. There, *Green Hornet* was known as *The Kato Show* after his character, and he already had a huge following. Hong Kong filmmakers like Chang Cheh and Lau Kar-Leung had revolutionized the martial arts film, replacing the female heroes of the fantasy-tinged swordplay genre with more "realistic" macho violence. Hit action movies like *Five Fingers of Death* and *One-Armed Boxer* were already making cult stars of actors like Lo Lieh and Jimmy Wang Yu even in the West, but the worldwide success of Lee's *The Big Boss* and *Fist of Fury* was unprecedented, and Lee rocketed to superstar-

Devil's Son-in-Law), in which Moore is forced to marry Lucifer's ugly offspring while battling rival comics LeRoy and Skillet; and *Disco Godfather* (1978), in which Rudy plays a disco security guard who goes gunning for drug dealers.

Home video has certainly helped Moore's popularity over the years, bringing him a whole new generation, and a new race, of fans. White hip-hop enthusiasts and aficionados of 1970s blaxploitation films have put Moore on a pedestal, saluting his no-holds-barred attitude, be it in the realm of movies, music, or stand-up performances. Audiences find his politically incorrect style refreshing and bask in his films' funky fashions, cartoonish ultraviolence, and good-natured but surprisingly raw sexuality.

At the same time, Moore still draws large crowds at live shows, and CD versions of his "party" albums have been reissued regularly. There's even been talk of a new *Dolemite* movie with *Undercover Brother*'s Eddie Griffith in the lead.

dom. Of course, someone at Warner Bros. mixed up the titles after they acquired these pictures for U.S. distribution, calling them *Fists of Fury* and *The Chinese Connection*, respectively, but that didn't seem to bother the thousands that lined up to buy tickets.

With *Kung Fu* a hit on TV and Bruce Lee exploding in theaters, producers all over the world (but especially in Hong Kong and Taiwan) rushed hundreds of martial arts films into production. Even Lee's death in 1973 didn't stem the tide—fans were crushed, of course, and producers worried that the popularity of Hong Kong cinema would fade, but Lee imitators were already becoming common. The kung fu craze continued unabated. Urban grindhouses began showing triple and even quadruple features to keep up with the constant stream of "chop socky" movies coming out of Asia. In the inner cities of America, theaters mixed together kung fu movies with the equally popular blaxploitation films of the day, creating a connection between Chinese kung fu and African American culture that has lasted into the current century. Blaxploitation stars such as Rudy Ray Moore and Jim Kelley pumped their action-packed cinematic funk with high kicking antics. Jamaican singer Carl Douglas had a number-one hit with his funky novelty song "Kung Fu Fighting," a quickly recorded intended B-side that took off after being discovered in the discos.

By the end of the 1970s, audiences began to tire of the huge banquet of kung fu choreography. Performers like Jackie Chan and Sammo Hung became stars in Asia by turning their talents to kung fu comedy and other styles of action pictures, but the movie business was quickly becoming overwhelmed by American blockbuster spectacles like *Star Wars* and *Jaws*. As the home video business boomed in the 1980s, most independent theaters closed down, leaving fewer avenues for imported action movies. However, as we all know, the United States finally caught up with Jackie Chan and Jet Li in the 1990s, and the Asian martial arts influence on Hollywood has never been stronger. With dozens of "old school" kung fu movies being rediscovered and released on video every month, new fans are being made every day, and a new generation is finding out what all the fussin' and fightin' was about.

In other words, the nerve-shattering, brain-battering, mind-splattering bad boy Moore plans to stick around.

1975 (R) 88m/C Rudy Ray Moore, D'Urville Martin, Lady Reed, Jerry Jones, Hy Pike, West Gale. **D:** D'Urville Martin. **W:** Rudy Ray Moore, Jerry Jones. **C:** Nicholas Josef von Sternberg. **M:** Arthur Wright. *VHS, DVD*

The Mack 🦴

This ode to pimps from former TV documentary specialist Michael Campus (*The Education of Sonny Carson*) has inexplicably picked up a cult following over the years, but it still remains one of the low points of classic blaxploitation. It's slow, senseless, and, despite the subject, surprisingly sexless.

Our hero is Goldie (Max Julien), a car thief who's sent to the slammer by a couple of crooked racist cops. Five years later, having acquired a questionable ovoid 'fro, he is released.

Goldie's driving ambition is to become a pimp. His mentor advises, "Anybody can control a woman's body, you see, but the key is to control their mind." Yeah, right. Moments later Goldie runs into Lulu (Carol Speed), an old flame and now a hooker who just happens to be in the market for representation. It's a little difficult to figure out exactly what happens next. Goldie experiences a fantasy where greenbacks magically rain down upon him and then, in the next scene—SHAZAM!—he's got it all: the pimpmobile, the cape, the funny hat. He's flashing a wad and spreading the wealth to neighborhood kids while cautioning them not to be like him. Is the cash a gift from God, or did Lulu decide to really throw herself into her work?

Who knows. After that, the action takes two directions. One follows the half-baked efforts of the gangster Fatman (B-movie stalwart George Murdock) to recruit Goldie. The second is a quasi-documentary look at the world of real pimps as they gamble, brag, strut, have picnics, and play softball. Really.

Both parts of *The Mack* have that rough-edged, shot-on-location (Oakland, California, in this case) grubbiness that makes '70s films so visually distinctive. The proceedings perk up occasionally with the aid of some gonzo humor. An underutilized Richard Pryor has some fine moments as Slim, Goldie's motor-mouthed sidekick. And Don Gordon, another veteran B-movie actor, performs an inspired drunken soliloquy during which he describes the differences between skinny people and fat people, relating them to giraffes and elephants. It's a moment that recalls his similar, deeply philosophical scenes in *The Last Movie*. And like Dennis Hopper's alternative western disaster, *The Mack* is interesting on a historical level but remains infuriatingly messy in the construction department.

In the end, *The Mack* simply doesn't deliver as a guilty pleasure. Goldie is an all-talk, no-action weenie. In the pantheon of the genre's heroes, he comes in dead last. Shaft, Slaughter, and Superfly wouldn't even acknowledge his existence. Coffy would kick his bony butt into next week. Cleopatra Jones would slice him a new orifice.

1973 (R) 110m/C Max Julien, Don Gordon, Richard Pryor, Carol Speed, Roger E. Mosley, George Murdoch. **D:** Michael Campus. **W:** Robert J. Poole. **C:** Ralph Woolsey. **M:** Willie Hutch, Alan Silvestri. *VHS, DVD*
AKA: *The Mack and His Pack*

—*Mike Mayo*

The Man ♫♫♪

The Man is one of those half-challenging, half-conventional oddities that could have been made only in the turbulent days of the late '60s and early '70s, when Hollywood didn't know how to appeal to a young audience.

James Earl Jones stars as New Hampshire senator Douglass Dilman. Dilman is serving as president pro tempore of the Senate, a largely ceremonial office, when the president and the Speaker of the House are killed in an unfortunate building collapse. The vice president, recovering from a recent stroke, refuses to accept the promotion. The order of succession being what it is, Dilman becomes, as he says, "the first Negro ever to hold this office."

The first half of the film is strong, as Jones is able to make Dilman's emotional combination of uncertainty, fear, and ambition seem completely real. But when more familiar plot complications unfold around the midway point, the story loses power. Members of his own party scheme to hamstring Dilman; racist Senator Watson (Burgess Meredith) is heard muttering that "the White House doesn't seem near white enough to me tonight"; a black American student (Georg Stanford Brown) is accused of attempting to assassinate a South African government official; and Dilman's own militant daughter (Janet MacLachlan) accuses him of not standing up for the right ideals.

The racial politics of the time were as important as the generational ones. But the side of the film that deals with race is almost cartoonish, particularly when Barbara Rush, as a senator's greedily ambitious wife, says, "The pity is that I'm married to a man whose principal accomplishment to date is to be kingmaker to a jigaboo."

Rod Serling's script is based on an Irving Wallace potboiler. Although it tends to come off as stilted, as happens with many political movies, the script has believable, human moments, too. Some of the scenes are charmingly dated. Upon first entering the White House, Dilman's daughter Wanda remarks, "This is quite a pad." Unfortunately, the most interesting elements of the plot never really take center stage, and the South African business is wrapped up rather too easily. The abrupt ending is—to use a phrase of the time—a cop-out. You come away feeling like the third act is missing.

The film was originally made for television by ABC, and the production values are not top drawer. But perhaps because Jones had been nominated for an Academy Award the year before for his role in *The Great White Hope,* it was given a theatrical release. Jones's performance is still the most compelling part of the film. Despite it, *The Man* plays more like a 1950s political melodrama than the consciousness-raising film it aims to be.

1972 (G) 93m/C James Earl Jones, Martin Balsam, Burgess Meredith, Lew Ayres, William Windom, Barbara Rush, Elizabeth Ross, Georg Stanford Brown, Janet MacLachlan. *D:* Joseph Sargent. *W:* Rod Serling. *C:* Edward C. Rosson. *M:* Jerry Goldsmith. *VHS*

—*Mike Mayo*

Original Gangstas ♫♫

This 1996 regrouping of top stars from the 1970s blaxploitation surge was something retro revelers and movie fans had been hoping for since Keenan Ivory Wayans gave the genre a kick in the booty with his right-on

PAM GRIER by Mike Mayo

Pam Grier

Pam Grier made an impressive screen debut against stiff competition in Russ Meyer's magnum opus *Beyond the Valley of the Dolls.* It's a small role in which she has barely a line, but she looks spectacular with her lush figure and a striking face that defies conventional standards of beauty. It is, somehow, an altogether appropriate beginning for a career that has progressed from low-budget horror to serious drama and mainstream acceptance as a legitimate actress.

Grier served her apprenticeship in a five-year stint with the famous exploitation houses American International Pictures and New World Pictures, where she made such seminal babes-behind-bars flicks as *Women in Cages, The Big Doll House, Black Mama, White Mama,* and *The Big Bird Cage.* In such films, she was usually cast as a black revolutionary (a popular stock character in the early '70s), an evil matron, a lesbian, or a singer. Her character was seldom alive when the closing credits rolled.

Later, she remembered that those movies "were my sounding board. I was green; I was hungry. These were my first roles so I made them as close to Shakespeare as possible. That's how I approached it and it got me work. The characters stood out. I got recognized."

She also had supporting roles in a couple of early black-themed crime dramas, *Cool Breeze* (a variation on *The Asphalt Jungle*) and *Hit Man* (an adaptation of the novel *Jack's Return Home,* which has also been filmed twice as *Get Carter*).

After all of that, she was ready for her close-up as the no-nonsense, gun-toting eponymous heroine of four blaxploitation classics.

- In *Coffy* she's a nurse who must avenge the death of her little sister at the hands of drug dealers.

- In *Foxy Brown*—originally a sequel titled *Burn, Coffy, Burn*—she must avenge the death of her boyfriend at the hands of drug dealers.

1988 spoof, *I'm Gonna Git You Sucka.* Director and producer Larry Cohen, who helmed *Hell up in Harlem* and *Black Caesar,* may have longed to be back in familiar territory, but he also found out with *Original Gangstas* that you can't go home(boy) again.

The story takes place in Gary, Indiana, where John Bookman (Fred "The Hammer" Williamson), a football coach in L.A., returns after his grocer father has been shot by thugs. Turns out Dad was shot because he blew the whistle on a gang of youths that Bookman actually helped start when he was

- In *Friday Foster* she is a photographer who must avenge the death of a black politician at the hands of white supremacists.

- In *Sheba Baby* she is a private detective who comes home to protect her father—who, breaking the cycle, is still alive—from gangsters. With a PG rating, it's by far the weakest of the bunch.

The films vary widely in quality. In all of them, the limitations of the budgets are obvious in every frame, but so is Pam Grier's appeal. She's beautiful, brassy, bawdy, and aggressive—a sexy heroine who is in charge of her own life. And, perhaps more important, she's alive and triumphant at the end. Pam Grier had a hand in the creation of the original *Coffy*, researching the character with an uncle who was a vice cop in Denver. All the other characters are variations on that prototype. Although the amounts of nudity and sexual activity were relatively restrained by today's standards, Grier proved she was not shy in showing off her voluptuous dimensions. It's doubtless that this display, coupled with her athletic prowess and "ain't gonna take no crap" attitude, had something to do with her tremendous popularity.

When the heyday of the genre passed, so did the starring roles. Still, Grier made strong impressions as a murderous psycho junkie whore in *Fort Apache: The Bronx* and as the Dust Witch, "the most beautiful woman in the world," in *Something Wicked This Way Comes.* But, like so many actresses, she ran into the problems that women face in Hollywood once they're past their twenties, and she was largely limited to typecast roles as a tough-talking authority figure—usually a cop. She found some of her best work on television, with recurring roles on *Miami Vice, Linc's,* and the 2004 series *The L Word.*

When Quentin Tarantino cast her as the lead in his adaptation of Elmore Leonard's *Rum Punch* in 1997, the resulting film was an affectionate homage to her earlier work. Her character was renamed and the film's title was changed to *Jackie Brown.*

Tarantino has never been reticent about admitting his fondness for the trashy escapism of his youth, and where Pam Grier's films are concerned, he's got nothing to be ashamed of. The best of them are fast-paced action pictures that remain ridiculously entertaining, due at least in part to the fact that Grier's sexy screen presence still smokes.

a teen. With uncaring police and sleazy politicians turning their backs on the situation, Bookman decides to take matters into his own hands. He joins forces with old pals Laurie Thompson (Pam Grier), Jake Trevor (Jim Brown), Slick (Richard Roundtree), and Bubba (Ron O'Neal) to get into shape and then meet the creeps head-on.

Original Gangstas has some exciting moments, and just seeing the aforementioned group (plus Paul Winfield and character greats Robert Forster, Charles Napier, and Wings Hauser) on the screen together is enough to give any fan of '70s action flicks a nostalgic jolt. What's been left out is the leering sexuality of the original blaxploitation films, which is probably for the best.

But a larger problem exists for *Original Gangstas:* can you be entertained by drive-by shootings or the killing of innocents when you read about the exact same incidents in the morning paper? It's one thing to make a serious film about these problems, but *Original Gangstas* wants it both ways, as the cast charismatically channel their '70s personas with a wink.

You soon become uneasy watching this film, and you realize that maybe the blaxploitation films are better enjoyed from afar, leaving them as a time capsule of the period from which they came. A few years later, a *Shaft* remake with Samuel L. Jackson proved that notion all over again.

1996 (R) 98m/C Fred Williamson, Pam Grier, Jim Brown, Ron O'Neal, Charles Napier, Wings Hauser, Paul Winfield, Isabel Sanford. **D:** Larry Cohen. **W:** Aubrey K. Rattan. **C:** Carlos Gonzalez. **M:** Vladimir Horunzhy. *VHS, DVD* **AKA:** *Hot City*

Shaft

If you had to pick the single biggest icon of the blaxploitation film, it would have to be Richard Roundtree as John Shaft—in his leather coat, turtleneck sweater, and neatly trimmed 'fro, striding tall and confident through the mean streets of New York.

That's how Gordon Parks introduces the character, in a series of high-angle telephoto shots, with Isaac Hayes's famous theme pulsating in the background. Right away we know that this is a man who's cool, who's in charge. In terms of character, locale, and profession, John Shaft is not far removed from Mike Hammer of the 1950s. The plot comes straight from the tough-detective playbook, with the first act being especially reminiscent of many crime movies.

As he's walking to his Manhattan office one cold January morning, John Shaft learns that a couple of suspicious characters from uptown are looking for him. After a slam-bang confrontation, he meets Harlem gangster Bumpy Jonas (Moses Gunn), who wants to hire Shaft to find a kidnapped daughter.

A black militant group led by Ben Buford (Christopher St. John) might be involved, and, given Bumpy's line of work, Italian mobsters could also be behind the snatch. Like the premise, the resolution is handled without many surprises, but the movie still works, primarily for two reasons.

First, Shaft is an engaging, attractive character. He doesn't come across as arrogant but rather, like the best detectives, as staunchly individualistic, a man who refuses to knuckle under to corrupt authorities, be they cops or crooks, black or white. Besides cop Vic Androzzi (Charles Cioffi), who's always honest and respectful in his dealings with Shaft, Shaft has few friends or personal attachments.

Richard Roundtree is the iconic supercool detective John Shaft in Gordon Parks's classic 1971 film, *Shaft*.

Second, New York City is a character in itself, and its bare winter landscape has seldom been captured so accurately on film. Director Gordon Parks (who appears in a cameo as a landlord) has a still photographer's eye for striking images. He simply gets things right, and by using long lenses for the street scenes, he gives the action a feeling of documentary-like accuracy.

This film was followed by two above-average sequels: *Shaft's Big Score* (1972), in which the detective discovers a recently murdered close friend was involved in dirty dealings, and *Shaft in Africa* (1973), which details Shaft's attempt to bust a slavery ring overseas. And let's not forget a short-lived 1973 TV series starring Roundtree and the 2000 "update" in which Samuel L. Jackson plays Shaft under the direction of John Singleton (*Boyz 'N the Hood*).

1971 (R) 100m/C Richard Roundtree, Moses Gunn, Charles Cioffi, Christopher St. John, Gwenn Mitchell. **D:** Gordon Parks. **W:** Ernest Tidyman, John D. F. Black. **C:** Urs Furrer. **M:** Isaac Hayes, J. J. Johnson. *VHS, DVD*

—*Mike Mayo*

SAMUEL L. JACKSON by Amy Longsdorf

The force is definitely with Samuel L. Jackson. Not only did he make his dreams come true by playing a Jedi master in the *Star Wars* prequels, but he also got the opportunity to embody the epitome of urban cool as the title character in John Singleton's remake of *Shaft*. During a 2000 interview in Beverly Hills, the actor contemplated his update of the '70s icon for modern audiences.

Q: Did you feel cooler while you were making *Shaft*?

A: No, not really. But it was strange being on the streets of New York. On the way to the *Shaft* set, I'd pass women and they'd go, "Oh Sam, you look so much better in person." I never realized that I was lookin' like a troll on screen before. It never occurred to me that I was this ugly guy in movies. It was a revelation to know that suddenly I'm a sex symbol.

Q: But you don't bag as many women as the original *Shaft* did.

A: Don't I know it. I did want one really hot love scene, but the studio thought in this age of AIDS, it wasn't appropriate for me to be bedding everyone. I remember saying, "Just give me one woman."

Q: How many times did you listen to that Isaac Hayes theme song before you went to work in the morning?

A: You know my agent sent me the soundtrack when I first got the job. And then people sent me so many copies of the damn CD that I was able to give them away as Christmas presents. Some people actually think I did sit in my trailer and say, "Let me play the *Shaft* theme song before I go out there today." Please. Give me a break.

Q: Richard Roundtree, who starred in the original *Shaft* (1971), played your uncle in the movie. Did you ask him for any advice?

A: We had absolutely no conversations about how he did *Shaft*. It's different times. Richard's demons were the Man and the System. I'm out there fighting race crime and drugs. Therefore my character is a bit more volatile. But my guy embraces the violence in a different way. When things start getting dangerous, my character keeps a smile on his face, like, "I know I can handle this."

Slaughter ♫♫♪

Slaughter's Big Rip-Off ♫♫

Jim Brown's acting career began before the rise of blaxploitation films and it has continued at a more leisurely pace since the genre ebbed. His first fame came as a football player for Syracuse and then for the Cleveland

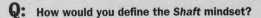

Q: How would you define the *Shaft* mindset?

A: John Shaft is about being calm in the skin you're in, having confidence bordering on arrogance, with a simple dollop of humility.

Q: You were a marine biology student at Atlanta's Morehouse college when you saw *Shaft* for the first time. Any reactions?

A: I was blown away by *Shaft* because here was a guy who looked like me, sounded like me, and dressed like I wanted to dress. And he was a hero. And he was black. That was new. He was also cool, sexy, and tough. *Shaft* also taught Hollywood that African Americans were a viable cinematic force. It was time they tailored movies to us.

Q: There were reports of constant battling on the set between you and *Shaft* director John Singleton. Any truth to those rumors?

A: Well, I didn't argue necessarily with John. First of all, the [studio] hired Richard Price [*Sea of Love*] to write the script. Richard writes really good cop stories. Fine. But he can't put certain kinds of words in my mouth. Still, the studio paid this guy a lot of money so occasionally there's a voice in John's ear going, "Make Sam say the lines we paid for." But I said, "I'm not saying that."

Q: Was it a race issue because Richard Price is white?

A: Sometimes, it came to that. I was like, "The black writer who wrote these lines doesn't talk like me." Then someone would say, "Uh, Sam, the writer is not black." I would be, like, "Exactly."

Q: If there were a sequel to *Shaft,* what would you like to see happen?

A: What I'd like is for Richard Roundtree to have a bigger role. We hung out a lot. I remember playing golf with him for the first time, whispering to myself, "I'm playing golf with John Shaft!"

Q: So, did the new Shaft let the old Shaft win?

A: Hell, no. I beat Sidney Poitier the first time I played golf with him, okay. It's not in my nature to be beat. *Shaft* has nothing to do with golf.

Browns. His transition to the silver screen is certainly one of the most successful of any athlete's.

After a supporting role in the little-known but well-regarded sagebrusher *Rio Conchos* in 1964, he really hit the big time in 1967 with *The Dirty Dozen,* in which he managed to stand out in a very crowded, very talented Oscar-class ensemble. Brown's final sprint with the grenades is the scene everybody remembers. After that, he starred in a series of low-budget action movies, all of them solid.

Based on a Donald Westlake novel, *The Split* (1968) features Brown as a professional thief, a character portrayed under a different name by Lee Marvin in the Westlake-adapted *Point Blank.* He had a then-scandalous, now-tame love scene with Raquel Welch in *100 Rifles* (1969). He was a southern sheriff dealing with racists in . . . *tick . . . tick . . . tick . . .* (1970). And he and spaghetti western regular Lee Van Cleef made three films together, the first being *El Condor* (1970), which was quite shocking in its day for Marianna Hill's nude scene.

When *Shaft* hit it big and the studios became interested in the urban ghetto genre, Jim Brown was ready, cranking out two to three titles a year throughout the 1970s. As often as not, his character wound up seeking vengeance against evil white gangsters who had killed his brother/father/friend.

The titular character of *Slaughter* is a Vietnam veteran whose parents are blown up by a Mexican-based mafia led by Hoffo (Rip Torn). Director Jack Starrett (*Cleopatra Jones*) makes full use of the south-of-the-border scenery and handles the generic revenge material with sufficient energy (though his penchant for the fish-eye-lens shot is curious—it's used so sporadically that it almost seems accidental). If Brown's acting chops are less than perfect, he does have undeniable screen presence and is able to carry the soggy plot over its slow patches. He also gets first-rate support from genre regular Don Gordon and a cheerful Stella Stevens as the obligatory beautiful blonde white chick who lusts after our hero and doffs her clothes to keep him interested.

The film is actually a little too well made to be great blaxploitation. It lacks the any-crazyass-thing-can-happen quality of the classics, and Slaughter's wardrobe borders on the tasteful. Also, considering the technical limits of the early 1970s, stuff blows up pretty good.

Slaughter's Big Rip-Off simply continues the first film's story in a Los Angeles setting. Slaughter has come back from Mexico and is having a picnic with his old friend Warren (George Gaynes, Commandant Lassard from the *Police Academy* series) when they're attacked by a biplane: the mob, now led by Mr. Duncan (Ed McMahon), is still after Slaughter. Again, cars go over cliffs, lots of stuff explodes, and Slaughter teams with a hard-nosed cop (Brock Peters) to rally against the mob.

Overall, *Slaughter's Big Rip-Off* is a more polished effort than the first film. But being slick isn't exactly the point of this genre, is it?

The rest of Brown's work in the '70s is made up of comparable low-budget action melodramas, all of which depend on his considerable physical presence—the same quality that made him a success on the gridiron.

> **It's not only his name, it's his business and sometimes—his pleasure!**
>
> —Tagline for *Slaughter*

Slaughter
1972 (R) 91m/C Jim Brown, Rip Torn, Stella Stevens, Cameron Mitchell, Don Gordon, Marlene Clark. *D:* Jack Starrett. *W:* Mark Hanna, Don Williams. *C:* Rosalio Solano. *M:* Luchi De Jesus. *VHS, DVD*

Slaughter's Big Rip-Off
1973 (R) 94m/C Jim Brown, Don Stroud, Ed McMahon, Brock Peters, Gloria Hendry, Dick Anthony Williams, Art Metrano. *D:* Gordon Fleming. *W:* Charles Johnson. *C:* Charles F. Wheeler. *M:* James Brown, Fred Wesley. *VHS, DVD*
AKA: Slaughter 2

—*Mike Mayo*

FRED WILLIAMSON

Like Jim Brown, Fred "The Hammer" Williamson successfully crossed over from the gridiron to the silver screen. A veteran of the Pittsburgh Steelers, Oakland Raiders, and Kansas City Chiefs, the former architecture student made two films in 1970, costarring as "Spearchucker" Jones in *M*A*S*H* and appearing opposite Liza Minnelli in *Tell Me That You Love Me, Junie Moon*. What may have brought Williamson even more exposure, however, was a recurring role as star Diahann Carroll's boyfriend in the TV series *Julia*, the first network show to feature a black performer in a lead role.

With blaxploitation films heating up, Williamson parlayed his brief on-camera experience into starring roles in films geared to black audiences. His debut effort in this realm was in the 1972 western *The Legend of Nigger Charley*, a low-budget effort with an in-your-face title that not only achieved box-office success but was accorded a sequel, *The Soul of Nigger Charley*, the next year.

With his chiseled body, athletic agility, and cool charisma, Williamson cranked out a series of violent hits in the early 1970s. Among them were *Hammer, That Man Bolt, Bucktown, Black Caesar* (an African American take on *Little Caesar*), and its same-year sequel, *Hell up in Harlem*, both directed by Larry Cohen (*Q, God Told Me To*).

Williamson decided to try his hand at writing, directing, and producing his own films, forming Po' Boy Productions in the mid-1970s. Portraying such heroes as Jess Crowder or Dakota Smith—black versions of Bronson- and Eastwood-style cops—the Hammer has delivered a parade of self-produced actioners, from *Death Journey* in 1974 through 2000's *Down 'N Dirty*.

Aside from his own self-produced efforts, Williamson has appeared in many ensemble action films. In 1974's *Three the Hard Way*, he teamed with Jim Brown and karate expert Jim Kelly to tackle a racist group tainting African Americans' water supply. *Three Tough Guys*, also from '74, featured Williamson with Italy's Lino Ventura as well as Isaac Hayes. And *Original Gangstas*, the 1996 reunion of 1970s rabble-rousers, showcased Fred with Pam Grier, Jim Brown, Richard Roundtree, and Ron O'Neal.

While most veterans of the blaxploitation scene rarely register blips on the radar screen, the Hammer still wields his cinematic muscles, whether it be in one of his own direct-to-video shoot-'em-ups, or playing supporting parts in such hip directors' projects as Robert Rodriguez and Quentin Tarantino's *From Dusk till Dawn* (1996), John Woo's *Blackjack* (1998), and Todd Phillips's *Starsky and Hutch* (2004).

Superfly 🦴🦴🦴

This low-budget blaxploitation winner from Gordon Parks Jr., son of *Shaft* helmer Gordon Parks, has everything you want from the genre, including: a fully realized sense of place and time—New York in winter; groovy

Ron O'Neal and Carl Lee wear groovy clothes and snort cocaine in Gordon Parks Jr.'s 1972 film *Superfly*.

Never a dude like this one! He's got a plan to stick it to the Man!

—Tagline for *Superfly*

clothes, including shirts with super-wide collars that look like they might be capable of flight; a brilliant, silky soundtrack from Curtis Mayfield; a slick, morally compromised hero; and perhaps the most magnificent pimpmobile ever to grace the silver screen.

Youngblood Priest (Ron O'Neal) is a coke dealer who has it all—"eight-track stereo, color TV in every room," as his partner puts it. But Priest wants to get out of the life, and he attempts to set up one massive, final deal that will net him a retirement fund of $300,000. First he has to persuade his mentor, Scatter (Julius Harris), to help him connect with a supplier, and then he has to deal with the corrupt cops who want a piece of his deal.

The film has a gritty, cinema vérité feeling, and Parks and director of photography James Signorelli make the alleys, apartments, bars, sidewalks, and restaurants of New York important elements of the story. Their gliding shots that follow Priest's chrome-heavy El Dorado through the neighborhood have their own rhythm. Near the film's middle, a sequence of still photographs depicting dope dealers, their customers, and the results of their transactions strikes the right note and sketches in the full social and racial impact of drug use. On the downside, a fight scene shot in slow motion fizzles, and some plotlines are left unfinished or unexplained.

The senior Gordon Parks worked with similar material in his 1971 film *Shaft,* but while the two title characters are comparable in many ways, Priest is really the antithesis of Shaft. The tough detective always maintains his own sense of honor. The drug dealer, who's feeding off his own people, is driven by self-loathing. Priest knows that he's involved in a destructive business and that he has his own problem with cocaine.

It's probably unfair to pile too much baggage onto escapist entertainment. The flaws are part of *Superfly*'s dated, politically incorrect charm. This movie is one of the greats, still as cool as it ever was.

The film spawned two sequels: *Superfly T.N.T.* (1973), which finds O'Neal's Priest living in Europe and trying to help overthrow nasty colonialists in Africa, and *The Return of Superfly* (1990), with Nathan Purdee, O'Neal's unmemorable replacement, stepping back into the drug world after an associate is murdered. The most notable thing about *Return* was an appearance by a young actor named Samuel L. Jackson—perhaps tuning up for his *Shaft* remake years later.

1972 (R) 93m/C Ron O'Neal, Carl Lee, Sheila Frazier, Julius Harris, Charles McGregor, Nate Adams. **D:** Gordon Parks Jr. **W:** Phillip Fenty. **C:** James Signorelli. **M:** Curtis Mayfield. *VHS, DVD*

—*Mike Mayo*

Sweet Sweetback's Baadasssss Song ♪♪♪

"Rated 'X' by an all-white jury!" proclaimed the ads for Melvin Van Peebles's landmark film. It's no surprise that this attention-grabbing line help launch a film that originally had no chance of being made, let alone becoming a sizable hit.

Then thirty-nine, the Chicago-born Van Peebles had already found some success in the arts. He had penned novels, directed award-winning short films, and, in Europe, written and directed an acclaimed autobiographical feature, *The Story of a Three-Day Pass.* The positive reaction that film received led to a studio directorial assignment, *Watermelon Man,* a sharp satire with Godfrey Cambridge playing a white insurance agent who turns black and has to deal with a new perspective on life.

Rather than continue to take on work he had little control over, Van Peebles decided to bankroll his next project independently. Armed with a tiny budget (somewhere between $150,000 and $500,000—the amount varies depending on the source—some of which was contributed by Bill Cosby), Van Peebles starred in, wrote, directed, edited, and composed the music for *Sweet Sweetback's Baadasssss Song.*

Although few theaters would originally book *Sweet Sweetback,* word-of-mouth spread quickly—*Ebony* magazine denounced it while the Blank Panthers applauded its radical point of view. As theaters wised up, the film

> **Dedicated to all the Brothers and Sisters who have had enough of the Man.**
>
> —Tagline for *Sweet Sweetback's Baadasssss Song*

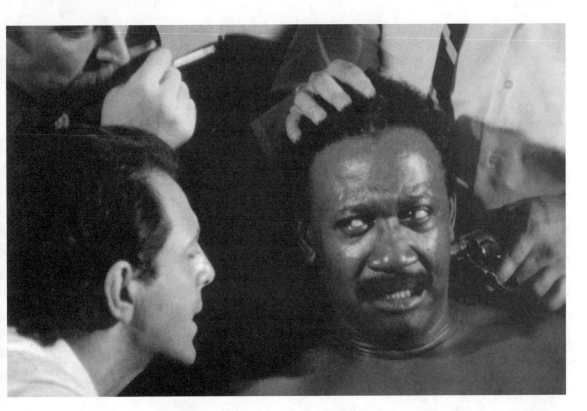

Melvin Van Peebles deals with a gun to the head and the Man in his face in *Sweet Sweetback's Baadassss Song.*

became a hit, almost exclusively with urban audiences. Like *Easy Rider,* released two years earlier, the film's enthusiastic acceptance and astonishing $16 million box-office take showed Hollywood that there was yet another ignored audience out there. The response from mainstream studios was quick, and big boys were soon churning out films for black audiences using some of *Sweet Sweetback*'s major elements as boilerplate features for blaxploitation films.

Sweet Sweetback begins in a most unsettling manner and remains disconcerting throughout. A young boy (played by Mario, Van Peebles's son) is called into a whorehouse bedroom and coerced by one of the prostitutes into having sex with her. During the act, the boy becomes an adult (now played by Melvin). As the woman reaches orgasm, she gives the boy the nickname "Sweetback."

As the plot unfolds, the solemn Sweetback is recruited by white cops to help them out by pretending to be a prisoner in a murder case. But, on their way to the station, he intervenes when the cops try to beat up Mu-Mu (Hubert Scales), a black man with revolutionary views. Provoked to violence by the cops' actions, Sweetback brutally thumps the men in blue, then runs for his life through the streets of Los Angeles.

Sweetback's run from the law—cops controlled by a racist white police commissioner (John Dullaghan)—makes up the rest of the film's running time. During his frenzied dash for the Mexican border and freedom, Sweetback encounters some former associates, as well as a gang of bikers and an old girlfriend (Rhetta Hughes) who calls on him for sexual favors.

The film displays a raw, explosive power. Sweetback is constantly facing off against nefarious white people and, in almost every circumstance, the blacks he meets become victims of the white man's violent racism. Van Peebles's in-your-face style is designed to elicit disgust from the audience as the camera lingers on the bloody consequences of white-on-black beatings and tortures.

Some of Van Peebles's visual stylings seem fresh and experimental; at other times they appear to be inspired by cash-strapped amateurishness. The images are muddy, the editing jumpy. He overdoes the visual tricks, using slow-motion, chroma-key effects, and superimposed images, which, at times, make the film come off like a project in a Filmmaking 101 course. Symbolic subtlety is not his strong suit: in one scene, Sweetback rides atop a van, his arms spread in a Christlike fashion. Get it? The non-union cast does what it can acting-wise, but the villainous white police rarely go beyond one dimension. The music is an offbeat combo of acid jazz (composed by Van Peebles), R&B (by Earth, Wind & Fire), and gospel. None of this, of course, mattered much in the end. Audiences got the message, and they loved it.

Sweet Sweetback's Baadasssss Song has some striking similarities to *Easy Rider,* aside from their miniscule budgets and surprise success. Essentially, both are anecdotal road movies about protagonists who run into alternately threatening and helpful characters as they flee from society. The ultimate goal of both protagonists is to attain independence.

But while *Easy Rider* ends on a note of total desperation, *Sweet Sweetback* leaves us with the possibility that, for Sweetback, there could be freedom and a life beyond what we're shown in the film. Or, as the movie warns before the credits roll: "WATCH OUT . . . A Baadasssss Nigger Is Coming Back to Collect Some Dues."

1971 (R) 97m/C Melvin Van Peebles, Hubert Scales, Simon Chuckster, John Dullaghan, West Gale, Mario Van Peebles, Rhetta Hughes, Max Van Peebles. *D:* Melvin Van Peebles. *W:* Melvin Van Peebles. *C:* Robert Maxell. *M:* Melvin Van Peebles, Earth, Wind & Fire. *VHS, DVD*

Chapter 6

Shocks to the System

T hanks to a 1950s resurrection, the traditional monsters that had shocked the world in the earlier decades of the twentieth century reentered filmgoers nightmares. Hammer Films, a British company, put a new spin on such creatures as Frankenstein, Dracula, and the Mummy, popularized in the 1930s by Universal Pictures, adding color, glossy production values, dollops of sex, and stars like Christopher Lee and Peter Cushing, who became new fan favorites.

Hammer continued pouring forth the horror throughout the 1960s and into the 1970s, when period bloodsucker Dracula, as played by Lee, was hurled head on into hippies and the psychedelic world with *Dracula A.D. 1972* and 1974's *The Satanic Rites of Dracula.*

Old blood did just fine in the case of Vincent Price, a veteran character actor who became the preeminent shock star of the 1960s. Young audiences first turned on to the erudite actor in 1959's *The Tingler,* one of the first films to depict the effects of LSD on the screen. Later, they followed Vinny through some of Roger Corman's American International Pictures–produced, Hammer-inspired Edgar Allan Poe interpretations, including *The Pit and the Pendulum* and *The Masque of the Red Death.* Fans even clung to Price when he slyly spoofed his mad-doctor persona in both the *Dr. Phibes* and *Dr. Goldfoot* movies.

The kids were certainly all right with horror throughout the 1960s. Drive-ins were still booming, and low-budget studios catering to open-air theaters gave the kids flocking to the shows exactly what they wanted. The old vampire tales were gussied up with counterculture types and gruesome gurus in the *Count Yorga* films and *The Deathmaster.* And for kids who weren't old enough to drive, every major city had a late-night horror show on the tube on Saturday nights, featuring old favorites hosted by buxom lady vampires and guys in capes to go along with that extra-cheese-and-pepperoni pizza ingested while watching the shock fests.

It was during the 1960s, however, that the nightly news became as horrifying as anything at the movies. Vietnam, race and campus riots, the generation gap, assassinations, the threat of nuclear annihilation, the ongoing Cold War: all were enough to give even non-horror-movie fans the heebie-jeebies.

Sometimes, these events subtly and not-so subtly found their way into films of the era. Unlike the 1950s, when the chief scaremeisters were mutated creatures or big bugs, during the 1960s and '70s humans were, or at least could become, the boogeyman. In Pittsburgh in 1968, documentary filmmaker George A. Romero resurrected zombies, best remembered from Val Lewton's films from the 1940s, for *Night of the Living Dead*. The low-budget B&W effort shocked audiences by presenting a paranoid scenario in which friends, neighbors, countrymen, and even children could transform into flesh-eating ghouls at the snap—or bite—of a finger.

Meanwhile, Wes Craven, a onetime college professor, delivered two unforgettable discourses on the darker side of humanity in the 1970s with 1972's *Last House on the Left* and 1977's *The Hills Have Eyes*. Inspired by Ingmar Bergman's *The Virgin Spring, House* portrays the counterculture's vulnerability in its tale of parents avenging the death of two flower children at the hands of psychopathic cretins. *Hills,* using the song "The Sound of Music" as the inspiration for its title, also saw a group of innocents resorting to violent means to fend off creeps, only this time the setting is a desolate desert, the innocents are a family headed by a racist, fundamentalist Christian father, and the creeps are a cannibalistic clan vying for possession of the family's infant.

Of course, not every horror flick during the era was as deadly serious as Craven's, even when they were tackling morbid themes. Psychological and gothic horror, mixed with doses of dark humor, were pioneered by Hitchcock in *Psycho* in 1960, and the formula became popular with mostly older audiences who could appreciate classy performers camping it up in deranged manners. For a hoot and horror, check out 1962's *What Ever Happened to Baby Jane?* with Bette Davis and Joan Crawford; 1969's *What Ever Happened to Aunt Alice?* starring Geraldine Page and Ruth Gordon; and 1971's *What's the Matter with Helen?* featuring Debbie Reynolds and Shelley Winters.

Prime examples of 1960s films that straddle reel and real horrors can be found in two of the most disturbing movies of the era. *Targets* (1968), Peter Bogdanovich's first feature, presents two stories that eventually conjoin: one concerns a young, emotionless serial killer (Tim O'Kelly) on a shooting rampage; the other focuses on a promotional appearance of a retiring horror star (played by eighty-one-year-old Boris Karloff) at a drive-in theater. Produced by Corman, the movie offers a powerful statement for gun control; it was released in theaters in the wake of the Robert Kennedy and Martin Luther King Jr. assassinations.

Also in 1968, Roman Polanski delivered a landmark horror film with *Rosemary's Baby,* an unsettling account of a struggling actor (John

Cassavetes) selling his soul, his wife (Mia Farrow), and his unborn child to the devil for a shot at stardom. A year later, in August 1969, Polanski encountered his own horrors in the guise of Charles Manson, who directed his demented minions to slaughter Polanski's pregnant actress wife, Sharon Tate, in their Southern California home. The incident was one of the most horrifying moments of the 1960s, inexorably linked to one of its scariest movies.

The Abominable Dr. Phibes 🦴🦴🦴

Dr. Phibes Rises Again 🦴🦴🦴

Vincent Price revived his career yet again for the "now generation" with these surprise horror hits—all the more impressive in light of the fact that Price's face remains immobile throughout both films.

In the first entry, twisted genius Dr. Anton Phibes (Price) is presumed dead after a freak car accident. Alive and well but quite disfigured with extensive facial scarring, he decides that members of a surgical team let his wife die, and each shall perish by a different biblical plague. One victim is devoured by locusts, another has his head crushed by a frog mask, and so on. Highly stylized, the murders have a ceremonial feel to them, with Phibes's mysterious, beautiful, and silent assistant Vulnavia (Virginia North) accompanying the gruesome deaths on her violin.

Music plays an important role in the film, with Phibes performing on a massive organ or dancing through his art deco mansion to the melodies of a mechanical band. As the London police, led by Inspector Trout (scene-stealing Peter Jeffrey), piece together the clues to Phibes's plan, the vengeful genius stays one step ahead of them while concocting a death trap to top them all: Dr. Vesalius (Joseph Cotton) is forced to operate on his own son to recover a key to the boy's shackles, all before a shower of acid rains down on both of them.

Although *The Abominable Dr. Phibes* is set in the 1920s, Phibes's equipment seems a bit ahead of its time—and where did he get a Frank Sinatra record? Never mind. This is one of those movies set in a world of its own, reminiscent of the strange European villages of the Universal Frankenstein movies, and it pays little heed to actual history or geography. High camp and good humor balance the suggested gore, mixing laughs and gasps with split-second timing. The veteran cast of British character actors is in top form, with Terry-Thomas oddly chilling as a pornography enthusiast who suffers the plague of blood. In the end, it's the sense of style that director Robert Fuest (TV's *The Avengers*) brings to the proceedings that triumphs.

Phibes was such a success that a sequel was hurried into production the following year. In *Dr. Phibes Rises Again,* Trout follows the doctor's trail to

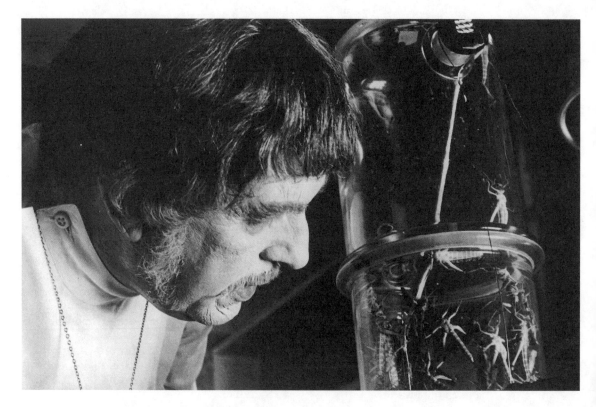

Vincent Price plays the title character in the campy 1971 film *The Abominable Dr. Phibes.*

Egypt. There, Phibes and his rival, Darius Biederbeck (Robert Quarry), are racing toward an arcane secret hidden in an ancient tomb. True to form, Phibes reacts by taking out the opposing team using various imaginative methods. While entertaining, *Rises Again* appears to have been hurriedly thrown together, and the pieces of the plot don't always fit. Price would have much better luck the following year with the similar *Theater of Blood,* this time playing a ham Shakespearean actor seeking revenge on his harshest critics.

The Abominable Dr. Phibes
1971 (PG-13) 94m/C *UK* Vincent Price, Joseph Cotton, Hugh Griffith, Terry-Thomas, Virginia North, Susan Travers, Alex Scott, Caroline Munro. *D:* Robert Fuest. *W:* James Whiton, William Goldstein. *C:* Norman Warwick. *M:* Basil Kirchin, Jack Nathan. *VHS, DVD*
AKA: *Dr. Phibes; The Curse of Dr. Phibes*

Dr. Phibes Rises Again
1972 (PG-13) 98m/C *UK* Vincent Price, Robert Quarry, Valli Kemp, Hugh Griffith, John Thaw. *D:* Robert Fuest. *W:* Robert Fuest, Robert Blees. *C:* Alex Thomson. *M:* John Gale. *VHS, DVD*

—Brian Thomas

Blue Sunshine 🎵🎵🎵

Where have all the flower children gone?

Well, according to this post-psychedelic shocker, a group of former hippie students who took acid at Stanford University in the '60s are going to hell. They're also losing large portions of their hair, experiencing bouts of irritability and brain-rattling migraines, and having extremely violent freak-outs.

The movie is called *Blue Sunshine,* and so was the acid Ed Flemming (*Lost in Space*'s Mark Goddard) sold around campus back in the day. Ten years on, Flemming is running for a seat in Congress and his former acquaintances are experiencing disturbing after-effects. Jerry Zipkin (*Red Shoe Diaries* creator Zalman King), a Cornell grad, decides to investigate.

Zipkin keeps showing up in the wrong place at the wrong time, and he becomes a murder suspect when some former LSD experimenters start kicking the bucket. When his old pal Franny (Richard Crystal, Billy's brother) wigs out and starts stuffing friends into fireplaces, Zipkin gets blamed. Soon, other Stanford alums begin losing their grip: Johnny (Bill Cameron), a cop, kills his wife, kids, and the family pooch, and Flemming's ex-wife (Ann Cooper) can't take the pressure of being a single parent and goes after the tykes with a knife. It's up to Zipkin, with some help from pals Alicia Sweeney (Deborah Winters) and Dr. Bloom (Robert Walden, Rossi from *Lou Grant*) to put a stop to the insanity.

Shot on a small budget, *Blue Sunshine* works surprisingly well as an intelligent, spare thriller in the creepy vein of early David Cronenberg flicks such as *Rabid* and *The Brood* or Larry Cohen's *It's Alive* and *God Told Me To.* And like Cronenberg's efforts, *Blue Sunshine* also finds horror in the idea of science gone awry. But this film effectively accents the psychological manifestations of horror, rather than the physical fallout, as the deranged protagonists' faces contort, inspiring genuine chills. They look like a cross between James Arness's interstellar carrot in the original *The Thing* and Marshall Applewhite, leader of the Heaven's Gate suicide cult.

Blue Sunshine's most disturbing scenes involve the drug-triggered violence directed at children. While the actual carnage is only implied, there is something undeniably disconcerting about watching a bald woman threaten her children with a huge carving knife when they won't stop chanting "Dr. Pepper, Dr. Pepper."

Writer and director Jeff Lieberman is best known for his 1974 mutant worm movie, *Squirm,* a fun, tongue-in-cheek endeavor that features memorable lines like, "Pardon me, but there's a worm in my egg cream." *Blue Sunshine* is a somber creation, with nary a joke or light moment in sight. The film barely got a theatrical release and was unavailable on video for years, partly because its negative was ruined in a flood at the film lab where it was being stored.

Resurrected on limited-edition DVD in early 2003, *Blue Sunshine* now stands as one of the most interesting, little-known horror films of the 1970s.

It's enough to scare the daisies out of college students who turned on and tuned out in the 1960s. A bummer of a trip, but that's the point.

1976 (R) 89m/C Zalman King, Deborah Winters, Robert Walden, Mark Goddard, Charles Siebert, Ann Cooper, Richard Crystal. *D:* Jeff Lieberman. *W:* Jeff Lieberman. *C:* Don Knight. *M:* Charles Gross. *VHS, DVD*

The Deathmaster 🦴🦴

Years after Charles Manson and his "family" committed their heinous crimes in and around Los Angeles in the summer of 1969, independent producers were still cashing in on Charlie and his murderous minions in such films as *The Manson Massacre, Angels' Wild Women,* and *Sweet Savior* (AKA *The Love-Thrill Murders*).

The Deathmaster stars veteran character actor Robert Quarry, who worked for Samuel Fuller in *House of Bamboo* and alongside Paul Newman in *WUSA* and *Winning.* Hot from the strong returns his stylish *Count Yorga, Vampire* collected at drive-ins, Quarry took the role of Khorda, a Manson-like figure who serves as gruesome guru to a group of hippies living on a Southern California beachfront commune.

Khorda's charismatic and New Agey sermons hypnotize the kids, who otherwise aimlessly smoke pot, drink booze, and enjoy free love. First to fall for Khorda is the dishy Esslin (Betty Anne Rees), a biker chick fed up with her boyfriend, Monk (William Jordan), a despondent fellow biker with a fondness for "steak and liquor." Once under Khorda's spell, she soon realizes that there's more to this guy than meets the eye. In fact, he's a vampire, and Esslin is the first counterculture gal on his menu.

By film's end, most of other commune dwellers fall prey to Khorda's appetite for plasma, but a few holdouts remain: Pico (Bill Ewing), a Billy Jack wanna-be who enjoys kung fu and wearing headbands; his girlfriend Rona (Brenda Dickson-Weinberg); and Pops, a local merchant (played by John Fiedler, a longtime character actor and the voice of Piglet from the *Winnie the Pooh* cartoons).

The Deathmaster has some genuinely hair-raising moments early on, thanks to Quarry's over-the-top turn. But by the time it's over, the vampire shtick, with the stakes and the mirrors, seems tired. Eventually you get the feeling you're watching another installment in the *Count Yorga* series—and the weakest one at that.

Still, there are enough interesting aspects to make *The Deathmaster* worthwhile, if for camp reasons alone. Hippie lingo is prominent, so you get "man" and "bummer" with great regularity. One irresistibly strange touch is the presence of Barbado (LaSesne Hilton), a Khorda associate who plays Zanfir-like tunes on the flute whenever the evil one appears. And then there are Khorda's long-winded words of advice and inspiration to his flaky followers, such as: "I saw it all. The rise and fall of Rome, Caesar trampled, gored,

Eyes Like Hot Coals ... Fangs Like Razors! Khorda the Deathmaster Has Left His Tomb

—Tagline for *The Deathmaster*

and ridden . . . Bonaparte, Hitler. I am like you, as other men, yet not. You number days of your few precious years; I count only centuries. Join us! We shall see! We shall see!"

Not many people actually went to see *The Deathmaster*; audiences preferred *The Return of Count Yorga* when it unspooled at drive-ins throughout America the following year. Despite his eerie presence, Quarry never became the horror "it" man that American International Pictures, the company that produced the *Count Yorga* films and distributed *The Deathmaster,* hoped he'd become. Still, for a few brief, shining years in the early 1970s, Quarry was top creep at movie theaters of the open-air variety.

1972 (R) 88m/C Robert Quarry, Betty Anne Rees, William Jordan, John Fiedler, Bill Ewing. *D:* Ray Danton. *W:* R. L. Grove. *C:* William C. Butler. *M:* Bill Marx. *DVD* *AKA: Deathmaster*

Dracula A.D. 1972

Dracula A.D. 1972 begins a century earlier than the date in the title, in 1872. Dracula (Christopher Lee) and primary agitator Abraham Van Helsing (Peter Cushing) are embroiled in a wicked fight aboard a horse-drawn coach. The altercation ends with Van Helsing dead and the infamous bloodsucker staked through the heart before he dissolves into dust. But as Van Helsing is being laid to rest, a Dracula fanatic (Christopher Neame) takes the vampire's dusty remains and plants them in the same cemetery.

Flash forward to 1972. We're now in mod London at a swinging, hoity-toity party. No one seems to be enjoying the performance of rock band Stoneground, but the booze is flowing freely, marijuana fills the air, and some of the younger people are intimately involved under tables.

The cops soon break things up, and a bored group of hippies, just bounced out of the party, gather at the Cavern, a local club. What to do for kicks now? Johnny Aculard (Neame again), a descendent of that Dracula fanatic, has an idea: why not perform a Black Mass and raise the spirit of the Devil himself? His friends are into it, except for one, who complains, "If we do get to summon the big daddy with the horns and tail, he has to bring his own liquor, his own bird, and his own pot." Good point.

Black Mass takes place next to the old burial grounds where Dracula's dust was earlier sprinkled. Johnny uses the blood of his willing pal Laura (Caroline Munro) to get the vampire back into business. The mass involves screaming, chanting, and a bubbling crude of blood. Then, poof! Drac is back.

Not one to let bygones be bygones, the bloodsucker intends to go after the Van Helsing family. Lawrence Van Helsing (also played by Cushing), the great-grandson of Abraham, is an anthropologist who knows everything there is to know about creatures of the night. And his granddaughter, Jessica (*Beverly Hills, 90210*'s Stephanie Beacham with a Jane Fonda *Klute*-era shag), is high on Drac's hit list.

> "There is evil in the world. There are dark, awful things. Occasionally, we get a glimpse of them. But there are dark corners; horrors almost impossible to imagine . . . even in our worst nightmares."
>
> —Peter Cushing as Van Helsing in *Dracula A.D. 1972*

Hardcore fans of the Christopher Lee–Peter Cushing Hammer fright films wanted to take a hammer to director Alan Gibson when *Dracula A.D. 1972* was released. The film probably seemed dated the day it was released. But Gibson, who also helmed the film's more successful, modernized follow-up, 1974's *The Satanic Rites of Dracula,* should be commended for trying to bring some new blood to an old formula. The contemporary music, oddball camera angles, and counterculture characters don't really click, but at least Gibson had the good sense to give us two vampires (Lee and the freshly dead Neame) and send them off to nasty battle royals against Van Helsing. Mirrors, stakes, a Bible, a cross, beams of light, a bathtub filled with water—you name it, and Van Helsing uses it to beat back the bloodsuckers and save his granddaughter. Although *Dracula A.D. 1972* aspires to be au courant, it doesn't quite hit the mark.

1972 (PG) 96m/C *UK* Christopher Lee, Peter Cushing, Stephanie Beacham, Christopher Neame, Caroline Munro, Michael Coles. *D:* Alan Gibson. *W:* Don Houghton. *C:* Dick Bush. *M:* Michael Vickers. *VHS*
AKA: *Dracula Today*

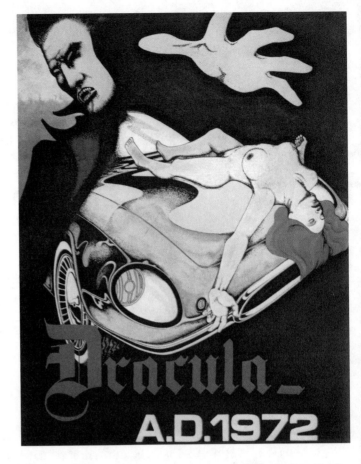

Poster for *Dracula A.D. 1972,* starring Christopher Lee

The Fearless Vampire Killers 🎵🎵🎵

Polish-born director Roman Polanski made his reputation with intense psychological thrillers like *Knife in the Water, Repulsion,* and *Rosemary's Baby,* but in between those highly praised pictures he directed *The Fearless Vampire Killers,* a surprising horror comedy. While its peculiarly European-flavored humor is a turnoff for many, the picture has nevertheless picked up a healthy cult audience over the years and even inspired an ill-fated Broadway production, *Dance of the Vampires,* in 2002. It may be unsophisticated, but its slapstick has an appeal similar to that of *Abbott and Costello Meet Frankenstein,* while offering wonderfully detailed art direction and costumes.

Crackpot Professor Abronsius (Jack MacGowran) and his naive assistant Alfred (Polanski) are traveling through the Carpathians in search of

ROMAN POLANSKI: FOREIGN FEAR FACTOR
by Laurence Lerman

With his recent Academy Award for Best Director for 2002's *The Pianist* and body of work that includes such classics as *Rosemary's Baby* (1968), *Chinatown* (1974), and *Tess* (1979), Roman Polanski can rightfully be considered one of cinema's great contemporary artists. In light of that status, it's fascinating to consider how a filmmaker whose works span more than forty years can be so immediately identified with a specific period of time. For Polanski, it's a ten-year stretch beginning with the 1967 release of the horror comedy *The Fearless Vampire Killers* and ending in 1977, when the Polish-born filmmaker unceremoniously fled the United States, a country to which he has yet to return.

The American Dream—Shattered

Roman Polanski's tango with the American dream back in the '60s was so vivid and colorful that it could have been its own movie. In 1967 he was happily enjoying the cult buzz of *Vampire Killers* and the love of his soon-to-be wife, starlet Sharon Tate (with whom he enjoyed the "unreality" of lovemaking and LSD, according to his 1984 autobiography, *Roman by Polanski*). His friendships in Hollywood were growing and solidifying—he met longtime friends Robert Evans and Jack Nicholson around this time—and the future classic *Rosemary's Baby* was in production, a film that would turn Polanski into a Hollywood golden boy overnight. A handful of fascinating directorial opportunities flew Polanski's way at that time, including such titles as *Downhill Racer* and *The Day of the Dolphin,* which ultimately were directed by Michael Ritchie and Mike Nichols, respectively. It was a happening time for the slight Polish émigré, and he dove into it head-on. The party came to a sudden and violent end on August 9, 1969, when Sharon Tate Polanski, eight months' pregnant, was ritualistically stabbed to death and mutilated by members of the notorious Charles Manson "family."

Many have proposed that Polanski's response to the tragedy can be seen in subsequent films. *The Tragedy of Macbeth* (1971), produced by none other than Hugh Hefner, is by far one of the most bloody, dank, and ugly adaptations of Shakespeare's Scottish play to ever hit the screen. As for the great *Chinatown,* Polanski famously altered the finale of Robert Towne's Oscar-winning script by having his leading lady, Faye Dunaway, die via a bullet through the eye. His argument for the rewritten ending? "That's life. Beautiful blondes die in Los Angeles," he reportedly said.

Trouble, On-screen and Off

Polanski's tragic life was tainted even further with scandal upon his 1977 arrest and imprisonment in Los Angeles on the charges of the alleged rape of a thirteen-year-old girl and his subsequent flight from the United States the following year. But it was the loss of his wife in the most notorious murder story of the era that still resonates in Polanski's work today. Witness two sequences in *The Pianist,* for which he won the Academy Award for Best Director. One depicts a very pregnant Jewish woman in Warsaw being herded onto a freight train for the camps, a Nazi roughing her up and holding a knife to her swollen middle; the other finds struggling-to-survive Jew Wladyslaw Szpilman sneaking several moments of peace playing a piano in front of a Nazi officer who has the power to kill him at will, if he so desires. These seconds-long shots effectively sum up the hell and hope that became part of Polanski's life one fateful day two years following the Summer of Love.

vampires when they note some sure signs of their quarry in a small mountain inn run by Shagal (Alfie Bass). Alfred is more interested in Shagal's gorgeous daughter, Sarah (Sharon Tate), but before the young man can woo her, she's abducted by the local undead royalty, Count Von Krolock (Ferdy Mayne). Although the vampire hunters fail in their efforts to destroy the vampirized Shagal, they do trail him back to the Count's castle and manage an attempt at rescuing Sarah. Unfortunately, the virginal maiden is set to be the main course at a vampire ball hosted by Krolock.

Cartoonish characters, dubbed dialogue, and an uneven pace may bother some viewers, but those who can get into the film's irreverent spirit will get a kick out of Polanski Lite. Some of the gags haven't aged well, but there's still a good deal of material that's on target, including the cinema's first Jewish and gay vampires, Tate's double entendre–filled bath spiel, and a cranky hunchback played by former boxing champ Terry Downes. As for Polanski, he hasn't stuck his neck out attempting this sort of foolishness since.

1967 108m/C Jack MacGowran, Roman Polanski, Sharon Tate, Ferdy Mayne, Alfie Bass, Jessie Robins, Iain Quarrier, Fiona Lewis, Terry Downes. *D:* Roman Polanski. *W:* Gerard Brach, Roman Polanski. *C:* Douglas Slocombe. *M:* Christopher Komeda. *VHS, DVD* *AKA:* Fearless Vampire Killers, or: Pardon Me, but Your Teeth Are in My Neck; Dance of the Vampires

—*Brian Thomas*

Ganja & Hess ♫♫♫♪

In 1972, actor-screenwriter Bill Gunn (*The Landlord*) was eager to direct his first commercial feature film. With *Blacula* and other blaxploitation movies making good at the box office, executives at low-budget Heritage Enterprises urged Gunn to make a "black vampire" movie. What they got back was a work of such depth and originality that they literally did not know what to do with it.

The film was ahead of its time in many ways. Gunn used the metaphor of vampirism as addiction—now a common element of movie mythology, seen in films from *Habit* to *Blade*—and ran with it. The common European interpretation of the vampire myth was avoided, supplanted by a more ancient African take. Instead of exploiting funky ghetto locations, Gunn chose to put black characters in luxurious and cultured environments, and he emphasized the film's romance as much as its horror.

The lead character, Dr. Hess Green (well played by Duane Jones of *Night of the Living Dead*), is a wealthy anthropologist who lives in a sprawling mansion in upstate New York and is chauffeured around in a Rolls Royce. But Hess guards a bizarre secret: while on an expedition to research primitive African tribes, he was stabbed with a ceremonial Myrthian dagger. The wound didn't kill him, but he became infected with a prehistoric virus from the blade, making him virtually immortal and in constant need of human blood. The doctor soon finds himself in unfamiliar and seedy neighborhoods in search of victims.

Shocks to the System

While a guest in Hess's house, psychotic George Meda (Gunn) dreams of stabbing the doctor, but instead commits suicide. Hess takes advantage of the situation for a meal and then conceals the corpse in his cellar freezer. Trouble arrives when George's wife Ganja (Marlene Clark) comes looking for her husband. Thrown off his game by this earthy, sexy woman, Hess takes her in until he can figure out what to do about the situation. Unexpectedly, the stuffy academic and the opportunistic Ganja become drawn together and fall in love. This circumstance creates a fresh dilemma for Hess: should he reveal, and even share, his curse with the woman he loves? If he does, will he create an even worse monster than himself? When Ganja discovers George's body in the freezer, Hess is forced to make a decision.

One of those premier works engulfed in fiery creativity, Gunn's film drew raves from critics and film festival audiences, but, sadly, the distributor couldn't see the value in it. With the distributor intending to sell it as another exploitation title for the urban grind-house market, the film was carefully but thoroughly recut by editor Fima Noveck to heighten the sex and violence angles. The new version showed up in theaters (and later, on video) in a seventy-eight-minute version as *Black Vampire* and, when the blaxploitation genre seemed to be dying out, under several other titles. Thought lost for many years, Gunn's original cut of the film was reassembled by the good folks at All Day Entertainment for an early DVD release, one that amply demonstrated the potential of that then-young format. The way the picture straddles the line between art film and horror show is still surprising audiences; we only hope it eventually acquires the status it deserves.

1972 (R) 110m/C Duane Jones, Marlene Clark, Bill Gunn, Leonard Jackson, Mabel King, Richard Harrow, Candece Tarpley, Sam Waymon. *D:* Bill Gunn. *W:* Bill Gunn. *C:* James E. Hinton. *M:* Sam Waymon. *VHS, DVD*
AKA: Blood Couple; Black Evil; Black Vampire; Blackout: The Moment of Terror; Double Obsession; Vampires in Harlem

—*Brian Thomas*

The Honeymoon Killers ♪♪♪♪

Many true-crime thrillers were produced in the wake of *Bonnie and Clyde,* but this unusual effort stands alone. The film is given extra depth thanks to the strength of its lead performances and an experimental atmosphere that feels like early John Cassavetes. The "Lonely Hearts Killers" case, as it came to be known, had been portrayed before, notably by Hitchcock in *Shadow of a Doubt* and in Frederic Brown's novel *The Far Cry,* but never before with such raw power.

The life of nurse Martha Beck (Shirley Stoler) takes a dramatic turn when her friend Bunny (*Everyone Loves Raymond*'s Doris Roberts) enrolls her in a Lonely Hearts pen pal service. Coerced into going along with the idea, Martha becomes entranced by the letters of Spanish immigrant Raymond Fernandez (Tony Lo Bianco), a handsome "importer." Unfortunately, Ray is a con man victimizing a parade of lonely women. But before he can get too far in

Tony Lo Bianco and Shirley Stoler cuddle and kill in the 1970 film *The Honeymoon Killers.*
ROXANNE PRODS / THE KOBAL COLLECTION

manipulating Martha, she begins to manipulate him. Before long, they team up in his business and add a more extreme element to the game: murder. While aiding in the seductions, Martha also becomes a jealous enforcer, preventing any of their conquests from getting too intimate with Ray. Of course, such goings-on can put quite a strain on a relationship.

One wonders throughout whether Martha and Ray are really in love or have entered into a contract of mutual obsession and desperation. It's easy to see why this film is one of John Waters's favorites—its influence on many of his films is obvious, what with its lurid atmosphere, tabloid storyline, and protagonist Martha, a 250-pound killer caregiver. (Martin Scorsese was originally scheduled to direct *The Honeymoon Killers,* an assignment that would have yielded fascinating results.) While it would be easy to camp up such material, all the characters are played straight, for the most part, and a slow-building tension lends each of the murder scenes a vivid intensity. Tony Lo Bianco is excellent as the crafty lothario, but Shirley Stoler is really sensational. Martha stalks through seedy apartments and hotel rooms like an Angel of Death, yet she never loses audience sympathy. Only the melodramatic Mahler score and a few other flaws resulting from a limited budget taint the production. It's somewhat disappointing that director Leonard Kastle didn't compose the music himself, as music was his true vocation. He had great success with his own orchestral compositions and in directing opera. But the real disappointment is that, despite this film's immediate and continued critical praise, Kastle chose never to direct again.

1970 (R) 115m/B Shirley Stoler, Tony Lo Bianco, Mary Jane Higby, Doris Roberts, Marilyn Chris, Dortha Duckworth, Ann Harris, Mary Engel, Mary Breen. **D:** Leonard Kastle, Donald Volkman. **W:** Leonard Kastle. **C:** Oliver Wood. **M:** Gustav Mahler. *VHS, DVD* **AKA:** *The Lonely Hearts Killers*

—*Brian Thomas*

I Drink Your Blood

One of many horror films inspired by the crimes of Charles Manson and his followers, this entry distinguished itself with its enthusiastic willingness to go violently over the top. Hippie Satanists, led by the hilariously ranting acid-head Horace Bones (Bhaskar), beat up and rape Sylvia (Iris Brooks), a teenage girl who witnesses their corny ceremony. The group's ancient van breaks down before they can leave the tiny mountain village of Valley Hills, so they settle in to terrorize the local population. When the girl's veterinarian grandfather (Richard Bowler) comes to settle accounts, they give him a drink spiked with LSD. To get revenge, the old codger's grandson, Pete (Riley Mills), sells the troublesome flower children meat pies injected with the blood of a rabid dog. But instead of just making them sick, the plot makes matters much worse by turning them into cannibalistic maniacs. Before the heroes or the authorities can act to contain the situation—and before the loonies can finish each other off—a crew of dam construction workers is infected, and the protagonists have to fight their way to safety through an army of psychopathic killers.

In this orgy of violence, a knife, a rifle, an ax, a dagger, a machete, an electric knife, a shotgun, a wooden stake, a pitchfork, teeth, a sword, a revolver, and a garden hose are all used as deadly weapons. The bloodbath is tempered with humor, both intentional and otherwise, as when the construction chief (John McCook) tells the leading lady (Elizabeth Marner-Brooks), who is seeking help for the assaulted girl, "Rape is a little outside of an engineer's domain." This comes after she'd complained about people leaving town because of his "damn dam." Producer Jerry Gross (*Girl on a Chain Gang, Black Godfather*) brought in a fortune, mostly at the drive-ins, by pairing this film with Del Tenney's seven-year-old he-man adventure flick *Zombies*, which he retitled *I Eat Your Skin*. Talk about your distasteful double features!

1971 (R) 83m/C Bhaskar, Jadine Wong, Rhonda Fultz, Elizabeth Marner-Brooks, George Patterson, Riley Mills, Iris Brooks, Tyde Kierney, John Damon, Lynne Lowry, John McCook. *D:* David E. Durston. *W:* David E. Durston. *C:* Jacques Demarecaux. *M:* Clay Pitts. VHS, DVD
AKA: Satan's Band

—*Brian Thomas*

Last House on the Left ♪♪♪

The film that boasted, "In order to avoid fainting, keep repeating . . . it's only a movie, it's only a movie," centers on pretty young Mary Collingwood (Sandra Cassel) and her best friend, Phyllis Stone (Lucy Grantham). While trying to score some weed on the way to a rock concert, the teens are kidnapped by a gang of escaped convicts led by the sadistic Stillo brothers (David Hess and Marc Sheffler). The brutal gang members abuse the girls for their own amusement—scenes of the ordeal are contrasted with Mary's parents preparing her birthday celebration—and eventually they take their victims out into the woods to murder them. Coincidentally, the murders are committed right across the street from Mary's home. When the gang attempts to hole up at the first convenient house, the Collingwoods (Cynthia Carr and Gaylord St. James) roll out the red carpet. But the quiet suburban parents soon discover the murders, turn commando, and exact bloody revenge (including a chainsaw massacre two years before Tobe Hooper's *Texas* one).

Last House on the Left's occasional tongue-in-cheek tone clashes with the repellent, drawn-out rape and torture sequences. For those who can stomach the hard-to-watch bits, the film is counterbalanced by the outrageous second half, during which the inept criminals and the local lawmen are given a humorous treatment. Adding to the lighter tone is a ridiculously cheery music soundtrack by Hess and an uncredited Steve Chapin, brother of Harry and Tom.

Ingmar Bergman's 1960 *The Virgin Spring* served as *Last House*'s inspiration, and *Last House* itself spawned a host of imitators. It also served as a springboard for its two creators as Wes Craven went on to direct *The Hills Have*

MONDO MOVIES: REAL FILMS FOR REEL PEOPLE
by Brian Thomas

Ever since exotic documentary features such as *Nanook of the North* and *Grass* made a hit with the public, less honest filmmakers have been rolling into theaters with documentaries of their own. Since directors could get away with greater nudity, sex, violence, and attention to lurid subjects under the "educational" guise of a documentary, staples of the roadshow circuits like *Ingagi* and *Forbidden Adventure* were built around footage filmed in distant locales by adventurous travelers and were spiced up with additional sensational footage faked in the director's backyard. Other shockumentaries emphasized gruesome true-crime elements.

Viva Italia!

In 1962 Italians Franco Prosperi and Gualtiero Jacopetti created a worldwide sensation with *Mondo Cane,* a mishmash of weirdness filmed all over the world, intended to illustrate the basic bestial nature of man. Although it's never been determined which sequences were real and which were faked, it's been accepted as fact from the beginning that a certain percentage of footage was fabricated—not that knowing this spoils its entertainment value. Since then, these "mondo movies," with their combination of sensational sights and snide narration, have been frequently imitated, from the scores of such films produced throughout the 1960s to today's "reality TV" epidemic. Prosperi and Jacopetti produced some of the harder-edged subjects themselves, following *Mondo Cane 2* (AKA *Mondo Pazzo*) with the controversial *Farewell Uncle Tom* and the repellent *Africa Blood & Guts,* while their associate Paolo Cavara made *Malamondo.*

Other Italians contributed *Mondo Balordo* (with narration by Boris Karloff), which begins with human oddities around Naples (lucky hunchback, a dwarf who lip-syncs to Louis Prima records), then spreads its view to Japanese bondage photography, French drag queens, African animal butchery and voodoo, Ecuadorian cocaine addicts, German lesbian bars, and Hong Kong strippers. The filmmakers even found an excuse to include clips and behind-the-scenes shots of Hercules movies. Some mondos, such as *Slave Trade in the World Today,* concentrated on a certain subject, while *Naked World, Go Go Go World, Taboos of the World* (narrated by Vincent Price), and others stuck to the general carnival-of-oddities format, skipping effortlessly from travelogue to freak show.

Mondo, American Style

With the success they were having distributing the Italian *Ecco* (narrated by George Sanders) in the United States, adult filmmakers Bob Cresse and Lee Frost (*House on Bare Mountain*) decided that they could cash in easily with their own mondo movie. After all, they were a stone's throw away from all the weirdness of Hollywood, and if they couldn't procure enough footage from elsewhere in the world, they could always fake it. With its peep show hidden-camera-in-a-dressing-room title sequence, *Mondo Bizarro* follows more in the spirit of the filmmakers' nudie pictures than in the shock territory of *Mondo Cane.* Attempting to give an impression of worldliness akin to their Italian models, Cresse and Frost cut in sequences from foreign shores, but most of the feature takes place in the United States. We see nude sunbathers, gay prostitutes, spring-break hedonism that goes beyond American International Pictures' *Beach Party* movies, modern art, and pinup photography. With this film, notes of relevance begin to creep into the festival of titillation, as the cameras capture billboards painted by artists protesting the Vietnam War, then veterans protesting against the artists, then other protesters protesting the veterans. Soon after, audio clips of interviews with kids bumming around on the beach play over film of the same, giving a portrait of the short period between surf culture and Summer of Love hippiedom.

But the taint of authenticity doesn't last very long in any mondo movie. One of the phoniest sequences in *Mondo Bizarro* is a long section that purports to be film of a slave auction in the hills of Lebanon, but it more likely took place in Hollywood's familiar Bronson Canyon. In fact, it looks much like the location where the "voodoo ceremony" was filmed. Cresse himself is recognizable as the auctioneer.

Frost and Cresse followed up on *Bizarro* a year later with *Mondo Freudo* (AKA *Sensuous Taboo*), this time more openly embracing the sexual theme, though hardly referencing Freudian psychology. We're shown Sunset Strip "watusi club" cruisers, London strip clubs, topless clubs, body painting (seemingly part of every other movie made in 1967), a "Satanic mass" in a New York City loft, German mud wrestling, and Japanese S&M performances. In Tijuana, there's a slave auction—which features some of the same slaves sold in *Mondo Bizarro*!—and a visit to a strip club fronting for a bordello. Comic highlights are provided by interviews with prostitutes at various sites (though, of course, the setting could be anywhere). One wonders whether the camera crew crossed paths with that of director Peter Perry (*Kiss Me Quick!*), who was covering similar territory for *Mondo Mod*—a collection of sequences about teen surfing, biking, and other common pursuits, highlighted by an interview with a guy purported to be on LSD—at about the same time, or whether they encountered crews making *Mondo Hollywood, Mondo Teeno,* or the more musical *Mondo Daytona.* Europeans teamed up with Hollywood for one of the strangest mondo movies, *The Wild, Wild World of Jayne Mansfield,* in which cameras accompany the statuesque star on a tour of Europe's sexy hot spots, climaxing with a sequence detailing her gruesome and fatal car wreck.

It's tough to say just how many scenes in these pictures were performed specifically for the cameras, but an estimate close to 100 percent wouldn't be too far off the mark. However, what they lack in authenticity is made up for in another kind of truth: they give a full glimpse of the exploitation business at that specific time period, along with a look at different cultures and fashions. Although sleazy, the mondo movies of the '60s retain a certain kind of charm that was quickly abandoned for further exploitation in the 1970s, when pictures like *Shocking Asia* and *Faces of Death* would leave no grotesqueries unexposed.

Eyes and *A Nightmare on Elm Street,* while producer Sean S. Cunningham created the *Friday the 13th* series. Three decades later, the effort seems more amateurish than when first released, but it remains effectively creepy.

1972 (R) 84m/C David Hess, Lucy Grantham, Sandra Cassel, Fred J. Lincoln, Gaylord St. James, Cynthia Carr, Mark Sheffler, Jeramie Rain, Marshall Anker, Martin Kove. **D:** Wes Craven. **W:** Wes Craven. **C:** Victor Hurwitz. **M:** David Hess, Steve Chapin. *VHS, DVD* **AKA:** *Krug and Company; Night of Vengeance; Sex Crime of the Century; Grim Company*

—*Brian Thomas*

Night of the Living Dead 🦴🦴🦴🦴

When TV-commercial director George Romero and Latent Image, his film company, decided that their first feature project should be a horror movie, the notion that it should involve a siege naturally came to mind. The TV news was full of footage of the war in Vietnam, riots, and civil unrest, and the fear of becoming overwhelmed by a group of people was very much on the public's mind.

So, in *Night of the Living Dead,* a group of desperate characters holes up in a remote farmhouse during a catastrophe. As a hostile horde tries to batter its way inside, the squabbling survivors attempt to save themselves any way they can. But one escape plan after another fails, and their numbers steadily dwindle. The horrific twist is that the attackers are actually walking corpses that have been reanimated by radiation from a fallen satellite. Twisting the knife even further, the ghouls are hungry for the flesh of the living. It's one thing to fear being killed by zombies, but to be killed and *eaten* by zombies multiplies the horror tenfold, at least.

Night of the Living Dead wasn't produced in a vacuum. The siege movie had been a popular subgenre for decades, stretching back to early sound films like *The Lost Patrol,* then through *Fort Apache* and *Zulu.* The zombie twist cropped up in 1959, when John Agar battled unseen aliens who had taken advantage of a nuclear accident in order to take possession of the bodies of dead earthlings in *Invisible Invaders.* Another model was the 1964 Italian film *The Last Man on Earth* (which was based on Richard Matheson's classic novel *I Am Legend*). In that film, a plague turns humanity into undead vampires, and scientist Vincent Price is the only one who is immune. Although Price was a great horror star, his marquee value was wasted in this outing, as his theatrical style is out of place. An earthier leading man would have served the film much better, but Price gives it his all, feverishly boarding himself up inside his house while an army of ghouls tears away at his defenses. Sound familiar? Even the early sequence of *Night* in which heroine Judith O'Dea finds a mutilated corpse inside the farmhouse apes a similar scene from Hitchcock's *The Birds.*

So what made *Night of the Living Dead* so different? Talent, for one thing. Romero's intellectual approach to the pulp material makes it shine. He craftily has some of the remote action play out in the form of news reports, which the trapped heroes watch on TV, much like people across America were

watching the war. The cast is a mix of amateurs and pros, but New York stage actors like Duane Jones manage to lift the level of performance, giving the film dramatic weight. The excellent B&W cinematography draws the viewer in, and the story's violent scenes deliver shock after shock. It's a gripping film that keeps its hold on you for weeks afterward.

Title card for George Romero's horror classic *Night of the Living Dead*

THE KOBAL COLLECTION

   Unfortunately for Romero and company, *Night* also pioneered a depressing business model: the creators made little money from their classic horror film and were ripped off by a long line of distributors. Other first-time horror projects such as Tobe Hooper's *Texas Chainsaw Massacre* and Sam Raimi's *Evil Dead* followed a similar creative and financial arc, making it necessary for all to produce sequels and remakes in order to see a profit. *Night* ended up in a legal gray area as well: despite the fact that Romero and coscriptor John Russo retained the rights to their screenplay, the film itself slipped into the public domain, resulting in countless inferior releases on home video until a superior laserdisc restoration (and subsequent DVD release) made all other versions moot. Like Romero's zombies, *Night of the Living Dead* seems to be unstoppable.

1968 96m/B Duane Jones, Judith O'Dea, Karl Hardman, Marilyn Eastman, Russell Streiner, Keith Wayne, Judith Ridley, Kyra Schon. *D:* George Romero. *W:* George Romero, John Russo. *C:* George Romero. *M:* Scott Vladimir Licina. *VHS, DVD*
AKA: *Night of Anubis; Night of the Flesh Eaters*

—*Brian Thomas*

Spirits of the Dead

The tales of Edgar Allan Poe had already been proven to be fertile ground for filmgoers with Roger Corman's stylish shockers throughout the 1960s, when Italian producer Alberto Grimaldi enlisted three acclaimed European auteurs to try their hands at adapting Poe for this anthology film.

Not surprisingly, the accent is on the sexual underbelly of the stories, and the results are a mixed bag. In the first entry, "Metzengerstein," director Roger Vadim casts his then-wife Jane Fonda in a tale of medieval debauchery and obsession. Fonda plays Countessa Frederica, a powerful and hedonistic woman unaccustomed to hearing the word "no" from anyone. She wants an orgy, she gets it. She wants to shoot arrows at a young squire just for fun, nobody's going to stop her. The only person beyond her control is Baron Wilhelm (played by Peter Fonda, Jane's brother), her cousin and an aristocrat of the neighboring estate. So annoyed is the countess at the baron's disregard that she has his castle burned down, killing him. But the act throws her into an emotional tailspin, leaving her almost catatonic. Even an orgy doesn't rouse the countess's normally lustful desires.

What does awaken the countess, in an unhealthy sort of way, is Wilhelm's most prized possession, a wild horse. She tames the animal and begins riding him around her estate. Oddly, after the fatal fire, a tapestry of the horse supernaturally disappears, and the countess oversees its painstaking recreation by an artist. Once the work is complete, Frederica takes the horse by the reins and faces her destiny.

Vadim, whose studies in sensuality include . . . *And God Created Woman, Charlotte,* and, of course, *Barbarella,* but who is really best known for his relations with Fonda, Brigitte Bardot, and Catherine Deneuve, treads on taboo territory here, tackling incest, a certain fondness for horses, group sex, and Jane Fonda speaking French. The result is an undeniably icky soufflé filled with pretentious symbolism, poor period sets and production design, and some far-out '60s-style costuming that puts not-so-plain Jane in yellow negligees. Equestrian fans may enjoy it, but it's no *Seabiscuit,* and Vadim ultimately proves that as a filmmaker, he made a great lover.

"William Wilson," the second segment, comes from Louis Malle, the French filmmaker of such sensitive, childhood-themed dramas as *Lacombe Lucien, Murmur of the Heart,* and *Au Revoir Les Enfants.* Later, Malle also gave us *Pretty Baby,* with Brooke Shields playing a child prostitute; "William Wilson" also hints at the director's kinkier side.

Here, French tough guy Alain Delon is the title character, an ill-mannered no-goodnik with an odd tale. During a confession to a village priest, Wilson admits to having killed someone and then launches into the strange story behind the murder. Since he was a young boy, Wilson has been shadowed by another William Wilson, a doppelganger, who steps in when he's about to take his sadistic behavior to the next level. As the story unfolds, we witness Wilson as a young boy in military school torturing a fellow student with rats; as a med-

Edgar Allan Poe's ultimate orgy

—Tagline for *Spirits of the Dead*

ical student preparing to perform an autopsy on a living woman; and, while in the Austrian army, cheating at cards and then whipping his female competitor (Brigitte Bardot, wearing a black wig and smoking cigars).

Does the other William Wilson really exist? Is he the physical manifestation of Wilson's conscience? Or is he simply a delusion, the result of heavy drinking and emotional instability? Well, that's for the priest and the audience to find out. In this disturbing segment, Malle, a filmmaker known for his gift of understatement even when tackling controversial subjects, offers us instead vivid images of stabbings, tortures, whippings, and other violent acts.

The final entry in *Spirits of the Dead* has become the most talked about of the trio. Federico Fellini's "Toby Dammit," liberally adapted from the Poe story *Don't Bet the Devil Your Head,* was made in 1968, his first work after the drug-influenced *Juliet of the Spirits,* and just before *Fellini Satyricon,* his most grotesque offering. So, it should come as little surprise that the segment serves as a bridge between those two mind-blowing efforts.

Terence Stamp is the title character, a pasty-faced, drunken British movie star in Rome to make a religious western. Sipping on a flask of the hard stuff, Dammit is taken from the airport to a TV studio by limo. During the ride, he encounters irate cab drivers, nuns, and a fortune-teller who refuses to read the actor's palm. On the set of the TV talk show, the actor is interrogated on religion, his bad reviews playing Hamlet, why he wants to make a western film (he was promised a Ferrari), and his use of LSD ("I use all types of drugs to get back to normal"). Afterward, Dammit is taken to the Golden She Wolf awards ceremony, where he is the guest of honor.

It's here that Fellini's trademark style shines through as he serves up a surreal, savage satire of Hollywood and celebrity adulation. On a spare, fog-enshrouded set, female groupies vie for the star's attention while a trippy fashion show takes place on stage. Soused and rumpled in his seat, the insolent actor pays little attention to the never-ending parade of nagging, adoring fans and industry workers. When the spotlight finds him to accept his award, he barely rises, then spits out some Shakespearean meanderings. All he cares about is that Ferrari and the recurring image he has of a young, blonde girl playing with a ball.

Dammit is finally given that Ferrari, but he takes it on a ride to hell from which there is no return. Driving the sports car at high speeds in search of Rome and, perhaps, his past innocence, Dammit appears to have entered another dimension, courtesy of Fellini. The car revs wildly down narrow streets, dodging pedestrians and skirting detour signs until Dammit reaches his ironic demise.

Despite the presence of three big-name international directors, *Spirits of the Dead* didn't fare all that well at the box office. In the United States, its artistic pedigree went by the wayside when the savvy exploitation pioneers at American International Pictures took on distribution chores, dubbing the picture and adding some narration by house favorite Vincent Price.

Actually, the film's production history could warrant a film in itself. Fellini signed on to direct "Toby Dammit" because he was told Ingmar Bergman and Orson Welles would be behind the cameras for the other segments. But

EUROHORROR: THE SCARES THAT CAME IN FROM THE '60S
by Brian Thomas

Barbara Steele in *Black Sunday*

GALATEA / JOLLY / THE KOBAL
COLLECTION

While the cinema of horror had its origins in the silent classics of Germany, what we think of as true Euro-Horror began in Italy in 1956. *I Vampiri*—a twisted tale of life extension, murder, and reanimated corpses—was Italy's first true horror picture, opening the floodgates to a wave of Old World nightmares that would haunt screens worldwide. Although the film's director, Riccardo Freda, was a great talent and would go on to create other fine spook shows such as *The Ghost* and *The Horrible Dr. Hichcock,* an even greater talent emerged from *The Devil's Commandment* (as *I Vampiri* became known in the United States) in the person of cinematographer and assistant director Mario Bava.

Super Mario

Bava, a visionary genius who could create amazing photographic effects with a few pieces of cardboard, went on to direct several milestones in horror cinema. Whether in grand, gothic, supernatural period pictures like the vampire classic *Black Sunday* (which made an icon of Barbara Steele) or the far future gothic sci-fi epic *Planet of the Vampires* (which would greatly influence *Alien*), Bava's sense of style always seemed perfectly in step with the go-go '60s. This was never more apparent than in his chilling tale of murder in the fashion world, 1964's *Blood and Black Lace.* This wickedly violent and stylish picture pioneered many of the elements of what became known as the "giallo" thriller—that peculiarly Italian brand of horror story named after a series of yellow-jacketed paperback novels.

Louis Malle substituted for Bergman when the Swedish filmmaker dropped out. And Vadim was brought in to replace Welles because Vadim guaranteed the pairing of Jane and Peter Fonda and a surefire distribution deal in the States. This development distressed Fellini to no end. And he found even more things to worry about when star Peter O'Toole bowed out from "Toby" at the last minute. Stamp, in Italy to film Pier Paolo Pasolini's *Teorema* at the time, filled in for O'Toole.

1968 (R) 117m/C *FR/IT* Jane Fonda, Alain Delon, Terence Stamp, Brigitte Bardot, Peter Fonda, James Robertson-Justice, Françoise Prévost. *D:* Roger Vadim, Louis Malle, Federico Fellini. *W:* Roger Vadim, Federico Fellini, Louis Malle, Daniel Boulanger, Pascal Cousin, Clement Biddle Wood, Bernardino Zapponi. *C:* Claude

While EuroHorror has its share of monsters and ghosts, *Blood and Black Lace* would be widely imitated a few years later—its nightmarish visual style, mysterious murderer, disturbing violence, and female victims—and the giallo would become the defining subgenre of Italian horror, with Bava protégé Dario Argento (*Suspiria*) becoming its foremost maestro and, eventually, a collaborator with Mario's son, Lamberto Bava.

The Pain in Spain

Meanwhile, over in Spain, Jesus Franco borrowed a few ideas from Georges Franju's *Eyes without a Face* to make his own more sensational version, which was released in the United States as *The Awful Dr. Orloff* in 1962. Franco possesses a form of genius diametrically opposed to that of Bava, favoring quantity over quality. *Orloff,* which treads the line between German weird-crime movies and the kind of colorful redressing of Universal horror classics coming from Britain's Hammer Films, was a career-making success for Franco, inspiring many other EuroHorror pictures (including several unofficial sequels, with and without Franco and his star Howard Vernon). Still going strong, Franco has directed over two hundred films to date, his 1960s output alone stretching from the sleazy *Sadistic Baron Von Klaus,* to the campy *Two Undercover Angels* movies, to *The Castle of Fu Manchu* and *The Blood of Fu Manchu,* two late-1960s entries in Harry Alan Towers's series starring Christopher Lee as Sax Rohmer's villain.

Another product of an era during which a tyrannical regime in Spain oddly promoted genre filmmaking was one of Europe's few truly international horror stars. A professional athlete and movie extra, Paul Naschy shot to stardom playing an energetic werewolf in 1968's *Mark of the Wolfman* (released in the United States under the misleading title *Frankenstein's Bloody Terror*). Naschy would go on to play most of the classic old monsters, from Dracula to the Mummy, but he'd always return to his "Waldemar Daninsky" wolfman character, even into the twenty-first century.

Whether the films portrayed supernatural beasts or psychopathic killers, the 1960s were the years in which these and other European filmmakers made their bloody mark on the world's movie screens.

Renoir, Tonino Della Colli, Giuseppe Rotunno. **M:** Diego Masson, Jean Prodromides, Nino Rota. *VHS, DVD*
AKA: *Histoires Extraordinaires; Tales of Mystery and Imagination; Tales of Mystery; Trois histoires extraordinaires d'Edgar Allan Poe*

Targets ♫♫♫♪

On August 1, 1966, a clean-cut young ex-Marine named Charles Whitman, the son of a well-off Austin plumber, changed forever how Americans would define the term "safe." After killing his wife and mother,

Peter Bogdanovich depicts the real-life horror of a serial-killing sniper in *Targets*, his directorial debut.

Whitman packed up a footlocker with guns, ammunition, and other supplies and drove to the nearby Texas Tower on the campus of the University of Texas. After killing any potentially troublesome witnesses on lower floors, he made his way to the top. From the observation deck he began a sniping spree, indiscriminately shooting anyone he could get in his sights. In all, he killed fourteen people and injured dozens more before police made their way past his barricades and shot him down. Whitman was suffering from depression and headaches and had confessed in therapy to fantasizing about such a killing spree, but the question of why Charles Whitman shot all those people was never really answered.

For his debut feature as director, Peter Bogdanovich took this real-world horror story and contrasted it with the kind of gothic terrors no longer considered relevant in modern movies. To do this, Bogdanovich employed horror legend Boris Karloff, casting him essentially as himself. Karloff plays an aging horror film star named Byron Orlock who decides to retire when he comes to recognize that his kind of films are now out of date. Despite the entreaties of an earnest young director (Bogdanovich himself), Orlock refuses to consider starting another picture, and he can't be talked out of a planned public appearance at the Reseda Drive-In, a symbol of receding Hollywood glamour. His story is juxtaposed with that of Bobby Thompson (Tim O'Kelly), a cheerful, all-American young man who hides deep psychological turmoil and an extensive arsenal. After gunning down his wife, mother, and a delivery boy,

Thompson stops by the freeway to test his sharpshooting skills from the top of a gas tower (a sequence recalling the close of *White Heat*). But when he finds his targets too difficult to hit—and when the police start closing in—Thompson retreats to another perch, behind the drive-in movie screen, bringing him face-to-face with horror icon Orlock.

Beginning the film with footage from AIP's crazy-quilt production *The Terror* (which turns up again at the drive-in premiere, further blending fact and fiction), Bogdanovich creates a sharp contrast to the gaudy castle sets by placing the rest of the picture against cool blues, whites, and grays (sharp photography courtesy of Laszlo Kovacs). He further heightens the division between real life and movie life by using only ambient music from radios, televisions, and the drive-in speakers to accompany his story. Another contrast is provided by Karloff's classical acting style, which is successfully played off of the more natural approach used by Bogdanovich and others in the film. The old veteran and the novice director are a touching pair, making the mayhem all the more chilling.

Many aspects of the picture struck uncomfortably close to the truth, and not just in a true-crime sense. Although Karloff always maintained a cheerful outlook in public, the fact was that low-budget studios like American International Pictures were the only ones offering him steady work in his later years, with parts that exploited his name in increasingly seedy productions. (Interestingly, despite the fact that this project was initially green-lighted because of its cut-rate budget, it was deemed of high enough quality that it was sold to Paramount for distribution, not AIP.) While essentially making a "message" picture promoting gun control, Bogdanovich still does a wonderful job creating tension throughout, especially in the climactic sequence, when you don't know where the sniper will strike next—just like in real life.

1968 (R) 90m/C Boris Karloff, Tim O'Kelly, Peter Bogdanovich, Arthur Peterson, Monte Landis, Nancy Hsueh, Sandy Baron. *D:* Peter Bogdanovich. *W:* Peter Bogdanovich. *C:* Laszlo Kovacs. *VHS, DVD*
AKA: Before I Die

—Brian Thomas

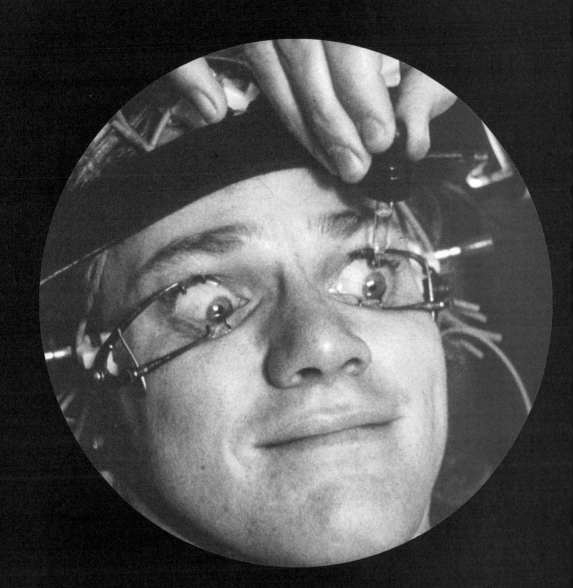

Chapter 7

Far Out, Man

Dum . . . dum . . . dum . . . DA-DUM!

Can you name that tune in four notes?

Sure you can. Those are the opening notes to Richard Strauss's *Also Sprach Zarathustra,* the song most closely associated with Stanley Kubrick's landmark 1968 science fiction film *2001: A Space Odyssey.*

After the film's release, everyone was humming those notes. Deodoto, a Brazilian musican, turned the music into a funky jazz fusion piece that hit the charts a bit later. It became the signature theme for any sort of space footage, perfectly timed for man's landing on the moon in '69. Hmmm. People couldn't get enough of a song composed in 1896 taken from a two-and-a-half hour philosophical space opera? But this was only one example of the impact of that watershed film.

The other was that sci-fi could be taken seriously on the big screen. Of course, *Barbarella* came along that same year, sending out a different set of space-age vibes with its satire, wildly colorful sets and costumes, goofy dialogue, and heavy exposure to lead actress Jane Fonda's skin.

So throughout the psychedelic era you could have your science fiction both ways: solemn or silly. But either way, your mind was going to be blown, and, in most cases, you were going to get more sophistication than from the 1950s-fueled sci-fi about space exploration (like *Destination Moon*), malevolent aliens (*War of the Worlds*), and big bald carrot monsters (*The Thing [from Another World]*).

Since the space race between the United States and Russia had accelerated and the Cold War continued to heat up, a display of the serious side of sci-fi was inevitable. The challenge of space exploration became the source of intense drama about both inner and outer space with films like *Marooned* and *Countdown,* tales that looked at the personal impact of getting sent into the wild black and blue yonder.

Kubrick came back to the future in 1971, shifting villainous gears from the totalitarian computer of *2001* to demonic British punks with *A Clockwork Orange.* Like Kubrick, who adapted the works of Arthur C.

Clarke (for *2001*) and Anthony Burgess (for *A Clockwork Orange*), other filmmakers based their tales of futuristic disharmony on literary works by such notable genre writers as Ray Bradbury (*Fahrenheit 451, The Illustrated Man*) and Richard Matheson (*The Omega Man*). Charlton Heston, who played *The Omega Man*'s smartass hero, moved from battling vampires to confronting sinister simians in the *Planet of the Apes,* which made people go bananas in such a big way, it was followed by sequel after sequel after sequel after TV series after remake.

The environment became a big issue during the 1970s, emanating from the counterculture consciousness that spawned Earth Day. *Silent Running,* from *2001* and *Candy* special-effects expert Douglas Trumbull and young writers Michael Cimino and Steven Bochco, features Bruce Dern as an astronaut transporting the last remaining forest on Earth to a brave new world. It elicited kudos for its dandy special effects and nature-friendly theme. Meanwhile, a steady flow of films tackled other pressing problems: *Soylent Green* confronted food shortage and overpopulation, *ZPG* took on just overpopulation, *The Andromeda Strain* encountered plague, *No Blade of Grass* delved into pollution, and *Glen and Randa* showed the after-effects of a nuclear bomb.

Except for *Planet of the Apes,* none of the science fiction films of the era could come close to *2001*'s groundbreaking achievements on a technical, attention-getting, or financial level. But *2001*'s studio, MGM, decided to give itself one more chance of finding *Space Odyssey*–style success on a grand scale in 1976. The result was *Logan's Run,* which supplanted Kubrick's intellectual approach with action-oriented chase sequences. But early disco-era costumes and sleek suburban mall surroundings were no match for the Star Child or the sight of space stations and rocket ships pirouetting poetically—even sexually—to Johann Strauss II's *Blue Danube.*

Alphaville ♩♩♩♪

American-born actor and singer Eddie Constantine had been playing tough-guy secret agent Lemmy Caution, or similar characters, since 1953's *Poison Ivy;* working primarily in France for most of his career, he was like the French James Bond to European film fans long before Sean Connery took his first starring role. Jean-Luc Godard was the darling of the French New Wave, best known for his American-influenced (but thoroughly French) romance *Breathless.* These two joined forces for *Alphaville,* a wondrous oddity that bent over backward to undermine itself.

Lemmy Caution, Secret Agent 003, is sent to Alphaville, that "whore of cities," on an undercover mission to abduct (or liquidate) a scientist, Professor Leonard Von Braun (Howard Vernon). Posing as a reporter, but making little effort to stay incognito, Caution's first order of business is to find his predecessor, Henry Dickson (Akim Tamiroff), who has become lost in Alphaville. Dickson warns Caution of the great Alpha 60 computer that runs the city, begging him to rescue "those who still weep."

Godard, who has said that to have feelings for a film is not possible— "You can't kiss a film"—perhaps wanted to confound us into agreeing with him by creating an unsolvable puzzle. Or perhaps the puzzle itself doesn't exist. *Alphaville,* a supposedly futuristic film, isn't set in the future at all, and employs only the barest of science fiction trappings. Godard seems intent on contradicting at every turn: a Ford Galaxy travels "intergalactically" along a seemingly regular highway; femme fatales are dispassionate and dull; our stone-faced hero answers questions that haven't been asked; and fight scenes are obscured behind doors and walls. Often, we only know that Caution is in danger because the soundtrack music tells us so. The Alpha 60 computer, which intends to destroy mankind for its illogic, is the most poetic and philosophical character in the film.

Audiences have been fascinated and amused by the trippy intricacies of *Alphaville*—or bored by its pretensions—ever since its release, and its influence has been felt far and wide, especially within the spy genre (such as the TV series *The Prisoner*). As for Constantine, one would think that *Alphaville*

PLANET OF THE APES

by Charles A. Cassady Jr.

Battle for the Planet of the Apes

20TH CENTURY FOX / THE KOBAL COLLECTION

Lance Link, Secret Chimp, was not the only eminent simian in the late 1960s. The King of the Jungle title goes to *Planet of the Apes,* first in a cycle of science-fiction epics that bowed in 1968.

That groovy annum is considered by genre authority Peter Nicholls as "the single most important year in science-fiction cinema." It heralded not only *POTA,* but also *Barbarella, Night of the Living Dead, 2001: A Space Odyssey, Yellow Submarine, The Illustrated Man, The Monitors,* and others, a diversity of flicks that not only raised the bar in terms of mind-expanding visuals and ideas, but also proved conclusively to Hollywood money men—guys who didn't know Orson Welles from H. G. Wells—that big-budget sci-fi could show a profitable return on investment and was worth doing even if they didn't understand it any more than they understood *Easy Rider.*

Gambling on Apes

POTA was indeed a gamble for 20th Century Fox, after Warner Bros. had rejected the property, not comfortable with the proposed $10 million budget (a mainstream feature at the time cost $2.5 million). Richard D. Zanuck, then a head of production at Fox, gave the property a launch. At the time, the studio was still feeling the hangover of having fruitlessly poured $40 million into the Liz Taylor flop *Cleopatra* five years earlier.

Blake Edwards, before typing himself as a farceur with *The Party* and *The Pink Panther* series, was originally attached to direct *POTA* (would Peter Sellers have gone ape?); he was replaced by *Patton* helmer Franklin J. Schaffner. Each successive *Apes* feature would have a different director; it was the witty scripts—the first by *Twilight Zone* founder Rod Serling, remotely based on a satirical novel by French author Pierre Boulle—that pushed all the buttons: creationism vs. evolution; space exploration; military force (the gorilla troops) vs. understanding and compromise (the chimpanzees); race relations; and, of course, the Bomb. On top of all this, *POTA* offered one of the greatest surprise endings of its time, a scene that sent people out of the theater chattering about its stunning revelation at fade-out.

Preproduction and production were bumpy. Edward G. Robinson was supposed to portray wily orangutan Dr. Zaius, but he couldn't handle the makeup (test photos of the veteran actor under the fur still exist); in a last-minute change, thespian Maurice Evans (TV's *Batman* and *Bewitched*) took over. The cosmic cosmetics were devised by John Chambers. Whereas previous creature flicks either used whole-head masks or layers of mascara, Chambers perfected "appliances," mask segments glued on the planes of an actor's face, that permitted a full range of motion and expression, and he won a special Oscar for his efforts.

Principal apes like Roddy McDowall remained encased in the things all day and had to eat using chopsticks. Still, for hundreds of extras—mostly gorillas—an unprecedented number of whole-head masks were made. Not until the Klingons in *Star Trek VI: The Undiscovered Country* were so many actors creature-costumed.

Simian Sequels

POTA was a hit with audiences and generated a 1970 sequel *Beneath the Planet of the Apes*, reuniting Charlton Heston (in a brief role), Kim Hunter, Linda Harrison (Mrs. Richard D. Zanuck at the time), and Maurice Evans (Roddy McDowall, off on another project, supplied a voice cameo). Some regard *BTPOTA* as a more challenging film, if only for new writer Paul Dehn's harsher judgment against war, society, and humanity, ending with the Doomsday-Bomb destruction of Earth.

Four months after *BTPOTA* premiered, Dehn got a famous telegram from Fox, reading: "Apes exist, sequel required." Under duress, he came up with *Escape from the Planet of the Apes*, with a reverse of the original's time-travel gimmick, enabling a spaceship of ape survivors (Roddy McDowall, Kim Hunter, and Sal Mineo) to end up martyred prisoners of xenophobic humans in late-twentieth-century Earth. In Dehn's script for *Conquest of the Planet of the Apes* (1972), Caesar (McDowall again), son of the back-from-the-future chimps, grows to adulthood in a world where pollution has killed off many other nonprimate species, and apes are enslaved; in a twist on blaxploitation, the minority species rise up against their oppressors in urban riots. *Battle for the Planet of the Apes* (1973) ties up loose ends but is universally regarded as the least interesting of the bunch. Still, watched in its entirety, the *Apes* cycle is a favorite for DIY movie-marathon-watchers, and it won't make you as late for work as all the 007 pics watched back to back.

In 1974 Fox, CBS, and British television launched a TV series modeled after the first movie, with a hirsute Roddy McDowall again helping a pair of fugitive human astronauts explore the planet of the apes. Weak ratings in the United States led to quick cancellation, but some of the fourteen completed episodes have been repackaged for cable with titles like *Back to the Planet of the Apes, Forgotten City of the Planet of the Apes,* and *Life, Liberty and Pursuit on the Planet of the Apes.* A *Return to the Planet of the Apes* TV cartoon aired Saturday mornings on NBC from 1975 to 1976. Thanks especially to the TV incarnations, a number of *POTA* action figures, comic books, and toys proliferated through the next decade.

As other movie franchises have come and (not frequently enough) gone, the *Apes* movies have held up nicely in retrospect. When Richard Zanuck produced a $100 million, supersized, deluxe *Planet of the Apes* remake, directed by Tim Burton and starring Mark Wahlberg, in 2001, the general reaction was that the '68 original was far and away the better movie.

would have been the last word on Lemmy Caution, but the actor returned to the role in several more films, fittingly bidding Caution adieu in 1991's *Germany Year 90 Nine Zero,* directed by Godard himself.

1965 100m/B *FR* Eddie Constantine, Anna Karina, Akim Tamiroff, Jean-Louis Comolli, Michel Delahaye, Howard Vernon. **D:** Jean-Luc Godard. **W:** Jean-Luc Godard. **C:** Raoul Coutard. **M:** Paul Misraki. *VHS, DVD*
AKA: *Alphaville, Une Étrange Aventure de Lemmy Caution; Alphaville, A Strange Case of Lemmy Caution; Tarzan vs. IBM*

—*Brian Thomas*

Barbarella ♫♫

Jane Fonda has said she will probably never live down *Barbarella,* the outré space spoof she made in 1968 with French filmmaker Roger Vadim. To the two-time Oscar-winning actress, former fitness guru, former antiwar leader, and former wife of Vadim, activist Tom Hayden, and media mogul Ted Turner, *Barbarella* is still a source of great embarrassment. But to people who remember the '60s—in spite of the drugs—it is Ms. Fonda's defining moment.

Face the facts, Jane. The rest of the movie may be a blur, but audiences will never forget *Barbarella*'s opening sequence. Designed by James Bond credit maestro Maurice Binder, it's an antigravity striptease in which Lady Jane doffs her metallic spacesuit and gets naked while floating midair. After jumbled letters come together to form the credits, one of the strangest theme songs (in an era of strange theme songs) makes the scene even more memorable. Sample line: "Barbarella psychedelia, there's a kind of cockleshell-a about you." So true, so true.

Based on a popular French comic strip by Jean-Claude Forest, *Barbarella* is set in the forty-first century. The lead character, a "five-star double-rated astronomical aviatrix," is called on by the President of Earth (Claude Dauphin) to find Durand Durand (yep, the character led to the band's name), a scientist who has been kidnapped after inventing a positronic ray. Dressed in a latex jumpsuit with a breastplate that resembles twin fish bowls, Barbarella sets off on an interstellar odyssey. During her journey, she hops from one futuristic city to the next, bedding down most of the human and nonhuman males with which she comes into contact.

By way of a spaceship with ugly orange shag carpeting and an imposing computer named Alfie, the star siren stops at the planet Lythion in the Tau Seti solar system. There she encounters blue bunny rabbits, an army of psychotic children, and some flesh-seeking dolls that make *Child's Play*'s Chucky look like Strawberry Shortcake. Saving her from the demented playthings is Mark Hand (Ugo Tognazzi), a burly kid-catcher with more hair on his chest than George "The Animal" Steele. She rewards him with a sexual encounter— the old-fashioned, flesh-on-flesh kind, not the "psycho-cardiogram" and pleasure pill routine that's used by most of the futuristic populace.

More hedonistic adventures occur in episodic fashion, and what they all have to do with finding Durand Durand and stopping the positronic ray from causing the destruction of the galaxy is, ultimately, beside the point.

Much of the movie was filmed on a stage at producer Dino de Laurentiis's Rome-based Cinematographica Studios. Mario Carbuglia, the production designer, and costumers Jacques Fonterey and Paco Rabanne (the designer and perfume guy) must have read issues of *Penthouse* before dropping acid, so filled with phallic symbols and orifices are the sets, so sexed up are the characters, and so colorfully out-of-sight is the wardrobe Fonda and company are forced to wear.

Barbarella was budgeted at a reported $10 million, a nice chunk of space change in 1968. In spite of abundant publicity, the mostly miserable reviews from Establishment critics resulted in a small $5 million take in its initial U.S. release. But the film was warmly received later, tickling the funny bones (and other body parts) of young, wasted audiences viewing it on the midnight movie circuit. Today, their grandchildren can watch the film freely since its "M" rating ("for mature audiences") has been inexplicably rerated a family-friendly "PG." Nothing says family entertainment like that CNN guy's ex-wife naked and intimately involved with half the film's characters and set pieces.

Despite the name of hip writer Terry Southern (*Dr. Strangelove, Easy Rider*) in the credits, *Barbarella* is a silly, often childish affair. Sure, it has some funny

John Phillip Law is Pygar and Jane Fonda, whether she likes it or not, is the title character in Roger Vadim's *Barbarella*.

moments, found mostly in Southern's self-effacing dialogue. But you can see the film's creative motors working overtime throughout, straining to be with-it in every imaginable way. In the end, the film falls flat. Along with Fonda's sex-kitten style and oft-displayed torso, we have to contend with her deer-in-the-headlights line readings, Vadim's clumsy and uninspired storytelling style, an awful (but campily enjoyable) Vegas lounge-act score, and the chintzy, self-consciously weird special effects that make an episode of *Lost in Space* look like *The Matrix* in comparison.

Barbarella psychedelia? Well, nobody can argue that fact. But does *Barbarella* make any sense-a? Not much, even in the forty-first century.

1968 (PG) 98m/C *IT/FR* Jane Fonda, John Phillip Law, Anita Pallenberg, Milo O'Shea, Ugo Tognazzi, Marcel Marceau, Claude Dauphin. **D:** Roger Vadim. **W:** Vittorio Bonicelli, Claude Brule, Brian Degas, Jean-Claude Forest, Tudor Gates, Clement Biddle Wood, Terry Southern. **C:** Claude Renoir. **M:** Bob Crewe, Charles Fox. *VHS, DVD* **AKA:** *Barbarella: Queen of the Galaxy*

A Clockwork Orange 🎵🎵🎵♭

It's amazing to think that, in the brief stretch of time from 1968 to 1971, one filmmaker—Stanley Kubrick—gave moviegoers two of the best-known and most diametrically opposed cinematic views of the future: *2001: A Space Odyssey* and *A Clockwork Orange.* The former presented man as a still-apelike savage reaching for the stars and the next evolutionary stage, while the decaying world of *Clockwork* finds a technologically advanced society living in mortal fear of its own young people and unable to offer them anything that will help them build a better world.

Based on Anthony Burgess's chilling 1962 novel set in a near-future England, the film opens memorably with one of Kubrick's patented "stare shots," taking the audience deep inside the character's soul. The character in this case is young psychopath Alex (Malcolm McDowell), nattily dressed in white shirt and trousers and black derby and boots. Alex and his similarly attired "droogs"—Pete, Georgie, and Dim—drink psychotropic-laced milk at their favorite watering hole before setting out for an evening of mayhem and violence. On this particular night, that means attacking a hobo, fighting a rival gang for the right to ravage an abducted young woman, and then invading an author's remote country house, beating the owner, and raping his wife to the tune of "Singin' in the Rain." The next morning, Alex returns to the decrepit apartment he shares with his factory-worker parents and, later, hangs out at the local record store in search of girls and recordings of his favorite composer, Beethoven. It seems to be a full life for him, but his mistreatment of his chums is beginning to cause friction within the group.

After breaking into the home of an artist and killing her with a phallus sculpture, Pete, Georgie, and Dim leave Alex to be apprehended by the police. Sentenced to fourteen years in prison, Alex is offered a chance at parole if he takes part in an aversion therapy experiment that will teach him to repress his criminal impulses. Conditioned to become nauseated at the very thought of vio-

lence (and, inadvertently, at the sound of his beloved Beethoven), the "cured" Alex goes from aggressor to victim: cast out by his parents, beaten by his former mates, and forced to seek refuge at, by coincidence, the home of the now-paralyzed writer whose wife died as a result of the gang's assault. When the writer learns his guest's identity, he plots with a radical group to drive Alex to suicide and use his death to discredit the government and its rehabilitation program.

Malcolm McDowell plays a young thug who likes a bit of the ultraviolence in *A Clockwork Orange*.

WARNER BROS. / THE KOBAL COLLECTION

Tribute must be paid to production designer John Barry and cinematographer John Alcott for depicting an urban landscape at once colorful and coldly sterile, and to synthesizer master Walter Carlos (later Wendy Carlos, following a sex change) for a score that mixes classical music with an off-putting electronic edge. Credit for the often disturbing, sardonic tone of the film, however, rests squarely on the star-making performance of McDowell, whose only other major role at that point was in Lindsay Anderson's 1968 antiauthority drama *If...*. As Alex, McDowell struts his way across the screen like an amoral Mick Jagger (who actually considered making the film along with his fellow Rolling Stones) and narrates the proceedings in the unforgettable pseudo-language of Nasdat, Burgess's at times baffling blend of British slang, Shakespearean flourish, and Russian ("Come and get one in the yarbles," Alex calls out to another gang leader, "if you have any yarbles, you eunuch jelly thou!"). As vicious as Alex is, we almost feel sorry for him when he is betrayed by his friends, subjected to an experiment that effectively removes his freedom of choice, and made to suffer, as he puts it, "the tortures of the damned."

As he did in such earlier works as *Paths of Glory* and *Lolita,* scripter/director Kubrick seems to be looking at how much "necessary evil" any society can tolerate, society in this case being a grimy and jaded world where sexuality is a packaged commodity (check out the milk bar's statues and dispensers and the lollipops the girls at the record store eat) and crime has escalated to the point where people are more than willing to trade liberty for a little security. It's a message that struck a chord in 1971 and is perhaps even more relevant now.

1971 (R) 137m/C Malcolm McDowell, Patrick Magee, Warren Clarke, Adrienne Corri, Miriam Karlin, Anthony Sharp, James Marcus, Michael Tarn. *D:* Stanley Kubrick. *W:* Stanley Kubrick. *C:* John Alcott. *M:* Walter Carlos. *VHS, DVD*

—Gary Cahall

The Day the Fish Came Out ♫♫

Call it *My Big Fat Greek Nuclear Disaster.*

After scoring an international success with *Zorba the Greek,* director Michael Cacoyannis decided to tackle the threat of nuclear annihilation with *The Day the Fish Came Out,* a delirious dose of 1960s madness that often plays like *Dr. Strangelove Goes to the Beach.*

With '60s classics *On the Beach, Fail Safe,* and *Strangelove* preceding him, the Cypress-born Cacoyannis decided to take a new approach to the end-of-the-world genre by focusing on how a group of people in and around Karos, an island in the Aegean Sea, react to the threat of annihilation.

Cool opening credits that mix cubist designs and modern architecture, created by Maurice Binder of James Bond fame, promisingly open the film. The story involves a NATO plane that accidentally loses some of its cargo over the island. When the navigator (Tom Courtenay) and the pilot (Colin Blakely) realize what has happened, they abandon their plane and land safely in the island's mountains. Having lost most of their clothing in the process, the two are reduced to wearing nothing but their skimpy underwear. This scares them into hiding and hinders them from acting promptly on what could be an impending disaster, as one of the lost items is a canister that contains highly radioactive material.

Meanwhile, James Elias (Sam Wanamaker), another NATO commander, is chosen to head the canister recovery mission. The plan is for Elias and a military crew to pose as hotel industry speculators looking to build a new resort in the area. But the sudden appearance of these disguised government types only brings chaos as the locals sense a business deal is in the works and tourists from around the world begin appearing in droves. While all this is going on, a local family finds the deadly cargo, believing it to be some sort of treasure. But when they discover balls of plutonium instead of pieces of eight, they unknowingly dump the balls in the sea, killing legions of fish and contaminating the island's water supply.

On paper, the story may not seem so out there. But it's the cinematic telling that takes *The Day the Fish Came Out* to a different planet. For starters, there's a homoerotic current running through the film that can't be denied. Courtenay and Blakely remain in tight, wet briefs throughout, made the most of through several low-level shots. When the government forces pose as hotel professionals, they dress like extras from *Can't Stop the Music,* donning feathery hats, fishnet shirts, and oversized white sunglasses. That's when they're not showing off their glistening biceps and tight swimwear. Cacoyannis, who produced, wrote, and directed the film, is also credited with creating its outrageous costumes.

It's not just the men, however, who shine in the costume department. At about the halfway point of the film, Candice Bergen, then twenty-one years old, shows up as Electra Brown, an assistant to archaeologist Mr. French (Tom Klunis). After sleeping with her boss, she pursues one of the younger military men. When he seems unwilling to take her up on her come-ons, she drops a "Don't you like women?" line on him, confusing the poor guy even more. Bergen is decked out in wildly suggestive outfits throughout, drawing the attention of nearly everyone on the island. Her most memorable get-up consists of lime green hot pants, an orange halter top, white knee-high go-go boots, and a white sailor's cap, all worn in what appears to be a 104-degree climate. Murphy Brown would most definitely disapprove of such a role (and pretty much every role Bergen played in the 1960s and '70s, for that matter).

It's a safe bet that audience members were rendered speechless by the film's dance numbers. In these sequences, the rabid, vacation-crazed tourists bump, sway, frug, and shimmy on the beach with wild abandon. They cluck like chickens, wear togas and skimpy bathing suits, and in general party like it's 1999. You practically expect to see *Beach Party* regulars Frankie and Eric Von Zipper twist by in cameos, hugging each other. The music, written by Mikis Theodorakis of *Zorba the Greek* fame, is ethnic electronica gone haywire, something like the Hellenic version of *The Twilight Zone* theme performed by the Ventures.

The Day the Fish Came Out is an example of immoderate '60s filmmaking at its dizzying, brain-fried heights, and the extra dollop of gay accoutrements makes things even more excessive. Coming off *Zorba the Greek,* his huge international success, Cacoyannis was given carte blanche to comment on nuclear disaster, restless youth, Greece, tourism, and, well, about 143 other subjects near and dear to his heart. The result is like feta cheese that's been lying out in the sun for a week: smelly and hard to forget.

1967 109m/C *GR/UK* Tom Courtenay, Colin Blakely, Candice Bergen, Sam Wanamaker, Ian Ogilvy, Patricia Burke, Tom Klunis. *D:* Michael Cacoyannis. *W:* Michael Cacoyannis. *C:* Walter Lassally. *M:* Mikis Theodorakis. *VHS*

Fantastic Voyage 🦴🦴🦴

"**B**ut I don't want to be miniaturized!" So declares government-agent-of-indeterminate-expertise Stephen Boyd when he learns that his latest assignment will have him joining a medical team

> "The medieval philosophers were right. Man is the center of the universe. We stand in the middle of infinity between outer and inner space, and there's no limit to either."
>
> —Dr. Peter Duvall (Arthur Kennedy), in *Fantastic Voyage*

Richard Fleischer takes viewers on a journey through the interior of the human body in *Fantastic Voyage.*

20TH CENTURY FOX / THE KOBAL COLLECTION

that will be shrunk down to microscopic size and injected into the bloodstream of a comatose defecting scientist. Once inside the patient, they have one hour to reach the brain, destroy a blood clot causing the coma with an experimental laser, and get out before automatically returning to normal size.

Joining Boyd on the subcutaneous surgical strike are doctors Arthur Kennedy and Donald Pleasence, medical technician Raquel Welch, and William Redfield as pilot of their submersible vessel, the Proteus. The reason the top-secret government agency behind the project wants Boyd along is because of fears that there's an enemy saboteur among the crew. There is, of course, and it becomes painfully clear during an evolution vs. God debate on the wonders of the human body who is the rotten apple. The team members have other things to worry about, though, as their journey is threatened by everything from an emergency detour through the heart to attacks by infection-fighting antibodies and white corpuscles.

Fantastic Voyage is probably one of the best-known science fiction films of the era, containing elements of both the "us vs. them" feel of 1950s Red Scare cinema (though where the scientist—or the enemy agents whose attack left him on death's door—came from is never specified, it was clearly from behind the Iron Curtain) and the meticulously detailed technology that was a hallmark of such late-'60s and early-'70s works as *Marooned* and *The Andromeda Strain.*

The Academy Award–winning special effects may seem a bit dated to today's CGI-accustomed audiences. At times the veins and arteries look as

RICHARD FLEISCHER: '60S SCI-FI ADVENTURER
by Lowell Goldman

"I thought [*Fantastic Voyage*] had great possibilities for an unusual science fiction film," declared director Richard Fleischer (*The Vikings*) in a 1989 interview. "I don't think there had been a big, important science fiction film until we made *Fantastic Voyage*."

"The picture was offered to me by Richard Zanuck [vice president in charge of production for Fox]," continued the director. "They had a film treatment and that was about all. The producer was Saul David [*Our Man Flint*]. Anyway, we went to work and developed a screenplay with Harry Kleiner [*Bullitt*]."

The film spent almost a year in preproduction. "The picture was very difficult to prepare and difficult to shoot. And the film was very scientifically accurate. We had plenty of technical advisers. It was all very thoroughly researched."

Fantastic Voyage (1966) was an excursion through inner space—the human body. "There were enormous enlargements of actual body parts. They were what I'd call macrotures," added Fleischer. "For example, the heart was the largest model of a heart ever made. It was about a hundred times larger than an actual heart. We also made macrotures of lungs, the inner ear, and so on."

Fleischer was very satisfied with the finished film. "Unfortunately, the picture didn't do as well [at the box office] as it could have done," revealed Fleischer. "The people who were trying to sell the film really didn't know how to handle it. They had simply never seen a movie like it before. The ads also didn't let the audience know that it was an intelligent science fiction film. Instead, the public probably had the impression that it was some sort of monster movie. Meanwhile, I was trying to impress the audience with the majesty of the human body."

Subsequent Fleischer films included *The Boston Strangler, Tora! Tora! Tora!* and *The New Centurions.* Then he was back into science fiction with *Soylent Green* (1973).

Soylent Green was loosely based on Harry Harrison's novel *Make Room! Make Room!* "The film was generally based on the idea of the book," noted Fleischer. "But we actually had very little to go on. The whole story had to be developed while using the book as a springboard."

Soylent Green takes place in the year 2022, and the setting is a smoggy, overpopulated New York City. Charlton Heston portrays a dogged detective and Edward G. Robinson his research assistant who shares a small apartment with him. This film marks Robinson's final screen performance; his character's touching death scene constitutes Robinson's last moments in a motion picture.

"You know, we really didn't know he was going to die so soon," recalled Fleischer. "He had been very, very ill. But we were still able to get insurance for him on the picture. He actually was very well during the shooting of the film."

Since the film's initial release, *Soylent Green* has developed a loyal following. "The charm of the picture to me was that I didn't use any scientific apparatus. The future isn't going to look like what everyone thinks it's going to look like. It's going to look like today, but much worse. The film's really a peek into the future."

though they're filled with lava lamp liquid (and why are the blood vessels so brightly lit, anyway?), and cell walls often resemble the painted canvases they really are, but the scenes of the miniaturized submarine traveling through the circulatory system are truly impressive. So impressive, in fact, that they often overwhelm the at-times stoic performances by leads Boyd, Kennedy, and Welch. Making her feature debut as a 20th Century Fox starlet, Welch spends her screen time in a white wetsuit that doesn't offer as much of her as did her next film costume, the fur bikini of *One Million Years B.C.*

As for the "science" part of the film, the editors of the *Harvard Lampoon* put it best in their 1966 Movie Worsts Awards when they awarded *Fantastic Voyage* the prestigious Piltdown Mandible Award "for assuming that the molecules which made up the submarine would not re-expand to normal size simply because said submarine had been devoured by a white corpuscle." Renowned author Isaac Asimov wrote a novelization of the screenplay that managed to explain away some of the story's inaccuracies, but for once even his colorful descriptions couldn't match the wonder of what's seen in this classic inner-space odyssey.

1966 (PG) 100m/C Stephen Boyd, Raquel Welch, Edmond O'Brien, Donald Pleasence, Arthur O'Connell, William Redfield, Arthur Kennedy, Jean Del Val. **D:** Richard Fleischer. **W:** Harry Kleiner. **C:** Ernest Laszlo. **M:** Leonard Rosenman. *VHS, DVD*
AKA: *Microscopia; Strange Journey*

—*Gary Cahall*

The Illustrated Man 🦴🦴

For a writer considered a titan in the science fiction field, and one whose works have often drawn upon the horror and fantasy films of his youth, it's disappointing that Ray Bradbury has not been better served by the big screen over the years. Two of the author's lesser short stories were transformed in 1953 into a pair of seminal drive-in creature features—*The Beast from 20,000 Fathoms* and *It Came from Outer Space*—but apart from French filmmaker François Truffaut's sterile 1966 adaptation of *Fahrenheit 451* and the overlooked 1983 chiller *Something Wicked This Way Comes,* the only other feature based on a Bradbury book was *The Illustrated Man,* an anthology centered around carnival roustabout-turned-living-canvas Rod Steiger.

Set, presumably, in the Depression-era Midwest of Bradbury's youth, the film opens with drifter Robert Drivas reluctantly sharing his open-air campsite with another wanderer, the short-tempered Steiger, who carries his pet dog in a sack and is looking for a mysterious woman whose house may or may not be in the area . . . or even in the present (Steiger claims she may have gone "back into the future"). When Drivas notices Steiger's colorfully decorated corpus (and yes, there's a little more Rod on view here than most moviegoers, even in 1968, wanted to see), Steiger grunts and rants his way through the story of how, one summer afternoon, he came upon the house of witchlike beauty Claire Bloom (then Rod's wife) and allowed her to begin covering his body with strange designs ("Dey are not tattoos!" he bellows to Drivas, "Dey are skin illustrations!"), designs that come to life and offer looks into the past, present, and future.

Thus the illustrated man himself serves as the framing device for a trio of tales that are more or less linked by themes of trust and betrayal and that feature the three stars in different roles. First, parents Steiger and Bloom are worried about the time their two children are spending in their holographic playroom's African jungle program, with Drivas as a mental health caseworker who reassures them that it's just an illusion . . . or is it? Next, Steiger and two others, all astronauts, are stranded on a rain-drenched planet where the very sound of the unceasing downpour on their helmets can kill them. Their only chance for survival lies with an emergency shelter dome twenty miles from their crash site, but getting there through the raging waters is no easy task. The final segment again finds Bloom and Steiger playing parents, this time faced with the choice of killing their children or allowing them to witness their dying world's final moments.

Bradbury's book features eighteen stories, and sci-fi fans have often debated why these three were picked for the movie translation. Thanks in large part to director Jack Smight's leisurely, if not glacial, pacing, none of them carries much dramatic weight, though the first, "The Veldt," does offer an intriguing pre-*Matrix* look at virtual reality. Another minus is Steiger's bellicose turn in the title role, where his histrionics at times threaten to overwhelm his psychedelically festooned features (the makeup job on Steiger's torso took ten hours to complete, with another day's work required on his arms and legs).

The movie's climax finds Drivas seeing his own brief and painful future in Steiger's skin illustrations. Since the actor's actual future would entail just three more film roles in the years to come, concluding with Larry Cohen's 1976 shocker *God Told Me To,* before returning to stage work, Drivas's on-screen reaction seems eerily prescient and perfectly understandable.

1968 (PG) 103m/C Rod Steiger, Claire Bloom, Robert Drivas, Don Dubbins, Jason Evers, Tim Weldon. *D:* Jack Smight. *W:* Howard B. Kreitsek. *C:* Philip H. Lathrop. *M:* Jerry Goldsmith. *VHS*

—*Gary Cahall*

> **The only thing you can't have in this perfect world of total pleasure is your thirtieth birthday.... Logan is twenty-nine.**
>
> —Tagline for
> *Logan's Run*

Logan's Run ♫♫

In 1975 MGM decided to produce a big-budget version of *Logan's Run,* the popular science fiction novel by William F. Nolan and George Clayton Johnson. Written in 1967, the book touches on several of the issues the counterculture was contemplating at the time: revolution, freedom, authority, draft dodging, making a better society, and so on, and so on. . . .

By 1976 the pertinence of these topics and the influence of the counterculture on youthful audiences was on the wane. But that didn't stop the

Logan 5 (Michael York) and Francis 7 (Richard Jordan) confront each other as Jessica 6 (Jenny Agutter) fearfully looks on in 1976's *Logan's Run.*

THE KOBAL COLLECTION

studio from going ahead with a special-effects-filled saga they had hoped would become a landmark of the genre in league with *2001: A Space Odyssey,* another MGM production. Choosing to highlight the effects and futuristic look of the production over some of the issues deftly probed in the source material, MGM went all-out marketing the movie. They pushed a *Logan's Run* line of space-age fashions and even hired models to dance for film critics at their annual studio press junket.

But *Logan's Run* wasn't the blockbuster MGM had hoped for, though the marketing blitz did pay off and the film tripled its impressive (for its time) $9 million budget. It also spawned a short-lived TV show the following year. Today, the film, at least in terms of visuals, works as a misguided link between the psychedelic '60s and the emerging '70s disco era. A tad dated, perhaps, but enjoyable for those who like seeing people with names like Francis 7 and Jessica 6 wear capes and tunics or soak in hot tubs in locations that look like the Cherry Hill Mall, escalators and all, circa 1976.

Thirty is the big number in *Logan's Run.* That's because when you hit the age of thirty you're through, done in during a weird ceremony called Carousel. The old geezers are outfitted with Tony Esposito–style hockey masks, dressed in capes, and hurled into midair where they're blown to bits in front of a large crowd. On the positive side, the dead are promised a form of reincarnation.

This practice keeps a lid on the population, most of which lives in huge geodesic domes. But things are cool: there is sex, those hot tubs work pretty well, and there's no trace of the Muzak version of "Norwegian Wood" heard in the Cherry Hill Mall during the mid-1970s. The one big problem is that all orders are given by the omnipotent Computer, a mysterious, mega-powerful machine that makes HAL of *2001* seem like a wuss.

Logan 5 (Michael York) is a Sandman, a member of the police force whom the Computer calls on with a special assignment: finding the Sanctuary, a place beyond the domes where thirty-year-old people flee in hopes of finding, well, sanctuary. These death-dodgers are called Runners, and Logan must impersonate one of them in order to carry out his mission. He soon befriends Jessica 6 (Jenny Agutter), a Runner, in order to find Sanctuary, but he falls in love with her instead. His feelings for Jessica 6, and his age, twenty-nine, spur him to become a Runner as well. The problem then becomes Logan's Sandman partner and best friend, Francis 7 (Richard Jordan), who is hot on their trail.

Logan's Run wants to have it several ways, but sometimes-reliable director Michael Anderson (*The Quiller Memorandum, Orca, The Killer Whale*) and usually reliable screenwriter David Zelag Goodman (*Straw Dogs, Farewell, My Lovely*) can't even get one right. The film tries hard to say something important about the value of individuality and the dangers of blind allegiance to authority, but it delivers the messages with a heavy hand and pretentious dialogue. As a chase movie, the film is a washout as well, giving us long scenes of characters running through corridors and across catwalks while fog machines roll out too much smoke. And the special effects—particularly judged against today's standards—look ultrachintzy, from the souped-up golf carts and phony matte paintings of a post-holocaust Washington, D.C., that looms beyond the domes to a metallic robot (Roscoe Lee Browne) and monorails that look like they were borrowed from Tomorrowland. And they were good enough to win the Academy Award for visual effects, just a year before *Star Wars* was released.

Not helping matters is the cast. The wide-eyed York's Logan sure looks like he should be running—to an acting school where he can learn some new expressions. Jordan makes a flaky nemesis, Agutter is a goner as the uninteresting and occasionally unclothed heroine, and Farrah Fawcett (credited in the movie as Fawcett-Majors), who shows up in her trademark '70s-era hairdo, acts terribly as a forgetful plastic surgery assistant and ally of Logan and Jennifer. Even the usually sublime Peter Ustinov, wearing lots of phony white hair and a silly beard, adds little charm.

The story is supposedly on the docket for a remake, and it could work well as an intense thriller with cutting-edge special effects à la *Minority Report* or *Total Recall*. The original *Logan's Run,* however, remains a movie that time has not been especially kind to, unless you're big on tunics and shopping malls.

1976 (PG) 120m/C Michael York, Jenny Agutter, Richard Jordan, Peter Ustinov, Michael Anderson Jr., Farrah Fawcett, Roscoe Lee Browne. *D:* Michael Anderson. *W:* David Zelag Goodman. *C:* Ernest Laszlo. *M:* Jerry Goldsmith. *VHS, DVD*

The Omega Man

It's hard to say whether his conservative brand of politics colored his choice of film roles or vice versa, but Charlton Heston's sci-fi and fantasy movies certainly contain some of the bleakest cinematic dystopias ever created. From the evolutionarily inverted *Planet of the Apes* to *Soylent Green*'s over-crowded supercities and even, tangentially, a Los Angeles destroyed by an *Earthquake,* the future worlds of the former screen Moses are anything but a Promised Land.

To this list is added *The Omega Man,* the second screen adaptation of Richard Matheson's novel *I Am Legend,* in which the sole remaining human on the postapocalyptic planet fights for survival against vampire-like mutants (a low-budget 1964 version, *The Last Man on Earth,* featured Vincent Price in the title role). Here it's Heston playing military doctor/lone warrior Robert Neville, who, thanks to an experimental vaccine, is immune to the biological warfare that wiped out nearly all of humanity and turned the others into slowly dying, light-shunning mutants.

Now Heston spends his days driving the deserted Los Angeles streets, scavenging for clothes and food in whatever stores are handy and going to a movie theatre where he powers up the generator-powered projectors to watch *Woodstock* (!) again and again. At night, though, Chuck holes up in his fortress-like home and defends himself against hordes of the sunglasses-and-monk's-robe-clad neo-zombies, who call themselves the Family (shades of Charles Manson). The Family's fanatical leader, Matthias (Anthony Zerbe), wants to eliminate Heston as one of the last vestiges of the civilization the technology of which led to the deadly pandemic and mankind's downfall.

Heston's solitary struggle is altered when he is rescued from Family captivity by ex-medical student Paul Koslo and two-fisted foxy mama Rosalind Cash, who serves as den mother to a band of children who have so far resist-ed the plague but will inevitably succumb to it. It's Heston's blood that carries the possible cure, if he and his newfound charges can perform the experiments necessary to develop it in time.

Coming as it did on the cusp of the free love era, *The Omega Man* con-tains commentary on the times, with the youngsters Heston fights to save as back-to-nature flower children whose dark side is represented by the technology-eschewing, cult-like Family. Also, as one might expect from a film starring the man who played Moses *and* John the Baptist on-screen, there's a lot of reli-gious symbolism, with Heston cast as humanity's second savior. That said, Heston offers a suitably sturdy performance mixed with bits of sardonic humor as he wanders his urban wasteland, and Cash lends fine support as his ass-kickin' love interest (even in 1971, their interracial romance caused some controversy). As the former TV newscaster-turned-Family-leader, veteran screen heavy Zerbe handles his at times hammy dialogue with gusto.

Matheson was not happy with either film version of his novel, but *The Omega Man* does have some things to recommend it, heavy-handed Christ analogies aside.

> "You know the old song? If you were the only girl in the world, and I was the only boy, well, okay, but until then, don't bother me? Well, I guess I'm the only boy...."
>
> —Charlton Heston, as Robert Neville, in *The Omega Man*

1971 (PG) 98m/C Charlton Heston, Anthony Zerbe, Rosalind Cash, Paul Koslo, Lincoln Kilpatrick, Eric Laneuville. **D:** Boris Sagal. **W:** John William Corrington, Joyce H. Corrington. **C:** Russell Metty. **M:** Ron Grainer. *VHS, DVD*

—Gary Cahall

Planet of the Vampires ♪♪♪

Italian cinemaestro Mario Bava (*Black Sunday*), who tried his hand at several genres during his long career, submitted this memorable entry, based on the story "One Night of 21 Hours," by Renato Pestiniero, into Italy's mid-'60s wave of science fiction pictures.

Planet of the Vampires stars Barry Sullivan as Mark Markary, captain of the exploratory spaceship *Argos*. While in orbit around the newly discovered fogbound planet Aura, the source of strange electronic signals, the *Argos* is overcome by radiation and forced into a bumpy landing. Immediately afterward, crew members begin attacking one another in seemingly random fashion; after the "mad" people are subdued, they retain no memory of their violent actions. Before they can puzzle over what's happened to them, they receive a distress call from their sister ship, the *Gallead,* which has also been forced to land. But the rescue party from the *Argos* arrives too late—the *Gallead*'s crew has already massacred one another. Things take an even more dire turn when the dead begin to rise from their graves to prey on the living, even as the survivors fight for control of their own minds against alien invaders.

Although not credited as cinematographer, Bava's distinctive candy-colored palette and creative camera tricks are much in evidence. He works low-budget miracles by using mirrored miniatures in place of expensive process shots as well as other simple, in-camera techniques. Memorable art direction also contributes to the film's atmosphere, as Giorgio Giovanni's sets create a surreal landscape and costume designer Gabriele Mayer dresses the entire cast in distinctively sexy black vinyl space suits.

Although the "haunted house in space" idea had been used before in films like *It! The Terror from Beyond Space,* a gothic atmosphere had never before been applied so completely to a futuristic setting. While a bit lacking in character development, *Planet of the Vampires* gave a whole generation enough matinee and late-show nightmares to influence scores of movies that came after it. Ridley Scott's classic *Alien* draws on it heavily, and that influence has been passed on to countless others. After decades in release in a variety of abbreviated versions, MGM restored the film in all its glory for a 2002 DVD release.

1965 (NR) 88m/C *IT* Barry Sullivan, Norma Bengell, Angel Aranda, Stelio Candelli, Evi Marandi, Mario Morales, Ivan Rassimov. **D:** Mario Bava. **W:** Mario Bava, Alberto Bevilacqua, Callisto Cosulich, Antonio Roman, Rafael J. Salvia. **C:** Antonio Perez Olea, Antonio Rinaldi, Mario Bava. **M:** Kendall Schmidt, Gino Marinuzzi Jr. *VHS, DVD*
AKA: *Terrore Nello Spazio; Demon Planet; The Haunted Planet; Haunted World; Outlawed Planet; Planet of Blood; Planet of Terror; Planet of the Damned; Space Mutants; Terror in Space*

—Brian Thomas

Seconds 🦴🦴🦴🦴

According to Thomas Wolfe, you can't go home again, but that's never stopped the human race from trying. This is especially true in *Seconds,* a terrifying meditation on the fact that it sucks getting old. When rolls of flab and thinning hair become your personal nightmare, *Seconds* offers an appealing alternative—at least at first glance.

Arthur Hamilton (John Randolph), a banker sound of mind but moldy of body, decides to undergo a radical surgical procedure that will allow him to look young and feel younger. Hamilton is a troubled man. Estranged from his daughter, his marriage an empty shell, he's coasting through by virtue of inertia. With little spark left in his existence, he turns to the dark side, here known as the Company, which arranges his convenient "death" via a fire. Carried off on a gurney to meet his re-maker, he emerges as the young and studly Tony Wilson (Rock Hudson). Wisely, director John Frankenheimer chooses to skirt the mechanics of this transformation, leaving the surgical and financial details on the cutting-room floor, so to speak.

The result is true noir ambience, where explanations serve no purpose in a malevolent universe. Aided by John Wong Howe's expert cinematography (through a dramatic wide-angle lens and B&W imagery), Hamilton's world appears to us as if through a funhouse mirror, minus the fun. But this is a situation the makeover will cure, right?

Of course not. There's no miracle life extension here—you look like a movie star, but the same old biological limitations and psychological baggage remain.

Apparently, the otherwise unnamed Company has something crucial invested in Hamilton/Wilson's transformation that goes beyond the operation proper. They set him up with an entirely new life as a moderately successful painter with an oceanside house. (How Wilson was infused with artistic talent also goes unexplained. Some may find this annoying, but the deeper meaning—intentional or not—suggests that creativity can be acquired just as easily as a new face. A comment on the burgeoning Pop Art movement of the time, perhaps?)

Adjusting to this carefree lifestyle is not so easy. As part of the Faustian bargain, Wilson is denied access to his past. Depressed, yearning for contact with old friends, he meets a beautiful young beachcomber (Salome Jens). This free spirit introduces him to a less uptight (read: hippie) life, taking him to a wine-making party where he gets to put his hip young self to the test in a vat full of grapes and naked bodies. (Note: The DVD version shows more nudity than the censored original theatrical release.) At first shocked by the sybaritic behavior, Wilson soon sheds his clothes, followed quickly by his inhibitions. In a scene laced with alcoholic symbolism, the goofy grape proves to be his undoing. Wilson's lubricated tongue loosens, and he reveals more than he should about his taboo secret. The Company most definitely disapproves. Suddenly, benign inhabitants of his new universe turn ugly (a page neatly lifted by Roman Polanski for *Rosemary's Baby*). The beach colony, his new girl-

> **What Are Seconds? . . . The Answer May Be Too Terrifying for Words!**
>
> —Tagline for *Seconds*

friend, and God knows who else are part of a vast conspiracy of transformed septuagenarians who rely on new recruits to solidify their ranks. Each new member is expected to become, in effect, another recruiter.

Free as the proverbial bird in the gilded cage, Wilson's justifiable confusion begins to eat at his fragile mind. After an unauthorized visit to his former wife, the machinery of the inevitable is set into action. The closing sequence (better left undisclosed) reveals the truly Orwellian intentions of the sinister Company. The viewer is inexorably pulled—just like Wilson—to a finale that is far more terrifying than the proceedings foretell. In this respect, *Seconds* resembles gothic chestnuts such as *Frankenstein.* One can only imagine how violated '60s audiences must have felt after seeing the star of fluffy Doris Day comedies dissolve into a paranoid heap. (Given what we know about Hudson today, the perspective is twisted even further.)

John Frankenheimer directed *Seconds* during his most fertile period, a four-year span in the early 1960s during which he also helmed *The Manchurian Candidate, The Train,* and *Seven Days in May.* Many of his cinematic flourishes, such as a subjective camera attached to an actor, have been used, ad nauseum, in contemporary films such as Darren Aronofsky's *Pi.* Given the context, it makes *Seconds* seem all the more fresh today.

1966 107m/B Rock Hudson, John Randolph, Salome Jens, Frances Reid, Will Geer, Jeff Corey. ***D:*** John Frankenheimer. ***W:*** Lewis John Carlino. ***C:*** James Wong Howe. ***M:*** Jerry Goldsmith. *VHS, DVD*

—Steven Austin

Silent Running ♫♫♫

As part of that relatively small subgenre of late-'60s/early-'70s cinema that could be called "ecology sci-fi"—a field that includes, among others, *Soylent Green* and *ZPG*—*Silent Running* stands out as perhaps the most notable of the lot for a variety of reasons. It marked the directorial debut of Douglas Trumbull, special effects supervisor for *2001: A Space Odyssey;* it was cowritten by, along with Deric Washburn, future *Deer Hunter* and *Heaven's Gate* bad boy Michael Cimino and *NYPD Blue* creator Steven Bochco; it offered Bruce Dern a chance to further hone his "barely suppressed psycho" screen image; and it showed that squat, nonverbal robots could easily steal a film (are you listening, R2-D2?).

In the year 2008 Earth has been environmentally ravaged after nuclear war, and the only remaining vegetation resides in huge orbiting greenhouse ships like the *Valley Forge,* whose four-man crew includes botanist/twenty-first-century hippie Dern. When the order is given to abandon the project and destroy the cargo, the already quirky Bruce goes off the deep end, killing his shipmates and setting out for deep space in the hopes of finding a place to transplant his beloved flora. Dern's only remaining companions are a trio of adorable mechanical helpers named Huey, Dewey, and (you guessed it) Louie. The interplanetary Johnny Appleseed and his metallic flunkies are happily

JOHN FRANKENHEIMER: '60S CINEMA ICON

by Lowell Goldman

"I thought [Richard] Condon's *The Manchurian Candidate* was one of the best books that I had ever read," declared director John Frankenheimer in a 1987 interview. "I just knew that I had to make a film from it. The book also had great social and political significance for me at the time."

According to Frankenheimer, who died in 2002, screenwriter George Axelrod had secured the film rights to the novel. Frank Sinatra was also an avid fan of the book. "As soon as we had Sinatra, we could have shot it at any studio in town," exclaimed the director. "You know, Frank was wonderful in that role. He worked really hard on that film too.

"Sinatra also had control of the distribution of *The Manchurian Candidate*," continued Frankenheimer. "He's also an equal [producer] partner with George Axelrod and myself. For reasons that I could not fully understand, he didn't want the picture shown on television or available on video. Anyway, I just want to get the film out there. After all, we have a whole new audience waiting to see the picture." The film's twenty-four-year absence from distribution has been attributed to Sinatra's regret over onetime pal JFK's death, but it's more likely due to Sinatra's dispute with distributor United Artists over his share of the profits.

The Manchurian Candidate was very faithful to the novel. "It's probably one of the best adaptations from a best-selling book to the screen. And I think we tend to forget George's contribution to the final film. It was also the first film that I had complete control over. It's exactly the film that I wanted to make."

After *The Manchurian Candidate*, Frankenheimer helmed the acclaimed political thriller *Seven Days in May*, with Kirk Douglas and Burt Lancaster, and the large-scale action epic *The*

tending their garden and playing cards until the ship is intercepted by the authorities near the moons of Saturn, where Dern must decide to continue his green rebellion or allow the trees, shrubs, grass, and stray bunny or two to be obliterated. Anyone paying attention to Dern's messianic characterization can see how it will play out, with the only suspense coming from wondering how many of the robots will survive.

The film is steeped in pro-environmental bias (it's never fully explained why the mission, which must have cost billions and already has ships scattered throughout the solar system, is being scrapped), but it nonetheless manages to get its point across without hitting the viewer over the head. Director Trumbull's effects expertise came in handy as he was able to create a sense of vastness and outer-space grandeur on a relatively modest (even

Train, with Lancaster. His next film, *Seconds,* received mixed reviews and poor box-office results, but it has gone on to gain a strong following.

"Yeah, *Seconds* is about the only movie that I ever heard of that has gone from failure to classic without ever being a success," stated the director. "Of course, it's become something of a cult film over the years."

Quite popular for playing light comedy parts, Rock Hudson was cast against type in a very intense role in *Seconds.* "I feel he did very well in the film," said Frankenheimer. "Yet, it was probably a mistake to cast him in *Seconds.* The people who would see a film like *Seconds* would not normally see a Rock Hudson picture. Meanwhile, the folks who wanted to see a typical Rock Hudson movie were shocked by the film. And remember, he was one of the top box-office draws at the time."

Frankenheimer's next big-screen effort was the auto-racing extravaganza *Grand Prix,* which featured an all-star international cast that included James Garner, Yves Montand, Toshiro Mifune, and Eva Marie Saint. It was also Frankenheimer's first film shot in color, employing elaborate split-screen sequences, sometimes with twenty-four images on the screen at the same time.

"I really loved *Grand Prix,*" exclaimed Frankenheimer about the film, which offered hair-raising racing sequences. "I also had more fun making *Grand Prix* than any other movie. The nice thing about it was that I knew it at the time."

Easily one of the director's most obscure films was a comedy entitled *The Extraordinary Seaman,* a bizarre misfire with Faye Dunaway, Alan Alda, and David Niven, about the crew of a ship during World War II that encounters a ghostly skipper in the Pacific.

"That's probably the worst movie I ever made," stated Frankenheimer. "I did it for all the wrong reasons. I did it for the money. You know, there are all kinds of humorous stories connected with that film. But I really don't want to dwell on it at this time."

for 1972) budget of $1 million, using the soon-to-be-scrapped aircraft carrier USS *Valley Forge* for scenes set onboard its extraterrestrial counterpart.

And while you never quite believe his character wasn't already unhinged—as with Jack Nicholson's turn in *The Shining*—Dern's sometimes manic persona serves him well as the man who knows the eventual cost of his quixotic mission. The most memorable portrayals in the movie, for most people, were the most anonymous. There were real-life multiple amputees inside the metallic exteriors of Huey, Dewey, and Louie, and these silent star turns were certainly an influence on another young filmmaker who was working on the Universal lot at the time: a film-school graduate named George Lucas.

It's hard not to like a movie that features a futuristic go-cart chase scene and a soundtrack that includes both Joan Baez and Peter (P. D.Q.

Bach) Schickele. If you watch only one sci-fi film on Arbor Day, make it *Silent Running.*

1972 (G) 89m/C Bruce Dern, Cliff Potts, Ron Rifkin, Jesse Vint. *D:* Douglas A. Trumbull. *W:* Deric Washburn, Michael Cimino, Steven Bochco. *C:* Charles F. Wheeler. *M:* Peter Shickele. *VHS, DVD*

—Gary Cahall

Soylent Green

It's generally accepted as bad form to reveal pertinent plot twists within a review. However, the "surprise ending" to *Soylent Green* is not only heavily foreshadowed throughout the film but also became common knowledge immediately after the picture's release. In fact, even folks who are unaware of the film probably know the ending, as Charlton Heston's final line "Soylent Green is people!" has become part of popular culture via frequent lampoons throughout the years.

Soylent Green was drawn from the novel *Make Room! Make Room!* by popular science fiction author Harry Harrison, best known for his stories of the Stainless Steel Rat. But this 1966 book stood in stark contrast to former cartoonist Harrison's usual lighthearted work. Inspired by forecasts of devastating overpopulation, Harrison wrote a grim tale of a crowded future world, comparable to Upton Sinclair's *The Jungle* in tone. Industrialized cannibalism, the focus of the movie, was only a minor note in the novel, which went on to describe steadily worsening conditions.

Stanley R. Greenberg's script moves Harrison's oppressive atmosphere into the background of this sci-fi mystery thriller set in the overcrowded New York City of 2022. Heston plays the lead role of the comparatively honest Detective Robert Thorn, who at first turns his latest murder assignment into an opportunity to ransack the classy apartment of politically connected millionaire William Simonson (Whit Bissell). But his own thievery only highlights the fact that the supposed burglar/killer took nothing after the murder, and Thorn refuses to dismiss the strange case. Thorn's research partner, Sol Roth (Edward G. Robinson), is a former detective, and he agrees that the two should continue digging into Simonson's connections for a motive even as their stubborn pursuit of the case puts them in danger. The only hope seems to be exposing the conspiracy before they're both erased by their powerful foes.

With attributes more akin to an intensified urban action movie like *Shaft, Soylent Green* offers little in the way of the f/x trickery found in other sci-fi features of the same period. Instead, director Richard Fleischer (*Fantastic Voyage*) concentrates on the performances and dialogue and making the most of the setting's close quarters. Heston, at the far end of his early-'70s revival built on science fiction pictures, delivers a refreshingly multilayered character. His Thorn may be the hero, but his motives are not that standard, ranging from self-protection to altruism. Robinson is a delight in his final role. Originally cast to support Heston in *Planet of the Apes* before having to bow out due to illness, Robinson displays real chemistry with Heston. Their scenes together are the emotional highlight of *Soylent Green,* and the relationship between the tough cop and the older former detective is genuinely touching. Far less successful are attempts to generate action and excitement through standard gunplay and fight scenes. And the film's insistent return to the detective story elements in spite of the rich opportunities presented by its setting gives it an uneven tone. So, in other words, *Soylent Green*'s best moments involve . . . people!

1973 (PG) 97m/C Charlton Heston, Edward G. Robinson, Leigh Taylor-Young, Chuck Connors, Joseph Cotton, Brock Peters, Paula Kelly, Mike Henry, Whit Bissell, Dick Van Patten. *D:* Richard Fleischer. *W:* Stanley R. Greenberg. *C:* Richard H. Kline. *M:* Fred Myrow. *VHS, DVD*

—*Brian Thomas*

The Tenth Victim ♪♪♪♥

A lethal mix of hide-and-seek and big-game hunting for the reality TV generation, "The Big Hunt," which asks participants to alternate between being hunted and playing the hunter, has taken the futuristic world by storm in *The Tenth Victim.* Winners get product endorsements, cool prizes, vacations, and a chance to win up to $1 million. The game is used as a way for people to unleash their violent, homicidal tendencies, thereby ridding the world of aggression and war. The hunters get to know everything about their prey; the hunted know nothing. The Big Hunt is particularly popular and ruthless in the United States, which is no surprise as this film was directed by an Italian.

Caroline Meredith (Ursula Andress), an American from Hoboken, has become a Big Hunt celebrity of sorts. She's knocked off nine contestants in a row and even received a bonus endorsement offer from the Ming Tea company after slaying an Asian gentleman with her double-barreled brassiere. Gunning for her next victim, with the chance to win the million bucks, she chooses Italy's Marcello Poletti (Marcello Mastroianni with blond hair), who has just assassinated *his* last victim with explosive footwear. Caroline will be the hunter; he, the unsuspecting hunted.

The plan is for Caroline to murder Marcello on TV. After much bickering among tea company executives, Rome's Temple of Venus is chosen as the venue, where both a commercial and the murder will be filmed simultaneously.

A slick, suntanned operator on the surface, prone to wearing sunglasses and driving fast cars, Marcello remains troubled in his personal life. He's broke, thanks to an ex-wife (Luce Bonifassy) who's been spending his money; he doesn't seem all that happy with his girlfriend (Elsa Martinelli); and he's the leader of a strange religious cult whose members worship the sun. He confesses to being involved in the latter simply for the money.

In order to find out all she can about her quarry, Caroline poses as a reporter. She intrigues Marcello, but he's got a hunch she's a player in the

She'd love to kill him—and kill . . . to love him!

—Tagline for *The Tenth Victim*

deadly game. The downside to killing her before he's proven correct is the small matter of a thirty-year prison term. Marcello and Caroline play a seductive cat-and-mouse game, eventually falling for each other.

Both the *The Tenth Victim* and Richard Sheckley's source story "The Seventh Victim" were inspired by "The Most Dangerous Game," the Richard Connell tale about the mysterious Count Zaroff, who gets his kicks bagging humans on a deserted island. While the story had been filmed before, in 1932 as *The Most Dangerous Game* with Leslie Banks and Joel McCrea (and would later inspire both *Hard Target* with Jean-Claude Van Damme and *Series 7: The Contenders*), the idea of taking a satiric stab at the material and transporting the events to the future works surprisingly well here. The link between violence and the media's coverage of it may seem like well-trod ground today, but *The Tenth Victim* still seems slightly ahead of its time with its spot-on premonitions.

Credit director Elio Petri (*An Investigation of a Citizen Under Suspicion*) and his team of writers for keeping *The Tenth Victim* spry in both the action and dialogue departments. Along with building genuine sexual intensity between Caroline and Marcello, the film manages to grab hold of the audience with its disturbing ideas about the future and the role the media can play in it. Also noteworthy is the work by the production team (which includes Fellini and Antonioni associates) for designing the film in an ultracool, distinctly '60s fashion. Along with Mastroianni's space-age apartment (orange furniture, aquarium-like lights, and hidden doors), there's Andress's wardrobe of barebacked outfits, bulletproof leather armor, and that ratta-tat-tat brassiere.

Andress, the Swiss actress of *Dr. No* and *Casino Royale* fame, acquits herself nicely in the acting department, though it would have been better to have her American character speak English rather than the disconcerting (and dubbed) Italian. Meanwhile, Mastroianni does a slight variation on his role as the free-spirited journalist in Fellini's *La Dolce Vita,* who was also named Marcello. *Victim*'s Marcello could be the same character a few years later, after alcohol, women, and cynicism have taken their toll.

The Tenth Victim isn't perfect. Along with Andress's annoying dialect, the final ten minutes, in which other players from the Big Hunt get involved in a shoot-out, is a little garbled, and some of the characters' motives are questionable. There's also an oddball score featuring a high-pitched female scat shriek over what sounds like a roller-skating-rink organ. Sure, it gives the film a frenzied, near-hallucinatory feel, but after an hour, it'll remind you of a wailing cat. Still, *The Tenth Victim,* with spunky humor and a sense of surprise, tackles questions about the media and violence that we ponder whenever we turn on the TV.

1965 (NR) 92m/C *IT* Marcello Mastroianni, Ursula Andress, Elsa Martinelli, Salvo Randone, Luce Bonifassy. **D:** Elio Petri. **W:** Ennio Flaiano, Tonino Guerra, Elio Petri, Giorgio Salvioni. **C:** Gianni Di Vananzo. **M:** Piero Piccioni. *VHS, DVD*
AKA: *La Decima Vittima*

2001: A Space Odyssey 𝄞𝄞𝄞𝄞

Stanley Kubrick's *2001* belongs to that rare class of films (*Lawrence of Arabia, Ben Hur, Once upon a Time in the West*) that cannot remain the same entity after the transition from their original theatrical medium to a television screen. When a vast canvas is reduced to the size of a postage stamp, it *becomes* a postage stamp.

If you've seen *2001* on the big screen—love it or hate it—you probably don't need much of a refresher course to recall its basic content:

1. Apes.
2. Big black thing.
3. Bone in the air.
4. Spaceships.
5. Another big black thing on the moon.
6. More spaceships.
7. Boring astronauts, interesting computer.
8. Light show.
9. Astronaut in hotel room.
10. Big fetus in space. Roll credits.

Why, for heaven's sake, would an uncomplicated laundry list of scenes like this generate some of the most voluminous criticism ever written about a single motion picture? Why do debates still rage over whether the movie is sterile or moving, meaningful or vacuous, significant or trivial? Because this

> "I know I've made some very poor decisions recently, but I can give you my complete assurance that my work will be back to normal."
>
> —HAL 9000 (the voice of Douglas Rain), in *2001: A Space Odyssey*

movie is uniquely open to interpretation, and an understanding of it has eluded many viewers, that's why.

The film's tank is not, as many of its most single-minded proponents insist, topped off with high-test philosophy. The message is being confused with the medium. Kubrick, one of the most aggressively intellectual directors of his time, made a conscious effort not to do what previous science fiction films had done (indeed, what most Hollywood films do): be literal, be expository rather than poetic. Instead, Kubrick adapted a deliberately straightforward tale (Arthur C. Clarke's "The Sentinel") but chose to take advantage of the medium and tell it *visually.*

Even though the events tend to have a miraculous bent, *2001* is most definitely not about mysticism. As Clarke himself wrote, "Any sufficiently advanced technology is indistinguishable from magic." Here is precisely what *2001* is about: alien intervention in the course of human evolution. That the effects of the intervention are seen while the aliens are not is one of the prime reasons for mass misinterpretation.

The alleged "plotlessness" of *2001* is utter nonsense. In fact, lest anyone have trouble discerning the beginning, middle, and end, Kubrick literally planted cue cards in the movie.

"The Dawn of Man" signals act one. In prehistoric Africa, a band of starving Australopithecus may not make it to another generation. Humankind is doomed . . . until a jet-black monolith mysteriously appears.

One ape-man who touches it inexplicably gains the ability to recognize that a formerly useless bone contains the potential to be both tool and weapon. (Blaring on the soundtrack, with all its Nietzschean implication, is Richard Strauss's *Also Sprach Zarathustra*.) Suddenly, the bone can be used to kill pigs for meat—and to protect against a warring tribe.

In one audacious moment—quite possibly the most notorious, clever, and oft-parodied in the history of cinema—the bone is tossed into the air and the screen jump-cuts to a spaceship, traversing millions of years in one-twenty-fourth of a second.

The ship's lone passenger docks with a space station revolving high above Earth. Nothing happens, in dramatic terms, but Kubrick's icily perfect visual effects—accompanied by strains of *The Blue Danube*—usher the sequence into the realm of the balletic. Heywood Floyd (William Sylvester), the traveler, spends a brief time aboard the midtransit point making small talk until the next leg of the journey takes him moonward.

It's nearly impossible to convince a contemporary, overadrenalinized, post–*Star Wars* generation of the overwhelming power of such scenes, particularly to a 1968 audience accustomed to the cinematic sci-fi of giant bugs and rubber-faced mutants. Mankind has not only survived, Kubrick suggests, we've conquered the impossible—and yet we're blind to the majestic beauty of, and our place in, the cosmos. This in itself implies an evolutionary dead end for our species.

After he docks on the moon, Floyd addresses the press and fellow scientists regarding the monumental discovery of an eons-old monolith deliberately buried under the moon's surface. It can only mean one thing: it was placed there long ago by an intelligent species patient enough to wait for man's ability to discover it. We're being tested; has their experiment in human evolution succeeded? Judging by Floyd's banal speech, the incomparable event isn't much more important than finding a prize at the bottom of a Cracker Jack box.

In a scene that recalls the prehistoric sequence, the scientists journey to the archaeological moon site and cautiously gather around the monolith. The slab suddenly emits a piercing radio signal directed toward Jupiter. In this case, the monolith is not a "big brain" machine; it's a cosmic security alarm.

"Jupiter Mission: Nine Months Later" is the title heralding act two. Aboard the *Discovery* ship, astronauts Bowman and Poole (Keir Dullea and Gary Lockwood) mark time as they gradually approach the giant planet in search of answers. The onboard computer, HAL 9000, clearly has more personality than do his human companions.

When HAL fails a crucial test, he decides (quite humanly) to murder Poole by cutting off his spacesuit's air supply rather than face the consequences of an electronic lobotomy. Decades before Kubrick conceived of the screenplay that became Steven Spielberg's *A.I.: Artificial Intelligence,* he was already making statements about the limitations of human thought and the ability of computers to display human consciousness.

Bowman eventually outsmarts HAL, unplugging his higher brain functions in a poignant scene that renders the computer unable to do much more than sing a simple song. Outside, yet another (gigantic) monolith beckons.

What follows is act three, a chapter called "Jupiter and Beyond the Infinite," where the infamous Ultimate Trip occurs. Here the monolith acts as a gateway to another dimension, province of the alien intelligence that had altered the course of human evolution. The effects in this psychedelic light show are the most dated in the film, if only because they've been imitated so many times.

Bowman travels through space and time, eventually coming to rest in a setting that resembles nothing more ordinary than a twentieth-century hotel room. His reason for being there is left open to interpretation: is he being held for observation—and judgment?

Kubrick reveals Bowman spending the rest of his life in this solitary existence through a series of cuts wherein Bowman grows into a frail old man. Another creative tour de force: the cuts act as both flashbacks *and* flash-forwards, sometimes placing two versions of his aging body in the same shot, observing each other with detached wonder.

Finally, with Bowman on his deathbed, the smallest (and most powerful) monolith appears. It transforms Bowman into a fetus, the "Star Child," who floats in space near Earth. The Star Child may be the next crucial step in human evolution.

When properly screened in a theater, *2001* remains *the* watershed film of the late '60s. It both defines and transcends a period fraught with anxiety for the future. Prosaic bromides are hardly Kubrick's bailiwick, but *2001* offers hope in place of answers.

1968 (G) 139m/C Keir Dullea, Gary Lockwood, William Sylvester, Daniel Richter. **D:** Stanley Kubrick. **W:** Stanley Kubrick, Arthur C. Clarke. **C:** Geoffrey Unsworth. **M:** Aram Khachaturyan, György Ligeti, Richard Strauss, Johann Strauss. *VHS, DVD*

—Steven Austin

Zardoz

A gigantic stone head floats along a futuristic countryside. "I am Zardoz!" it booms in a voice that makes James Earl Jones sound like Betty Boop. "The gun is good, the penis is bad," it intones through a grimacing maw, burping up a cache of rifles. What the heck is this thing, anyway? A twenty-third-century incarnation of the NRA? Charlton Heston himself? Kind of. It's God. Maybe. As writer, producer, and director of this misbegotten flick, only John Boorman can say for sure, and even that's debatable. *Zardoz* is awash in allegory, steeped in symbolism, and mired in metaphor. The result is a Dagwood-sandwich-sized parable—pretentious as a Moby CD but fun to watch on an enjoyably bad level.

Take a typical postapocalyptic world, neatly subdivided into two landscapes: the elite Vortex and the ruddy Outlands. Roaming the barren Outlands on horseback, wearing two-faced masks, and worshiping the giant rock-faced god are the savage Brutals (as opposed to the brutal Savages).

Here comes Zed, our champeen (Sean Connery), a brute among Brutals. Zed's so brutal the bloody adjective has become a noun—and all the while his participle dangles out of his drawers. (It should be noted that the main appeal of *Zardoz* is watching a portly, post-007 Sean Connery cavort around in a long ponytailed wig and a short red diaper.) His opponents are the ruling class—skinny, asexual immortals called the Eternals. A squirrelly Eternal with facial hair tattooed on his mug (don't ask) is charged with keeping order in the Outlands. He controls the nifty Zardoz head, turning fun-loving Brutals like Zed into deadly Exterminators, who control the savage population with their big, phallic guns.

But, as rifle-wielding savages go, Zed is a thinking man. Sick of the 'burbs, he stows away in Zardoz's mouth for a Perillo cruise tour of the Vortex. (Apparently, minimum-wage security guards are a concept of the distant past.) He's disappointed to find Vortex citizens are a supercilious and condescending bunch—twenty-third-century Republicans, no doubt, albeit ones graced with superior genes and psychic powers. The problem with these so-called Eternals is that they're all bored with being immortal. Without procreation or sex to keep them busy, Eternals get their kicks by being really mean to the oldest and craziest of their own race. Obviously, Boorman's political and allegorical roadmap leans a little to the left. The women of the Vortex do tend to fall out of their tops a lot; gratuitous nudity, for some viewers, is the film's saving grace.

Here comes Zed, that hairy, half-naked fish out of water, to upset the status quo. Are the Eternals grateful for some authentic stimulation, even if it's buried behind a thick Scottish burr? No, they'd rather (telekinetically) beat Zed into submission, experiment on his rudimentary brain, and figure out why he seems so interested in Charlotte Rampling.

Thus far, *Zardoz* has tossed together Jungian psychology, Greek mythology, mysticism, and Marxism like a wilting Waldorf salad of freshman liberal arts courses. But then things just get weird. Zed climbs into a wedding dress and begins to spout aphorisms that would make L. Ron Hubbard proud, like, "An old man calls me. The voice of the turtle is heard in the land." Zed, we learn, is not really a brutal exterminator channeling a fortune-cookie scribe. He's a super-brained mutant of vastly untapped potential. Will Zed break the cyclical bonds of Eternal boredom, instill the muse of creative human thought, and save a dying race? And will any members of the audience be there to care?

As *Zardoz* (the movie, not the giant stone idol) veers off into a never-*NEVER* land of high-minded solipsistic hooey, any intentions that Boorman may have entertained about lifting the mind(s) of the audience go right out the bathroom window. More strange than the film itself is the fact that Boorman also directed *Point Blank, Deliverance, Excalibur, Hope and Glory,* and *The General*—five certifiable classics of genuine wit, adventure, compassion, and drama. Chalk it up to the '70s. Take my dystopia, please.

A near-naked Sean Connery as Zed battles the Eternals in John Boorman's *Zardoz.*

1974 (R) 106m/C Sean Connery, Charlotte Rampling, Sara Kestelman, Niall Buggy. *D:* John Boorman. *W:* John Boorman. *C:* Geoffrey Unsworth. *M:* David Munrow. *VHS, DVD*

—Steven Austin

Chapter 8

Don't Bogart That Trip

Yesterday's warnings often turn into today's camp. Never has this been more apparent than in films dealing with pot, weed, reefer, marijuana, acid, dope, pills, uppers, downers, bennies, 'ludes, smack, "H," coke, crank, speed, and so on. You know—drugs.

Witness *Cocaine Fiends, Reefer Madness, Marihuana,* and *Marijuana: Assassin of Youth,* all films from the 1930s intent on scaring the bejesus out of audiences with their depiction of the antisocial, psychotic, and criminal after-effects of a drag on a joint or a sniff of some white powder. In the late 1960s and into the 1970s, these older films drew enthusiastic crowds, especially on college campuses and in repertory houses. At such venues, young audiences laughed hysterically, secure in the knowledge that they would not be afflicted in the same way the on-screen protagonists were. After all, they had passed around a reefer or snorted a line just before the movie's screening. Meanwhile, newfangled drugsploitation flicks like *Maryjane* and *The Hooked Generation* invaded drive-ins, providing cautionary tales while the smell of those funny scented cigarettes filled the night air.

In the 1950s, directors turned to realism rather than propaganda to depict drug use, a trend marked largely by two acclaimed films. Leading director Otto Preminger teamed with star Frank Sinatra in 1955 for *The Man with the Golden Arm,* a then-harrowing look at the world of drug addiction with Sinatra as a wanna-be jazz drummer and failed gambler whose life spins downward when he gets hooked on the hard stuff. The scene in which Frank tries to kick his habit still elicits shudders. The project received a great deal of flack, and Preminger sent it to theaters without the seal of approval from the Production Code, an antiquated list of cinematic "don't"s, hatched in 1930, that clearly stated "illegal drug traffic must never be presented." Disturbing in a similar way is 1957's big-screen translation of *A Hatful of Rain,* based on Michael V. Gazzo's acclaimed autobiographical play, in which Don Murray's character's heroin dependency takes its toll on him, his pregnant wife (Eva Marie Saint), and his understanding brother (Anthony Franciosa).

LSD was probably first seen in movies in *The Tingler,* William Castle's 1959 shocker, with Vincent Price as a demented scientist looking into how people react to fear in extreme situations. Castle's desire to scare audiences resulted in a gimmick of wiring theater seats to give patrons minor electrical shocks. On-screen, Price wires himself by injecting LSD into his veins and tripping out, experiencing visions of skeletons and moving walls and a general feeling of claustrophobia.

It was not a good trip, nor were many of them throughout the next decade. Pot smoking and, to a lesser extent, acid dropping, became mainstays in many flicks geared to the youth market in the 1960s. It was one way to bond with the kids—and scare them at the same time.

Producer-director Roger Corman, a filmmaker with a sixth sense of how to give young audiences what they wanted, offered some trippy visual work in his Edgar Allan Poe movies earlier in the decade. With help from screenwriter Jack Nicholson, Corman really flew high with *The Trip* in 1967, in which troubled TV producer Peter Fonda becomes enmeshed in the hallucination generation in an attempt to clear up personal problems. Corman's own experiments with LSD inspired the wild trip sequences in the film. American International Pictures, the filmmaker's home base throughout the '60s, cranked out such LSD-laced 1968 favorites as *Psych-Out,* with Nicholson leading Susan Strasberg to Haight-Ashbury to find her hippie brother Bruce Dern, and *Wild in the Streets,* with Christopher Jones as a rock idol who uses his clout to throw everyone over thirty years old into concentration camps and doses the water supply with mind-altering drugs.

It was not only the kids who were turning on, either. *Skidoo* (1968) presented Jackie Gleason—"The Great One"—as a mobster who drops acid while serving time behind bars. What would Trixie say? And Peter Sellers was a straitlaced lawyer who got a dose of hashish along with the fudge when he tried some brownies in *I Love You, Alice B. Toklas!*

While *Psych-Out* was mostly melodramatic and *Wild in the Streets* addressed its subject in satiric tones, trip films subsequently got pretty serious again. *Easy Rider* (1969) may have made heroes or even martyrs of the lead characters played by Peter Fonda and Dennis Hopper, but the film did not paint a particularly positive picture of their all-American odyssey, especially with its ominous New Orleans trip sequence. In 1971 *Panic in Needle Park* made a star of Al Pacino as a New York City junkie and *Dusty and Sweets McGee* took an unflinching pseudo-documentary look at the L.A. drug scene. Meanwhile, TV movies like *Maybe I'll Come in the Spring* and *Go Ask Alice* brought the not-so-idyllic side of the drug-influenced counterculture into homes across America.

Toward the end of the decade, drug use got cooler again. Cheech and Chong, the comedy team whose routines were based on praising and participating in pot smoking, brought their act to the big screen in 1978's

Up in Smoke, a sloppy, low-budget farce that made audiences laugh at the duo's dopey exploits and rejoice in the film's antiauthoritarian hijinks. *Up in Smoke* amassed an incredible $44 million at the box office, opening the stash for more stoned sold picnics.

Chappaqua ♫

Siddhartha ♫♫♫♪

One of the oddest footnotes in trip-movie history, Conrad Rooks made only two movies, the almost unwatchable *Chappaqua* and the visually sublime *Siddhartha.* The son of the CEO of Avon, Rooks has led a most peculiar life: alcoholism and drug addiction at a young age, marriage to a Romanov princess, an affinity for Eastern religions years before it became fashionable, and friendships with everyone from Bollywood stars to beat icon William S. Burroughs. Friendships were the key to the creation of his films—the high caliber of "guest stars" in the first and his collaborators on the second are the reason the films were saved from utter obscurity and underwent restoration in the 1990s.

Regarding *Chappaqua,* imagine being locked in the mind of a pretentious drug addict trying to detox. Picture said junkie being a wealthy dilettante encountering a host of musical and literary 1960s icons, and there you have Rooks's abrasive debut feature. The central problem is Rooks's decision to cast himself as himself. As an actor, he comes across as Dennis Hopper without talent, drifting through the movie wearing a cowboy hat and dancing convulsively. While there are precedents for his blissed-out, nearly infantile method of acting (one thinks of Taylor Mead in the films of Warhol and of Ron Rice), Rooks's style is unsettling. The film's continent-jumping proves to be jarring as well, calling attention to the obviously sizable budget allotted to this "underground" film (Rooks reportedly used—you guessed it—his inheritance to fund the project). The film moves in no particular order from footage of the baby-faced, all-American-looking Rooks rambling around New York City in biker leathers, to what appear to be beautifully shot home movies of him learning devotional practices in India, to stray shots of an American black church service and Stonehenge, to the central setting, a small-town French sanitarium where Rooks undergoes a "sleep cure" administered by a playful doctor (*Children of Paradise*'s Jean-Louis Barrault).

Rooks's film debut winds up being so obtuse it almost appears to be a parody of better-executed avant-garde movies. However, he did have the services of the supremely talented Robert Frank (*Pull My Daisy, Cocksucker Blues*) as his main cinematographer, so the film contains some memorable images of the cities Rooks flits through. The musical and literary names also make the film truly "historical" by today's standards. Allen Ginsberg is seen chanting by the Central Park Reservoir, while William Burroughs appears in several scenes (in one with his gangster henchman, Hervé Villechaize!) as "Opium Jones," a menacing undertaker-like figure. Rooks attends a New York gig by the Fugs early on (sucking up crushed LSD cubes from the carpet) and later is present at a Paris concert by Ornette Coleman. The Avon heir's most interesting coup: getting Ravi Shankar to do his soundtrack (and make a brief onscreen appearance) around the same time that Shankar was making the acquaintance of Beatle George Harrison.

Where *Chappaqua* is the ultimate act of self-indulgence, *Siddhartha* is a cinematic ode to self-denial and the common-sense truths to be found in Eastern spirituality. Rooks's adaptation of Herman Hesse's college-student favorite is a subtle, mature film that uses no cinematic tricks or guest stars to pull the narrative along.

Siddhartha (Shashi Kapoor), a Brahmin's son, leaves his father's house to search for truth. He watches his friend Govinda (Romesh Sharma) become a disciple of the Buddha and continues on his way alone. A courtesan (Simi Garewal) indoctrinates him into the art of love; his subsequent work for a merchant (Pincho Kapoor) teaches him the art of commerce. As he gains worldliness, he loses his spiritual direction, until he meets a philosophical ferryman who leads a thoroughly contented life.

Made a few years after the vogue for all things Eastern had died down, *Siddhartha* qualifies as the ultimate coming-of-age tale. Our hero goes from callow youth to a wise old man in the space of ninety-four minutes, his search for spiritual enlightenment ending with what many would consider a dull, repetitive life as an impoverished ferryman, studying the ways of the river. Herman Hesse's compact 1922 novel attracted a cult following in the 1960s, presenting as it did a Westerner's look at Eastern spirituality.

Rooks overcame major obstacles making the film, as the Indian government opposed its production. It wound up being shot in Northern India and in the holy city of Rishikesh (garden spot of the maharishi), as well as on the private estate of a maharajah (a friend of Kapoor's superstar brother Raj). The film contains "the first screen kiss filmed on the subcontinent," according to press releases, and it represented the first time Bollywood stars (Kapoor and Garewal) were seen nude in a film; the scene is infinitely demure and tasteful. The film's main triumph is the crystal-clear, radiant cinematography of Bergman stalwart Sven Nykvist. The widescreen compositions show placid, sun-drenched Indian landscapes—perfect settings for this leisurely but by no means dull allegory.

Kapoor is one of the few Bollywood stars to have an extensive Western filmography (*Sammy and Rosie Get Laid, Shakespeare Wallah*). Here, he and the rest of the cast seem occasionally to give flat line-readings. This style is a by-product of the fact that, as written by Hesse and adapted by Rooks, the characters are defined primarily by their dialogue. They outline their beliefs in poetic utterances that are crammed to capacity with epigrams—"The cause of suffering is craving," for example.

Siddhartha is such a masterfully executed work that it can scarcely be believed it was made by the person responsible for *Chappaqua.* One can easily speculate that if Rooks had passed on *Chappaqua*, produced only *Sid-*

dhartha, and then quit filmmaking, today he would be considered one of the most important "lost" directors of all time. His earlier film has no doubt harmed his reputation as a mystery man—sometimes it's best *not* to film yourself dancing like a fool in a cowboy hat.

Chappaqua
1966 (NR) 82m/C/BW Conrad Rooks, Jean-Louis Barrault, William S. Burroughs, Allen Ginsberg, Ravi Shankar, Ornette Coleman. *D:* Conrad Rooks. *W:* Conrad Rooks. *C:* Robert Frank, Étienne Becker, Eugen Schüfftan. *M:* Ravi Shankar. *VHS*

Siddhartha
1972 (R) 94m/C Shashi Kapoor, Simi Garewal, Romesh Sharma, Pincho Kapoor. *D:* Conrad Rooks. *W:* Conrad Rooks, Paul Mayersberg. *C:* Sven Nykvist. *M:* Hemant Kumar. *VHS, DVD*

—Ed Grant

Cisco Pike 🦴🦴🦴

"**H**e's a poet / He's a picker / He's a prophet / He's a pusher." Those lyrics from "The Pilgrim: Chapter 33," one of four Kris Kristofferson songs heard in *Cisco Pike,* pretty much sum up the title character, played by the singer/songwriter/actor in his first starring role.

When we first meet up with him in seedy Venice, California, Cisco is trying to sell his guitar, which was signed by old acquaintances like Bob Dylan and Janis Joplin when Cisco and his former musical partner, Jesse Dupre (Harry Dean Stanton), were close to grabbing the brass ring themselves. They never quite made it, with Cisco sidelined by two drug busts and Jesse by addiction to a variety of illegal substances. Realizing that if he gets busted a third time, it'll be "a long time between drinks" and he'll lose his live-in old lady, Sue (Karen Black), Cisco has quit his drug-dealing ways.

Unfortunately, Cisco's music-biz cronies don't care about his demo tape of old songs, made without Jesse; they are only interested in him for the grass he insists he can no longer supply. Fortunately, there are some meager signs of hope in Cisco's life. The owner of the music store where Cisco is attempting to sell his guitar holds the performer's talent in such high regard that he refuses to buy the instrument. It turns out that Jesse's on his way to Los Angeles to reunite with Cisco. And in Sue, Cisco has a loving, supportive, true believer. So maybe he's still got a chance.

Alas, Sergeant Leo Holland (Gene Hackman), the psychotic cop who busted Cisco previously, sees the still-aspiring rock star as his chance to score some badly needed money. He blackmails Cisco into selling, over one weekend, at least $10,000 worth of grade-A grass he's confiscated from a recent bust.

Over two days, Cisco visits homes, offices, diners, recording studios (to pitch Rex, a hyperactive musician played by Sir Douglas Quintet leader Doug Sahm), beaches, clubs, and canyons—wherever his customers want to meet to sample and purchase this incredible grass. Trouble is, the tightly wound Holland is tailing him to make sure Cisco neither rips him off nor lets him down, even if that means scaring off customers and making Cisco's task tougher. During this weekend activity, Jesse returns, still addicted, insecure, and too wobbly to seriously resume his musical pursuits with Cisco. When he re-enters the picture, he brings with him a sense that tragedy is inevitable.

A young, clean-shaven Kristofferson plays Cisco with a mix of inner strength, sensitivity, and vulnerability. Never issued on video by its studio, *Cisco Pike* has not made it beyond fringe cult status, but Kristofferson's acting career certainly did, and you can see his talent quite clearly here. You can hear it, too, in the soundtrack, which includes Kristofferson's classic, "Loving Her Was Easier (Than Anything I'll Ever Do Again)." Hackman brings to this film the same ferocious intensity he brought to his Oscar-winning performance as Popeye Doyle in *The French Connection* a year earlier, while Stanton adds a doomed sensitivity to his turn as Jesse. Additionally, the film features a gallery of talented character actors from the '70s, such as Roscoe Lee Browne (*Logan's Run*), Severn Darden (*The President's Analyst*), Allan Arbus (*Greaser's Palace*), Antonio Fargas (Huggy Bear on TV's *Starsky & Hutch*), Hugh Romney (AKA *Woodstock*'s "Wavy Gravy"), and Andy Warhol party perennial Viva.

Director Bill L. Norton (*More American Graffti*) applies a minimalist flair to the film, which lies somewhere between the blurry semisurrealism that Dennis Hopper brought to *Easy Rider* and the more natural style with which Bob Rafaelson helmed *Five Easy Pieces*. *Cisco Pike* isn't in the same league as either of those classics, of course, but as a look at the seedy underbelly of the fast-lane life that was L.A. in the '70s—or just as a thriller laced with humor, pathos, character, and music—it's a very cool ride. It certainly ranks among the very best titles in Kristofferson's admirable filmography and among the most criminally underrated in Hackman's.

1972 (R) 94m Kris Kristofferson, Gene Hackman, Harry Dean Stanton, Karen Black, Viva, Joy Bang, Allan Arbus, Severn Darden. *D:* Bill L. Norton. *W:* Bill L. Norton. *C:* Vilas Lapenieks. *M:* Kris Kristofferson. *VHS*

—Barry Gutman

The Hooked Generation 🦴

A prime example of how psychedelia invaded every corner of American moviemaking, *The Hooked Generation* is a standard backwoods-fugitive saga that, if it weren't so poorly paced and abysmally acted, could have qualified as a hallucinogenic *High Sierra*. Instead, it is notable only for the sight of some very visibly stoned actors playing visibly stoned crooks, and for an amusingly dippy scene set in a Coral Gables commune (an earthly "Nir-vein-a," as one resident puts it).

Three perpetually high drug smugglers—Daisey, Acid, and Dum Dum—do business on their fishing boat in the Everglades. After ruthlessly killing their Cuban suppliers, the trio unwisely kills an entire boatload of Coast Guard officers, ensuring that they will have to flee for their lives for the rest of the picture. Along the way, they abduct a clueless young blonde in a bikini and her stoic boyfriend; the girl is forced at gunpoint to go-go dance for the smugglers and is eventually raped (offscreen), while the boyfriend attempts a number of escapes from the clutches of the trio and is soundly beaten every time. The smugglers continue to indulge their craven appetites until they are cornered in the Florida swamps by the cops.

The Hooked Generation is about twenty minutes longer than it should be. You can virtually *feel* events being dragged out as we move from mode to mode. First there are slam-bang action sequences shot on location in the Everglades, then we're trapped in claustrophobic indoor sets (giving the film the feel of the B&W "roughie" sex flicks made in the mid-'60s), and then the finale finds the characters back out in the swamps exchanging taunts and bullets. Director William Grefé (*Death Curse of Tartu*) allocates a good amount of time to the smugglers' exploits in the bog, but this isn't surprising, considering that he was a specialist in waterlogged adventures—among his best-remembered movies are those that deal with snakes, alligators, and sharks. Perhaps the Grefé feature best known to cult audiences these days, however, is the wonderfully overwrought William Shatner opus *Impulse* (AKA *Wanna Take a Ride, Little Girl?*).

Grefé's flair for casting authentic performers (read: those who'd work cheap) is seen throughout the film, as nonactorly hippies and Seminole Indians populate the sequences that require extras. The leads go through their paces with varying degrees of success: onetime swinging TV host Steve Alaimo (*Where the Action Is*) is fairly credible as the erstwhile hero/punching bag; Jeremy Slate (*The Born Losers*) acts cool as the self-assured Daisey; and John Davis Chandler incarnates Acid as a jittery addict, the kind who would kiss a girl on the mouth after he'd just finished killing her. Former light heavyweight champion Willie Pastrano gives the movie's Method performance, as there is not a *second* he's onscreen that he doesn't look genuinely stoned out of his mind.

The movie has its share of sordid thrills, but both of the standout moments center around Acid. The first finds him struggling to shoot up right in the middle of the smugglers' gun battle with the Coast Guard—he winds up exiting the boat's cabin and rolling on the deck, attempting to tie off as the bullets whiz around him. The other unforgettable sequence occurs when Acid is gunned down by police while visiting the Coral Gables commune. Grefé segues into a montage that's supposed to visualize Acid's parting thoughts, finding time for a shot of a monkey, several glimpses of the sexy hippie chicks seen earlier on, a portrait of Jesus (for more of Grefé's fun with religious icons, see the review of *The Psychedelic Priest* in this chapter), and a candle being blown out. Death truly *is* the final freakout.

1968 (R) 94m/C Jeremy Slate, Steve Alaimo, John Davis Chandler, Willie Pastrano, Cece Stone. *D:* William Grefé. *W:* Quinn Morrison, Ray Preston, William Grefé. *C:* Gregory Sandor. *M:* Chris Martel. VHS, DVD

AKA: Alligator Alley

—*Ed Grant*

I Love You, Alice B. Toklas! ♫♫♫

There is a far-fetched but irresistible story that in two separate incidents, on the sets for *What's New Pussycat?* and for *Casino Royale*, Peter Sellers was mistaken for Woody Allen. On both occasions, the

"I've got pot, I've got acid, I've got LSD cubes. I'm probably the hippest guy around here. I'm so hip, it hurts!"

—Harold Fine (Peter Sellers), in *I Love You, Alice B. Toklas!*

people making the mistake confided in "Woody" what an absolute pain Peter Sellers was. Sellers, supposedly, did a dead-on impersonation of Allen and played right along.

In *I Love You, Alice B. Toklas!*, Sellers seems to be channeling Allen again, in spirit and mannerisms if not in vocals. He portrays Harold Fine, a straitlaced Jewish attorney in Los Angeles who reluctantly acquiesces to demands by his lover, Joyce (Joyce Van Patten), that they get married. While she and his mother (Jo Van Fleet) dicker over details of a big celebration with two hundred guests and twin cantors, Harold's brother Herbie (David Arkin), a blissed-out beach-bum hippie, introduces him to Nancy (Leigh Taylor-Young), a sensual flower child. Harold lets Nancy stay at his apartment and, in a famous sequence that lends the picture its title, some hash-laced Alice B. Toklas brownies she makes in gratitude give a hilarious buzz to the oblivious Fine clan and their future in-laws.

When the time comes for the wedding to Joyce, a smitten Harold ducks out of the ceremony instead

Uptight lawyer Harold (Peter Sellers) contemplates his interests in the counterculture in *I Love You, Alice B. Toklas!*

and completely changes his life for Nancy, making himself over with beads, long hair, and a guru (played by Louis Gottlieb, bassist for the folk group the Limeliters). His comfy apartment becomes a hippie crash pad, replete with animals and scruffy strangers freeloading in the kitchen and bathroom. Although he tries to adopt a mellow peace-and-brotherhood attitude, the novelty wears off quickly—especially when he realizes that Nancy still extends her charms to other men in the name of free love. So where to turn when even the counterculture becomes a drag?

Screenwriters Paul Mazursky and Larry Tucker don't know, and they're willing to admit it in the picture's frustratingly open ending. The duo contributed much to the canon of late-'60s films, penning everything from the television pilot of *The Monkees* to *Bob & Carol & Ted & Alice* (which Mazursky also directed, subsequent to this picture's success). And while strong finishes are not Mazursky's greatest asset, he certainly knew his way around the fringe vests and Hopi Indian tchotchkes of the day—not to mention the disillusionment phase, in which Harold Fine realizes that yoga poses and the Tibetan Book of the Dead don't necessarily hold all the answers.

Don't Bogart That Trip

The lead character is, in fact, a materialist who is drawn into the Age of Aquarius by his gonads and not much else, and the self-centered likes of Harold will be the ones to endow the subsequent 1970s with the sobriquet of the Me Generation. Sellers, adopting a flat American intonation, is just fine as Fine, slightly nebbishy and Allen-like right down to psychosomatic asthma attacks and an attraction to shiksas. This film is a reminder of Sellers's skills as a master of nuance and characterization, going well beyond the slapstick bumbler of *The Party* and the *Pink Panther* series.

1968 (R) 92m/C Peter Sellers, Leigh Taylor-Young, Joyce Van Patten, David Arkin, Herb Edelman, Salem Ludwig, Jo Van Fleet, Louis Gottlieb, Grady Sutton. **D:** Hy Averback. **W:** Paul Mazursky, Larry Tucker. **C:** Philip H. Lathrop. **M:** Elmer Bernstein. *VHS*

—Charles A. Cassady Jr.

Koyaanisqatsi ♫♫♫♫

Powaqqatsi ♫♫♫

Naqoyqatsi ♫♫♫

One of the strongest legacies passed down from the movies of the '60s is the idea of a film as a sensory experience. Underground directors had been pursuing this idea since the 1940s (overseas, it had been around since the days of the silent movie), but in the '60s both the major studios and independent exploitation producers began to include introspective, trippy sequences in their movies to attract younger viewers who might want to turn on in the relative safety of a darkened theater. With the advent of the music video in the '80s, this sort of visual and aural experimentation was used for everything from hyping bands to introducing news programs to selling soda. Moviegoers and couch potatoes became so used to these technologies that a "shock" was needed to bring them back around to the naive, receptive state that made the initial underground movies so effective back in the '60s.

That shock appeared in the form of the last great art-house "head" movie, the dialogue-less, narrative-less *Koyaanisqatsi*. "Presented" by Francis Ford Coppola in 1983, the film was a sensory creation of the first order—the kind of work that had been shown on gallery walls and in video installations was now available in 35 millimeter, with mesmerizing music by neoclassical composer Philip Glass and unforgettable images by cinematographer Ron Fricke. Best of all, linking this film indelibly with the genuine '60s mindset was the fact that director Godfrey Reggio was a socially conscious individual who was using his mind-altering combination of visuals and music not only to offer the viewer a new perspective on objects and locations from the everyday world, but also to convey a message about the way technology has overwhelmed nature to become the dominant force in American life.

Reggio's unusual background has made him acutely aware of the conflict between the spiritual and the secular world. Throughout his teens and early twenties he studied to become a monk in the Christian Brothers order; he quit the priesthood after only three years at the age of twenty-eight to work with youth groups in New Mexico. He came to filmmaking by way of a public service campaign he directed in the early '70s to inform the citizens of New Mexico about the government's part in recent invasions of privacy. Given this history, it's no surprise that while he maintains that *Koyaanisqatsi* and its two increasingly complex follow-up films are "deliberately wrapped in ambiguity," the astute viewer can readily detect a number of overt messages in the films' flow of imagery.

The first of what Reggio now refers to as "the Qatsi trilogy" is still the most effective film. *Koyaanisqatsi,* titled for the Hopi Indian phrase meaning "life out of balance," begins with majestic images of landscapes in the Southwestern United States and slowly, insidiously, begins to speed up as it presents daily activities in New York City and Los Angeles. The film offers the best-ever visualization of the "rat race," as Reggio uses time-lapse photography to slow down and then speed up the motion of cars on L.A. freeways, workers tending to production lines, and Manhattan commuters making their way to work. As the pace becomes more and more frenzied, the key component kicks into high gear: the hypnotically repetitive music of Philip Glass makes the film akin to a scientist's study of modern life, with humans viewed as little more than ants. Reggio's head-spinning look at mall and moviehouse leisure-time activity shows the same physical gestures that are present in the work sequences. The film was soundly lauded by the critics and became so influential that Reggio's time-lapsed view of city life (especially certain breakneck driving scenes) was instantly duplicated in a number of music videos.

Reggio's second film, *Powaqqatsi* (Hopi for "life in transformation"), offered little for music-video directors to pilfer, as it moves at a slower, more studied pace. This installment of the series focuses on the effect of technology on the Third World, examining in particular the contrast between smaller villages (where people are poor and harmonious) and cities (where people are poor and miserable). Presented this time by Coppola and George Lucas, the film often resembles an ethnographic documentary—in fact, some of its thunder was stolen by the equally hypnotic 1992 image-fest *Baraka,* a documentary made by Reggio's former cinematographer, Ron Fricke. Reggio and company's eye for mind-boggling visuals and Glass's flawless scoring distinguish *Powaqqatsi* as the deliberately slow second "movement" of the Qatsi trilogy.

The third film, *Naqoyqatsi* (Hopi for "life as war"), is the densest and the most high-tech of the three entries (ironic given Reggio's emphasis on the pitfalls of technology). While the first two films were constructed almost entirely out of footage shot by Reggio and his crew, a good deal of *Naqoyqatsi* consists of images that he and his collaborators altered with digital technology—including numerous technological phenomena rendered with CGI animation. The result is a barrage of imagery that is certainly "cold" (but still mesmerizing to watch), counterpointed with "back to basics" scenes in which Reggio shows the work of legendary photographer Eadweard Muybridge (a progenitor of the motion picture who photographed images of horses in motion) and super-slo-mo sequences of athletes in action.

With Coppola and Lucas seemingly off the case, filmmaker Steven Soderbergh stepped in to present *Naqoyqatsi,* which solidly connects Reggio's concerns and his approach to filmmaking with the '60s tradition. Although technology is viewed as a benevolent force in the film's initial images (logarithms, animated transistors, tunnels composed of endless zeroes and ones), the film's last third focuses on its application in combat, offering the single most kinetic war montage to appear in a movie since Nixon left the White House (discounting those "tribute" pieces that cropped up in films set during the period). Reggio's inclusion of a digitally composed *2001*-esque "starchild" image brings it all back home quite nicely. His initial work with Philip Glass may have inspired countless music videos and the ever-so-tame documentaries currently shown in the IMAX format, but at heart Reggio is a purebred product of the '60s, the era that proposed viewers turn on, tune in, and . . . try to change things while they still could.

Koyaanisqatsi
1983 (NR) 87m/C D: Godfrey Reggio. **W:** Walter Bachauer, Ron Fricke, Michael Hoenig, Godfrey Reggio, Alton Walpole. **C:** Ron Fricke. **M:** Philip Glass. *VHS, DVD*

Powaqqatsi
1988 (G) 97m/C D: Godfrey Reggio. **W:** Godfrey Reggio, Ken Richards. **C:** Graham Berry, Leonidas Zourdoumis. **M:** Philip Glass. *VHS, DVD*

Naqoyqatsi
2002 (PG) 89m/C/BW D: Godfrey Reggio. **W:** Godfrey Reggio. **C:** Russell Lee Fine. **M:** Philip Glass. *DVD*

—Ed Grant

The Love-Ins 🦴

Ever channel-flip to a really embarrassing rerun that grappled with '60s culture? Like when Lucille Ball and Vivian Vance clowned at a psychedelic happening? Or when Ironside disdainfully investigated crime in the decadence of "Hashbury?" Or when the USS *Enterprise* got hijacked by Eden-seeking space hippies?

Hold that vibe for the *The Love-Ins,* a stilted and unintentionally hilarious examination of San Francisco flower children under the spell of a charismatic, Timothy Leary–style guru. As the movie begins, he's upstanding college professor Jonathan Barnett (Richard Todd), who defends an underground newspaper, the *Tomorrow Times,* before a stuffy dean. The dean wants to expel students Larry (James MacArthur) and Patricia (Susan Oliver)—both looking well past their student years—unless they stop publishing the rag. In protest, Barnett resigns, an act that makes him a hero to the local summer-of-love youth. Barnett moves into a hippie pad in Haight-Ashbury, adjacent to Larry and Patricia, and the academic adapts instantly, presiding over rallies and love-ins in shamanic white robes, eventually starting his own peace-and-brotherhood cult.

"Be more! Sense more! Love more!" goes Barnett's mantra, and he promotes consciousness-exploration via LSD and cohabitation. Larry has doubts when Patricia freaks while tripping out, and he tries to unmask Barnett as a phony in the *Tomorrow Times.* Alas, the hippie element now turns against the paper. Patricia learns she's pregnant with Barnett's child, but bliss turns to despair when Barnett coldly orders her to get an abortion—he's too busy with cult business to be bothered. Patricia attempts suicide; Larry saves her, but the baby does not survive. The clumsy and abrupt wrap-up occurs in Candlestick Park, where Larry gets revenge but also "creates a martyr" in the process.

The lurid synopsis doesn't do justice to the unremittingly square flick, which is shot in bright, happy colors with the production values and broad acting of a TV *Batman* episode. MacArthur, adopted actor-son of Helen Hayes and playwright Charles MacArthur, would subsequently play Detective Danny Williams on *Hawaii Five-O,* and Mark Goddard (as a Barnett loyalist) battled long-haired galactic bikers, among other phenomena, on the tube's *Lost in Space.* But it's Richard Todd, a dignified British actor exuding civility and authority, who is the best thing on display, though he's more Oxford headmaster than Leary-esque San Francisco guru. Unfortunately, there's no evolution or insight in Barnett's arc from articulate free-speech champ to megalomaniacal cult chieftain, and campy dialogue and melodramatics don't help. A druggy Barnett disciple taking a fatal head-first dive out a window is eerily prophetic of the real-life 1969 suicide plunge of Diane Linkletter in West Hollywood. Her famous father, TV host Art Linkletter, singled out Leary and LSD, perhaps unjustly, as being responsible for her death (inspiring *Pink Flamingos* teammates John Waters and Divine to make a scabrous underground short subject, *The Diane Linkletter Story*).

Haight-Ashbury here is a nonstop street party of bongo drummers, flutists, and go-go chicks, with visiting tourist buses coming under siege from groovy hipsters the way visitors' cars at safari parks are mobbed by monkeys. But the most indelible imagery in *The Love-Ins* has to be Susan Oliver's LSD hallucinations, consisting of a gauzy dream ballet with dancers costumed as creatures from *Alice in Wonderland* (including "the sacred mushroom") while an audio track supplies chants of "Mellow yellow, mellow yellow. . . . Take the acid! Take the acid!"

Producer Sam Katzman had established himself as a prolific low-budget mogul, wringing screen material out of fads from flying saucers to calypso to Elvis. With director Arthur Dreifuss he pumped out a quick succession of late-'60s hippie-sploitationers: *Riot on the Sunset Strip, The Love-Ins,* and *The Young Runaways.* But their naive filmmaking style proved particularly ill-suited to *The Love-Ins,* though seekers of pop-culture time capsules may hearken to the likes of the Chocolate Watch Band (who also guested in *Riot on the Sunset Strip*), the UFOs, and abrasive talk-show host Joe Pyne. A forerunner of Wally George, Morton Downey Jr., and Bill O'Reilly, Pyne portrays himself, raging at Barnett in a broadcast debate and successfully duping the viewer into rooting for the wrong crank.

1967 (R) 85m/C Richard Todd, James MacArthur, Susan Oliver, Mark Goddard, Carol Booth, Michael Evans, Marc Cavell, Joe Pyne. *D:* Arthur Dreifuss. *W:* Hal Collins, Arthur Dreifuss. *C:* John F. Warren. *M:* Fred Karger. *VHS*

—*Charles A. Cassady Jr.*

Don Johnson plays the directionless Stanley in *The Magic Garden of Stanley Sweetheart.*

The Magic Garden of Stanley Sweetheart WOOF!

Were the '60s really this boring? You'd sure think so after watching this dull, aimless mess, the sole redeeming feature of which is a few good Bee Gees songs on the soundtrack.

Don Johnson, making his film debut at age twenty-one (he's so young, he hasn't even had his teeth fixed yet), plays the eponymous Stanley, a Columbia University student who wanders around Morningside Heights scoring dope and sleeping with whatever women are available.

Chief among the latter are Cathy (Diane Hull), a "straight" type he deflowers, and Fran (future folk singer Holly Near), Cathy's roommate, whom Stanley winds up sleeping with after he makes a movie of her masturbating.

Groovy! It's the '60s, people, with all the sex, drugs, and tie-dyed clothing you can possibly stand. There are psychedelic light shows, "happenings," and the kind of dialogue that makes you wonder how we got through the decade:

Cathy to friends she's just met: "Hi."

Musician friend Danny (Michael Greer): "No, but we're getting there."

Danny in response to Stanley's tale of woe involving dropping out of school and having to deal with competing girlfriends: "Just be, man. Just be."

Stanley when he finds out an acquaintance once worked as a model: "It's a groovy thing, being a model."

Far freakin' out! Movies like *Stanley Sweetheart* weren't any good when they first came out, and they definitely haven't improved with age. Untalented director Leonard Horn, a TV veteran who worked on shows like *Wonder Woman* and *Mannix,* tries to inject style—or at least weirdness—into the visuals but fails every step of the way. The acting, by a group of nobodies who went nowhere, is at the level of high school senior play at best. And the storyline? What storyline? Stanley hangs out. Stanley gets high. Stanley gets laid and has strange dreams. You just want to scream, "Luis Buñuel, where are you when we need you?"

Stanley Sweetheart and its ilk are to the counterculture what blaxploitation films were to the civil rights movement: an attempt to make some quick bucks out of a true social phenomenon. But most of these movies lacked either political awareness or cinematic style or both. *Stanley Sweetheart* just happens to be the bottom of a very deep barrel.

1970 (R) 117m/C Don Johnson, Linda Gillen, Michael Greer, Holly Near. *D:* Leonard Horn. *W:* Robert T. Westbrook. *C:* Victor J. Kemper. *M:* The Bee Gees. *VHS*

—*Lewis Beale*

Maryjane 𝄞𝄞𝄢

When you're looking for a powerful, real-life drama about how troubled youths are abusing marijuana, you know you can't go wrong with a film written by Hymie the Robot from "Get Smart" and the host of *Hollywood Squares.*

At least that's the case with *Maryjane,* a supposed exposé of the evil of pot penned by Dick ("Hymie") Gautier and Peter ("Here's the Secret Square") Marshall.

Produced with drive-in theaters in mind by exploitation wizards American International Pictures and directed by Maury Dexter (*The Mini-Skirt Mob*), *Maryjane* features former South Philly teen idol Fabian as Phil Blake, a young teacher and assistant football coach at Oakdale High School. A recent car accident has the school administrators and local police in a tizzy because they have reason to believe pot smoking played a part in the crash. Students are suspected of using reefer, and the Oakdale principal and authorities want Blake and other teachers to spy on the kids. Although John Ashcroft would undoubtedly approve of such action, Blake says that would make him a fink, compromising the all-important teacher-student relationship, so he just says "no" to spying. Then he fesses up that he actually tried marijuana—even inhaled—and he becomes the scourge of the town in the eyes of anyone over the age of eighteen.

Later, Mr. Blake gets in a lot of trouble when marijuana is found in his cool sports car, which is searched by the cops. To jail he goes, suspecting a setup. Once bailed out by Ellie (Diane McBain), a pretty blonde teacher, he searches for the creeps who did him wrong and are behind the rampant doobie-rolling going on, particularly among Oakdale's top football players.

Maryjane has been compared to *Reefer Madness,* the campy potboiler from the 1930s that became a midnight hit for college kids and stoned repertory-house audiences in the late 1960s and 1970s. Granted, *Maryjane* has some of that antiquated classic's charm, particularly regarding its wrong-headed warnings about becoming a pothead. Here, the police chief spouts that "'marry wanna' leads to LSD, cocaine, STP, and heroin." Not true. Everyone knows that excessive "marry wanna" use leads to eating greasy tacos,

Yodels, and onion rings at 3 A.M. And as depicted in *Maryjane,* teenage dope addicts act like energetic goofballs who get off on making out, gallivanting in public fountains, and riding carousels late at night. Another fallacy. Studies have actually shown that smoking weed leads to in-depth discussions about belly button lint and whether side two of the Grateful Dead's *Blues for Allah* is better head music than side one of Pink Floyd's *Dark Side of the Moon.*

But *Maryjane* has some of its own idiosyncratic—and idiotic—charms as well. First and foremost is how the dope deals go down. Here an ice cream truck pulls up behind the bleachers during football practice. Like the Pied Piper of Hamelin, the truck's dulcet bells attract the crème de la football team, who then purchase pints or quarts—containers that are actually stuffed with pot. Wouldn't the team's clueless coach question why the ice cream never melts? Isn't he suspicious that everybody buys pints and quarts and never, ever a fudgesicle or ice cream sandwich? This unique way of dealing drugs also makes one wonder: did Cheech & Chong watch *Maryjane* before they made *Cheech & Chong's Nice Dreams,* a film with essentially the same premise? I'd bet Tommy Chong a bong that they did.

Along with the future "Golden Boy of Bandstand," the pompadour-coiffed Fabian, and screenwriters Marshall and Gautier (who also adds comic relief as a flaky jailbird hippie), a number of other pop-culture icons can be found scattered throughout *Maryjane*'s cast. Keep your eyes peeled for future *Pretty Woman* director Garry Marshall, actress Teri Garr, *Jaws* screenwriter Carl Gottlieb, *The Bad Seed*'s Patricia McCormack, *American Hot Wax* helmer Floyd Mutrux, and—"eww, eww"—Joe E. Ross, Officer Gunther Toody of *Car 54, Where Are You?*

Maryjane has a bad rep, but despite its sanctimonious sermonizing, some wooden dialogue, and a ridiculous final reel, the film flies by, delivering the sort of thrills and el-cheapo shocks and a shred of social message the kids expected from an American International Picture release at the time. Why expect anything less from *Hymie and Pete's Excellent Drug Adventure*?

1968 95m/C Fabian, Diane McBain, Michael Margotta, Kevin Coughlin, Patricia McCormack, Baynes Barron, Garry Marshall, Teri Garr. *D:* Maury Dexter. *W:* Dick Gautier, Peter Marshall. *C:* Richard Moore. *M:* Lawrence Brown, Mike Curb. *VHS*
AKA: Mary Jane

The Psychedelic Priest

The combination of antidrug propaganda and a Christian message is irresistible to fans of camp cinema. It was not as appealing a prospect, though, to drive-in and grindhouse audiences, which is why *The Psychedelic Priest*—AKA *Jesus Freak,* AKA *Electric Shades of Grey*—was never released when it was made. It's a shame, since the film contains one of the most genuinely silly freakout-in-a-church sequences ever filmed, as well as an "upbeat" conclusion that makes a return to the Church seem about as dismal a prospect for a young person as a life spent "on the needle."

The plot concerns young Father John, who one afternoon tries to talk sense to a group of teens playing hooky (and smoking some devil-weed). The naive young priest accepts the offer of a cup of Coke from the devious young stoners, and he's off on a trip.

When next seen, John has deserted the priesthood, is living out of his car, and says things like "Far out. . . . I dig ya, man." John picks up a hitchhiker named Sunny, who immediately feels a kinship with the grubby young ex-priest. When she reveals her infatuation for him, he rejects her, which causes Sunny to go back on the road, do a lot of illegal stuff (all spoken of but not seen, in the truest no-budget tradition), and winds up a suicide statistic. A distraught John turns to alcohol and eventually heroin, until . . . a local church group saves his life. The moviemakers attempt some severe symmetry as John, back in the priesthood, once again makes a move to caution some druggin' young'uns.

The above description makes the movie sound like a tidy little feature, but it actually is a meandering, episodic mess. Director William Grefé has stated that when production began, there was no script or shooting schedule. At that point, nonprofessionals (including the two leads) were recruited, local hippies were pressed into service as crew members, and the dialogue was, for the most part, improvised.

Grefé refused a direction credit for the movie because when it was made he was working in an important capacity for the Ivan Tors Studio, which produced family fare like *Gentle Ben* and *Flipper*. Scripter-producer Stewart "Terry" Merrill was credited instead, but it's important to note that a veteran low-budget auteur like Grefé was really at the helm, if only because the movie brazenly mimics the gloomy, end-of-the-dream ambience of *Easy Rider* (Grefé was known for following trends—he made *Stanley* after *Willard* and *Mako, Jaws of Death* after *Jaws*). A noble black doctor is beaten to death by rednecks, Sunny tells about being raped in a graveyard while stoned (the overlaid visuals reek of *Easy Rider*'s famous cemetery sequence), and our collarless hero in one scene decides to hop a late-night freight train to take his smack-snack.

Priest's haphazard creation is best reflected by Grefé's inclusion of countless nature sequences (perhaps a lesson learned on Tors productions) in which our two leads wander through Southern California's picturesque countryside. Of course, sloppily made "message pictures" always contain special delights. Here, a scene where boozehound John is harassed by a barroom loudmouth has the pungent aroma of the best '60s drive-in films—the heckler calls our hero a "whiffenpoof" and defines a hippie as someone who "looks like a Jill but smells like a john." The most repeat-worthy sequence, however, is the aforementioned church-set acid trip. Darrell gives a Bill Shatner-esque, head-clutching, face-twisting turn, while he views his surroundings as if through the wrong end of a telescope. The Virgin Mary statue, altar, and votive candles are all real, as Grefé and crew "stole" shots one night without authorization in a local Southern California church. The very fact that John returns to the bosom of the church, and is *still* eager to caution another group of sinning young folk at the movie's end, proves that, despite his travails, he never learned the cardinal rule of tripping: a little dose'll do ya.

1971 (R) 81m/C John Darrell, Carolyn Hall, Joe Crane, Ken Keckler, Larry Wright. **D:** William Grefé (credited to Stewart Merrill). **W:** Terry Merrill. **C:** William Grefé. *VHS, DVD* **AKA:** *Electric Shades of Grey; Jesus Freak*

—Ed Grant

Psych-Out ♫♫♫♪

All hail Dick Clark! He was the producer and guiding force behind this film, which, flaws, kitsch, and all, must rank as the *Citizen Kane* of the late-'60s Haight-Ashbury scene, a groovy movie par excellence.

Deaf teen runaway Jennie (Susan Strasberg) arrives in the wild youth-whirlpool of San Francisco, trying to find her artist brother Steve, alias "the Seeker," who left a clue to his whereabouts in a postcard reading "God is alive and well inside a sugar cube." Police are looking for the AWOL juvenile, but Jennie is saved from the dragnet by members of Mumblin' Jim, a rock band fronted by ponytailed Stoney (Jack Nicholson) and backed up by Ben (Adam Roarke) and Elwood (Max Julien). They welcome Jennie into their Victorian-style crash pad and a vehicle that looks like the same multicolored van the Scooby Doo gang would later drive as the Mystery Machine.

> "Reality is a deadly place. I hope this trip is a good one."
>
> —Dave (Dean Stockwell), in *Psych-Out*

Stoney agrees to help seek the Seeker, and at the same time he readies his bandmates for a major gig. He finds himself falling for innocent Jennie, even though his dropout buddy and self-appointed spiritual adviser, Dave (Dean Stockwell), looks down on both material success and sexual attachments. "It's all a plastic hassle," he declares.

The elusive Steve briefly materializes, trying to take back his sculptures from an art gallery. It's Bruce Dern, in a stringy Apache wig the filmmaker's wardrobe department borrowed from a western. He promises Stoney he'll reunite with Jennie at the big Mumblin' Jim concert, but the rendezvous is foiled by a marauding pack of right-wingers—heavy-handed villains-of-convenience whose existence seems to revolve around beating up the Seeker for earlier verbal endorsements of peace and love. Their pursuit accidentally starts a fire. Dave, putting his own moves on Jennie, turns her on to the latest drug craze, a cocaine/LSD/meth cocktail called STP. Jennie wanders the streets, tripping. By the end of the eventful night, two of the major characters are dead. As Dave observes, "Reality is a deadly place."

For budgetary reasons, Clark and director Richard Rush orchestrated most of the shooting in Los Angeles rather than San Francisco, but they still managed to capture the seductive excess of Bay Area counterculture in full head-shop flower, an eye-popping display of acid-influenced poster art ("God Grows His Own"), bead webs, public "happenings," and lycanthropic sideburns. Yet what sounds like pure camp comes across on-screen as a savvy and effective look at the lifestyle, with its ecstatic highs, devastating lows, and ultimate disillusionment. Sharp dialogue, clever camerawork, snappy pacing, pure goofiness (in the midst of a junkyard tussle with the Nixonian hardhats, Julien suddenly dreams he's a knight, fight-

ing a dragon), and Laszlo Kovacs's celebrated cinematography keep things moving along at a nice clip.

Nicholson and Adam Roarke were both coming off leads in the Richard Rush biker flicks *Hell's Angels on Wheels* (Roarke and Nicholson) and *The Savage Seven* (Roarke), and there was no way they would be caught playing flower-power weenies; instead they infused their characters with restlessness, humor, and anger. Susan Strasberg, daughter of famed Method-acting coach Lee Strasberg (and, briefly, wife of *Wild in the Streets* actor Christopher Jones), does what she can in the more-symbolism-than-substance role of the deaf teen (the actress was actually pushing thirty) who uses no sign language and seems to have little difficulty communicating otherwise. Late in the story we learn that her hearing loss is psychosomatic, à la *Tommy,* the legacy of an abusive mother. Henry Jaglom and Gary Marshall, later better known as directors, have small parts respectively as a freaking-out hippie and a plainclothes (and thus painfully obvious in Haight-Ashbury) cop.

Music-wise, the Seeds and the Strawberry Alarm Clock provide most of the tunes, including the latter's classic "Incense and Peppermints." Mumblin' Jim's sound is credited to a group named Boenzee Cryque, though their big instrumental in the movie is a blatant ripoff of Jimi Hendrix's "Purple Haze."

Dick Clark originally wanted to call the movie *The Love Children,* but he was told audiences would believe it was a film about illegitimate babies. The

Jack Nicholson plays Stoney and Dean Stockwell is Dave, his spiritual adviser, in the Dick Clark–produced *Psych-Out.*

DARREN ARONOFSKY: DREAM WEAVER by Lou Gaul

If Darren Aronofsky earned his living as a boxer, he'd never be allowed to participate in an exhibition match. This guy just can't hold his punches.

After gaining international attention with his fascinating $60,000 debut film, *Pi,* the director decided against going Hollywood. Instead, the Harvard graduate opted to make *Requiem for a Dream,* an extremely hard-edged $4.5 million film based on Hubert Selby Jr.'s 1978 novel about ill-fated Coney Island addicts hooked on heroin and speed. With its graphic shots of people shooting up and working in the sex trade to support their habits, Aronofsky knew the members of the Motion Picture Association of America's ratings board might be shocked, but he still expected an "R" rating.

Rating Game

The MPAA, however, kept slapping *Requiem for a Dream* with an "NC-17," an action that prompted Aronofsky and his distributor, Artisan Entertainment, to release it unrated.

"There's a lot of shortsightedness with the ratings board," Aronofsky said during an interview at the time of the film's release. "When you show something real and intense, like drug addiction and its effects, they just can't deal with it.

"My film is psychologically intense, and it has a supercharged climax [involving Jennifer Connelly as a heroin addict who performs sex acts for entertainment at an all-male party] that a lot of people respond to in a very strong way."

Final Cut

For many young directors, a failure to obtain an "R" rating from the MPAA would result in the studio taking away the film and cutting it. According to Aronofsky, that was never the case with the executives at Artisan.

"The studio really understood the nature of the film and understood that it would be undermined and damaged if it wasn't released in an uncut form," he said. "From the beginning, it was pretty clear that this was the film I wanted to make. It's intense, sometimes surreal.

"*Requiem* is not necessarily a traditionally commercial movie, but there's an audience that hungers for this type of [no-holds-barred] film."

With *Requiem for a Dream,* the Brooklyn native had the opportunity to work with veteran actress Ellen Burstyn. He credited the Oscar-winning actress, who plays a woman obsessed by her weight and hooked on diet pills in *Requiem,* for teaching him more about acting than any other performer.

"Every five minutes she was on the set, I learned something from Ellen," he said. "During my career, capturing Ellen on screen is the greatest thing with which I've ever been involved.

"It was amazing to watch her work."

title *Psych-Out* came courtesy of American International Pictures exec Samuel Z. Arkoff, who saw dollar signs in the phonetic echo of Hitchcock's *Psycho.*

1968 (R) 82m/C Susan Strasberg, Jack Nicholson, Dean Stockwell, Max Julien, Adam Roarke, Bruce Dern, Henry Jaglom. ***D:*** Richard Rush. ***W:*** E. Hunter Willett, Betty Ulius. ***C:*** Laszlo Kovacs. ***M:*** Ronald Stein. *VHS, DVD*

Requiem for a Dream ♫♫♪

Jared Leto, in the role of Harry, is a junkie on a downward spiral in Darren Aronofsky's *Requiem for a Dream.*

Drugs aren't just for kids anymore. That could be taken as the moral of Darren Aronofsky's showy '60s-style junkie saga *Requiem for a Dream.* The film is based on a 1978 novel by one of the bards of addiction/paranoia literature, Hubert Selby Jr. (*Last Exit to Brooklyn*). Aronofsky's gritty, hyperkinetic visuals make the film largely a triumph of style over substance. Certain two-character scenes are extremely effective, however, which makes it all the more disappointing when Aronofsky resorts to gimmicky editing, camerawork, and framing to drive home a scene's point.

The screenplay is uncommonly faithful to the book; in fact, a good deal of the dialogue comes directly off the page. Structured as a group character study, *Requiem* centers around a quartet of drug addicts. Harry (Jared Leto) and Tyrone (Marlon Wayans) are junkies who are scrounging to stay supplied and nurturing a dream: to score "a pound of pure," which they can resell at exorbitant prices to local addicts. Harry's artistically inclined girlfriend Marion (Jennifer Connelly) shares this dream, but she often has to be the source of funds for the project, earning money by supplying favors to her lust-filled therapist. In the meantime, Harry's mother, Sara (Ellen Burstyn), a TV-addicted senior citizen, becomes hooked on diet pills after receiving notification that she's been chosen to appear on a game show. The parallel plotlines chart a downward course as the junkies break the dealer's first law—never sample thy own stash—and Sara becomes a remarkably thinner, and unbelievably wired, old lady. She thrives on her memories, while her son and his friends dwell in their dreams.

TUESDAY WELD: NOT EVERYTHING WAS PRETTY

by Ed Grant

Tuesday Weld

THE KOBAL COLLECTION

Many actresses in the '50s and '60s swiftly moved from playing nymphets to tackling more adult roles, but none did it with the exuberance, talent, and surprisingly eccentric indifference of Tuesday Weld. Weld's progress as a performer is best illustrated by her filmography: from *Sex Kittens Go to College* (1960) to *Play It As It Lays* (1972) in twelve years is a stunning trajectory that shows Weld's strength of character and her interesting preference for noncommercial projects.

Susie's Cue

Born Susan Ker Weld, the New York City native's early life was difficult. She once declared to an interviewer that she had a nervous breakdown as a nine-year-old child model, was frequently drunk at age ten, and made her first suicide attempt at age twelve. By age fifteen, she had moved to Hollywood, where she appeared in Bob Hope and Danny Kaye vehicles, then graduated to "Elvis's girlfriend" status (in *Wild in the Country,* 1961) and did a memorable stint as the money-hungry Thalia Menninger on the *Dobie Gillis* TV series. She began playing serious romantic leads when she costarred with Steve McQueen in *Soldier in the Rain* (1963) and *The Cincinnatti Kid* (1965), but she cut loose from the "good girl" stereotype in George Axelrod's delightfully dark 1966 satire of teenage fads, *Lord Love a Duck.*

In *Duck,* Weld plays a greedy, self-centered high school senior courted by a lovesick teenager (Roddy McDowall) with a wild imagination. As the film proceeds, McDowall finds a way to get her everything she wants, including stardom in films made by an upscale exploitation producer (Axelrod's spot-on spoof of the mentality that produced William Asher's *Beach Party* movies), yet she still remains out of his reach. The film is a smart social satire dressed up as a wistful, swingin' teenage love story. Axelrod's inclusion of dramatic elements amidst the broad comedy underscores the fact that Weld's character isn't simply a bitch, she's also a trendaholic who believes what the media has taught her about happiness.

Poisoned Parts

Weld's cult status solidified with the critically lauded 1968 sleeper *Pretty Poison.* A perfect '60s allegory about the nature of evil, the film cast Weld as a high school majorette whose wholesome veneer conceals her violent, scheming tendencies. Her newfound older boyfriend (Anthony Perkins), considered a "threat to society" due to his pyromaniac past, is revealed to be nothing more than a neurotic dreamer. In 1968, *Poison* effectively functioned as both sordid entertainment and searing social satire: the fact that its all-American heroine is more volatile than her "weirdo" boyfriend was a potent metaphor for the straight/"freak" division being made among American youth at the time. The film was the finest achievement of its scripter, Lorenzo Semple Jr. (whose more memorable efforts include the *Batman* feature, *The Parallax View,* and the dreaded '76 *King Kong*), and director, Noel Black (whose other best-known titles are the '80s make-out movie *Private School . . . for Girls* and the TV movie *The Quarterback Princess*). The rave reviews the film received put the spotlight on Weld, ensuring that her "sexpot" days were over, and she was ready for meatier roles.

Oddly enough, shortly before *Poison,* Weld began a trend that looms large in her legend: turning down lead roles in films that were destined to be hits. *Bonnie and Clyde, Rosemary's Baby, Bob & Carol & Ted & Alice*—Tuesday rejected them all outright. The movies she *did* choose to act in during this period were downbeat character pieces, like John Frankenheimer's *I Walk the Line.* As in her previous two films, Weld's performance as a moonshiner's daughter who seduces a Tennessee sheriff (Gregory Peck) was an inversion of the *Lolita*-like roles she had played prior to *Lord Love a Duck;* the finale of *Line* is a stark bit of violence that doubtless left the average viewer with a bad aftertaste, but it was perfectly in keeping with the grimly authentic tone Frankenheimer maintains throughout the picture.

Weld graduated to fully adult parts in the early 1970s, when she played women suffering identity crises in Henry Jaglom's *A Safe Place* and Frank Perry's *Play It As It Lays.* The former is a bumpy affair about a free spirit who is defined by the men in her life—to the extent that she is trippily called different names in different sequences. The film is composed mostly of dreamlike two-character scenes in which Weld interacts with costars Philip Proctor, Jack Nicholson, and Orson Welles; the stars are often photographed looking directly into the camera, thus offering the chance for Welles and Weld to overwhelm the viewer with both profoundly poignant sentiment and overtly hammy behavior (which means they're still both thoroughly charming). *Play It As It Lays* is a terrific actor's showcase in which Weld plays a washed-up actress who experiences a nervous breakdown. The strongest sequences reunite her with Tony Perkins, playing one of his most demanding, least Norman Bates–like characters. The two performers had seemingly grown up considerably on-screen and off in the four short years since *Pretty Poison,* and thus their scenes together betray a shared cynicism that is both wryly amusing and deeply moving.

In the years after *Play It,* Weld's career choices continued to be erratic: fans would sit through her TV movies (including stylish but pointless remakes of *Diabolique* and *Madame X*) for the occasional flash of brilliance, but her sole performances of note were in two uncommonly intelligent action pictures, Karel Reisz's *Who'll Stop the Rain?* (1978) and Michael Mann's *Thief* (1981); the very funny "me generation" spoof *Serial* (1980); and *Looking for Mr. Goodbar* (1977). *Goodbar* is a tough, grim film that offered Diane Keaton a tour de force lead role, but Weld steals every scene she's in, playing Keaton's ultracynical sister.

These days, Weld continues to turn in the occasional supporting performance, but it became evident in the 1980s that she wasn't interested in pursuing the sort of demanding, often alienating roles that cemented her reputation amongst critics and what she herself once sarcastically referred to as "the Tuesday Weld cult." Whatever Weld's feelings about her past work may be, she remains one of the most intriguing and luminous actresses of the late '60s and "maverick" '70s. Her ability to shed her sex kitten image and then effectively incarnate a series of complex, urban women in crisis made her deserving of a cult. It appears that the lady herself wouldn't have had it any other way.

Certain sequences in *Requiem* are sublime, most notably an encounter between Harry and Sara in which the son notices that his mother has some sort of drug dependency. Sara's heartbreaking loneliness is conveyed through the combination of Selby's declarative, slang-ridden dialogue and Burstyn's impeccable acting. The sequences that grate are those in which Aronofsky settles for an attention-getting technical touch to convey an action. For example, to avoid showing the characters shoot up time after time, he concocts a quick montage of close-up shots (hypo, flame, blood cell, eye dilating) punctuated by a rapid series of popping, burning, and hissing sounds. The MTV-style montage merely distracts from the drama.

The film's casting is intriguing but inconsistent. Leto and Connelly are altogether too picture-perfect to play junkies effectively. Not only are their freak-out sequences largely illustrated through Aronofsky's moody visuals rather than straightforward acting, but their fresh, movie-star faces make them wildly inappropriate choices to play seasoned junkies. Wayans acquits himself nicely in the underwritten role of Tyrone; surprisingly, his character becomes the most human at the film's conclusion, his personal "dream" being the simplest and most touching of all. Ellen Burstyn does wonders with Sara. Clearly not as old or as overweight as the role requires, she still renders Sara a three-dimensional being, despite the plethora of filmic techniques that Aronofsky trots out during her "speed freak" sequences.

Aside from its gaudy, film-school attitude, *Requiem* is a film that does linger in the memory, with Aronofsky's more placid, static images of the cherished dreams and memories of his characters carrying much more weight than his jump-cut montages. (Viewers interested in a less distracting rendition of Selby's trendsetting fiction, though, are referred to Uli Edel's starkly disturbing adaptation of *Last Exit to Brooklyn*.) Even with its relentless tragedy and despair, *Requiem* does boast one rather positive side effect for viewers: after seeing Sara's descent into madness come about largely as a result of her son's neglect, adults everywhere will feel compelled to phone home and check in on Mom.

2000 (R) 102m/C Ellen Burstyn, Jared Leto, Jennifer Connelly, Marlon Wayans, Christopher McDonald, Louise Lasser. **D:** Darren Aronofsky. **W:** Hubert Selby Jr., Darren Aronofsky. **C:** Matthew Libatique. **M:** Clint Mansell. *VHS, DVD*

—Ed Grant

A Safe Place

Most people today know Henry Jaglom as the independent auteur who, for decades, has cast himself, friends, girlfriends, wives, and ex-wives in touchy-feely, improvisational relationship movies such as *Eating, Venice/Venice,* and *Festival in Cannes.* But Jaglom got his start as part of the crew at BBS, the influential late-'60s/early-'70s production company that gave the world *Head, Five Easy Pieces,* and *Easy Rider,* which Jaglom reportedly helped shear down to a palatable length.

In 1971 Jaglom made his directorial debut with *A Safe Place,* an experimental fantasy that plays like an *Annie Hall*–era Woody Allen movie on acid.

But unlike a vintage Allen movie, there are few laughs here. Instead, Jaglom and his eclectic cast want to keep things mysterious and fanciful, which means the film doesn't unfold in any sort of conventional style. The whole confounding enterprise doesn't really add up to much, but you sure can't beat it for old-fashioned hippie-era weirdness.

Tuesday Weld, at the height of her beauty, is the focal point of the film, playing a woman who is sometimes called Susan, other times Noah. Susan/Noah hangs out in and around Central Park. In a high-rise apartment, some of her friends sit around and smoke pot, while another rides a hobby horse and two women make out. Meanwhile, Susan/Noah talks about a magical box that has some link to her childhood. She also likes staring into a mirror. In the background, we hear music from the 1940s and Charles Trenet's "La Mer," the French version of the song that was later Americanized as "Beyond the Sea," recorded by Bobby Darin. Nostalgic stuff, but not exactly the sort of thing the counterculture was listening to at the time.

Susan/Noah continually rejects the advances of sincere and strait-laced Fred (Philip Proctor of the Firesign Theatre comedy group), a man who desperately wants to be her boyfriend. She has a recurring fantasy involving Mitch (Jack Nicholson), a raffish past boyfriend, coming on to her on a rooftop. After Nicholson throws that patented "Jack grin" in short segments whenever Susan/Noah thinks of him, he and Susan/Noah hook up for an extended make-out session that leads nowhere. Ah, fantasy.

At the same time, a magician, played by Orson Welles affecting a Russian accent that makes him sound like he's playing Tevye in a third-rate dinner-theater production of *Fiddler in the Roof,* fools around doing magic tricks in the park. He makes a huge silver ball float in the air and moves things around. When he attempts to make llamas and other animals disappear from the zoo, however, he comes up short. At one point, he holds the box that has fascinated Susan/Noah and makes a plastic rainbow appear from it, but he seems to have trouble finding out what's inside.

OK. We know what you're saying: "Huh?!" Well, join the club. Who can say what all of this means. Several themes are definitely present here, including Susan/Noah's desire to return to her childhood (or a child-like state), elusive loves and lovers, the need for wish-fulfillment, and the preference of fantasy to reality. But they remain just themes—none is explored in any linear, sensible manner. Making matters worse is Jaglom's fragmented, frazzled structure, a definite salute to French New Wave masters, especially Jean-Luc Godard. With a plethora of zoom shots, scenes where characters address the camera, choppy editing, odd juxtapositions, and actors going on improvisatory jags, babbling on but not making a whole lot of sense (Weld and Proctor have an endless conversation about phone exchanges), you have to believe Jaglom either wanted to alienate his audience or is trying for some groundbreaking form of cinematic poetry that simply does not translate onto the big screen. Or maybe a little of both.

In a 1987 interview, Jaglom claimed *A Safe Place* ran for seven years in Europe but didn't get a fair shake in America because Columbia Pictures promoted it as a romance in the tradition of *Love Story.* It was this experience, Jaglom said, that made him steer away from major studios, finding

PREMINGER PROBED BY THE FEDS

The FBI was so unhappy with a scene in *Skidoo* in which Jackie Gleason's gangster is pursued by G-men after stealing a filing cabinet from the FBI building in Washington that they investigated Gleason and producer-director Otto Preminger. While Gleason was given a clean bill of health from the bureau, they discovered Preminger had ties to the Communist Party in the 1950s and to blacklisted writer Dalton Trumbo (who scripted Preminger's *Exodus*). Although noting the scene's comedic nature, the FBI strongly urged in a memo that it be excised from the completed film. Preminger responded with a letter, claiming he had "the utmost respect for FBI Director [J. Edgar Hoover], whom he had personally met . . . and that he would not present anything unfavorable to the Bureau in any picture." The filmmaker even took it a step further, stating that "the FBI should see the humor in the sequence" and that he would "welcome a test of the law in this case if the Department of Justice was so inclined." The Feds backed off, the scene was left intact . . . and the film did a "23 skidoo" anyway.

financing from independent sources instead. Strangely enough, *A Safe Place* was adapted as a play that opened in Los Angeles in 2003.

Over the years, Jaglom's films have divided audiences, but none of them has come close to *A Safe Place* in terms of all-out weirdness. No wonder they loved it in Europe.

1971 (R) 91m Tuesday Weld, Philip Proctor, Jack Nicholson, Orson Welles, Gwen Welles, Sylvia Zapp, Richard Finocchio. *D:* Henry Jaglom. *W:* Henry Jaglom. *C:* Richard C. Kratina. *VHS*

Skidoo ♪♪♪

In the late 1960s and early 1970s, veteran Hollywood directors were afraid of losing touch with the youthful ticket-buying public. So, they decided to meet the younger generation of moviegoers head-on, talking the talk and walking the walk of the times. Otto Preminger, the testy, head-shaven producer-director of such classic films as *Laura* and *Anatomy of a Murder* and such large-scale epics as *Exodus* and *The Cardinal,* decided that the time was ripe not only to chronicle the contemporary world of sex, drugs, and rock 'n' roll, but also to experience it personally. Preminger—hubby of famed stripper Gypsy Rose Lee and best known to the in crowd as "Mr. Freeze" on the *Batman* TV series—had a nifty idea: hang out with counterculture guru Timothy Leary and drop some acid in the name of research for his newest project.

Skidoo, the result of his exploratory efforts, makes perfect sense in the scheme of things: it's an old pro's hunch at what would make the kids feel groovy at the time. Preminger decided to dose a gangster flick starring stalwarts from his generation with hippies, rock music, and dope. So he has Jackie Gleason at his most dour playing Tony Banks, a midlevel gangster facing a midlife crisis. Unhappily married to the flirtatious Flo (Carol Channing) and father to vacuous, free-spirited teenager Darlene (Alexandra Hay), Tony gets an assignment to kill old friend "Blue Chips" Packard (Mickey Rooney) in prison. In order to ensure the job gets done, Banks's superiors have him arrested and thrown into the pokey. While Banks fumes about his fate behind bars, his wife and daughter try to arrange his release by seducing Angie (Frankie Avalon), a smarmy mobster who has pull with God (Groucho Marx)—that is, the lead mobster in this racket. In the meantime, Banks plots an escape plan with a young radical prisoner named the Professor (Austin Pendleton). The plan? Have everyone in prison dosed with acid as Jackie scoots away in a balloon.

This storyline certainly guarantees *Skidoo* as a candidate for the most asinine plot in cinematic history. But a summary of the plot doesn't begin to describe how enjoyably demented the film can be at times. For starters, you have Jackie Gleason—Ralph Kramden, folks—taking LSD. And away he goes, hallucinating about machine guns, eyeballs, and numbers while swatting imaginary flies coming right at him. Ultimately, the trip leads to his fateful decision that it's time to give up a life of crime. See, acid is good, youngsters.

Then there's Groucho Marx, in his last screen appearance, as a no-nonsense gangster chief who lives on a yacht, smokes joints, and can't stay away from his mistress, a statuesque black model. Reportedly, Groucho tripped out for research as well. Is that the most ridiculous thing you ever heard?

Not yet. Because in *Skidoo,* say "Hello, Dolly" to middle-aged Carol Channing, stripping down to her bra and panties in order to seduce mustachioed beach-party king Avalon! Frankie doesn't even list the film on his official biography.

Certainly it would be tough to top this crazed cast that also includes two—count 'em!—*Batman* villains (Frank "The Riddler" Gorshin and Cesar "The Joker" Romero), Arnold Stang (the voice of cartoon character "Top Cat"), Roman Gabriel (quarterback of the Los Angeles Rams), Richard Kiel ("Jaws" of the James Bond movies), Rat Pack member Peter Lawford, tough guy George Raft, good ol' boy Slim Pickens, and "Everybody's Talkin'" singer-songwriter Harry Nilsson, appearing as a prison guard as well as singing the entire—including "key grip"—end credits!

When *Skidoo* opened, it bombed at the box office, probably because the kids didn't care about Gleason, Channing, and company, while the older audience couldn't relate to the drug and hippie references. Today, it stands the test of time as a fascinating generation-colliding wonder, masquerading, of course, as insightful social satire. Maybe, just maybe, that's exactly what acid-ingesting Otto ordered.

1968 (PG) 97m/C Jackie Gleason, Carol Channing, Frankie Avalon, Groucho Marx, Alexandra Hay, Mickey Rooney, Frank Gorshin, Arnold Stang, Peter Lawford, John Phillip Law, Cesar Romero, Roman Gabriel, George Raft, Slim Pickens, Harry Nilsson, Richard Kiel. **D:** Otto Preminger. **W:** Doran William Cannon. **C:** Leon Shamroy. **M:** Harry Nilsson. *VHS*

DRUG WARNING FILMS: LOOK OUT FOR POT, PILLS, AND PSYCHEDELICS
by Bruce Klauber

Reefer Madness poster

THE KOBAL COLLECTION

Drugs. Controlled substances. Weed. Blow. Pot. Reefer. Hollywood moviemakers have been saying the same thing about "the stuff" for over fifty years: use drugs and you'll go blind and/or insane, and then you'll probably die. Never mind that the same good people making these films were probably stoned out of their collective gourds when they made these pictures.

In terms of rotten movies, *Reefer Madness* still stands as the granddaddy of them all, often named on "ten worst films of all time" lists, right next to *Bela Lugosi Meets a Brooklyn Gorilla*. This 1936 opus is still a howler when viewed today, with the focus being "the devil weed with its roots in hell." See young high schoolers get turned on by stoned, adult pushers. Watch teens go nuts after taking one puff of the weed. See them dance faster and faster. Watch them go insane and die. And dig that crazy piano solo. The alternate titles say it all: *The Burning Question* and *Tell Your Children*.

Weed and Coke Are It

With all the deserved acclaim that *Reefer Madness* got on the midnight cult circuit, it wasn't the first film of its kind. In 1933 the exploitation team of Dwain and Hildegarde Esper (best known for *Maniac* from the following year, fondly remembered for the "eating the cat's eye" segment) produced something called *Narcotic*. This movie told the tale of a medical student who starts smoking pot, then opium. Eventually, he starts frequenting houses of ill repute. While we hate to give away any film's ending, it's pretty clear that only death can be the end result.

Marihuana (film's original spelling) from 1936 and *Marijuana: Assassin of Youth* from 1935 were two almost-forgotten quickies released before *Reefer Madness* that cover the same ground. *Assassin of Youth* is the story of a young lady, played by Luana Walters, whose life is destroyed after she smokes a reefer. And this thing clocks in at seventy-four minutes! The message of *Marihuana* is simple: "Did you know that the use of marihuana is steadily increasing among the youth of this country?" For shame. And what will this increase mean? According to this picture, what started out as a teenage pot party will lead to insanity, murder, pregnancy and . . . insanity.

Reefer wasn't the only drug danger out there in the 1930s. *Cocaine Fiends* from 1937 spells out just what will happen if you happen to sniff that white powder. In the course of fifty-seven minutes, this film makes it clear that using coke will make users want to listen to hot swing music, have sex, and then, of course, die.

After *Cocaine Fiends,* the drug-film novelty wore off for a time, but in 1942, Hollywood covered the subject again with the release of something called *The Devil's Harvest.* This one actually had a plot, as incoherent as it was. Seems that high school students buy pot from a hot dog vendor, who obviously had more to offer than Hebrew Nationals. Everyone then must answer to a higher authority when a girl is accidentally killed in the midst of a reefer and booze party. The plot thickens when one of the girls' friends goes undercover as a showgirl. Remember, we did say "incoherent."

Just Say "No"

In 1949 film star Robert Mitchum was arrested for possession of pot, which caused quite a furor in the press. The young lady who was with Mitchum at the time of the bust, an actress by the name of Lila Leeds, saw a real chance at making a few bucks out of the mess, so she appeared in a picture called *She Shoulda Said No*. Leeds maintained that she would be personally and professionally "redeemed" by appearing in this film, which is the tale of a chorus girl who ends her "addiction" to the weed. Unfortunately, no one cared too much about Leeds or this film, which later carried the more sensational title of *Wild Weed*.

Lotus-land producers saw great opportunities in the 1950s, by combining aspects of juvenile delinquency with drugs. In *The Flaming Teenager* from 1956, half of the story deals with booze, the other half with drugs. The plot of the drug section is simple: a drug addict becomes an evangelist. Who woulda thought?

What better element to add to the drug and delinquency mix than motorcycle gangs? This combo was actually achieved in 1956 via a film called *One-Way Ticket to Hell*. A disturbed teen girl (Barbara Marks) hangs out with a cycle gang, becomes addicted to pills, pot, and smack, and then is forced to become a dealer on behalf of "Mr. Big." But she takes the cure in the end by going cold turkey in Mexico. The alternate title is even better than the original: *Teenage Devil Dolls*.

Two years later, *The Narcotic Story* told the tale, in pseudo-documentary style, of the whole sordid business of controlled substances. The whole business, of course, includes drug addicts, pushers, all kinds of dope, and the police who attempt to save these juvenile delinquents from a terrible, terrible fate.

Some of these projects must have made money, if even only at the drive-in, because film studios (however small) continued to grind these things out. *Curfew Breakers* from 1958 follows a narc in action as he rips the lid off on drugs and the questionable goings-on at everything from pool parties to taprooms with jukeboxes.

Taking Trips

The '60s had their share of drug message movies centering on the most popular artificial stimulants of the day. LSD was represented in a number of offerings. In *The Weird World of LSD*, the frightening effects of dropping acid are shown. Did you know when you eat a sandwich you can turn into a Roman emperor scarfing down a leg of mutton? *The Acid Eaters*, a 1968 offering produced by exploitation king David F. Friedman, shows how taking LSD affects a group of bikers and their chicks when they go out ot the country. And *Alice in Acidland* tells the cautionary tale of a a young girl named Alice and her journey to hippiedom, which is laced with LSD experiences.

Of course, acid was not the only drug of choice in the 1960s. Opium and its dangers were the focus of *Poppies Are Also Flowers*, a big-budget all-star propaganda outing that's known by about seven different titles on home video, including *The Opium Connection*. Produced for TV by the United Nations, the film boasts an international cast that includes Yul Brynner, Stephen Boyd,

Trevor Howard, E. G. Marshall, Angie Dickinson, Rita Hayworth, Omar Sharif, and Grace Kelly (who provided the introduction). The story deals with drug-smuggling espionage in the Middle East and special UN agents' attempts to halt it. The film has many James Bond connections, including direction by Terence Young (*Dr. No, From Russia with Love, Thunderball*), a story by Ian Fleming (penned shortly before his death), and an appearance by Harold "Oddjob" Sakata around the same time of his commercials for Hai Karate, a man's aftershave. With stilted dialogue, wooden performances by that all-star cast, and annoying moralizing about the dangers of drugs, *Poppies* is also a snoozer, much less entertaining than those Hai Karate commercials.

The Trip ♫♫♫

Just say yes/no/maybe to drugs. Roger Corman figured, accurately, that while many people would never take LSD, everyone was curious about what a hallucinatory "trip" would be like. So he sought to give ticket-buyers this vicarious thrill in the comfort of their own theater seats. This minimally plotted, quintessentially psychedelic feature resulted.

Paul Groves (Peter Fonda), a West Coast director of TV commercials, faces an impending divorce from his wife Sally (Susan Strasberg), among other pressures. He decides to sort himself out by experimenting with LSD, under the supervision of drug guru John (Bruce Dern, who, in full beard and gentle demeanor, looks uncannily like Muppet creator Jim Henson). Paul's visions begin serenely, with brilliant colors and idyllic landscapes (scenes shot in Big Sur). Gradually, however, spectral *Lord of the Rings*–type horsemen and death-like figures appear in his vision, sweeping Paul up in a procession that takes him to an inquisitor figure (Dennis Hopper, who also directed a few sequences), and, ultimately, Paul's own funeral and cremation.

At one point a paranoid Paul thinks he's seen John murdered, and he bolts into the night, blissfully staring at washers in a laundromat, trespassing in a family home, and watching Vietnam bulletins on TV with a little girl. In a Sunset Strip music club, the wanderer is recognized by a casual acquaintance, Glenn (Salli Sachse), a sexy blonde who gets off being around people tripping out. They make love at her place, and in the morning Paul feels reborn and renewed. However, due to some last-minute tinkering—against Corman's objections—by *The Trip*'s nervous producers, a closing shot, as well as an opening disclaimer, leave in question whether Paul's trip was a good one or a bad one after all.

Although it promises to be über-camp, especially when "groovy" seems to turn up in every line of the script penned by actor Jack Nicholson, a longtime Corman cohort, *The Trip* plays surprisingly well even decades later, with the actors gamely hitting their marks in a sincere manner. Fonda, Nicholson, and Hopper all had prior LSD experience, but ironically, the movie's Timothy Leary stand-in, Dern, was actually a straight arrow who refused to get into the narcotics scene. Director Corman famously dropped acid, under close supervision, to research the effects firsthand. His visions, of a ship in the clouds turning into jewels, which turned into a beautiful woman, sound like something that computer-generated special effects three decades later could have realized. But in the 1960s such mind-blowers were practically unfilmable, especially on an American International Pictures budget. In fact, some might notice a resemblance between the mock-medieval costumes and props in Paul Groves's visions and those in the Edgar Allan Poe chillers Corman had wrapped for AIP.

Some psychedelic effects were created by multifaceted filters, strobes, and projected patterns put together by special-effects techs who normally specialized in light shows for rock concerts. Some of the imagery is quite startling, while some of it looks like soft-focus tinsel, Lite Brite, and secondhand Vincent Price dungeons. One could argue that the non-narrative *Head* (also written by Nicholson) or parts of *Chappaqua* are trippier than *The Trip,* but at least Corman's intentions seem good. Peter Fonda in particular was bummed out by the finished film's more conventional elements and publicly called the ending a "cop-out." His disappointment with compromises on the picture fueled his outlaw enthusiasm for his next collaboration with Hopper and Nicholson, the classic *Easy Rider.*

Meanwhile, for a sort of index of *The Trip*'s potency, note that this 1960s classic was officially banned in Britain until 2003.

1967 (R) 79m/C Peter Fonda, Bruce Dern, Dennis Hopper, Susan Strasberg, Salli Sachse, Barboura Morris, Luana Anders. *D:* Roger Corman. *W:* Jack Nicholson. *C:* Archie R. Dalzell. *M:* Barry Goldberg. *VHS, DVD*

—*Charles A. Cassidy Jr.*

Poster for Roger Corman's *The Trip*

AIP / THE KOBAL COLLECTION

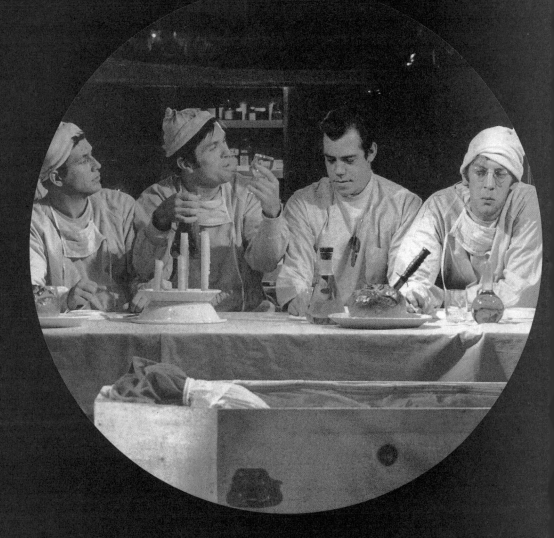

Chapter 9

Military Madness

War is hell and Vietnam was certainly no picnic, but you'd barely have known the conflict in Southeast Asia existed if you were watching films from the late 1960s to the early 1970s.

The conflict in Southeast Asia was actually depicted first in the 1950s. Samuel Fuller's two-fisted *China Gate* (1957) told of racist American and Korean War vet Gene Barry's involvement in the Vietnamese-Chinese conflict. A year later, Oscar-winning director Joseph L. Mankiewicz (*All about Eve*) was the first to tackle Graham Greene's *The Quiet American,* with Audie Murphy as the title character, a Yank economic adviser whose interests in covert arms dealing and a beautiful Vietnamese woman in Saigon draw the attention of Michael Redgrave, a British journalist married to that woman. Unlike the controversial 2002 version of the story with Brendan Fraser and Michael Caine, the 1958 film softens the author's criticism of American involvement in that region of the world.

For most of the 1960s, Hollywood was gun-shy about portraying a bloody, unpredictable war that frightened and divided a nation. Throughout the decade, the studios had no problem churning out expensive, war-related sagas such as *The Longest Day, The Dirty Dozen, Battle of the Bulge,* and *Tora! Tora! Tora!* as long as they were about World War II, a conflict all Americans could get behind.

It wasn't until *The Green Berets* (1968) that the public was given a film that directly dealt with the Vietnam War. Pulling in an impressive (for that time) $8 million at the box office, John Wayne's jingoistic, let's-kick-Commie-ass effort may have scored with older audiences who supported the war (and saw everything Duke starred in), or kids younger than draft age who could whistle the catchy Sergeant Barry Sadler tune or who thought the bamboo stick deaths looked wicked. But with over 200,000 troops "over there," body bags coming home every day, and television bringing the horrors into homes on a regular basis, *The Green Berets* angered many. It's hawkish approach wasn't going to make it with the angrier and more politicized young moviegoers who were taking part in protesting against the Vietnam War. The war had turned into a minefield that Hollywood decided was best left unexplored, at least directly.

Instead, the Vietnam War became an indirect presence—revealed in varying degrees—in a number of movies ostensibly tackling different subjects altogether. Counterculture hero John Lennon got a shot at acting in *A Hard Day's Night* and *Help!* director Richard Lester's *How I Won the War*, a 1967 World War II–based antiwar satire that openly referenced Vietnam. Robert Altman's *M*A*S*H*, from 1969, may have been set during the Korean War, but everyone knew the film was addressing the military protocol and bloody everyday events being played out in Vietnam. The satiric, antiauthoritarian spin of *M*A*S*H* proved to be an enormous success, leading director Mike Nichols to take a similar approach with *Catch-22*, an expensive all-star version of Joseph Heller's World War II–based novel, adapted for the screen by Buck Henry, *The Graduate*'s coscreenwriter. Again, the futility of war—and Vietnam in particular, in the shadows—was on the screen, but this time, despite its popular source material, the project didn't click with counterculture theatergoers, resulting in an expensive flop.

The failure of *Catch-22* didn't bode well for other war movies during the Vietnam era, but occasionally a small-scale film would slip through the cracks. Combat was avoided, but the plight of returning veterans became the focus of 1972's *Limbo*, concerning three wives of MIA soldiers in Florida; Robert Wise's 1973 film *Two People*, with Peter Fonda as an army deserter romantically involved with fashion model Lindsay Wagner in Marrakesh; and *Tracks*, Henry Jaglom's 1976 drama starring Dennis Hopper as a paranoid vet escorting his buddy's casket on a cross-country train ride. Meanwhile, 1976's *Taxi Driver* and 1977's *Rolling Thunder*, both penned by Paul Schrader, showed how the anger of troubled, returning vets fuels violent actions.

Aside from the controversial *Taxi Driver*, these well-intentioned films didn't draw large audiences, and *Limbo* was unceremoniously shelved by its studio. That's why *Coming Home*, the first studio release focusing on Vietnam to find a sizable audience, made such an impact. Hal Ashby's 1978 picture not only did well at the box office, it won Oscars for its screenplay and for stars Jane Fonda and Jon Voight.

Later that same year, Michael Cimino's sprawling and unsettling *The Deer Hunter* was released to critical praise and five Academy Awards, followed by Francis Ford Coppola's long-in-production *Apocalypse Now*. It took some time, but finally, with some distance, the Vietnam War was deemed a subject worthy of exploration, and American movies continued the fascination with that conflict with such films as *Platoon, Born on the Fourth of July*, and *Heaven and Earth* (all three from Vietnam veteran Oliver Stone), as well as *Hamburger Hill, The Hanoi Hilton, We Were Soldiers, Full Metal Jacket*, and many other notable efforts.

Apocalypse Now Redux ♫♫♫

Apocalypse Now was already a pretty terrific film when it was first released in 1979. But by adding fifty-three minutes of footage, Francis Ford Coppola turned it into a masterpiece.

Apocalypse Now was already a pretty terrific film when it was first released in 1979. But by adding fifty-three minutes of footage, Francis Ford Coppola turned it into a masterpiece.

Not that everything in *Redux* works. It's just that the passage of time and some of the new scenes make the film a richer, more meaningful experience. It now has the classic feel of historical epics like *Lawrence of Arabia.*

Of course, Coppola's first masterstroke was to take Joseph Conrad's innocence-lost masterpiece, *Heart of Darkness,* and transpose it to the Vietnam War. Coppola instinctively understood how that divisive conflict had corrupted nearly everything it touched, from the political process to personal morality. So the character of Marlon Brando's Colonel Kurtz, a brilliant officer who has apparently gone insane and set up his own private army in Cambodia, is a metaphor for America itself. And Martin Sheen's Captain Willard, the tortured officer sent upriver to terminate Kurtz "with extreme prejudice," is every soldier forced to do ugly things for reasons he can barely understand.

Redux follows a story arc that is as creepy as it is fascinating to watch. The film is a case study on the surreal experience of Vietnam: Willard freaking out in his Saigon hotel room; a *Playboy* Playmate show in the middle of nowhere; the "Ride of the Valkyries" helicopter attack sequence; the incredibly effective usage of the Doors' eerie "The End" on the soundtrack.

But wait, there's more. Almost two hours into *Redux,* Coppola has restored a twenty-five-minute sequence in which Willard and his men stumble upon some French colonials still living on a plantation upriver. The best part of this new footage involves a political lecture given by de Marais (Christian Marquand), the leader of the group, who runs through the disastrous French history in Vietnam and wonders why the Americans can't learn from their mistakes. This historical context is a wonderful addition to the film, and the setting—a cultured dinner party in the midst of a war zone—fits perfectly with *Redux*'s bizarre tone.

Other additions don't work as well, particularly a sequence in which Willard's men hook up for some sexual dalliances with the Playmates. But

> "We train young men to drop fire on people. But their commanders won't allow them to write 'fuck' on their airplanes because it's obscene!"
>
> —Colonel Kurtz (Marlon Brando), in *Apocalypse Now Redux*

Marlon Brando (as Colonel Kurtz) and Martin Sheen (as Captain Willard) star in Francis Ford Coppola's Vietnam War classic, *Apocalypse Now.*

ZOETROPE / UNITED ARTISTS / THE KOBAL COLLECTION

another scene, in which Brando reads an article from *Time* magazine that claims the U.S. is finally winning the war, shows just how deluded U.S. leaders really were.

Despite its massive running time, *Apocalypse Now Redux* moves along very well. But the film is also a sad reminder that such a quirky, iconoclastic, challenging, and over-the-top project like this could never be made in today's Hollywood. More's the pity.

2001 (R) 203m/C Marlon Brando, Robert Duvall, Martin Sheen, Frederic Forrest, Albert Hall, Sam Bottoms, Laurence Fishburne, Dennis Hopper, G. D. Spradlin, Harrison Ford, Colleen Camp, Christian Marquand, Aurore Clement. *D:* Francis Ford Coppola. *W:* Francis Ford Coppola, John Milius. *C:* Vittorio Storaro. *M:* Carmine Coppola, Francis Ford Coppola, Mickey Hart. *VHS, DVD*

—*Lewis Beale*

Coming Home ♫♫♫♪

Director Hal Ashby, actress Jane Fonda, and cinematographer Haskell Wexler were three of Hollywood's leading liberals during the late 1960s and early 1970s. So it came as no surprise that they would collaborate

THE ABC MOVIE OF THE WEEK: TURNED-ON TUNE-INS

With Hollywood studios usually timid during the 1960s and 1970s about tackling such topical subjects as the Vietnam War, homosexuality, drugs, and feminism, television often filled the void. In 1969 the ABC Movie of the Week debuted, based on an idea by programming honcho Barry Diller. Each week, the network broadcast an original ninety-minute movie, made with relatively low budgets (compared to big-screen features) and with performers who were either TV staples or up-and-coming screen performers. Many of these films were actually quite solid and offered viewers the opportunity to see professional treatments of subjects Hollywood found verboten. Among the most memorable entries were:

That Certain Summer (1972): Hal Holbrook was the father who had to come out of the closet to son Scott Jacoby and ex-wife Hope Lange. His lover was played by Martin Sheen.

Tribes (1970): Jan-Michael Vincent is a hippie drafted into the military who goes head-on against tough drill instructor Darren McGavin.

Maybe I'll Come Home in the Spring (1972): After spending time in a commune, hippie chick Sally Field gets bad vibes when she returns home to her alcoholic parents Jackie Cooper and Eleanor Parker and her drug-addicted sister.

Go Ask Alice (1973): With a title taken from Jefferson Airplane's drug anthem "White Rabbit," this preachy drama tells of a teenage girl's descent into the world of drugs. William Shatner plays her father and Andy Griffith is a priest.

The Feminist and the Fuzz (1972): Light comedy tale in which Barbara Eden plays a feisty liberated woman rooming with cop David Hartman. The supporting cast alone makes it a happening: Julie Newmar, John McGiver, Joanne Worley, Herb Edelman, Farrah Fawcett, and Harry Morgan.

The Ballad of Andy Crocker (1969): Lee Majors is the brooding Vietnam vet who returns home and finds girlfriend Joey Heatherton about to marry someone else. The eclectic supporting cast includes sausage king Jimmy Dean, singer Marvin Gaye, and *Bewitched*'s Agnes Moorhead.

Three's a Crowd (1969) Bigamy done cute as pilot Larry Hagman tries to balance the affections of two women (E. J. Peaker, Jessica Walter) in different cities.

The Astronaut (1972): After an astronaut dies on a mission to Mars, NASA uses a stand-in to fool the public as well as the real space traveler's wife. The cast includes Monte Markham, Jackie Cooper, and Susan Clark.

The Desperate Miles (1975): While making a 180-mile trip by wheelchair, handicapped Vietnam veteran Tony Musante is stalked by a deranged trucker.

on *Coming Home,* one of the first Hollywood studio productions to deal directly with the Vietnam War. Curiously, the trio—with Fonda shepherding the project—decided to tell a story concerning the after-affects of the conflict on its veterans, rather than a combat tale. The result is a film that, though it has lost some of its impact over the years, remains a stirring human story, even for conservatives—if they are willing to overlook the liberal undercurrent.

Set in Los Angeles in 1968, *Coming Home* tells of Bob Hyde (Bruce Dern), a patriotic Marine captain who has shipped to Vietnam for active duty. Bob's absence leaves wife Sally (Jane Fonda) home by herself. Sally is essentially apolitical but believes she can help out with the war effort by taking a volunteer position at a veteran's hospital. There Sally befriends Vi (Penelope Milford), a nutritionist whose brother (Robert Carradine) has returned home from Vietnam severely depressed. Sally is soon given an eye-opening introduction to the consequences of the war, witnessing the physically and psychologically incapacitated veterans at the hospital.

At the hospital Sally meets Luke Martin (Jon Voight), once a jock at her high school, now a paraplegic due to war injuries. At first their relationship is uneasy, as Luke's bitterness about his condition consumes him. Eventually, as the two begin to connect, Sally develops a romantic interest in Luke.

A furlough in Hong Kong for Bob brings Sally to the Far East, but their reunion proves uncomfortable. He appears distant and distressed. Upon returning to the States, Sally acts on her desires and sleeps with Luke after he locks himself and his wheelchair to the entrance of a Marine recruiting station. As their relationship deepens, Bob returns home injured, even more unhinged than before, and obsessed with being recognized as a war hero. It's not long before Bob learns of the affair, and he goes off the deep end, threatening violence.

When it was first released in theaters, *Coming Home* was considered gutsy for grappling with touchy subjects. Its unflinching depiction of the trials of handicapped vets undoubtedly paved the way for Oliver Stone's *Born on the Fourth of July* years later. Employing jittery cinema vérité–style camerawork, Ashby and Wexler want to get under your skin—and they do. The film also received a lot of attention for the fairly explicit lovemaking scene between Fonda and Voight. The sequence seemed corny to some, sensitive and erotic to others.

An iffy project from the get-go despite the presence of marquee names, *Coming Home* did well at the box office and received eight Academy Award nominations, including Best Picture and Best Director. It took home three Oscars, for Fonda and Voight and for the original screenplay by Nancy Dowd, Robert C. Jones, and Waldo Salt. The acting throughout is exceptional. Voight forcefully runs the gamut of emotions, but he really nailed his Best Actor statue with an impassioned antiwar address near the film's end. Meanwhile, Fonda believably moves from naive military wife to politicized, three-dimensional woman. Dern, also Oscar-nominated, brings a sense of melancholy to his patented characterization of a man on the edge. Of special note are Wexler's cinematography and the classic-rock soundtrack that finds many unique ways to use popular songs, particularly the Rolling Stones' "Out of Time" ("You don't know what's going on / You've been away for far too long / You can't come back and think you are still mine / You're out of touch, my baby / My

"I have killed for my country, or whatever, and I don't feel good about it. 'Cause there's not enough reason, man, to feel a person die in your hands, or to see your best buddy get blown away."

—Jon Voight, as Luke Martin, in *Coming Home*

poor discarded baby / I said, baby, baby, baby, you're out of time").

In some ways, *Coming Home* plays as an updating of *The Men*, Fred Zinneman's 1950 drama with Marlon Brando as the World War II vet returning home as a paraplegic, crossed with *The Best Years of Our Lives*, William Wyler's Oscar-winning chronicle of a trio of returning World War II servicemen. The fact that *Coming Home* tackles the war in Vietnam—finally!—with such requisite skill makes it a worthy addition to a mantel lined with those classics. But be forewarned: *Coming Home* is likely to tip the mantel to the left.

1978 (R) 125m/C Jane Fonda, Jon Voight, Bruce Dern, Penelope Milford, Robert Carradine, Robert Ginty, Mary Gregory. *D:* Hal Ashby. *W:* Robert C. Jones, Nancy Dowd, Waldo Salt. *C:* Haskell Wexler. *M:* The Beatles, Tim Buckley, Buffalo Springfield, the Chambers Brothers, Aretha Franklin, Richie Havens, Janis Joplin and Big Brother and the Holding Company, Jefferson Airplane, the Rolling Stones, Simon & Garfunkel, Steppenwolf. *VHS, DVD*

Luke (Jon Voight) and Sally (Jane Fonda) make love, not war, in Hal Ashby's 1978 film, *Coming Home*.

F.T.A. ♫♫

Designed to raise awareness of American policies during Vietnam, *F.T.A.* was a traveling vaudeville show led by Jane Fonda and Donald Sutherland that staged live performances near military bases in the United States and overseas in the early 1970s. This documentary chronicles the group's trip to various locales where the performers preach against the U.S. government's involvement in the war through songs, comedy skits, dramatic readings, and stories addressed directly to the military audience.

The film is a mixed bag, alternating boring, heavy-handed sequences with genuinely fascinating footage of the troupe in action. Filmed shortly before Fonda was pegged "Hanoi Jane" after venturing to North Vietnam in support of the country's Communist regime, *F.T.A.* shows us what may have inspired Fonda's subsequent trip.

Fonda takes a low-key spot in the quasi-U.S.O. tour that most assuredly made Bob Hope ill. She joins in on a few protest songs, takes part in some fairly dated sketches, and is seen making organizational decisions in the background. Joining her are a scruffy Donald Sutherland—whose best moments find him relating the story of Dalton Trumbo's *Johnny Got His Gun* to an audience of soldiers (he had just played the role of Christ in the film version)—folk singer Holly Near, and funnyman Michael Alaimo.

The film begins with a stop on the battleship USS *Coral Sea,* then proceeds to the Pacific, where Fonda and company make stops in Okinawa, the Philippines, Hawaii, Japan, and other locations. Uninteresting travelogue footage of each locale is occasionally interspersed with such events as a demonstration against U.S. imperialism in the Philippines, a disturbing stop at a photo exhibit of the bombing of Hiroshima, and talking-head interviews with American servicemen disillusioned with Uncle Sam's foreign policies, the ongoing war, or racism. Occasionally, one of the F.T.A. all-stars talks to the servicemen.

The more interesting moments of *F.T.A.* turn up during unscripted conflicts the group encounters. Ninety minutes of the same message can get tiresome, so when there's a problem with visas at the airport or hecklers taking offense at F.T.A.'s antigovernment rants, the incidents are almost a relief.

What's most amazing about *F.T.A.,* however, may be that this film was actually produced and released to theaters—albeit for an extremely brief period—by the exploitation specialists at American International Pictures. One cannot even imagine a documentary such as this, one that shows members of the military enthusiastically supporting a movement against the government's role in a major conflict, seeing the light of day in contemporary times.

F.T.A. has rarely been shown since its initial release and has never been issued by a video company. Interested parties may have to take to the Internet to find a copy from an independent source. Reportedly Fonda, the former champion of free speech, has put the kibosh on the film. There's nothing in this messy but intriguing time capsule that she should be ashamed of, especially considering that *Barbarella* is readily available around the corner at Blockbuster.

1971 (R) 97m/C Jane Fonda, Donald Sutherland, Holly Near, Michael Alaimo, Paul Mooney, Pamela Donegan, Len Chandler. *D:* Francine Parker. *W:* Michael Alaimo, Pamela Donegan, Robin Menken, Holly Near, Dalton Trumbo. *C:* Juliana Wang, Joan Weidman. *M:* Aminadov Aloni. VHS
AKA: Free the Army; Fuck the Army

How I Won the War 🦴🦴

Pity Fab Four fans who rent *How I Won the War* expecting a swinging, comic romp à la *A Hard Day's Night* and *Help!* Instead, *How I Won the War*—from the writing and directing team of Charles Wood and Richard Lester, with John Lennon second-billed in a nonmusical role—is a jaunty but oft-impenetrable spoof of English manners and attitudes in the face of battlefield horrors.

Ernest Goodbody (Michael Crawford) is an eager young twit whose main enjoyment in life is playing cricket. Nonetheless, in the Second World War his social standing puts him in charge of a small squad of men from the lower classes, including the amiable, rotund Clapper (Roy Kinnear), the manic Juniper (Jack MacGowran, right out of *The Fearless Vampire Killers*), the sardonic Gripweed (Lennon), and other chaps, all of whom are sent to North Africa.

There, Lieutenant Goodbody tries to seize a German fuel depot with disastrous results, then leads his infuriated men to build a cricket pitch for the arriving reinforcements. Their only real victory comes when they shoot down an attacking plane, only to find out it's a British aircraft. The group proves to be an odd, ill-prepared lot as Juniper starts dressing like a music-hall comic (complete with blackface and baggy pants), Gripweed sweetens his tea with spoonfuls of sand instead of sugar, Clapper obsesses over his wife's infidelities back home, and Goodbody fumes and sputters at them all.

Whenever a soldier dies, the unfortunate fellow (or his ghost, or something) subsequently reappears as a quiet, faceless, monochromatic figure; these red, green, or yellow apparitions are haunting visuals, even for viewers watching during the age of computer graphics. But some of the characters appear to die more than once as Lester's narrative marches backwards, forwards, and sideways through time, from the African desert to France—where Goodbody's clownish crew, now part of the D-Day invasion, run into jarring, violent skirmishes—and to Germany, where a captured Goodbody establishes a closer rapport with a pleasant Nazi officer than any he ever had in his now-annihilated battalion ("Does this make me a fascist?" he wonders). Thanks to the cooperative German, Goodbody is indeed able to help Allied forces cross the Rhine and win the war.

Characters frequently address the audience, *Alfie*-style, some even begging for the movie camera to be switched off. "You just knew this would happen to me, didn't you?" laments a mortally wounded Gripweed. Well, no, we didn't actually, since it's hard to get a handle on just what is going on at any point. Lester blends realistic combat scenes, stock footage, and social satire in an energetic but atonal frenzy that's more often confusing than provocative. At least Lennon underplays his role—that, or he isn't enough of an actor to ham it up like the rest of the thespians. Crawford, a Richard Lester regular long before his triumphs in stage musicals, is fittingly but excessively annoying as Goodbody, his reedy *Phantom of the Opera* voice a shrill insect buzz as he harangues his underlings or philosophizes on the English fighting man.

How I Won the War was part of a fashionable platoon of often inventive mock-epics (such as Tony Richardson's *The Charge of the Light Brigade,* also written by Wood, and released a year later) that contrasted the tally-ho and stiff-upper-lip attitude of yesteryear's British Empire with the '60s realization that war was no gentleman's game but rather a gory, unfair mess in which the best or righteous don't necessarily win and the wealthy have a much better chance of surviving than do the working-class folk.

Leaving no doubt what was actually on the filmmakers' minds in *How I Won the War,* two of the deceased soldiers at the end discuss shipping out to Vietnam.

1967 111m/C *UK* Michael Crawford, Roy Kinnear, John Lennon, Michael Hordern, Jack MacGowran, Lee Montague, Karl Michael Vogler, Ewan Hooper, Ronald Lacey. **D:** Richard Lester. **W:** Charles Wood. **C:** David Watkins. **M:** Ken Thorne. *VHS*

—*Charles A. Cassady Jr.*

ROBERT ALTMAN: TROUBLE-MAKING AUTEUR

Robert Altman

DR T INC / SANDCASTLE 5 PROD. /
THE KOBAL COLLECTION /
ROSENTHAL, ZADE

Robert Altman has always been the outsider, the non-conformist, the director who managed to have a long and colorful career while pointing his middle finger at the Hollywood Establishment. Constantly saying incendiary things about the way Tinseltown does business, making headline-grabbing political statements about such hot topics as the United States' 2003 invasion of Iraq, and continually squabbling with producers and money men, Altman has remained a cantankerous filmmaking force for five decades.

The Kansas City native and army veteran got his start by making dozens of documentaries in the early 1950s. He parlayed some of his earnings into *The Delinquents* in 1957, a juvenile-delinquent drama he helmed starring Tom Laughlin, the future Billy Jack. The documentary *The James Dean Story* followed, as did hours of directing such TV dramas as *Combat!* and *Bonanza*. He returned to the big screen with 1967's *Countdown,* a suspenseful space drama with Robert Duvall and James Caan, but he got into trouble with the studio when he refused to cut it down. *That Cold Day in the Park,* a baffling psychodrama with Sandy Dennis, followed.

After it had been rejected by many directors, Altman took on *M*A*S*H,* a loose adaptation of Richard Hooker's satiric novel about medics during the Korean War. Although the script was credited to Ring Lardner Jr., it was Altman's baby all the way. The film's improvisational style, anti-authoritarian stance, overlapping dialogue, blend of comedy and gore, and allusions to Vietnam proved an immediate international sensation, spawning a long-running series (of which he had no financial part). Ignoring the more mainstream projects handed to him, the iconoclastic Altman settled on *Brewster McCloud* as his next project.

The far-out fantasy detailed the adventures of a young man (Bud Cort) obsessed with flying in the Houston Astrodome. Offbeat to the extreme, the film boasted a guardian angel with wings

Kelly's Heroes ♫♫♫

This enjoyable, if overlong, World War II heist pic (from the scriptwriter of *The Italian Job,* Troy Kennedy-Martin) earns its peace-sign stripes thanks to an anti-Establishment 'tude and Donald Sutherland's notoriously anachronistic turn as a bead-wearing pre-hippie who drives a tank and spouts Peter Maxisms ("Positive waves, man, positive waves!") not long after D-Day.

(played by Sally "Hot Lips" Kellerman), a romantic interest essayed by a debuting Shelley Duvall, a ribbing of *Bullitt* and other cop movies, and lots of bird droppings. *Brewster* crashed at the box office.

This disappointment, of course, led Altman to continue experimenting, this time with the western genre. He delivered *McCabe and Mrs. Miller* in 1973, a moody rumination on capitalism and its discontents highlighted by ace performances from Warren Beatty and Julie Christie, Vilmos Zsigmond's striking photography, and Leonard Cohen's dirge-like score. Altman tried his hand at Hitchcockian psychological horror with *Images,* an unsettling study of a schizophrenic essayed by Susannah York. His genre samplings continued brilliantly with *The Long Goodbye,* featuring Elliott Gould as a modern variation of Raymond Chandler's Philip Marlowe, now a rumpled detective caught up in some contemporary L.A.-based danger.

With the exception of 1977's dreamlike *Three Women,* Altman spent the rest of the 1970s showing us the dark side of genre movies, critically examining social institutions and exploring avenues that other filmmakers shied away from. *Thieves Like Us* took the stark, unromantic approach to the gangster film, the opposite route *Bonnie and Clyde* traveled, while *Buffalo Bill and the Indians,* with Paul Newman and Burt Lancaster, traced the roots of show business to the phony razzle-dazzle of the legendary Wild West shows. The frantic, darkly comic world of compulsive gamblers took center stage in *California Split,* while the lives of twenty-four characters tied in one way or another to the country-western music world formed 1975's *Nashville,* arguably Altman's masterwork. The inventive, multicharacter, let-the-actors-do-what-they-damn-well-please technique Altman pioneered was used less successfully in *A Wedding,* a cranky celebration of a messed-up wedding party, and in *H.E.A.L.T.H.,* a look at a health-food convention with a large cast headed by Carol Burnett, which bypassed theaters for cable.

Aside from one box-office triumph and some smaller successes (like 1992's *The Player* and 2002's *Gosford Park*), Altman's name has never been bankable and is often seen as a deterrent for making money. The frisky poobah of actors, of improvisational techniques, and of bold technical experimentation continues to scare the hell out of Hollywood, even as he approaches the age of eighty. He is still making movies the only way he knows how, eager to dazzle even while walking on a tightrope. And for that we should all be grateful.

During the liberation of France, Lieutenant Kelly (Clint Eastwood, playing it even more coolly detached than usual) learns from a captured Nazi that 14,000 bars of gold, worth millions, lie relatively unprotected in a bank in a battle-ravaged town that Allied forces haven't yet reached. At a time when preppy officers are loading entire yachts on board planes to take back as souvenirs, the bullion makes a tempting target for Kelly, his blustering sergeant (Telly Savalas), and his dogface G.I.s. "The perfect crime," beams an army black-marketeer played by Don Rickles.

Kelly and select members of his platoon embark on an unauthorized sortie behind enemy lines to steal the treasure, first securing the services of "Oddball" (Sutherland) and his handy Sherman tank. It is a rather long and cumbersome journey to the gold—but dig the homage to the Italian westerns Eastwood had been doing for Sergio Leone when the fortune-hunters face off against an unexpected set of defending Panzers.

If universal love and brotherhood don't exactly prevail, good old-fashioned greed does the trick, and the conflict-weary Germans and Americans declare an armistice long enough to divide the booty.

Comical business, most of it provided by Sutherland, mixes with customary depictions of mass destruction, horror, and the absurdity of war. Familiar faces in the cast include *The Love Boat*'s Gavin McLeod, the future Archie Bunker, Carroll O'Connor, future *Rockford Files* second banana, Stuart Margolin, and a then-unsung Harry Dean Stanton. You can compare this caper to David O. Russell's critically acclaimed *Three Kings* from 1999, which had Gulf War commandos George Clooney, Ice Cube, and Mark Wahlberg helping themselves to Saddam Hussein's stolen gold, but it just wasn't the same without Oddball.

1970 (PG) 145m/C *US/YG* Clint Eastwood, Telly Savalas, Donald Sutherland, Don Rickles, Carroll O'Connor, Stuart Margolin, Gavin McLeod, Harry Dean Stanton, Hal Buckley, Len Lesser, Gene Collins. *D:* Brian G. Hutton. *W:* Troy Kennedy-Martin. *C:* Gabriel Figueroa. *M:* Lalo Schifrin. *VHS, DVD*

—*Charles A. Cassady Jr.*

> "Why don't you knock it off with them negative waves? Why don't you dig how beautiful it is out here? Why don't you say something righteous and hopeful for a change?"
>
> —Oddball (Donald Sutherland), in *Kelly's Heroes*

M*A*S*H

Arguably the greatest antiwar comedy ever made (*The Americanization of Emily* gives it a run for its money), *M*A*S*H* put director Robert Altman on the map and established a style that has been seen in dozens of pictures since.

It's all there: the ensemble cast, overlapping dialogue, and hip cynicism. Plus, *M*A*S*H,* which spawned one of the most popular series in TV history, contains any number of sequences that have become iconic in their familiarity: the Last Supper for dentist Walter "Painless Pole" Waldowski (John Shuck), who's about to commit suicide; "Trapper" John (Elliott Gould) and "Hawkeye" Pierce's (Donald Sutherland) golf trip to Japan; the meltdown of Major Frank Burns (Robert Duvall); and "Hot Lips" Houlihan's (Sally Kellerman) ultimate humiliation in the shower.

It's all quite funny and cleverly done, and the fact that the film is set in a mobile army hospital during the Korean War only adds to the surreal tone. After all, this is the "forgotten" war, which makes it seem particularly absurd. Altman's success with the film is all the more astonishing given its anachronistic tone. *M*A*S*H* is obviously a product of the countercultural '60s, not the conformist '50s. Let's face it: no doctor in 1951 would ever look or act like the walrus-

mustached Gould, and the kind of antiauthoritarian hijinks on display would have gotten our heroes a quick trip back to the States, if not a swift court-martial.

But that seems neither here nor there. *M*A*S*H* works because it is swift and witty, and because it manages to plug into essential truths about the idiocy of war and the military mindset. But the film has a major flaw, one that pops up in much of Altman's subsequent work—it is unreservedly misogynist.

Every female in this movie has a nickname like Hot Lips, Dish, or Knocko. Their main purpose is to act as subservient screw bunnies for the male members (double entendre intended) of the hospital unit. And Hot Lips's treatment borders on the sadistic. It's true that she's a prude and a bore. But there's no indication that she's anything less than a good nurse. Yet that's not good enough for the guys on staff. Hot Lips can only become fully accepted when she's caught naked in the shower in a prank engineered by Trapper and Hawkeye and, thus humbled, comes over to "the other side." By the end of the film, she's become a compliant cutie, like every other woman in the picture.

*M*A*S*H* is terrific in many ways, but, ultimately, it would be even better if it weren't so darn sexist.

1970 (R) 116m/C (uncut), (PG) 112m/C (edited) Donald Sutherland, Elliott Gould, Tom Skerritt, Sally Kellerman, Robert Duvall. *D:* Robert Altman. *W:* Ring Lardner Jr. *C:* Harold E. Stine. *M:* Johnny Mandel. *VHS, DVD*

—*Lewis Beale*

Carl Gottlieb, David Arkin, Tom Skerritt, John Schuck, Donald Sutherland, and Elliott Gould form part of the ensemble cast of Robert Altman's *M*A*S*H*.

20TH CENTURY FOX / ASPEN / THE KOBAL COLLECTION

"This isn't a hospital! It's an insane asylum!"

—Hot Lips Houlihan (Sally Kellerman), in *M*A*S*H*

Chapter 10

Road Rules

Blame it on Brando.

The mumbling rabble-rouser caused all sorts of trouble in 1953's *The Wild One.* With a leather jacket, a biker hat, and a cigarette dangling from his mouth, Brando electrified the screen as Johnny, leader of the Black Rebels, a gang of cyclists causing conniptions among the townsfolk in a small California town. When a girl asks him "What are you rebelling against?" he answers, "Whaddya got?" Cool as a cucumber.

Then, in '54, James Dean, another disciple of the same Method Brando followed, was the *Rebel without a Cause,* detesting parents and authority, taking part in a death-defying "chicken race," a drag tourney to oblivion in glorious Cinemascope.

There was always something cool about fast wheels, an open road, and rebellious youths with devil-may-care attitudes. Four years after *Rebel without a Cause,* heavy-lidded Hollywood bad boy Robert Mitchum took to the dirt roads of Appalachia in *Thunder Road,* playing a Korean war vet who gets back into the family moonshine business. Eventually, he has to make one last run in his loaded 1950 Ford Coupe, dodging the feds and rival 'shiners along the way. The film was made cheaply, but it was compelling enough to bring people to the 3,000 drive-in theaters that populated the United States at the time. And later, it even inspired a Bruce Springsteen song or three.

More movies of various octanes and vehicles followed, gassed up to deliver the goods primarily for open-air auditoriums throughout America. Sleek sports models, heavy-duty Harleys, souped-up muscle cars: the wheels didn't matter as long as they were fast, the antiheroes bucked authority, and the proceedings were decorated by some nice scenery and cute girls. Adding further fuel to the road fire was the fact that young Americans were keeping the beat with Jack Kerouac's *On the Road.*

Motorcycles blossomed as the vehicle of choice in the '60s. Hell's Angels, the California-based bad-ass biker gang, were in the news, causing troubles like Brando and his men. So Roger Corman, opportunistic filmmaker par excellence, decided to cash in. Writer Charles N. Griffith spent some time with the Angels and leader Sonny Barger. The experiences led Corman to film *The Wild Angels* in 1966 for exploitation studio American International Pictures. It may not have been the first of the motorcycle gang flicks, but it was the most unusual, an impressionist look at the bikers' violent, unsavory world and ways with Peter Fonda, Bruce Dern, and Nancy Sinatra in the leads and brutal fights, orgies, swastikas, and drug-taking in the story. The low-budget offering was a smash and was even well-received at the Cannes Film Festival.

Other indy companies followed AIP's lead, cranking out biker flicks with incredible regularity in the latter part of the 1960s. Leather-clad, Harley-handling congregations of all sorts permeated the screen. There were blacks, women, football players, werewolves, nuns, vampires, gays.

At the same time, the road rules were changing and serious filmmakers were taking shots at road themes. *Easy Rider,* intended as an AIP project, was rejected by the low-budget specialists and then landed at Columbia. Dennis Hopper and Peter Fonda, two vets of the cycle trade, played the hippie bikers who came up short of fulfilling their dreams. The cash registers went cha-ching as the film garnered serious attention and landmark audience appreciation. Meanwhile, two years later, Monte Hellman recruited rock stars James Taylor and Beach Boy Dennis Wilson to play the leads in *Two-Lane Blacktop,* a movie about life on the road filled with heavy philosophical musings. This movie was serious stuff and, though it ultimately arrived with an empty tank at the box office, it got rave reviews and magazine covers for its unique approach to the road-movie genre.

Dodging the fuzz with a strong dose of nihilism was the main ingredient for two drive-in muscle-car fantasies in the 1970s: *Vanishing Point,* featuring Barry Newman as an ex–auto racer coerced onward by blind disc jockey Cleavon Little in a high-speed cross-country trip to deliver a car; and *Dirty Mary Crazy Larry,* with Peter Fonda as an ex–race car driver on a high-speed just-for-kicks whirlwind, outracing cops and helicopters and acting as a sounding board for the frustrations of fellow passengers Adam Roarke and Susan George.

As drive-ins faded, so did the biker films, and zippy cars with the men in blue in pursuit found their place in action-packed cop movies of the 1970s like *The Seven-Ups;* Corman and company's *Grand Theft Auto* and *Eat My Dust,* both directed by Ron Howard; and *Death Race 2000,* a satiric sci-fi take on the formula. Certainly good ol' boy Burt Reynolds got lots of mileage out of his *Smokey and the Bandit* and *Cannonball Run* chase comedies.

America wasn't the only country fascinated with adventures on the road. In the 1970s, the Road Warrior emerged out of Australia. *Mad Max,* a cop played by Mel Gibson, seeks revenge for the hardships inflicted upon his family by futuristic thugs. Mel's Max faced off against other colorful creeps in *The Road Warrior* and *Mad Max beyond Thunderdome.* The trilogy (with a reported fourth film in the works), conceived and directed by former doctor George Miller, won fans of both exploitation films and artier fare thanks to its frenzied, eccentric take on action and characters.

Since the 1960s, interest in road movies has appeared to come, appropriately, in cycles. *The Fast and the Furious* and its sequel, *2 Fast 2 Furious,* two big hits of the early twenty-first century, used the essentials put forth in the '60s motorcycle movies and even *The Wild One* and *Rebel without a Cause* of the 1950s, proving that wheels are always in—provided they're cool and very fast.

Angel Unchained

Hate Was the Chain That Linked Them Together! God Help the One Who Broke It!

—Tagline for *Angel Unchained*

By the time the biker genre had established itself, it was already starting to lose steam. But the films managed to hang on for a few years by adapting the general structure of westerns. *Angel Unchained* takes on some of the plot attributes of *The Magnificent Seven* and *Seven Samurai*.

Former surfing champ Don Stroud mumbles his way through the lead role as Angel, vice president of the Nomads motorcycle club, who has been feeling "strung out" lately. After saving the life of Pilot (Larry Bishop), the group's leader, during a rumble at an amusement park, Angel is allowed to leave to ride the highways alone. Eventually, he stops in at an Arizona commune run by Tremaine (Luke Askew), allowed to stay primarily because of the invitation by cute hippie chick Merrilee (Tyne Daly). But Angel brings added heat on the commune from the hostile locals when he takes action to defend his new friends. When the town's redneck mob gives the commune a week to pack up and leave, Tremaine asks Angel to call on his biker buddies to help them out. Angel refuses to bring in his dangerous ex-comrades, but he has to think twice when his attempts to make peace with the townsfolk are met with further violence. Pilot and the rest of the club are finally brought in, but, as Angel feared, their arrival threatens to destroy the community he's trying to save.

Although there are some traditional biker fisticuffs during the first hour, most of the attention is focused on showing the clash between the various lifestyles depicted in the movie and trying to flesh out the otherwise one-note characters. Producer and director Lee Madden (*Hell's Angels '69*) keeps the tone relaxed for far too long, letting his cast improvise lines and try to stay cool in the hot locations.

All the laid-back talk gives way to some fine stunt driving in the third act, when the bikers meet the dune-buggy-riding rednecks for a big battle. The bikes and buggies bouncing around the desert locations raise the excitement level somewhat, but it comes a bit late, rendering *Angel Unchained* one of the tamer biker pictures. Tyne Daly, long before TV stardom, looks a bit too fresh for her role, chastely hiding behind a fence during her topless scene. Aldo Ray

supplies an interesting bit as the laconic local sheriff who, sharing a chat with Pilot while the two gangs fight, recognizes that the bikers are much like the cowboys, only in different garb. And Askew, a folk singer and activist when not acting, practically repeats his *Easy Rider* role as the commune leader.

1970 (PG-13) 86m/C Don Stroud, Luke Askew, Larry Bishop, Tyne Daly, Neil Moran, Jean Marie, Bill McKinney, Aldo Ray. *D:* Lee Madden. *W:* Jeffrey Allan Fiskin. *C:* Irving Lippman. *M:* Randy Sparks. *VHS, DVD*
AKA: *Hell's Angels Unchained*

—*Brian Thomas*

Susan George and Peter Fonda take to the road—and to thievery—in *Dirty Mary Crazy Larry.*

Dirty Mary Crazy Larry 🎵🎵🎵

Dirty Mary Crazy Larry is an anomaly, a cult film that is practically impossible to see. Unavailable on video for at least two decades and rarely shown on TV, the film still boasts a large following and has even inspired entire websites dedicated to its vrooming pleasures. At first, you might wonder why all this slavish attention is being paid to what is essentially a low-budget chase flick. But after a second viewing the film takes hold of you as its charms kick into high gear.

Cut from the same racing-stripe cloth as *Vanishing Point, Dirty Mary Crazy Larry* graduated from the school of devil-may-care road flicks in which

PETER FONDA by Lowell Goldman

" **E** asy Rider seems dated to a degree," admitted Peter Fonda in a 1990 interview. "But, I tell you the trip is not to watch it on television. You have to see it on a big screen with an audience. Then you'll remember why it was so powerful."

After starring in *The Trip* and *The Wild Angels* for Roger Corman, Fonda formed his own production company (Pando) to make *Easy Rider*. He also cowrote the film with Terry Southern and Dennis Hopper. Hopper helmed the low-budget flick. *Easy Rider* was released by Columbia to outstanding reviews and huge box-office returns.

"You know, we were filming in Texas in 1968 when we got the news that Robert Kennedy had been shot," revealed Fonda. "I recall the mood on the set was really down at the time."

Torn Away

Rip Torn was set to play the lawyer role that eventually went to Jack Nicholson. "Rip Torn wanted a certain amount of money for some unknown reason. I forget why he needed the money," said Fonda. "Anyway, I told Torn that we really weren't taking salaries. We were working for scale. Although he was from Texas and really wanted to play the part, he passed on it because we couldn't pay him. Yet, we still remained friends."

Meanwhile, they still needed an actor to replace Torn. "I suggested Jack [Nicholson] to play the lawyer," related Fonda. "Then Dennis [Hopper] said that Jack might not be right for the role. After all, he's not from Texas."

"'Come on Dennis, give me a break,'" continued Fonda. "'He can play a Texan. He's a fine actor.' You know what? Jack was outstanding and almost stole the film."

the zippy car chases come with an air of fatalism, some snappy and occasionally deep dialogue, and a downer of an ending.

Dirty Mary Coombs, played by British actress Susan George (*Straw Dogs*), is a hitchhiker with a criminal record from a small Southern town. Crazy Larry Rayder (Peter Fonda behind the wheel once again), a former drag racer, tries to compensate for his failed career by driving too fast. Deke Sommers (*Psych-Out*'s Adam Roarke), Larry's friend, is a mechanic who has trouble staying sober. The three get involved in a kidnapping and robbery during which they retrieve $150,000 from a supermarket owner (an unbilled Roddy McDowall). What makes it annoying to the police is that it was all done without a gun.

Calling the shots for the law is Everett Franklin (Vic Morrow), a cranky lawman constantly at odds with Carl (Kenneth Tobey), the local sheriff. There's plenty of tension between the two men as the hot-tempered Franklin becomes increasingly bemused at the police department's inability to catch the trio. Meanwhile, relationships are touchy among the outlaws as well. Larry and Mary don't get along, and Deke can't seem to put his fondness for their

Solo Direction

After playing a cameo in Dennis Hopper's ill-fated *The Last Movie,* Fonda went on to direct and star in a western entitled *The Hired Hand.* "We made a darn good film for nine bucks," he said with an uneasy laugh. "*The Hired Hand* was a classic when it hit the stands. The picture was very well received in Europe and at film festivals. But, Universal dumped the movie. They never really promoted it or gave the film a wide release." The film finally saw a high-profile DVD release in October 2003.

Idaho Transfer, an environmental science-fiction film, was another lost Fonda film for some time. "The movie was in release for only three weeks when the distributor [Cinemation] went bankrupt. The banks had the film for years." This movie has resurfaced in video stores in recent years.

Fonda was soon back at Universal as an actor in Robert Wise's 1973 romantic drama *Two People,* in which he played a Vietnam veteran who deserts the army and gets romantically involved with fashion model Lindsay Wagner. "We shot the film in sequence. It was designed by Bob [Wise, the director]. It was simply the best way to shoot the film. You know, we spent five weeks on the Marrakesh Express. And it worked out pretty well."

Road Warrior

Dirty Mary Crazy Larry was a huge drive-in hit for Fox in 1974. "That movie was an incredible success," exclaimed Fonda. "It made a ton of money. We also shot that film pretty much in sequence. There were lots of exciting stunts and about five minutes' worth of acting. Adam Roarke, Susan George, and myself were sort of like the Three Stooges. We had to make our scenes count.

"You know, I couldn't believe that so many moviegoers had seen the film four or five times," added Fonda. "I could understand them seeing *Easy Rider* four or five times or maybe even *The Hired Hand.* But why *Dirty Mary Crazy Larry*?"

gal-pal into words. The internal tensions, combined with the anxiety of pursuit by the law, causes Larry's driving to get wilder and more death defying.

Ditching their blue Chevy for a lime green 1969 Dodge Charger, Larry confounds everyone—including his two passengers—by hurtling recklessly through intersections, dodging pedestrians, skidding loudly, making 360-degree turns, and even keeping pace in a parallel showdown with a helicopter. And, as if to rub salt into the befuddled police department's wounds, Larry and company nonchalantly stop by a pool hall for a drink mid-pursuit.

What the halter-topped and not-to-be-trusted Mary, wiseacre Larry, and depressed Deke are going to do with the cash when the chase is over isn't exactly clear, but that's one of the movie's points. Although Mary and Deke seem to be forming a bond, nobody has any precise future plans. Everything is being done for kicks, the thrill of living on the edge.

The film certainly delivers the racing thrills fans of this genre demand, as a high-speed, nonstop chase takes up the better portion of the film's final half. Music is kept to a minimum, allowing the sound of the car's engines to dominate. Director John Hough (*The Legend of Hell House*) places the camera both in and alongside the careening cars, getting maximum jolts out of these scenes. And when the helicopter flies low at the same level as the Charger, it's way cool. Look, Ma, no rear-screen projection or CGI effects!

1974 (PG) 93m/C Peter Fonda, Susan George, Adam Roarke, Kenneth Tobey, Eugene Daniels, Vic Morrow, Lynn Borden, James Gavin, Roddy McDowall. *D:* John Hough. *W:* Leigh Brackett, Antonio Santean. *C:* Michael D. Margulies. *M:* Jimmie Haskell. *VHS*

Easy Rider

Easy Rider gave the finger to Hollywood, and it sent a seismic wave through the entire industry. "Hey, dude," it seemed to say, "we got a revolution going on here and you better take notice or it's gonna sneak up on you and bite you on the ass."

Other movies made during the era contained elements also found in *Easy Rider*. Pot smoking, hippie communes, the wide-open road, a rock score, rebellious heroes—none of these were startlingly new to the screen. But *Easy Rider* put them all together in a hip, palatable package and sent it special delivery straight to its youthful audience. It was a film made by young people who were the same age as the intended audience, an unusual circumstance at that time in Hollywood.

Easy Rider chronicles the adventures of two bikers on the road from Los Angeles to New Orleans. After cashing in big-time on a drug deal at an L.A. airport, Billy (Dennis Hopper) and Wyatt, AKA "Captain America" (Peter Fonda), roll their cash into a plastic tube, insert it into their gas tank, and head to the Big Easy to blow some of their dough on debauchery. The journey takes them through some visually stunning parts of the country and into the paths of the people who populate it. Two of those they encounter end up tagging along for the ride: a philosophical hippie (Luke Askew) who invites Billy and Wyatt back to a commune and George Hanson (Jack Nicholson), a drunken ACLU lawyer who helps them get released from prison after they're booked on a bogus charge of "parading without a permit" in a small town. Along the way, the two bikers are also confronted by angry racists and lawmen who don't like their looks or what they think they stand for.

Seen today, *Easy Rider* is, in spots, comically dated. Hopper says "man" at least thirty-five times. And Fonda is so emotionless that it's difficult to get a handle on his character: is he just perpetually zonked on weed or is this what passed for deep thinking back then? The stop at the hippie commune, in which a makeshift theatrical troupe sings groovy kiddie songs and the men and women practice free love, plays like a *Saturday Night Live* sketch.

On the other hand, parts of *Easy Rider* remain surprisingly potent. The scenes of small southwestern towns run by redneck sheriffs and filled with nefariously prejudiced townspeople still disturb. And the film's violent outbursts are sudden and unsettling. One gets the sense that not much has

changed since 1969. While you may laugh at Billy's "man"s and Wyatt's stoned glaze, the characters still command viewers' empathy.

Easy Rider is remembered as a pro-counterculture film, yet its attitude seems downright critical of the free-love generation and its ideals. Although he appears freaky with his shaggy mustache, long hair, buckskins, and Australian bush hat, Hopper's Billy is never comfortable with the hippie types he meets. When he and Wyatt are taken to the commune by the hitcher, he wants to ride away, practically begging Wyatt to leave. An LSD trip in a New Orleans cemetery is also a bummer as Wyatt, Billy, and two hookers (Karen Black and Toni Basil) experience images of death and despair. Then there's the case of Nicholson's Hanson, the one person Billy and Wyatt truly befriend during the film. After he's beaten at a campsite, the bikers react by taking a business card advertising a New Orleans whorehouse from his wallet, then heading back out on the road. Next, they're pigging out in a fancy restaurant and then hanging out in the baroque brothel, waiting to be serviced. Are these script inconsistencies or intentionally satiric jabs at '60s culture, pointing out hypocrisy and callousness? These questions are what make *Easy Rider* so fascinating to watch today.

Of course, there are other points of interest as well. Nicholson steals the picture as the winning, grinning, alcoholic attorney who wants a part in Billy and Wyatt's upcoming New Orleans party. Nicholson swigs Jim Beam for breakfast, wears a gold football helmet while riding on the back of a chopper, and

Peter Fonda and Dennis Hopper ride down the roads of America—and into pop-culture history—in *Easy Rider*.

COLUMBIA / THE KOBAL COLLECTION

wins us over by being a cool lawyer, a profession usually portrayed as being populated by uptight Establishment types. Nicholson's Oscar-nominated supporting turn jump-started the career of the thirty-two-year-old journeyman actor and writer, establishing him as the movie world's best-liked authority-shunning wiseass.

Like most movies set on and around the road, *Easy Rider* is anecdotal, but director Hopper and his team should get credit for making Billy and Wyatt's ride smooth. Despite limited directing experience (he shot some footage for Roger Corman's *The Trip*), Hopper gets the most of the riding sequences, photographed by Laszlo Kovacs against such auspicious backdrops as Monument Valley, made famous by *The Searchers* and other John Ford westerns. He also brings a realistic, documentary-like feel to the confrontational moments between the rednecks and Wyatt, Billy, and Hanson. Quick flash-forwards preceding the location shifts add both a European feel and an eerie tone to the film. Hopper originally delivered a cut of the film that was four hours long. After deliberation with Fonda, among others, the director whittled it down to just under three hours. Additional excising had to be done, and, according to many reports, the movie was whipped into watchable shape by editor Donn Cambern, who was assisted by "adviser" Henry Jaglom. The soundtrack, now considered a landmark, is highlighted by Roger McGuinn and the Byrds' flavorful country rock, Jimi Hendrix's electric guitar riffs, the Band's classical biblical allegory "The Weight," and Steppenwolf's anthems "Born to be Wild" and "The Pusher."

The story about the making of *Easy Rider* could be a film in itself. Legend has it Hopper and Fonda took the project initially to American International Pictures, the low-budget specialists behind many of the biker flicks of the era. The company balked at the price tag, so Fonda sought independent financing from producers Bert Schneider and Bob Rafelson. After the film was bankrolled for under $400,000, Columbia Pictures picked up the distribution rights. It became an instant sensation, winning critical favor in the United States and overseas, eventually returning over $20 million in America alone. Who did what and who owed who became important issues almost immediately. Hopper claimed he wrote most of the script, while Fonda attested that he and Terry Southern were at least equal to Hopper in that department. Later, Hopper would sue Fonda over royalties he thought were owed to him from the film's earnings. Years later, Rip Torn took legal action against Hopper after Hopper told a story on a talk show about why Torn was replaced by Jack Nicholson. Whatever happened to flower-power unity?

Perhaps the passage of time offers an opportunity to reinterpret *Easy Rider*. When Billy talks about the easy times ahead of them following their New Orleans sojourn, claiming they really "made it," Wyatt responds, "We blew it, Billy." And Billy's idea of utopia after making the big drug deal? Jumping on those choppers and heading out to retirement in . . . Florida? Kinda square, isn't it? Shudder at the thought of Billy and Wyatt, a few years down the line, working at a certain theme park, operating the "Wild Tea Ride" or "Spaced Mountain."

1969 (R) 94m/C Peter Fonda, Dennis Hopper, Jack Nicholson, Luke Askew, Karen Black, Toni Basil, Luana Anders, Sabrina Scharf, Phil Spector, Robert Walker Jr.

D: Dennis Hopper. **W:** Dennis Hopper, Peter Fonda, Terry Southern. **C:** Laszlo Kovacs. **M:** The Band, the Byrds, the Electric Flag, the Electric Prunes, the Fraternity of Man, Holy Modal Rounders, Jimi Hendrix, Little Eva, Roger McGuinn, Steppenwolf. *VHS, DVD*

Faster, Pussycat! Kill! Kill! ♫♫♫♫

For bodacious superbabes, overwrought psychodrama, and hardboiled mid-'60s sleaze, it just doesn't get any better than this Russ Meyer classic. Meyer had recently completed a biker picture called *Motor Psycho* in an attempt to switch from sexploitation to straight action. After finding that project's final results unsatisfying, he came up with a brilliant idea. Why not make the brutal biker villains statuesque and equally violent women?

Three tough go-go dancers—savage karate expert Varla (Tura Satana), vicious lesbian Rosie (Haji), and girl-next-door-gone-bad Billie (Lori Williams)—get their after-work kicks by hot-rodding their "bombs" across the California desert. They soon find themselves enveloped in murder, kidnapping, lust, and robbery after an impromptu desert race gets out of hand. Psychotic Varla, always on the lookout for someone or something to dominate, challenges clean-cut car-club president Tommy (Ray Barlow) to a race. When she discovers that nearly wrecking his car isn't enough to incite him, she openly attacks him. Before anyone can stop her, she snaps the teen's back like a twig. The girls keep Tommy's girlfriend, Linda (Sue Bernard, *Playboy*'s Miss December 1966), on sleeping pills until they can think of a way to dispose of her. The answer to their problem comes from an expository gas station attendant (Meyer regular Michael Finn). He tells them of a hateful old man in a wheelchair (Stuart Lancaster, another Russ fave) who lives on a desert ranch with his two grown sons. The old lecher is rumored to be hiding a fortune somewhere on the property, and Varla sees in their virginal captive a chance to finagle their way into the old man's house. Before long, the trio is engineering various wiles in an effort to remove all obstacles between them and the loot. Of course, everything goes violently wrong—for everybody.

Faster, Pussycat! Kill! Kill! is an exploitation masterpiece that takes the Bad Girl persona and raises it to operatic proportions. The three leads, all well-known exotic dancers when they weren't appearing in films, gnaw on their insane roles with gusto. Williams perfectly embodies the self-destructive child of privilege willing to go to any length in her pursuit of kicks. At the other end of the spectrum is Haji's vaguely Italian cauldron of hatred. At the apex of this triangle stands Tura Satana, an instant exploitation icon in low-cut black outfits and a Bettie Page hairdo. As narrator John Furlong intones at the very beginning, "Welcome to Violence!" Whether you love the film for its obvious cheap-thrills value or as an underappreciated piece of camp noir, you have to admit, *Pussycat* is a classic.

> **"Women! They let 'em vote, smoke, and drive—even put 'em in pants! And what happens? A Democrat for president!"**
>
> —Old Man (Stuart Lancaster), in *Faster, Pussycat! Kill! Kill!*

Tura Satana plays the insatiably violent Varla in Russ Meyer's camp classic *Faster, Pussycat! Kill! Kill!*

EVE PRODUCTIONS INC / THE KOBAL COLLECTION

1965 83m/BW Tura Satana, Haji, Lori Williams, Sue Bernard, Stuart Lancaster, Paul Trinka, Dennis Busch, Ray Barlow, Michael Finn. *D:* Russ Meyer. *W:* Russ Meyer, Jack Moran. *C:* Walter Schenk, Russ Meyer. *M:* Paul Sawtell, Bert Shefter. *VHS* *AKA: Leather Girls; Pussycat; Mankillers*

—*Brian Thomas*

Hot Rods to Hell ♪♪♪

I n the annals of "so good it's bad" cinema, seldom has the blending of a preposterous plot, bad acting, and all-around cheese been as gloriously seamless as in *Hot Rods to Hell,* a 1967 flick starring Dana Andrews as the victim of joy-riding teens.

Based on a story ("Fifty-Two Miles to Terror") published in 1956 in the *Saturday Evening Post, Hot Rods to Hell* tells the tale of a ridiculously straight-arrow and uptight Boston family bedeviled by a posse of hot-rod-driving rich-kid thugs in the California desert. It was originally produced as an ABC-TV "movie of the week," but it was deemed too hot for prime time. Ouch.

The perverse joys of *Hot Rods* are many and diverse. The acting, especially by Andrews—light-years removed from his 1940s heyday as the star of

BRUCE DERN by Brian Thomas

There always seemed to be something not quite right about Bruce Dern. Like many young actors in Hollywood during the 1960s, he took on a variety of bit parts and supporting roles in movies and TV shows playing soldiers, cowboys, and so on, but with his stringbean physique and that wild look in his eye, he was usually cast as a heavy. Sci-fi fans remember him as a crook in the classic "The Zanti Misfits" episode of *The Outer Limits*—a good performance in a good series, typical for Dern at the time.

Corman Character

He was a regular outlaw in westerns, but it took a motorcycle and not a horse to make Bruce Dern a star. A younger breed of Hollywood filmmakers began to update the western genre, replacing "nags" with "hogs" and cowboys with Hell's Angels, and Dern became a key performer in these pictures. Although Peter Fonda took the lead in Roger Corman's *The Wild Angels,* it was Dern as Loser who drew the most attention, leading to roles in *Cycle Savages* and *Rebel Rousers.*

The Wild Angels and *Rebel Rousers* gave Dern a chance to act beside his wife, Diane Ladd. Dern and Ladd divorced a few years later; their daughter, Laura Dern, has subsequently become a star. The couple reunited on-screen in *Mrs. Munck* (1995), which Diane Ladd produced, wrote, and directed.

Good at Bad

By the late 1960s, Dern had become a regular member of Corman's American International Pictures troupe, fielding good parts as a gangster in *The St. Valentine's Day Massacre,* as a Timothy Leary–like guru in *The Trip,* and as a lost hippie in *Psych-Out.* With each film he built on a screen persona as a frequently drug-addled bad egg and all-around nut case. He even played a mad scientist in a landmark of the bi-cranial horror genre, *The Incredible Two-Headed Transplant.*

Deepening his reputation as a screen villain, Dern, a fitness enthusiast who is the grandson of former Secretary of War George Dern and nephew of poet/playwright Archibald MacLeish, was one of the few actors to ever kill John Wayne on-screen, gunning down the Duke in *The Cowboys.* Despite attempts to expand his range playing good guys in *Silent Running* and Alfred Hitchcock's *Family Plot,* and alongside Jack Nicholson in *The King of Marvin Gardens* and for Nicholson as director in *Drive, He Said,* the general public probably still remembers Bruce Dern best for his scary unpredictability—especially as the crazed Vietnam vet trying to destroy the Super Bowl in 1977's *Black Sunday* or as the unstable soldier returning from Vietnam in 1978's *Coming Home,* a role that earned him an Oscar nomination for Best Supporting Actor.

such A-list films as *Laura* and *The Best Years of Our Lives*—is wooden enough to cause splinters. He plays Tom Phillips, who, with his 1960s standard-issue family, is headed West to assume ownership of a neon-bedecked Sodom called the Arena. The club, where underage drinking and wild dancing are the order of the day, is the center of the social universe for the bored teens of the surrounding area.

Tom's journey is interrupted by a brat pack of motor hoods. The kids who menace the family—especially Tom's overly ripe and oh-so-innocent daughter, Tina (Laurie Mock)—do so in the belief that it will save their beloved hangout from the scourge of Puritanism. And that ethic is embodied by Andrews, who plays his character as if a steel rod was welded up his rear.

In an early encounter with the punks, led by the malevolent, 'Vette-driving Duke (Paul Bertoya), the Phillips' Squaremobile (a pale green '61 Plymouth Fury, easily the uncoolest car of the tailfin era) is run off the road. In the most unintentionally funny moment in a film filled with them (and perhaps in cinematic history!), Andrews asks rhetorically, "What kind of animals are those?" in the excruciatingly precise tones of a thespian.

Still, Andrews looks brilliant next to Paul Genge, who plays a highway patrolman who apparently works twenty-four hours a day. It's not often you see an actor who makes Jack Webb in *Dragnet* look like Al Pacino in *The Godfather II*. Genge is a hoot as he spouts monosyllabic cop propaganda as if he's in one of those 16-mm "don't smoke dope and drive" educational films they showed at 1960s school assemblies.

To be fair, though, George Ives rules as Lank Dailey, the Hawaiian-shirt-wearing sleazeball who sells the Arena to Tom. The goggle-eyed Ives fairly oozes off the screen in all his slimy glory. And that the lowlife local kids, whose ranks include too-much-is-never-enough bad girl Gloria (played by B-movie fave Mimsy Farmer), are all essayed by actors far too old for their roles only adds to the fun. As does the hoods' absurdly conservative wardrobe: they apparently bought their threads at the same place Chip and Ernie Douglas of *My Three Sons* got theirs.

But there's more to *Hot Rods to Hell* than lame casting, questionable acting, and bizarre costuming. For instance, there's surrealism that would confound Salvador Dali; in exactly what part of the Mojave Desert would you find a picnic area that looks like an ad for Wisconsin tourism? And, of course, there's the soundtrack, a marvel of "far out" garage rock performed by the inimitable Mickey Rooney Jr. and His Combo. "Do the Chicken Walk." Say no more!

A production of noted schlockmeister Sam Katzman (*Riot on Sunset Strip*), *Hot Rods to Hell* adds up to a wonderfully weird and wigged-out trip, baby. Dig it if you can.

1967 100m/C Dana Andrews, Jeanne Crain, Mimsy Farmer, Laurie Mock, Paul Bertoya, George Ives, Gene Kirkwood, Tim Stafford. *D:* John Brahm, James Curtis Havens. *W:* Robert E. Kent. *C:* Lloyd Ahern. *M:* Fred Karger. *VHS*
AKA: 52 Miles to Terror

—*Chuck Darrow*

The Jesus Trip

Remember those bumper stickers that read, "Honk if you love Jesus"? The advertising line for this oddball biker-by-baptism flick could be "Rev your Harley if you love Jesus."

The bikers in this case are a group of scruffy riders, led by Waco (Robert Porter), who have received some hot vehicles from across the border. Rather than stop at the customs checkpoint at the authorities' request, the gang flees, prompting a shooting spree that leaves Waco with a nasty wound. Hoping to get Waco some needed care, the bikers stop at a convent where Sister Anna (Tippy Walker, who played precocious teenager Val in *The World of Henry Orient*), a pretty young nun, takes care of him. A bond develops between the caregiver and the patient, and when the lawman (Billy Green Bush) shows up looking for the outlaw cyclists, Sister Anna tries to cover for them. Soon, Sister Anna is so impressed by the gang's free-spirited ideals and disinterest in bathing that she doffs her habit and joins up with them.

In the wake of *Easy Rider*, motorcycle movies looking for a fresh angle abounded. Religious symbolism overwhelms *The Jesus Trip*, a truly misguided meshing of exploitation cycle-cinema and religious parable. Director Russ Mayberry, whose credits include episodes of *The Flying Nun*, a TV movie about the Osmond family, and the Disney feature *Unidentified Flying Oddball*, goes cuckoo for crosses, adding simple symbolism when the script or actors can't supply in-depth characterizations or believable dialogue, or when the mock Doors score can't quite get you to believe you're listening to Jim Morrison.

Porter's Waco is obviously the Christ figure here, with his facial hair, a degree of suffering from those bullet wounds, and his final call for martyrdom, but he's in need of some charisma. Meanwhile, the other gang members are generic biker types and, while Walker's Sister Anna is a potentially interesting character, her conversion from religion to cycle chick remains a long stretch.

The best moment of *The Jesus Trip* comes when three members of the gang are buried up to their necks and then terrorized by enemy bikers who closely buzz by their heads with their cycles. There's genuine tension and a sick thrill here that's absent from the rest of the film. A subplot involving the gang members unknowingly transporting drugs hidden in their bikes is reminiscent of *Easy Rider*, but it is barely explored.

The flick is a real curio. It's not everyday you get to see a religious biker movie. And after genuflecting in the house of *The Jesus Trip*, you'll know why. And to that we say amen.

1971 (PG) 84m/C Tippy Walker, Robert Porter, Billy Green Bush, Carmen Argenziano, Virgil Frye, Alan Gibbs. **D:** Russ Mayberry. **W:** Don Poston. **C:** Flemming Olsen. **M:** Bernardo Segall. *VHS*
AKA: *Under Hot Leather*

> Waco's bunch rode hard and fast to meet their fate ... and Sister Anna rode with them!
>
> —Tagline for *The Jesus Trip*

The Losers ♪♪♪

What do you do with Hell's Angels once you've starred them in a few hit movies? Why, send them to Vietnam, of course!

When a top CIA adviser to the president is captured by Viet Cong and held prisoner across the Cambodian border, an army major (Dan Kemp) calls in his biker brother, Link (William Smith)—along with his veteran buddies Limpy (Paul Koslo), Duke (Adam Roarke), Speed (Eugene Cornelius), and Dirty Dan (Houston Savage)—on a mission to get him back. While holed up in a village garage rigging their motorcycles with silly-looking armor and weaponry, the filthy quintet takes time out to make themselves as conspicuous as possible by engaging in barroom brawls, ill-advised love affairs, and other diversions from the plot. They even build a nifty scale model of the camp they have to storm. With all this time spent on buildup, and little action to pick up the slack, there's no chance that the action-packed climax will be able to make the wait worthwhile. Inevitably, despite a large number of exploding huts and bamboo towers, there are only enough thrills here to make this a semi-decent time-waster.

Not that many of the film's faults can be blamed on director Jack Starrett (*Cleopatra Jones*), who also turns up at the end to play the captured government agent. He's saddled with a script that has too many speeches for its own good and not enough ridin' and fightin'. He handles what action there is pretty well—in an emulation of Sam Peckinpah, just about everybody dies in slow-motion—and the crew creates as much authentic 'Nam atmosphere as the Philippines can provide. Among the standard themes on the soundtrack, you can hear Joan Baez and CCR knockoffs.

1970 (R) 95m/C William Smith, Adam Roarke, Paul Koslo, Houston Savage, Bernie Hamilton, Eugene Cornelius, John Garwood, Jack Starrett, Paraluman, Vic Diaz, Paquito Salcedo, Paul Nuckles, Alan Caillou, Dan Kemp. **D:** Jack Starrett. **W:** Alan Caillou. **C:** Nonong Rasca. **M:** Stu Phillips. *VHS, DVD*
AKA: *Nam's Angels*

—*Brian Thomas*

They Play Around with Murder Like They Play Around with Men!

—Tagline for *The Mini-Skirt Mob*

The Mini-Skirt Mob ♪♪

If you think hell hath no fury like a woman scorned, wait until you see what kind of fury hath a biker chick.

The biker chick in this case is Shayne, a platinum-blonde hussy played by Diane McBain. This gal is all venom, a member of the Mini-Skirts, a biker gang led by Lon (Jeremy Slate). The gang includes gals and guys—but there's no question who wears the real leather pants in this group.

Shayne's in a tizzy because her former beau, a rodeo rider named Jeff Logan (Ross Hagen), just got hitched to Connie (Sherry Jackson), a pretty brunette who works at a bank. The newlyweds are enjoying postnuptial bliss in their camper (this is a low-budget movie, after all) when Shayne and the

WARREN OATES   by Brian Thomas

Although almost always cast as a tough guy, grifter, or outlaw, there was something indefinable in Warren Oates's character that added subtle depth, humanity, and a bit of humor to every role he took on. Just look at him in *The Split,* a relatively minor heist thriller: in that film he plays a tough thief who finds himself in a trap at one point that requires him to lose his pants to escape. Not exactly glamorous; definitely down to earth.

After kicking around New York's theater and TV world in the 1950s (he took over James Dean's old job of testing gags for *Beat the Clock*), Oates found that his puffy face and Kentucky accent didn't fit in well with the Broadway set, but he thought it might make him a natural for the scores of western movies and TV shows being made in Hollywood at the time. A key turning point in his career came when Sam Peckinpah gave him a small but important role in *Ride the High Country.*

Wild Oates

The individualistic Peckinpah was fiercely loyal to those that could maintain their professionalism on one of his difficult shoots, and Oates became a regular member of the Peckinpah troupe until the mid-'70s. Directors Leslie Stevens and Burt Kennedy were also fond of using Oates, but it was the Peckinpah films that made him a cult favorite, with roles in *Major Dundee* and *The Wild Bunch.* Oates's final teaming with Peckinpah was for the classic *Bring Me the Head of Alfredo Garcia,* a near-hallucinatory road movie in which Oates plays a Mexican-based American expatriate lounge owner. Hidden early on behind huge sunglasses and cocktails as he croons at a piano, Oates is forced to go on the title quest to save his own skin from the Mexican mob.

During the late '60s he also struck up a fertile professional relationship with another Hollywood outsider, director Monte Hellman. Starting with 1967's *The Shooting,* Oates starred in a string of Hellman pictures that quickly became cult favorites, including the existential road movie *Two-Lane Blacktop, Cockfighter* (based on Charles Willeford's noirish novel), and the European western *China 9, Liberty 37* (which features Peckinpah in a supporting role).

Steady Character

By the late '70s, many filmmakers had discovered Oates, even if he was still not quite a household word. Several attempts were made to acquaint larger audiences with Oates's chameleonic charms through television remakes; he took John Wayne's role in *True Grit,* Humphrey Bogart's role in *The African Queen,* and prominent parts in miniseries versions of *Black Beauty* and *East of Eden.*

But Warren Oates only gained true international stardom in the eyes of his loyal fans. A new generation of filmmakers, who loved him for his Peckinpah and Hellman movies, cast him in iconic roles in movies like *Stripes, 1941,* and *Blue Thunder.* Those that worked with him could only confess that he was a hard man to know, but maybe they were looking in the wrong direction. The true Warren Oates could likely only be known by watching him on-screen, where a squint of the eyes or a crooked grin spoke volumes.

Mini-Skirts arrive at the front dirt patch. Soon, the gang members are swigging beers, grooving to loud music, screwing all over the grass, and making life miserable for the newlyweds. Bob Eubanks would not approve.

What follows are tussles, catfights, gunplay, cycle crashes, and a nasty face burn, topped off by Harry Dean Stanton making it with two biker chicks. Not bad for an eighty-eight-minute movie.

The cast of the film is game and a real treasure for schlock aficionados. Slate and Hagen are old standbys at this sort of thing, but the female performers are what make this enterprise of special interest. McBain (*I Sailed to Tahiti with an All-Girl Crew*) is juiced up and having a grand old time as the Queen Meanie; Jackson, formerly Danny Thomas's daughter on *Make Room for Daddy,* is all hubba-hubba, even while being terrorized; and Patricia McCormack, *The Bad Seed* herself, does well as the sympathetic Mini-Skirter.

The Mini-Skirt Mob was produced by American International Pictures as part of their popular and seemingly unending series of biker pics. But the film is not exactly what one expects. Cycle stunts and scenes of the Mini-Skirts on the road are sadly limited, and much of what passes for action involves scenes in the camper and the ho-hum mountain terrain. Applaud director Maury Dexter (*Hell's Belles*) for taking a different approach to the genre and attempting to make a psychological biker flick. But the story and tension don't rise to the level of *The Wild One* or even *The Wild Angels.* The spirit is willing, but *The Mini-Skirt Mob* just doesn't have the right wheels.

1968 (PG) 88m/C Jeremy Slate, Ross Hagen, Diane McBain, Sherry Jackson, Patricia McCormack, Harry Dean Stanton, Ronnie Rondell Jr. *D:* Maury Dexter. *W:* James Gordon White. *C:* Archie R. Dalzell. *M:* Les Baxter. *VHS*

Satan's Sadists ♪♪♪♥

Sam Sherman and Al Adamson launched Independent International Pictures with this rude and raw-boned biker movie after the western picture they'd planned to make in Europe collapsed. Their aim was to make a picture that included as much sex and violence as they could afford, aimed squarely at the drive-in audience, and they succeeded brilliantly.

Former child star and dancer Russ Tamblyn plays against type as Anchor, leader of the vicious Satans outlaw motorcycle gang. Hitchhiking Vietnam veteran Johnny (Gary Kent) gets picked up by vacationing cop Charlie (Scott Brady of *Mighty Gorga* and *Operation Bikini*) and his wife Nora (Evelyn Frank), and they soon happen upon a desert diner (run by Kent Taylor of *The Crawling Hand* and the *Boston Blackie* TV series) just in time for the Satans' arrival. The outlaws' rude behavior doesn't sit well with the other patrons, and it's not long before an altercation occurs. While Anchor and most of the Satans are outside amusing themselves with the captive diner patrons, Johnny manages to kill two of the bikers and escape with waitress Tracy (Jackie Taylor, who was actor Chuck Connors's secretary at the time). The Satans trail the pair into the nearby hills and, after spending some time hassling a trio of sunbathing beauties, close in on Johnny for a showdown.

Although the plot is paper thin, *Satan's Sadists* nevertheless plays well as a western updated for the late 1960s, mostly on the strength of Adamson's well-framed direction and the movie's violent action scenes. The imaginative camera angles on picturesque desert locations (courtesy of B-movie stalwart Gary Graver and future Oscar-winner Vilmos Zsigmond) help heighten the tension and increase production values. Several of the actors outclass the basic genre material, especially Tamblyn, who is so understated that he's almost hidden. He and Bud Cardos (as Firewater) come alive for a terrific fight scene near the end, doing all their own tough stunts. Regina Carrol, a popular Las Vegas singer and dancer (billed by Sherman as the Freak-Out Girl), also stands out in her role as a brokenhearted biker chick. After the film, she married Adamson and went on to appear in most of his subsequent movies.

In all, *Satan's Sadists* works as a solid little action item with just a touch of social commentary. Sherman and Adamson built on the cachet created by this picture to successfully run Independent International through the end of the 1970s, and their library of films is still popular on home video.

1969 (R) 87m/C Russ Tamblyn, Scott Brady, John "Bud" Cardos, Robert Dix, Gary Kent, Greydon Clark, Kent Taylor, Regina Carrol, Jackie Taylor, William Bonner, Bobby Clark. **D:** Al Adamson. **W:** Al Adamson, Greydon Clark. **C:** Gary Graver, Vilmos Zsigmond. **M:** Harley Hatcher. *VHS, DVD*
AKA: *Nightmare Bloodbath*

—*Brian Thomas*

She-Devils on Wheels ♫♫♫

Shot for peanuts (and it shows), this drive-in classic from Herschell Gordon Lewis (*Blood Feast*) kicked off the female biker genre, and it cleaned up at the box office. Keeping his priorities straight, Lewis cast women who were bikers first, actresses second, rather than casting actresses who might be able to ride, and he was wise to stress authenticity over stagecraft.

Queen (Betty Connell) is the tough leader of an outlaw, female motorcycle gang known as the Man-eaters on Motorbikes. The Man-eaters terrorize citizens of the small Florida town of Medley, even dominating the local male bikers. Typical activities of the gang are shown via the initiation of their little mascot, Honey-Pot (Nancy Lee Noble). The girl who wins the opening bike race has first pick of the "stud line," bedding down with her choice of men. When a male biker gang rides into town for a challenge, the Man-eaters promptly thrash them. Seeking to get back at the ladies, the guys kidnap and beat up Honey-Pot, but the Man-eaters launch a plan to get more than even with them. The climactic revenge sequence is one of the most memorable in the annals of biker cinema.

Lewis was never the most polished of filmmakers, but he made a career out of breaking new ground in the field of exploitation, and *She-Devils* is no exception. It contains scenes of assault, kidnapping, torture, robbery, murder, and disturbing the peace, but it's really not as harsh as some of Lewis's other films. Except for a few scenes of mayhem, all the sex and violence is suggested rather than shown. The flick is finely honed by Lewis—there's not a

MONTE HELLMAN by Brian Thomas

I n need of young, cheap talent to help fill the demand they'd helped create for low-budget drive-in fare in the 1950s, Gene and Roger Corman mined the talent pool of UCLA's film school and struggling stage productions, coming away with quite a few individuals that went on—quite unexpectedly—to change the shape of American cinema.

Monte Hellman got his big chance as part of the crew traveling to South Dakota with Corman's Filmgroup company to help shoot the quirky war movie *Ski Troop Attack.* The Cormans, ever ready to squeeze a production dollar, had Hellman film a second picture using basically the same cast and locations for a very different script. Hellman made his debut with *Beast from Haunted Cave,* a monster movie that overcomes its low budget and structure as the horror version of *Key Largo,* set in the snow to generate eerie shocks, genuine drama, and suspense. Hellman may have only had a guy in a rickety spider-monster suit covered in phony cobwebs, but he managed to make it all darn creepy, especially in scenes set in the monster's lair (which subsequently inspired *Alien*).

Bumpy Rides

Now highly regarded by a growing cult of fans, Hellman's career did not skyrocket after this respectable first film, and ever since his career has been frustratingly bumpy (frustrating both for himself and for his fans). In a pattern that would be duplicated for much of his career, he spent many of the following years doing piecemeal work: he and director Jack Hill were both hired to prepare expanded versions of Filmgroup B-movies for television distribution. Such patchwork filmmaking reached its acme with Corman's 1963 feature *The Terror,* the final version of which included footage shot by Hellman, Hill, Francis Ford Coppola, and others.

foot of film wasted. There may not be anything fancy about it, but the crude performances and home-movie framing give it a raw immediacy. He even has the local cops playing themselves. And don't leave when you reach "The End": a coda appears afterward that's one of the kookiest scenes in the picture.

1968 82m/C Betty Connell, Christie Wagner, Pat Poston, Nancy Lee Noble, Ruby Tuesday. *D:* Herschell Gordon Lewis. *W:* Allison Louise Downe. *C:* Roy Collodi. *M:* Larry Wellington, Herschell Gordon Lewis. *VHS, DVD*
AKA: Maneaters

—*Brian Thomas*

Two-Lane Blacktop 🎵🎵🎵🎵

A n existential road movie that gearheads can get into, *Two-Lane Blacktop* was the legendary lost film of the early 1970s. Talked about but rarely seen since its 1971 theatrical run, the film practi-

After shooting a pair of adventure films in the Philippines, Hellman saw his career take an upswing with the creation of two philosophical westerns, *Ride in the Whirlwind* (starring and written by Jack Nicholson) and *The Shooting* (also with Nicholson). In between, Hellman edited Corman's *The Wild Angels*, a project that only increased Hellman's and Nicholson's high regard for each other. However, it was another actor in *The Shooting* who has become inextricably linked to Hellman: Warren Oates, who would star in three of Hellman's best films: *Two-Lane Blacktop* (1972), *Cockfighter* (1974), and *China 9, Liberty 37* (1978).

Road Ruler

Two-Lane Blacktop, a surprisingly existential road-race feature that rose above its drive-in target market, has had a growing reputation as a cult classic for decades, with only its relative scarcity accounting for a following considerably smaller than that for *Easy Rider. Cockfighter,* a dusty suspense drama drawn from a fatalistic novel by Charles Willeford, ably illustrates the desperation of its seedy characters via the repellently bloody "sport" through which they make their living. And *China 9, Liberty 37* is another western, this time one of a more challenging stripe, shot with an international cast.

Sadly, *China 9* is the last of Hellman's more personal film work, with the remainder of his resumé taken up with editing, second-unit work, and half-credits in which he was either brought in to hack together an unfinished work or had someone else hack together his own unfinished assignment. However, ever since he served as a producer for Hellman fan Quentin Tarantino's breakthrough picture *Reservoir Dogs*—a film that at one time Hellman was to direct—rumors have persisted that Hellman is at work on one project or another. Fates willing, we'll one day have another Hellman classic to enjoy.

cally disappeared from sight, its video release held up because of Univesal Studios' lack of interest in clearing the film's musical rights. Finally, in 1999, *Two-Lane Blacktop* resurfaced with a video release by independent Anchor Bay, and it quickly cemented its status as one of the great road movies of all time.

The film features two rock stars and one neophyte actress in the lead roles. James Taylor, with the long hair of his solemn "Sweet Baby James" stage, plays the Driver, the owner of a souped-up '55 Chevy in primer color. Along with his closest ally, known only as the Mechanic (charismatic Beach Boy Dennis Wilson), the Driver tools around the country competing in races against fellow hot-rodders willing to put up a couple hundred dollars as prize money. Joining the two on the road is the Girl (first-timer Laurie Bird), a hippie hitchhiker who has no problem swapping sex for a good ride.

While on the road in Arizona, the three encounter G.T.O. (Warren Oates), the weird and wired owner of an orange 1970 Pontiac "Goat." G.T.O, who likes to make up stories about his life for all who will listen, decides to take on the Driver in a cross-country competition that will end in Washington,

D.C. The high-stakes prize is the biggest the Driver has gone for yet: If he wins, he gets the Goat. If he loses, goodbye '55 Chevy.

The race is a methodically paced journey through roadside America, with stops at gas stations, tiny diners, and swap meets along the way. There are encounters with cops and other hitchhikers, including a cowboy (Harry Dean Stanton) who makes sexual advances to G.T.O.

At times, *Two-Lane Blacktop* plays more like a documentary—even a painting—than a feature film. Detailed attention is paid to the composition of scenes, rather than how or where the camera moves. As a result of this cinematic self-consciousness, the characters are explored through their movement in scenes and how they relate to each other and to their environment. Complementing this style, the film's soundtrack consists mostly of "driving" songs played on car radios (the Doors' "Moonlight Drive," Chuck Berry's "Maybellene").

The script, penned by Rudy Wurlitzer (*Pat Garrett and Billy the Kid*) and Will Corry, is sparse and low-key with an offhand, wise-guy humor to it. When the Girl asks the Mechanic, "Which way are we going?" he replies, "East." The Girl says, "I've never been east before."

The jarring, surprising ending of *Two-Lane Blacktop* baffled audiences and movie projectionists alike. But it makes one think: Is this whole thing a dream? One also wonders if the film could have inspired a Bruce Springsteen song or two. Was the Boss thinking of *Two-Lane Blacktop* when he wrote "Racing in the Streets"?

The labeling of characters in lieu of names adds a mythical quality to the film. But it makes sense that these characters don't have real names— they don't seem to exist for reasons other than what they do. Driving and working on cars define the Driver and the Mechanic completely. The Girl could be any girl of the era, a prototypical flower child in search of herself. And like his beloved hot wheels, G.T.O is bigger than life and flashy. One would think that this technique would depersonalize the characters, but the film is extraordinarily personal in many ways. After watching it, one has the sense of knowing everything there is to know about the four protagonists. Except, of course, their real names.

Director Monte Hellman brought a similarly enigmatic and intellectual quality to two low-budget westerns with Jack Nicholson, *Ride the Whirlwind* (1965) and *The Shooting* (1967). Before *Two-Lane Blacktop* opened, it was primed to become the Next Big Thing, Univeral Studios' answer to Columbia's counterculture smash *Easy Rider*. *Esquire* magazine, then the hippest publication around, not only featured it as a cover story but hailed it as a masterpiece, reprinting the script in its entirety. However, the film unceremoniously belly-flopped, as critics and its young target audience found it slow-moving and remote. Taylor and Wilson, both giving fine performances here, never appeared in a film again, while Bird, a girlfriend of Art Garfunkel, went on to act in just two other movies before committing suicide in 1979 at the age of twenty-six.

The passage of time has been kind to *Two-Lane Blacktop*. It has been rediscovered, its nuts and bolts reevaluated. Although it hasn't been an easy ride, the engine's still in good shape.

"If I'm not grounded pretty soon, I'm gonna go into orbit."

—G.T.O. (Warren Oates), in *Two-Lane Blacktop*

1971 (R) 102m/C James Taylor, Warren Oates, Dennis Wilson, Laurie Bird, Richard Ruth, David Drake, Alan Vint, Harry Dean Stanton. *W:* Rudy Wurlitzer, Will Corry. *C:* Jack Dearson. *M:* Billy James. *VHS, DVD*

Warren Oates (G.T.O.) looks askance at the road-racing trio of Dennis Wilson (the Mechanic), Laurie Bird (the Girl), and James Taylor (the Driver) in Monte Hellman's *Two-Lane Blacktop.*

Vanishing Point 🦴🦴🦴🦴

Part smash-'em-up car-chase flick, part religious parable, and part hip counterculture statement, *Vanishing Point* has amassed a strong cult of followers over the years. After the film initially came up with an empty tank at the box office, fans of muscle cars subsequently caught on, digging the star of the show, a kick-ass 1970 Dodge Challenger 440. And those not into hot cars heralded the film's spiritual vibes and antiauthoritarian sentiments.

The film is filled with flashbacks (title cards that read "Two days earlier," for example), an oddball soundtrack (boasting gospel, bluegrass, soul, and rock), and lots of camera trickery, all designed to make it feel "now." In other words, *Vanishing Point* was dated the day after it opened in theaters. To its credit, the film remains highly watchable today, and it still delivers a high-octane kick.

The simple storyline posits Barry Newman as Kowalski, a lonely former race-car driver and ex-Marine who now makes a living driving cars from Denver to San Francisco. Kowalski places a bet that he can guide that white Challenger 440 R/T on that route in fifteen hours. Despite his boss's doubts, he's off, figuratively and literally. Kowalski starts popping speed to get him out of the starting gate, and it doesn't take long for him to put his pedal to the heavy metal.

Kowalski's fast driving gets him into big trouble with the law, and he's soon dodging cops of all sorts during his seemingly impossible trek. He also encounters an unusual group of characters along the route, including a demented snake wrangler (an enjoyably wigged-out Dean Jagger), two homosexuals who have it in for him, some hippies, and a biker chick (Gilda Texter) aping Lady Godiva, riding naked on a cycle.

Vanishing Point is filled with hair-raising stunt sequences, with Newman reportedly behind the wheel for many of them. There's lots of lane shifting and criss-crossing with parallel traffic, most of it done with the Rocky Mountains and the Nevada deserts as backdrops.

As Kowalski's trip gets increasingly dangerous, blind disc jockey Super Soul (Cleavon Little), a precursor of sorts to *Do the Right Thing*'s Radio Raheem, begins following the action on a police monitor, offering Kowalski advice and turning him into "the last American hero," a man taking on the "blue meanies" all by himself. Whether Kowalski actually hears the DJ's advice is another story, as the film doesn't care much about coordinating Super Soul's voice and Kowalski's radio listening. But the vibes are where it's at, after all.

Kowalski is defined via fragmented flashbacks: a screwed-up romance, a failed stint as a cop, military service, some time spent behind the wheel of a race car. He's a loner now, and the hint in the beginning of the film is that this Denver–San Francisco sojourn could be the last ride of his life. The manhunt for Kowalski and the speed freak himself have become big enough stories that even CBS News is covering it.

With his long '70s sideburns and his relatively cool demeanor, Barry Newman doesn't really make a convincing Christ figure, but *Vanishing Point* is adamant about the audience accepting him as, at the very least, a really cool martyr, a man who sacrifices his life for the simple love of the open road and the sheer joy of going very, very, very fast. If you can't get behind that, man, what can you get behind?

Director Richard C. Sarafian (*Man in the Wilderness*) and cinematographer John A. Alonzo (who would photograph *Chinatown* so masterfully a few years later) use lots of unnecessary zoom shots, giving the film a true 1970s look. The musical mix is odd, with Delaney & Bonnie & Friends (including Rita Coolidge) appearing briefly in the film and on the soundtrack, which also includes some generic rock tunes, quick-picking bluegrass instrumentals, Mountain's "Mississippi Queen," and gospel numbers used to add an exclamation mark to the religious imagery.

Against the wishes of Sarafian, *Vanishing Point*'s studio, Fox, cut the film by about nine minutes prior to its release. The excised footage, featuring Charlotte Rampling as a joint-toking hippie hitchhiker picked up by Newman,

Tighten your seat belt. You never had a trip like this before.

—Tagline for
Vanishing Point

was featured in the British version of the film, which is included, along with the original American release print, in the 2004 DVD of the film.

Many films have tried to emulate *Vanishing Point*'s rebel-takes-on-whomever-in-a-high-speed-car-chase motif over the years, including *Gone in Sixty Seconds* (the original and the remake), Ron Howard's *Grand Theft Auto,* the *Smokey and the Bandit* movies, and even *Thelma and Louise.* For sheer muscle power and authentic '70s ambience, however, you can't beat *Vanishing Point,* a film that floors it from the get-go. Meep-meep.

1971 **(R)** **107m/C** Barry Newman, Cleavon Little, Victoria Medlin, Dean Jagger, Paul Koslo, Timothy Scott. *D:* Richard C. Sarafian. *W:* Guillermo Cain, Malcolm Scott. *C:* John A. Alonzo. *M:* Jimmy Bowen. *VHS, DVD*

Chapter 11

Radical, Man

"**T**he whole world is watching!" "Down with the Establishment!" "Make love, not war!" "Burn the bra!"

The signs were visible everywhere throughout the '60s and into the '70s. People were angry and confused over a variety of things: the war, the generation gap, the sexual revolution, the country's leaders. You name the topic and someone, somewhere was livid about it.

At the movies, Hollywood tried to tackle some of the injustices the kids were upset about. Studio execs wanted to speak to America's youth—and thereby make a buck off of them—but they were only willing to go so far. For example, the Vietnam War itself was a topic virtually ignored by the studios, but the stateside reaction to the war did find its way onto the big screen in films like *The Strawberry Statement,* based on the student riots that took place at Columbia University and featuring Bruce Davison as a newly radicalized student, and *Getting Straight,* with Elliott Gould as a legendary revolutionary torn between joining the Establishment and helping a new generation of kids follow in his rebellious footsteps. Interestingly, the protagonists of both of these films used their protesting as a way to score with their respective chicks. In American studio-backed films, it simply wasn't enough to delve into the politics of the troubled times. "Getting some" had to be on the agenda as well, especially with all the free love expressed on college campuses in those days. In other words, the kids may not have been all right, but the sex sure was.

Sometimes more daring films were made, but the filmmakers encountered difficulties getting studios to distribute them. Haskell Wexler, a cinematographer with an Academy Award under his belt for *Who's Afraid of Virginia Woolf?,* made *Medium Cool* without studio interference. He then sold it to Paramount, who sat on it for a year until dumping it in theaters with little advertising and an "X" rating. The studio suits were fearful that Wexler's landmark mix of fiction and factual footage from the turbulent '68 Democratic convention in Chicago would provoke rioting. Had *Medium Cool* been issued a year earlier, it may have had some impact, both in enlightening the public and in showing Hollywood that unconventional, politically charged films could be made in the same manner as they were being done in Europe.

In Europe, after all, there were few restrictions on filmmakers willing to create challenging films that made audiences question their own government's motives or ponder the politics of contemporary times. These films eventually crossed the Atlantic and, flying in the face of conventional Hollywood wisdom, won great acclaim with critics and college-age crowds who simply weren't getting the same kind of challenging fare from American filmmakers. For example, Greece's Costa-Gavras boldly depicted political skullduggery and assassination in *Z* in 1969, while earlier, in 1967, Italy's Gillo Pontecorvo surveyed the complexities of the French-Algerian war in *The Battle of Algiers*. Bernardo Bertolucci, another Italian, explored the seeds and impact of fascism in his native land in *The Spider's Stratagem* and *The Conformist*. And the ever-defiant Gallic filmmaker Jean-Luc Godard joined fellow French New Wavers Chris Marker, Alain Resnais, and Agnès Varda for the 1967 antiwar anthology *Far from Vietnam*. Unlike their American counterparts, these filmmakers didn't need to include a sappy love story, sex scenes, or recognizable pop tunes in their efforts in order to have the privilege of making salient political statements.

Then as now, young, politically motivated American filmmakers knew that if they wanted to speak to the public through their films, they would occasionally have to do so through non-studio financing. New York–based Brian De Palma tackled the Vietnam War, racial inequality, the draft, and the impact of these troubling topics on others of his generation through his independently financed *Greetings* (1968) and the 1970 sequel, *Hi, Mom!,* both starring a young Robert De Niro. De Palma's experimental, satiric works had enough impact on the moviegoing public that the Hollywood Establishment could not fail to notice that kids were not necessarily seeking escapism in theaters during the troubled times—and that the country didn't devolve into an anarchic mess just because a film dared to confront volatile issues.

So Hollywood did depict the unsettling current of the counterculture in a number of films, but, predictably, these subjects were treated in a fairly conventional manner. The most radical—in style and content—came from Arthur Penn, hot off his *Bonnie and Clyde* success. In 1969 the TV-trained director brought *Alice's Restaurant,* Arlo Guthrie's lengthy musical narrative, to the screen. Among the subjects touched on in this free-spirited, anti-Establishment film are Vietnam, draft dodging, communal living, and Arlo's own life as son of folksinger Woody Guthrie.

Scoring was a big part of the much-anticipated American debut of Italian filmmaker Michelangelo Antonioni, whose *Zabriskie Point* boasted a hallucinogenic lovemaking scene amidst natural rock formations in Death Valley. The rest of the expensive, highly hyped message film from the *Blow-Up* director proved to be a bummer to counterculture audiences confused over his languid, antinarrative style and to critics, who panned it. Influential critic Pauline Kael, writing for the *New Yorker,* called it "A pathetic mess . . . a huge, jerry-built, crumbling ruin of a movie."

Zabriskie Point certainly didn't help the cause for serious-minded, overtly political filmmaking, but John Avildsen's *Joe,* a low-budget production released the same year, addressed a central issue concerning many Americans: the depth of the chasm between the countercultural youth and the Establishment. This downbeat exploration of generational tensions left young and old audiences alike in a deep funk. *Joe* tells of Manhattan executive Dennis Patrick, who brutally attacks hippie daughter Susan Sarandon's drug-dealing boyfriend, then teams with Peter Boyle, a working-class bigot, to try to track Sarandon down among the pot-smoking flower children in Greenwich Village. The journey is filled with fear and loathing from all sides, ending on a hopeless note for the Establishment, the younger generation, and the entire country, for that matter. With *Joe,* the hopes and dreams of the Woodstock Nation were flushed down the toilet. And once those dreams had expired, Hollywood could sigh with relief and go back to safer territory.

Alice's Restaurant ♪♪♪♪

Sing along now! "You can get anything you want / At Alice's Restaurant."

Arlo Guthrie's hit eighteen-minute talking blues song "The Alice's Restaurant Massacree," an underdog ditty of how a silly police hassle allowed the vocalist to 4-F himself out of the Vietnam War, inspired this melancholic ode to fading '60s counterculture idealism. Part of the song's sly humor is that it never got around to telling you much about Alice and her restaurant. Director Arthur Penn, right between *Bonnie and Clyde* and *Little Big Man,* fills us in.

Arlo Guthrie ably plays himself, footloose son of folksinger Woody (Joseph Boley), now dying in a hospital from Huntington's chorea. To rednecks and authority figures, Arlo's just another long-haired freak. Leaving behind bad scenes in Montana and at his stuffy music college, Arlo plays a few gigs (turning down offers from groupies), visits his father, and stays in a nearby Massachusetts town with old friends Alice (Pat Quinn) and her common-law husband Ray (James Broderick). The couple bought a deconsecrated church and turned it into a hippie crash pad, which attracts a variety of young people, including Shelly (Michael McClanathan), Alice's twitchy, heroin-using ex-flame, whose presence causes Ray some discomfort. Alice also starts up her own restaurant (Arlo records his catchy jingle as a radio ad).

As if he's afraid of getting too commercial (or lighthearted), Penn hastily rushes through narrative chapters that recap the song: a Thanksgiving feast leaves a pile of trash that Arlo heaves off a rural hillside when he finds the town dump closed for the holiday. Local cops treat this infraction as a major incident, though their case unravels as a fiasco in court. Subsequently, when Arlo shows up for his draft physical he tries to act like a psycho killer, unfit for service in Vietnam. That doesn't work, but he's got an arrest record (albeit for littering), which puts him in "Group W," along with "mother-rapers . . . father-stabbers . . . father-rapers!" This gets him off the hook, rendering him morally unsuitable for the army.

Back at the commune Alice gripes that her flower children guests are more like freeloaders; neither they nor a boozy Ray help much with the running of the restaurant. Shelly's caught stealing from the group, hiding his drug stash in mobiles he creates to decorate the homestead (meanwhile the movie smiles on casual marijuana use, applying the usual "dope good"/"smack bad" dichotomy). The addict flees to NYC and fatally overdoses, and at the same time Woody Guthrie succumbs to his illness. Alice and Ray lift the gloom by throwing a groovy wedding ceremony for themselves, but the commune's days are numbered. Like the Age of Aquarius itself, *Alice's Restaurant* ends with a puzzled, sad shrug. The long closing shot is of Alice, all by herself, the party over.

Actual hippies filled out most of the cast, including the real Alice Brock (as Suzy) and Officer William Obanhein, the tune's Obie, as himself. They blend well with the professional actors, except maybe in the "Group W" sequence wherein M. Emmett Walsh is encouraged to really ham it up as a sergeant. McClanathan certainly seemed to have a lock on junkie roles in the early '70s, with his part in this film plus *Jennifer on My Mind* and *The Panic in Needle Park*. Folkie Pete Seeger also shows up, comforting the stricken, speechless Woody with a bedside concert, with Arlo on backup guitar. The real Woody Guthrie died in 1967, but this picture's vibe is more like three years later, when the Woodstock generation had a last hurrah, then looked around bewildered and couldn't figure out what to do next. The film is worth seeing—just don't let its elegiac tendencies keep you from enjoying the song.

1970 (R) 111m/C Arlo Guthrie, Pat Quinn, James Broderick, Michael McClanathan, Tina Chen, Geoff Outlaw, Sylvia Davis, Pete Seeger, M. Emmett Walsh, Kathleen Dabney. *D:* Arthur Penn. *W:* Venable Herndon, Arthur Penn. *C:* Michael Nebbia. *M:* Arlo Guthrie. *VHS, DVD*

—*Charles A. Cassady Jr.*

Between the Lines ♫♫♫

The scrappy alternative weekly that came of age in the 1960s is now almost extinct. Some larger cities still have a weekly newspaper marketed toward college kids and hip urbanites, but in most cases these are owned by large corporations or media conglomerates. Heck, the *Village Voice,* the granddaddy of all alt-weeklies, is owned by a big company and was once even controlled by Hartz Mountain, the pet-food giant.

Between the Lines, a lively and insightful comedy, concerns a Boston newspaper called the *Back Bay Mainline,* a publication that made its name covering the turmoil of the 1960s but can't seem to adapt to the 1970s. The paper's once-committed readers have grown older and are now less interested in revolution than in revolutionary tips for interior design. Harry (John Heard), the crusading editor, cut his teeth on breaking stories of importance to the counterculture and now feels deeply troubled by the possibility of seeing his beloved *Mainline* acquired by a company with deep pockets. Harry simply can't face the fact that his brand of muckraking journalism—and possibly his career—is being ushered out the door.

The small but colorful staff of the *Mainline* have their own problems and personality quirks. Harry's girlfriend, Abbie (Lindsay Crouse), the paper's head photographer, isn't sure where the relationship with her stubborn boyfriend is going. Michael (Stephen Collins), a former star writer and Harry's rival, is ready to leave the paper when he takes an advance on a novel; Laura (Gwen Welles), Michael's wife, is a little uncertain of her husband's fidelity. There's also Max (Jeff Goldblum), the motor-mouthed rock critic who meets chicks by giving them private rock journalism lessons, and David (Bruno Kirby), a novice reporter who's doing everything in his power to track down a notorious record bootlegger in order to get a big story.

It should come as no surprise that *Between the Lines* director Joan Micklin Silver (*Hester Street, Crossing Delancey*) once wrote for the *Voice* and that coscreenwriter Fred Barron spent time at the *Boston Phoenix*. They pepper the film with wry observations of life in the world of a weekly and successfully capture the odd assortment of characters that make their living there.

Like *American Graffiti,* another ensemble-oriented coming-of-age movie that aimed to chronicle the end of an era, *Between the Lines* boasts a terrific supporting cast, many of whom make their screen debuts here. Along with the aforementioned performers, there's Jill Eikenberry as the loyal secretary, Lewis J. Stadlen as the bottom-line business manager, and Marilu Henner playing a stripper who gets interviewed for one of the *Mainline*'s new, trendy articles.

While the film handles some of the personal drama in simplistic and often clumsy ways, *Between the Lines* is mostly knowing, funny, and honest, and many of the problems faced by the film's characters ring true today. To sell out or not to sell out? That was the question. Now, in the days of Jayson Blair, Stephen Glass, and numerous one-newspaper cities, the answer seems all too clear.

1978 (R) 101m/C John Heard, Lindsay Crouse, Stephen Collins, Jeff Goldblum, Gwen Welles, Jill Eikenberry, Bruno Kirby, Marilu Henner, Lewis J. Stadlen, Joe Morton, Lane Smith. **D:** Joan Micklin Silver. **W:** Fred Barron, David Halpern. **C:** Kenneth Van Sickle. **M:** Michael Kamen. *VHS*

> "I try, I really try ... but when I see this girl of such a beautiful spirit suffer this indignity ... I just go BERSERK!"
>
> —Tom Laughlin, *Billy Jack*

Billy Jack 🦴🦴🦴

In *Billy Jack,* Tom Laughlin resurrects his ex–Green Beret antihero from 1967's *The Born Losers* to take on an even bigger target than the outlaw biker gangs he faced the first time out. Now it's the Establishment he's after, and by the time Billy Jack gets through with them, we had a drive-in classic and box-office legend.

Billy Jack, now in touch with his Indian heritage, has appointed himself protector of the reservation, giving him the opportunity to face off against crooked local officials who have been poaching wild horses to butcher for dog food. When Barbara (Julie Webb) returns home pregnant after running away to Haight-Ashbury, she is beaten and then abandoned by her police officer father (Kenneth Tobey). When she's taken in by the reservation's "freedom school," run by Billy Jack's girlfriend, Jean (Delores Taylor), the friendly relationship the Indians have with the sheriff (Clark Howat) and the town begins to break down. It briefly appears that an improvisational comedy group led by Howard Hesseman will bring peace to the community, but the deputy and the evil councilman's son (David Roya) go too far, making it necessary for Billy Jack to go berserk.

The secret of *Billy Jack*'s success is in its paradoxes. By portraying young people living uncomplicated lives as they explore spiritual values, Laughlin targeted the growing flower-power segment of the moviegoing market. But instead of holding the pacifists to the standards of Gandhi, the filmmaker exploits the anger on both sides of the generation gap with a Wild West–style two-fisted action hero capable of kicking asses and taking names if provoked. The film even scored on the music charts—both with the original release and again during the film's 1974 re-release—with Coven's rendition of "One Tin Soldier" (previously a hit for Original Caste in 1969).

Budgeted at around $800,000, *Billy Jack* would have sat on the lower rung of drive-in triple bills if Laughlin hadn't rescued it from Warner Bros. and taken over its marketing campaign. His efforts resulted in an astonishing $98 million take, making it one of the most successful independent features ever made. It also paved the way for two controversial and financially disastrous *Billy Jack* sequels (*The Trial of Billy Jack* and *Billy Jack Goes to Washington*) and Laughlin's western, *The Master Gunfighter*.

1971 (PG) 114m/C Tom Laughlin, Delores Taylor, Clark Howat, Victor Izay, Julie Webb, David Roya, Debbie Schock, Stan Rice, Lynn Baker, Howard Hesseman, Kenneth Tobey. **D:** Tom Laughlin. **W:** Tom Laughlin, Delores Taylor. **C:** Fred J. Koenekamp, John M. Stephens. **M:** Mundell Lowe. *VHS, DVD*

—*Brian Thomas*

End of the Road ♫♫♪

As a college graduation ceremony erupts into joyful chaos, a professor wanders away from the crowd in a zombified state; news photographs show antiwar protests and Vietnam atrocities; the American flag is bathed in Dayglo red. These images set the stage for this exceptionally well-acted, unremittingly depressing account of a college prof's identity crisis. The filmmakers use John Barth's 1958 novel of the same name to craft an all-purpose parable about the end of the '60s. Like its hero, the film is bathed in an air of melancholy.

Professor Jacob Horner (Stacy Keach), after walking away from his college teaching job, stands immobilized on a suburban train platform until the mysterious Doctor D (James Earl Jones) comes to his aid. The doctor takes

TOM LAUGHLIN by Brian Thomas

A young actor named Tom Laughlin met a young lady named Delores Taylor and began to court her. Reacting to the treatment of Native Americans living on a reservation near her home, Tom and Delores began to write a story about a hero who defended the peaceful tribe. Laughlin went on to carve out a career in TV and movies—an episode of *Wagon Train,* his first starring role in Robert Altman's *The Delinquents,* as "Lover Boy" in *Gidget*—but his ambition was to write and direct his own films. Within a few years, he'd begun making low-budget pictures of his own, starting with the juvenile-delinquent dramas *The Proper Time, Like Father Like Son,* and its sequel, *The Young Sinner.* Eventually, though, he left Hollywood to run a Montessori school. But that reservation story wasn't forgotten.

A New Kind of Hero

Midway through the '60s, Roger Corman created the biker movie craze, and Laughlin joined in with *Born Losers,* which pitted an ex–Green Beret half-Indian karate expert named Billy Jack, who is trying to leave war behind, against a monstrous outlaw motorcycle gang. Released through American International Pictures in 1967, the picture did terrific business. Along with Bruce Lee's Kato on the *Green Hornet* television show, Billy Jack represented a kind of hero that Americans hadn't seen before and presaged the coming age of martial arts movies. Tom moved on to direct some exploitation films under the name Don Henderson (one of many pseudonyms he used), but when the *Born Losers* receipts began to pile up, he and Delores felt the time was right to make the movie they'd been planning for over a decade.

Billy Jack, which was both a low-budget drive-in action picture and a social commentary film, went on to become a major phenomenon, grossing nearly $100 million to date. With a major hit on their hands, Tom and Delores went to work on a sequel that would contain everything but the

Horner to his Institute of Psychic Remobilization, where he "reconnects" Horner to the human race by bombarding him with sights, sounds, and sudden commands. Horner emerges a new man: he acts like a normal person, affecting a witty and urbane persona and eventually scoring a new teaching post at another local college. While there, he makes his first important emotional connection by embarking on an affair with Rennie (Dorothy Tristan), the wife of fellow teacher Joe Morgan (Harris Yulin), a forthright, uptight, gun-toting Scoutmaster and fascist.

Given Aram Avakian's expert work as an editor on films like *Mickey One* and *You're a Big Boy Now,* it comes as no surprise that most of the memorable moments in *End of the Road* contain startling juxtapositions of iconic sights and sounds of the '60s. Horner's reprogramming sessions allow Avakian and writers Terry Southern and Dennis McGuire to let their imaginations run wild while presenting a *1984*-style cautionary tale. (Director Nicolas Roeg, no stranger to the themes explored in *End of the Road,* placed one of kitchen sink, touching on every volatile subject they could think of in those very volatile times. *The Trial of Billy Jack* turned out to be heavy-handed, preachy, and, at 170 minutes, in dire need of editing, but Laughlin made it a hit by regaining control of *Billy Jack* and releasing both pictures together, mostly in theaters he had rented. The critics thumped Laughlin's films, but that just made the counterculture kids want to see them more.

Beyond Billy Jack

Laughlin's love of westerns is apparent in his work, and he tried to create a western hero similar to Billy Jack (and surely inspired by Clint Eastwood's spaghetti westerns) with *The Master Gunfighter* (1975), in which he plays Finley, an outlaw defending Mexican peasants using a custom-made gun and a samurai sword. But the market for westerns was on the wane, and when the picture disappointed at the box office, Laughlin returned to what was considered surefire territory. Emulating Frank Capra's classic (and working with Frank Capra Jr. as producer), Laughlin got his hero out of prison and appointed to a U.S. Senate seat by scheming politicians in *Billy Jack Goes to Washington.* If the growing martial-arts-movie audience that had cropped up since the release of *Billy Jack* was disappointed by the relative lack of action in *Trial,* they must've really felt cheated by this latest effort, which has the hero wearing a suit and tie most of the time with only minimal karate. By this time, theaters were ruled by blockbusters like *Jaws* and *Star Wars,* and *Billy Jack Goes to Washington* barely received a release. Meanwhile, Laughlin cried conspiracy, blaming politicians and Hollywood alike.

Only occasionally making film and TV appearances since the '70s, Laughlin has spent most of his time researching Jungian psychology and investigating alternative cancer therapies, but he caused a stir in 1992 by expressing an interest in running for president. He has since refused credit for the success of *Billy Jack,* claiming that a lot of fortunate talents and circumstances came together at the right time, guided by a higher power.

these reprogramming scenes on one of the televisions David Bowie watches in the 1976 film *The Man Who Fell to Earth.*)

The film's main strength is its uniformly excellent cast. Keach has the most difficult challenge: bringing an essentially comatose character to life. James Earl Jones plays the good doctor as an insidiously charismatic figure, a stern father who's forcing Horner to grow up. The movie's tragic finale puts the doctor's stability into question (and strengthens the film's insistent Doctor D=Uncle Sam/Horner=counterculture metaphor). Yulin makes the most of his one-dimensional role, but it's Avakian's real-life wife, Tristan, who, in her film debut, makes a great impression, quickly becoming the linchpin of the entire piece. As Rennie, she's the only genuinely likable character in the film, and she comes by her emotions genuinely. The final sequence (which garnered the film its "X" rating), in which a traumatic and illegal abortion takes place, finds the viewer truly concerned for her welfare. The scene is devastating—and quite politically pointed—but it comes so late in the film that many viewers will simply be left with a very bad aftertaste.

Southern (who also produced) waved goodbye to the '60s in high style with his screenplay for *Easy Rider*. Here, he and his cowriters explore the mental and physical wounds of the period. Southern's gloomy tone was no doubt a result of his having recently covered the disastrous 1968 Democratic convention in Chicago (*End of the Road* was shot in Massachusetts in late '68). Avakian adds an ironic coda when the film's final trauma is followed by joyous newsreel footage of the Apollo 11 moon landing—the upbeat, approved-by-the-Establishment conclusion to the decade. But Horner sums up the whole film (and, presumably, the thoughts of a generation) when, after making love to Rennie, he wonders aloud, "Where do I go from here?"

1970 (NC-17) 110m/C Stacy Keach, James Earl Jones, Harris Yulin, Dorothy Tristan, Grayson Hall. *D:* Aram Avakian. *W:* Dennis McGuire, Terry Southern, Aram Avakian. *C:* Gordon Willis. *M:* Teo Macero, Johann Sebastian Bach, Pyotr Ilyich Tchaikovsky. *VHS*

—Ed Grant

Gas-s-s-s! ♫♫♪

Roger Corman directed *Gas-s-s-s!*—a surreal phantasmagoria that could only have happened in the late '60s—as though he were still under the influence of the acid he dropped while researching *The Trip*. That, or he was working with an unfinished script, impossible deadlines, and a balky production outfit. Guess which?

Following a clever cartoon prologue (from the animation studio Murakami-Wolf, creators of *The Point*), we discover that an experimental U.S. military nerve gas has accidentally been let loose, causing the rapid aging and death of everyone over the age of twenty-five—a twist on the youth-protest motto "Don't trust anyone over thirty." But now that everyone over twenty-five is gone, absurdist anarchy, not peace, reigns. A motorcycle-riding Edgar Allan Poe (Bruce Karcher), like an American International Pictures guardian spirit, predicts that these young inheritors of Earth won't find their job too easy.

Indeed, a pair of hippie lovers (Robert Corff and Elaine Giftos) hit the Texas highway in an Edsel in search of a utopian commune in New Mexico. When not dreaming up poetic new terms for lovemaking ("arrowfeather" wins out), their postapocalyptic odyssey brings them into contact with a number of strange and pointedly symbolic characters, including a neo-cowboy who calls himself Billy the Kid (George Armitage); a very pregnant girl named Marissa (Cindy Williams) who cheerfully resists giving birth and thrills over discovering retro rock music; her African American boyfriend, Carlos (Ben Vereen); and others.

They finally locate the commune at the Taos Pueblo, the famous Acoma Indian complex (and the oldest continuously inhabited community in North America). But the sanctuary comes under threat by two barbaric enemy tribes in athletic gear, one a fascistic football team, the other a group of Hell's

Angels bikers who have inexplicably upgraded to their parents' golf carts and country-club manners. Just when it looks like war will consume this brave new world, the hippies trick their foes into a peaceful truce in a fashion that even Poe respects.

Corman started shooting the picture with just an outline and supporting actor George Armitage (who would later direct *Miami Blues* and *Grosse Pointe Blank*) scribbling the script along the way. To make matters worse, gloomy winter weather and money woes demanded further rethinks. Because Corman had committed to direct a World War I flick, *Von Richtofen and Brown*, he was out of the country when the more conservative American International Pictures honcho James Nicholson drastically re-edited *Gas-s-s-s!*, excising, for example, a dialogue between God (reduced to a gag voice cameo) and Jesus, and lopping off a closing shot that Corman considered one of his finest. In the aftermath, Corman severed his relationship with AIP and opened his own production-distribution company, New World Pictures, during the 1970s.

Whether viewers consider *Gas-s-s-s!* a mangled masterpiece or a huge misfire, they're unlikely to see the film as Corman intended. As it exists now it's a broadly comic curio, alternatively goofy and groovy, with more sloganeering and anti-Establishment punch lines than solid characterization. Some jokes are pretty rich, in a Monkees-meet–*Mad Max* way, such as scenes of the football team practicing pillaging as though it were a just another strategy in the playbook (though the rape humor doesn't sit so well). The Grateful Dead were booked for a musical guest spot in the film but wanted too hefty a payout. Instead, Corman got Country Joe & the Fish, billed as "FM Radio," for a very psychedelic concert sequence at a drive-in. Talia Shire, sister of budding director (and Corman associate) Francis Ford Coppola, portrays a supporting flower child under her maiden name, Talia Coppola. Watch also for cameos by Johnny and the Tornadoes, some lucky members of a New Mexico high school marching band, and *Mad* magazine mascot Alfred E. Newman.

1970 (PG) 79m/C Robert Corff, Elaine Giftos, Pat Patterson, Ben Vereen, George Armitage, Alex Wilson, Bud Cort, Cindy Williams, Talia Shire, Bruce Karcher, Country Joe & the Fish. **D:** Roger Corman. **W:** George Armitage. **C:** Ron Dexter. **M:** Barry Melton. VHS

AKA: *Gas-s-s-s . . . or, It May Become Necessary to Destroy the World in Order to Save It*

—Charles A. Cassady Jr.

Getting Straight ♫♫♫♪

When it comes to early-1970s authority bucking, it doesn't get any better than Elliott Gould. Following his star-making turn as "Trapper" John in Robert Altman's *M*A*S*H*, Gould took on a series of roles playing poor, opinionated schlemiels who use their wit and sarcasm to battle the Establishment. Some of these roles were in superior films, like *Little Murders, The Long Goodbye,* and *California Split,* and some of them were in dreck, like *Move, S*P*Y*S,* and *Whiffs.* One of Gould's best efforts of the peri-

In *Getting Straight* (1970), director Richard Rush examines the tensions between the counterculture and the Establishment on a college campus.

od is also his most underappreciated—*Getting Straight,* an unusually ambitious campus comedy-drama that holds up surprisingly well today.

Gould plays Harry Bailey, a former radical who dropped out of society after a stint in Vietnam. Now, at an unnamed campus (actually filmed in Eugene at the University of Oregon), he's returned to society and academia, teaching basic English to college kids while trying to get his master's degree in American literature.

But Harry is his own worst enemy. He has problems with Jan (Candice Bergen), his gorgeous girlfriend, because she aspires to middle-class values. He has problems with the school's stuffy faculty members, some of whom don't want him to be part of their staff. And while he's looked up to by his students as the resident radical, Harry is constantly criticizing their political efforts, unfavorably comparing them to his own experiences in the '60s. On top of all this, Harry is broke, his decrepit convertible belches black fumes, and Nick (Robert F. Lyons), his hippie friend, threatens to squeal on him to the administration for cheating on an important exam. Compounding Harry's personal problems are a standoff between angry students and the National Guard, his position as liaison between the youthful demonstrators and the stodgy board of university trustees, and his upcoming master's degree oral exam.

Getting Straight is a surprisingly accomplished and complex film for its time, especially when stacked against the likes of *The Strawberry Statement* and even *Zabriskie Point.* Director Richard Rush and screenwriter Robert Kaufman (adapting a book by Ken Kolb) attempt to have it both ways, presenting the counterculture in both positive and negative lights. The film succeeds admirably, painting Harry as an underground icon and as a hypocrite. As played by Gould, Harry is a likable smartass, a former rabble-rouser stuck between his past and his future, between a dying idealism and an Establishment lifestyle he both shuns and pursues. Gould makes the unlikable crank likable.

Throughout, Gould ably recites Kaufman's sharp, politically spiked monologues, and we get to watch him freak out during his oral exam when a prodding professor poses questions about *The Great Gatsby* and F. Scott Fitzgerald, Harry's hero. Also strong in the cast are Bergen as the perpetually conflicted Jan; Lyons, whose darkly humorous attempts at dodging the draft eventually turn pitch black when he gets gung-ho and enlists in the Marines; and Cecil Kellaway (in his last role), Jeff Corey, and Jon Lormer as faculty members Harry faces off against.

Director Rush (*Psych-Out, The Stuntman*) does a bang-up job, especially when meshing Harry's personal story with the on-campus unrest, which builds in the film's background, eventually exploding into an all-out riot in the finale. And the expert cinematography of Laszlo Kovacs (*Easy Rider*) is as jarring as any news footage of similar upheavals during the time.

Getting Straight turns clunky at times, mostly a result of taking on too much. Harry's liaison with a black student (Brenda Sykes) effectively demonstrates his character's lack of sensitivity, but the intimate rapport between the two suggests there should be more here. In need of more depth, too, are Harry's brief gig as a campus recruiter and his involvement as a negotiator between the school and the students.

Still, *Getting Straight* should be praised, not condemned, for introducing us to Harry Bailey, warts and all.

1970 (R) 124m/C Elliott Gould, Candice Bergen, Robert F. Lyons, Cecil Kellaway, Jeff Corey, Jon Larmer, John Rubinstein, Brenda Sykes, Jeannie Berlin, Max Julien, Leonard Stern, Harrison Ford. *D:* Richard Rush. *W:* Robert Kaufman. *C:* Laszlo Kovacs. *M:* Ronald Stein. *VHS*

Greetings ♫♫♫

Hi, Mom! ♫♫♫

Whether or not you think Brian De Palma an heir to Hitchcock's throne as the master of suspense, it's likely you'll find *Greetings* and *Hi, Mom!,* two of his earliest efforts, fascinating to watch. For one thing, you'll get a glimpse of Robert De Niro before he was Robert De Niro. For another, a veritable catalog of De Palma's trademark techniques and themes—long tracking shots, voyeurism, conspiracies, and obsession—can be found in these low-budget New York–based productions. The only thing missing is the split-screen shot, so prevalent in *Carrie* and *The Fury,* the absence of which can probably be chalked up to budgetary restrictions.

Greetings is a freewheeling comedy full of skits and parables centering on the concerns of the counterculture, circa 1968. The film begins with a television news report about the recent casualties in Vietnam, then shifts to LBJ promising no letup to the fighting in Southeast Asia. Johnson then claims that Americans' quality of life is better than ever before. That's what *he* thinks. To a trio of friends living on the fringes of Greenwich Village, things look much different.

Paul (Jonathan Warden) is so anxious about his impending draft exam that he tries to pick a fight in a Harlem bar in the hope of getting beat up so badly that he won't be selected to go overseas. Lloyd (Gerrit Graham) is a conspiracy enthusiast who, in one of the film's funniest scenes, demonstrates the ridiculousness of the JFK assassination single-bullet theory by drawing the projectile's supposed trajectory on the body of his naked girlfriend with a magic marker. Jon (De Niro), meanwhile, gets an opportunity to make his voyeuristic hobby a vocation when he meets Joe Banner (Allen Garfield), a pornographer, who enlists him to make short sex films.

Even as it tackles Vietnam, the draft, and the JFK assassination, *Greetings* remains breezy, thanks in part to the way De Palma calls attention to the film medium and to his own interests as a film buff. For instance, we see the influential Hitchcock/Truffaut interview book make a cameo appearance; there's a discussion of Antonioni's *Blow-Up,* a film that De Palma would remake thirteen years later as *Blow Out*; and silent-movie-style title cards introduce the film's different sequences. You can tell how much fun he's having when the twenty-eight-year-old De Palma, in his second feature film, gets to self-consciously show off his cinematic range with De Niro's porno film-within-a-film sequence and some handheld Vietnam combat footage in the film's ironic ending.

Originally rated "X" (for some full-frontal but harmless nudity) and produced for a miniscule $45,000, *Greetings* drew solid reviews and a sizable young crowd when it was first released. Its success led to 1970's *Hi, Mom!,* a sequel put together by De Palma, cowriter and producer Charles Hirsch, and De Niro.

In the equally episodic sequel, De Niro's Jon is just back from his tour of duty in Vietnam. He rents a disgusting Greenwich Village apartment (from a young and slim Charles Durning) located across the street from a middle-class co-op. With the intention of making it in the porn world, with financing help from the surly Banner (Garfield again), Jon plans to secretly observe and film the apartment's tenants in different stages of undress, then market the peepshows to theaters.

When Jon can't get footage risqué enough to sell, he schemes to get his lonely neighbor Judy into compromising positions by posing as her computer-matched date. When he begins to fall for his intended victim, Jon abandons his nascent career altogether and winds up in a completely different kind of performance, playing a cop in a play called *Be Black, Baby* that's showed on an early form of cable-access TV.

Taking up more than fifteen minutes of *Hi, Mom!, Be Black, Baby* is a "Living Theatre"–type production that intends to scare the hell out of the white audience members by giving them a firsthand demonstration of what it's like to be black in America. The production's black actors appear in whiteface, then proceed to browbeat, scream at, and throw black paint on the theatergoers, causing them to panic, as they're unable to discern between reality and a planned theatrical experience. When it all ends, the cast members (including the white Gerrit Graham from *Greetings*) give hugs to the audience, reassuring them it was only make-believe. After regaining their composure, the frazzled theatergoers rave about their "black" experience.

Following this sequence, Jon appears to have been shaken to the point of turning his entire life inside out: overnight, the former hippie and Vietnam vet has become a full-fledged member of the Establishment, happily married to the pregnant Judy, selling insurance for a living, and smoking a pipe in a comfortable chair in a Manhattan co-op. But, of course, something's amiss about this radical transformation. After reading the book *The Urban Guerilla,* Jon destroys the entire scene, blowing his co-op to smithereens, wife and unborn child included.

There is no clear explanation for such an act. Did the *Be Black, Baby* experience push him over the edge? Or is this Jon's—and De Palma's—ultimate rejection of the middle class and its values? If the latter, the resolution is strikingly similar to the explosive fade-out of *Zabriskie Point,* another examination of America's underground released the same year.

After the incident, Jon shows up in military regalia near the building's rubble, at which point he's interviewed by a newscaster. When the microphone is put to his face, Jon talks about how in Vietnam he helped "clean up the country" and now, upon returning to America, he has to face "this big mess." When the newscaster asks if there's anything else he'd like to add, he looks into the camera with a maniacal grin and says, "Hi, Mom!"

It's only then that something that's been in the back of your mind comes into focus: it's clear that Jon is, in fact, the pre–*Taxi Driver* Travis Bickle.

Greetings
1968 (R) 88m/C Jonathan Warden, Robert De Niro, Gerrit Graham, Richard Hamilton, Megan McCormick, Allen Garfield, Bettina Kugel. *D:* Brian De Palma. *W:* Brian De Palma, Charles Hirsch. *C:* Robert Fiore. *M:* Eric Kaz, Stephen Soles, Artie Traum. *VHS*

Hi, Mom!
1970 (R) 87m/C Robert De Niro, Jennifer Salt, Lara Parker, Gerrit Graham, Allen Garfield, Paul Bartel, Charles Durning. *D:* Brian De Palma. *W:* Brian De Palma, Charles Hirsch. *C:* Robert Elfstrom. *M:* Eric Kaz. *VHS*
AKA: Blue Manhattan; Confessions of a Peeping John; Son of Greetings

If.... 🎵🎵🎵🎵

indsay Anderson's cult favorite breaks neatly into two halves. The first is a documentary-style examination of life at an English public school (the American equivalent of an exclusive prep school); the second is a wish-fulfillment revenge fantasy against the bullies and blowhards who run such

BEATNIK BEAT   by Charles A. Cassady Jr.

"'Beat' and 'hippie' are all yesterday's headline bullshit."
—Allen Ginsberg, 1969

Before there was "groovy," there was "cool." Before Jimi Hendrix, there was Miles Davis. Before Haight-Ashbury, there was Greenwich Village. Before flower children, there was the Beat Generation, the precounterculture counterculture whose adherents were fondly known as "beatniks."

Pop historians date the American beatnik era as beginning around 1957, the year author Jack Kerouac's *On the Road* was published. Kerouac and his contemporaries, like the poets Allen Ginsberg, Gregory Corso, and Lawrence Ferlinghetti; writers Ken Kesey, William S. Burroughs, and Paul and Jane Bowles; musicians Thelonious Monk and Charlie Parker; and all-around Beat icon Neal Cassady, ushered in an era of restless experimentation—in lifestyles, literary expression, music, and art—as a reaction against post–World War II disillusionment and the rampant Squaresville of the Eisenhower years.

Maynard Rules

The cartoon beatnik stereotype should be familiar, even if you've never seen Bob Denver's famous supporting role as hep-cat sidekick Maynard G. Krebs on the late-'50s/early-'60s TV sitcom *The Many Loves of Dobie Gillis.* The beret, the goatee, the black pullover, the "funny cigarettes," the vast collection of jazz LPs, bongo drums, coffeehouse hangouts, vaguely leftist-fringe politics (which most media Beats seemed to politely keep to themselves), and a syncopated vocabulary laced with "crazy, man." You dig?

For the most part, the bourgeois public perceived beatniks and their nonconformist attitudes more with amusement than alarm. But following in the Beats' footsteps came others who turned their backs on conventional society: not much later, the long-haired "freaks," tuned in, turned on, and dropped out. Doubtless the Beats had an immense influence on the late '60s—why do you think the Fab Four called themselves Beat-les anyway? And the Beat went on. . . .

So why didn't Hollywood serve up an *Easy Rider* or *Monterey Pop* a decade earlier, as a manifesto for the Beat Generation? Psychedelic movies heralded the Age of Aquarius; why not an Age of . . . Capricorn?

Maybe because the essence of the Beats was a difficult thing to capture dramatically. Exploring free verse and atonal sax riffs is an endeavor that can't be forced into a three-act scenario. Maybe the Woodstock Generation simply had more obvious antagonists to face in their own pop mythology—the Vietnam draft, reactionary bigots, hostile parents, cops and/or National Guardsmen, and the U.S. government itself. And, you could dance to their music.

Sour Notes

In any case, mainstream Hollywood dropped the ball. *The Beatniks* (1960), about a delinquent turned crooner, doesn't have a single beatnik in it. That same year MGM tried a big-budget approach, assigning the Arthur Freed unit (the talent behind such classic musicals as *Singin' in the Rain* and *Gigi*) to adapt another Kerouac opus of Bay Area Beats, *The Subterraneans.* The film features George Peppard as a writer who falls in with a group of daddy-Os, eventually cozying up to French girl Leslie Caron. A critical and commercial flop, the rarely seen film's coolest elements were the appearances of such jazz greats as Art Farmer, Red Mitchell, Carmen McRae, and Gerry Mulligan. *The Beat Generation,* also distributed by MGM, was a crime melodrama about a serial rapist with a jazz-club backdrop. Produced by exploitation maestro Albert Zugsmith, the sleazefest does boast an astonishing mish-mash of a cast that includes sexpot Mamie Van Doren, Ray ("Legs Diamond") Danton, Louis Armstrong, Jackie "Uncle Fester" Coogan, accordionist Dick Contino, Irish "Sheena, Queen of the Jungle" McCalla, Charles Chaplin Jr., and Maila Nurmi, AKA "Vampira" of Ed Wood movie fame.

Roger Corman, who would later depict feral bikers, LSD users, and hippies, at least tapped a humorous vein in his made-for-pennies 1959 dark comedy *A Bucket of Blood,* wherein murderous coffeehouse busboy Dick Miller finds fame as a sculptor after people go crazy for his grotesque works of art—actually victims' bodies covered in clay. Corman also produced an unheralded, affectionate remake, *The Death Artist,* for the straight-to-tape market in 1997.

Movie history to this day is littered with the occasional stabs at Beat Generation flicks, from *Greenwich Village Story* (1963), to the attempted Jack Kerouac memoirs *Heart Beat* (1979) with John Heard and Sissy Spacek and the pseudo-documentary *Kerouac* (1985), to the Neal Cassady–inspired *The Last Time I Committed Suicide* (1997) with Keanu Reeves, Adrien Brody, and Thomas Jane as Jack Kerouac. Then there's David Cronenberg's semi-coherent junkie nightmare *Naked Lunch* (1991), with Peter Weller, Judy Davis, and lots of icky bugs. It's comforting for us to note that addled source author Burroughs would sometimes toss his manuscript pages and reassemble them in whatever random order they fell.

On the Beaten Track

The Beats were also capable of making films themselves, with low-budget indies such as *The Flower Thief* (1961), *The Flaming City* (1963), *The Square Root of Zero* (1964), the 1958 shorts *Pull My Daisy* and *Beat,* plus numerous abstract, animated, and avant-garde pieces by Harry Smith, Hy Hirsch, and the brothers John and James Whitney (influences of the latter group can be seen prominently in the creative opening-credit sequences designed for numerous Hollywood blockbusters by Saul Bass).

One suggestion for a new generation's introduction to the Beat Generation: Chuck Workman's aptly titled 1999 docu-feature *The Source* (with Johnny Depp, Dennis Hopper, and John Turturro in chief roles). A book that sheds valuable light on the underground world of Beat filmmaking is Wheeler Winston Dixon's *The Exploding Eye: A Re-Visionary History of 1960s American Experimental Cinema.*

And we can't forget the ongoing saga of *On the Road,* Kerouac's seminal Beat book from 1957. The rights have been owned by Francis Ford Coppola for years, but the film- and winemaker hasn't been able to get the project rolling as of this writing. The latest word was Brad Pitt as the Neal Cassady–inspired Dean Moriarty and Billy Crudup as Kerouac, with Joel Schumacher directing a script by novelist Russell Banks (*The Sweet Hereafter*). Sounds hip, but is it too far-out for Hollywood to handle?

places. Seen that way, the film is a curious prototype for another great anti-Establishment movie, Robert Altman's *M*A*S*H*. It also sets the stage for more violent films that would follow.

Anderson eases into this challenging tale with an ironic on-screen epigram:

> Wisdom is the principal thing:
> therefore get wisdom:
> and with all thy getting
> get understanding.
> —Proverbs

(Or as Emil Faber, founder of *Animal House*'s Faber College put it, "Knowledge is Good.")

The opening scenes introduce College House as the students are returning. The place is pure pandemonium as seen through the eyes of Jute (Sean Bury), a new boy who doesn't know the ropes. Our hero is Mick Travis (Malcolm McDowell). He and his two friends Johnny (David Wood) and Wallace (Richard Warwick) are about as rebellious and nonconformist as the school will allow. In place of conventional pinups, they plaster images of war and violence on their walls. They smuggle in vodka, smoke cigarettes, and refuse to cut their hair. Their nemesis is Rowntree (Robert Swann), leader of the whips—senior students who, under the pretense of supervision, act as casual sadists and pedophiles, doing the dirty work for the faculty and administration. Other bad guys include the Chaplain (Geoffrey Chater), a warmonger in a stiff, white collar; and the Headmaster (Peter Jeffrey), a smug windbag who spouts glib nonsense every time he opens his mouth.

It's a world—think *Lord of the Flies* in a boys' school—where the acts of cruelty range from petty pranks to real torture, and Anderson presents them with an assurance that must have come from his own experiences. (The film was made on location at Anderson's old school, Cheltenham.) The famous beating scene is brilliantly staged. It begins with one long take during which only sound is used to build suspense. Then the scene expands to encompass the whole school. For better or worse, that is essentially the last "realistic" moment in the film.

Midway through the film, the tone shifts. The dramatic change is introduced in a long fantasy sequence involving a motorcycle and a character called simply the Girl (Christine Noonan). Such inventive, imaginative moments become increasingly important in the second half as *If. . . .* builds to its grandly violent conclusion, perhaps the most partisan dramatization of the '60s generational conflicts ever put on film. Even presented as fantasy, it's something that no filmmaker would attempt today.

Much has been said about Anderson's shifting between color and B&W throughout the film. Conventional wisdom has it that Anderson was filming out of chronological order, ran out of money for color stock, and had to switch to B&W. Not so. According to Gavin Lambert's biography, *Mainly about Lindsay Anderson,* near the beginning of the production, cinematographer Miroslav Ondříček said that the lighting limitations in the dark interior locations wouldn't allow him to use relatively slow color film. The director responded that since they couldn't afford more lights, they'd use faster B&W film in those shots, and then slip it into a few others as well. It's one of those moments where a tight budget led to an artistic revelation, as the first B&W scene, about fifteen minutes into the film, lets the viewer know that something unusual is going on.

In all, *If. . . .* works well on its own terms, even though it's clearly politically biased. Anderson and cowriter David Sherwin were just finishing the script when the upheaval of 1968 seemed to be at a breaking point, with the riots at the Democratic convention in Chicago and student takeovers at Princeton, Harvard, and the Sorbonne. Few other films have expressed so much rage so well.

Of course, three years later Malcolm McDowell starred in Stanley Kubrick's *A Clockwork Orange.* Mick, Johnny, and Wallace are clear prototypes for Little Alex and his Droogs, though *Clockwork*'s violence is much more difficult to endorse. McDowell's Mick Travis became Anderson's protagonist in two other films: 1973's epic musical satire *O Lucky Man!,* which found him as a coffee salesman embracing capitalism, and 1982's *Britannia Hospital,* with the character as a documentary filmmaker.

1968 (R) 111m/C *UK* Malcolm McDowell, David Wood, Richard Warwick, Christine Noonan, Rupert Webster. *D:* Lindsay Anderson. *W:* David Sherwin, John Howlett. *C:* Miroslav Ondrícek. *M:* Marc Wilkinson. *VHS, DVD*

—Mike Mayo

Joe 🦴🦴🦴🦴

Few films presented the generational conflicts of the 1960s with more perception and prescience than this low-budget masterpiece from John G. Avildsen (six years before he gave us the adrenaline-rush uppercut of *Rocky*). At a time when the movies were trying to reach a young, hip audience, *Joe* exposed the discontent and rage of an older, blue-collar America.

The opening scene brutally deromanticizes the whole hippie/druggie/peace-love-and-rock-'n'-roll myth. Frank (Patrick McDermott) and Melissa (Susan Sarandon) live in a squalid Greenwich Village apartment. He's a wanna-be artist turned pusher. She's the daughter of a well-to-do Manhattan family. Both are shooting heroin, though his addiction is more serious than hers. (When Frank can't get a fix he turns abusive, and she takes it.) Frank's goal is to make just a little more money from one last score before he retires from the trade and returns to painting.

When an overdose lands Melissa in the hospital, her parents are brought into the picture. Her father, William Compton (Dennis Patrick), is appalled at his daughter's living conditions; when he meets Frank, his reaction is predictably violent.

To reveal any more of the plot to those unfamiliar with it would spoil the surprises in the deceptively realistic script by Norman Wexler (*Saturday*

As the title character in John G. Avildsen's *Joe,* Peter Boyle expresses the anger and alienation of the working class in an unsettling film about the generation gap and class divisions.

Night Fever). Suffice it to say that for completely legitimate reasons, Mr. Compton meets Joe Curran (Peter Boyle). Joe is a World War II veteran and factory worker who hates virtually everyone and, after a few beers at his favorite bar, loudly vents his anger.

Under other circumstances, Joe and Compton would probably never have reason to speak to each other. But they're forced together, and through their relationship the roots of Joe's discontent are exposed. He's a fascinating character—the spiritual father of *Taxi Driver*'s Travis Bickle. In many ways, Joe is completely repellent. But he has his sympathetic moments, especially when you come to see that his many resentments are born of, at least in part, a need for recognition and respect.

America has passed him by. On one side are rich guys with connections—men like Compton and Joe's own union bosses; on the other side are the good-for-nothing kids and the welfare queens (not the term Joe uses) who are freeloading on his tax money. As Joe muses aloud, "What's that word they got? Groovin'? Groovy? When they're not screwin', they're groovin'. Screwin' and groovin'." But the key to understanding Joe's discontent is more subtle and easy to miss. We learn through conversations that he is estranged from his two grown sons. It's not hard to imagine that he's driven them away and still refuses to admit that failure. This combination of powerlessness, rage, and bafflement is what fuels the second half of the film, as Joe and Compton work their way toward a conclusion that's both surprising and inevitable.

The acting, like the winter locations, is understated but powerful. Dennis Patrick (a character actor whose face is more recognizable than his name and who appeared in dozens of movies and TV series, including *All in the Family*) puts in a superb performance. But the film belongs to Peter Boyle. In the hands of a lesser actor, Joe might easily have become a caricature, but Boyle's performance is perfectly nuanced. He doesn't mean for viewers to sympathize with Joe, but he does want them to understand what drives him.

Although many of the details are dated now, the statements *Joe* makes about the social and economic divisions in America haven't changed at all, and the film remains one of the most original and haunting of its time.

1970 (R) 107m/C Peter Boyle, Dennis Patrick, Aubrey Claire, Susan Sarandon, Patrick McDermott, K. Callan. **D:** John G. Avildsen. **W:** Norman Wexler. **C:** John G. Avildsen, Henri Decae. **M:** Bobby Scott. *VHS, DVD*

—Mike Mayo

Last Summer ♫♫♫

Beach Blanket Bingo it ain't. *Last Summer* is a beach movie that starts out as wholesome and all-American as it can be and then slowly, insidiously, turns into a parable about the "evil within," the pettiness and brutality that can be found under a civilized veneer. The film might be described as a teenage *Lord of the Flies,* but its sharply defined upper-middle-class milieu makes it a pure product of the '60s. Like the impressive *Pretty Poison* (1968), *Last Summer* reflects on a changing America by focusing not on kids who were "dropping out," but on active, intelligent young people—young people who are immoral and surprisingly violent.

Three teens bond when their families vacation at adjoining summer houses along a beach. Dan (Bruce Davison) and Peter (Richard Thomas) are red-blooded guys who like to talk and goof around with the flirtatious, whimsically bitchy Sandy (Barbara Hershey). The three spend a better part of the summer getting drunk, having their first experiences with pot, and engaging in a series of "projects." These include taking care of (and torturing) an injured seagull they come across; finding a computer date for Sandy (whom she maliciously intends to humiliate); and teaching their introverted neighbor Rhoda (Catherine Burns) how to swim and get drunk. Rhoda, the only one of the fun-loving group with a conscience, remains an outsider. Her crush on Peter makes her especially vulnerable to the cruel condescension of these new-found friends.

Frank and Eleanor Perry were an uncommonly talented husband-and-wife filmmaking team who turned out a number of influential, highly metaphorical character studies in the 1960s. They focused on the younger set in their groundbreaking independent feature *David and Lisa* (1963) and again in *Ladybug Ladybug* (1963), then put financially comfortable middle-aged folk under the microscope in *The Swimmer* (1968) and *Diary of a Mad Housewife* (1970).

It was a summer of shared friendship . . . and lost innocence.

—Tagline for
Last Summer

ROBERT FORSTER

Thanks to the efforts of a young writer-director, Robert Forster pulled himself out of a vocational abyss. Before Quentin Tarantino came along, the near-forgotten, barely employed middle-aged actor was struggling to make a living.

Tarantino had just about cast him for the role of Joe Cabot, the blustery ringleader of a group of thieves in 1992's *Reservoir Dogs,* when Lawrence Tierney, a film-noir regular from the 1950s and 1960s, was given the part.

"Quentin told me he was a big fan of my work in the TV show *Banyan* in the 1970s," recalled Forster. "But when Lawrence became available, he decided to use him instead. I understood that. But Quentin did promise that we'd work together one day, and though it took several years, he held to that promise."

Forster almost got the role of a menacing, expletive-spewing mobster in the Tarantino-scripted *True Romance* in 1993. But that, too, went to another actor: Christopher Walken. When Tarantino was looking for someone to play burned-out bail bondsman Max Cherry in 1997's *Jackie Brown,* he remembered Forster and granted him the role that helped revive his career with an Academy Award nomination for Best Supporting Actor.

The Oscar went to Robin Williams for *Good Will Hunting,* but Forster doesn't consider himself a loser by any means. "The difference between being nominated for the Oscar and winning the Oscar to me was the difference between a twenty-two-pound box of chocolates and a twenty-five-pound box of chocolates," says Forster. "It's mighty sweet either way."

Since the recognition for *Jackie Brown,* the Rochester, New York, native has been one of Hollywood's busiest character actors, nabbing key roles in such high-profile Hollywood films as *Me, Myself and Irene, Mulholland Drive,* the 1998 remake of *Psycho, Like Mike, Confidence,* and *Charlie's Angels: Full Throttle;* acclaimed independent efforts such as *Outside Ozona, Lakeboat,* and *Diamond Men,* which he helped produce; and the TV series *Karen Sisco.* Not bad for a guy who had just about given up on acting and had taken to the motivational-speech circuit to make a living after appearing in such fare as *Maniac Cop 3, Scanner Cop 2,* and *The Kinky Coaches and the Pom Pom Pussycats.*

"I thank Quentin for helping me out," said Forster. "I had a great career, starting out, for about five years. Then I had a cold streak that lasted twenty-seven years . . . until *Jackie Brown.*"

With Eleanor serving as screenwriter and Frank as director, the Perrys produced a remarkably powerful body of work. Just as John Cassavetes had done with *Faces* (1968), his study of a dying suburban marriage, the Perrys steered clear of politics and overt social commentary but still wound up delivering scathing statements about alienation and conformity.

Their films were also perfect showcases for actors. *David and Lisa* made stars out of Keir Dullea and Janet Margolin, while *The Swimmer,* the

After attending the University of Rochester and doing some acclaimed work on Broadway, Forster made an immediate impression in his film debut, sharing the screen with Marlon Brando, Elizabeth Taylor, and Julie Harris in John Huston's kinky 1967 adaptation of Carson McCullers's *Reflections in a Golden Eye*. Forster plays a young army private who rides around naked on horses, sniffs Liz's underwear, and attracts the romantic attention of Brando.

A few years later, Forster took the part of John Cassellis, the news cameraman covering the 1968 Democratic convention in Chicago, in Haskell Wexler's highly charged *Medium Cool*.

Like his character in the film, Forster was unaware what he was getting into, but he received a wake-up call once filming began, having to improvise some of his lines and finding himself in the middle of actual demonstrations and riots involving police, the National Guard, and protestors on the Windy City streets.

"The film was as adventurous for me as it was for Haskell and the crew," said Forster. "I didn't know films could be shot in which actors were expected to improvise, but much of the stuff in the film was improvised. Let's just say I got a crash course in the process."

"Luckily, John Huston taught me well before we started *Reflections in a Golden Eye*," added Forster. "He told me that the way to create a character, to make it believable, was just to be the character within the frame of the movie camera. That was all screen acting was all about, he said. If I could do that, I'd do fine. So, I just followed his advice for the part in *Medium Cool*."

For the film, Forster said he "felt responsible for bringing a frame of reference to the material, and, especially in this case, being myself was a key to creating this character."

As for the drama unfolding in the streets, Forster had an eye-opening experience.

"The film was being shot near where we were staying, and a lot of the activity was happening there," he recalled. "I remember the actress [Verna Bloom] wearing a yellow dress, so Haskell and the crew could follow her. She was really in the middle of it all, more than me.

"I remember that Haskell and I had press credentials and we were actually on the convention floor, shooting. That stuff's all in the movie, and shot exactly as it happened.

"I'm pretty sure the term 'the whole world is watching' came from the film, in the scene where the military was attempting to separate the crowd from the press. You can hear the people yelling the chant, 'Don't leave us, the whole world is watching.'"

Perry film closest in tone to *Last Summer,* offered Burt Lancaster one of his most challenging roles. *Last Summer*'s lead trio—Davison (pre–*Strawberry Statement*), Thomas (pre–"John Boy" Walton), and Hershey (pre–*Boxcar Bertha*)—does marvelous work, with the actors expertly showing their characters' playful sides, then slowly lowering their masks. Burns has an easier job, since Rhoda is marked as a victim from the start, but her sympathetic portrayal makes the final atrocity all the more disturbing.

Radical, Man

The Perrys were often criticized, and just plain mocked, for their overly metaphorical storylines (see the abuse heaped on *David and Lisa* in Brian De Palma's *Hi, Mom!*). *Last Summer* has a good amount of corny symbolism—most prominently the aforementioned seagull the teens maliciously keep tethered to the ground (perhaps the inspiration for actress Hershey's name change to Barbara Seagull for a short time in the early '70s?). Evan Hunter, he of *Blackboard Jungle* and *87th Precinct* fame, wrote the novel upon which the film was based, so some of the blame for the film's ham-handedness can be laid on his doorstep. Still, his basic scenario is riveting: one knows something unpleasant is bound to occur to sacrificial lamb Rhoda, and yet it's hard to turn away.

Last Summer stands as a fine example of the late-'60s "bummer" dramas—films that were exquisitely acted, written, and directed, and certain to end in tragedy. The creators made statements about the period (*Easy Rider*'s "We blew it" being the tersest message) by depicting characters who were either unable to function at all in society (*Little Murders, End of the Road*) or who became the victims of violence (*Easy Rider,* the films of Sam Peckinpah). *Last Summer* is a perfect example of this movement. Hunter's storyline may be timeless, but the film is very much of its era, due to various cultural signposts. (The "first turn-on" pot-smoking scene is a particular delight.) Luckily, the film's palpable sensuality (swimsuits and libidos are constantly on display) contributes to its complexity—the movie's final, violent act is all the more disturbing to the viewer because he or she has responded to the attractiveness of the characters. This element also underscores the talent of the cast members. Who would have suspected that John Boy could be such a convincing heel?

1969 (R) 97m/C Barbara Hershey, Richard Thomas, Bruce Davison, Catherine Burns, Ernesto Gonzalez. *D:* Frank Perry. *W:* Eleanor Perry. *C:* Gerald Hirschfeld. *M:* John Simon. *VHS*

—*Ed Grant*

Medium Cool 🦴🦴🦴

In one of those rare, right place/right time circumstances, cinematographer Haskell Wexler was in Chicago during the 1968 Democratic convention making *Medium Cool,* his first feature film, when all hell broke loose. Young people took to the streets to demonstrate against the Vietnam War, police brutality, and racism. Chicago mayor Richard Daley, hosting the convention, fanned the flames, making coarse remarks about the unrest and calling out the police and National Guard. Protestors were clubbed and tear-gassed, and the whole world watched as the United States seemed to crack under the strain of its problems.

At the center of all this, observing with his camera, was Wexler, the Academy Award–winning cinematographer of *Who's Afraid of Virginia Woolf?* and later, *Bound for Glory.* When he scheduled *Medium Cool* to be shot in his hometown of Chicago during the convention, he had a hunch there would be problems, but what unfolded was a sobering wake-up call, which happened to be perfect for his film.

In *Medium Cool,* Robert Forster plays a TV news cameraman caught in the chaos of massive demonstrations (and their aggressive repression) during the 1968 Democratic convention in Chicago. PARAMOUNT / THE KOBAL COLLECTION

HASKELL WEXLER:
SHOOTING STAR

Haskell Wexler has had several brilliant careers. He's best known as one of Hollywood's greatest cinematographers, winning Academy Awards for *Who's Afraid of Virginia Woolf?* and *Bound for Glory,* with other credits including *In the Heat of the Night, The Thomas Crown Affair, Coming Home,* and *Matewan.* As a director, he's taken on politically charged projects, including *Medium Cool,* set against the turbulent backdrop of the 1968 Democratic convention in Chicago, and *Latino,* about the war between the Sandinistas and the American-backed Contras in Nicaragua. Wexler also teamed with the late Conrad Hall to direct and photograph many popular TV commercials for such companies as Schlitz and STP. And as a documentarian, he's worked on scores of factual films including a trilogy about bus drivers in L.A. that spans several decades and, with Emile de Antonio, *Underground,* a controversial study of the Weather Underground, the radical 1960s group.

Sitting in the lobby area of a Philadelphia hotel during the Philadelphia Film Festival one morning in 2003, the ever-active seventy-seven-year-old Wexler talked about different facets of his career. Occasionally, he would peer up at a TV monitor, where CNN broadcast images from the Middle East during the first days of "Operation Iraqi Freedom" and the subsequent protests against the actions. For what it's worth, Wexler said the images reminded him of the '60s and Vietnam.

Q: Do you like having the reputation of being an activist and bringing activism into your filmmaking?

A: Let's say I was always socially aware. I hesitate to use the word "activism." It's a way of categorizing things like "normal" and "abnormal."

Q: When did you first get interested in making movies?

A: I remember first shooting while traveling with my family when I was ten years old. I had a Bell & Howell camera that somebody graciously gave me. I was quickly attracted to capturing images. I grew up in Chicago. My first films with a Bell & Howell 16-mm camera were of a crippled children's hospital and a meat-packing plant.

Q: Can you talk about the problems you had with getting *Medium Cool* released?

A: Paramount held the film for over a year before they released it and that was because they were obliged to release it. I used my own money and money from investors to make it and Paramount had a "negative pickup" on it. They were obliged to open it. But Gulf & Western [the studio's parent company] induced an insurance company to say we didn't have the proper clearances from all the people in it to keep it away from the public. The studio said they thought the film should be more balanced and "show the other side." Then, when it did come out, it got an "X" rating, which meant people under the age of eighteen weren't allowed to see it, although this was probably the ideal audience for it. Then, despite great reviews, the studio didn't publicize it.

Q: Why do you think the studio was so skittish?

A: Well, the people I worked with like Peter Bart [a production executive on the film, now the editor of *Variety*] were supportive and sensitive. But like many corporations, there was pressure. There was a lot of pressure on Gulf & Western from the Democratic Party, and [Chicago] Mayor Daley's son was involved somehow. They actually said they thought people would do violent acts after they saw it. It's funny, but for six years after the film's release, I had my taxes audited by the IRS.

Q: Was a lot of *Medium Cool* shot on the fly, capturing things at the 1968 Democratic convention unrehearsed, as they were happening?

A: Actually, 90 percent of the film is scripted. We knew things were going to go on there, but we were surprised as to what extent. I knew that if the government ignored the antiwar protestors, there would be some kind of conflict. And I knew about certain things I wanted to shoot, like the rehearsals of the National Guard. I had worked with Appalachians before and I was aware of the Appalachian population in Chicago, which was part of the film as well.

Q: A year earlier, you were director of photography for *The Thomas Crown Affair,* recognized as one of the most stylish films of the 1960s. You previously worked with Norman Jewison on *In the Heat of the Night,* your first color film. Was *Thomas Crown* a determined effort to do something lighter?

A: Yes. The game plan was "style" from the start, a slick movie—or at least as much as you can make it slick during shooting.

Q: Whose idea was it to use all the split-screens during the film?

A: Norman, Hal [Ashby, the film's editor and producer], and I went to Canada in 1967, I think it was Expo '67 [the world's fair]. We saw a film there in this huge room that was projected on different panels. When we left, Norman and Hal decided they wanted to try something like that. I shot incredible polo scenes for the movie. I remember riding on a polo pony. I dug holes to shoot in and invented things for certain shots.

Q: Steve McQueen, the film's star, has a reputation for being difficult or a loner. What was he like during filming?

A: Steve was a friend. We both were interested in race cars. I remember taking a drive with him in one of the dune buggies in the film. He was nervous and upset because he was unsure how he was coming across in the role. The part was so different from anything else he had done before.

Q: Have you seen the remake of the film with Pierce Brosnan?

A: I've never seen it. I can tell you the script of the original was lousy. It was written by a lawyer from Boston.

Medium Cool is the story of Chicago TV news cameraman John Cassellis (Robert Forster, in a role originally intended for John Cassavetes). Caught in the middle of the turmoil, Cassellis is nonetheless able to maintain his journalistic objectivity. Even a fiery car crash has little affect on him. Instead of offering help, he films the accident scene, then nonchalantly dials for an ambulance.

His first step toward waking up to the turbulent times he's living in comes when he finds himself in the middle of a controversy while covering a story about a black cab driver who has returned a bag of lost money. The cabbie refuses to cooperate, claiming he's being used as a puppet by the media, and he is ostracized by his radical friends. Not only does this episode make Cassellis uneasy, but the sequence makes the audience uneasy, too, as the ghetto residents talk directly into the camera about racial differences and how they're being exploited by white America. Reality and fiction blend, and we're never sure where one begins and the other ends.

Later, Cassellis's eyes are further opened by a number of events: he learns that his TV station is in cahoots with the FBI, giving them news footage upon request; and the assassinations of RFK and Martin Luther King are in the media spotlight. The flurry of events make Cassellis question the role of the media, leading to his dismissal from the TV station, where his bosses claim the cameraman is getting too caught up with unnewsworthy events.

Cassellis's transformation takes another step forward when he begins dating Eileen (Verna Bloom), a struggling teacher and single mother from Appalachia who has a young son to whom Cassellis gets close. When the son is lost, Eileen frantically tries to find him. Wearing a bright yellow dress, the woman searches the streets of downtown Chicago; in the midst of this scene, the line between fiction and reality blurs as the actress finds herself in the middle of the genuine, increasingly violent altercations between protestors, cops, and the National Guard. Director Wexler also finds himself in danger at the ensuing brawl where, in the background, someone yells, "Look out, Haskell, it's real!"

Even in its scripted scenes, *Medium Cool* has an immediate, documentary-like feel, and Wexler builds drama steadily, particularly while ominously capturing six thousand National Guardsmen preparing for the eminent showdown. He alternates between fiction and reality, mixing the narrative with shots of the protestors battling for their lives in the streets. The irony of all this is that behind closed doors, the Democratic delegates chose Lyndon Johnson's vice president, Hubert H. Humphrey, over liberal favorite Eugene McCarthy to run for president against Richard Nixon in 1968. And it was McCarthy's supporters who were getting the tar kicked out of them just outside the closed convention doors.

Because of its unvarnished liberal—some would say "radical"—politics, *Medium Cool* ran into myriad problems when it was to be released in theaters. First, the MPAA slapped it with a ridiculous "X" rating, making it difficult for the young, political-minded audience to see it. Then, reportedly under pressure from political contacts, the studio waited an entire year to release it, dumping the film unceremoniously into a handful of venues. *Medium Cool,* then, became a film that few people saw, but somehow it still managed to make several "best of the year" critics' lists.

The story behind the making of the film, briefly chronicled on the special-edition DVD and in a 2001 documentary called *Look Out, Haskell, It's Real* adds to the mystique of *Medium Cool.* "The whole world is watching" was chanted by protestors in the streets of Chicago during the '68 convention, and *Medium Cool* confirms it.

1969 (R) 110m/C Robert Forster, Verna Bloom, Peter Bonerz, Marianna Hill, Peter Boyle, Charles Geary. *D:* Haskell Wexler. *W:* Haskell Wexler. *C:* Haskell Wexler. *M:* Mike Bloomfield. *VHS, DVD*

The Revolutionary 🦴🦴

Jon Voight's wholesome, boy-next-door good looks were used to terrific effect in *Midnight Cowboy.* But Voight appeared in a number of less successful movies around the same time that showcased the young actor's versatility.

The Revolutionary is an adapatation of a late-'60s allegorical novel set in an unnamed European city. The author, Hans Koningsberg, adapted his novel for the movie (he did the same for John Huston's similarly allegorical *A Walk with Love and Death* [1969], a look at a star-crossed peace-and-love couple who live in the fourteenth century). Voight stars as "A," a university student who, in short order, goes from belonging to his school's "radical committee," to teaming with a cell of communist labor unionists, to allowing himself to be drafted into the army (he refuses his rich father's offer to help him evade). As his political activities become more and more extreme, he pursues a rich girl (Jennifer Salt), who is attracted to his dangerous beliefs and tattered appearance. "A" has his moment of truth after he leaves the army (a clear desertion, but with no repercussions!) and must decide whether to take the life of a judge who may approve the execution of some of his labor-union colleagues.

Unlike other college protest movies of the period, *The Revolutionary* is an artsy endeavor that conveys a general message about revolution rather than addressing any actual events of the day. The film never explicitly establishes the film's setting, but it's clear that this isn't 1960s America: Voight's appearance and several cultural touchstones seem to indicate the 1920s or 1930s.

The Revolutionary is a film that most folks watch these days simply to get a glimpse of its stars in their formative periods. Voight (who had worked for director Williams previously in *Out of It*) does his best, but "A" plainly is a bore. Costarring as the head of the radical labor-union sect, the always reliable Robert Duvall (who had played opposite Voight in a celebrated 1965 off-Broadway production of *A View from the Bridge*) is caught in the same bind as Voight: his character is meant to represent a certain element of the working class, which prevents him from acting like a real human being. The only performer allowed to shake things up is the John Cassavetes stalwart Seymour Cassel, who vibrantly plays Leonard, an eccentric, unpredictable radical.

Director Paul Williams, who also helmed the offbeat counterculture crime film *Dealing: Or the Berkeley-to-Boston Forty-Brick Lost-Bag Blues,* ultimately communicates that revolutionaries are the product of privilege and ennui (Voight) or of discontent (Duvall). Either way, the characters' efforts are fruitless gestures, quickly crushed by government and police suppression.

1970 (PG) 100m/C Jon Voight, Seymour Cassel, Robert Duvall, Collin Wilcox-Horne, Jennifer Salt. **D:** Paul Williams. **W:** Hans Koningsberg. **C:** Brian Probyn. **M:** Michael Small. *VHS*

—*Ed Grant*

The Strawberry Statement ♫♫

The year was 1970, and MGM, the studio that once specialized in grand musical entertainment, was feeling the pinch. Youthful audiences didn't know Fred Astaire from Fred Flintstone. Seizing on the popularity of films like *2001: A Space Odyssey* and *Blow-Up,* executives adopted a new counterculture-friendly policy, which resulted in films like *The Strawberry Statement.*

Inspired by a best-selling book by James B. Kunen, a sophomore who kept a journal of the unrest at Columbia University during the legendary 1968 campus takeover, *The Strawberry Statement* purports to tell it like it is from the student's perspective. A pre-*Willard* Bruce Davison plays Simon, a student at a nondescript San Francisco college who's oblivious to the anti-Establishment sentiments swirling around him. All he really wants to do is row with the school's crew team and maybe get laid once in a while.

Simon's friends, including Elliott (*Harold and Maude*'s Bud Cort), want him to open his eyes and get involved with the demonstrations against the plan to turn a children's playground into an R.O.T.C. center. But his most political gestures include listening to Neil Young on the radio and pinning a picture of Robert F. Kennedy to his dorm wall.

All of this changes, however, when Simon meets Linda (Kim Darby of *True Grit* fame), a cute, politically motivated coed. With hopes of winning her over, Simon begins demonstrating against the R.O.T.C. situation, racism, and Vietnam. He even puts his photography hobby to good use, shooting photos of the ongoing campus rebellion.

Eventually, the protestors take over the school, and Simon, newly sensitive to the plight of his fellow students, becomes one of the campus's fearless leaders: protesting, going head-on against the billy-club-wielding "pigs," and, of course, winning over the affections of Linda in the process.

The Strawberry Statement tries to paint the revolution that was going on at college campuses in the late '60s in human terms, but director Stuart Hagmann (whose best work can be seen in TV episodes of *Mannix*) and scripter Israel Horovitz (now a prolific playwright as well as a screenwriter) use simplistic, Hollywood strokes. For example, Simon's budding relationship with Linda is sweet, but his political awakening is downright bizarre. It's only when Linda is temporarily elsewhere that Simon becomes interested in what's going on around him. Amazingly, the revelatory moment comes when, during a student takeover of administrative buildings, a buxom protestor appears out of nowhere, flashes Simon her breasts, and performs oral sex on him. Simon smiles, looks at a poster on the wall of Che Guevara, and, in the next scene, he's practically Abbie Hoffman.

Many other scenes are just as poorly thought out. Take Simon's angry rallying cry at the final demonstration: "Bullshit! Nobody cares, from the president to the local thugs! The cops are beating up on the peace demonstrators and protestors when they should be beating up on the criminals and the haters! It's all bullshit, man! Bullshit!" Couldn't have said it better ourselves.

So, was *The Strawberry Statement* an honest attempt to reflect the real-life unrest occurring regularly on college campuses? (It did, after all, win some international awards, including the Grand Jury Prize at the Cannes Film Festival in 1970.) Or was the film simply a ruse—a cynical attempt by Hollywood to cash in on a hot issue? More than likely, it was a little of both, with the accent on the latter. One thing's for sure, though—we're dusting off those Che Guevara posters.

1970 (R) 109m/C Bruce Davison, Kim Darby, Bud Cort, Murray MacLeod, James Coco, Bob Balaban. **D:** Stuart Hagmann. **W:** Israel Horovitz. **C:** Ralph Woolsey. **M:** Iain Freebairn-Smith. *VHS*

Wild in the Streets ♪♪♪♪

P ity Jonathan Swift didn't live to rent *Wild in the Streets*. Of course, if he had, he'd be reeaally old, and that's not cool, man. Not cool at all.

This ultimate satire of '60s generation-gap warfare begins with a brisk recap of the maladjusted childhood of Max Flatow (Christopher Jones), alternately smothered and shunned by an overbearing California bourgeois mom (Shelley Winters). After learning to home-brew drugs and explosives in his basement, Max splits for good, becoming Max Frost, rock superstar. Max's with-it entourage includes lover Sally LeRoy (Diane Varsi), a former Hollywood child star turned decadent groupie; flip backup man Stanley X (Richard Pryor), a teen-prodigy accountant; and a trombone player with a hook for a hand. Max Frost's music is laced with political screeds skillfully aimed at disaffected youth, his "troops." After a backstage reunion with the incorrigible Mrs. Flatow turns into a calamity, Max's disdain for his elders knows no bounds.

When the segment of under-twenty-fives in the general population reaches 52 percent, Max is approached by Kennedyesque politician John Fergus (Hal Holbrook), who sees the rock star as key to his plan to get elected to the U.S. Senate by lowering the voting age from twenty-one to eighteen. For Max, however, that's not enough; he wants fourteen-year-olds to be eligible as well. Even after Fergus's victory at the polls, Frost's "Fourteen or Fight!" push puts millions of teen demonstrators in the streets and succeeds in getting spacey Sally into public office. Even Fergus's own rebellious kids defect to Frost's camp. The brainstorm of putting LSD in the Capitol Hill water supply finally gets the new

"America's greatest contribution has been to teach the world that getting old is such a drag."

—Sally LeRoy (Diane Varsi), in *Wild in the Streets*

voting-age law rubber-stamped by an addled Congress. Soon Max Frost is elected president by a landslide and withdraws the United States from international affairs, as similar youth revolutions sweep through the Iron Curtain and China. Escaping an assassination attempt by Fergus, Max orders mandatory retirement by thirty, with everyone thirty-five or over rounded up and sent to internment camps where they are perpetually pacified with LSD—with no exemption for Max's mother. The only dark cloud on the horizon is that kids around the age of ten might be contemplating their own movement.

Viewers may be put off by the ambiguous conclusion, but American International Pictures put this package together with an adroit mixture of dark humor, good music performed by the principals (the soundtrack spawned one bona-fide hit, "The Shape of Things to Come"), and the deft use of docudrama news footage of '60s demonstrations and marches on Washington. *Wild in the Streets*'s editing, in fact, received an Oscar nomination. Narration by Paul Frees (the ubiquitous voice-over artist behind Boris Badenov) and cameos by Dick Clark, lawyer Melvin Belli, Pamela Mason (Herriman), Walter Winchell, and Army Archerd also help out, while Shelley Winters, who spent most of her career playing over-the-top matriarchs, gamely shrieks her way through a performance as the parent responsible for Max Frost's reign of terror. Campy psychedelia, the downfall of so many groovy movies, is saved for the concert scenes; the real money shots here are the lampoons of youth culture and ageism, flung around like Marx Brothers Molotov cocktails. Referring to a sexagenarian incumbent in the Oval Office, the future President Frost declares, "What do you ask a sixty-year-old man? 'Do you want your wheelchair facing towards the sun or away from the sun?'" The hip script by Robert Thom (who had earlier worked on a notoriously bowdlerized Jack Kerouac adaptation, MGM's *The Subterraneans*) persuasively directs the "Don't trust anyone over thirty" argument at Fergus, Mrs. Flatow, and other gray-haired, starched, war-stirring, and scotch-swilling Establishment figures, but he doesn't let the youth movement off easily either.

Sequences of staid U.S. senators tripping out inspired real-life threats and attempts by hippies to dope water supplies across the country. Thom would later collaborate on several Roger Corman projects, while Jones would make only a few more features, like *Three in the Attic,* before he, like Varsi, dropped out of the Hollywood scene.

1968 (R) 96m/C Christopher Jones, Shelley Winters, Hal Holbrook, Richard Pryor, Diane Varsi, Millie Perkins, Ed Begley, Kevin Coughlin, Larry Bishop. **D:** Barry Shear. **W:** Robert Thom. **C:** Richard Moore. **M:** Les Baxter. *VHS, DVD*

—Charles A. Cassady Jr.

Zabriskie Point 🦴🦴

Armed with a huge wad of cash handed to him by MGM (the studio that released his surprise hit *Blow-Up* in 1966), Italian director Michelangelo Antonioni took his cameras to America to see what he could see. And all he could see was trouble, so he filmed it.

On paper, the project made perfect sense for a filmmaker whose reputation was based on an ability to relate his characters' alienation to an audience. So, with help from five screenwriters (including a young playwright
named Sam Shepard and future director Clare Peploe), Antonioni decided to
stuff all of his observations into one movie. Not surprisingly, the result,
Zabriskie Point, is a bloated but not uninteresting mess.

The film centers on a college dropout and young radical named Mark
(Mark Frechette). Tired of toiling as a forklift operator, Mark decides to join
some of his student roommates in "the movement" occurring on their Los
Angeles campus. Packing a gun, Mark joins in on a chaotic campus demonstration. When a cop is shot and Mark is accused, he splits the scene.

Rather than leaving L.A. quietly, Mark decides to go out making a statement. He steals a small airplane from a local airport (where a young Harrison
Ford works) and flies it out toward the desert. When Mark is forced to land and
refuel, he happens upon Daria (Daria Halprin), a pretty hippie romantically
involved with her real-estate-mogul boss (Rod Taylor), who happens to be scouting desert locations for development. The two hit it off as they discuss the state
of the world and take in the scenery near Zabriskie Point, a spot located near
Death Valley that offers picturesque views of natural, permanent sand dunes.

To its credit, *Zabriskie Point* bravely attempts to take the pulse of an
America in disarray. The fifty-eight-year-old Antonioni's prognosis, based on

Mark Frechette and
Daria Halprin explore
the desert, each other,
and the sociopolitical
landscape of America
in Michelangelo
Antonioni's sprawling
Zabriskie Point.

MGM / THE KOBAL
COLLECTION

what he (and his screenwriters) observe, is decidedly negative. The downside to this pulse-taking is that too many issues are introduced. The conflict-heavy script, combined with Antonioni's impressionistic (and oversimplified) approach, keeps the film from being the freewheeling, shoot-from-the-hip flick it wants to be.

Which is not to say *Zabriskie Point* doesn't have some memorable moments, including scenes of Taylor's desert oasis, an artificial environment where mannequins, ominously serving as stand-ins for humans, enjoy sunbathing and fishing; a segment in which Daria is aggressively pursued by a group of local children with learning disabilities; and a mind-blowing lovemaking scene (which nearly earned the film an "X" rating) that cross-cuts Mark and Daria's sexual liaison with other couples and threesomes (played by members of an experimental theater group) groping and engaging in foreplay among the sand dunes. And who can forget the infamous finale, in which Daria wishes an apocalyptic destruction to all material things within her reach—and gets it, at least on-screen, as houses, appliances, and various products blow up while Pink Floyd performs "Come in Number 51, Your Time is Up" on the soundtrack.

Zabriskie Point would have been helped by compelling performances. Unfortunately, Antonioni purposely chose two novices for the starring roles. His gamble hurts the film, even though Frechette and Halprin were called on to do little more than play themselves. Frechette appears uneasy and, while compellingly edgy, brings little compassion to his role. We never buy that he believes in what he's doing. Halprin, meanwhile, can't pull off the complexities of a character trying to come to terms with her confused ideals. More interesting than the performances of these two former commune dwellers are their offscreen life stories. After appearing in two post-*Zabriskie* films in Europe, Frechette robbed a Boston bank, claiming political motivations, and was sentenced to fifteen years in prison. He died behind bars at the age of twenty-six after a freak weightlifting accident. Halprin, a onetime member of Frechette's commune, wed Dennis Hopper two years after *Zabriskie Point*'s release. They remained married for four years.

Viewed today, *Zabriskie Point* isn't as awful as its wretched reception and disastrous box office would suggest. But it's obvious that this is one case where a foreign director's unfettered perception of the American landscape didn't prove to be as insightful or enlightening as everyone had hoped. Still, Antonioni serves up some indelible images in *Zabriskie Point* that are hard to shake—even thirty years after they originally appeared.

1970 (R) 110m/C Mark Frechette, Daria Halprin, Rod Taylor, Paul Fix, G. D. Spradlin, Kathleen Cleaver, Harrison Ford. *D:* Michelangelo Antonioni. *W:* Michelangelo Antonioni, Fred Gardner, Tonino Guerra, Clare Peploe, Sam Shepard, Harrison Star. *C:* Alfio Contini. *M:* Pink Floyd, Jerry Garcia, the Grateful Dead. *VHS*

Chapter 12

Foreign Affairs

I t could never be said that American films had the market cornered for the weird, wild, and trippy during the 1960s and 1970s.

Speaking English wasn't a requirement for understanding the universal language of "psychedelic." Foreign filmmakers could get just as wigged out as their American counterparts—and sometimes even more so.

With far less emphasis on box-office returns—like Jean-Luc Godard's going to care if *Vivre sa vie* makes more money in its opening weekend than François Truffaut's *Jules et Jim*—international filmmakers were generally given more freedom to journey into new cinematic frontiers. And during the '60s and '70s, they sure did plenty of that.

Consider Federico Fellini. The Italian maestro tried LSD before filming 1965's *Juliet of the Spirits,* his first color film. The effects of the drug put the already out-there auteur even more out there. *Juliet,* featuring his spouse Giulietta Masina as a wealthy, troubled wife, boasted several mind-bending fantasy scenes. The film was followed by such other drug-inspired works as the surrealistic, satiric "Toby Dammit" segment of the *Spirits of the Dead* anthology and *Fellini Satyricon,* a free-form, brain-frying excursion into the decadence of ancient Rome.

In France, Jean-Luc Godard continued the bold experimentation— not with drugs, but with cinematic form, blasting all that was conventional at the time. After *Contempt,* his 1963 reflection on filmmaking with Brigitte Bardot, Godard cranked out such well-regarded efforts as the existential chase film *Pierrot Le Fou* and *Alphaville,* the threadbare sci-fier with Eddie Constantine as detective Lemmy Caution. Godard's indoctrination into the world of Maoism by new wife Anne Wiazemsky in the mid-1960s led to the filmmaker's most overtly political period, during which he directed such extremist films as *Weekend, Sympathy for the Devil* (AKA *One Plus One,* with the Rolling Stones), and, in tandem with his newly formed Dziga Vertov group of politically minded filmmakers (a sort of Dogma 95 of its day), *Tout Va Bien* and *A Letter to Jane,* two showcases for Jane Fonda's radical politics at the time.

Of course, Godard wasn't the only filmmaker concerned with the turbulent politics of the time. Fellow French New Wave director Alain Resnais, who contributed with Godard and five other filmmakers to *Far from Vietnam,* the seven-part love letter to North Vietnam, delivered *La Guerre Est Finie* with Yves Montand as a Spanish Communist party official. Greek director Costa-Gavras won acclaim with such probing political films as *Z, The Confession,* and *State of Siege.* And Italy's Bernardo Bertolucci explored both contemporary and past political dilemmas with 1965's *Before the Revolution* and 1970's *The Conformist,* respectively.

Many foreign filmmakers who weren't concerned with politics were making movies about mind expansion or sex—and sometimes both. Consider the counterculture ideals, drug use, and sex in exotic settings with the Iranian-born, France-based filmmaker Barbet Schroeder's *More* and *La Vallée.* Or Wojciech Has's 1965 film *The Saragossa Manuscript,* an epic, multistory piece of Polish psychedelia set during the Napoleonic Wars, beloved by the Grateful Dead's Jerry Garcia. Or the works of Alejandro Jodorowsky, whose violent 1970 hallucinogenic western *El Topo* became a staple at midnight screenings in the United States during the early 1970s. John Lennon became such a big fan of the surreal spaghetti western that he had the Beatles' Apple Records back *The Holy Mountain,* Jodorowsky's even wilder, peyote-inspired 1973 follow-up. Much tamer but welcoming *El Topo*–like adoration from young audiences in the latter part of the '60s was *King of Hearts.* In Philippe de Broca's gentle tale of lunatics taking over an asylum in a French village, the setting may have been World War I, but counterculture audiences took the messages of antiwar and nonconformity as relevant for all seasons.

And the film that made the biggest splash—at least financially—among foreign films shown in the States during the '60s? *I Am Curious (Yellow),* of course. The cheaply made sexual/political Swedish import's chronic controversy assured box-office notoriety to the tune of an astounding $20 million. Many other sex-related items from all over the world filtered into America throughout the late 1960s and 1970s. In 1975, *Emanuelle,* France's erotic, exotic, and far less talky answer to *Yellow,* asked whether Americans were still curious. The answer? A resounding *oui.*

El Topo ♫♫♫

The Holy Mountain ♫♫♫

Alejandro Jodorowsky: visionary genius filmmaker or shaman-like schemer? The lines are sharply drawn between the two camps. On one side, the fans of the Chilean director of such way-out works as *El Topo* and *The Holy Mountain* claim he's a mystical mastermind whose disturbing, symbol-laden films are surrealistic pillars of mind-expanding cinema. On the other side are those who pooh-pooh Jodorowsky as a lunatic let loose with a camera, shooting whatever deranged vision, fantasy, or fear comes into his twisted mind.

Whatever your opinion, after seeing one of his disturbing odysseys—particularly *El Topo* or *The Holy Mountain*—you're not likely to forget it. Jodorowsky was one of the founders of the Panique movement of the 1960s, staging wild sexual and political performance-art happenings around Europe. He once requested that cast members drink each other's blood in order to get to know one another better. On top of that, he had a close association with mime master Marcel Marceau, so what do you expect?

El Topo is a psychedelic, violence-strewn spaghetti western that spaghetti-western specialist Sergio Leone might have experienced as a nightmare after consuming three plates of pasta and a bottle of wine. The film begins with a definition of *el topo* (the mole), describing it as "an animal that digs tunnels under the ground, searching for the sun. Sometimes his journey brings him to the surface. When he sees the sun, he's blinded."

This bit of allegorical info relates to the particulars of the film, though you don't realize it until the finale. The actual story concerns El Topo (Jodorowsky), a clad-in-black cowboy who, along with his naked young son (Brontis Jodorowsky, the director's real son), rides into a town right after most of its inhabitants have fallen victim to a bloody gun battle. After allowing the boy to shoot the only survivor of the massacre, El Topo encounters the people responsible for the bloodshed and castrates their leader, the Colonel. Before the Colonel commits suicide, he asks the cowboy who he is. "I am God," El Topo answers. From there it's off to the sadistic, sacrilegious races.

Alejandro Jodorowsky directed and starred as the title character in the head-tripping western *El Topo*.

The Colonel's girlfriend, Mara (played by Mara Lorenzio, a real-life drug addict), decides she wants to ride with El Topo on his journey. So, after irresponsibly dumping his son off with a group of monks, El Topo and Mara wander into the desert. While attempting to prove himself a god to Mara, El Topo is eventually shot and crucified. Resurrected twenty years later, he is reacquainted with his vengeful, now-grown son, meets and prepares to marry a dwarf known as the Small Woman (Jacqueline Luis), and builds a tunnel to help free a group of deformed dwarves stuck in a cave.

While the plot summary gives you a taste of the weirdness that permeates *El Topo,* its over-the-top images are really what set the film apart and what gave it its "must be seen and seen again" reputation for college students, pot-smoking curiosity seekers, and heady cinephiles who attended the midnight movie circuit in the early 1970s. Peckinpah, Eastwood, Leone, and Altman may have breathed new creativity into the genre, but even they didn't dare serve up women fornicating with penis-shaped rocks, a parade of deformed supporting players, Zen-like philosophizing, mime performances, ultra-ultraviolence, and enough perverse psychosexual dynamics to confound Sigmund Freud.

El Topo's rapid acceptance in New York, where it packed the Elgin Theater each weekend, prompted Allen Klein, the Apple Records honcho, to get involved with the film at the behest of John Lennon, an *El Topo*-aholic. Klein's ABKO Films took on the distribution, bringing the film around the country and

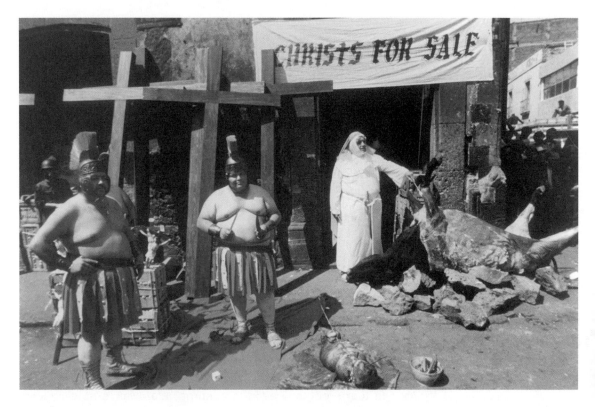

achieving great success at campuses and repertory theaters. And it was *El Topo*'s popularity that prompted Klein to back Jodorowsky's next effort with a more lavish budget. The result was 1974's *The Holy Mountain,* perhaps the most notorious but rarely shown film in history (next to, perhaps, Jerry Lewis's Holocaust drama *The Day the Clown Cried*).

Religious symbolism and bizarre satire collide in Alejandro Jodorowsky's *The Holy Mountain.*

ABKCO FILMS / THE KOBAL COLLECTION

The Holy Mountain received spotty exposure in U.S. theaters, but those who did manage to catch it likened *El Topo* to an episode of *Love, American Style* in comparison. The general consensus was that Jodorowsky, armed with stepped-up production resources and his magically mushrooming ego, went bonkers, bringing personal cinema to new and unparalleled psychedelic heights and depths. Or, as Jodorowsky himself put it in a 2003 interview with the British newspaper *The Guardian,* "El Topo was normal; *The Holy Mountain* was abnormal. I wanted to make a picture like you make a holy book, like the Bhagavad Gita or the Tao Te Ching. I went very far."

Like *El Topo, The Holy Mountain* takes the form of a quest film and is presented in three distinct parts. We're first introduced to the Alchemist (Jodorowsky, in a role that Lennon once considered), a spooky, black-clad figure who we witness shaving the heads of two women. Then we meet the Thief (Horacio Salinez), a Christlike character who, along with a limbless dwarf, wanders the streets of what appears to be Mexico City, witnessing murders, executions, rapes, and animal annihilation.

Eventually, the Thief is used by a group of drunken Romans as a mold for the figure of Jesus Christ. He's then lifted to the top of a monolith-like tower where, inside, he meets the Alchemist, now dressed all in white. An odd experiment involving the Thief's excrement follows (we'll spare you the details). Then he's introduced to the "disciples," a group of local wheeler-dealers who have profited from deception and nefarious dealings. In these segments, Jodorowsky's satire is focused, and he proves himself capable of doing funny things on an outré scale; the work of Terry Gilliam and David Lynch come to mind.

An ornery crew is recruited by the Alchemist to join the Thief for a journey to the Holy Mountain, where they have to prove they are worth of immortality. How to achieve this? First, the Alchemist informs them, "give up your friends, your past, and your self." Then they must kill the nine masters who reside on the mountain.

The final part of The Holy Mountain jarringly jumps from unsettlingly satiric to downright trippy. The journey to the masters is filled with disturbing situations for all involved, as the disciples are put through a series of trials that test their desire for immortality. Along the trek, the Alchemist dispenses instruction (heavy with Eastern philosophy) on how the disciples can conquer their fears.

During this journey up the holy mountain, the disciples meet some lost souls who didn't quite make it to the top. Among them is a meandering man who states, "The cross was a mushroom and the mushroom was the tree of good and evil. The philosophical stone of the Alchemist was LSD and the Book of the Dead was a trip. The Apocalypse described a mescaline experience."

As if further proof is needed to confirm Jodorowsky's drug-induced state (he later admitted to using mushrooms and LSD during the shoot), the final showdown between disciples and masters—the reason the audience has endured the last two hours of this hallucinogenic starship enterprise—never really occurs. It turns out that, like, the entire film was, like, a joke. Was this Jodorowsky's original intention, or did his creativity run out as his artificial stimulants wore off?

A nasty, decades-long feud with producer Klein has made both El Topo and The Holy Mountain virtually unavailable in any format to viewers in most of the world. And the filmmaker, now in his seventies, has had a bizarre career since The Holy Mountain. Aside from an aborted, big-budget attempt to film Dune—a project that involved Salvador Dali, Orson Welles, and Dan O'Bannon—his only film of note has been 1989's Santa Sangre, a return to the El Topo tunnel with some of Tod Browning's Freaks, Alfred Hitchcock's Psycho, and John Waters's Desperate Living thrown in for good measure. Occasionally, however, there's discussion about Jodorowsky returning to the material that really made his career. The project? A sequel to El Topo called The Son of El Toro, with the name change due to his legal battles with Allen Klein.

El Topo
1970 125m/C MX Alejandro Jodorowsky, Mara Lorenzio, Brontis Jodorowsky, Jose Legaretta, Alfonso Arau, José Luis Fernandez. **D:** Alejandro Jodorowsky. **W:** Alejandro Jodorowsky. **C:** Rafael Corkidi. **M:** Alejandro Jodorowsky, Nacho Mendez. VHS **AKA:** The Gopher; The Mole

The Holy Mountain
1973 114m/C *MX/US* Alejandro Jodorowsky, Horacio Salinas, Zamira Saunders, Juan Ferrera, Burt Kleiner, Valerie Jodorowsky, Richard Rutkowski. *D:* Alejandro Jodorowsky. *W:* Alejandro Jodorowsky. *C:* Rafael Corkidi. *M:* Don Cherry, Roger Frangipane, Alejandro Jodorowsky. *VHS*
AKA: The Sacred Mountain; La Montana Sagrada

Max Born (left) plays Gitone, the boy over whom Encolpio and Ascilto argue, in Federico Fellini's first-century romp through Rome, *Fellini Satyricon*.

Fellini Satyricon 🦴🦴🦴

A s defined by world cinema experts, the term "Felliniesque" became, in the words of Gary Morris from the online magazine *Bright Lights Film Journal,* "a common synonym for the grotesque, the satirical, and the surreal," qualities that are readily visible in Italian master Federico Fellini's classics from the 1960s such as *La Dolce Vita* (1960) and *8½* (1963). But the term should really refer to the entire breadth of his multifaceted career, encompassing his earliest, earthier works, films from the '50s that were story- and character-driven—including *The White Sheik* (1952), *La Strada* (1954), and *Nights of Cabiria* (1957)—as well as his later works. What "Felliniesque" really points to is the inimitable, self-referential takes on the social and sexual mores of Fellini's beloved homeland and the art of cinema, and these can be found in all of his films.

The term became popular after 1965's *Juliet of the Spirits,* which showed young audiences that Fellini was hip to their scene. In the film, his wife, Giulietta Masina, plays a confused housewife who believes her husband is having an affair. Fellini's first color film, *Juliet* was partially inspired by his own experiences with LSD and offered delirious dream sequences and dazzling color schemes. The film is Felliniesque in the fullest sense of the term. And that term suits 1969's *Fellini Satyricon,* the director's notorious adaptation of the Petronius classic, to a tee.

Leading lads Encolpio (Martin Potter) and Ascilto (Hiram Keller, who several years earlier became the toast of a generation with his star turn in Broadway's *Hair*) are Italian party boys who embark on a series of often-debauched adventures in first-century Rome. And while the scenarios that the '60s poster boys find themselves in are certainly epic, erotic, and engaging, it's the images conjured by Fellini and his remarkable crew of production artists that grab our attention foremost. *Satyricon*'s mise-en-scène is so over the top and saturated with color that Nero's Rome and Fellini's '60s seem like two sides of the same coin.

Giuseppe Rotunno's sensational cinematography, Luigi Scaccianoce's imperial production design (which must have put a financial stranglehold on Rome's Cinecitta Studios), Danilo Donati's hippie-flavored costume designs, and Rino Carbuni's masquerade-style makeup were all served up at the peak of their creators' powers, fueling Fellini's free-flowing amalgam of tales about hermaphrodites, homosexuals, lesbians, emperors, harlots, slaves, poets, minotaurs, thieves, virgins, nymphomaniacs, ghosts, soldiers, widows, and actors, all of whom traverse a sea of suicide and spirited sexuality. The whole shebang culminates in an earthquake, in Rome, circa the time of Jesus Christ. If it all seems like too much, that's because it is.

Petronius Arbiter's *Satyricon* was lost for centuries and exists only in fragments, one of the many elucidations Fellini used to explain his audaciously fragmented movie. Like the tome, the film ends in midsentence, which makes the freakish, phantasmagorical affair even more . . . well, Felliniesque.

1969 (R) 138m/C *IT/FR* Martin Potter, Hiram Keller, Max Born, Salvo Randone, Magali Noel. **D:** Federico Fellini. **W:** Federico Fellini, Brunello Rondi, Bernardino Zapponi. **C:** Giuseppe Rotunno. **M:** Tod Dockstader, Ilhan Mimaroglu, Nino Rota, Andrew Rudin. *VHS, DVD*
AKA: *Satyricon; The Degenerates*

—*Laurence Lerman*

I Am Curious (Yellow) ♫♫♪

Throughout the spring of 1969, protesters were commonplace at movie theaters across the country. Carrying signs that read "Dirty Movie" and "Shame on You!," the demonstrators were showing their displeasure concerning *I Am Curious (Yellow),* "that Swedish sex film" that was playing at their local movie houses, a film they were certain was going to poison the minds of Americans everywhere.

SERGE GAINSBOURG: THE FRENCH EVERYMAN by Ed Grant

Serge Gainsbourg was a uniquely French phenomenon. Well schooled in painting and litera-ture, he wound up having the equivalent of three careers in music: first as a "musician's musician," a jazz pianist and sad *chanteur* à la Jacques Brel; next as the tunesmith who blessed numerous female pop artists with unforgettable bubblegum hits; and finally, as an older, audacious singer-songwriter who was as well known for his provocative actions on French TV talk shows as for his innovative, uncommonly poetic albums.

All throughout his career, Gainsbourg worked steadily in the movies as an actor, an occasional director, and, most prominently, a composer. He was first cast in starring roles in the late 1960s, but the true turning point occurred when he was paired with English model Jane Birkin (*Blow-Up, Wonderwall*) for the love story *Slogan* (1969). The film includes a tune that Gainsbourg later reworked into his only international hit song, the orgasmic, organ-driven "Je T'Aime, Moi Non Plus" (a duet with Birkin). Jane and Serge married; their daughter, Charlotte Gainsbourg, is a present-day French film star.

Gainsbourg scored or contributed theme songs to over fifty movies. His scores are mesmerizing and evocative. He has admitted to using soundtracks as his "laboratories" for working in different musical genres. *Cannabis* (1970) boasts a super-catchy psychedelic rock soundtrack that is the only reason to see the mediocre Gainsbourg/Birkin crime thriller. Serge played with marching-band music and soul for the soundtrack of William Klein's 1968 superhero fantasy *Mister Freedom* (in which he also had a small role); used a sitar on the soundtrack of the Jean Gabin vehicle *La Pacha* (1968); employed country harmonica-and-banjo melodies for the first film he directed, *Je T'Aime, Moi Non Plus* (1976); and did a Walter Carlos–style turn on the Moog synthesizer for the crime comedy *Too Pretty to Be Honest* (1972). One of Serge's strangest-ever assignments was to adapt Rod McKuen's lyrics for the French-dubbed version of the cartoon feature *A Boy Named Charlie Brown* (1970).

Gainsbourg produced dozens of "publicity films" and music videos during his more than three decades in show business, but his most memorable efforts are two prime swingin'-'60s arti-facts. The first is *Anna* (1967), a delightful TV movie musical starring Jean-Claude Brialy and Anna Karina as star-crossed lovers. The vibrantly colored film, which seems like a "mod" variation on both *Funny Face* and *The Umbrellas of Cherbourg,* includes supporting turns by Gainsbourg himself and a dulcet-voiced Marianne Faithfull.

The other mega-mod musical item, much bootlegged on these shores, is *Le Bardot Show.* A 1967 New Year's Eve special, the program features Brigitte Bardot in a series of short music video–like segments created to accompany new Gainsbourg songs. Highlights include Brigitte straddling a "hog" while warbling "Harley Davidson"; Serge and Brigitte duetting on the classic doomed-lovers lament "Bonnie and Clyde"; and Brigitte, Serge, and guest Sasha Distel performing a *très* psychedelic tune about the joy of kissing hippies(!). Gainsbourg, who died in 1991, collaborated musically with quite a few female movie stars—from *Orpheus*'s Juliette Greco to Isabelle Adjani and Vanessa Paradis—but nothing compares to his short idyll with the luscious B.B.

But the dissenters had little effect (or at least not the effect they hoped to have). People gladly paid the special trumped-up admission prices to see the film everyone was talking about, a movie that had roused American authorities so much that it was almost banned and branded obscene. When the moviegoers walked out of the theater, in spite of disappointment that the film failed to live up to its erotic hype, they rushed home to tell their friends and neighbors (but probably not their spouses) that they, in fact, were no longer curious about *Yellow*. They had become part of history by seeing the most controversial film to ever play around the corner—a film that scored astoundingly well at the box office.

Shot free-form without a script, *I Am Curious (Yellow)* features an entire cast of people who pretty much play themselves. Lena Nyman is a twenty-two-year-old woman who keeps a file on a number of subjects important to her, including "Franco" and "men." She regularly takes to the streets in protest and poses questions to random people regarding racism, politics, the military, women's liberation, and Spain's General Franco. Most of the interviewees respond with confusion or disinterest, or they simply don't respond at all.

Lena is also interested in sex, which annoys Vilgot Sjöman, the movie's real director, who also plays a filmmaker here. He makes no secret of his feelings for Lena, but Lena becomes involved with the younger Börje Ahlstedt, whose conservative politics alternately repel and attract her.

Lena's sexual and political awakening are the focus of *I Am Curious (Yellow),* but neither issue is explored in a satisfying fashion. The film does supply some nudity, but the supposedly frank sex sequences are dreary, shot in gritty, B&W, handheld, cinema vérité style. The film does raise serious and troubling political issues, but in a disturbingly matter-of-fact way. Celebrity appearances by Martin Luther King Jr., Russian poet Yevgeny Yevtushenko, and Olof Palme, the controversial Swedish minister of transport (who was critical of U.S. involvement in Vietnam and apartheid policies in South Africa and backed the Palestinian Liberation Organization and Fidel Castro), add little to the proceedings. For all of her concern and awareness, Lena, and by extension the film itself, never gives us any insight.

Viewed from a historical perspective, *I Am Curious (Yellow)* was an important film not so much for what it contained but for the hoopla it created. Grove Press, the publishers responsible for such landmark works as *Lady Chatterley's Lover* and *Naked Lunch,* piloted the film's troubled theatrical release, which even involved a hearing before the U.S. Supreme Court (a hearing that Grove won). At the box office, Grove cashed in big, as *I Am Curious (Yellow)* became the highest-grossing foreign film of all time, taking in over $20 million (it cost less than $500,000 to produce). Despite its shortcomings, *I Am Curious (Yellow)* remains worth seeing, if only for its place in cinema history.

1968 (NC-17) 121m/B *SW* Lena Nyman, Vilgot Sjöman, Börje Ahlstedt, Marie Göranzon, Olof Palme. *D:* Vilgot Sjöman. *W:* Vilgot Sjöman. *C:* Peter Wester. *M:* Bengt Ernryd. *VHS, DVD*
AKA: Jag är nyfiken—en film i gult

King of Hearts ♪♪♪

Essentially an antiwar morality play based on a simple idiom ("the lunatics have taken over the asylum"), *King of Hearts* mixes equal parts farce, slapstick, and melodrama. Perhaps the first true cult film—or, more accurately, the first repeatedly screened midnight movie—*King of Hearts* still brings a warm smile to the faces of those who initially viewed it as a communal experience.

The World War I setting plays metaphorically as the then-current insanity occurring daily in Vietnam. Private Plumpick (Alan Bates), a low-level British officer, is ordered to defuse a bomb, left behind by evacuating Germans, in a tiny French village. After the doors to the local asylum are accidentally opened, Plumpick finds himself surrounded by the merry madcaps, who soon crown him "King of Hearts." They completely disregard his warnings of a possible explosion, taking him as seriously as the Cheshire Cat regarded Alice.

Lurching between Monty Python-esque gags (one inmate claims he's the pope, another plays chess with a chimp) and moments of lyrical poignancy (the prostitute choir), *King of Hearts* cannot fail to stir the emotions. But as an intellectual exercise, it's like dissecting a golf ball with a plastic spoon.

The "ticking clock" plot was already creaky by 1966, but in *King of Hearts* it simply provides a springboard from which to launch grenades of whimsical satire at the Establishment—a point not lost on young viewers of the day. Nonconformity is embraced like Abbie Hoffman might bear-hug Jerry Rubin.

Once the bomb is defused, the wacky patients decide that a three-year celebration is in order. Plumpick seizes the opportunity to depart, but his attempts are thwarted by Coquelicot, who fancies herself an apprentice prostitute and tightrope walker (which is, coincidentally, also a pretty good analogy for a U.S. senator). The fact that Coquelicot is played by twenty-four-year-old Geneviève Bujold is reason enough for a sane man to hang around with lunatics. In fact, while Bates is the film's protagonist, Bujold is its heart, and her performance is filled with magical, wide-eyed wonder.

Irony abounds in *King of Hearts,* and it's doled out liberally: the good guys are named for flowers (General Geranium) and the bad guys are named for meats (Lieutenant Hamburger), with carnivore being code for "capitalist" and vegetarian code for "socialist."

Having spent some quality time with the deranged, Plumpick is slowly but surely drawn into their make-believe world. Unfortunately, British and German troops are still fighting—albeit in a stylized, highly comical manner. Inevitably, Plumpick finds the "real" world outside the village far less palatable than the carefree lifestyle the lunatics lead. The final shot of Bates—naked, carrying a birdcage, and pleading for "acceptance" from the asylum patients—is a classic image of international cinema.

Contemporary audiences may wiggle uncomfortably on their IKEA sofas as the story rambles toward an open-ended finale, but back in the mid-'60s, *King of Hearts* was—or at least passed for—hip entertainment with a heady message.

1966 102m/C *FR* Alan Bates, Geneviève Bujold, Pierre Brasseur, Adolfo Celi, Michel Serrault, Jean-Claude Brialy. **D:** Philippe de Broca. **W:** Maurice Bessy, Daniel Boulanger. **C:** Pierre L'homme. **M:** Georges Delerue. *VHS, DVD*
AKA: *Le Roi de Coeur*

—Steven Austin

More 🎵🎵

La Vallée 🎵🎵🎵

Undoubtedly two of the most mind-expanding celluloid collaborations to emerge from the drug-drenched psychedelia of the late '60s and early '70s, *More* and *La Vallée* brought together the formative talents of Iranian-born, Sorbonne-educated filmmaker Barbet Schroeder, scenarist Paul Gégauff, cinematographer Nestor Almendros, and rock outfit Pink Floyd. Together, they explore the joys and dangers embodied in the hippie culture of sex, rock 'n' roll, and, particularly, drugs. They don't preach "Just Say No," nor do they evoke the "heroin chic" music-video-slick attitude that one sees in many of today's contemporary films. Labeling a film as "dated" is too easy— indeed, all films are products of their time. And one might take a quick look at these two and dismiss them as another couple of '60s druggie youth flicks. But the step-by-step precision of their narratives—though obscured by the clouds of spirited nudity, open-minded sex, unregulated drug usage, and an appropriately trippy soundtrack by the Floyd—reveal that *More* and, to an even greater extent, *La Vallée* were essentially metaphors for the final curtain falling on the freewheeling idealism of '60s cinema.

Both films revolve around protagonists who set out on journeys of the body, mind, and soul. *More* concerns a German college student, played by Klaus Grünberg, who falls for earthy American ex-pat Estelle (Mimsy Farmer, the peroxide-blonde leading lady of countless '60s youth and biker flicks), who subsequently introduces him to the mind-opening possibilities of drugs. Following Estelle to sun-drenched Ibiza, Grünberg (his name is never revealed, presumably so we can refer to him as an Everyboy) and his gal up the ante and begin to ingest LSD and heroin. Their relationship soon deteriorates and Estelle takes off, leaving Grünberg to overdose all by his lonesome.

Bulle Ogier portrays the journeywoman of *La Vallée*. Her Viviane is a restless French fashionista in New Guinea, the wife of a diplomat, who encounters a colorful group of hippie adventurers loosely led by Gaetan (Jean-Pierre Kalfon). It doesn't take long for Viviane to ditch her husband and other bourgeois amenities and join the spirited little commune. The group heads to the highlands in search of a secluded valley that legend suggests may be the Garden of Eden.

More and *La Vallée* are taking-it-on-the-road pictures of a distinctly psy-chedelic bent, wherein the filmmakers seem as obsessed as the film's characters. In fact, Schroeder's dedication to hauling an entire crew to the New Guinea highlands to shoot *La Vallée* immediately calls to mind Werner Herzog's schlep to the jungles of Peru for *Aguirre: Wrath of God* and *Fitzcarraldo*. The difference in this case is that the ends do not justify the means, even if there are a lot of pretty pictures and landscapes to take in along the way, most of which are set to the always-soothing if somewhat creepy hum of Pink Floyd's score. *More* becomes less when Grünberg dies of a heroin overdose; *La Vallée* becomes crystal clear when our pilgrims reach the mythical site at the film's close and it looks like, well, what every artist since the dawn of time has ever imagined paradise on Earth to look like. The overdose, the discovery of a rather ho-hum valley. FIN. It just ends. Just like the '60s.

More
1969 117m/C *LG/WG/FR* Klaus Grünberg, Mimsy Farmer, Michel Chanderli, Heinz Engelmann. *D:* Barbet Schroeder. *W:* Barbet Schroeder, Paul Gégauff. *C:* Nestor Almendros. *M:* Pink Floyd. *VHS, DVD*

La Vallée
1972 105m/C *FR* Bulle Ogier, Valerie Lagrange, Michael Gothard, Monique Giraudy, Jean-Pierre Kalfon. *D:* Barbet Schroeder. *W:* Barbet Schroeder, Paul Gégauff. *C:* Nestor Almendros. *M:* Pink Floyd. *VHS, DVD*
AKA: The Valley (Obscured by Clouds); The Valley

—Laurence Lerman

The Saragossa Manuscript ♪♪♪

Can a "head" movie get a better recommendation than being noted as the favorite film of late Grateful Dead leader Jerry Garcia? *The Saragossa Manuscript,* a 1965 Polish film that won a small cult following in and around Haight-Ashbury when it was first released and then practically vanished, received just such an honor.

In the years after its initial showing, truncated versions of this three-hour epic occasionally showed up in repertory houses. Garcia, who had seen it in the mid-1960s, was in the process of overseeing the film's restoration before his death in 1995. After Garcia passed away, Martin Scorsese and Francis Ford Coppola took on the project, and, in 2001, it resurfaced briefly in art-house theaters.

It's easy to see why Garcia—AKA Captain Trips—was drawn to the material. Strikingly shot in B&W, the movie is based on a novel by nineteenth-century mystic Count Jan Potocki. Like the book, titled *The Manuscript Found in the Saragossa,* the film is filled with eerie imagery, starkly surreal moments, some surprising lighthearted humor, and a structure that employs a story-within-a-story-within-a-story-within-a-story motif guaranteed to confound and amuse at the same time.

The setting for the interwoven tales is Spain during the Napoleonic Wars. Young Belgian Captain Alphonse Van Worden (Zbigniew Cybulski, AKA

the James Dean of Poland), heading toward Madrid along with his regiment, discovers an antique book in an old inn. As he reads, Van Worden realizes sections of the book actually involve his grandfather. From that point on, several tales from the book—involving possession by demons, sexual infatuation, and ghostly sisters—are visualized in the film.

Either you'll get the point thirty minutes in or you won't get it at all. Following all of these plotlines takes some getting used to, and even savvy filmgoers may find this element of *Saragossa* exasperating. If so, they can simply soak up the stunning visual style, the splendid classical score, and some of the stranger side journeys director Wojciech Has has dreamt up. Another saving grace is the film's subtle, deadpan humor. A particularly funny bit involves Van Worden, a possessed man, and a pail of milk that Van Worden just doesn't want, no matter how many times it's offered.

The film is definitely influenced by the Luis Buñuel brand of surrealism. Like the great Spanish director's work, it pokes fun at social institutions, the military, sex, family relations, and, of course, religion. It should comes as no surprise that Buñuel was a big fan of *The Saragossa Manuscript,* claiming to have seen it several times. Visually, though, the film most resembles the efforts of Guy Maddin, the innovative Winnipeg-based director of the shadowy, off-kilter *Tales of the Gimli Hospital, Careful,* and *Archangel.* Like Maddin's work, *The Saragossa Manuscript* takes you to an alternative, dreamlike universe where reality is uncertain. At the end of this 180-minute excursion into

Polish psychedelia, you're likely to echo Jerry Garcia's sentiments and agree that it has indeed been a long, strange trip.

1965 124m/B *PO* Zbigniew Cybulski, Iga Cembrzynska, Kazimierz Opalinski, Gustaw Holoubek. **D:** Wojciech Has. **W:** Tadeusz Kwiatkowski. **C:** Mieczyslaw Jahoda. **M:** Krzysztof Penderecki. *VHS, DVD*
AKA: *Rekopis znaleziony w Saragossie*

W. R.: Mysteries of the Organism 🎵🎵🎵

It was produced in 1971 and much of its subject matter concerns the 1940s and '50s, but Dusan Makavejev's *W. R.: Mysteries of the Organism* is an undeniable product of the sexual enlightenment of the 1960s.

The film's subject is Wilhelm Reich, the Marxist psychoanalyst and onetime associate of Freud who fought against pornography while arguing that by embracing the joys of sexuality, a better society could be created. But what begins as a straightforward documentary, albeit on a rather saucy topic, gets put through the auteur's grinder when Makavejev throws in a fictionalized narrative at the half-hour mark. The story concerns always-game sexpot Jagoda (Jagoda Kaloper) and politically charged Milena (Milena Dravic), two young Yugoslavian women who slip in and out of a variety of sexual and political situations. ("The October Revolution was ruined when it rejected Free Love!" proclaims Milena at one point, as Jagoda engages in some explicitly photographed copulation with a fellow "rebel.")

By the time the story of Milena and Jagoda takes off, Makavejev has added a handful of running commentaries, which include sequences of the American poet Tuli Kupferberg running around New York clad in military regalia, *Screw* magazine publisher Al Goldstein talking about his periodical as one of his staffers has his schlong cast in plaster, and Andy Warhol Factory regular Jackie Curtis whining poetic about genital-to-genital contact.

W. R. grew out of a Ford Foundation grant that Makavejev obtained to research the life and works of Reich. Snaring additional funds from German television producers, Makavejev decided to turn the project into a fictional feature, grafting together the documentary footage with a narrative story that he shot in Yugoslavia. The result is a memorably fragmented but undeniably provocative and uninhibited pastiche celebrating the joys of eroticism, as put forth by Reich in his preachings about the parallels between sexual liberation and political freedom. It's no surprise that the explicit *W. R.* was immediately banned in Makavejev's native Yugoslavia, deemed politically offensive in Moscow, and given an "X" rating in the United States.

1971 (NC-17) 89m/C *YG/WG* Wilhelm Reich, Milena Dravic, Jagoda Kaloper, Ivica Vidovic. **D:** Dusan Makavejev. **W:** Dusan Makavejev. **C:** Aleksandar Petkovic, Pega Popovik. **M:** Bojana Marijan. *VHS*

—*Laurence Lerman*

Weekend 🦴🦴🦴🦴

One of the most accessible and angrily enjoyable works by the always eye-opening Jean-Luc Godard, a chief architect of the French New Wave movement, *Weekend* is a colorful, almost comic book–style attack on the bourgeois and their values. Its spirit of political, sexual, and, most important, cinematic revolution remains as sincere and inspired today as when it first knocked over audiences some thirty-five years ago.

After talking about sex and murder for a spell, married couple Roland (Jean Yanne) and Corrine (Mireille Darc) set out on a weekend drive across the French countryside to see Corrine's dying mother and confirm their status in the will. (It's important to keep in mind that Roland and his unseen mistress are plotting his wife's murder postinheritance, and that Corrine appears to have a lover or two with whom she engages in threesomes.) Moments after they hit the road, the fun begins—fun being what appears to be the collapse of Western civilization, which kicks off with the mother of all traffic jams.

Rightfully, the film's centerpiece and highpoint for many is the remarkable eight-minute-long tracking shot of the highway traffic, which is filled with bumper-to-bumper cars and a host of extras trying to cope with the situation as Corrine and Roland squeeze into the left lane and putter past them all. Set to the glorious "music" of piercing car horns, the traffic jam remains one of Godard's best-mounted and most indelible sequences. Pissed-off (and pissing!) motorists, Catholic school girls, a couple playing checkers, zoo animals on flatbed trucks, a Shell Oil tanker—a healthy dollop of the Western world's most banal images—litter the highway, the virtuosity of the tracking shot representing the only glory to be seen on this stretch of road. Ever the provocateur, Godard inserts a title card in the middle of the gorgeous shot, an interruption that only adds to the frustration.

Following the traffic backup, the narrative structure of *Weekend* begins to tear away as Corrine and Roland's getaway deconstructs into a series of vignettes that include more car crack-ups, rape, murder, fire, thievery, philosophical rantings, and a roadside encounter with Emily Brontë. Lost in the countryside, the unhappy couple ultimately hooks up with a band of wandering terrorists, leading to the final shots of Corrine apparently *eating* her own husband, who's become the primary ingredient in a cauldron of bubbling revolutionary stew!

The finale isn't nearly as shocking as it reads, but, for Godard, it marked an end to any formal narrative accessibility in his work, which proceeded to become as fractured as it was political. Via the film's last two title cards, Godard appears to acknowledge that a radical change was on the horizon for both his own universe and the one that surrounded him: "End of Film." "End of Cinema."

1967 105m/C *FR/IT* Mireille Darc, Jean Yanne, Jean-Pierre Kalfon, Valerie Lagrange. *D:* Jean-Luc Godard. *W:* Jean-Luc Godard. *C:* Raoul Coutard. *M:* Antoine Duhamel. *VHS*

—Laurence Lerman

Chapter 13

Out of the Underground

There was a whole lot of shaking going on in the 1960s from the underground. On occasion, mainstream films issued a mild jolt, but for the most part, the shock waves that registered on the cinematic Richter scale throughout the decade originated underground.

Anyone from young kids to college students could suddenly get their paws on cameras in the 1950s and early 1960s, whether they be in the 8-mm or 16-mm format. Budding cinephiles just started shooting stuff, and eventually, if the finished product had any merit, film clubs, collectives, or museums in places like New York and San Francisco would show it.

A movement was afoot to make films as remote from Hollywood as possible. Attention to such elements as story, plot, acting, or photography was considered beside the point. This was the cinema of personal expression, and individual exploration and revelation were of primary importance in the eyes of the filmmakers and their supporters.

It was in the early 1960s that interest in an alternative form of cinema really bloomed, as Jonas Mekas and others wrote in the *Village Voice* and *Film Culture* magazine about the works of such underground directors as Ken Jacobs, Jack Smith, Stan Brakhage, Stan van der Beek, George and Mike Kuchar, Carolee Schneemann (known for painting and scratching her films), and Dov Lederberg, who, according to an article in *Bright Lights Film Journal,* "cooked his films in ovens until they assumed the texture of eggplants." But experimental cinema had been around since the movies' earliest days. A young Spanish director named Luis Buñuel teamed with surrealist artist Salvador Dali for 1928's scandalous *Un Chien Andalou* and then went on to make a prodigious career with films tweaking religion, sexual obsessions, the differences between the classes, and men's and women's delicate psyches until his death in 1983.

In the 1940s, Russian émigré Maya Deren introduced the world to what would become known as "dream" or "trance" films with her eighteen-minute *Meshes in the Afternoon,* a mysterious, meditative cinematic poem involving a woman's inner thoughts. And in 1947, Kenneth Anger, a former child actor, directed *Fireworks,* a free-form look at a gay man's fantasy of being beaten by a group of sailors. Anger, an advocate of the teachings and writings of occultist Aleister Crowley, included gay-related imagery of bikers and other (sometimes nude) macho men in such films as *Scorpio Rising* and *Lucifer Rising* over the next several decades.

Anger's works were revered by such film aficionados as Martin Scorsese, Roger Corman, and John Waters, who began shooting his own 8-mm shorts in Baltimore in the late 1960s. He graduated to 16 mm with such features as *Multiple Maniacs* in the early 1970s, and, in 1972, he had a bona fide cult hit with *Pink Flamingos,* which ran for years on the midnight circuit. Featuring Divine, a three-hundred-pound transvestite, *Flamingos'* story of feuding families attempting to gross each other out took cinematic weirdness to the outer limits. Along with subsequent films *Female Trouble* and *Desperate Livng,* the filmmaker simultaneously delighted and disgusted audiences with his outré view of the world.

Waters's Dreamland Studios—really nothing more than a bunch of his eccentric acting friends who hung around together—was fashioned after Andy Warhol's Factory. And like the Waters films, such Factory productions as *Flesh, Trash,* and *Heat* took a satiric approach to the stark realities of everyday life. With Paul Morrissey directing stud-like star Joe Dallesandro and scenemakers Holly Woodlawn and Candy Darling in the casts, the films found comedy in the sometimes sordid, always highly dramatic worlds of drug addiction, sexual dysfunction, prostitution, and homosexuality. Earlier, of course, Warhol's name had helped bring crowds to such experimental works as 1966's methadone-fueled *The Chelsea Girls,* a three-and-a-half-hour epic about Factory members hanging out at the famed Chelsea Hotel in New York, and *Lonesome Cowboys,* 1968's incomprehensible, drug-fueled western.

Another New York–based artist drawing attention to the underground circuit during the '60s was Robert Downey Sr. In 1966 he made *Chafed Elbows* for $25,000, a film about a male welfare recipient who marries his mother. Downey's next film, 1969's *Putney Swope,* a scathing satire about the aftermath of a black takeover of a Madison Avenue advertising agency, became a hit with counterculture and mainstream audiences alike. Unfortunately, Downey was unable to equal *Putney Swope*'s success with *Pound,* in which human actors (including his young son, Robert Downey Jr.) portrayed dogs at a city pound, and *Greaser's Palace,* a zonked-out religious allegory with Jesus as a vaudeville performer who parachutes into a western town wearing a zoot suit.

Almost every person who has become a filmmaker has begun as an amateur dabbling with the camera in his or her formative years. Some, like the aforementioned artists, have won acceptance by their peers, critics, and sometimes even audiences. But remaining "underground" has always been a tricky thing. Seeking wider acceptance and, consequently, finding greater financial rewards by making films that appeal to more mainstream tastes, directors like Downey, Waters, Morrissey, and other more recent underground "graduates" (like E. Elias Merhige and Todd Haynes) have had the term "sell-out" applied to them on occasion. Theirs is the same old art-vs.-commerce story that serious filmmaking talents have wrestled with for ages. Some directors have used increased funding to broaden and deepen their vision, while others have been unable to work on broader cinematic canvases with the added financial pressure. And then there are those who are perfectly content with eggplants.

Chafed Elbows ♫♫♫

Putney Swope ♫♫♫

Pound ♫♫♫

Greaser's Palace ♫♫

Perhaps the rawest comic filmmaker of his age, Robert Downey—now known as Robert Downey Sr. because of his actor son's high-profile career—made a name for himself with a trio of wildly anarchic, gag-riddled social satires and one trippy allegory. In the decades since, he has completed only a few films, none of which has an ounce of the innovation and ballsiness that characterized his early work.

After a few "underground" short-film efforts, Downey made his break-through feature, *Chafed Elbows* (1966). A pure product of the era, when the Marx Brothers and Lenny Bruce were the dominant comic influences, the film is an outrageous account of a few days in the life of a New York City drifter, Walter Dinsmore (George Morgan). Walter's biggest fear is that he has impregnated his mom (the two sleep together on a regular basis); he blows off steam by strolling around Manhattan wearing a police uniform he obtained for an acting job.

The film's dialogue is Groucho-esque in the extreme ("Everything you just said has a universal ring to it, or is it Warner Brothers?"), and Lenny Bruce's influence is felt in the taboo-busting, anti-Establishment plot twists (found here and in Downey's other early films). Bruce's desire to demystify racial epithets is reflected by a barrage of ethnic jokes aimed at Jews, Italians, and blacks. *Elbows*' greatest triumph, however, is its imaginative approach to no-budget filmmaking. Downey uses the technique French film-maker Chris Marker innovated in his sci-fi short *La Jetée* (1962) and tells the bulk of his story through "kinetic" still photographs. The film was shot in easily accessible locations (most of them outdoors) with a very small cast (Elsie Downey, the director's then-wife, plays every female role, and Lawrence Wolf overdubbed a record thirty-four voices).

The most dated of Downey's quartet of oddball classics is ironically also his most vibrant and enduring work. *Putney Swope,* spoofing the advertising business, depicts a token black employee accidentally ascending to CEO status and, in an attempt to add honesty to TV sales pitches, creating "Truth and Soul Advertising." The film's highlights are spot-on spoofs of late-'60s TV commercials, replete with idyllic visuals and trite lyrics (an interracial couple hawking a blemish-cream warbles, "You gave me a soul kiss / boy, it sure was grand / You gave me a dry hump / behind the hot dog stand / oh yeah"). The other central component is a series of scenes in which Swope's employees, especially a gonzo Muslim (Antonio Fargas), argue about whether or not he has sold out. The scenes deftly reflect (and tweak) black militant attitudes of the time. Not bad for the white Downey, who was also such a control freak that he supplied the gravelly voice for the actor playing Swope, Arnold Johnson.

Downey followed *Putney* with his weirdest-ever creation, *Pound,* in 1970. Based on his off-Broadway play, the film focuses on an N.Y.C. dog pound and its inhabitants, who are cute canines when brought into the building but then transform into chatty men and women when locked up in the main cell. While the "dogs" wait to be adopted or gassed, a murderer, nicknamed "The Honky Killer," is disposing of Manhattanites. A terrific ensemble cast makes the most of Downey's alternately hysterical and maddening dialogue. The "breeds" accounted for are incarnated by Downey regulars Lawrence Wolf, Stan Gottlieb, and Elsie Downey, as well as character actors like Don Calfa, Antonio Fargas, and Marshall Efron. The most delightfully strange sequences are the interlude in which the "dogs" all dance to the film's obscene theme song clad in tutus (a truly enjoyable bit of '60s indulgence), and the introduction of a "puppy," played by a very young Robert Downey Jr., who gets to ask the bald Borscht Belt comic (Wolf) serving as a Mexican hairless, "Have any hair on your balls?" (Is it any wonder Downey Jr. grew up to have so many problems?)

Downey's golden era ended with the anachronistic western *Greaser's Palace* (1972). Made with a decent-sized budget, the film takes place in a frontier town run by a sadistic villain (Albert Henderson). Enter a zoot-suited messiah (Allan Arbus) who has the power to heal the sick and resurrect the folks the villain has killed, and you've got one seriously druggy sagebrush saga (sample utterance from a resurrected character: "I was swimming in a rainbow . . . all of a sudden I turned into a perfect smile."). Less dialogue-dependent than any other Downey film, *Greaser's* has the feel of a Robert Crumb comic, with Arbus spouting hep talk ("[I'm journeying] to Jerusalem . . . the agent Morris awaits me!"), walking on water, and performing a musical

Up Madison Ave.

"PUTNEY SWOPE"

The Truth and Soul Movie

Poster for Robert Downey Sr.'s *Putney Swope*

HERALD /THE KOBAL COLLECTION

KENNETH ANGER: THE DEVIL GOES UNDERGROUND
by Ed Grant

Kenneth Anger

Best known for his notorious gossip compendium *Hollywood Babylon*, Kenneth Anger is one of the most important figures in the history of American underground film. His lushly stylized, dreamlike short films have influenced generations of avant-garde, exploitation, and porn filmmakers in the United States and overseas, and his pioneering use of rock music to accompany fragmented images qualifies him as one of the forefathers of the music video. Maverick-turned-Hollywood-auteur Martin Scorsese has testified to Anger's importance for his generation, and countless gay filmmakers have also cited his *Fireworks* (1947) as a seminal work of queer cinema.

Before he became a filmmaker, Anger had a brief career as a child actor, but his only documented movie appearance is as the Changeling Prince in the gossamer 1935 adaptation of *A Midsummer Night's Dream.* He shot a few home-movie productions in his teens, but he made his legitimate underground debut with *Fireworks,* a symbol-laden, Jean Cocteau–style short that introduced his distinct style. Anger's films unfold like a dream—or a drug-induced nightmare—but are executed with a silent movie–like simplicity that makes them both understandable and involving. His taste for gaudy color schemes, costuming inspired by ancient mythology, and pop-culture artifacts also makes his films seem "lighter" and more humorous than those of his contemporaries. Anger's work remains eminently rewatchable, in contrast to the free-floating abstractions of underground pioneer Stan Brakhage and the static "real-time" experiments of Andy Warhol, which are strictly one-time affairs.

On the strength of *Fireworks*, Anger was able to find patrons in Europe and the United States who funded his films for the next three decades. He worked with ultralow budgets, but his propensity for using his financing to re-edit and retool his older titles, plus his strange personal

number in the local saloon. Many events can be written off as weirdness for its own sake, as when our jivin' Jewish hero encounters a flirty pioneer woman (played by the bearded Stan Gottlieb) and "her" lover (a sombrero-wearing Hervé Villechaize!). The cast put the esoteric material across, but *Greaser's* has none of the anarchic enthusiasm of its three predecessors. The allegorical storyline may limit the number of quick one-liners, but the closing shot of a sunset accompanied by electronic noise classifies the film as a bona fide product of the Aquarian Age.

pursuits—including a major devotion to the work of legendary occultist Aleister Crowley—ensured that he spent a great deal of his professional life scrounging for completion money. This circumstance may explain his authorship of the books *Hollywood Babylon, Hollywood Babylon II,* and a long-in-the-works unpublished third entry in that series.

The first truly mind-warping Anger creation was the thirty-eight-minute *Inauguration of the Pleasure Dome* (1953), a hypnotic film that features mythological characters posed in tableaux vivantes and taking part in odd ceremonies that play like Anger's demonic reenvisionment of a Hollywood biblical epic. *Pleasure Dome* was shown during the 1960s in a San Francisco art house as part of "Acid Test" happenings, and it truly does qualify as one of the first "head" movies. Anger himself is featured in drag as Hecate, the goddess of witchcraft; his circle of friends from the period—including author Anaïs Nin and director Curtis Harrington (*Night Tide*)—fill out the cast.

Anger's undisputed masterwork is *Scorpio Rising* (1964). Here he combines the nightly activities of a biker with images that evoke homosexuality, S&M, Satanism, and Nazism—with the Sunday funnies and wind-up toys thrown in for good measure. Anger edits his characters' activities to tunes by Elvis, Ricky Nelson, Ray Charles, and others, creating amusing juxtapositions (B&W footage of a silent-movie depiction of the Last Supper set to Claudine Clark's "Party Lights") and genuine pre–Richard Lester music-video set pieces (a motorcycle race and inevitable crash set to the Surfaris' classic "Wipe Out"). Due to the below-the-radar distribution patterns of underground films, Anger successfully used major artists' music in *Scorpio* without paying large sums of money (he claimed in interviews to have spent a one-time sum of $12,000 for royalties). This practice caught up with him in the 1990s when music publishers protested, and the film was pulled from the VHS release of Anger's collected works, entitled the Magick Lantern Cycle.

Scorpio made an immediate impact on its viewers and soon became one of the few underground films that was shown outside of art houses and college auditoriums. In his well-researched biography *Anger,* Bill Landis examines the way that the film created a vogue for underground features, which generally contained only a few seconds of explicit material, to be booked into porn theaters. Anger's inclusion of gay images made the film a "quality" item on the fledgling gay porn circuit in the mid-1960s. In the meantime, his celebration of the biker lifestyle, along with Hunter Thompson's book *Hell's Angels,* jumpstarted the biker movie genre—exploitation mogul Roger Corman being one who never let a trend pass unnoticed.

After *Greaser's Palace,* Downey was involved in a number of movie comedies, all of which had respectable budgets and "name" talent; each and every one is a disappointment, from *The Gong Show Movie* (1980) and *Mad* magazine's *Up the Academy* (1980) to *Too Much Sun* (1991) and the Alyssa Milano vehicle *Hugo Pool* (1997). His move to the West Coast marked a decisive break with his "underground" roots (though his sensibility was always far more mainstream than contemporaries like the Kuchar brothers and Paul Morrissey). His lacerating, anything-goes humor gave way to a mellower, character-based style of farce. In the case of the '60s-style porn spoof *Rented Lips* (1988), talented performers (Dick Shawn, Martin Mull) are given too little to work with, while Downey Jr. is given free rein to expand his screen time (prone to overacting, the *Less Than Zero* star is unforgivably hammy in his dad's productions). Downey Sr.'s lean and hungry years were undoubtedly his best.

Chafed Elbows
1966 83m/B George Morgan, Elsie Downey, Tom O'Horgan, Lawrence Wolf. *D:* Robert Downey Sr. *W:* Robert Downey Sr. *C:* Stanley Warhow. *M:* Tom O'Horgan. *VHS*

Putney Swope
1969 (R) 84m/C Arnold Johnson, Allan Arbus, Alan Abel, Mel Brooks, Antonio Fargas. *D:* Robert Downey Sr. *W:* Robert Downey Sr. *C:* Gerald Cotts. *M:* Charles Cuva. *VHS, DVD*

Pound
1970 92m/C Lawrence Wolf, Stan Gottlieb, Elsie Downey, Don Calfa, Antonio Fargas. *D:* Robert Downey Sr. *W:* Robert Downey Sr. *C:* Gerald Cotts. *M:* Charles Cuva. *VHS*

Greaser's Palace
1972 91m/C Allan Arbus, James Antonio, Luana Anders, Toni Basil, Don Calfa, Woody Chambliss, Elsie Downey. *D:* Robert Downey Sr. *W:* Robert Downey Sr. *C:* Peter Powell. *M:* Jack Nitzsche. *VHS, DVD*

—Ed Grant

Every Picture Tells a Story
—Tagline for *CQ*

David Holzman's Diary 🦴🦴🦴

CQ 🦴🦴🦴

Two films in which the protagonists decide to make documentary films about themselves and then think better of it at the end, *David Holzman's Diary* and *CQ*, may have been produced thirty-five years apart, but they share many similarities. After all, both attention-getting efforts use distinctive styles (and B&W stock) to show how personal filmmaking projects initially bring delight—and then disillusionment—to their sad-sack protagonists.

David Holzman's Diary, the first effort from then twenty-six-year-old Jim McBride, takes the form of a documentary in which aspiring filmmaker David Holzman (L. M. Kit Carson) decides it's time to chronicle his life on celluloid. Quoting French director Jean-Luc Godard, Holzman states that, after all, "film is truth at twenty-four frames per second."

The young filmmaker starts things off with a tour of his neighborhood, Manhattan's Upper West Side, where he films neighbors, shows us elderly people sitting on benches in the park, and points out such landmarks as the "Red House" building that William Randolph Hearst constructed for Marion Davies and the Dakota Hotel, where "Humphrey Bogart and Zachary Scott

once lived." Holzman begins the project with the enthusiasm of a kid in a candy store, eager to shoot everything and anything that touches his life.

Holzman talks on-screen of his girlfriend Penny (Eileen Dietz), a model who he claims is something of a slob. He holds up her photo and points out some dirt beneath her chin to underline his point. When Penny stops by his apartment, David continues his filming, thinking nothing of including her in his elaborate home movie. But trouble begins—Penny doesn't want to be part of the project. David relents, but then he later films her as she sleeps naked in his bed. When she awakes and sees David with the camera, she flips out.

This marks the beginning of the end of their relationship and David's film project. Penny bolts, and David's attempts to win her back are ineffective simply because he can't shake his filmmaking fever. So he turns his attention to other subjects—a female neighbor across the street whom he observes and then calls to get her reaction on film. He also shoots a brassy nympho-maniac he meets in front of his apartment.

CQ, written and directed by Roman Coppola (the son of Francis Ford, who coproduced, and brother of Oscar-nominated director Sofia), helmer of music videos for Matthew Sweet, Moby, and Fatboy Slim, takes a different approach to the predicaments of personal cinema, but he finds time to directly salute *David Holzman's Diary.* Here, Paul Ballard (Jeremy Davies) is an American film editor in France toiling over a space-age spy thriller called *Dragonfly* in 1969. Ballard,

David Holzman (L. M. Kit Carson) ponders his unraveling life on camera in Jim McBride's *David Holzman's Diary.*

who lives in a Paris flat with Marlene (Élodie Bouchez), a French flight attendant, decides he needs a more fulfilling outlet for his artistic urges and decides to shoot his own 16-mm personalized documentary. Soon he's pontificating about life, art, and other pretensions for the camera and sticking his lens in the increasingly aggravated Marlene's face. Meanwhile, *Dragonfly* is experiencing a number of production problems and Paul becomes enamored of Valentine (Angela Lindvall), the knockout actress and model playing the lead in the production. As if that's not enough, students are protesting in the streets of Paris.

There's little doubt that *David Holzman's Diary* served as an inspiration for Coppola. But affectionate homages to other movies and movie personalities of the psychedelic era abound in *CQ*. There's *Dragonfly*'s heroine, who looks and dresses like Barbarella; a storyline out of *Modesty Blaise*; and specific scenes that smack of *Danger: Diabolik*. Served with extra relish are caricatures of *Barbarella* and *Diabolik* producer Dino de Lauentiis (played by Giancarlo Giannini), William Friedkin (Jason Schwartzman, Coppola's cousin), and a character combining Jean-Luc Godard and François Truffaut (Gérard Depardieu). For good measure we get cameos from *Diabolik* and *David Holzman* actors (John Phillip Law and Carson, respectively). Coppola is right-on with the sleek, Euro-flavored pop-period score and *Dragonfly*'s appropriately ostentatious futuristic production design.

Granted, these are two films from different times, made under different circumstances, and taking different approaches to the subject matter. But both *David Holzman's Diary* and *CQ* explore the pitfalls of filmmakers making statements on celluloid that are so personal they come back to bite them on the ass. *David Holzman's Diary* was photographed in B&W (by *Woodstock* director Michael Wadleigh) on a miraculously low budget of under $5,000 by first-timer McBride (who went on to make the Richard Gere *Breathless* remake and *The Big Easy*). Threadbare but undeniably provocative, the movie essentially takes place in and around the lead character's apartment and presents him either talking directly to the camera or making phone calls. The power of the film comes from the fact that we believe what we're seeing is real. Like David, the audience becomes wrapped up in watching "real" events unfold no matter how mundane they might seem on paper.

CQ, from the son of a world-renowned filmmaker, was made on a modest budget (reportedly in the $3–$4 million range), but it offers a more elaborate way of going about its business with its film-within-a-film-within-a-film motif, the mixing of garish color and gritty B&W, a plethora of in-jokes, and a spiffy sound and visual design scheme. While not totally successful—lead actor Davies comes off as a drone at times and Coppola's pacing could use some more snap and crackle to go with the pop—the film shows that in the world of moviemaking, as Davies's character discovers, total freedom may be more a hindrance than a blessing.

David Holzman's Diary
1967 77m/B L. M. Kit Carson, Eileen Dietz, Lorenzo Mans, Louise Levine, Fern McBride. *D:* Jim McBride. *W:* Jim McBride. *C:* Michael Wadleigh. *VHS*

CQ
2001 (R) 88m/C/B Jeremy Davies, Angela Lindvall, Élodie Bouchez, Giancarlo Giannini, Gérard Depardieu, Jason Schwartzman, Dean Stockwell. *D:* Roman Coppola. *W:* Roman Coppola. *C:* Robert D. Yeoman. *M:* Mellow. *VHS, DVD*

I Shot Andy Warhol ♪♪♪♪

Valerie Jean Solanas decided she wanted more than fifteen minutes of fame, so she shot Andy Warhol in his office in the hopes of killing him.

Warhol, the '60s icon to beat all '60s icons, survived the near-fatal gunshots, but he never fully recovered. Solanas, a radical lesbian and wannabe writer, wound up in a mental hospital, then spent years as a lost soul until she died penniless in San Francisco in 1978. The irony of all this is that Solanas's book, *The SCUM Manifesto,* became an important work heralded by radical feminists. (SCUM, incidentally, stands for Society for Cutting Up Men.) *I Shot Andy Warhol* provides the backstory of the Solanas-Warhol gundown, and what a story it is.

Helmed by first-timer Mary Harron, who went on to direct *American Psycho,* the film is a vividly realized character study of Solanas's dreams, aspirations, and mental illness. Lili Taylor turns in a sensational performance as Solanas, an unbalanced woman who proudly describes herself as a "butch dyke"—though her lesbianism doesn't deter her from making ends meet by turning tricks with men.

Solanas comes from a broken family and a terrible childhood, but she manages to make it to the University of Maryland, where she works on the school newspaper. It's there that the seeds of her manifesto take root. In biology class, she believes she has discovered that men's chromosomes are damaged and that there's no need for the male sex to exist. Later, while living in flophouses in Manhattan, she bangs out her antimale rants on an old typewriter, then photocopies the collected pages and tries to sell them on the street for spare change. She also writes a play called *Up Your Ass,* which echoes many of the sentiments concerning men written about in the manifesto.

A close friend, transvestite Candy Darling (Stephen Dorff), begins to get interested in acting and introduces Solanas to the world of Andy Warhol and his fabulous Factory crowd. Valerie wants Warhol (Jared Harris) to produce *Up Your Ass,* and after a group reading, he actually considers it. His female associates reject the idea, claiming it's too dirty (but Solanas does get to act in a Warhol film or two). At the same time, Solanas meets Maurice Girodias (Lothaire Bluteau), a publisher specializing in controversial works by the likes of William Burroughs and Henry Miller—or "high-class porn," as Solanas puts it. Always on the lookout for the next big thing and facing financial problems, he signs Solanas to a two-novel contract and a $500 advance. But in Solanas's twisted mind, what seems like a big break becomes a conspiracy involving Warhol and Girodias.

I Shot Andy Warhol began life as a documentary, but Harron and her collaborators had trouble finding footage of Solanas, and few people would talk about her. With this in mind, Taylor's performance seems even more remarkable, as it plays as if she's channeling a character she knows intimately. Dressed like a man, chain-smoking cigarettes, and appearing in desperate need of a shower, Taylor is totally convincing. Sure, Solanas is mentally unhinged, but Taylor makes us aware that, behind the jittery, desperate, and confrontational surface, there's a talented, driven person in need of acceptance.

> **"You got to go through a lot of sex to be ready for anti-sex."**
>
> —Valerie Solanas (Lili Taylor), in *I Shot Andy Warhol*

JUST THE FACTS, MAN:
THE 1960S, DOCU STYLE

Real and reel mesh in the following don't-miss documentaries covering different aspects of the psychedelic era:

New York in the Fifties (2001): This film constitutes a primer on the hip happenings in the Big Apple during the decade that bridged the gap between World War II and the way-out '60s. Special focus is placed on Greenwich Village, scene of the early folk rock movement, beatniks, and the *Village Voice* newspaper. Lots of interviews and great clips help tell the story, adapted from Dan Wakefield's book.

Grass (1999): This superior overview of the United States' uneasy association with marijuana is filled with incredible footage, much of it stingingly funny. Presidents make themselves look foolish, the government contradicts itself on several occasions, and archival footage humorously underlines Uncle Sam's on-again off-again hatred of pot. Woody Harrelson (of course) narrates this film from Ron Mann (*Comic Book Confidential*).

Berkeley in the Sixties (1990): The hotbed of radicalism comes alive again in this insightful study of the University of California campus that provided a stamping ground for Black Panthers, the antiwar movement, and some of the era's most famous student demonstrations. While decidedly one-sided, the Oscar-winning film takes audiences into the vortex of political and social upheaval in a most turbulent time.

Smothered: The Censorship Struggles of the Smothers Brothers Comedy Hour (2002): On the surface, it looked like an old-fashioned, squeaky-clean variety show, but a closer look tells us that *The Smothers Brothers Comedy Hour* was, in fact, a sneakily subversive attack of the Establishment—critical of the Vietnam War, big business, and religious hypocrisy. Of course, CBS, its studio, eventually pulled the plug because of the controversy and outside pressures. But, as evidenced in this first-rate docu, what went on behind the scenes with such guests as Joan Baez, Pete Seeger, and Harry Belafonte and with staffers Rob Reiner and the brothers Smothers was more than some hot-shot yo-yo tricks and yet another version of folkie standard "Tom Dooley."

Hearts and Minds (1974): A lacerating, Academy Award–winning look at the Vietnam War, this film moves from American leaders' unsettling attitudes toward the country's involvement in Southeast Asia to the full-blown fighting in Vietnam and its effects on the soldiers and the country. Disturbing

As compassionately as Solanas is portrayed, Warhol comes across as the exact opposite. He's a sponge who casually soaks up others' ideas and talents, then squeezes them out as his art. Harris is memorable as the detached artist who appears either totally zonked out or so aloof that he doesn't want to bother with anything—even a gun pointed at his body at close range. Other real-life roles are filled out nicely, too, from Dorff's sexually ambiguous Darling to Factory regulars like starlet Viva (Tahnee Welch), director Paul Morrissey (Reg Rogers), and actor Ondine (Michael Imperioli), whose insensitive taunting helps drive Solanas over the edge.

combat images are used unsparingly while interviews with and archival footage of American military leaders are often equally appalling. When he won the Oscar, director Peter S. Davis thanked the North Vietnamese government, causing an uproar and creating one of the most controversial moments in Academy Award history. This should give you an idea where the film is coming from politically.

A Decade Under the Influence (2003): Shown in theaters in a truncated version, this three-hour study of some of the prime films and filmmakers of the late 1960s and 1970s is a must-see for anyone interested in the period. The film overlaps with Peter Biskind's book *Easy Riders, Raging Bulls* and its subsequent documentary, but *Decade* has enough interviews and film clips to give a uniquely full picture of what could be the last great era in American filmmaking. Paul Schrader, Martin Scorsese, Dennis Hopper, Julie Christie, and others discuss the period and their work. Directed by Richard La Gravenese and Ted Demme, who died during postproduction, the film suggests that this golden era was undone by *Jaws* and *Star Wars* and the onslaught of the blockbuster movie mentality.

Timothy Leary's Dead (1997): The life and times of LSD advocate Timothy Leary are presented with a plethora of great footage, period music, and interviews with drug-culture spiritual spokesman Ram Dass and others in this well-rounded portrait. Visionary genius or total flake? Well, the movie has you believing that the former Harvard psychology professor was a little of the former and a lot of the latter. It follows Leary from his early days of 1960s LSD experiments to his somewhat decadent lifestyle as spokesperson for a generation of acid-takers, who said the way to find God was through chemical infusion in the body (and he claimed to have taken that trip over five hundred times). Startling and sad are the final parts of the film, featuring the folly of Leary's debating G. Gordon Liddy on tour and showing Leary's noggin being taken from his body in order to be cryogenically frozen for future placement inside another body. Now that's what you call a head movie.

Underground (1976)/*The Weather Undergound* (2003): These two accomplished documentaries about the radical antiwar activist group called the Weather Underground were made twenty-five years apart. *Undergound,* from filmmakers Haskell Wexler, Emile de Antonio, and Mary Lampson, depicts the Weather Underground as a group that took its politics seriously, bombing and threatening to destroy government sites. Sam Green and Bill Siegel's *The Weather Underground* shows how the guerrilla activists, formed in 1969 from Students for a Democratic Society, were heavily influenced by the acts of foreign revolutionaries. They were fueled by drugs and group sex and by their desire to use violence acts at home to stop the violence of war overseas.

I Shot Andy Warhol may not be the last word on the artist, but it offers a fascinating peek into a near-forgotten incident of 1960s subculture. It's one walk on the wild side you're not likely to forget.

1997 (R) 103m/C Lili Taylor, Jared Harris, Stephen Dorff, Martha Plimpton, Lothaire Bluteau, Tahnee Welch, Reg Rogers, Michael Imperioli, Donovan Leitch. *D:* Mary Harron. *W:* Mary Harron, Dan Minahan. *C:* Ellen Kuras. *M:* John Cale. *VHS, DVD*

Lion's Love 🦴🦴

I f Robert Kennedy hadn't been assassinated, one wonders what the hell *Lion's Love* would've wound up being about. The film is a free-form exercise that combined the talents of individuals from various important '60s art "scenes": the French New Wave, the Warhol Factory, the off-Broadway theater world, and the New York underground film movement. The result, naturally enough, is a mess. The fact, however, that the performers experience the RFK assassination the way most Americans did—on television—and that filmmaker Agnès Varda (unlike, say, Warhol) had an idea as to what direction she wanted her improvised film to go in, makes it a valuable document of a time, a place, and an attitude.

Warhol superstar Viva and the scripters/lyricists of *Hair,* Gerome Ragni and James Rado, move into a house in the Hollywood hills. They lounge around, mostly naked, and then play host to New York filmmaker Shirley Clarke (*The Cool World, The Connection*), who is visiting L.A. to nail down a deal with a Hollywood producer. Clarke's deal falls apart, which causes her to attempt suicide—but only after she's argued with Varda about whether or not she would actually do such a thing. Viva, Ragni, and Rado are disturbed by this clearly fictional "tragedy" but are soon paying more attention to real-life events, including Valerie Solanas's shooting of Andy Warhol and the assassination of RFK.

The only woman filmmaker to be part of the loosely defined French New Wave of the 1960s, Varda has made a point throughout her career of working in different genres. *Lion's Love* was her American-style underground film, an evocation of the improvised, rambling works of Warhol and Morrissey. Thus, we are treated to the sight of Viva, Ragni, and Rado lying in bed arguing over who will make coffee, watching television for long periods of time, playing with their dope-smoking kids, and cleaning their gaudily decorated house (wall hangings include posters of Jimi Hendrix, Frank Zappa, and Varda pal Jim Morrison, who reportedly appears as an extra in the film's first scene, set in a theater).

The film goes nowhere fast until the performers learn of the shooting of Robert Kennedy. They then take part in what they call "televised death," as the networks broadcast a national deathwatch, statements of consolation from public figures (President Johnson, Coretta Scott King), and Kennedy's funeral. This segment of the film provides a realistic window into the average viewer's perception of the events of early June 1968. The three leads continue to make comments throughout their TV viewing, but they seem to have abandoned all pretense. Viva may not shed a tear on camera for her mentor Andy, lying near death in a Manhattan hospital (two somber phone calls appear to suffice), but her sad response to the murder of the charismatic, movie-star-like RFK seems thoroughly genuine.

These scenes aren't the film's only saving grace. The sequences in which film historian Carlos Clarens drives Clarke around L.A., and his later lecture on the town's lack of a sense of history, give the viewer a fascinating glimpse of Tinseltown at the exact moment that Hollywood's old guard was collapsing. Varda focuses on a nostalgia bookshop in great detail, showing how the town's legends now reside there and not on studio sets.

Those interested in seeing the best work by Varda, her actors, and Shirley Clarke can surely take a pass on *Lion's Love.* Those who'd like to see the beginnings of today's "couch potato" phenomenon—as well as the ways in which real history can wind up trumping thinly scripted fiction—will be more richly rewarded.

1969 (PG) 110m/C Viva, James Rado, Gerome Ragni, Shirley Clarke, Carlos Clarens, Eddie Constantine. *D:* Agnès Varda. *W:* Agnès Varda. *C:* Steve Larner, Lee Alexander, William Weaver, Rusty Roland. *M:* Joseph Byrd. *VHS*

—Ed Grant

Pink Flamingos 🦴🦴🦴🦴

> **"I guess there's just two kinds of people, Ms. Sandstone; my kind of people and assholes. It's rather obvious which category you fit into. Have a nice day."**
>
> —Connie Marble (Mink Stole), in *Pink Flamingos*

Through a thick marijuana haze in repertory houses all over the country, midnight moviegoers laughed, cheered, and often got sick while watching *Pink Flamingos.* Throughout the 1970s, the notorious film packed in brave souls and treated them to the sight of demented people licking furniture, an anal cavity "singing" "Poppa Oom-Mow-Mow," cannibalism, simulated sex with chickens, and a three-hundred-pound transvestite ingesting . . . well, you know—if, that is, they didn't run for the exit before film's end.

As if these elements aren't disturbing enough, other factors almost ensure queasiness. The film looks like it was shot on 8-mm stock, the acting is either profoundly over-the-top or junior-high-school-play bad, the scratchy oldies music sounds like it is being played on the Flintstones' phonograph, and perhaps worst of all, the cast's distinct Baltimore accents are painfully obvious.

In the film, writer/director/producer/perpetrator John Waters, AKA the Prince of Puke, displays his demented view of the world, where everybody is a pervert or a freak or a creep. But within his cinematic psychoses, there's also lots of chutzpah, as well as some talent. After all, a certain degree of talent is needed to induce moviegoers to watch, open-mouthed, in awe and/or disgust, over and over.

Babs Johnson (Divine), a large transvestite in a tight pink dress, high heels, and ornate facial makeup, is the heroine of the story—particularly in scenes such as the one when she goes into a corner grocery store and shoves what looks like a piece of liver up her crotch. She also has an incestuous relationship with Crackers (Danny Mills), her son, while her disturbed, snaggle-toothed mother, Edie (Edith Massey), lives in a playpen, dressed in bra and panties, and has an unhealthy obsession with eggs. In the film, Connie (Mink Stole) and Raymond Marble (David Lochary) challenge Divine for the title of "Filthiest Person Alive." In their bid for the crown, the Marbles have

Channing (Channing Wilroy), their degenerate butler, impregnate hitchhikers, then sell their babies to childless lesbian couples to fund the Marbles' drug operation (in which they sell heroin to schoolchildren). Swell.

The gross-out goings-on are episodic, but what do you want for a budget of $12,000? Waters modeled the film after such Warhol Factory productions as *Lonesome Cowboys* and *The Chelsea Girls.* Like the Warhol Factory, Waters's Dreamland Studio players, an ensemble of hippies, amateur performers, and just plain weirdos, deliver their lines with gusto; they are more than willing to do what is asked of them in front of the camera, acting or otherwise.

Beneath the surface of this disturbingly hilarious debacle, you'll find antibourgeois themes in the tradition of Luis Buñuel, as well as a love of tabloid sensationalism and an unabashed willingness to shove the middle finger up the rear of mainstream America and all that it stands for. There's a ringing endorsement for the Manson family here, a cannibal cookout there, and a call to arms for the put-upon lovers of filth and denizens of trailer parks to commence the revolution.

Pink Flamingos, billed matter of factly by distributor New Line Cinema as "an exercise in poor taste," made Waters and Divine hero and heroine of the midnight circuit. Following it, each consecutive project that Waters turned out targeted the same midnight moviegoers who brought *Pink Flamin-*

gos into the black, and each received progressively more attention from mainstream audiences. Eventually, even Universal Pictures and Ron Howard—Opie himself—backed one of his pictures (*Cry Baby*). Meanwhile, notable Hollywood stars like Kathleen Turner, Sam Waterston, and Melanie Griffith joined the likes of former Symbionese Liberation Army member Patricia Hearst, former Hollywood heartthrob Troy Donahue, future talk-show host Ricki Lake, and punk rocker Iggy Pop in Waters's casts as he gained respectability.

The ultimate acceptance of John Waters occurred, of course, when *Hairspray,* a musical based on his 1988 film, became a Broadway smash and multiple Tony Award winner. One wonders what the notorious Babs Johnson would have thought of this turn of events.

1973 95m/C Divine, David Lochary, Mink Stole, Mary Vivian Pearce, Edith Massey, Danny Mills, Channing Wilroy. **D:** John Waters. **W:** John Waters. **C:** John Waters. *VHS, DVD*

Trash 🦴🦴🦴

Although you won't find it on as many video-store shelves as *Easy Rider, Trash* was a top ticket-seller in 1970 and almost as defining a motion picture of the counterculture. A pitch-black comedy shot on jerky 16 mm by Paul Morrissey and featuring habitués of Andy Warhol's Factory, the movie plays like a John Waters farce relocated from Baltimore to the scummier edges of Manhattan. And, as with Waters, the nudity and degradation are more than equitable between the sexes.

Joe (Joe Dallesandro), butt-naked from the outset, is a sullen but mostly passive junkie. Joe is apathetic about his inability to become sexually stimulated due to his addiction, but it disturbs the assorted Times Square lowlifes who take him in, aroused by his muscular body—or the thought that he might have some acid stashed away somewhere.

Joe gets passed around like an impotent joint, from a go-go dancer to an LSD-obsessed rich girl to a creepy married couple from Grosse Pointe, Michigan, whose spartan apartment he halfheartedly attempts to rob. The only stable relationship in Joe's life is with Holly (Holly Woodlawn), a trash-diving transvestite who supplies high schoolers with drug fixes. Holly's career goal is to get on welfare, and she tries to pass herself and Joe off as a deserving and expectant couple (it's really Holly's strung-out sister who's pregnant, and she's also just about the only female who can raise Joe's libido). A natty claims investigator (John Sklar) on their case turns out to harbor a shoe fetish, and for a moment it looks like Holly and Joe have him under their heel. But never underestimate the ability of these folks to screw up a sure thing.

While "Andy Warhol Presents" shows up in the opening titles of *Trash* (spelled out in lights on the Times Square ticker), the eccentric multimedia artist and avant-garde impresario was not really involved in the film's production; he had nearly been assassinated by a man-hating Factory regular

> "Just because people throw it out and don't have any use for it, doesn't mean it's garbage."
>
> —Holly Woodlawn, in *Trash*

Warhol regular Joe Dallesandro (left) takes direction from filmmaker Paul Morrissey during the production of *Trash*.

(see *I Shot Andy Warhol*) and, during his recovery, stopped directing his own motion pictures. The working title of this project was *Drug Trash,* and it mirrored what Warhol biographers have seen as Morrissey's contempt for the narcotics-gobbling, late-'60s crowd in which he and Andy were immersed. Practically everyone in *Trash* is damaged goods, some hilariously so—a nice way to disguise bad acting as brilliance, incidentally. While watching a parade of freaks whose thoughts seldom stray beyond the next needle-stick may sound like a tedious and depressing experience, Morrissey's mordant wit lurks continually around the edges, be it in Woodlawn's monologue about being a lifelong welfare case (a cathartic release for Morrissey, who once studied to be a social worker) or in "superstar" Jane Forth's slurring statement, "They say people who take drugs have warped minds? Is that true? I graduated from high school with honors!" The 110-minute running time goes by surprisingly fast.

1970 110m/C Joe Dallesandro, Holly Woodlawn, Jane Forth, Geri Miller, Andrea Feldman, Michael Sklar, Bruce Pecheur, Diane Podel. *D:* Paul Morrissey. *W:* Paul Morrissey. *C:* Paul Morrissey. *VHS, DVD*

—*Charles A. Cassady Jr.*

PAUL MORRISSEY:
THE FACTORY LIFE

With hopes of make more conventional—and, possibly, commercial—films, pop artist Andy Warhol enlisted Paul Morrissey to take over the directing chores of his film projects in the mid-1960s. Using realistic settings and situations and employing Warhol's Factory non-actor players as drug addicts, fag hags, and transvestites (which they often were), Morrissey managed to bring the out-there dramas "in" enough to be financially successful and to garner critical acclaim.

Morrissey worked in tandem with Warhol on the three-and-a-half-hour, two-projector epic *The Chelsea Girls* in 1965 and on the druggy sagebrush saga *Lonesome Cowboys* in 1968. But Warhol eventually handed over the directing chores and distribution responsibilities on future productions to the conservative Fordham literature grad so he could concentrate on other things.

Morrissey's first true solo effort was 1968's *Flesh* with Joe Dallesandro, a hunky actor Warhol idolized. Dallesandro and his deadpan delivery scored in more ways than one as a drug-addicted bisexual hustler trying to make enough cash for his lesbian wife's lover's abortion. Morrissey found humor in the direst situations along with surprisingly strong box-office receipts with *Trash,* the 1970 effort with Dallesandro as a heroin addict constantly looking for a fix and transvestite Holly Woodlawn as his trash- and sex-addicted pseudo-wife. For 1972's *Heat,* Morrissey used Dallesandro yet again, this time in a subtle send-up of *Sunset Boulevard* with Joe as a desperate actor willing to jump into the sack with anyone he thinks could help his career. Sylvia Miles, an Oscar nominee for *Midnight Cowboy* (in which Morrissey made a cameo), plays the fading Norma Desmond–style movie star with whom Dallesandro gets entangled.

Seeking something different and attempting to draw an even larger audience in the process, Warhol stepped even further back from his film operation, sending Morrissey and Dallesandro to Europe for two horror films that were to be shot back-to-back with many of the same cast members. *Andy Warhol's Frankenstein* (AKA *Flesh for Frankenstein*), released in 1974, was an outrageously gory epic shot in 3-D that offers German character actor Udo Kier as the demented doctor out to make a human race of superbeings and Dallesandro as the stable boy who takes care of the doctor's wife/sister in the sack. Body parts and blood ooze off the screen and sexual kinkiness abounds. Those who weren't getting ill at the theaters were having a great time with the film's campy dialogue and tone. The equally outré and often hilarious *Andy Warhol's Dracula* (AKA *Blood for Dracula*) features Kier as the plasma-seeking count who hopes to find new "wirgin" blood in Italy among four young women who reside in a small village. The count, however, doesn't count on local communist servant Dallesandro deflowering the women he has targeted.

Following the international success of the two horror projects, Morrissey and Warhol parted company, leaving Jed Johnson to direct 1977's *Andy Warhol's Bad,* the last Warhol-sponsored feature film. Morrissey went on to write, direct, and produce a number of less experimental but decidedly offbeat films over the years on his own. Among the most interesting works have been 1985's *Beethoven's Nephew,* a look at the odd relationship between the composer and his young relative, and 1988's *Spike of Bensonhurst* (1988), an energetic, darkly comic look at an amateur boxer who falls for his mobster guardian's daughter.

Wild 90 ♪

Beyond the Law ♪

Maidstone ♪♪

Author Norman Mailer was a ubiquitous presence during the Vietnam era. The middle-aged enfant terrible made numerous appearances on TV talk shows (usually in an argumentative mood); sparred with prizefighters; was arrested for taking part in antiwar demonstrations; conducted a heated, nearly surreal debate with feminist leaders at Manhattan's Town Hall; and even ran for the office of mayor of N.Y.C. His mayoral run was perhaps his biggest failure, but running a close second are his three forays into experimental cinema.

Mailer's triumphs during this period were a series of magazine articles in which he recounted key political and social events of the day in a terse, novelistic style. His genius for crafting characters and sketching situations barely factored, however, into the production of his films. The first two were each shot in four evenings and the third took a full five days. As a filmmaker, he chose to emulate Andy Warhol in that he refused to shoot retakes. Unlike Warhol's minimalist efforts, though, Mailer's movies contain characters and storylines, with the director himself (sometimes visibly under the influence) in the lead roles. The first film is a completely forgettable effort about three hoods who've been in hiding in a loft apartment for three weeks. Shot on 16 mm by the great documentarian D. A. Pennebaker, 1967's *Wild 90* is a barely audible affair (the title is a reference to its running time) that stars Mailer and his actor friends Buzz Farbar and Mickey Knox as the three crooks. Pauline Kael put her finger on the film's god-awful yet compulsively watchable quality when she dubbed it "the worst movie I've stayed to see all the way through."

Beyond the Law (1968), Mailer's second effort, was a slightly more sophisticated affair that still amounted to little more than an elaborate ego trip. Norman and his cohorts are cops this time, police detectives in a fictitious N.Y.C. precinct. The cast includes Rip Torn, poet/playwright Michael McClure, various Hell's Angels playing criminals, and George Plimpton as the mayor. *Law* found Mailer using a three-camera set-up (with Pennebaker again helping out), but the results were the same—Mailer aimed for a "gritty" feel and so has his cast indulge in pointless hardboiled banter. The film thus consists of numerous dialogue-heavy sequences, the most notable of which has Norman himself, speaking with a ridiculous Irish brogue, hitting on a young woman played by Marsha Mason (her name spelled "Marcia" in the film's credits). Although Mailer was in favor of the homemade method of filmmaking, Pennebaker has noted that Mailer was not a hands-on editor of his "personal" creations. In fact, he set *Law* completely aside for a number of months as he attended the march on the Pentagon and chronicled that protest in his first influential piece of "new journalism," *The Armies of the Night*. The book, which began as a magazine article, went on to win the Pulitzer Prize and was hailed by many as his finest since his debut novel, *The Naked and the Dead.*

The third Mailer opus is the wildly ambitious *Maidstone* (1971). In this case, he concocted an imaginative, playful scenario and assembled a very large cast for a low-budget feature. Once again, though, he chose not to script the film in advance, and he had only an inkling of a finale in mind. The result is a social satire so mannered and intentionally arty that audiences usually find it funny. Mailer's imperious on-screen attitude and his stunningly misguided attempts at a performance (best exemplified by a silly seduction scene in which he flirts with an actress by way of making strange noises with his mouth) moves *Maidstone* into the realm of unintentional camp.

Like many of Mailer's projects, the film was conceived with the noblest of intentions. He wanted to fashion a response to the violent events of 1968—including the police riot at the recent Democratic convention—with a fantasy about the upcoming presidential election (though shot in '68, the film wasn't shown publicly until '71). In his scenario, he assumed the role of Norman T. Kingsley, a veteran movie director who is filming a male version of *Belle De Jour,* about a bordello in which women can select the hustler of their choice. As Kingsley is directing his movie he is simultaneously running for president and is rumored to be the target of an assassin. Thus Mailer divided the film's cast into two camps: potential assassins and members of a fictitious government agency ("a combination of the CIA and the FBI and the Secret Service," according to Mailer) who have sworn to prevent Kingsley's murder. Certain characters, like the director/candidate's half-brother, interpreted in a delightfully damaged manner by Rip Torn, seemingly belong to both camps.

Thus the film was conceived both as a work of social commentary and as a party game. What wound up on-screen, though, was something decidedly different. Mailer intended to achieve his grandiose goal of making the film nothing less than a full-scale "attack on the nature of reality" by allowing his actors to improvise and his cameramen to film the action wherever they deemed appropriate. This reliance on chance makes the film the crazy quilt that it is, with some performers hamming it up and others taking their roles seriously, while not a single soul (including Mailer himself) had any idea what *Maidstone* would wind up being about.

In the book version of the film's script, Mailer admits that his movie "kept promising developments of plot which never took place." He had expected that a cast member would try to "assassinate" his character, but no one did. (The truth is that the party atmosphere that surrounded the film's shoot in the Hamptons rendered such "inspiration" unlikely.) Thus was born *Maidstone*'s only riveting moment, a scene that truly makes the movie come alive: Rip Torn decided to playfully attack Mailer with a hammer on film, in order to provide the movie with its assassination. Mailer, ever on guard, took the attack seriously, and the scene becomes a messy brawl in which the two-time Pulitzer Prize winner actually bites off part of the future *Larry Sanders Show* star's ear (the fight with Mailer became a staple of Torn's late-night talk show patter for years). The fight takes place in front of Mailer's wife and fairly traumatized children, so it crackles with electricity—and trash-talk, as Torn declares that Norman is "the champ of shit." It's been noted by D. A. Pennebaker (once again serving as cameraman) that Mailer initially left the scene out of the film. He finally saw the light, though, and the scene was included, granting us a candid look at Mailer's violent side (and Torn's insane gutsiness) during this volatile period.

Mailer made one additional film, years later: the gonzo noir *Tough Guys Don't Dance,* which was fully scripted in advance and has gained a small cult following, thanks to its frenzied dialogue and wonderfully melodramatic acting from straight-to-video action star Wings Hauser and tough guy emeritus Lawrence Tierney. Mailer also acted again, in Milos Forman's *Ragtime* (1981), Jean-Luc Godard's *King Lear* (1987), and Matthew Barney's *Cremaster 2* (1999). But the single best portrait of the author on film is *Town Bloody Hall,* a documentary by (who else?) D. A. Pennebaker of the aforementioned 1971 Mailer/feminist showdown at Manhattan's Town Hall. Norman never comes to blows with any of his very calm and caustic opponents, but when he nicknames one verbal antagonist "Cunty," one knows that the Eloquent One's smart retorts have all dried up.

Wild 90
1967 90m/B Norman Mailer, Dick Adler, Beverly Bentley, Harold Conrad, Mickey Knox, Buzz Farbar, Milt Machlin, Jose Torres. *D:* Norman Mailer. *W:* Norman Mailer. *C:* D. A. Pennebaker. *M:* Charlie Brown. *VHS*

Beyond the Law
1968 87m/B Norman Mailer, Rip Torn, Mickey Knox, George Plimpton, Michael McClure, Beverly Bentley, Mary Lynn, Marsha Mason. *D:* Norman Mailer. *W:* Norman Mailer. *C:* D. A. Pennebaker, Jan Welt, Nicholas Preferes. *M:* Frank Conroy. *VHS*

Maidstone
1970 110m/C Norman Mailer, Rip Torn, Jean Campbell, Joy Bang, Beverly Bentley. *D:* Norman Mailer. *W:* Norman Mailer. *C:* Jim Desmond, Richard Leacock, D. A. Pennebaker, Jan Welt, Nicholas Preferes, Sheldon Rochlin. *M:* Isaac Hayes. *VHS*

—Ed Grant

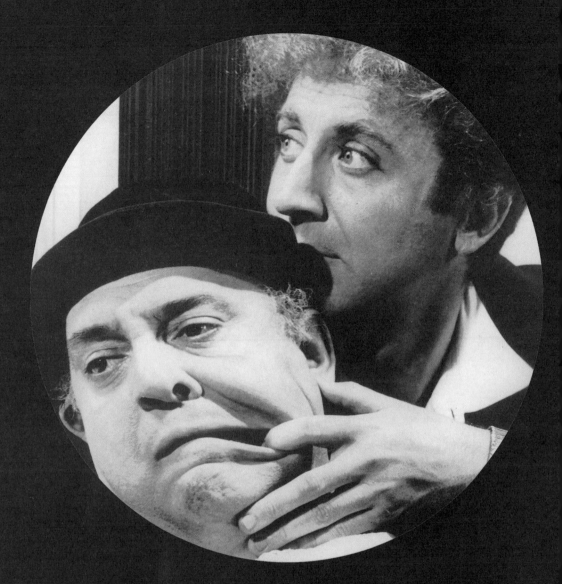

Chapter 14

Laughing on the Outside

"**W**hat's going on with those wacky kids?" was probably the question probed more often than any other in the comedies of the '60s.

They weren't "those little scamps" any more. The younger generation struck confusion, even fear, into the hearts and minds of their parents. And the youngsters were equally baffled by their elders.

What better way to bring this misapprehension out than through laughter? After all, if theatergoers young and old couldn't laugh at themselves, what were they going to laugh at? Certainly not at other hot-button topics of the day.

Francis Ford Coppola impressed some people with 1967's *You're a Big Boy Now,* a breezy extension of his thesis film at the University of Southern California, in which Peter Kastner deals with the eccentricities of New York City with the help of pal Tony Bill, their actions heightened by a soundtrack from the Lovin' Spoonful and some "nice try" camera tricks by the twenty-seven-year-old director.

Big Boy had the right idea—the hip music, the quirky supporting characters, the young protagonist's sexual awakening—but it didn't quite put it all together. Mike Nichols's *The Graduate,* released in 1967, brought much more to the party, proving that kids liked to see themselves on the screen and that adults could even manage to watch a depiction of youth rebellion, as long as the younger generation depicted in the movies looked unthreatening—in other words, "normal." Dustin Hoffman's Benjamin Braddock sported no beard, beads, tie-dyed shirts, or peace signs. He was still a rebel, though, sleeping with Mrs. Robinson, his parents' friend, then dumping her for Elaine, her daughter. Takes guts. The kids could buy into that sort of rebellion, especially when grooving to Simon & Garfunkel's soundtrack. No wonder the film quickly became one of the most popular ever released.

Hollywood got the hint. *The Landlord,* editor Hal Ashby's 1970 indoctrination into directing, features Beau Bridges as a rich kid who takes over a tenement building and gets a crash course in sensitivity from his ghetto tenants. Ashby went the youth route again the following year, but in a decidedly different and daring way, with *Harold and Maude,* a film that details the kooky romance between twenty-year-old death-obsessed Bud Cort and an elderly, life-loving Ruth Gordon.

Ashby also played a crucial part in making one of the '70s' most highly regarded movies, taking his insightful, subtle way with comedy to a more adult level in *Shampoo,* with Warren Beatty as a super-stud hairdresser who, with Julie Christie, Goldie Hawn, and Lee Grant, finds that sex and politics make strange but often necessary bedfellows.

Along with Ashby, Coppola, and Nichols, the 1960s and early 1970s saw the breakout of other notable talents in the comedy realm. TV comedy writer and stand-up comic Woody Allen penned the screenplay for the sex farce *What's New, Pussycat?* (1965), oversaw the redubbing of a Japanese secret-agent movie to hilarious effect with *What's Up, Tiger Lily?* (1966), and directed and starred in his first feature, *Take the Money and Run* (1969). Mel Brooks, another TV comedy veteran, wrote and directed *The Producers,* a hilarious film about Broadway schemers that offers one of the greatest spoofs of flower children in the guise of Dick Shawn's hippie-freak Hitler nicknamed LSD. And *The Manchurian Candidate* screenwriter George Axelrod pitched in with the 1966 film *Lord Love a Duck.* Axelrod's first—and last—directing assignment, *Duck* was a trenchant look at high school students Roddy McDowall and Tuesday Weld and their Southern California environs.

The most prominent, albeit ever-changing, face in comedies of the period was that of Peter Sellers. The prolific British comic changed like a chameleon throughout the era, dazzling audiences in four roles in Stanley Kubrick's *Dr. Strangelove;* tickling funny bones as bumbling French detective Inspector Clouseau in Blake Edwards's *Pink Panther* series and as a blundering Indian actor in Edwards's *The Party;* going weird as a sex-crazed psychiatrist in *What's New, Pussycat?;* showing off his eccentricities as the richest man in the world in *The Magic Christian;* playing an ill-fated James Bond in *Casino Royale;* and essaying a straitlaced attorney turned on to hash brownies and the counterculture in *I Love You, Alice B. Toklas!* Whew! And that's not to mention the other nineteen films Sellers made in the 1960s alone, a decade that should always be remembered as a Sellers market for comedy.

B.S. I Love You 🎵🎵

Early-'70s trappings and too-familiar elements (most of them from *The Graduate*) lend this comedy the odor of stale patchouli.

Paul (Peter Kastner), a New York–based enfant-terrible director of TV commercials, is so unenthusiastic about his engagement to boring Connecticut girlfriend Ruth (Louise Sorel) that he forgets their wedding date. While flying back and forth on business between the Big Apple and California, he flirts with Marilyn (JoAnna Cameron), a hippie-type chick. He: "Do you believe in free love?" She: "I don't believe in paying for it." Later he bumps into her in N.Y.C., where her addled, unpredictable behavior (in a dance club she suddenly accuses him of molesting her, getting poor Paul roughed up and ejected) adds spice to their whirlwind affair.

At work, Paul reluctantly takes the rap for some questionable expenditures by his boss, and he gets rewarded with a plum job at another ad agency, run by the imperious Jane (Joanna Barnes). She seduces him, Mrs. Robinson–style, even though he's queasy about her advanced age—she's thirty-seven, divorced, and even a mom. Their affair blows up when Paul finds out that the mysterious Marilyn is none other than Jane's daughter. Both young folks freak out, but Jane takes the grotesque news very much in stride, even offering to let Paul continue working for the agency. Instead he races through the city, seeking a reconciliation with the departing Ruth, whom he has finally grown to appreciate.

And race he does. It's an annoying trope in the English-speaking world that every romantic comedy must climax with a frantic chase scene (compare *The Impossible Years* with *Notting Hill* to see that not much has changed), and the unnecessary specimen here hardly uplifts the weak, derivative material. While Simon & Garfunkel wanna-bes on the soundtrack harmonize that Paul is "just an average man / doing the best he can," Kastner (who toplined *You're a Big Boy Now*) comes across as an overprivileged and callow repository of selfishness, regrettable early-'70s clothing ensembles, and unflattering facial hair. Much more should have been done, *Putney Swope*–fashion, with the decidedly subversive ads the hero concocts to peddle various consumer products that he clearly disdains. As a bonus this film also offers Gary Burghoff of *M*A*S*H* as Paul's best buddy and confidant, for you Radar O'Reilly completists out there.

1971 (R) 99m/C Peter Kastner, Joanna Barnes, Louise Sorel, JoAnna Cameron, Gary Burghoff, Richard B. Schull. **D:** Steven Hilliard Stern. **W:** Steven Hilliard Stern. **C:** David Dans. **M:** Jim Dale, Mark Shekter. *VHS*

—*Charles A. Cassady Jr.*

The Graduate ♫♫♫♫

H e didn't wear love beads or granny glasses or a ponytail. He didn't protest against the war and didn't even smoke pot. No, the top rebel of the '60s was a nebbish, a guy more comfortable in a suit and tie than tie-dye. His name was Benjamin Braddock.

"Hello darkness, my old friend," Simon & Garfunkel sing at the opening of *The Graduate,* as Benjamin (Dustin Hoffman) goes through an airport terminal to meet his future. The problem is he doesn't have any idea what that future will be. A recent college grad, Ben is going to stay at his parents' house in suburban Southern California until he sorts it all out.

He doesn't say much, but it's obvious he hates his preening parents (William Daniels and Elizabeth Wilson). They make a big deal out of his graduation and throw a party attended solely by their alcohol-swigging friends. In one of the film's most famous lines, one of them tells Ben that the future can be summed up in one word: "Plastics." Instead of laughing, we should all have taken notes.

At the party, Benjamin spots Mrs. Robinson (Anne Bancroft), an old-time pal of his folks, married to his father's law partner (Murray Hamilton). Later, her college-aged daughter, Elaine (Katharine Ross), comes up in conversation, but Mrs. Robinson quickly changes the subject. She's interested in Benjamin, and after some advances—including one in which she undresses in front of him in a bedroom—he gives in. An affair ensues, with Benjamin a somewhat reluctant and guilt-ridden participant. Over time, his interest fades. Eventually, after spending some time with Elaine, Ben finds himself in love with her, much to the chagrin of Mrs. Robinson.

On the surface, *The Graduate* seems like a competent coming-of-age film about a confused kid trying to make a place for himself in the world. But that's not what made Hoffman a star, turned the film into a sensation, and garnered it classic status over the years. Here was a movie that was funny, expertly written, superbly acted, wonderfully scored, mature in theme, and technically superior—and it was about people who were screwed up and indecisive. Where were the '60s and its idealism heading as the decade faded? Nobody knew, and this film showed it.

"For God's sake, Mrs. Robinson. Here we are. You got me into your house. You give me a drink. You … put on music. Now you start opening up your personal life to me and tell me your husband won't be home for hours. … Mrs. Robinson, you're trying to seduce me."

—Benjamin Braddock (Dustin Hoffman), in *The Graduate*

Along with Benjamin's confusion over where the road to adulthood may lead him, there's Mrs. Robinson, a woman stuck in a loveless, sexless marriage but lacking the courage to leave her well-off husband and comfy surroundings. Instead of making a meaningful change, she rebels by having an affair with a man half her husband's age—and the son of her husband's business partner to boot! Then there's Elaine—wishy-washy Elaine—a beautiful role-model student who seems to go with the tide, unable to decide on her own what she wants, unable to figure out how she feels. When faced with the possibility of being with Benjamin for life, she thinks about it and bam!—heads out of town to marry another boyfriend. Certainly her mother, fuming over Ben's rejection of her, plays a part in the decision, but one has to ask: Does Elaine totally lack a backbone to the point of being an emotional jellyfish? Or is she meant to be a satiric creation, a stand-in for other young women churned out of suburbia during an era when young people's desire to please their parents led them to become Stepford children? Elaine's ultimate decision, however, in the film's famous church finale, proves that at least she's with Benjamin in spirit, if not necessarily in sickness and in health, 'til death do they part.

Of course, Benjamin's decision to have an affair with Mrs. Robinson in the first place is a sign of rebellion, however ambivalent. He is flouting his parents' cloying upper-middle-class conventions, and certainly his parents would disapprove. But isn't Mrs. Robinson, in many ways, just a reminder of his parents' "plastic" ways? In one sense, by sleeping with her, Benjamin

Mrs. Robinson (Anne Bancroft) has her way with the clueless Benjamin Braddock (Dustin Hoffman) in *The Graduate.*

EMBASSY / THE KOBAL COLLECTION

BEACH PARTY MOVIES: SAND-DRENCHED CINEMA

by Bruce Klauber

In 1963 American International Pictures' honchos Samuel Z. Arkoff and James H. Nicholson came up with what turned out to be a brilliant idea. Pair an ex–Mickey Mouse Club heartthrob (Annette Funicello) with a popular rock singer from South Philadelphia (Frankie Avalon), put them on the beach, have them surf and sing, add some "name" comic and character actors to the mix to appeal to the older crowd, and just let them run loose. The concept turned out to be more successful than anyone anticipated. *Beach Party* inspired dozens of sequels, rip-offs, and homages. Some were good, some were not; none was as good as the original.

Beach Party stars Bob Cummings as an anthropologist who studies allegedly "wild" teen behavior. And that's about it for the plot. Still hilarious after all these years is Harvey Lembeck's legendary, Marlon Brando–esque portrayal of the infamous Eric Von Zipper. Look for Morey Amsterdam from television's *Dick Van Dyke Show,* the influential rockers Dick Dale and the Del-Tones, and, of all people, veteran actress Dorothy Malone. One important bit of trivia is the fact that Funicello actually had to get permission from Walt Disney himself to appear in a film wearing a bathing suit. Uncle Walt reluctantly agreed, but he did stipulate that Annette wear a one-piece outfit.

Sandy Sequels

Beach Party was such a hit that it spawned a sequel, *Bikini Beach,* the following year. Arkoff and Nicholson discovered that teen moviegoers really responded to the music in these films, so in this and future sequels, they added more star rockers to the mix. *Bikini Beach* is about a wealthy newspaperman who wants to turn the teen beach hangout into a home for senior citizens. Look for Avalon in a dual role as the regular Frankie and as an English rock star called the Potato Bug (an oh-so-clever allusion to the Beatles). Look for an interesting cast of on-their-way-up and on-their-way-down Hollywood actors, including Keenan Wynn, Martha Hyer, a hilarious Don Rickles, a return role for Lembeck, Meredith MacRae, and the first screen appearance of future rock star Stevie (then "Little Stevie") Wonder.

Also released that year were *Pajama Party* and *Muscle Beach Party.* Frankie Avalon must have had a better-paying job elsewhere, as he only makes a cameo appearance in the former. His role was taken by Tommy Kirk. Annette returns, as does Lembeck, as the beach party moves indoors. *Pajama Party* focuses on a Martian teenager named Go-Go (Kirk) who comes to Earth and is confused by the behavior of all these "Earth teens." Look for more performers on the downside of their careers here, including former *Road* movies leading lady Dorothy Lamour, silent comedy genius Buster Keaton, and Elsa Lanchester, *The Bride of Frankenstein* herself.

Meanwhile, *Muscle Beach Party* took the action to, well, Muscle Beach and boasted most of the gang's regulars along with Brian Wilson–penned tunes, European sexpot Luciana Paluzzi, funnymen Buddy Hackett and Morey Amsterdam, future *Mission: Impossible* member Peter Lupus and, in his last role, Peter Lorre.

Beach Blanket Bingo (1965) is probably the most fondly remembered of the *Beach* bunch. Frankie, Annette, and Lembeck are all there, and they're joined by Paul Lynde and a returning Don Rickles and Buster Keaton, who must have really needed a break back then. Along with the expected surf activities, skydiving was introduced to the gang, and the music was supplied by the Hondells and Donna Loren. Look for a very young future television superstar named Linda Evans in the cast.

Hoping there might still be life left in the series, the filmmakers distributed *How to Stuff a Wild Bikini* the same year. Avalon returns in a cameo, with Dwayne Hickman (television's Dobie Gillis) taking over the lead opposite Annette. It's pretty clear that things were starting to run out of steam with this one. Buster Keaton plays a witch doctor called upon to ensure that Hickman won't hook up with Funicello while Avalon is on navy reserve duty. Mickey Rooney is in this one, too, as is Beach Boy Brian Wilson playing an actual beach boy. The infamous Kingsmen of "Louie Louie" fame contribute some of their three-chord numbers.

The Ghost in the Invisible Bikini from 1966, an unsuccessful attempt to mesh the sun-and-fun flicks and horror movies, was the last beach movie outing produced by American International, and it was none too soon. Tommy Kirk is back among a new cast of characters, with only Lembeck a holdover from the other films. The cast is absolutely unbelievable, with Boris Karloff, Basil Rathbone, Jesse White, Patsy Kelly, Francis X. Bushman, and Benny Rubin among them. Nancy Sinatra takes over where Annette left off, and look for Dean Martin's daughter, Claudia, in a small role.

Sons of the Beach

A few other film companies tried to cash in on the beach craze while the AIP series was in full swing and for a few years after its prime. *Beach Ball* from 1965 stars Edd Byrnes (Kookie from television's *77 Sunset Strip*), but it remains best known today for appearances by a number of pop groups, including the Four Seasons, the Supremes, and the Righteous Brothers. *The Beach Girls and the Monster,* from the same year, combines scares and scanty swimsuits and is deservedly long-forgotten. The cast includes Frank Sinatra Jr. and Jon Hall (who played Ramar in several movies and in TV's *Ramar of the Jungle*). Also from 1965 was a quickie rip-off called *The Girls on the Beach,* which serves mainly as a musical revue for the Beach Boys, Leslie Gore, and the Crickets. Among the last of the beach movies was *It's a Bikini World* from 1967. Tommy Kirk appears in this one, and his female costar was Deborah Walley, who had appeared in several of the original beach movies in a smaller role. Again, this film was not much more than an excuse to present popular musical groups of the day. Look for the Toys, the Gentrys, the Castaways, and the Animals (performing "We Gotta Get out of This Place").

Twenty years later, in 1987, Frankie and Annette were reunited for *Back to the Beach.* Here, they're presented as a happily married couple with a punk rocker son (Demian Slade) and a grown daughter (Lori Loughlin) who is engaged to a guy (Tommy Hinckley) who just loves to surf. Everyone does end up on the beach at one time or another, and along the way, the stars run into a bunch of veteran television stars in cameo roles, including O. J. Simpson, Connie Stevens, Tony Dow, Barbara Billingsley, Edd Byrnes, Pee-wee Herman, and even *Gilligan's Island* stars Bob Denver and Alan Hale Jr. *Back to the Beach* may have captured some of the nostalgia of the earlier offerings, but it proved that the beach movies are better off left in a cinematic time capsule nestled in some warm sand.

gets to test out his parents' way of life. He doesn't like what he sees, and he is chilled by this bitter, emotionally detached middle-aged woman. She, and what she stands for, fail the test, so Benjamin finally decides to take a chance, strike out on his own—anything but become like his parents or the Robinsons.

Charles Webb's novel served as the source material for Buck Henry and Calder Willingham's smart adaptation. Mike Nichols, hot after *Who's Afraid of Virginia Woolf?,* directs, successfully using a host of unusual techniques to bring out the humor and complications of the story and characters. The director employed zooms, hand-held camerawork, expansive aerial photography, shots filtered through an aquarium, quickly edited montages, back-to-back musical sequences, and a whole lot more to deliver one of the most daring technical films of the '60s, all in the guise of a relatively small-scale comedy.

The Graduate was an immediate success, drawing repeat viewers from the get-go. Young audiences who could relate to Benjamin's turmoil as well as older audiences who wanted a laugh at the expense of the younger generation's confusion lined up in droves. While the last twenty minutes of the film, with the broader "Benjamin racing-against-the-clock" sequences, prove somewhat tiresome, the rest of *The Graduate* is a gem, a masterfully funny and insightful film about a rebel without a clue.

1967 (PG) 105m Dustin Hoffman, Anne Bancroft, Katharine Ross, William Daniels, Elizabeth Wilson, Murray Hamilton, Buck Henry. **D:** Mike Nichols. **W:** Calder Willingham, Buck Henry. **C:** Robert Surtees. **M:** Paul Simon. *VHS, DVD*

Harold and Maude

Hal Ashby's bizarre black comedy was one of those rare movies that tapped directly into the spirit of its time—at least for a college-aged audience. While most moviegoers paid little attention to the movie that *Variety* famously labeled as being as funny as a burning orphanage, kids flocked to it. The tale of a romance between an octogenarian woman and an immature twenty-year-old manchild enjoyed record runs in university towns and at midnight showings in big-city repertory houses.

Part of the movie's success stemmed from the small but enthusiastic cult following that star Bud Cort had earned from Robert Altman's 1970 avian fantasy *Brewster McCloud*. He plays a similar character here—Harold Chasen, a vacant, round-faced youth who bears a slight resemblance to the Pillsbury Doughboy with a bowl haircut. Harold is the son of a wealthy woman (Vivian Pickles) who pays no attention to his many feigned suicides. Thinking that it's high time he married, she arranges a series of computer-assisted blind dates to visit them at their mansion. Harold sees those meetings as the opportunity for more acting out, and the whole matchmaking scheme ends with one of the film's most surprising and funny moments.

But Harold's fixation with death takes him in other directions. He drives a hearse and attends strangers' funerals. At one such event he first

encounters Maude (Ruth Gordon), a wizened free spirit who takes the boy under her wing and tries to help him break out of his shell. Together, they embark on a series of adventures, all designed to show Harold the joy in life.

That description makes the movie sound hokey, and at times it is, but it became a hit and remains at least watchable because Ruth Gordon's performance is so fearless, touching, and believable, even in the most ridiculous moments. She's nothing less than excellent and always remains aware of the delicacy of the material, particularly when it threatens to become queasy, as it does in the bedroom scene. In some ways, Maude is an expanded version of the memorable character Gordon played in *Inside Daisy Clover,* the overblown 1965 Hollywood potboiler with Natalie Wood and Robert Redford.

Harold and Maude is similar to Ashby's debut, *The Landlord,* in plot and protagonist, though it's a solid step up stylistically. Much of the credit for that goes to cinematographer John A. Alonzo, who makes sure that every scene is properly lit, with the action clearly visible even in dim interiors. And certainly Cat Stevens's sensitive score moves things along and, at the time, helped capture the youth market.

The film's main problem is that the script by Colin Higgins (which he adapted from his own student short film) reduces all of the supporting characters to caricature: cops are bumbling, officious oafs; the blind dates are dull plodders; Harold's mother is a shallow society twit; Harold's Uncle Victor

Death-obsessed Harold (Bud Cort) forms an unusual relationship with lover-of-life Maude (Ruth Gordon) in Hal Ashby's *Harold and Maude.*

(Charles Tyner) is a militaristic martinet. Whenever the film moves beyond the central relationship, it becomes undernourished. At such moments, the tone shifts, and the humor becomes sarcastic and harsh, though it did not seem as extreme at the time. In its somewhat naive antimaterialism, the film is saying this: anyone who works—policeman, soldier, feed store file clerk—is a dim-witted jerk, while those who are free and open their hearts to beauty and joy are above such drudgery. To paraphrase the Lennon/McCartney song, all you need is love—and a trust fund, at least in hapless Harold's case.

1971 (PG) 91m Ruth Gordon, Bud Cort, Vivian Pickles, Cyril Cusack, Charles Tyner, Ellen Greer. **D:** Hal Ashby. **W:** Colin Higgins. **C:** John A. Alonzo. **M:** Cat Stevens. *VHS, DVD*

—*Mike Mayo*

The Hospital ♪♪♪♪

If you or someone you love is about to have an operation, make sure you don't see *The Hospital* beforehand. The film's hairstyles, militant-protester characters, and drug references may be dated, but scripter-producer Paddy Chayefsky's merciless, spot-on satire of the confusion and apathy that can reign in big-city hospitals is as relevant and disturbing today as it was back in '71. Unlike *M*A*S*H, The Hospital* has the look and feel of a drama; the humor creeps in through absurd plot twists and unforgettable lines of dialogue ("the patient was . . . was forgotten to death") that make the film one of the sharpest, grimmest medical movies ever.

Chief surgeon Dr. Herb Bock (George C. Scott) is going through several crises at once. His marriage has ended, he's drinking heavily, he suffers from impotence, and the hospital he works at is under siege by protesters angry that the hospital has purchased and intends to shut down their apartment buildings for purposes of expansion. Worse yet, a number of patients at the hospital are being "mislaid" and later found dead in their beds or the emergency room. Herb and hospital authorities soon discover a pattern: the deceased are actually doctors and nurses who were knocked unconscious and substituted for patients. As "patients," these medical personnel are subjected to unnecessary surgeries, neglect, and fatal mismanagement. Herb's life changes for the better when he takes an interest in Barbara (Diana Rigg), a patient's daughter. Barbara prevents Herb from committing suicide one evening, and the two make love, thereby curing Herb's impotence problem. Barbara invites Herb to return with her and her father to Mexico, where the two serve as missionaries. Herb mulls this over as he attempts to unmask the killer.

Paddy Chayefsky made a name for himself in '50s television with a series of understated, downbeat plays about marginalized characters, the best known being *Marty* (1953). By the '70s, he had begun to situate his alienated antiheroes in a broader social context. His most celebrated work, *Network* (1976), is a brutal, timeless commentary on American popular culture. *Network* has a slightly cartoonish edge to it, whereas *The Hospital* is a sober-minded attack on the apathetic, money-minded methods that began to control medical care in the latter half of the twentieth century.

Chayefsky had a masterful touch with dialogue, but he was remarkably unsubtle. Here, Herb's confusion about his life is rendered in the most bluntly metaphorical fashion imaginable: he's impotent and drunkenly boasts about it to his intimates. What rescues the film from descending into the realm of pure metaphor is Chayefsky's incredible attention to detail. The dialogue is filled with precise medical information and the "villains" of the piece—nurses who demand personal information from patients who appear to be dying, administrators who attempt to keep the protesters from disrupting the daily activities of the hospital—are each given a chance to complain about their untenable situations.

Director Arthur Hiller, who had just come off of one mega-hit (*Love Story*) and two Neil Simon comedies, counters the antiseptic *Medical Center* look of the era by showing Bock's hospital in all its drab glory. *ER* and other current-day medical series adopt this approach as a matter of course, but in its time *The Hospital* represented a break with the lusher, brighter hospitals seen in Hollywood melodramas like *Magnificent Obsession* (1954).

Chayefsky's dedication to detail is the primary reason that the film has such an emotional impact. Another key factor is its excellent ensemble cast: among the staff of the *The Hospital* are seasoned pros Frances Sternhagen, Barnard Hughes, Robert Walden, and Walden's later *Lou Grant* costar (and murderous *Sopranos* mama) Nancy Marchand. *The Avengers* cult figure Diana Rigg decisively stepped away from the action genre with her turn as Barbara. Her character may be one of the few "cultural signposts" in the movie (she makes much of her experiences with hallucinogens and swiftly becomes sexually involved with Herb), but Rigg takes care to incarnate her as a three-dimensional human being despite the on-again, off-again appearance of the actress's own British accent.

The willfully intense George C. Scott sets the tone for the entire movie. His work here seems like an elaboration on the "concerned social worker" character he played earlier in the groundbreaking but short-lived TV series *East Side/West Side* (1963). A few years, and several bureaucratic conflicts, down the line, Herb is the same sort of liberal freethinker as that earlier character. His alcoholism and impotence make the character something of a stereotypically tragic figure (akin to his jaded divorcé in *Petulia*), but his longing to reconnect with his emotions makes him a seminal Nixon-era hero. Scott's turns as a no-B.S. military man in both *Dr. Strangelove* (1964) and *Patton* (1970) might be more iconic, but Herb Bock qualifies as one of the larger-than-life actor's strongest and most sympathetic screen performances.

The Hospital remains a touchstone of early-'70s cinema, a film that didn't do exceptional business at the box office but has burnt itself into the memory of all who have seen it. It functions on several levels at once, with Chayefsky supplementing his social commentary with the oldest narrative hook in the business, a murder mystery. The murderer is eventually unmasked, and his discussion of his methods is one of the blackest touches in the picture—he killed his targets by simply arranging "for the doctors to become patients" in their bedeviled institution.

Chayefsky's portrayal of the chaos and high mortality rate in city hospitals may be seen as a comedic overstatement, but the end credits reveal that his N.Y. C.-shot production had the full cooperation of the New York City Health and Hospitals Corporation and the Department of Public Works. Evidently some real-life experts didn't feel his dark depiction of hospitals was that exaggerated after all.

1971 (PG) 103m/C George C. Scott, Diana Rigg, Barnard Hughes, Richard A. Dysart, Stephen Elliott, Andrew Duncan, Nancy Marchand, Frances Sternhagen, Robert Walden. *D:* Arthur Hiller. *W:* Paddy Chayefsky. *C:* Victor J. Kemper. *M:* Morris Surdin. *VHS, DVD*

—Ed Grant

The Impossible Years ♫♫♪

The generation gap and its malcontents were examined in comedic form in *The Impossible Years,* a hit 1965 Broadway play by Bob Fisher and Arthur Marx, Groucho's son, that boasted an eclectic cast, including comic Alan King, future outstanding character actor Scott Glenn, and future quiz-show master Bert Convoy.

In 1968, a year after the play ended its theatrical run, Hollywood turned *The Impossible Years* into an entertaining movie that plays to both sides of the gap, appealing to the befuddled parents trying to make sense of their kids and to the kids who can't deal with their parents' old-fashioned reaction to the burgeoning counterculture.

In the film, David Niven is Jonathan Kingsley, a college psychiatry professor working on a book with his associate, Richard Merrick (Chad Everett), on how to raise teenagers. Happily married to Alice (Lola Albright), Kingsley is having trouble dealing with seventeen-year-old Linda (Cristina Ferrare), the eldest of his two daughters.

The shapely, independent-minded young lady has been arrested for defending student rights with an obscene placard on Kingsley's college campus. After the proper, *veddy* British Kingsley bails her out of jail, he's hit over the head with the realization not only that Linda isn't a child anymore, but also that his potential job as head of the school's new psychiatric center is now in jeopardy.

Dad thinks the problems are linked to Linda's choice in men—all creeps, in his opinion—who range from Freddy (Rich Chalet), the dim-witted, trumpet-playing son of physician neighbor Herbert Fleischer (Ozzie Nelson), to a horny surfer dude (Michael McGreevy), to an older biker/artist (Jeff Cooper), who paints a nude portrait of Linda. So Kingsley decides to take matters into his own hands and do something about the men in his little girl's life. Things get even kookier when father discovers daughter is no longer a virgin. Now he must also find out which suitor is responsible for deflowering her and punish him accordingly. Of course, Dad overlooks the potential wild card in the whole situation.

Directed in pedestrian fashion by Michael Gordon (Doris Day's *Pillow Talk*, the neo–Rat Pack vehicle *Texas across the River*), *The Impossible Years* is a mildly diverting parents-versus-kids jest-fest that was considered somewhat bold when released because of its taboo sexual subject matter. Its laugh level may have dipped over the years because much of the material is handled in what now seems like a leering style, but for some viewers this approach will only enhance its material, making it a campy pleasure. In fact, the film—now ridiculously rated a family-friendly "G"—was such a hoot among hipsters even in the early 1980s that it inspired a Philly-based pop band called the Impossible Years.

Unintentional laughs aside, the film does get solid backing from a decent cast. Niven, fresh from his turn as Sir James Bond in *Casino Royale*, does a nice slow-burn routine as the put-upon shrink father whose scotch intake gets greater as his daughter's predicaments get more complex. In her debut film role, Ferrare, the future ex–Mrs. John DeLorean and TV talk show host, does a decent job when called on to emote, but she has really been cast to fill out her fringed bikini and loose sweatshirts, which she does perfectly. Cooper is a hoot as bearish Bartholomew Smuts, the hippie-beatnik artist who talks in jive lingo and analyzes situations better than "Daddy-Bear" psychiatrist Niven. And Darleen Carr has some endearingly precocious moments as Niven's boisterous young teen daughter. An example of the film's brand of humor has her getting a kick out of reading *Fanny Hill*. We don't think Uncle Walt would have approved.

The Impossible Years may not be particularly innovative or even especially funny, but it serves as a solid example of how Hollywood could turn such potentially serious subjects as the generation gap and the sexual revolution into enjoyable '60s sitcom silliness—all while trying to appeal to youngsters and their Mommy and Daddy-Os alike.

1968 (G) 92m/C David Niven, Lola Albright, Cristina Ferrare, Chad Everett, Ozzie Nelson, Jeff Cooper, Darleen Carr, John Harding, Rich Chalet, Michael McGreevy. **D:** Michael Gordon. **W:** George Wells. **C:** William H. Daniels. **M:** Don Costa. *VHS*

The Landlord ♪♪

All of the flaws and excesses of the late '60s are in full flower in former film editor Hal Ashby's directorial debut. At heart, *The Landlord* attempts to do for race relations what *The Graduate* did for romance. But that's where any comparison ends.

Our feckless hero is Elgar Enders (Beau Bridges), the unambitious son of a wealthy New York family. His mother (a brilliant Lee Grant) is a clueless social climber. His father is a right-wing racist. Played by Walter Brooke, he's also the film's most overt connection to *The Graduate*; Brooke played Mr. Maguire in that film, the character who gave Benjamin Braddock that famous one-word tip: "Plastics."

For reasons that are never completely clear, Elgar purchases a Harlem tenement. One sunny morning, he drives over in his VW convertible to introduce himself to his tenants and to spruce up the place with potted plants. Looking like a Tom Wolfe wanna-be in his white suit, lavender shirt, and flowered tie, Elgar is greeted with hostile derision by the black residents, who steal his hubcaps, trash his rhododendrons, and chase him into a laundromat.

But Elgar perseveres and eventually even moves into the place; "I'm twenty-nine years old and I've run away from home!" he declares.

Among his neighbors are Marge (Pearl Bailey), who meets him with a shotgun, and Fanny (Diana Sands), who's having trouble coming up with the rent but might be willing to work out a special arrangement because she's having problems with her husband Copee (Lou Gossett Jr.). At the same time, Elgar falls for Lanie (Marki Bey), a beautiful mixed-race dancer.

Apparently the various problems and conflicts that follow are meant to comment on the state of racial matters during those troubled years. As such, the film is very much a liberal Hollywood take on ethnic politics. It divides white characters into two camps: insensitive racists and well-meaning innocents. Black characters understand the realities of the situation, but they never emerge as fully formed individuals. Ashby attempts to break out of the conventional narrative structure with fleeting flashbacks to Elgar's youth and the odd moment or two when he addresses the camera directly. This technique ultimately proves frustrating, because the film could use more about Elgar's background, especially regarding the motivation for his decision to purchase the building in the first place.

A few highly emotional scenes are extended long past their effectiveness, and Ashby and cinematographer Gordon Willis undercut themselves by attempting to use only natural light in most of the interior shots. Even important scenes of physical action are staged in virtual darkness, making it difficult to understand what's happening and nearly impossible to tell what the characters are feeling because their faces are obscured. No wonder Willis, who shot *The Godfather* films, got the nickname "Prince of Darkness."

That same cinema-vérité technique was much more successful a couple of years later when Ashby made *The Last Detail,* but there he had Robert Towne's superb screenplay and Jack Nicholson's breakout performance to carry the film over the rough patches. Like virtually all directors, Ashby was seldom much better than the script he had to work with, and this one, adapted from Kristin Hunter's novel by Bill Gunn (*Ganja and Hess*), with its lapses and a too-convenient ending, is far from perfect.

To be fair to *The Landlord,* the strident politics displayed in this movie were not uncommon, and in those days, many young filmmakers wanted to rid themselves of conventional Hollywood glamour and to break the restraints of traditional storytelling techniques. They wanted their movies to be real, to be "relevant." That sense of immediacy is the best part of the film. The New York locations appear absolutely authentic. Some of the acting is excellent. Lee Grant's performance really stands out, but perhaps that's because most of her scenes are properly lit.

In the end, for better and for worse, *The Landlord* is a product of its times.

1970 (R) 112m/C Beau Bridges, Lee Grant, Diana Sands, Walter Brooke, Louis Gossett Jr., Marki Bey, Melvin Stewart, Susan Anspach, Robert Klein, Pearl Bailey. **D:** Hal Ashby. **W:** Bill Gunn. **C:** Gordon Willis. **M:** Al Kooper. *VHS*

—Mike Mayo

Little Murders ♫♫♫♫

Cartoonist Jules Feiffer presents a wildly funny vision of urban chaos in this pitch-black comedy based on his play of the same name. The city "under siege" that the characters inhabit may seem like a flat-out nightmare, but it's an accurate depiction of how many city-dwellers felt about their environment back in the late '60s and early '70s. The movie is brimming with sharp, caustic dialogue that the impeccable cast does full justice to.

Photographer Alfred Chamberlain (Elliott Gould) roams the streets of New York photographing dog crap (his latest obsession) and being pummeled by the gangs of teens who inhabit the city. Patsy Newquist (Marcia Rodd) saves him from one such beating and decides he's a sorry soul, but one worth salvaging. Patsy pressures Alfred to put his trust in her, hoping to help him reconnect with his own emotions. In the process, the couple visits Patsy's family, with Alfred undergoing interrogations from Patsy's uptight father (Vincent Gardenia), her house-beautiful homemaker mom (Elizabeth Wilson), and her repressed homosexual brother (Jon Korkes). After a bumpy courtship and an even more disastrous wedding ceremony, Alfred opens up and tells Patsy he's ready to "feel" again, at which point a random, senseless crime changes Alfred's life for good.

The characters in *Little Murders* live in a city that's beset by rampant crime, blackouts, break-ins, obscene phone callers, and snipers—in short, an only mildly exaggerated version of New York City (and any other major urban center) post-1968. The love story that blossoms in this setting is a perfect metaphor for the times, as self-proclaimed nihilist (and full-time coward) Alfred is a beaten-down former radical who only comes back to the land of the living when clear thinker (and protofeminist) Patsy reminds him of the importance of being active. Feiffer wisely avoids including the world at large in his portrait—for instance, Patsy's other brother flew bombing missions in Vietnam, but it's noted that his premature death came when he was an innocent bystander during a street shooting.

The only quibble one can have with *Little Murders* is that it is essentially a filmed play. With the exception of the amusing sequence where Patsy takes urban neurotic Alfred to a resort in upstate New York in an effort to tap into his emotions, the sequences shot in broad daylight (especially a later scene set in Central Park) do appear to have been grafted on to "open up" the play.

The extraordinary performances of all concerned more than compensate for what could have been a claustrophobic viewing experience. Seen here during his short post-*M*A*S*H* heyday, Gould (who also produced the movie) proves he was an exceptional talent. Alfred is mostly called upon to react to the other characters, but at two points he delivers monologues that are important in defining his character. The first involves his disgust with his career as a commercial photographer ("I've been shooting shit for over a year, and I've already won a half-dozen awards. . . . *Harper's Bazaar* wants me to do its spring issue"). The second is a brilliant piece about his "connection" to the FBI agent who was reading his mail when he was a radical. Rodd, playing the only sane character, imbues Patsy with a kind of friendly aggression that makes it clear how she has been able to "mold" her boyfriends into the form she wants them to take.

Director Alan Arkin clearly understood that the play functions as a nightmare rendition of the conventional family sitcom of that era (Feiffer wrote his theater piece before the rambunctious, socially conscious Norman Lear–Bud Yorkin sitcoms—like *All in the Family* and *Sanford and Son*—began airing). Thus the first section highlights the family itself with Vincent Gardenia and Elizabeth Wilson perfectly incarnating Patsy's middle-class parents. The second half introduces a series of notable guest stars. Lou Jacobi is a showstopper as a judge who lectures Alfred and Patsy on the reasons they need to mention God in their wedding ceremony. Gould's *M*A*S*H* cohort Donald Sutherland is wonderfully mellow as the hippie priest who marries the couple. Like Jacobi, he delivers a brilliantly written speech: "Last month I married a novelist to a painter. Everyone at the wedding ceremony was under the influence of an hallucinogenic drug. The drug quickened our mental responses, slowed our physical responses, and the whole ceremony took two days to perform. Never have the words had such meaning!" And Arkin himself plays the shaky, dictatorial homicide detective who visits the Newquists in the latter section of the film. One imagines he plays his character with such broadly comic flourishes because his appearance follows the movie's most strongly dramatic moment, a horrifyingly sad interlude where Alfred rides the subway in a shirt covered with Patsy's blood, his fellow passengers taking no notice of him.

Little Murders' devastating conclusion—in which our damaged leads learn to meet violence with violence—connects the film to later landmark works of urban paranoia like *Death Wish* and *Taxi Driver*. In its best moments, however, the film tells a simple story about a depressive being drawn out of his shell by a vital, intelligent woman. The fact that the city's atmosphere of violence wins out in the end and we're still able to laugh is a testament to Feiffer and Arkin's ability to perfectly mix comedy and drama.

1971 (PG) 110m/C Elliott Gould, Marcia Rodd, Vincent Gardenia, Elizabeth Wilson, Donald Sutherland, Lou Jacobi, Alan Arkin. *D:* Alan Arkin. *W:* Jules Feiffer. *C:* Gordon Willis. *M:* Fred Kaz. *VHS*

—Ed Grant

Mister Freedom 🦴🦴🦴

This wildly imaginative, delightfully unsubtle spoof of American patriotism plays like an unholy union of a Roy Lichtenstein painting, one of Jean-Luc Godard's mid-'60s color features, and Norman Mailer's gonzo novel *Why*

Are We in Vietnam? Celebrated photographer William Klein fashions a live-action comic-book adventure out of sports equipment, brightly colored sets, and ridiculously attired go-go dancers. Now what could be wrong with that?

When Capitaine Formidable (Yves Montand in an unbilled cameo) is killed, American superhero Mr. Freedom (John Abbey) travels to France at the order of his superior Dr. Freedom (Donald Pleasence). The gung-ho superhero tells the French that they "live like pigs" and sets about setting them straight. He soon tangles with the deceitful Moujik Man (Philippe Noiret) and fearsome supervillain Red China Man (played by a giant inflatable balloon). Mr. Freedom's biggest trouble comes, however, from sultry double agent Marie-Madeleine (Delphine Seyrig), who might be willing to sell him out.

Mister Freedom covers a lot of territory—it's an art-house feature, overflowing with ideas and jarring images, that just happens to move along at a fast clip and contain large doses of Hollywood-style turgid dialogue. The fact that Klein used elements of both "high" and "low" culture qualifies the film as a true work of pop art; in fact, it has more to do with that movement than any of the films made by pop artist extraordinaire Andy Warhol. Klein, a Manhattanite who has lived in Paris since the 1950s, also uses his knowledge of typical American points of pride to criticize U.S. foreign policy in the late 1960s: Mr. Freedom's indoctrination film for the French is a brilliant montage of cheerful American magazine ads intercut with violent imagery, summarizing America in a far harsher tone than the more famous clip-reel shown to Warren Beatty in *The Parallax View.*

One doubts that Klein was a regular reader of comic books, however, as *Freedom* has more in common with '60s Euro sci-fi titles like *The Tenth Victim* and *Alphaville* than it does with the average issue of *Captain America* or *Superman* (the two obvious models for Klein's flag-waving hero). The film drags whenever Freedom confronts his propaganda-spouting enemies, but even the slower patches dazzle the eye, thanks to the primary-colored sets and the insanely detailed, makeshift costumes (the superheroes are attired mostly in different pieces of sports uniforms, though Noiret resembles the Michelin Man). The funniest moments occur when our hero lectures on the joys of America. At such moments, hard-core expat Klein mocks the up-by-your-bootstraps aspect of the U.S. worldview: "Yeah, I was poor, dirt poor. My father worked in the sewers. Then the Depression came, and they closed down the sewers. No more school. We ate meat once a year."

Abbey, an actor picked by Klein primarily for his size and stature, succeeds admirably with Klein's stylized speeches. The rest of the film is peppered with major French stars who seem eager to "slum" in Klein's oddball costumes. The dignified Seyrig and Noiret play their characters with tongue-in-cheek aplomb. Pop star/cult hero Serge Gainsbourg supplied the film's campy soundtrack and appears at Freedom's political rallies as the piano-playing Mr. Drugstore.

Klein's film output has been sporadic; he has made only twelve features in forty-five years, including his other outrageously innovative '60s chronicle, the fashion-world satire *Who Are You, Polly Maggoo?* (1966). In this B&W, behind-the-scenes "peek" at the life of a model, Klein combines spoofs of unwearable '60s fashions, mock TV commercials, collage animation, faux documentary sequences, and some ultramod minidress-clad models wearing the requisite amount of eyeliner.

1968 105m/C John Abbey, Delphine Seyrig, Donald Pleasence, Philippe Noiret, Catherine Rouvel, Sami Frey. **D:** William Klein. **W:** William Klein. **C:** Pierre L'homme. **M:** Serge Gainsbourg. *VHS*

—Ed Grant

The Party 🦴🦴🦴🦴

I n 1961 Blake Edwards revolutionized the Hollywood sophisticated comedy with his film version of Truman Capote's novel *Breakfast at Tiffany's.* Among the devices he created for the film was a fifteen-minute party sequence that dazzled audiences at the time and caused a copycat stir among the many comedies in production. As if by a sudden mandate, all comedies, it seemed, were now obliged to offer a party scene.

The biggest party scene of all came in 1968, with director Edwards's enduring comic masterpiece, *The Party.* With an ad that proclaimed, "If you've ever been to a wilder party, you're under arrest," Edwards and co-conspirator Peter Sellers set out to meet a challenge that had been germinating in the director's head since *Tiffany's:* to make a movie that was simply one long party, and to be able to sustain laughs and interest without breaking away from the party's single location, a Beverly Hills/Bel Air mansion.

The Party casts Sellers as Hrundi V. Bakshi, a clueless Clouseau-esque character who's been imported from his native India to be a featured actor in a *Gunga Din*–like epic shooting on the backlot of a fictitious Hollywood studio. When Bakshi causes the (hilarious) downfall of the production, he's told he'll never work in this town again. "Does that include television?" he sheepishly inquires.

In the wake of said destruction on the movie set, General Clutterbuck (J. Edward McKinley), the man who runs the studio, mistakenly puts Bakshi's name on an invitation to a huge gathering his wife has planned at their estate. This prologue is simply the setup for what follows, which is one big uninterrupted gala.

The Party plays like an elongated two-reeler of yesteryear. Gags are carefully constructed, and each one acts as a peg upon which the next joke is built. (Edwards once acknowledged that a former mentor was the director Leo McCarey, who honed his trade working with Laurel & Hardy and reached his own comic pinnacle with the Marx Brothers' riotously anarchic *Duck Soup.*) The screenplay, by Edwards and coscripters Tom and Frank Waldman, concocts a veritable gallery of comic invention, and Sellers, in one of his most indelible and likable performances, radiates mischief and an endearing sense of innocence.

Peter Sellers (Bakshi) woos Claudine Longet (Michele) in Blake Edwards's 1968 comedy, The Party.

UNITED ARTISTS / THE KOBAL COLLECTION

Edwards's standout sequence occurs midway through the film, when all the guests are summoned to the dinner table. In a nonstop barrage of gags that could easily be mounted into a separate comic short, Edwards plows through every calamitous possibility of the dining experience, aided immeasurably by Sellers's deadpan expressions and a surprising comic turn from the underrated Steve Franken, here playing the most drunken of drunken waiters. (Also notable is former Tarzan Denny Miller, terrific in an on-target turn as a cowboy star named Wyoming Bill Kelso.) Edwards's cinematographer, the great Lucien Ballard (The Wild Bunch), frames each shot so that every angle achieves full comic potential.

Sellers's love interest in the film, played by Claudine Longet, is an unusual but inspired piece of casting. Longet, whose personal life would later be tarnished in a scandal involving her shooting of her lover, skier "Spider" Sabich, was, at this point in her career, a singer with a perceived persona of innocence, which works well in her scenes with Sellers. Although not really an actress, she's captivating throughout, and she has real chemistry, in a sweetly comic way, with Sellers.

Sweetness, in fact, is what's really at the heart of The Party. After a full hour of nonstop visual and verbal assaults, the movie settles in for a late-'60s coda in which the house is destroyed, but not before an elephant (don't ask) is painted with psychedelic colors and encoded with the peace symbol. But Edwards bravely puts aside the comedy to finish his film on a romantic note, bringing a satisfyingly quiet finish to the raucous proceedings. He's aided in his task by the sentimental scoring of longtime collaborator Henry Mancini. His terrific music provides the opportunity for Longet to sing one of his best songs, "Nothing to Lose," and it simultaneously provides Mr. Sellers with a convulsively funny bit of business while she's singing it.

A failure at the box office in 1968, today *The Party* is well regarded, and rightfully so. The more you see it, the better it gets.

1968 (PG) 99m/C Peter Sellers, Claudine Longet, Marge Champion, Steve Franken, Dick Crockett, J. Edward McKinley, Denny Miller. *D:* Blake Edwards. *W:* Blake Edwards, Tony Waldman, Frank Waldman. *C:* Lucien Ballard. *M:* Henry Mancini. VHS, DVD

—Alan Cylinder

Petulia ♪♪♪

An American who made some of the most influential British comedies of all time, Richard Lester had a cynical side that surfaced in his more surreal farces like *How I Won the War* and *The Bed Sitting Room. Petulia,* his first film featuring more drama than comedy, is also the most extreme expression of his cynicism and his first American movie. Considering its commercial failure and its dark subject matter, it's no surprise that this Philadelphia native subsequently went back to being a "British" director for the rest of his career.

At an upper-crust charity benefit in San Francisco, physician Archie (George C. Scott) is flirted with by society wife Petulia (Julie Christie), who assures Archie, "We're about to become lovers." The affair doesn't take off, but Archie begins to care for Petulia when she shows up at his apartment with a broken rib, the result of a beating by her hot-tempered husband, David (Richard Chamberlain). Archie's status as a recently divorced man makes him wary of being involved with Petulia, but he is shocked to find her unconscious and bleeding in his apartment one afternoon. He rushes her to the hospital, and later is disturbed to find that she joins with her in-laws in shielding David from any blame for the incident. David offers profuse apologies to Petulia for his behavior, but Archie fears for her safety as she checks herself out of the hospital and embarks on a sailing trip with her husband.

Petulia's first half is unique in movie history: it contains all the hallmarks of a classic screwball comedy (except for the abusive husband), but it is played in classic "alienated" '60s fashion. The film's second half is a more conventional doomed love story, albeit one with a Grateful Dead performance and light show. Petulia, labeled an "arch-kook" in the novel on which the film is based, is the '60s equivalent of Katharine Hepburn's characters in movies like *Bringing Up Baby* (1938). Here, her impetuous behavior seems sad and pointless rather than vivacious and endearing. Lester establishes a downbeat mood early on and maintains it throughout the film; to illustrate Archie and Petulia's addled states of mind, he inserts a number of flash-cuts to Archie's memories of his once-happy family, his fantasies of Petulia, and her own recollections of a young Mexican boy she brought home one day to compensate for the child she and David never had. Always in favor of experiments, Lester (a year before *Easy Rider*) also flash-forwards to events we haven't yet seen, like a roller derby match attended by Archie and his family, and gives the viewer disorienting glimpses of such things as the light show that accompanies the Dead performance.

The film's storyline could've taken place in any city at any time, but Lester and his screenwriters make a point of emphasizing that these upper-class characters dwell in San Francisco, in the period right after the Summer of Love. The stock image of the Haight/Ashbury sign is thankfully absent, but several picturesque travelogue-type shots are included. The truest symbols of the era can be found in the supporting cast. Members of the comedy troupe the Committee (including Howard Hesseman) appear as extras. Big Brother and the Holding Company, with Janis Joplin on lead vocals, perform at the charity benefit in the opening scene ("Down on Me" is virtually drowned out by acerbic dialogue). And the Grateful Dead are not only seen playing onstage but are also extras in the grim scene in which the bloodied Petulia is carried out of Archie's apartment on a stretcher (in a show of big-city callousness, the onlookers make sarcastic remarks about the situation, with Jerry Garcia's dialogue being the absurd farewell to the unconscious Christie: "Write if you get work").

Christie incarnates Petulia perfectly, but it's hard to become emotionally attached to the character. Her victimization is such an important and unpleasant aspect of the story that one can't help but view her as Archie does in his flash-cut fantasies: as a beautiful woman ruined by her own choices. The casting of George C. Scott is the linchpin of the entire movie. Although he showed a flair for comedy in one of the best satires of the '60s, *Dr. Strangelove,* his trademark intensity and dead-serious demeanor ensured that *Petulia* would play as a satire. Scott sets the tone for the movie; the opening may seem to signal the sort of lighthearted romantic farce that Peter Sellers made a specialty of in the decade, but Scott's no-nonsense responses to Christie's seduction establish the desperate nature of Petulia's behavior.

Heartthrob actor Chamberlain, who played Dr. Kildare on TV and was a dashing D'Artagnan in Lester's *Musketeers* movies, has the most clearcut role in the film: David is evil, pure and simple, the kind of coward who beats on Petulia rather than confront her "suitors" like the redoubtable (and much bigger) Archie. Like many dramas of the period, the film functions as a metaphor for the era, and here too, David is the most clear-cut sign of the times. He's an attractive, charismatic figure who conceals sadistic and cruel inclinations. The message that short-haired "Establishment" types could be more dangerous than the "freaks" inhabiting the Haight was undoubtedly understood by younger viewers at the time. While the movie was not well received upon release, it has since become a cult favorite and is hailed by many as one of Lester's finest. There's no doubt about it: *Petulia* was a unique moment in the career of Lester, the man now proclaimed to be "the father of music videos" thanks to his work on the Beatles' *A Hard Day's Night* and *Help!*

1968 (R) 105m/C Julie Christie, George C. Scott, Richard Chamberlain, Arthur Hiller, Pippa Scott, Joseph Cotton. *D:* Richard Lester. *W:* Lawrence B. Marcus. *C:* Nicolas Roeg. *M:* John Barry. *VHS, DVD*

TERRY SOUTHERN: MR. HIP GOES TO THE MOVIES
by Ed Grant

"It was a magical era, an era of change and astonishment," said writer Terry Southern of the 1960s. Southern began his career as a novelist, but he left an indelible imprint on the '60s through two trendsetting movie scripts he collaborated on, *Dr. Strangelove* (1964) and *Easy Rider* (1969).

Southern's deliciously warped sense of humor, as evidenced by his writings, influenced filmmakers, authors, and musicians (the Beatles included him on the cover of the *Sgt. Pepper* album) throughout the decade, though it was his decision in 1963 to turn his energies away from fiction and devote himself to screenwriting full-time that made him a seminal figure in the pop culture of the period. He quickly went from being a talented American expatriate living in Paris—attending school on the G.I. Bill after fighting in World War II—to a "scenester" who hung out with the hippest folk imaginable, from William Burroughs and Samuel Beckett, to Dennis Hopper and Jane Fonda, to Mick Jagger and Keith Richards.

The Write Stuff

An uncategorizable writer, Southern belonged to several different "schools"—he was at once a Beat, a supreme practitioner of black humor, and one of the very first of the "new journalists." His literary legacy is assured by a small handful of books, among them the best-selling, pseudonymous porn satire *Candy*, the brilliant greed fable *The Magic Christian*, and a terrific collection of his short fiction and journalism, *Red Dirt Marijuana and Other Tastes*. His movie legacy is a mix of bona-fide classics, bloated productions that were sunk by "too many cooks" behind the scenes and awful casting, and an underrated gem or two.

Dr. Strangelove is the undisputed masterpiece, a fusion of Stanley Kubrick's social and technological concerns and Southern's satirical view of bureaucracy and the military. The film's "tense

The Producers 🦴🦴🦴🦴

The Producers is a film that was once a novel, then a play, then a film, then a Broadway musical, and now it's going to be a movie musical. You got all that?

Writer-director Mel Brooks, a former staff member of Sid Caesar's *Your Show of Shows* in the golden days of TV, originally envisioned his story, "Springtime for Hitler," as a book. He started writing it; things didn't work out. He shifted gears with the form, thinking, the idea may jell as a play. No go. Frustrated, Brooks said, "What the hell" and turned it into his first feature-film screenplay, which also became his first directorial assignment when independent producer Joseph E. Levine decided to bankroll the project. Over thirty comedy" benefits not only from Peter Sellers's expert improvs, but also from Southern's unforgettable dialogue ("You wanna know what I think? I think you're some kind of deviated pre-vert"). Director-star-cowriter Dennis Hopper and star-cowriter Peter Fonda have maintained that *Easy Rider* was based on their own collaboration, but the film's only eloquently scripted scene (the campfire talk) has the undeniable sound and feel of Southern's other work. In his Southern biography (*A Grand Guy*), Lee Hill provides a convincing argument that Southern provided the structure and sensibility for that milestone end-of-the-'60s movie.

Southern Discomfort

Southern's other screenwriting work in the '60s includes the uneven but often hilarious *The Loved One* (1965) and the stone-cold-sober Steve McQueen gambling fave *The Cincinnati Kid* (1965). *Candy* (1968) showed scripter Buck Henry overwriting an adaptation of Southern's tight, terse little piece of porn dementia, while for the appropriately anarchic *The Magic Christian* (1969) Southern adapted his own novel, albeit with contributions from other writers (including future Pythons Graham Chapman and John Cleese). Southern's influence is felt in certain bizarre moments in *Barbarella* ("De-crucify the angel or I'll melt your face!"), for which he was one of several scripters. Right after Southern had the ultimate '60s journalistic assignment—covering the 1968 Democratic convention for *Esquire*—he cowrote his other end-of-the-'60s movie, the darkly allegorical drama *End of the Road* (1970). The film boasts impressive acting by Stacy Keach and James Earl Jones, but its story of a man mentally "programmed" by a mysterious doctor is so despairing it makes *Easy Rider* look positively cheery.

Southern spent the 1970s continuing the high life he began in the '60s (attested to by an appearance in the Rolling Stones' notorious documentary *Cocksucker Blues*). In the 1980s and early '90s, he wrote screenplays that sadly went unproduced and an elegiac, compact novel (*Texas Summer*). He also taught screenwriting before his death in 1995 at the age of seventy-one. Southern's produced movie work is sparse compared with that of other scripters, but his finest satiric work lives on in such immaculate dialogue as *Easy Rider*'s "They're scared of your freedom" and *Strangelove*'s "You can't fight in here—this is the War Room!"

years later, the idea metamorphosed yet again when Brooks successfully transformed it into a smash Broadway musical. Its success prompted Brooks to take the movie route once again, only this time with music, in a big-screen collaboration with Broadway stars Nathan Lane and Matthew Broderick, and with director Susan Stroman.

For a film with women wearing pretzels and beer steins on their boobs, that's a pretty good run.

"The movie to offend everyone," read one movie poster. "Inspired lunacy," shouted another. The pitchmen were right on both counts. Before there was the phrase "politically incorrect," *The Producers* was politically incorrect. Hell, it may have even invented the concept.

In a nutshell, the film is about Max Bialystock (Zero Mostel), a has-been Broadway producer reduced to seducing little old ladies and then bilking them out of their savings while wearing a cardboard belt. Neurotic accountant Leo Bloom (Gene Wilder) realizes that if Max can raise lots of dough and then produce a flop production, none of the investors will get paid. With the surplus money he raises, Max, accompanied by Leo, can then take off to South America with the cash and live the good life.

The surefire disaster Max and Leo mount is *Springtime for Hitler,* a musical love letter to the Führer penned by a Nazi-worshipping lunatic named Franz Liebkind (Kenneth Mars). To ensure disaster, Max and Leo hire effeminate cross-dresser Roger De Bris (Christopher Hewett) to direct and Lorenzo St. Dubois (Dick Shawn), a spaced-out flower child nicknamed LSD, to star.

Everything in this movie screams bad taste. Consider the sight of the rotund Bialystock playing touchy-feely with elderly women. Or Liebkind's perverse passion for pigeons. Or Max hiring a buxom secretary who can't speak English but can sure move her outrageous body while frugging wildly to music. Or the elaborate "Springtime for Hitler" production number in which Nazis sing and goose-step to form swastikas, Busby Berkeley–style, with Aryan enthusiasm.

Subtle? Not a chance. Sloppy? Kind of. Funny? Absolutely.

While Brooks's Oscar-winning screenplay hits its satiric targets—Nazis, gays, hippies, New Yawkers, Broadway snobbery—with gusto about 95 percent of the time, it's the casting and characters that really make *The Producers* click. Veteran funnyman Mostel, winner of three Tony awards and best known as Tevye in the original Broadway cast of *Fiddler on the Roof,* is perfect as the sweaty, rotund "Bialy." Wilder, in his first screen role following *Bonnie and Clyde,* won a well-deserved nomination for Best Supporting Actor for his hysterical security blanket–nuzzling Leo. In a part that was originally to be played by Dustin Hoffman, Mars turns grotesquerie into hilarity as the nutsy Nazi Liebkind, and Shawn's LSD (a part dropped from the Broadway musical) is a perfect caricature of a counterculture hipster, made riotous when filtered through Brooks's Boscht Belt sensibilities. Wonderful, too, is the score, highlighted by John Morris's zippy incidental music, the comically portentous "Springtime for Hitler" centerpiece spectacle, and Shawn's solo moment: clanging mini-cymbals, gyrating, and talkin' about "'Love Power,' the power of a little flower."

Made for a little under $1 million, *The Producers* did decent business when first released. Those who got to the theaters to see the film loved it, and the movie eventually turned into a cult favorite. Thirty-some years later, drawing huge audiences on Broadway and in touring companies all over the place, it's difficult to imagine the project started life as that outrageous "little movie that could." But its reception over the years in whatever incarnation reflects its brilliant not-quite-original concept. Or as Max Bialystock would say, "When you got it baby . . . flaunt it . . . flaunt it!"

1968 (PG) 88m/C Zero Mostel, Gene Wilder, Kenneth Mars, Dick Shawn, Estelle Winwood, Christopher Hewett, Andreas Voutsinas, William Hickey, Renee Taylor. *D:* Mel Brooks. *W:* Mel Brooks. *C:* Joseph F. Coffey. *M:* John Morris. *VHS, DVD*

"Will the dancing Hitlers please wait in the wings? We are only seeing singing Hitlers."

—Roger De Bris (Christopher Hewett), in *The Producers*

The Projectionist ♫♫♫

T he nostalgia craze of the 1960s and early '70s is delightfully reflected in this imaginative, surprisingly touching tribute to the heroes of Hollywood's Golden Age.

Kiddie-show host Chuck McCann plays a projectionist who works for tyrannical theater manager Rinaldi (Rodney Dangerfield, who, in a change of pace, *demands* respect in the role). While the film is rolling, Chuck sits in the projection booth, dreaming of his alter ego, the superhero Captain Flash, who aids a damsel (Ina Balin) abducted by the nefarious villain, the Bat (Dangerfield). When Captain Flash is down for the count and the Bat has the upper hand . . . a couple of screen heroes help out (via playful editing by director Harry Hurwitz). Humphrey Bogart, James Cagney, Gary Cooper, John Wayne, and even Sam Jaffe as Gunga Din rout the Bat's minions, which include not only evil aliens, but also hordes of Nazis and the KKK from *Birth of a Nation*. Chuck's own existence may be lonely, but in his dreams the world is safe from evildoers.

A Vietnam-era update of Buster Keaton's *Sherlock Jr.* (a still of Keaton hangs in Chuck's booth), *The Projectionist* is an unabashed valentine to the movies of the 1930s and '40s. It also contains a number of very modern scenes in which Chuck is seen as a solitary figure staying up late to watch his favorite movies on TV and wandering through the Times Square area. Director Hurwitz had a very uneven career, cranking out a number of soft-core features and other low-budget genre movies in between labor-of-love nostalgia comedies. *The Projectionist* is not only his take on Golden Age fanboys like himself and McCann, but also a recognition of the kinds of viewers who came to see his own movies.

The *Midnight Cowboy*–esque solemn moments aside, the film is a vibrant comedy. A great impressionist, McCann is able to slip in some of his improvised shtick between the fantasy sequences. Dangerfield, on the other hand, plays his villain role to the hilt and never resorts to his tie-tugging stand-up persona. The purest joy of Chuck's B&W dreams is the sight of these two hefty gents battling it out in true Flash Gordon/Ming the Merciless style.

Hurwitz's most startling accomplishment, given that the film is not a major studio feature like the later *Zelig* (1983) and *Dead Men Don't Wear Plaid* (1982), is the fact that Chuck's fantasies contain scenes from a host of classic movies, including *Citizen Kane, The Maltese Falcon, Sergeant York,* and *Casablanca* (Chuck visits Rick's Café Américain to find out the Bat's plans and stands "across the room" from Bogart and Lorre). The finale, in which our chubby hero summons Hollywood's finest fightin' men to help him take on the forces of evil is incredibly silly, but it's also strangely heartwarming. If Woody Allen could summon up Bogart to help him with his love life in *Play It Again, Sam* (1972), why can't Captain Flash have Bogey, the Duke, and Cagney help him dispose of the bad guys?

Chuck's fantasies aren't the only montages in the movie. True to the 1960s kitchen-sink ethic, Hurwitz includes a number of dazzlingly assembled "coming attractions" for movies like *The Terrible World of Tomorrow* that include newsreel footage and humorous superimposed titles (one snappy edit has JFK's "Ask not what your country can do for you" speech coming from the mouth of a wildly gesticulating Hitler). In this way, presumably, Hurwitz was linking Chuck and his superhero double to the counterculture and the evil Rinaldi (who likes nothing better than to salt the popcorn to make patrons buy more soda) to then-president Nixon.

Hurwitz made two later '60s-style nostalgia comedies. The sadly unreleased *The Comeback Trail* (1982) has a plotline that resembles *The Producers* (1968) but contains wonderfully improvised routines by McCann and comic Robert Staats. *That's Adequate* (1989) is an episodic spoof about an awful movie studio that features early performances (the film was released years after it was shot) by Bruce Willis and Robert Downey Jr. (easily outclassed by comedy vets like Brother Theodore and Irwin Corey).

Hurwitz's films stand head and shoulders above the most astoundingly misguided nostalgia comedy, *The Phynx* (1970), a stunningly unfunny combination of *The Monkees* and *The President's Analyst* (1967) in which a prefab rock band infiltrates a Soviet-bloc country to set free abducted American "icons." The kidnap victims include Edgar Bergen and Charlie McCarthy, the Lone Ranger and Tonto, Busby Berkeley, Butterfly McQueen, Johnny Weissmueller, and Leo Gorcey and Huntz Hall (old men dressed in their Bowery Boy outfits). *The Phynx* has, no surprise, never gotten a video or DVD release.

1970 (PG) 88m/C/B Chuck McCann, Ina Balin, Rodney Dangerfield, Jara Kohout. *D:* Harry Hurwitz. *W:* Harry Hurwitz. *C:* Victor Petrashevic. *M:* Igo Kantor, Irma E. Levin. *VHS, DVD*

—*Ed Grant*

Shampoo 🦴🦴🦴🦴

The years have been kind to this sharp comedy, a perceptive look at the turbulent sexual/political/social whirl of the late '60s. Unlike so many movies of those groovy times, *Shampoo* understands that casual sex really is impossible, and it says so without preaching. It's a subtle "message" movie that makes its points through its surprisingly complex characters and their nuanced interactions with each other.

Although a synopsis makes the film sound like a typical sex farce, *Shampoo* is a serious story that makes its curious way to a conclusion that's dead solid perfect. The setting is Los Angeles, election eve, 1968—the dawning of the Age of Nixon. George Roundy (Warren Beatty) is a hairdresser who's constantly in demand, both professionally and personally. Women of every age flock to him for attention, and George is just a boy who can't say no. If almost any other actor were playing the role, he would likely turn George into a caricature or a male fantasy figure, but given Beatty's reputation as a man about town, he's completely credible. He was also one of the major creative forces behind the camera, credited as producer and cowriter.

Jackie (Julie Christie) is just one of many women complicating the life of hairdresser George (Warren Beatty) in *Shampoo*. COLUMBIA / THE KOBAL COLLECTION

George has a live-in girlfriend, Jill (Goldie Hawn), an actress who's considering a job that would take her out of the country. He's also seeing Felicia (Lee Grant), who's married to Lester (Jack Warden), a rich, well-connected Republican. Jackie (Julie Christie) is Lester's mistress, and she's also one of George's old flames. George is so skilled and popular as a hairdresser that he's ready to open his own shop, but he's having trouble persuading a bank to lend start-up money. Perhaps, George wonders, Lester would be interested in investing.

As it happens, Lester needs help, too. He has to attend to a political function that night. If George, whom Lester assumes is gay, could escort Jackie, Lester could make an appearance with Felicia. Of course, George has to do all the women's hair. (At some time in the future, popular-culture historians may trace the roots of the stiff blonde helmet hair favored by certain conservative Republican women to the 'do that George creates for Jackie.)

Thousands of sex farces have been based on flimsier premises, and, like most, this one becomes more and more complicated as it goes along. But the film never descends into who's-been-sleeping-in-my-bed farce, and it changes course radically but realistically toward the end.

Shampoo's real strength is accuracy. It gets the fashions and the sexual attitudes right, and despite the artifice of the plotting, the characters remain realistic. Because their flaws are so visible, they're a remarkably sympathetic group. Also, *Shampoo* has that raw, unpolished immediacy that makes '70s movies memorable and "real" compared to the glossy slickness of today's studio releases.

It's difficult to say exactly how credit for the movie's effectiveness should be divided. Beatty and screenwriter Robert Towne came up with the idea together. Beatty pitched the idea to different studios. Director Hal Ashby was brought in after the deal had been signed. The three men worked on the script together, and once they began filming, Ashby was anything but the stereotypical '70s auteur. His collaborators and studio executives were looking over his shoulder constantly. They demanded more takes than Ashby felt necessary and restaged key scenes. Even so, the film has the relaxed feel of some of Ashby's best work, like *The Last Detail* and *Coming Home.* He's completely comfortable with the characters and never shows off with intrusive camera moves.

In the end, regardless of who deserves the credit, *Shampoo* is one of the most accomplished works of the decade.

1975 (R) 109m/C Warren Beatty, Julie Christie, Lee Grant, Goldie Hawn, Jack Warden, Tony Bill, George Furth, Luana Anders, Carrie Fisher. *D:* Hal Ashby. *W:* Robert Towne, Warren Beatty. *C:* Laszlo Kovacs. *M:* Paul Simon. *VHS, DVD*

—*Mike Mayo*

Taking Off 🦴🦴🦴🦴

It was a double bummer, to put things mildly, when the USSR invaded its satellite state of Czechoslovakia in August 1968. With all due respect to Peter Boyle in *Joe,* Moscow was the ultimate 1960s uptight parent here, using military might to crush the "Prague Spring"—a '60s period of liberal politics and culture that the Kremlin could not tolerate.

As Red Army tanks rolled in, one rising Czech filmmaker was out of the country, scouting locations for a never-completed project in Paris. Milos Forman, who had established himself in international cinema with witty and popular critiques of Czech life (*Loves of a Blonde, Firemen's Ball*), decided to stay in the West. He settled in the United States, where he would later direct *One Flew over the Cuckoo's Nest* and *Hair,* among other films. *Taking Off* was his first American feature, a deadpan comedy that turns a quizzical lens on a hot-button subject Forman had been addressing back in Eastern Europe: the generation gap. In suburban Queens, Larry Tyne (Buck Henry) and his wife Lynn (Lynn Carlin) are frantic because their daughter Jeannie (Linnea Heacock) is gone. In fact, she's absconded to New York City to audition as a singer, but the tryout is a fizzle. The Tynes seek comfort from neighbors and follow up fruitless leads. Larry discovers the existence of an organization called S.P.F.C., the Society for Parents of Fugitive Children, where other families of runaway teens can pool information and seek support.

Jeannie briefly shows up, silent and enigmatic. Mom thinks she's on drugs, dad loses his temper and smacks her. The girl vanishes again, and the Tynes eventually attend a crowded S.P.F.C. meeting. There, in an attempt to better understand contemporary youth, the entire assembly smokes marijuana, under supervision of a rather seedy character named Vincent Schiavelli (portrayed, fittingly enough, by character actor Vincent Schiavelli). The Tynes and another couple, the Lockstons (Audra Lindley, Paul Benedict), go back to the Tynes' place, all higher than kites. They play strip poker, sing, and are edging toward an orgy when Jeannie walks in. The parents sober up rather suddenly. More diplomatic now, Larry and Lynn get Jeannie to open up (a little) about her life and to introduce her musician boyfriend, who, to Larry's partial relief, has a $290,000 yearly income to go along with his Charles Manson looks.

Forman's subtle narrative does not so much conclude as just cease, leaving the viewer suspended in ambiguity. But that also preserves a vital sense of impenetrable mystery about Jeannie and her circa-1971 peers—kids from well-to-do families, suddenly dropping out of sight, jumping aboard motorcycles with scruffy guys, or darting out the coffeehouse door in the company of surly hippies. At the S.P.F.C. meeting, right before Forman offers up the funniest dope sequence in movie history ("This . . . is . . . a joint"), the ballroom full of worried, Rotary Club types queue up to ask a returned runaway if she has any news about their own prodigal progeny, as though young people, like the psychic extraterrestrial children in the sci-fi pic *Village of the Damned,* are a whole separate species, in tune with one another via collective unconscious. When Jeannie does make her furtive appearances, she's just like someone who has been abducted to a UFO, probed by aliens, and left in a trance on the side of a road. Sure, we can relate to the silly but comprehensible Tynes (who, it turns out, don't have a single photo of their daughter taken in the past four years). Youth is another country. This isn't a generation gap—it's a trackless chasm.

Viewers of a later generation will note supporting roles by '70s sitcom mainstays Georgia Engel (*The Mary Tyler Moore Show*), Benedict (*The Jeffersons*), and Lindley (*Three's Company*), as well as Ike and Tina Turner, who are onstage at an upstate New York roadhouse where the Tynes stay during their pursuit of Jeannie. Carly Simon also appears and performs in the lengthy audition sequence that opens the film.

1971 (R) 99m/C Buck Henry, Lynn Carlin, Tony Harvey, Georgia Engel, Audra Lindley, Paul Benedict, Vincent Schiavelli, Linnea Heacock, Gail Busman, Allen Garfield, Ike Turner, Tina Turner, Carly Simon. **D:** Milos Forman. **W:** Milos Forman, John Guare, Jean-Claude Carriere, John Klein. **C:** Miroslav Ondricek. *VHS*

—*Charles A. Cassady Jr.*

What's New, Pussycat?

It's an old Hollywood legend that "What's new, pussycat?" was the greeting that Warren Beatty used whenever he saw one of his many girlfriends in the early 1960s. Beatty was even considered for the lead of this comedy, but he backed out, and the role went to Peter O'Toole, who wanted to stretch his acting muscles with lighter material after appearing in *Lawrence of Arabia, Becket,* and *Lord Jim* in succession.

O'Toole plays Michael James, a guy who not only has incredible luck with the ladies, but also has the world's most perfect job, editing a fashion magazine. Michael lives in France and is getting close to settling down with longtime girlfriend Carole (Romy Schneider), but he just can't shake his desire to hop into bed with other women. In order to get help for his problem, Michael goes to Dr. Fritz Fassbender (Peter Sellers), a German quack psychiatrist. The problem is that the good doctor is as infatuated with women as his new patient is; in Fassbender's case, however, he not only has a nagging opera-singing wife at home (Edra Gale), but he also displays absolutely no luck at scoring on the side. Things have gotten so bad for him, he begins targeting his patients as potential pick-ups.

It seems the more Michael wants to curtail his tomcatting, the more he's put to the test. And he fails miserably time after time. Among the women he gets involved with while Carole awaits word on a serious commitment are Renee (Capucine), a sex addict, and Liz (Paula Prentiss), a tall, flaky drink of water who repeatedly tries to commit suicide by popping pills.

After proposing to the ever-patient Carole and telling her parents of their impending wedding, Michael heads to the Chateau Chantelle, a small hotel in the countryside, where all hell breaks loose. Every woman Michael has been intimate with shows up there, including Rita (Ursula Andress), a gorgeous parachutist in a jumpsuit who falls out of the sky and into his antique roadster. Also arriving at the spot is Victor (Woody Allen), Michael's nerdy friend who works at the Crazy Horse club helping strippers in and out of clothing.

What's New, Pussycat? is best known for its bouncy, Oscar-nominated title tune, written by Burt Bacharach and Hal David and memorably belted out by Tom Jones. The film, alas, is not as well remembered, though it did well at the box office and maintains a corps of feverish followers. This film marks Woody

Allen's first screenplay and first screen appearance, but while the effort does have some choice one-liners (and at least two great in-jokes), the comedic elements are often labored or uneven. One of the problems is that once the film gets comfortable with a tone, it shifts gears, and British journeyman director Clive Donner (would you believe *The Nude Bomb*?) is not so smooth at steering.

What's New, Pussycat? starts out like one of Allen's later cerebral New York–set romantic comedies, with O'Toole seeking help from crackpot shrink Sellers and Allen appearing every once in a while to add Woodyisms. The movie then becomes a bedroom farce with confused characters frantically running in and out of hotel rooms. It then changes course once again with the slapstick hijinks of a high-speed escape from gendarmes via go-kart, a chase that ends abruptly in a nearby farmyard.

On the plus side, the film makes no excuses for its politically incorrect nature. It's hard to recall an effort so blatantly lecherous.

In the acting department, O'Toole fits comfortably into a less serious role, Edra Gale is a hoot as Sellers's Wagner-obsessed, Viking-helmeted spouse, and the sets and fashions (catch the culottes on Paula Prentiss!) are pure '60s wow. Then there's Sellers. Wearing his trademark glasses with a mop-top wig and red velvet caftan, the British comic looks like a brunette version of Dana Carvey's Garth from *Wayne's World* in drag. His Germanic accent is tough to decipher at times, and he never seems totally comfortable as the screwy shrink, alternating between over- and underplaying the part. He's just not sure which way Dr. Fritz Fassbender should be going, so he sort of prowls all over the place. Much like O'Toole's lead character and the rest of *Pussycat.*

1965 108m/C *UK* Peter Sellers, Peter O'Toole, Woody Allen, Romy Schneider, Capucine, Paula Prentiss, Edra Gale, Ursula Andress, Howard Vernon, Katrin Schaake. *D:* Clive Donner. *W:* Woody Allen. *C:* Jean Badel. *M:* Burt Bacharach. *VHS*

Who Is Harry Kellerman and Why Is He Saying Those Terrible Things about Me? ♫♫♫

Moviegoers in 1971 didn't know what to make of this brilliantly written, undeniably schizophrenic character study. It's a movie about a rock musician that has little to do with music; a movie starring the hottest young actor of the day that finds him ruminating about old age and memory; a movie sporting a "black humor"–style title and premise that quickly veers off into dialect comedy and a series of poignant two-character scenes.

Georgie Soloway (Dustin Hoffman) is a rock-music phenomenon whose string of hit records has made him a national celebrity. A hard-core insomniac who attempts suicide on a regular basis, the reclusive Georgie spends his nights cooped up inside his luxury high-rise apartment thinking about his past and imploring his friends, his therapist (Jack Warden), and his accountant (Dom DeLuise), to talk to him. The musician's emotional problems are compounded by an unusual situation: a man named Harry Kellerman has been calling Georgie's dates and telling them Georgie's true (negative) feelings about them. Georgie's downward spiral continues until he meets Allison Densmore (Barbara Harris), an aspiring actress who is prone to making sad, sardonic statements ("I feel like I just auditioned for the part of human being and didn't get the job").

The late playwright Herb Gardner (*A Thousand Clowns*), screenwriter of *Harry Kellerman,* once stated that he's not a fan of rock music. His lack of knowledge about the genre becomes apparent as the movie goes along, since Georgie is depicted as, simultaneously, a Phil Spector–like producer/composer, a Dylanesque figure who writes vibrant rockers and tender ballads, and a sort of Brill Building songwriter who will work for the government or anyone else who has the dough. Gardner's musical confusion isn't a major problem, as the film is not about the music industry; it's primarily a study of fame and the toll it takes on the unwary artist.

It is also a surprisingly sentimental study of a man experiencing a mid-life crisis. Gardner's writing is often compared to that of the '60s' hottest comic playwright, Neil Simon. Gardner's output was smaller (only five plays and the *Harry Kellerman* script by the century's end), but his dialogue is incredibly honed and a good deal more quotable than Simon's. The "neurotic poetry" that punctuates his characters' conversations is, in fact, the main reason to see *Harry Kellerman;* the cast give it their all, and the results are unforgettable.

The key sequence is the beautifully acted first encounter between Georgie and Allison, in which Hoffman, at the top of his form, is called on to do little more than listen as the exquisite Harris offers Gardner's sublime observations on the process of aging: "Time, mister, it's not a thief at all like they say—it's something much sneakier. It's an embezzler, up nights juggling the books so you don't notice anything's missing."

Like Gardner, director Ulu Grosbard, who later worked with Hoffman on the ex-con drama *Straight Time,* is a theater veteran. He deftly transforms *Harry Kellerman* into an actor's showcase. Whether it's a light comic scene with Warden or DeLuise, a bit of "color" from former Dead End Kid Gabriel Dell as Georgie's playboy pal, or touching moments with Georgie's first wife (Grosbard's real-life wife Rose Gregorio) and his workaholic father (David Burns), the performers sketch their characters perfectly in the short time provided them. Harris is the standout, delivering an Oscar-caliber turn in a mere four sequences, while Hoffman's transformation from cheerful guitar-picker to jaded, unbalanced recluse demonstrates why he was one of the most important actors of the era.

The other individual who sets the tone for *Harry Kellerman* is only on-screen for one three-minute live performance (shot at the legendary Fillmore East in New York City): composer-author-wildman Shel Silverstein. The triple-threat Silverstein essentially was a real-life Georgie Soloway who wrote top-forty tunes for acts as diverse as Johnny Cash ("A Boy Named Sue"), Marianne Faithfull ("The Ballad of Lucy Jordan"), the Irish Rovers ("The Unicorn"), and Dr. Hook and the Medicine Show ("Cover of the Rolling Stone"). Silverstein was better known in later years as a writer of children's books, though those who heard his own LPs or read his work in *Playboy* were familiar with his raunchier "freaker" persona. He was a natural to supply Georgie's music, and he works wonders with the two melodies that crop up throughout the film. The final sequence, in which Georgie and his therapist are seen skiing down deep slopes (don't ask), wouldn't be as resonant if it weren't accompanied by the Dr. Hook rendition of Silverstein's mournful "Last Morning."

On reflection, it's easy to see why viewers were turned off by this movie at the time of its release. *Harry Kellerman* is a tale of a demented rich guy who is his own worst enemy (oops, did we blow the "surprise" denouement?), and whose suicide attempts turn into trippy fantasies. A few decades down the line, the film is still a peculiar commodity, but its sterling dialogue and extraordinary performances make it a relic of an age when major studios took chances on very strange material—with unwieldy titles, to boot.

1971 (R) 108m/C Dustin Hoffman, Barbara Harris, Jack Warden, Dom DeLuise, David Burns, Gabriel Dell, Betty Walker, Rose Gregorio. *D:* Ulu Grosbard. *W:* Herb Gardner. *C:* Victor J. Kemper. *M:* Shel Silverstein. *VHS*

—Ed Grant

You're a Big Boy Now ♫♫♪

A certain nostalgic affection prevents this early Francis Ford Coppola coming-of-age comedy from fading into oblivion, despite its forced charms. Based on one of Coppola's student film projects, *Big Boy* is a low-budget absurdist look at the floundering life of Bernard Chanticleer (Peter Kastner), a callow nineteen-year-old who is sent by his well-to-do parents to live in his own Lower Manhattan apartment (it's absurdist, remember) in order to realize his manhood.

That Bernard is a nebbish is clearly the fault of his smothering mother (Geraldine Page) and neurotic librarian father (Rip Torn, Page's real-life husband). Also urging Bernard to experience life—that is, pursue women—is a fellow underling at the New York library where Bernard works for his dad. Played by Tony Bill, this self-styled poet with a smug persona is a comment on '60s peacock narcissism.

In due course Bernard becomes smitten by the beautiful aspiring actress Barbara Darling (Elizabeth Hartman), and when he writes her a love note after seeing her in a dismal off-off-Broadway play, she invites him to her dressing room and eventually to her apartment. The vain and distracted Barbara, a Holly Golightly in a miniskirt and go-go boots, toys with Bernard while the Lovin' Spoonful sing "Darling Be Home Soon." Bernard, full of self-doubt, cannot finish what he has started, and Barbara eventually loses interest and rejects him.

All the while, Bernard has been rejecting a fresh-faced library worker (Karen Black, in her film debut) who clearly yearns for him and has visited his apartment in violation of house rules. When his mother hears about this illicit

Julie Harris chides young would-be lovers Amy (Karen Black) and Bernard (Peter Kastner) in *You're a Big Boy Now,* an early effort from Francis Ford Coppola.

visit from the eccentric landlady (Julie Harris), the chain of events leads to an unlikely confrontation at the New York Public Library and a chase on foot involving all the characters in Bernard's life. Of course young love triumphs, and, we presume, Bernard's sexual deficiency heals itself.

Despite the sprightly Spoonful tunes, the proceedings are surprisingly dull. Even the forays through Manhattan look less photogenic than one would expect. The night scenes near Times Square are annoyingly underlit and grainy, making one wonder if the director was "stealing" his shots without a permit. Kastner, looking somewhat like Elton John in heavy specs, brings little charisma to the role, and his cipher stands in contrast to the professional troupe of colorful types cavorting around him.

Big Boy is so labored that it can't enjoy its own humor. Coppola, still learning his craft, indulges in all manner of arty camera stunts, from negative film to jump cuts to titles superimposed over the action. Effects like these seemed much more fun in the playful hands of Richard Lester in his ground-breaking Beatles films *A Hard Day's Night* and *Help!* Here they remind us constantly and pointlessly that we are watching a dated fable.

1966 96m/C Peter Kastner, Elizabeth Hartman, Karen Black, Geraldine Page, Julie Harris, Rip Torn. **D:** Francis Ford Coppola. **W:** David Benedictus, Francis Ford Coppola. **C:** Andrew Laszlo. **M:** Robert Prince. *VHS*

—*Andy Wickstrom*

Chapter 15

Do They Make You Horny, Baby?

The movies were not shy anymore.

No longer did they have to disguise suggestions of sex behind veiled references or secret codes. This was the 1960s, baby, and the sexual revolution was on. Right on!

Or was it? Certainly long-banned books like Henry Miller's *Tropic of Cancer* and D. H. Lawrence's *Lady Chatterley's Lover* were now obtainable at most local bookstores. But they sure had to go through a lot to get there—protests, legal battles, obscenity charges, and, for many such works, outright bans.

The same was true of many of the groundbreaking films of the swinging '60s. Pioneering sexploitation filmmakers like Russ Meyer and Radley Metzger faced their share of difficulties from authorities, legal eagles, politicians, and citizens of sheltered communities, all of whom claimed that such works as *Lorna* and *Carmen, Baby* were not worthy of the celluloid they were developed on. So, the filmmakers fought the law and eventually, the filmmakers won.

Hollywood always knew that sex sold, but they wondered how much sex was too much. When the Motion Picture Association of America (MPAA) unveiled a rating system that placed all films into one of four categories—"G," "M," "R," or "X" (currently known as "G," "PG," "PG-13," "R," and "NC-17")—filmmakers began to explore the boundaries of these ratings. *Candy,* the screen adaptation of Terry Southern and Mason Hoffenberg's best-selling novel of the *Candide*-like adventures of a teenage nymph, was one of the first potentially problematic projects out of the chute. While rated "R" and fairly tame, the film still ran into problems in Mississippi, where it was deemed obscene and seized.

The "X" rating could have been interpreted as a scarlet letter at the time, but its very existence also reflected a new brashness and a ticket to artistic freedom for studios and filmmakers. And in fact, studios hoped an "X" rating would stir up the right kind of controversy and help bring people into theaters. In 1969 entertainer Anthony Newley was afforded a large budget by Universal Pictures for his "X"-rated *Can Hieronymus Merkin Ever Forget Mercy Humppe and Find True Happiness?,*

Do They Make You Horny, Baby?

a nudity-and-burlesque-spiked bit of ego-trippiness that was previewed in an expansive *Playboy* magazine spread. The movie flopped, however, and the studios got nervous. But the anxiety didn't last long, because the Swedish import *I Am Curious (Yellow)* became a much-debated sensation, and the high-profile, "X"-rated *Midnight Cowboy* not only made money and drew high praise but took home the Best Picture Oscar to boot.

Twentieth Century Fox, a struggling studio hampered by some old-fashioned bombs, took *Midnight Cowboy*'s success as a green light to get down and dirty, so they OK'd production on the expensive adaptation of Gore Vidal's best-selling *Myra Breckinridge* and on skinflick maestro Russ Meyer's inexpensive first "mainstream" picture, *Beyond the Valley of the Dolls.* The former, pairing Raquel Welch and Mae West, sex sirens of two different generations, bombed big-time; the latter, cast with unknowns, did well despite negative reviews.

Hollywood was still unsure of how to deal with "X"—the rating was slapped on everything from serious dramas like *Last Summer* and *End of the Road* to mondo exploitation films like *Goodbye, Uncle Tom* and *Censorship in Denmark,* and from Andy Warhol's drug-dosed *Trash* to such sex imports as Argentina's *Fuego.*

One segment of Tinseltown that figured out how to stop worrying and love the rating was the nascent hard-core porn industry. In 1970 Bill Osco, a member of the family that owned the Osco Drug chain, produced and directed *Mona, the Virgin Nymph,* a fairly explicit study of a woman obsessed with oral sex. The groundbreaking effort offered close-ups of sexual acts similar to the amateurishly produced, cheapie "smoker" shorts that came before it, but now the story unfolded in feature-length time with professional photography and editing. *Mona* was a hit that ran for months in the theaters that would play it, paving the way for such crossover "porno chic" hits a few years later as *Deep Throat, The Devil in Miss Jones, Behind the Green Door,* and Metzger's own leap into hard-core with *The Opening of Misty Beethoven.*

Behind the Green Door 🎵🎵🎵

The saying on the detergent box said "99 and 44/100% pure," though Marilyn Chambers was anything but.

She was the woman pictured on the Ivory Snow Laundry Detergent box, an attractive dirty blonde hugging a cute baby. A beacon of wholesomeness on a product that was as pure as the newly fallen snow and as all-American as apple pie.

Then word got around that the pretty-mother-next-door image was just an illusion. In fact, Chambers was an actress featured in a film called *Behind the Green Door,* a "dirty" movie in which she did all sorts of wild, kinky things.

The curious public left the supermarket aisles and laundromats en masse and headed out to the theater to see what this archetypal young mom was up to. Everything they had heard was true. There she was, being groped by nuns who had no problem making a habit out of their actions. Then she's servicing a black stud (former boxer Johnny Keyes in tribal makeup) to a funky bass-inflected beat. And in the film's most talked-about sequence, she takes care of three men on flying trapezes and another underneath her. Eat your hearts out, Great Wallendas.

Somebody should have tipped off Procter & Gamble, Ivory's manufacturer, that their soapbox derby could become a soapbox dirty. Chambers, it turned out, was no goody two-shoes. She had posed for the Ivory photo when she was just seventeen years old. After that, she accumulated other modeling and acting credits, including a small role in the Barbra Streisand comedy *The Owl and the Pussycat* and a nude scene in *Together,* a 1971 sexploitation hit directed by Wes Craven, future creator of the *Nightmare on Elm Street* and *Scream* franchises.

Even before Marilyn Chambers became infamous, *Behind the Green Door* was making waves. The filmmakers were Jim and Artie Mitchell, San Francisco–based siblings who owned and operated the O'Farrell Theater, a popular venue for strippers and sex shows in the Bay Area during the late

1960s and early 1970s. But word was out in the burgeoning sex movie industry that the adventurous Mitchells were getting into a new can of worms by producing a feature film. They invested $50,000 in the project, a large sum by porn standards at the time.

The result is a relatively slick, sex-drenched odyssey that has a story—sort of. A trucker at a lunch counter tells his friend, the cook, about an unusual experience he had. He was invited with a friend to a secret show during which he and his pal had to wear masks to disguise themselves. An abducted woman (Chambers) was given an opportunity to experience complete ravishment. (The morning following the show, we're told, the woman was to be set free.) The "secret show" scene reveals the woman being led onstage by a group of women dressed like nuns. Her clothes are taken off, and then she participates in a series of sexual acts in front of the trucker and other mesmerized onlookers. As the stage show goes on, the audience gets so turned on they have to let loose, and an orgy breaks out.

Behind the Green Door was unique because it was technically better than the rest of the porno pack at the time. *Deep Throat,* also released in 1972, looked or felt like most of the other adult films being made at the time: poorly lit, erratically photographed, choppily edited, and downright silly in tone. But *Green Door* boasted slick photography and, in the film's epic trapeze sequence, such techniques as slow motion, weird camera effects, alternating colors, and other sorts of trippy visuals. It was also deadly serious in tone and had little dialogue, though sometimes groans, weird electronic music, and the sounds of cats broke up the long periods of silence. It's no surprise that the movie came out of San Francisco, the center of flower power in America.

Like *Deep Throat, Behind the Green Door* crossed over, drawing mainstream audiences curious to find out what the hubbub was about. With Chambers gaining incredible media exposure, the film played for months in many theaters, while the Mitchell brothers (who play kidnappers in the film) and Chambers, who earned part of the proceeds, raked in the dough. A year later, the producer-directors teamed with their star again for *Resurrection of Eve,* another serious effort, this time focusing on the ups and downs of a couple experimenting with the swingers scene. *Resurrection* drew fairly well, but when the Mitchells paired it with *Green Door* and managed to book it into colleges, repertory cinemas, and mainstream (non-adult) movie theaters, the double feature became a sensation.

Thanks to *Green Door*'s notoriety, Chambers was able to command large salaries and a percentage of future films' profits, and she occasionally worked in non-adult films such as David Cronenberg's grotesque shocker *Rabid.* The Mitchell brothers kept a close hand on profits by distributing their films in theaters and later on video by themselves. In 1991 Jim Mitchell shot and killed Artie Mitchell during a supposed intervention for Artie's drug and alcohol problems.

Behind the Green Door has more to offer than most of the so-called classics of adult cinema. Sure, in many ways it's primitive and dated (check out the mime, Marilyn's opening act onstage), but that's part of the novelty. It also has ample kink, a modicum of style and, of course, Marilyn Chambers, in all her impure and simple glory.

1972 (NC-17) 72m/C Marilyn Chambers, George S. McDonald, Johnny Keyes, Yank Levine, Ben Davidson, Jim Mitchell, Artie Mitchell. *D:* Artie Mitchell, Jim Mitchell. *W:* Jim Mitchell. *C:* Jon T. Fontana. *M:* Daniel Le Blanc. *VHS, DVD*

Beyond the Valley of the Dolls ♪♪♪♪

T wentieth Century Fox must have had some idea of what they were getting into in 1970 when they handed Russ Meyer a three-picture deal.

It was, after all, the box-office returns from *Vixen!,* the sexploitation king's torrid tale of sexuality and politics in the Great White North, that reeled 20th Century Fox in. The film—highlighted by a scene known as "the fish dance," featuring an erotic dance involving buxom star Erica Gavin and a dead fish—was made for a pittance, somewhere under $100,000, but it brought in $20 million. The desperate studio, hoping to get back on track after mega-bombs like *Doctor Dolittle* and *Hello, Dolly,* wanted a surefire money-maker. With Meyer, noteworthy for getting more bangs for his bucks than anyone, they got their money-maker—and a whole lot more.

Working with twenty-nine-year-old Chicago film critic Roger Ebert, Meyer was given Jacqueline Susann's novel *Valley of the Dolls* to use as a starting point. Fashioning an in-name-only sequel to the trash classic depicting the pill-induced downward spiral of a group of actresses, Meyer and Ebert played up the lurid elements, goosing their tale of female rock stars on the road to ruin with enough excessive nudity, sex, drugs, rock 'n' roll, and violence to earn an easy-to-market "X" rating. Although Susann sued the studio and Fox practically denied making the film, *Beyond* went on to become one of Fox's most profitable films of the era, taking in close to $10 million on a budget just below $1 million.

The audiences who saw *Beyond the Valley of the Dolls* when it was first released fell primarily into three camps. A large percentage of the public went to the theater actually expecting to see a sequel to Susann's story. Another portion of the audience were the male Russ Meyer fans—"raincoaters"— tuned in to the filmmaker's brand of macho men and women with mammoth mammaries, figures they'd seen in *Lorna, Cherry, Harry & Raquel,* and other ogling opuses. And the third segment of theater attendees comprised the pot-smoking, drug-ingesting kids the movie was mocking.

What this means, of course, is that a huge percentage of people just didn't get *BTVD* when it first issued. Today the film works, often brilliantly, as the ultimate parody of the high life of the '60s, a not-so-gentle ribbing of flower children, LSD, groovy lingo and fashions, free love, psychedelic music, and the Charles Manson massacre. Audiences may have been hip to the scene, but they were likely unaware that the film was out to make mincemeat of that scene. It's astonishing in many ways that *BTVD* was produced at the height of the era it was spoofing. Twenty-first-century audiences should bear in mind that this film wasn't meant as a straightforward reflection of the far-out happenings of the time. This

> **The world is full of them, the super-octane girls who are old at twenty. If they get to be twenty.**
>
> —Tagline for *Beyond the Valley of the Dolls*

This time...
**they've
really
gone
Beyond
the Valley
of the
Dolls**

A Russ Meyer Production

The world
is full of them,
the super-octane
girls who are
old at twenty

If they get to be twenty.

Poster for Russ
Meyer's *Beyond the
Valley of the Dolls*

20TH CENTURY FOX / THE
KOBAL COLLECTION

film was a satiric chronicle of a lifestyle Meyer and Ebert saw every-day and deemed worthy of ripping apart with a cinematic buzzsaw.

In *BTVD,* three young female musicians head to L.A. to find fame and fortune. Kelly (Dolly Read), Casey (Cynthia Myers), and Petronella (or "Pet," played by Marcia McBroom) are the stunning trio who grab the attention of legendary music producer Ronnie "Z-Man" Barzell (John Lazar) at a party. After they're dubbed the Carrie Nations, they cut an album that soars to the top of the charts, and their troubles begin. All three members of the Carrie Nations are drawn into the decadence of Holly-wood. Kelly dumps Harris (David Guri-an), the band's manager, so she can go out with Lance Rock (Michael Blodgett), a bed-hopping actor-gigolo. Casey recognizes she has no interest in men, so she gets intimate with Roxanne (Erica Gavin), a lesbian fash-ion designer. Pet begins dating Emer-son (Harrison Page), a mild-mannered law student, but sleeps with Randy Brown (James Inglehart), a boister-ous heavyweight boxing champ.

If it seems like you need a scorecard to keep track of all this, just wait. We haven't even mentioned Ash-ley St. Ives (Edy Williams), a porn star obsessed with fornicating in large luxu-ry cars! Or Kelly's long-lost rich relative, Aunt Susan (Phyllis Davis), who wants to renew her relationship with her ex, Baxter Wolf (Meyer regular Charles Napi-er), and count Kelly in on her inheritance! Or Porter Hall (Duncan McLeod), the shyster lawyer who doesn't want Kelly to get the inheritance money! Or Otto (Henry Rowland), Z-Man's trusty German servant!

Whew. Now, take all these characters, dose them with a tab or two of acid, let them smoke a couple joints and kick down a couple glasses of Scotch, throw in some '60s-style rock music, and add to the mix one sword-wielding psy-chopath in the midst of a sex-change operation. Now it's showtime!

The approach Meyer takes in capturing all of the perverse proceedings can only be categorized as "type A-plus." You get a sense subtlety isn't going to be one of *BTVD*'s strong points when it begins, *Memento*-style, with a scene that occurs near the story's ending: a woman in a deep sleep is awak-ened by a gun being moved up her body until it's phallically placed in her mouth; a finger pulls back on its trigger; the woman's face freezes in horror at the thought of what's going to happen next. The sound of the gun's blast bleeds into the shrill scream of a female rock singer and we're suddenly thrust into the middle of a wild '60s high school party scene.

Meyer's visuals are hyperactive throughout. The frenzied editing style proves hard to get a handle on at first, especially when mixed with the severe camera-angle curveballs he delights in using. Sometimes it appears he leaves key shots and set-ups out to either increase the film's tempo or catch the audience off guard. He also throws in some prime references to other films and real people. *Citizen Kane* and Douglas Sirk's *Written on the Wind* are the films he and Ebert salute, while Phil Spector and Muhammad Ali are the real-life personalities thinly fictionalized by the characters Z-Man and Randy Brown, respectively.

And if this approach weren't enough to confuse the unhip masses at the time, Stu Phillips's overly ripe dramatic score offers a kaleidoscope of oddball sound effects, audio puns, and a soundtrack that includes original songs by the Strawberry Alarm Clock (performing "Incense and Peppermints") along with memorable pop ballad/acid rock originals "performed by" the Carrie Nations. It's no wonder original *BTVD* soundtrack albums go for big bucks on eBay these days.

Much of the work in *BTVD*'s acting department is purposefully deadpan, a good thing considering the actresses who play the Carrie Nations were best known as *Playboy* models with little acting experience and little depth to add to their roles other than their impressive chest measurements. But juicy theatricality is also in abundance as well, with the spotlight on Lazar's Z-Man, spouting soliloquies like he's either William Shakespeare or an extra at a Renaissance fair; Williams's man-hungry adult-movie-star slut; and Blodgett, perfecting the sleazeball stud role.

The dialogue, penned in six weeks by Ebert and Meyer, remains dementedly purple or mockingly "with it" throughout. A bevy of great lines populate the script. They're delivered with the utmost conviction, most of them probably too hip for the room when *BTVD* initially came out. A sampling: "In a scene like this, you get a contact high!"; "You're a groovy boy—I'd like to strap you on sometime!"; "Don't bogart that joint!"; and the ever-popular "This is my happening and it freaks me out!"

After a gruesome hallucinogen-fueled bloodbath that looks like *Alice in Wonderland* meets *The Texas Chainsaw Massacre* and would make Sam Peckinpah wince, the film winds down with an upbeat fairy-tale double wedding. A solemn narrator recaps the characters' fates in flowery soap-opera style and suggests that audiences should take what they've just seen as a cautionary tale. One senses that, in the early 1970s, this finale was followed by the sound of heads being scratched. Now, people who get *BTVD* laugh hysterically, recognizing the vibe Russ Meyer was sending out when he made the film. It was his happening and he freaked everybody out.

1970 (NC-17) 109m/C Dolly Read, Marcia McBroom, Cynthia Myers, John Lazar, Michael Blodgett, Erica Gavin, Edy Williams, Phyllis Davis, David Gurian, Harrison Page, Duncan McLeod, Charles Napier, James Inglehart, Henry Rowland. **D:** Russ Meyer. **W:** Russ Meyer, Roger Ebert. **C:** Fred J. Koenekamp. **M:** Stu Phillips. VHS **AKA:** *Hollywood Vixens*

RUSS MEYER: BEYOND THE VALLEY OF THE BOOB-OBSESSED DIRECTOR

Russ Meyer was given a movie camera by his policeman father and nurse mother when he was eight years old, and the world has never been the same since. Meyer began to shoot whatever he could in and around his Oakland, California, neighborhood. When he got older and World War II began, he became a member of the Army Signal Corps, the division of the military assigned to photograph the war. Russ graduated to 16 mm and helped capture the landing of Normandy and other key events in Europe.

After the war, Meyer settled in Los Angeles and took jobs working in the publicity departments of Warner Bros. and other studios. At night he'd moonlight as a fashion photographer, clicking pictures of near-naked and naked women for a host of cheap girlie 'zines. Eventually he found work shooting layouts for Hugh Hefner's young but classy *Playboy* magazine.

Teasing the Audience

But there was still something about movie cameras and the movie industry that intrigued Meyer. With help from a friend named Peter DeCenzie, a burlesque entrepreneur in San Francisco, Meyer made his first film in 1959, a nudie-cutie called *The Immoral Mr. Teas*. The movie centers on a dental appliance salesman who keeps imagining he sees women in the buff. A playful naiveté permeated the often-naked proceedings, helping *Teas* become a hit on the art-house circuit. Meyer went into the movie business full-time, cranking out low-budget and highly profitable skin flicks like *Eve and the Handyman,* featuring his wife, former *Playboy* Playmate Eve Meyer, and *Naked Gals of the Wild West.*

After a handful of these live-action burlesques, Meyer, along with his now-producer wife, turned his attention to more dramatic tales, focusing on overheated melodramas like *Mudhoney* and *Lorna.* These B&W films boasted big-breasted heroines with big sexual appetites. As the films played around the country, they often ran into legal troubles, and Meyer found himself battling obscenity charges on several occasions.

After knocking out a sexed-up cycle flick called *Motor Psycho* in '65, Meyer delivered *Faster, Pussycat! Kill! Kill!*, a twisted tale of a trio of leather-clad strippers on a sadistic rampage in the desert. Later in the decade, Russ aroused studio interest in Hollywood when the "X"-rated *Vixen!*, a tale of a nymphomaniac running rampant in the Great White North, brought in $7 million on a budget of $76,000.

Establishment Calls

Major studios came calling, and Meyer signed on to a three-picture deal at 20th Century Fox. Quickly, he caused a ruckus, teaming with young Chicago film critic Roger Ebert to write *Beyond the Valley of the Dolls,* a spoof of Jacqueline Susann's best-selling novel *Valley of the Dolls,* a property Fox owned. Susann and husband-manager Irving Mansfield sued, but the film went into production anyway. Meyer's take on the project was to put the basic story-line—a trashy soap opera of pill-dependent actresses—through a satiric, "X"-rated '60s kaleidoscope fueled by LSD, cult murders, and rock music. The result was an ahead-of-its-time masterpiece that had studio suits and unhip audiences scratching their heads. But an "X" rating, prerelease ballyhoo, and young audiences who wouldn't have been caught dead watching the schmaltzy soap opera *Valley of the Dolls* helped the $1 million production rake in more than $9 million at the box office.

Meyer's next studio effort, an "R"-rated adaptation of Irving Wallace's best-seller, *The Seven Minutes,* features such veterans as John Carradine and Yvonne De Carlo, but this film about an obscenity trial never took off. Fox subsequently bought Meyer out of his contract, allowing the filmmaker to return to his personal brand of down-and-dirty self-financed filmmaking. Meyer also divorced Eve (who died in 1977 in a plane crash) around this time and began a tumultuous five-year marriage to actress Edy Williams, best known for her long-running, paparazzi-pleasing, near-naked appearances at Oscar ceremonies and at the Cannes Film Festival.

Back in the Indie Saddle Again

Supervixens, Meyer's first film upon returning to independent turf, marked the beginning of a new period for the filmmaker. While his directing style has never been subtle, this 1974 effort plays like a live-action "X"-rated Li'l Abner cartoon on Viagra and espresso. The editing is maniacally quick, the female characters display ludicrously large bosoms, the sex scenes are grunt-a-thons that take place on mattress coils or scenic mountaintops, and the violence goes way over the top. No wonder Meyer, a no-nonsense taskmaster on the set, was gaining such detractors as critic John Simon, who characterized the director, his fans, and his films as "demented hillbillies." Spokespeople of the women's movement also cried foul, claiming Meyer's films were sexist works portraying women in an ugly, unrealistic light. Of course, this had little effect on Meyer, who pointed to *Pussycat* as an example of a film where women were not only strong, positive role models, but they could also kick the stuffing out of men if necessary.

So Meyer continued the *Supervixens* pattern of outrageousness with *Up!* and *Beneath the Valley of the Ultravixens,* both featuring real-life girlfriend Kitten Natividad, and both coscripted anonymously by Ebert.

Over the years, Meyer has had several projects that looked great on paper but never got off the ground. At one time, he was to make a film with the Sex Pistols called *Who Killed Bambi?,* based on a script he cowrote with Ebert, but problems with the notorious punk group's manager Malcolm McLaren derailed it. An Edy Williams vehicle called *Foxy, The Jaws of Lorna,* a sequel to *Supervixens,* and a documentary he began shooting about his life never saw the light of day either.

Writing in his classic book *Adventures in the Screen Trade,* screenwriter-novelist William Goldman called Russ Meyer Hollywood's "only true auteur." Goldman pointed out that for his independent projects, Meyer handled all creative and business aspects of filmmaking—editing, cinematography, producing, directing, theatrical distribution, and video distribution—something few in the movie business have ever attempted. And, except for one of them (1973's racial potboiler *Blacksnake*), all of his indie films turned a tremendous profit. Not bad for a kid from Oakland who started out with a crank-it-up 8-mm camera.

Bob & Carol & Ted & Alice

Whee, four stars in bed together! Moviegoers in 1969 had every hope of a hot time when Paul Mazursky brought *Bob & Carol & Ted & Alice* to the screen. Trailing in the wake of sexually daring movies like *I Am Curious (Yellow)* and tapping into the rebellious spirit of *Easy Rider,* this examination of couples experimenting with "free love" or "open marriage" looked at the time like a champion taboo-breaker.

Well, curb your "R"-rated enthusiasm. This gentle comedy—like the good girl next door—doesn't go all the way. Despite Natalie Wood and Dyan Cannon parading around in underwear in the "orgy" scene, this film shows less raunch than the average *Friends* episode. In fact, the movie is so innocuous, it inspired a 1973 TV sitcom. *B&C&T&A* is, at heart, just an old-fashioned tease.

Still, as a comedy of '60s manners, the movie makes sharp observations, helped along by solid performances. Robert Culp and Natalie Wood portray Bob and Carol, an adventurous L.A. couple who visit an Esalen-like self-actualization retreat where people "get in touch with their feelings," a popular activity during the Age of Aquarius. They emerge from the inevitable group dynamic of sobs, laughter, and embraces with the determination to always be truthful with each other. They try to share these beautiful feelings with friends Ted and Alice (Elliott Gould and Dyan Cannon), who react with uptight trepidation, especially when told that Bob has just admitted to Carol that he had an affair. Carol, carefully nonjudgmental, declares Bob's honesty to be deeply moving. Hey, it was just physical, and what's so wrong about that?

Then Bob, returning early from a business trip, discovers that Carol is having a one-night stand of her own. His initial troglodyte shock and outrage comically give way to the serene realization that Carol is simply pursuing unfettered joy, just as he did in his dalliance. Ashamed of his own behavior, he even ends up serving the astonished interloper a scotch.

The group's delicate dance culminates in a Las Vegas suite where Carol reveals her affair to an approving Alice, who, in her forced delight almost fails to hear Ted's blurted admission that he too has strayed. In a state of mild hysteria, Alice begins disrobing and demands a friendly orgy, but once in bed and after initial kisses, the enormity of it all overwhelms the foursome. They next are seen exiting the hotel, at first somber, then with tentative smiles as Jackie DeShannon sings "What the World Needs Now."

So the powder keg of emotions never explodes, and the overall innocent tone (all transgressions are conducted discreetly offscreen) means the viewer is never quite sure what Mazursky and cowriter Larry Tucker are saying about sexual opportunism, except to recognize that it's dangerous territory. The danger is also softened by the clearly affluent status of these handsome couples. It would take more than a little cheating and pot smoking to shatter their comfortable Beverly Hills universe.

Surely the production gloss of *B&C&T&A* and its marquee names were intended to help the distasteful idea of wife-swapping go down more easily at

> **"First, we'll have an orgy. Then we'll go see Tony Bennett."**
>
> —Elliott Gould as Ted, in *Bob & Carol & Ted & Alice*

the time, but the film's very trendiness works against it in the long run. Today's audiences are likely to be more amused by the period hairstyles (Gould's sideburns!) and clothes (dig those ever-present love beads on Culp!) than by the clever dialogue. In the end, the movie is a somewhat dry artifact, a study of a certain time and place in popular culture when we got too groovy for our own good.

1969 (R) 101m/C Natalie Wood, Robert Culp, Dyan Cannon, Elliott Gould. *D:* Paul Mazursky. *W:* Paul Mazursky, Larry Tucker. *C:* Charles Lang. *M:* Quincy Jones. *VHS, DVD*

—Andy Wickstrom

Camille 2000 ♪♪♥

The Lickerish Quartet ♪♪♪

After breaking into the New York adult-film business, Radley Metzger acquired the U.S. distribution rights to the groundbreaking Scandinavian film *I, a Woman,* which opened his eyes to the possibilities represented by this new breed of European erotica. He then went to Europe to make films himself for the international market. Metzger sought to make sex films for the people who read the articles and fiction in *Playboy* magazine. In some ways, his films in this period resemble those of Russ Meyer, but his characters are more twisted and desperate, and his style lacks Meyer's cartoonish sense of outrageous fun.

Camille 2000, a modern update of the Alexandre Dumas *(fils)* story, reveals its Fellini-inspired pretensions with its first shot, which starts with the film's clapper board. Armand Duval (Nino Castelnuovo, also the star of *The Umbrellas of Cherbourg*), on a business trip to Rome for his rich father's company, soon gets caught up with the depraved jet-set crowd. He finds himself helplessly drawn to the mysterious and morose beauty Marguerite Gautier (Daniele Gaubert). However, Marguerite is the mistress to a duke, which makes starting an affair with her complicated and ill advised.

The Lickerish Quartet begins with multilevel voyeurism, as we spy on a jaded family getting their limited kicks by watching a B&W "smoker" (underground sex film). The family consists of a rich man and woman (Frank Wolff and Erika Remberg) and her grown son (Paulo Turco). As the bickering three prepare to leave their castle in search of new thrills, the film turns silent and B&W, foreshadowing the way their lives are about to meld with the film they were watching. At a carnival, they're surprised to discover the blonde star of the smoker is also the star of a motorcycle thrill show. The family lures the woman back to the castle, and the fun and games begin in earnest; this time there's a different woman in the film and the family members see their own faces there. The visitor makes strange statements implying second sight, and at one point she rewinds the film to change a conversation. Each member of

BRIGITTE BARDOT: THE FRENCH SEX KITTEN
by Ed Grant

Less neurotic than Marilyn, more accessible than Liz, and far livelier than Raquel, Brigitte Bardot was the supreme international sex symbol of the '60s, France's greatest pop-culture export then and now. Her superstar allure has only increased since her retirement in 1973, at which point she became the Gallic Greta Garbo, one of the few stars who chose to call it quits while she was still in demand.

Roger and Her

Bardot's emergence as a sex bomb is invariably attributed to producer-director Roger Vadim, who started packaging her when she was still a teen—and swiftly married her when she came of legal age. Clearly, Vadim had a Svengali-like talent when it came to showcasing Bardot's luscious good looks and carefree—and clothes-free—sensibility, but Bardot was such an eye-catching lass that surely some other entrepreneur would have come along and molded her had Roger been preoccupied. Although Brigitte first trained as a dancer (and throughout her working life seemingly preferred working as a dancer and singer over acting), she first attracted Vadim's attention as a fourteen-year-old model on the cover of *Elle.* He was recruited by his boss, director Marc Allegret, to find the girl dubbed "B.B." Bardot's mother, meanwhile, wanted her daughter's identity kept a secret, for propriety's sake.

Within four years, Bardot was one of the most photographed model-actresses in France, and by 1956, Vadim had devised the film that would thrust her into the consciousness—and arouse the libidos—of the rest of Europe, the U.K., and America: . . . *And God Created Woman.* One of Vadim's standard, overheated sensual dramas, this movie would have been forgotten had it not been for Bardot's presence. Projecting an image that is at once wholly innocent and delightfully debauched, she seduces her male costars and tops Monroe's famous skirt-raising in *The Seven Year Itch* with a devilish samba that brings the movie's plotline to a kitschy simmer. Bardot was not shy about showing her body, but in the tradition of other classic sex symbols, she was rarely seen completely nude from a head-on perspective on-screen; Vadim's film began the canny process of giving the viewer just enough of La Belle Brigitte to get him to attend her next film.

B.B. Gets Reel

Like those of many other sex symbols, the majority of Bardot's films are forgettable affairs, memorable only for certain moments: a dance, a bathtub scene, or a moment in which her character surrenders to her passions (that, and the inevitable change to another tight-fitting outfit). Some of the leering pictures that followed . . . *And God Created Woman* were a cut above the rest, particularly the wildly farcical *Naughty Girl* (AKA *Mam'zelle Pigalle* and *Cette Sacrée Gamine*) and the evocatively titled *Plucking the Daisy* (AKA *Please, Mr. Balzac* and *Mademoiselle Striptease* on U.S. video). As B.B. became more and more of a media phenomenon and was continually stalked by paparazzi, she sought more challenging roles. Her self-proclaimed favorite role was in *La Vérité* (1960), directed by Henri-Georges Clouzot (*Diabolique*). This stark drama about a free spirit arrested for killing her sister's fiancé utilized Bardot's own personal traumas; her character attempts suicide just as she herself was to do in real life shortly after the film's release (the event became a media circus, as did all things Bardot at the time). The film's more serious Bardot was rejected by movie-goers, but art-house audiences embraced her next attempt at "legit" acting.

Jean-Luc Godard's *Contempt* (1963) is one of the influential direc-tor's most accessible films. Bardot gives her finest performance as a wife who has grown to loathe her husband (Michel Piccoli), whom she believes has sold out his ideals. Her presence may have attracted audiences, but she truthfully was the icing on the cake: the film is an adaptation of a novel by prestige author Alberto Moravia (*Two Women*) by director Godard during his most prolific, critically heralded period; it features other "name" stars (Jack Palance, Piccoli, legendary director Fritz Lang); and it was sumptuously shot on the island of Capri. Godard and cinematographer Raoul Coutard crafted a number of unforget-table images, not the least of which was the famous opening in which Bardot lies nude on a bed. Forced by producer Carlo Ponti to include more B.B. nudity, Godard has her ironically asking hus-band Piccoli about his opinion of her body parts, one by one.

Bardot's other memorable roles all came courtesy of director Louis Malle. In *Vie Privée* (1961), she essentially plays herself, a dancer-turned-model-turned–movie sensation. Malle's *Viva Maria* (1965) is a rambunctious farce that pairs B.B. with Jeanne Moreau; the movie is an adorable period piece about showgirls caught up in a Mexican rebellion, marred only by the leaden presence of male lead George Hamilton. The anthology *Spirits of the Dead* (1967) found Bardot wearing an unbecoming black wig in Malle's sadistic and slightly off-kilter adaptation of the Poe tale "William Wilson."

Throughout her career, whether her European producers cast her in flops or in monster hits, Bardot wisely avoided "going Hollywood." Although she appeared in a few films in English (starting with the Dirk Bogarde British farce *Doctor at Sea* in 1954), she escaped the trap that befell so many other European screen sirens of the '50s and '60s, never shooting a film in the United States. Even her appearance in the 1965 Jimmy Stewart family comedy *Dear Brigitte* was shot in Paris.

Singing Siren

Bardot may have been the hottest female screen star of the '60s, but the only time she really was in sync with the tenor of the times was on her recordings (yes, she sang) and in a series of French TV specials. The single finest example of Bardot's special place as a peace-and-love-era icon is *Le Bardot Show,* a 1967 New Year's Eve television special created to accompany a group of songs written for her by singer-songwriter extraordinaire Serge Gains-bourg, with whom she had a short-lived personal relationship. Bardot makes an indelible impres-sion straddling a motorcycle as she warbles "Harley Davidson" (the scene spawned a "pop poster" that sold steadily throughout the late '60s); duets with Gainsbourg in full Faye Dunaway finery on his impeccable "Bonnie and Clyde"; and delivers Roy Lichtenstein–style exclamations ("Shebam! Pow! Blop! Wizz!") in a superheroine outfit as Serge strolls calmly behind her during the arch-camp "Comic Strip." Bardot's music career continued on through the 1970s, but with-out Gainsbourg's clever tunes her admittedly pleasant singing voice was consigned to items like a French cover of Stevie Wonder's "You Are the Sunshine of My Life." Gainsbourg, in the meantime, had a huge French hit with his ode to the end of his relationship with Brigitte, "Ini-tials B.B."

Brigitte Bids Adieu

In the 1970s, Bardot was fed up with the movie business, and it showed in her performances and choice of roles. In most instances, the best sequences in these movies were an extension of the aforementioned TV special (and her earlier career as a model). B.B. played "dress-up" in *Les Novices* (1970), as a nun who wears a bikini underneath her habit; *The Ballad of Frenchie King* (1971), as a cowgirl who has a bruising, lengthy fistfight with her slumming sister glamour gal Claudia Cardinale; *L'Histoire Très Bonne et Très Joyeuse de Colinot Trousse-Chemise* (1973), as a medieval courtesan; and the best of the bunch, *Rumrunners* (1970), as a 1920s movie star who in one scene wears a jungle-girl outfit.

The final sign that B.B. stood for "bored Brigitte" was Vadim's *Don Juan* (1973). The movie offered Bardot the chance to be a female version of the famous sexual predator, but Vadim's skittish approach to the sex scenes (which reaches its peak in a lesbian interlude with Jane Birkin that begins *after* the two women have finished making love) proved awfully tame in the "porno chic" era when *Deep Throat, Behind the Green Door,* and movies by Radley Metzger were delivering much, much more.

Bardot quit the movies in 1973 after *Colinot Trousse-Chemise* (literally translated "Colinot the Skirt-Lifter," the film wasn't widely distributed in the U.S.) to devote her attention to her favorite charity, animal rights. She has remained a newsmaker in the decades since, due to her intrepid work on behalf of her furry friends and her still-active love life (she caused a scandal by marrying right-wing politician Bernard d'Ormale in 1992). As time moves on and it becomes apparent that new-model sex symbols can barely hold a candle to B.B. in her prime, one can argue that Brigitte gave her fans the greatest gift a star can give: she opted out of growing old on-screen and left show business before she became either a "relic" or a cosmetic-surgery curiosity.

the family has an intimate encounter with their visitor, but it's unclear who the seducer is and who is the seduced. And just who is this visitor, really—a whore the man knew during the war? A saint the son saw as a boy? And is she there to destroy them or save them? Metzger mixes editing tricks with psychobabble and even indulges in some literal navel gazing in one of his most interesting films.

Metzger's films are more than a little melodramatic—and the sex scenes are much tamer than their early "X" ratings would indicate in retrospect—but they stand in sharp contrast to the seedy, unhealthy atmosphere of American adult films of the time, signaling an end to the "roughie" era. With their relatively high budgets and the stunning beauty of their casts, his films stood out among their European contemporaries as well. But, more than other attributes, it's Metzger's sense of visual flair that makes his films memorable. *Camille 2000*'s bedrooms of the ultra rich are shining white temples resembling the Krypton sets in *Superman*—one is surrounded by mirrors, with a bed in a womb of Plexiglas columns, and a bondage theme party is set in the glitziest dungeon ever. The centerpiece of *Lickerish* is a seduction set in the 700-year-old castle's over-the-top oval library, which features a floor decorated with oversize dictionary definitions of "dirty" words in several languages. Such flourishes likely alienated the usual adult-theater raincoat crowd, but they opened up the market to dating couples looking for some sophisticated thrills.

Camille 2000
1969 (NC-17) 96m/C *IT* Daniele Gaubert, Nino Castelnuovo, Eleonora Rossi Drago, Roberto Bisacco, Massimo Serato. *D:* Radley Metzger. *W:* Michael DeForrest. *C:* Ennio Guarnieri. *M:* Piero Piccioni. *VHS, DVD*
AKA: *Erotic Illusion; Erotic Instinct; Erotic Quartet; Hide and Seek*

The Lickerish Quartet
1970 (NC-17) 89m/C *US/IT/WG* Silvana Venturelli, Frank Wolff, Erika Remberg, Paulo Turco. *D:* Radley Metzger. *W:* Michael DeForrest. *C:* Hans Jura. *M:* Stelvio Cipriani. *VHS, DVD*

—Brian Thomas

Can Heironymus Merkin Ever Forget Mercy Humppe and Find True Happiness?

One of the biggest ego trips in movie history, as well as one of the '60s' weirdest sex comedies, *Heironymus Merkin* is a tribute to the many talents (and big-time neuroses) of singer-songwriter Anthony Newley, made by a properly worshipful . . . Anthony Newley. Newley stars as his fictional alter-ego, but the fever-dream quality of the film, plus later interviews with Newley's ex-wife/costar Joan Collins, indicate that this was one of his most personal works. Uncomfortably confessional at times—Newley could've easily left his meditations about lusting after teenage girls on the therapist's couch—the film remains compulsively watchable, due to the fact that *no one* seems to have told Newley he was going overboard.

Heironymus Merkin (Newley) brings his two children (Sasha and Tara Newley) and his mother (Patricia Hayes) to a secluded beach to tell them the sordid story of his life. His tale unfolds in a surreal, storybook fashion. Heironymus began as an insecure young man, but the discovery of his musical talent leads to a career in British music halls and eventual pop stardom. With stardom comes a seemingly endless stream of sexual encounters—at one point so many women want to sleep with him, they're lined up for miles outside his bedroom (in a home conveniently located on the same beach that serves as the picture's main setting). Merkin ends his womanizing ways when he meets Polyester Poontang (Joan Collins), whom he marries. The couple have two children, but Heironymus strays from the marital bed when he meets the nubile young Mercy Humppe (*Playboy* Playmate Connie Kreski). At this point, the film's title becomes the central dilemma—though most viewers will be too shell-shocked to care.

Newley was an impressive presence on the British music scene in the '60s. He had a steady string of hit songs that became variety-show/nightclub-act staples for other singers even as he continued to have a solid career singing his material himself. *Heironymus Merkin,* his only directorial effort, is the first full-fledged, feature-length homage to (read: rip-off of) Federico Fellini's *8½,* in which Newley was allowed to fully indulge himself by the British arm of Universal Pictures. *Playboy* praised the film thoroughly ("like a Marx Brothers movie shot in a nudist camp"), but the critics as a whole were savage. This reaction was no problem for Newley, as his "modernist" strategies attempted to one-up Fellini: Heironymus's storytelling is often interrupted by a shadowy figure named Tony (Newley), who is directing the very film we're watching; two scripter characters (Stubby Kaye and Ronald Rubin) break up the narrative with story conferences; and *A Hard Day's Night*'s Victor Spinetti, playing the stuttering member of a team of on-screen movie critics, spells it all out for the dumb folks in the audience by proclaiming at one point, "I lie awake at night and curse the name Fellini—he started this whole autobiographical, soul-searching bit."

Newley might have made the movie a profitable sex farce if he'd assembled a hipper cast. Collins (then Mrs. Newley) most likely had no other choice but to appear in the film, but casting Borscht Belt comic-actor emeritus George Jessel as the specter of Death was a dementedly inspired move that most assuredly turned off both the youth market and any male attending the movie to catch a glimpse of some skin. Much like Fellini's vision of Death (the absolutely gorgeous Claudia Cardinale), Jessel pops up every few scenes to needle Newley; unlike Cardinale, Jessel is truly frightening to look at (the old gent sports what looks to be a shoe-polish dye job) and tells the worst old jokes in an attempt to sober up Heironymus. Not content to have alienated his audience with Jessel, Newley decided that Heironymus should be led on by the Devil himself, in the form of Good Time Eddie Filth, played by Milton Berle. Berle does his usual shtick (way out of date by swinging '69), encouraging Newley to be as bad as he'd like to be. He is frequently seen egging on the already middle-aged, frequently nude Newley as he receives gratification from a sweet young thing. A more revolting sight cannot be imagined.

Given Newley's history, the single most curious thing about the movie is that it has no memorable songs. With his partner Leslie Bricusse, Newley had three hit songs emerge from each of his first two West End hit shows, wrote the best-remembered Bond theme song ("Goldfinger"), and crafted one of the most enchanting non-Disney children's movie scores of all times, *Willy Wonka and the Chocolate Factory.* (The swingin'-est of all '60s belters and "Candy Man" himself, Sammy Davis Jr., was the premier U.S. interpreter of the Newley canon.) Here, the best tunes are a trio of oddities: the ridiculous "Chalk & Cheese," sung by Collins to the once again very nude Newley on a trippy astrological set (each dancer represents a different sign of the Zodiac); "I'm All I Need," Newley's well-written but completely unhummable salute to atheism; and the jaw-dropping "Once upon a Time." The latter is a ribald fairy tale about a girl named Trampolena Whambang (yet another example of Newley's Ian Fleming–style female character names) that has no connection whatsoever to the film's plotline but is presented by Heironymus to the *Heironymus Merkin* film crew at the ninety-minute mark. The song is extremely catchy, but its theme of royal bestiality (not to mention its wretched last-line pun) most likely made it a key reason that the film received an "X" rating.

Heironymus Merkin isn't all pretension and flat-out weirdness; it also has its disturbing moments. Newley includes his own children in the film's most thoroughly uncomfortable scenes, one in which he reveals his secret misogyny ("Not only do I have no respect for women, I may very well hate them . . . ") and another in which his daughter is the victim of a child-touching lecher. Daddy Merkin punches out the offensive chap, but the scene leaves an unpleasant aftertaste—even though it serves as the catalyst for Heironymus to realize that his own affection for teenage girls is a problem (again, one feels as if Newley's therapist's notes were transcribed for the screenplay). Newley's final victory over good taste is the inclusion of some delightfully dated '60s staples: silent movie footage used to punctuate comedy sequences, a *Sound of Music* crane shot showing a character singing while communing with the elements, and carefully situated sitar music.

In terms of star power, *Heironymus Merkin* is surely surpassed by mind-blowing flops like *Skidoo, Candy,* and *Myra Breckinridge. Hieronymus Merkin* is the winner, however, in terms of sheer surreal navel-gazing. Anthony Newley was a solidly talented musical artist, and to the relief of many, after this film he left the director's chair and went back to the recording studio and concert halls.

1969 (NC-17) 108m/C *UK* Anthony Newley, Joan Collins, Milton Berle, George Jessel, Connie Kreski, Stubby Kaye, Ronald Rubin, Bruce Forsyth, Victor Spinetti. *D:* Anthony Newley. *W:* Anthony Newley, Herman Raucher. *C:* Otto Heller. *M:* Anthony Newley. *VHS*

—Ed Grant

Candy 🎵🎵

Terry Southern and Mason Hoffenberg's novel *Candy* was a sensation in the early 1960s, a sexual spoof of Voltaire's *Candide* that turned into a genuine phenomenon and captivated many people who had never read a "dirty" book before. When it came time to cast the lead for the film, a blonde and busty Swedish former teenage-beauty-contest winner named Ewa Aulin was recruited to play the title role of the naive nymph who can't seem to avoid having close encounters with every male member of society she meets. Add a script by screenwriter Buck Henry, hot off his work on *The Graduate,* and a big-name cast of Hollywood talents to play Candy's suitors, and you have what could have been a seminal film of the late 1960s.

Unfortunately, actor-turned-director Christian Marquand took his source material too literally, and the story's satirical elements are replaced by

Ewa Aulin plays the title role in *Candy,* a sexual romp based on a novel that is based on Voltaire's *Candide.*

a leering, dirty-old-man attitude toward the sexual situations. When filtered through a haze of cinematic psychedelia that includes odd-angled camerawork (by Fellini collaborator Giussepe Rotunno), a score with songs by the Byrds and Steppenwolf, and sleek, hyper-stylized production design, you get something like *Playboy*'s "Little Annie Fanny" on acid. This means, of course, that *Candy* may be a botched mess of a movie, but it is a must-see misfire.

Consider the cast of big-name stars, all mugging for the camera, all cinematically involved with a seventeen-year-old Swede whose accent makes Zsa Zsa Gabor sound like James Earl Jones. Among them are Richard Burton as a pompous, whiskey-swigging Welsh poet (parodying himself, no doubt) who lives in . . . New Jersey; Marlon Brando playing a hairy spiritual adviser, dispensing wisdom from a traveling guru-mobile; Walter Matthau as a befuddled military man, reminiscent of characters out of Southern's *Dr. Strangelove* script; Charles Aznavour as a French hunchback in Central Park; Ringo Starr as a studly Mexican gardener; James Coburn as a brain surgeon with a feverish rock star–style following; and John Astin—Gomez Addams, himself—in dual roles, playing Candy's teacher father *and* her sleazeball uncle.

While strobe lights swirl in the background, Candy manages to consummate one liaison after another, remaining oblivious to the primal motivations of the men around her. Her final encounter is a jaw-dropper, too, an unnerving blast of incest wrapped in a cosmically delivered message. Candy's odyssey ends in a dilapidated underground temple, where she meets a masked holy man who embraces her. As the temple falls around her, the holy man's mask crumbles to reveal the face of her true love: Daddy!

The meeting underlines the film's point that all men are, at heart, slime buckets—ready, willing, and occasionally able to make it with a hot chick as long as she is oblivious to their motives, even if the chick is their daughter. After Candy and father grope each other, Candy walks through a field, passing all of the men she encountered during her adventure. As the theme song by Roger McGuinn and the Byrds plays in the background, Candy evaporates into space, taking her place among the other heavenly bodies in the galaxy.

Trying very hard to be profound but coming off as nonsensical and flaky, the finale, like the rest of the film, proves that *Candy* is dandy only if you're looking for a true time-warped capsule from the era of sexual awakening.

1968 (R) 123m/C *FR/IT/UK/US* Ewa Aulin, John Astin, James Coburn, John Huston, Walter Matthau, Marlon Brando, Charles Aznavour, Richard Burton, Ringo Starr. **D:** Christian Marquand. **W:** Buck Henry. **C:** Giuseppe Rotunno. **M:** Dave Grusin. *VHS, DVD*

Carnal Knowledge ♫♫♫♪

U ntil Neil LaBute delved into similar turf with *In the Company of Men* and *Your Friends and Neighbors* in the late 1990s, Mike Nichols had cornered the market in devastating black comedies about the sexes with *Carnal Knowledge.* Although the film boasted major stars and an Oscar-winning director, the film ruffled enough feathers that it was labeled obscene and banned in certain parts of the country.

Written by cartoonist/satirist Jules Feiffer, *Carnal Knowledge* offers snapshots of the sex lives of its two lead characters, Jonathan (Jack Nicholson) and Sandy (Art Garfunkel), through different eras of their lives. The glimpses viewers get are often scathingly funny but not very pretty.

The film introduces the men as roommates attending college in New England in the 1940s. Sandy is quiet and naive, desperately wanting his first real sexual encounter. Jonathan remains technically a virgin, though he has had some encounters with women. Even with his limited experience, however, Jonathan has theorized that women are little more than sexual partners who become problematical when they desire more than a roll in the sack. A woman's looks to him are everything.

Both men lose their virginity to the same woman: Susan (Candice Bergen), a pretty coed Sandy meets at a social. Their dating becomes troublesome because Sandy wants "it" badly, while the virginal Susan appears ready, willing, and able to wait for it. Sandy tells Jonathan about his frustrations, prompting his calculating, caddish pal to secretly start to date and bed Susan. Eventually, Susan's lack of emotional attachment to the increasingly demanding Jonathan and her fear of hurting the vulnerable Sandy leads her

"Why don't you leave me? ... For God's sake, I'd almost marry you if you'd leave me."

—Jonathan (Jack Nicholson), in *Carnal Knowledge*

Ann-Margret (Bobbie) and Jack Nicholson (Jonathan) play a bitterly unhappy couple in Mike Nichols's *Carnal Knowledge.*

to break up with Jonathan. Sandy never learns of Susan's fling with Jonathan, and we find out later that he and Susan eventually get married.

In the early 1960s, Jonathan, now a successful accountant, gets involved with voluptuous actress-model Bobbie (Ann-Margret). Even a mention of marriage or kids sends the commitment-phobic Jonathan to a cold shower. Eventually, however, Jonathan yields and marries Bobbie. A few years pass, and Bobbie becomes a depressed, pill-popping mess who spends most of her days sleeping.

When Sandy, now a doctor and divorced from Susan, comes to visit Jonathan and Bobbie with current girlfriend Cindy (Cynthia O'Neal), Jonathan suggests he and Sandy swap partners. Sandy buys the idea, but when Jonathan approaches Cindy, she rejects him. Meanwhile, Bobbie overdoses on pills in her bedroom and Sandy attempts to save her life.

The final segment of *Carnal Knowledge* takes place in the late 1960s. Sandy, now in his forties, is involved with Jennifer (Carol Kane), a hippie teenager less than half his age. They visit the now-single Jonathan, who entertains them with a slideshow chronicling his misadventures with women called "Ballbusters on Parade." Jonathan comments on each on-screen picture as Sandy and the saddened Jennifer look on. Except for one shot of his daughter, Jonathan's comments about the women in his life are thoroughly nasty. He shows Sandy and Jennifer all of his sexual conquests through slides, almost giving away his clandestine romance with Susan at one point. The night ends with the two friends coolly saying goodbye in downtown Manhattan; Nicholson then visits a prostitute (Rita Moreno) for a sexual interlude designed to make him feel manly.

The ending starkly reveals that Jonathan has never outgrown his misogynist views, which have left him lonely and cynical. The final, stinging irony of an irony-laden film is in the last scene, when we see that the self-assured sex expert is now reliant on a scripted role-playing game to achieve pleasure.

Carnal Knowledge features only seven characters and was an attempt by director Mike Nichols (*The Graduate*) to make a film on a smaller but not necessarily simpler scale than that of his big-budget, multicharacter adaptation of Joseph Heller's *Catch-22,* a box-office dud of the previous year. This film is a self-consciously spare production with no musical score, sparse sets designed by Richard Sylbert, earthy cinematography by Fellini collaborator Giuseppe Rotunno, and Feiffer's acerbic dialogue. No wonder *Carnal Knowledge* often resembles a filmed version of a play that hasn't been entirely opened up for the screen.

Nichols gets tremendous acting across the board, with Garfunkel (who made his screen debut for Nichols in *Catch-22*), Bergen, and Ann-Margret turning in their best performances ever. All have complex roles. Garfunkel has the difficult task of being smart *and* naive at the same time; Bergen is called on to show how Susan feels about both men in two key close-up shots, one of which captures her laughing (at a bar with Nicholson and Garfunkel on opposite sides of her) and the other crying (by herself, on the telephone). She goes deep to find her character's desires and ambiguities. Ann-Margret, given a rare serious role, was nominated for an Oscar for Best Supporting Actress for showing the world the vulnerable side of an idealized woman.

Carnal Knowledge also introduced viewers to Nicholson's marvelous hothead-goes-berserk routine. Catch some of the explosives Jonathan dishes out in the unsettling scene when he recognizes how Bobbie, his dream girl, has turned out: "You want a job? I got a job for you. Fix up this pigsty! You get a pretty goddamned good salary for testing out this bed all day! You want an extra fifty dollars a week, try vacuuming! You want an extra hundred, make this goddamned bed! Try opening some goddamned windows! That's why you can't stand up in here, the goddamned place smells like a coffin!"

Carnal Knowledge received mixed reviews from critics. The negative notices pointed to the film's detached style, the idea of buying Nicholson and Garfunkel as college students (a bit of a stretch), and the unlikable characters that populate the proceedings. Fans of the film loved the performances, Feiffer's pungent dialogue, and Nichols's gutsy approach to the war between the sexes.

It surprised many when this high-profile, "R"-rated film ran into censorship problems. After turning up on some top-ten lists for 1971, a criminal jury declared the film obscene in Albany, Georgia, in March 1972. A theater owner was arrested, the film was seized, and a judge ordered the owner to pay $750 and serve a sentence of twelve months' probation. After an appeal, the supreme court of Georgia upheld the charges. A later appeal to the U.S. Supreme Court eventually reversed the decision.

ANN-MARGRET: HOW SWEDE IT IS
by Brian Thomas

I f discussion turned to "sex kittens" during the 1960s, one of the first names to
come up would inevitably be Ann-Marget. With her sparkling looks, sassy personality, bright red hair, and incredible figure, the dynamic singer/dancer made a sensation wherever she appeared—but it hadn't always been that way. Early in her career,
Swedish-born former Winnetka, Illinois, cheerleader Ann-Margret Olssen traded
more on her wholesome image than on that of a sexpot. Soon after comedian
George Burns discovered her singing in cabarets, she was making appearances as
a fresh new face on his television show, as well as singing to Burns's pal Jack
Benny on his show.

But before long, the pretty teenager in sweaters and poodle skirts went through a transformation, blossoming from the farm girl next door in *State Fair* to a vivacious rock 'n' roll fan in *Bye
Bye Birdie* who rivaled lead Janet Leigh in the sex-appeal department. By 1964 she'd graduated to
full sex-bomb status, outshining the king of rock 'n' roll himself in the Elvis Presley vehicle *Viva
Las Vegas.* In this movie, one of his best, Elvis plays waiter Lucky Jackson, who dreams of winning
the Las Vegas Grand Prix but takes time out to woo Rusty Martin (who is likely the sexiest hotel
pool manager ever). Ann-Margret matches him song for song throughout, and for many fans this is
an "Ann-Margret movie" and not an "Elvis movie."

Most of her films from the '60s exploit the natural heat she provided, reflected even in their
titles. Along with roommates Pamela Tiffin and Carol Lynley, she prowled the streets of Madrid in
The Pleasure Seekers. As *Kitten with a Whip,* her escaped juvenile delinquent con gets her kicks
kidnapping uptight politician John Forsythe (a '60s icon of an entirely different kind). In *The
Swinger,* she plays a magazine writer (named Kelly Olssen) out to prove to her editor, Tony Fran-
ciosa, that she's sexually liberated. In *The Tiger and the Pussycat* (an Italian predecessor of Blake
Edwards's *10*), she's an irresistible temptation to married man Vittorio Gassman. For Dean Martin's second foray as silly secret agent Matt Helm in *Murderers' Row,* she adds to the fun as Suzie
Solaris, daughter of a kidnapped scientist and implied romantic interest for the twice-her-age star.
Even in the 1966 all-star remake of *Stagecoach,* she looks like a go-go girl dropped into the previous century. Perhaps it was in reaction to this overly simplified reputation that she decided to
take on the role of Jack Nicholson's lazy wife in *Carnal Knowledge.* As one of the first actors to
purposely get *out* of shape for a part, she was rewarded with a Best Supporting Actress Academy
Award nomination and Golden Globe Award.

Ann-Margret survived a serious fall from a stage in 1972 that could have ended her life, as
well as her career—and again, a motorcycle crash in 2000—to carry on in a variety of roles. But
to many, she perfectly represents a certain aspect of the 1960s, such an amazing presence that
she was even immortalized as a cartoon character on *The Flintstones.*

Astute producer Joseph E. Levine, who also produced *The Graduate* with Nichols, used the censorship trial to reissue the film in theaters with a new ad campaign bringing attention to the controversy. The ploy worked, as *Carnal Knowledge* eventually brought in an impressive $29 million at the box office, a fitting coda to a film with the chutzpah to tackle a difficult subject head-on.

1971 (R) 97m/C Jack Nicholson, Art Garfunkel, Ann-Margret, Candice Bergen, Cynthia O'Neal, Carol Kane, Rita Moreno. *D:* Mike Nichols. *W:* Jules Feiffer. *C:* Giuseppe Rotunno. *VHS, DVD*

The Girl on a Motorcycle

Male viewers with an Emma Peel fixation will be entranced by this delightfully trippy road movie about a chopper-ridin' woman who is, as the film's U.S. title put it, *Naked under Leather.* Women viewers will be fascinated by the movie's protofeminist stance—the lead character is eager for sexual fulfillment and will let nothing stand in her way—as well as the laughably florid dialogue.

Rebecca (Marianne Faithfull), a dissatisfied newlywed, flees the marital bed early one morning to visit her lover and mentor Daniel (Alain Delon). Dressed entirely in leather, she rides her Harley Davidson from France to Germany, all the while fantasizing about her eventual meeting with Daniel. She also mulls over the early stages of her wimpy husband's courtship and takes brief breaks for roadside naps, during which she has surreal dreams; one such Felliniesque scene takes place in a circus where Daniel is removing her leather bodysuit with deft strokes of a whip.

Both profoundly beautiful on a visual level and deeply corny on a narrative one, *Girl on a Motorcycle* is at its best when it is a sensory experience. Director Jack Cardiff made over a dozen films, but it is as a cinematographer that he did his finest work. He began working regularly in the silent era and hit his peak with masterworks made by Michael Powell and Emeric Pressburger (*Black Narcissus, The Red Shoes*). Cardiff's later work-for-hire on big-budget action tripe (*Conan the Destroyer, Rambo: First Blood Part II*) has done nothing to diminish his incredible legacy behind the camera. It's no surprise therefore that the most memorable moments in *Girl* are all visual. Eighty percent of the film was shot on location in France, Germany, and Switzerland, and so Faithfull's long, liberating journey is awash in gorgeous scenery and local color. Cardiff's neatest visual trick, however, was making his star appear as if she were a diehard biker—Faithfull had no "hog"-smarts and was in fact towed around the location, her hair blowing in the wind and her wheels barely touching the ground.

In her autobiography, Faithfull refers to *Girl* as a "terrible" film, mocking a choice howler: Delon's declaration that she (in her skintight leathers) resembles a "violin in a velvet case." Director Cardiff, who has stated that he rewrote a large portion of the script, notes in his own autobiography that that

Rebecca (Marianne Faithfull) rides her Harley across Europe, engaging in liberating sexual fantasies along the way, in *Girl on a Motorcycle*.

MID-ATLANTIC / ARES / CLARIDGE / THE KOBAL COLLECTION

particular line (also singled out for derision by a London film critic at the time of the film's release) isn't as corny as it might sound, since it occurs in a *fantasy* dreamt up by Rebecca. Cardiff does seem to be splitting hairs here, especially because lines said by Rebecca when she is in the real world are just as ripe. One would be hard pressed to pick the most unforgettable lines when faced with the choice between truly purple prose ("I'm a bit like a leaf myself, green, very supple and young, bendable . . . ") and Russ Meyer–worthy insanity (Faithfull to her Harley on her impending reunion with Daniel: "Take me to him, you black pimp!").

The film remains eminently watchable because of its photogenic leads and Cardiff's visual experimentation. Due to a busy schedule, Delon was only able to spare Cardiff a few days for shooting his sequences, but his iconic, pretty-boy good looks are well used. Faithfull may look down on the film, but it's a helluva showcase for her winsome good looks and fine physique. Best known in '68 for being Mick Jagger's "old lady," she is both properly rebellious and innocently sweet enough as Rebecca to carry off the many sequences that require her to laugh happily as she rides down the Autobahn.

Cardiff has stated that the original French novel was quite sexually graphic; he had to discover a way to present the sexual interludes without getting the film censored or consigned to the adult category. (It was branded "15" in Britain, the equivalent of an "R" rating.) Thus, his creative use of the "solarization" process, which changes *Girl* from a dreamlike film to an honest-to-god *trip*. Viewed today, the sex scenes seem like outright cheats (all one can see are brightly colored shapes as the two leads commingle), but at the time of *Girl*'s release moviegoers hadn't been exposed to the technique, which flourished after *2001: A Space Odyssey* (1968). Despite all of Cardiff's precautions, the film had to be drastically re-edited (and retitled) to get an "R" rating for the American release, under the assumption that a reshuffling of the film's random-seeming elements would make it seem less . . . dirty.

The European cut of *Girl on a Motorcycle* is still a delightfully disjointed viewing experience, which, as already noted, does have a pre–women's lib message about the importance of the female libido. It's interesting to note, however, that Rebecca, like many lead female characters in late-'60s dramas (i.e., *Petulia, Little Murders, End of the Road*) is the true "life force" of the film but winds up being the victim of violence before the rather somber finale. One can only conclude that young women took home a daunting message from these movies: have your fun while it lasts, because as soon as the Establishment gets wind of your independent lifestyle, you'll be ground underfoot.

1968 (R) 91m/C *UK* Marianne Faithfull, Alain Delon, Roger Mutton, Marius Goring. *D:* Jack Cardiff. *W:* Ronald Duncan, Jack Cardiff. *C:* Jack Cardiff. *M:* Les Reed. *VHS, DVD*
AKA: Naked under Leather

—*Ed Grant*

The Harrad Experiment ♪♪♥

Part drive-in exploitation flick, part social drama espousing revolutionary ideas on human sexuality, *The Harrad Experiment* is an example of oddball cross-pollination that remains cheesily entertaining and somewhat nostalgic, a reminder of the good old carefree days before things got scary, sexually speaking.

Based on Robert H. Rimmer's immensely popular novel of the same name, the film takes place at fictional Harrad College, situated on the New England estate of married couple Philip and Margaret Tenhausen (James Whitmore and Tippi Hedren). The Tenhausens are Masters and Johnson–style psychologists who preach sexual freedom. Their specialty is placing male and female students together in dorms, letting them cohabitate, then allowing their libidos to take over. Helping to steer the kids in the right direction are counseling sessions administered by the Tenhausens as well as group therapy boondoggles, naked yoga classes, and games of "Zoom," a touchy-feely version of the Macarena. Oh, yes: after a month of living together, couples are allowed to break apart and choose other sexmates.

Most of the focus of *The Harrad Experiment* is placed on Sheila Grove (Laurie Walters) and Stanley Cole (Don Johnson). Sheila is a sweet, innocent virgin, Stanley a young whippersnapper who may look like he's just getting over acne but who actually has a resumé Hugh Hefner would be proud of. The Tenhausens pair the two seemingly incompatible students together and we watch the fireworks begin.

Along with Sheila and Stanley, the film introduces us to two of the other duos chosen for the experiment, while the remaining ten or so couples remain in the background throughout. There's Beth (Victoria Thompson), with loads of sexperience under her belt, and self-conscious neophyte Harry (Bruno Kirby). We also meet the experienced Barbara (Sharon Ullrick) and Wilson (Elliott Street), who hates taking his clothes off because of his portly framework.

It's no surprise that Stanley turns out to be an insensitive S.O.B., and we can't wait until he learns his lesson. He disses sweet Sheila for her closed-mindedness, then suggests they change partners; he hopes to hop into the sack with the sex-savvy Beth. While the couples try to find a happy medium of coexisting and fulfilling their sexual needs, Philip Tenhausen puffs on a pipe, lecturing on the dangers of monogamy and his belief that marriage is a useless, antiquated institution. The kids seem to be buying the old man's spiel; doesn't anyone wonder why the hell he is married?

Stanley eventually gets his comeuppance when he makes a move on Mrs. Tenhausen. Her reaction? Stripping down to her bra and panties in the middle of Harrad's lawn and daring the student to do the nasty with her right in the middle of campus. This embarrasses poor Stanley—and later, we presume, Hedren, who became Johnson's mother-in-law after the actor married her daughter, Melanie Griffith, twice. Mrs. T.'s daring act sends Stanley away from Harrad for a while and into a state of solemn self-reflection. Will he emerge a new, sensitive person from the experience? Duh.

The Harrad Experiment proves that Johnson's smarminess on-screen started at an early age; that Bruno Kirby was always a likable character actor; that Laurie Walters, Joanie on quintessential '70s sitcom *Eight Is Enough,* was pretty well built (she has some nude scenes in the unedited video version of the film); that Ted Cassidy was more than Lurch on *The Addams Family* (he cowrote the script); and that improv comedy groups have never been funny (The Ace Trucking Company with Fred Willard are featured).

Also proven was that *The Harrad Experiment* was successful for one semester only. Walters and Thompson returned for a sequel, *Harrad Summer,* a year later. The innocuous and questionably comedic follow-up boasted funnymen Bill ("Jose Jimenez") Dana and Marty Allen in the cast, but it barely matriculated in theaters and later turned up on video under such titles as *Love All Summer* and *Student Union.*

The Harrad Experiment would neatly fit into a time capsule for movies made in the 1970s. Along with sideburns, psychobabble, and terrible anthemic ballads on the soundtrack, the film's view of the self-help movement and the sexual revolution plays as parody today. At the time, however, this film was taken as a fairly honest examination of what college-aged kids were thinking about. To young audiences who read the book or saw the movie, the notion of a school where, sexually speaking, "anything goes" (except, oddly enough, never-broached homosexual encounters) was a potent fantasy at the onset of the era of EST-like human potential programs, bra burning, and porn films.

1972 (R) 97m/C James Whitmore, Tippi Hedren, Don Johnson, Laurie Walters, B. Kirby Jr. (Bruno Kirby), Victoria Thompson, Elliott Street, Sharon Taggert (Sharon Ullrick), Robert Middleton. *D:* Ted Post. *W:* Michael Werner, Ted Cassidy. *C:* Richard H. Kline. *M:* Artie Butler. *VHS, DVD*

Midnight Cowboy ♪♪♪♪

Title card for *Midnight Cowboy*, starring Dustin Hoffman and Jon Voight

UNITED ARTISTS / THE KOBAL COLLECTION

Midnight Cowboy is the ultimate "I hate New York" movie.

In this movie, the Big Apple looks like a pigsty. Trash litters the crowded streets where busy pedestrians pass dead bodies lying on the sidewalks and dodge reckless taxi drivers. The city is populated by a host of unsavory characters: sex fiends, religious nuts, hookers, druggies, or just plain freaks. And that's not to mention the film's two lead characters: Joe Buck (Jon Voight), a naive male prostitute just off the bus from small-town Texas, and Enrico "Ratso" Rizzo (Dustin Hoffman), a sickly, handicapped con artist.

In other words, New York in *Midnight Cowboy* is the kind of place a guy like *Taxi Driver's* Travis Bickle could call home.

For a movie with abundant urban, social, and sexual blight, however, *Midnight Cowboy* remains dazzling, daring, and yes, touching, thirty-some years after its initial release.

To capture the low-lifes of America's top city, John Schlesinger (*Billy Liar, Darling*) was recruited as director. The Englishman working in New York brilliantly captured the underbelly of the streets thanks to his bold approach,

Do They Make You Horny, Baby?

419

THE CELLULOID CLOSET OPENS
by Charles A. Cassady Jr.

"**A**s for overt homosexuality in pre-1960s films, it was not attempted and not possible," said author/screenwriter Gore Vidal, accurately. Hollywood's self-regulating Production Code, in effect since 1934 to enforce general morality in studio releases regarding vice, crime, violence, revenge, eroticism, and other spicier ingredients in storytelling, spelled things out: "Sex perversion or any [reference] to it is forbidden."

By the 1960s the changing social climate and a few taboo-pushing productions—not to mention a marked drop in cinema attendance—had steadily worn away the power of the code. In October 1961 it was amended to permit "tasteful" depictions of homosexuality (supposedly to allow for the plot in Otto Preminger's Capitol Hill melodrama *Advise and Consent*), and the code itself would be abandoned entirely by the end of the decade. So the rallying cry of the 1960s might have been: Let the Gays Begin!

Well, yes, and no. For an adventurous movie era that saw enthusiastic depictions of drugs, heists, outlaw bikers, black power, war protests, leftism, sticking it to the Man, and, of course, heterosexual sex, the gay/lesbian experience seemed to be discomforting subject matter. Oh, homosexual characters were there, but as Vito Russo pointed out in his landmark book *The Celluloid Closet,* they were shown in ways that were seldom flattering or favorable.

Laughs and Death

Comedy, always a great equalizer, permitted nonthreatening, funny queers and trannies in *The Producers, The Day the Fish Came Out, The Fearless Vampire Killers, Myra Breckinridge* (based on a novel by Vidal), *The Magic Christian,* and others. Even the high-profile underground flicks of John Waters, Paul Morrissey, Andy Warhol, and Ralph Bakshi allowed straight audiences to digest such lurid cases as obese cross-dresser Divine (star of *Pink Flamingoes* and many other films) with a spoonful of satire to help the medicine go down.

More typical were screen portrayals that admitted homosexuality existed but treated it as a malediction, curable by death. Queer eyes meant dead guys in *Advise and Consent* itself (a senator blackmailed over a homosexual past commits suicide), and more toe tags were to come in *Caprice, Midnight Cowboy, The Detective, P. J., Tony Rome, Play It As It Lays, Deadfall, Villain, The Sergeant,* and *Reflections in a Golden Eye.*

fusing a daring technical command of the medium to Waldo Salt's masterful adaptation of James Leo Herlihy's novel and a gallery of great performances.

Midnight Cowboy centers on the affecting friendship between Joe and Ratso. Wearing a cowboy hat, boots, and a fringed jacket, Joe leaves his haunted past in Texas, where he worked as a dishwasher, and arrives in the big city with transistor radio in ear and high hopes of making it big as a male

It makes a neat segue to note that Carson McCullers's novel on which this last picture was based helped inspire Goldeneye, the name of Ian Fleming's Caribbean hideaway. In fact there were a few instances where movies featuring James Bond, the ultimate heterosexual, also offered on-screen depictions of homosexuality, however subtle. In Fleming's book *Goldfinger*, heroine Pussy Galore is, until she meets 007, a lesbian (hints of this are discernible in the blockbuster movie). Bond villainess Rosa Klebb in *From Russia with Love* has lesbian bull-dyke attributes—but Sean Connery makes no effort to convert *her*. In *Diamonds Are Forever*, 007 sends two gay hit-men/lovers to that Great Bathhouse in the Sky.

Getting Serious

"Serious" explorations of gay/lesbian life came along after the famous Stonewall Riots in Greenwich Village in 1969, when gay activists rose up in protest against police harassment, just as the yippies and African Americans had done previously. Nonetheless, many major post-Stonewall releases were tinged with pity, self-loathing, and pathos, such as *Staircase*, directed by Stanley Donen and featuring the not-so-dynamic pairing of Rex Harrison and Richard Burton; the lesbian-themed *The Fox*; and even *The Boys in the Band* (1970). The latter release, directed by William Friedkin and adapted from the play by Mart Crowley, was notable for an American film in that it not only portrayed homosexual men as something other than psychos, it also studied their mature, consenting relationships with other gay men. "It was not positive," writes Russo, "but it was fair."

Other features from that era that lean toward balance include a lesbian actress in professional and personal decline in *The Killing of Sister George* (helmed by, of all people, "macho" director Robert Aldrich of *The Dirty Dozen* fame) and a gay/straight/bisexual love triangle in John Schlesinger's *Sunday, Bloody Sunday*. And one can't get sunnier than this aside in *Little Big Man*: a Native American tribe accepts and embraces a gay Indian.

In 1980, when *Boys in the Band* director Friedkin turned being gay into an M.O. for murder in *Cruising*, gay activists protested and audiences rejected it (on a lesser scale, the same happened to the lesbian-stalker flick *Windows* that same year). Clearly, there was no turning back at this point.

Home video has helped audiences rediscover many additional obscurities and believe-it-or-not curios of psychedelic-era queer cinema, including the gay-biker opus *The Pink Angels*, love among California frontiersmen in *Song of the Loon*, and the Japanese *Black Lizard*, about a supercriminal who's an international transvestite of mystery. An excellent assessment of the cinematic depiction of homosexuality is *The Celluloid Closet*, the high-profile 1995 documentary based on Vito Russo's book.

hustler. His first experiences prove disastrous—he ends up paying one client, a prostitute (Sylvia Miles), for sex.

After he meets Ratso in a seedy bar, the two strike up a friendship, and Ratso suggests he get his own manager. But the pimp Ratso recommends, Mr. O'Daniel (John McGiver), turns out to be a religious fanatic, and Joe flees his crucifix-adorned apartment. Things get tougher for Joe, and he finds himself in a movie theater bathroom engaging in sexual relations with a student (played by twenty-four-year-old Bob Balaban) for cash. Joe and Ratso move in together in a dilapidated building, where their bond grows stronger as the times—and Ratso's hacking, tuburcular cough—worsen. Ratso's dream of moving to Florida becomes Joe's dream as well. He decides to risk what he still begrudgingly views as a career opportunity in prostitution to help his new friend find a better life in Miami. But just as the men are about to get a dose of that Florida sunshine, tragedy occurs.

Few would argue that *Midnight Cowboy* is a depressing movie, but it could have been torturous if it weren't for Schlesinger's ability to draw compassion and even humor from the direst circumstances. At the center of the story are two down-and-out losers, but Schlesinger is able to make us sympathize with the characters and their plight. To color the characters and add humanity, he gives us disturbing flashbacks of Joe's screwed-up past deep in the heart of Texas, where his girlfriend (played by Jennifer Salt, daughter of screenwriter Waldo) was sexually assaulted and his grandmother's regular dalliances with different men confused and psychologically damaged him at an early age. We're also presented hopeful flash-forwards of Joe and Ratso taking in the good life in Miami, scenes that offer some semblance of hope for the guys.

The director elicited two Oscar-worthy performances from his leads. With slicked-back hair, a stubbly face, and a pronounced limp, Hoffman's Ratso showed that after the smash-hit *Graduate,* the actor was not content playing clean-cut-kid roles. He was willing to go the character-actor route and meet tremendous challenges in the process. *Midnight Cowboy* was Voight's first major effort after his turn as a satiric superhero in the little-seen *Fearless Frank,* and he makes an indelible impression as the hayseed wanna-be stud. Both Hoffman and Voight were nominated for Academy Awards for Best Actor, but they lost to another type of cowboy—John Wayne in *True Grit.* They were also joined by a terrific supporting cast, including Oscar nominee Miles and Brenda Vaccaro; she plays Joe's only true female paying customer, Shirley, who suggests he may prefer men after he has trouble satisfying her.

There are any number of memorable lines and moments throughout *Midnight Cowboy:* Ratso staking his turf against an approaching car with the now-famous "I'm walking here" diatribe; a desperate Joe smashing the face of Towny (Barnard Hughes) to a pulp, then stealing his money; and the two men at a wild party in a Warhol "Factory" loft (populated by such "Factory" workers as Taylor Mead and Paul Morrissey) at which Ratso explains the gay context of the Hansel and Gretel fairy tale and stuffs cold cuts in his clothes while Joe gets high and meets Shirley. Also memorable is the score: John Barry's haunting music, "Toots" Thielemans's poignant harmonica playing, and, of course, Harry Nilsson's "Everybody's Talkin'" tune.

Midnight Cowboy sparked lots of controversy when released, not only because it portrayed such subjects as prostitution, homosexuality, and drugs with a gutsy, unflinching, "adult" approach, but also because it was a major film that received an adults-only "X" rating and then went on to win Oscars for Best Picture, Best Director, and Best Screenplay. Although it has since been re-rated "R," *Midnight Cowboy* still packs a punch. It's an unforgettable vision of a desolate urban landscape where buddies bond together in search of peace and comfort that appear obtainable but are, ultimately, just out of reach.

1969 **(R)** **113m/C** Dustin Hoffman, Jon Voight, Sylvia Miles, John McGiver, Brenda Vaccaro, Barnard Hughes, Ruth White, Jennifer Salt. *D:* John Schlesinger. *W:* Waldo Salt. *C:* Adam Holender. *M:* John Barry. *VHS, DVD*

Myra Breckinridge   WOOF!

Even diehard fans of bad cinema must admit that *Myra Breckinridge* scrapes the bottom of the barrel of American filmmaking. Yes, the movie was professionally photographed and slickly produced, but it was also poorly scripted, terribly acted, somewhat incomprehensible, and incredibly annoying to boot. Yes, Mae West appears in this film—her first in decades—but she's in her eighties here, and with a platinum blonde wig and lips that barely move even as she mouths her suggestive double entendres, she looks like a wax figure in dentures and a cheap Halloween wig. Yes, Raquel Welch is certainly pleasing to watch, especially when she wears her patriotic red, white, and blue sequined getup in the film's "big" scene—you know, the infamous one in which she straps on a dildo and surprises some guy up the hoo-ha. But Raquel's dreamily voiced dialogue is even less understandable than what she was given to recite in *One Million Years B.C.* You may recall that, in this dinosaur epic, the actress got to speak such memorable lines of dialogue as "Tumak!" And if that wasn't memorable enough, there was always the line, "Tumak!"

For the uninitiated, *Myra Breckinridge* is based on a best-selling novel by Gore Vidal. Film critic Rex Reed plays Myron, a movie buff, who undergoes a sex change in Denmark at the hands of a cantankerous, cigarette-smoking, octogenarian superstar surgeon (John Carradine). Before the doctor proceeds with the surgery, he warns Myron, "You realize, once we cut it off, it won't grow back. I mean it's not like hair or fingernails or toenails, you know." But Myron says Myra's waiting, and the procedure begins as Myron sings "Secret Love" to himself.

Upon returning to America, the newly christened Myra (now played by a va-va-voom Welch) decides she's going to wreak havoc on the male gender just to prove some obscure point. Her first stop is Hollywood, where she poses as the wife of pre-op Myron. Claiming her hubby died, Myra attempts to collect a $500,000 inheritance from relative Buck Loner (an irritable John Huston), a libidinous old western movie star who now runs an acting school. While Loner bucks Myra's attempt to collect inheritance money, the old codger compromises by offering Myra a position at the school, acting as a teacher of "posture and empathy."

Around this time, we're introduced to Letitia Van Allen (West), an elderly, perpetually randy casting agent whose hobbies include sleeping with young studs (including Tom Selleck!), cracking sexy double entendres, and croaking songs (such as the Ides of March's "Vehicle" and Otis Redding's "Hard to Handle") in showy production numbers. Her office resembles a whorehouse,

> "My purpose in coming to Hollywood is the destruction of the American male in all its particulars."
>
> —Raquel Welch, in *Myra Breckinridge*

and man after man passes through her door, all seemingly ready, willing, and able to succumb to her sexual hankerings.

Meanwhile, Myra does little teaching, but she trudges on, trying to achieve her goal of crushing all men. Her first target for seduction and ridicule is Rusty Godowski (Roger Hedden), a handsome, ultramacho student at the school. The dildo intrusion is the plan for him. And just for kicks, Myra sets her sights on attractive blonde student Mary Ann Pringle (Fawcett), who happens to be Rusty's girlfriend. Myra's goal? Turning the young woman on to lesbianism so Mary Ann will turn off to regular hetero sex with Roger.

As incoherent and tasteless as it sounds, this is how the film's main plot goes. Of course, these atrocities would be more than enough for the average film and the average director, but not for *Myra Breckinridge,* and not for director Michael Sarne, who co-adapted Vidal's novel with David Giler (*Alien*). Sarne just doesn't know when to leave things alone, no matter how overdone they already are. He's like the cook who comes in and starts a fire, trying to cook a steak that's already well done.

You want examples? We have examples. In what he must have sensed was a bold move at the time (though John Frankenheimer's misfire *The Extraordinary Seaman* tried a similar tactic a few years earlier), Sarne repeatedly injected old movie clips into the picture, hoping to up the laugh quotient. With access to the 20th Century Fox vaults, Sarne inserts clips of Marlene Dietrich in drag, Laurel and Hardy doing schtick, Richard Widmark in *Kiss of Death,* Dorothy Dandridge singing, and abundant stock footage in a weary attempt to inject humor into the proceedings. Simply put, he failed miserably.

Not one to leave well enough alone, Sarne—who claimed he wanted to ape his idol, Federico Fellini (no doubt during his acid-dropping *Juliet of the Spirits* years)—added all sorts of characters that show up in a scene or two, then disappear. Among them are some old B-movie western stars (played by Andy Devine and Grady Sutton); Irving Amadeus (Calvin Lockhart), Loner's effeminate cohort; and a noted dental-psychiatrist (played by Roger C. Carmel of *The Mothers-in-Law* TV show fame) whom Myra pays to testify on her behalf in a kangaroo court to decide her inheritance. Lest we forget, Rex Reed's preening Myron appears sporadically throughout, adding commentary and engaging in philosophical discussions with his female alter ego.

Like *Beyond the Valley of the Dolls, Myra Breckinridge* was part of 20th Century Fox's plan to click with young audiences who had stayed away from such big-budget family entertainments as *Star!* and *Doctor Dolittle,* the poor showings of which had the once-mighty studio teetering on the brink of bankruptcy. But problems plagued the production of *Myra Breckinridge* from the beginning. Mae West, feeling she was going to be upstaged by Welch, refused to share the screen with her costar. Extras had to be commingled in their scenes together. Reportedly, director Sarne would space out for hours while he was supposed to be shooting. Rex Reed, in one of the film's major roles, couldn't act. Worried studio executives reportedly pulled the plug on director Sarne's runaway production before the film was completed. They allowed Sarne to edit it but didn't afford him the opportunity to shoot an ending, a fact that explains

MICHAEL SARNE: MYRA MAKER

Raquel Welch in *Myra Breckinridge*

Michael Sarne, a British actor, came out of nowhere to direct two landmarks in groovy movie history: *Joanna* (1968), a topsy-turvy tale of a pretty art student in swinging London and her amorous, fantasy-fueled adventures with men set to the beat of Rod McKuen's music, and *Myra Breckinridge* (1970), the notorious big-budget bonanza about transsexuality boasting Mae West, Raquel Welch, Rex Reed, and soon-to-be emerging stars Farrah Fawcett and Tom Selleck.

School of Fellini

While Sarne seemed schooled in the Ken Russell style of filmmaking, punctuating both pictures with elaborate fantasy sequences, kooky camerawork, and sledgehammer-like delivery of messages, the young filmmaker was actually trying to emulate Italian maestro Federico Fellini.

"I thought, 'I can't be the greatest director around, because there's Fellini,'" he said in a 1989 interview in a video documentary called *Cult People.* "Then I was amazed to find out that not everyone loved Fellini. I didn't understand how people could not recognize his greatness."

As for *Joanna,* Sarne said, "I wasn't consciously trying to make it a piece of psychedelia; it was just that this trend was hitting at the same time we were making the movie. It was supposed to be like looking through the world in rose-colored spectacles. I wanted it to be intentionally misleading, that you have this girl who gets most things wrong but sees the world in a tremendously romantic way. That's why I wanted her fantasies to look like commercials, like a young girl's fantasies."

Vidal Signs

Sarne labeled his decision to come to the United States to adapt Gore Vidal's best-selling novel *Myra Breckinridge* "a big mistake."

"I inherited some very bad press because things were cut [by the studio] and not done as delicately as I wrote them.

"Still," he said, "the lines that I put in that are intentionally corny played great with audiences."

Despite a troubled production topped by a much-publicized feud between his two sex-symbol leads and a critical and financial drubbing that put a temporary halt to Sarne's once-promising directing career, Sarne said working with the legendary West on *Myra Breckinridge* was a memorable experience.

"I remember that I wrote her a letter to be in the film," he said. "She gave the letter to her spiritualist. 'What do you think?' she asked him. He said, 'This man is quite determined to get you in the picture.' Mae said that the letter was vibrating in his hand. She then decided to make the movie."

Since *Myra Breckinridge,* Sarne has directed a few movies (1993's *The Punk* and the 1995 rockumentary *Glastonbury the Movie* among them). But no matter what he does, Sarne will always be remembered as the man who brought the one-of-a-kind *Myra Breckinridge* to life on the screen—for better or worse.

the movie's abrupt fade-out. The film didn't come close to getting its $10 million budget back. Reviews were horrendous. *Variety* said the movie's "bad taste is beyond belief," while *Time* called the movie "some sort of nadir in American cinema." Vidal headed out of the country midway through production and disowned the film entirely, while Reed said he had no idea what the filmmaker was up to, claiming he was told the movie was akin to *The Secret Life of Walter Mitty*. Meanwhile, both Loretta Young (who sued) and Shirley Temple were appalled that clips of their films were used in such a trashy effort.

While designed for youthful audiences, *Myra Breckinridge*'s film clips, references to old movies, and lavish production work (which includes costumes by Edith Head) are definitely from the traditional Hollywood mold. So why did Fox bother in the first place?

Today, *Myra Breckinridge* remains as notorious as when it was released, though it could be said that its notoriety is a vestige of its original reception. Websites admonishing and admiring the picture at the same time can be found on the Internet. The gay community seems to love the picture, particularly for its camp content.

But while it played periodically on cable, it wasn't available on home video for decades. This issue has been remedied with a deluxe DVD edition issued by Fox in 2004, complete with a pristine, widescreen version of the film and commentaries by Welch and Sarne. Lovers of bad cinema can now have a field day with the film's torrent of terribleness, again and again, in all of its rancid glory. Being a masochist will definitely have an effect on where you stand on the *Myra* meter.

1970 (R) 94m/C Raquel Welch, Mae West, John Huston, Rex Reed, Farrah Fawcett, Roger Herren, Roger C. Carmel, John Carradine, Tom Selleck, Andy Devine, Grady Sutton, Calvin Lockhart. *D:* Michael Sarne. *W:* Michael Sarne, David Giler. *C:* Richard Moore. *M:* Lionel Newman. *VHS, DVD*
AKA: Gore Vidal's Myra Breckinridge

Three in the Attic ♪♪♥

How can one discard a semi-hip lava-lamp relic like *Three in the Attic* as mere sexploitation sleaze when it quotes Kierkegaard, Zola, and Genet? Or when the leading man shows more flesh than his three fantasy love interests?

"My name is Paxton Quigley. I'm the first casualty in the sexual revolution," narrates actor Christopher Jones from his attic prison at the beginning of the movie. At an eastern college, WASPy Paxton is a guitar-toting campus Casanova, but, unlike his frat-house brothers, he's not without an intellect. When he sees beautiful coed Tobey (then-twenty-six-year-old Yvette Mimieux), his ability to rattle off famous philosophers and their views on marriage (mostly against) wins the girl's ardor. Their summer idyll—note on-location footage of counterculture hub Provincetown, Massachusetts—turns uncomfortable for Paxton when Tobey's uptight parents intrude and when Tobey starts shopping around for an apartment in hopes of settling down.

Paxton then meets Eulice (Judy Pace), an African American–Southern belle–progressive-hippie–social worker (quite a combo, even for the '60s) from a nearby women's college who finds him a refreshing alternative to strident black militants and "white Negro" wanna-bes. He poses nude for a portrait she paints and gives in to her honey-dipped flirtations. Then the hero literally stumbles across another student at the women's college—Jan (Maggie Thrett), a neurotic but sexually available Jewish boho chick. For a time Paxton carries on regular liaisons with all three—until Tobey spots Eulice's painting and puts the pieces together. The three betrayed women lock Paxton in an attic and try to pleasure the cad to death with too much sex, conveyed through trippy montage sequences that are more suggestive than explicit. When school administrators figure out what's going on, the girls show mercy to their captive and release him. Paxton staggers out of an infirmary bed and after the one he really loves: Tobey.

If this seems like a job for some hip, New Hollywood filmmakers to bring to the screen, you're right—it is. Behind the camera, however, were a few old schoolers: director Richard Wilson (*Invitation to a Gunfighter*), a protégé of Orson Welles, and cinematographer J. Burgi Contner, whose career dated back to the 1930s. Their involvement with the swinging material makes for an uneasy alliance. No wonder screenwriter Stephen Yafa did not appreciate the eventual treatment of his work and disassociated himself from the results, despite surprisingly witty dialogue and an intelligence that plays today on a higher cerebral level than the whole *American Pie* series put together. Still, even the original distributor didn't know how to pitch *Three in the Attic*. This ambivalence comes across in a cartoon coda, obviously tacked on as an afterthought over the end credits, in which abstract line drawings show a middle-aged husband and his kvetching wife heading home after watching the movie. Imagine the Flintstones in a bull session after *The Graduate*.

How much you like *Three in the Attic* probably depends on your reaction to Paxton himself, a rake who shows signs of vestigial conscience but really sees himself more as a victim of the three girlfriends than their offender. *Wild in the Streets* star Jones, once married to *Psych-Out* leading lady Susan Strasberg and considered an inheritor of James Dean's rebel mantle, largely withdrew from film activity after the Charles Manson murders that claimed the life of another one of his offscreen associates, Sharon Tate.

Three in the Attic was enough of a success for the distributor, American International Pictures, to repackage a 1970 satire of sex and politics, *Up in the Cellar*, as *Three in the Cellar*, promoting it as a follow-up to *Three in the Attic*. The only pure link in this film, directed by Theodore J. Flicker (*The President's Analyst*) and featuring Larry Hagman and Joan Collins, was cast member Judy Pace.

1968 (R) 90m/C Christopher Jones, Yvette Mimieux, Judy Pace, Maggie Thrett, Nan Martin, Michael Beck. **D:** Richard Wilson. **W:** Stephen Yafa. **C:** J. Burgi Contner. **M:** Chad Stuart. *VHS*

—*Charles A. Cassady Jr.*

Wonderwall 🦴🦴🦴

The Peeping Tom is a time-honored figure in soft-core porn movies. In the '60s and early '70s, the British cinema had a particularly privileged relationship with the character, producing one of the best-ever voyeur thrillers (*Peeping Tom*) and a series of saucy (read: tame) sex farces (*Confessions of a Window Cleaner, Adventures of a Taxi Driver*). A few years before the confessions and adventures began, *Wonderwall,* a wondrously hallucinatory little number, appeared at British cinemas. It's best known for its score by the "quiet Beatle"—to the extent that one early home-video release titled it *George Harrison's Wonderwall*—but its cartoonlike psychedelic visuals and brash ogling of its minidress-clad star Jane Birkin make it well worth checking out.

Absent-minded professor Collins (Jack MacGowran) centers his whole life around his studies. One day he hears Indian music coming from the apartment next door, and he discovers a hole in the wall that allows him to observe his neighbor, a fashion model named Penny Lane (Jane Birkin). The professor begins to stay home from work and create more holes in his wall, all the better to study Penny's activities: photo shoots, parties, and making love with her photographer boyfriend (Iain Quarrier). The two don't cross paths until the mock-melodramatic climax, in which a distraught Penny attempts suicide, but the chameleon-like model stars in all the professor's dreams and fantasies—he even sees her floating on the slides he studies under his microscope.

Wonderwall does benefit greatly from Harrison's jubilant, sitar-drenched soundtrack, which was released in 1968 as the first album on the Beatles' Apple label. The music, in fact, provides the first sign that *Wonderwall* won't be just another Peeping Tom farce: as director Joe Massot's visuals turn more and more psychedelic, Harrison's hypnotic sounds—supplemented by Eric Clapton's guitar in one photo-shoot sequence—convey the nature of the internal "trip" the professor has embarked upon. A standard orchestral score wouldn't have cut it, for instance, in the scene where the professor's butterfly collection comes back to life (via animation) and flies away, or during the dream duel he has with Penny's boyfriend in which both yield consumer products (cigarettes, tubes of lipstick) as weapons.

The film's connection with the Fab Four having been thoroughly established (one gets the impression George winced at Birkin's character name), it must be noted that *Wonderwall* also has strong ties to the work of Roman Polanski. First, MacGowran and Quarrier had starred in both *The Fearless Vampire Killers* and *Cul-de-sac*. Also, the film's scenario was devised by Gerard Brach, Polanski's coscripter for most of the '60s and '70s.

Structured like many other "conceptual" mind-benders of its time, *Wonderwall* benefits from Massot's singularly bizarre imagination; the director contributed to the script of *Zachariah* and later helmed *The Song Remains the Same* (1976) and the ska chronicle *Dance Crazy* (1982). From the premise (a reserved intellectual breaks down the wall that serves as a barrier to uninhibited behavior—get it?) to the inclusion of silent-film slapstick to the open-ended finale (in which space *is* the final frontier), *Wonderwall* is a quintessential '60s flick. The crowning glory is its psychedelic intertitles, which also evoke silent movies ("What the Young Man Doesn't Know..."); these intertitles come courtesy of "the Fool," a Dutch collective of artists who designed clothes for the Beatles and painted the facade of the short-lived Apple Boutique in London.

MacGowran delivers a fine comedic performance as the Einstein-coiffed Collins, but a film about a voyeur wouldn't be any fun without someone nice to spy on. Birkin fits the bill quite well, as she looks splendid in the ultramod fashions designed by the Fool. She appears here during an interesting point in her career: right between her "dolly bird" phase (which culminated in a memorable supporting turn in *Blow-Up*) and her rebirth as the Lolita-like muse of French musical genius Serge Gainsbourg. The eye-catching tableaux in which Massot places Jane guarantees MacGowran has a lot more to gape at than your average window cleaner or taxi driver.

1968 (NR) 85m/C Jack MacGowran, Jane Birkin, Irene Handl, Richard Wattis, Iain Quarrier, Beatrix Lehmann. *D:* Joe Massot. *W:* Gerard Brach, G. Cabrera Infante. *C:* Harry Waxman. *M:* George Harrison. *VHS, DVD*
AKA: Wonderwall: The Movie

—*Ed Grant*

Chapter 16

England Swings

New York had Andy Warhol and the Factory scene, the underground film movement, and Greenwich Village. San Francisco had the hippies, acid rock, and Haight-Ashbury. And London? Well, London had lots of the above, along with mods and rockers, trendsetting fashions, gorgeous female models and handsome up-and-coming male scenemakers, wild discotheques, the Beatles, the Stones, Carnaby Street. London had it all as well as its own identity. London swung.

In terms of filmmaking, England's postwar cinematic movement began to shake things up almost overnight. The late 1950s and early 1960s saw a renaissance of British filmmaking. New, talented directors such as Tony Richardson, Karel Reisz (a Czech émigré), John Schlesinger, and Lindsay Anderson began making serious, personal pictures concerning "moral realism," often focusing on troubled youth and social problems typically ignored by British filmmakers in the past. Their efforts, which include *Look Back in Anger* (1958), *Room at the Top* (1959), *Saturday Night and Sunday Morning* (1960), *The Loneliness of the Long Distance Runner* (1962), and *This Sporting Life* (1963), were part of the "Free Cinema" movement, nicknamed "kitchen sink" films because of their focus on working-class problems in domestic settings.

Further into the decade, the vitality of the increasingly swinging city of London was finding its way into numerous films. Ironically, one of the leading pioneers of all this newfound energy was an American: director Richard Lester, whose two hits with the Beatles, 1964's *A Hard Days' Night* and 1965's *Help!,* led the way, boldly meshing style, technique, and the fresh enthusiasm of a younger generation. Lester's successful work also inspired the now-established veterans of the Free Cinema movement to set their cameras on youth as well. Anderson's *If. . . .* delivered a powerful indictment of the British school system, Schlesinger's *Darling* captured the decadence of London through the actions of sexually adventurous model Julie Christie, and Reisz's *Morgan: A Suitable Case for Treatment* looked at the offbeat foibles of a working-class artist trying to win back his much-loved former wife. Richardson also helped get things rolling, pre-dating the Beatles films with the Oscar-winning *Tom Jones,* which applied many forms of technical trickery to Henry Fielding's eighteenth-century source material.

Along with such up-and-coming directors, British cinema offered a dazzling array of young acting talent, most classically trained, who quickly found popularity and, in many cases, international success. In addition to the daughters of British actor Michael Redgrave—Vanessa, winning accolades for her work in *Morgan: A Suitable Case for Treatment* and *Blow-Up,* and Lynn, a picture of confused youth in *Georgy Girl* and *Smashing Time*—there were such talented up-and-comers as Oliver Reed, Albert Finney, Alan Bates, David Hemmings, Michael Crawford, Albert Finney, former roommates Michael Caine and Terence Stamp, Rita Tushingham, Susannah York, Judy Geeson, Jacqueline Bisset, Suzy Kendall, and party girl/Mick Jagger girlfriend/actress/singer Marianne Faithfull.

As Richard Lester proved, you didn't have to be British to capture the flavor or energy of London in the '60s. With *Blow-Up,* Italy's Michelangelo Antonioni soaked up all the decadence of the city in '65, but he also burst its bubble in his depiction of David Hemmings's jaded fashion photographer, a bloke who has it all at his fingertips but has grown numb from the hedonism playing out all around him. On a lighter note, American Stanley Donen's *Bedazzled* found London, circa 1967, a place of great opportunity for depressed short-order cook Dudley Moore—provided he makes a deal with the Devil (Peter Cook) to give up his soul in order to win the hand of a waitress he's in love with. Well, at least he had Raquel Welch in red lingerie as Lilian Lust to introduce him to the Seven Deadly Sins.

Austin Powers would've certainly approved.

Alfie 🎵🎵🎵🎵

"I suppose you think you're going to see the bleedin' titles now. Well you're not. So you can relax." From the opening scene when Michael Caine, as cockney rake Alfie Elkins, coshes his way through the Fourth Wall and starts speaking directly to the viewer as if to a drinking buddy in the local pub, you know you're watching a star in the making. Caine went from supporting player to durable international lead thanks to his work in this tragicomic morality tale about amorality, set in a gritty, jazzy 1960s London.

Alfie has its origins in a stage play by Bill Naughton. Actors had been addressing audiences from the proscenium even before Shakespeare came along, but the technique was relatively new and fresh in cinema. Director Lewis Gilbert (*You Only Live Twice, Educating Rita*) exploited it well. Indeed, it's hard to tell whether Caine is talking to the audience or to another character in the film.

Alfie Elkins is a charming but self-centered bloke who, in the prologue, is compared to a scruffy alley dog that goes from bitch to bitch. A Rolls Royce chauffeur and casual gigolo, Alfie drifts from one love affair to another, concerned primarily with his own pleasure and trying to avoid anything like emotional entanglement with his "birds."

He keeps working-class Gilda (Julia Foster) stringing along as his fall-back girl. When she gets pregnant and gives birth to a boy, Alfie becomes a doting but strictly part-time father. Due to his refusal to commit, Alfie loses Gilda (and the kid) to a more marriage-minded suitor. Diagnosed with a lung infection, Alfie spends time in a country sanatorium. Here he archly observes other invalids and their spouses and cheekily seduces both the nursing staff and Lily (Vivien Merchant), the wife of a patient he has befriended.

"It don't do to get attached to nobody in this life," says Alfie, who uses rampant womanizing to stave off his own fear of pain and betrayal. So 'ard-'earted is this ladies' man that he refers to women throughout with the pronoun "it," never "she." "She or it, they're all birds," he declares. And in Alfie's (feeble) defense, the majority of females he comes across seem pliant, spirit-

Michael Caine happily goes from bird to bird, including Shelley Winters, in his star-making turn in *Alfie*.

less creatures who willingly turn into doormats for him and show whining concern for his welfare even as he chases them out the door. The one exception to all this is Ruby (Shelley Winters), a rich American who uses Alfie strictly for bedroom fun. "She don't ever mention love," he says, admiringly.

There are times when Caine looks utterly demonic, a walking pool of lust in a picture without nudity or overt sex. But his comeuppance arrives, more or less. After one of his pickups (played by Jane Asher, who offscreen was a longtime steady of Paul McCartney) walks out, Lily reappears, inconveniently pregnant with Alfie's baby. Alfie finds a seedy specialist (Denholm Elliott) who illegally performs an abortion, a painful ordeal that leaves Alfie himself deeply shaken. He goes back to Ruby, only to find she's replaced him with a younger, long-haired musician. Alone and rejected, Alfie admits that despite his protective layer of hedonism, "I ain't got me peace of mind. And if you ain't got that, you ain't got nothing. So what's it all about?"

Caine took the lead role after it had been turned down by a number of rising British stars, including Terence Stamp (Caine's former roommate) and Anthony Newley. The actor was nominated for an Academy Award, as were Merchant, Naughton, and the film itself (the latter lost to *A Man for All Seasons*). Alfie Elkins is a character for all seasons, evidenced by word of an *Alfie* remake in the works, starring Jude Law. But can the character survive feminism and political correctness? And will we be able to erase Caine from our cinematic consciousness? Unlikely, but we'll have to wait and see the new version of the story to know what it's all about.

1966 (R) 114m/C *UK* Michael Caine, Shelley Winters, Millicent Martin, Jane Asher, Julia Foster, Shirley Anne Field, Vivien Merchant, Eleanor Bron, Denholm Elliott, Alfie Bass, Graham Stark. *D:* Lewis Gilbert. *W:* Bill Naughton. *C:* Otto Heller. *M:* Sonny Rollins. *VHS, DVD*

Bedazzled ♫♫♫♪

Bedazzled is a deliciously *Devil and Daniel Webster*–ish tale. On the surface it's a snapshot of the mod London scene, but underneath lies a timeless—if sometimes inconsistent—screwball comedy in the vein of Preston Sturges's *Unfaithfully Yours* (which, coincidentally, Dudley Moore remade in 1984).

Short-order cook Stanley Moon (Moore) pines for waitress Margaret Spencer (Eleanor Bron), but he's much too timid to act on his desires. Moore, who made a career out of playing hapless twits (think *10*), is ideal for the role, especially since this early interpretation of the proverbial lovelorn chump employs few of the thespian ticks he would trot out later in his career.

Suicide looks like a tempting solution to Stanley's woes, but then the Devil appears in the form of George Spiggott (Peter Cook), who offers Moon the sun and the stars—in other words, seven wishes. Stanley uses the wishes to further his love for Margaret, but Spiggott's clever interpretation of the pact manages to defuse every love bomb that Stanley lobs at his potential mate. And, naturally, a soulful IOU is attached to the bargain.

Literally damned if he does and damned if he doesn't, Stanley continues to pursue his fruitless wish list, whittling down his options as he wastes precious time as a rock star, a fly on the wall, and—vainly grasping for some peace and quiet—a nun.

While Stanley's spiraling vortex of wish-unfulfillment provides situation-driven amusement, there's another level of humor at work here, in the form of philosophically pointed barbs of dialogue exchanged between Spiggott and Moon.

In the '60s, this kind of cheeky comedy was considered big-screen controversy. And though Moore and Cook (along with Spike *The Goon Show* Milligan) pioneered such off-kilter humor (clearly laying the foundation for *Monty Python's Life of Brian*), the irreverent duo split the team before they could hatch a truly comic masterpiece.

Coyly skirting what could have been patently offensive material, director Stanley Donen (previously known for stylish thrillers like *Charade* and classic musicals like *Singin' in the Rain*) deftly handles the playfulness with his customary light touch. This accomplishment becomes even more impressive when you compare this film to its clunky 2000 remake with Brendan Fraser and Elizabeth Hurley.

> **"You see, a soul's rather like your appendix: totally expendable."**
>
> —Peter Cook as George Spiggott (the Devil), in *Bedazzled*

RICHARD LESTER: THE SCREEN JESTER

Even with an impressive list of credits behind him, Richard Lester will always be known as "the man who shot the Beatles."

A Philadelphia native who relocated to Europe in the 1950s, Lester directed the Fab Four films *A Hard Day's Night* and *Help!* and since then his name has been synonymous with John, Paul, George, Ringo, and London in the swinging '60s. Before 1964's *A Hard Day's Night*, Lester made a name for himself in British TV, working with Peter Sellers, Spike Milligan, and others on the popular *Goon Show* and its spin-offs, as well as hosting his own show called *The Dick Lester Show*. His first cinematic experience came with *The Running, Jumping & Standing Still Film*, a frantic eleven-minute short that saluted silent comedies and garnered an Oscar nomination.

Meeting the Beatles

After helming the hip mix of fiction and rockumentary called *It's Trad, Dad!* in 1961 and 1963's *The Mouse on the Moon*, a pseudo-sequel to the Sellers smash *The Mouse That Roared*, Lester's energy and inventiveness helped get him the plumb assignment from producer Walter Shenson of making a movie about and starring the Beatles. As he began to film 1964's *A Hard Day's Night* with a script by old pal Alun Owen, Beatlemania broke out. Lester decided to include the public's fanaticism over the boys from Liverpool in the story involving Paul's fictitious "clean old man" grandfather. The B&W mix of make-believe scenes, musical sequences, press conferences, slapstick shtick, cinema vérité footage of the band on the run, and the Beatles' charisma turned it into a smash hit and a classic rock film.

Lester got the call from Shenson for a follow-up, which he delivered in the form of *Help!* the very next year. Shot as the Beatles began to experiment with drugs, the colorful comic fantasy focuses on an ancient religious cult's attempt to get a ring worn by Ringo. Along with its bouncy soundtrack, the film boasts chase hijinks in London, the Alps, and the Bahamas, and was enlivened by the band as well as by such talented British performers as Leo McKern, Victor Spinetti, Roy Kinnear, Eleanor Bron, and Alfie Bass.

Discussing the Beatles' approach to acting while making *Help!* Lester told author/director Steven Soderbergh in his book-length interview *Getting Away with It: Or, the Further Adventures of the Luckiest Bastard You Ever Saw:* "Ringo, because his was the showy part, was always the odd one out, so he was given characteristics that were more sympathetic. John, I don't think, was interested, and didn't even bother. Paul was interested and tried too hard, and George was always the one that was forgotten. He just did it and got on with it."

The Knack . . . and How to Use It, also released in 1965, was Lester's satiric tale of bachelorhood at the dawn of swinging London. It won critical and audience favor, winning the coveted Palm d'Or prize at the Cannes Film Festival.

After Beatlemania

Riding high on a series of commercial and critical hits, Lester ventured into larger-budget territory with his adaptation of the Broadway musical farce *A Funny Thing Happened on the Way to the Forum.* The filmmaker's love for silent comedy is evident throughout the frenetic proceedings, which feature Zero Mostel as a wheeling-dealing slave in ancient Greece as well as Lester's idol, Buster Keaton. Mixed reviews and lukewarm box office greeted the project, which dismayed fans of the play because it ditches a portion of Stephen Sondheim's award-winning score.

Two antiwar satires followed: the Vietnam-influenced *How I Won the War,* with John Lennon and future *Phantom of the Opera* (and *Knack* and *Forum*) star Michael Crawford, and *The Bed Sitting Room,* a post–World War III journey into surrealism with comedy team Peter Cook and Dudley Moore. Neither clicked, but sandwiched between them in 1968 was the more successful *Petulia.* Lester returned to the States to make this edgy San Francisco–based seriocomedy about screwed-up relationships, featuring Julie Christie, George C. Scott, and Richard Chamberlain. Although garnering mixed reviews at the time, it is now considered to be one of Lester's best pictures.

Swords and Superman

With none of his recent efforts drawing crowds, Lester found work directing TV commercials in Italy until he got the assignment of helming the all-star swashbuckler yarns *The Three Musketeers* and *The Four Musketeers* for producers Ilya and Alexander Salkind. Despite a flap with the siblings over payment, the Salkinds later recruited Lester to help out on the *Superman* movies: Lester served as an adviser on *Superman,* handling postproduction chores on the film when original director Richard Donner bid adieu, and then he directed the cartoonish second and unsuccessful third entries in the popular series.

Over the years, Lester has brought his talents to a wide range of genres, including disaster pictures (*Juggernaut*), westerns (the prequel *Butch and Sundance: The Early Years*), period romances (*Robin and Marian* with Sean Connery as Robin Hood and Audrey Hepburn as Maid Marian), and historical dramas (*Cuba,* also with Connery).

Lester's final two credits were 1989's *Return of the Musketeers,* his third "all for one/one for all" epic (his friend Roy Kinnear died of an accident during production) and 1991's *Get Back,* a concert film of Paul McCartney. Now in his seventies, Lester lives comfortably in Europe in self-imposed retirement.

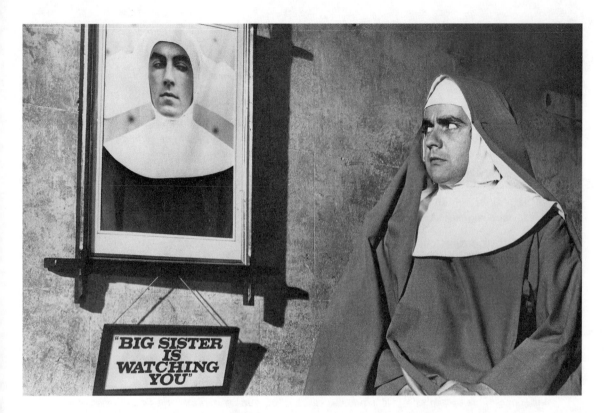

Although the screenplay tends to meander now and again, so did Cook and Moore, and *Bedazzled* remains a testament to their droll sensibilities. Lucky for us, it's also a nostalgia trip through the swinging London of the '60s—a time long before Austin Powers had his first pair of paisley diapers.

1967 104m/C *UK* Peter Cook, Dudley Moore, Eleanor Bron, Raquel Welch, Michael Bates, Alba, Barry Humphries. *D:* Stanley Donen. *W:* Peter Cook, Dudley Moore. *C:* Austin Dempster. *M:* Dudley Moore. *VHS, DVD*

—*Steven Austin*

Blow-Up 🦴🦴🦴

f it weren't for *Blow-Up,* we would have never had Francis Ford Coppola's *The Conversation,* Brian De Palma's *Blow Out,* Austin Powers's shutterbug antics, or any of the hundreds of direct-to-video erotic thrillers.

So, we can either thank or hiss at director Michelangelo Antonioni, the Italian master behind *L'Eclipse, L'Aventura,* and *Red Desert,* who decided to make *Blow-Up* his first English-language project. Bringing his studied and enigmatic style to a mod, mod, mod world, Antonioni fashioned a film that inspired many of the key young filmmakers coming of age in the 1960s and continues to intrigue audiences today.

The setting is swinging London. Thomas (David Hemmings), an arrogant fashion photographer, doesn't care if success has left him passionless. Even a seductive shoot with a gorgeous model (played by real-life poser Veruschka von Lendhorff) and a coterie of young woman begging for him to capture their beauty with his camera can't inspire Thomas, who takes no pleasure in and receives no sense of accomplishment from his work.

While out strolling one afternoon, the photographer spies a middle-aged man and younger woman embracing in a nearby park. Thomas begins clicking pictures of them. When the woman approaches him, asking him to stop, he continues snapping more photos. She claims she has the right to privacy. His rebuttal is that since taking pictures is his occupation, he has every right to do what he's doing. She demands the negatives, but he refuses.

The woman, whose name we learn is Jane (Vanessa Redgrave), later pays a visit to Thomas, again requesting the negatives. He tries to ignore her, but Jane means business this time and appears willing to seduce him to get what she wants. Not to be outdone, Thomas agrees to give Jane the negatives—duplicate negatives. But before the seduction is consummated, an interruption sends her out the door.

The episode seems to awaken the twin sleeping giants of artistry and passion in Thomas. Upon inspecting the photographs, he notices something in one of the bushes in the background. He blows the images up larger, suddenly seeing things he hadn't before—perhaps a gun? Thomas feverishly reconstructs the photos, closely inspecting one after another, soon believing he has accidentally photographed a murder. Obsession takes over. He now realizes why Jane was so adamant about retrieving the negatives, but he can't contact her—the phone number she left him is wrong.

A trip to the park where Thomas shot the photos leads to the discovery of a man's dead body. Did Thomas witness a murder? And, if so, can he prove it? Even his photographic evidence can't provide answers he desperately needs.

The film inspires these and many other questions but supplies precious few resolutions. Making things even more frustrating for those looking for definitive explanations is the film's memorably weird ending, which involves mimes, an invisible tennis ball, and a thoroughly bewildered Thomas. Such open-endedness was new to mainstream American audiences who, in 1966, were not used to vague, interpretive entertainment. Also new was Antonioni's intense attention to detail and color. *Blow-Up* divided critics in the United States (after mostly pans in England) but proved to be a box-office success stateside by giving college audiences, sophisticates, and older moviegoers a cerebral experience while also offering them a peak at the decadence of London with its drugs, rock music (the Yardbirds appear in a nightclub in the film), eye-opening fashions, and casual attitude toward nudity and sex. In many ways, *Blow-Up* was the "it" movie of its time, a thriller without many thrills, a mystery with no clear solution.

Antonioni's previous works had been deemed impenetrable to American movie fans, except for a select group of cinephiles. So it made sense for MGM to market the film on its sex quotient, with images of Redgrave's naked

torso covered by her crisscrossed arms displayed prominently in posters. But the scene in which the actress—who was just coming into her own with key roles in *Anne of a Thousand Days* and *Morgan: A Suitable Case for Treatment*—tries to seduce Hemmings doesn't even rate as a tease. Meanwhile, the other talked-about "adult" scene—featuring Jane Birkin and Gillian Hills as wanna-be models who tumble around on a paper photo backdrop before bedding Hemmings—offers little more than brief nudity.

While not as steamy as promised, *Blow-Up* proved provocative in other ways—ways that clicked with a new generation of moviegoers who settled for foreign food-for-thought in lieu of the promised sizzle.

1966 111m/C *UK/IT* David Hemmings, Vanessa Redgrave, Sarah Miles, John Castle, Jane Birkin, Gillian Hills, Veruschka von Lendhorff. **D:** Michelangelo Antonioni. **W:** Michelangelo Antonioni, Tonino Guerra. **C:** Carlo Di Palma. **M:** Herbie Hancock. *VHS, DVD*

Georgy Girl ♫♫♫

"Hey there, Georgy Girl / Dreaming of the someone you could be. . . ." Boasting one of the catchiest movie themes of the 1960s, *Georgy Girl* blends the "kitchen sink" genre (no angry young men on display here, however) with class-conscious British comedy and a healthy dose of girly romanticism. Various critics—and the folks on the brilliant *SCTV*—have noted that the most common plot twist in British dramas of the 1960s involved the antihero accidentally impregnating his girlfriend. *Georgy Girl* tells the story of a young woman who'd *love* to have a "bun in her oven" but will settle for raising her friend's baby.

Dowdy Georgina (Lynn Redgrave) is the twenty-something daughter of two servants who work for millionaire James Leamington (James Mason); though nearly three decades her senior, Leamington has eyes for Georgy. A nursery school teacher, our heroine rooms with her bitchy violinist friend, Meredith (Charlotte Rampling), who casually dates the preternaturally jolly Jos (Alan Bates). When Meredith declares that she's pregnant, Jos dutifully marries her, but he soon discovers that he likes Georgy a whole lot better. In a mercenary deal, Georgy agrees to become Leamington's mistress if he will pay for Meredith's delivery. Georgy and Jos become involved while Meredith is in the hospital, but it's no matter—upon coming home, the violinist announces her intention to split the scene and abandon her newborn daughter. Georgy is left with two options: try to hang on to the affectionate but commitment-phobic Jos or opt for the stable and very dull Leamington, whose newly widowed status would make him a proper "father" for Georgy's infant charge.

In *Darling* (1965), Julie Christie may have played the jaded, fashionable kind of girl that many young women wanted to be, but Redgrave's Georgy was intended to be a reflection of the way they really *felt*. The film is essentially a fairy tale, and so ugly ducklings everywhere can take heart in Georgy's blossoming during her relationship with Jos. She is never completely "transformed,"

David Hemmings plays a jaded fashion photographer who gets caught up in a murderous mystery in Michelangelo Antonioni's *Blow-Up*. MGM / THE KOBAL COLLECTION

Lynn Redgrave (flanked by James Mason, left, and Bill Owen) searches for a measure of happiness as the title character of *Georgy Girl*.

though, as is the case in numerous similar tales—compromises are a fact of life for our girl, and she continually endures put-downs from her parents, Meredith, and even her beloved Jos, who tells her, "You just missed being beautiful."

The kitchen-sink film that best presents the female perspective on the unintended-pregnancy issue was *A Taste of Honey* (1961). *Georgy Girl* offers a very different take on the problem (in this case, the female lead isn't even the "afflicted"). Yet the fact that Georgy is an unconventional heroine, a plus-size girl who has a solid working-class background, links the film to *Honey* and several other bun-in-the-oven classics like *A Kind of Loving* (the 1962 movie that featured one of Bates's first starring roles). Director Silvio Narizzano walks a fine line between humor and sentiment throughout, making it all the more surprising and disappointing that he never again made a film that received as much international favor as this one. His only other notable works are *Die! Die! My Darling* (1965) and the movie version of Joe Orton's *Loot* (1970).

One of Narizzano's greatest triumphs is the film's casting. Mason is both sleazy and sadly sympathetic as Leamington, while the three young leads are nothing less than dazzling. Rampling is uncommonly sexy and lacer   atingly evil as Meredith, and Bates exudes youthful energy as he simultaneously romances Georgy and strings her along. Redgrave makes the greatest impression in her star-making turn as she conveys Georgy's subtly willful side as well as her vulnerability. And then, of course, there's that theme song. A number-one hit in the United States, written by Tom Springfield and actor Jim

Dale, it deftly encapsulates the movie's entire plot in a few unforgettably bouncy verses: "You're always window shopping / But never stopping to buy / So shed those dowdy feathers and fly / A little bit."

1966 100m/B *UK* Lynn Redgrave, James Mason, Alan Bates, Charlotte Rampling, Bill Owen. **D:** Silvio Narizzano. **W:** Margaret Foster, Peter Nichols. **C:** Ken Higgins. **M:** Alexander Faris. *VHS, DVD*

—Ed Grant

I'll Never Forget What's 'isname ♪♪♪

F ew actors get to make as spiffy an entrance as Oliver Reed does in this very British sod-the-rat-race drama. Striding purposefully through 1960s London in his business suit with a gleaming axe over his shoulder and a twangy Francis Lai score in the background, Reed enters a high-rise office building and promptly smashes a hardwood desk to bits.

Reed plays Andrew Quint, a successful director of commercials for a giant ad agency run by the domineering Jonathan Lute (Orson Welles). At thirty-two, Quint has decided he's had enough and wants to quit. That decision includes separating from his dispirited wife (Wendy Craig) and breaking up with various free-spirited mistresses (one of whom is played by singer and actress Marianne Faithfull, then notorious as Mick Jagger's girlfriend and partner-in-decadence).

Quint tries to adapt to a satisfying, downscale job at *Gadfly,* a literary journal run by his old school buddy, Gerald (Harry Andrews). But there he meets Georgina (Carol White), a friendly secretary, and even though she's already engaged—and he's supposedly put his philandering ways behind him along with everything else—they wind up falling for each other. Meanwhile, Lute can't abide his star employee running out on him, so the ad baron merely takes over *Gadfly* and all its assets. To free himself once and for all, Quint creates a subversive commercial for a new Japanese 8-mm movie camera, full of disturbing Felliniesque imagery, revenge fantasies, and cruel ambushes on his exes. Just like in *The Producers,* what was meant to be a surefire flop instead becomes a hit, earning the Lute Agency a long-sought award. (Of course, it helps that Jonathan bribed the judges.) Alas, tragic circumstances ensue, and the toll of what has occurred to Quint leads to a troubling, ambiguous ending.

Director Michael Winner's quirky, jumpy camera edits enliven a witty script that somewhat falls between the seats of the "angry young man" school of realistic British drama and the burgeoning "tune in, turn on, drop out" psychedelia that was starting to juice the U.K. films of the time. Without a commune or a cause to cling to, Quint's one-man revolution looks pretty bleak, and the hero's determined attempts to shed the banalities of his comfy, modern metropolitan existence and find himself amount to revisiting the English schools he attended as a youth. Once there, Quint finds that the bullies of yesteryear are still bullying today, while his old teachers and mentors are either perverted poltroons or doddering deans who can't even remember his name—

Andrew Quint (Oliver Reed) tries to run away from his comfortable existence and into the arms of Georgina (Carol White) in *I'll Never Forget What's 'isname.*

UNIVERSAL / THE KOBAL COLLECTION

though the movie's title, according to director Winner, does not refer to this scene but rather was cooked up apropos of nothing by a cameraman on another project and sold to the filmmaker right off for fifty quid.

The great Orson Welles, top-billed in a supporting part, has one of the better roles of his later career; certainly there's more thespian meat to Jonathan Lute than there was to Le Chiffre in *Casino Royale.* The movie's parade of glamorous, pliant females, adorned in the latest "dolly bird" fashions, smacks of male wish-fulfillment sexism, but it's par for the period. As Georgina, despite her availability to Quint, is also sexually uptight (go figure), Reed indulges in some off-camera stimulation of her erogenous zones; this and other instances of immorality led to *I'll Never Forget What's 'isname* being condemned by the Catholic Legion of Decency in the United States. That seal of disapproval and the film's innate Britishness mean the film isn't particularly well known on Yankee soil, but the curious, and all fans of Reed and Welles, should dig it up. The DVD version includes the original trailer and a generous '60s London 101 commentary by the urbane director, who later found his greatest fame with the very un-British *Death Wish* movies.

1967 97m/C *UK* Oliver Reed, Carol White, Orson Welles, Wendy Craig, Harry Andrews, Michael Hordern, Marianne Faithfull, Ann Lynn, Frank Finlay. **D:** Michael Winner. **W:** Peter Draper. **C:** Otto Heller. **M:** Francis Lai. *VHS, DVD*

—*Charles A. Cassady Jr.*

The Magic Christian ♫♫♫

Surely one of the strangest films to be shown at a gala premiere for Britain's royal family, this proto-Pythonesque adaptation of Terry Southern's semi-free-form short novel tells the tale of the ultimate Merry Prankster, Guy Grand (Peter Sellers). Sellers sedately portrays the obscenely rich magnate, whose morning routine in Mayfair is contrasted with the vagrancy of a young tramp (Ringo Starr) brushing his teeth in the Buckingham Palace fountain. Grand happens upon the youth and impulsively adopts the lad, naming him Youngman Grand. What passes for plot more or less involves Youngman's apprenticeship, as he witnesses Dad's idea of fun.

Guy Grand proves that money can and does corrupt everybody, and he exhibits it by using suitcases of cash to stage perverse practical jokes on society, creating a sort of anti-Establishment guerrilla theater. There's not much room for character development, then, in what amounts to a scatter-shot but sometimes hilarious series of satirical blackout sketches, staged on a rickety framework of greed and punctured pretense. Actor Laurence Harvey (as himself) and a stage troupe doing *Hamlet* turn the Bard's most famous soliloquy into a male striptease act. To upstage a fellow aristocrat during a grouse hunt, Grand brings soldiers and an antiaircraft cannon ("Over to you, Red Leader One!"). At an auction house he buys a Rembrandt from a snobby dealer (John Cleese) and cuts it up for the one bit he likes—the nose. In his biggest jape, Grand tricks the jet-set and vulgar nouveau riche onto the maiden voyage of the *Magic Christian,* the world's most modern luxury liner. During the trip, however, terrorist attacks, power failures, leftist graffiti, a vampire (Christopher Lee), and a rampant gorilla send panicked passengers fleeing to the engine room, which is full of naked slave women rowing under the domination of the Priestess of the Whip (Raquel Welch). Finally the victims discover that the entire ship is a mockup; it never left port.

This project clearly reflected Peter Sellers's cynical worldview. "People will swim through shit if you put a few bob in it," he often said, and that's exactly what happens here in Youngman's one prank. Such pop gems as Thunderclap Newman's Pete Townshend–produced "Something in the Air" (later used effectively in *Almost Famous*) and Badfinger's Paul McCartney–penned "Come and Get It" pulsate on the soundtrack. Starr's easygoing persona makes him a surprisingly good straight man while Sellers, also getting script credit, flaunts his repertoire of funny voices and disguises (the star reportedly had Cleese's part trimmed down because he feared the younger comic would upstage him). Cleese and fellow Cambridge classmate Graham Chapman (who appears briefly in the film) were then coming into their own with *Monty Python's Flying Circus* airing on the British telly.

Were some opportunistic producer to reissue *The Magic Christian* as *Monty Python's Swinging London,* audiences would have little objection (though they'd miss Michael Palin, Terry Gilliam, and Terry Jones). The film also contains compensatory cameos by Roman Polanski, Yul Brynner, Ferdy Mayne, Richard Attenborough, Laurence Harvey, and others.

PETER SELLERS: THE ECHO CHAMBER

by Charles A. Cassady Jr.

Peter Sellers in *The Bobo*

There was a catchphrase during the silent era—"Don't step on it: it might be Lon Chaney!"—referring, of course, to the phantom screen star who hid his unremarkable appearance behind a bewildering number of make-up guises and grotesque characterizations. Even a bug scuttling on the ground might have been the master thespian.

In the '60s, the successor to the "Man of a Thousand Faces" was Peter Sellers, a Brit who went Chaney one better: Sellers seemed to be the man of a thousand psyches as well. In addition to his acting skills, he was an adept mimic, so skilled that, like Woody Allen's fictional Leonard Zelig, he was able to transform his voice, physiology, and mannerisms into whomever he was around at the moment. He imitated superior officers back when he served in the Royal Air Force during WWII (a potential court-martial if he'd ever been caught) and, when he was getting started in show business, he aped powerful talent agents, inevitably recommending an up-and-comer named "Peter Sellers" over the phone. Cohorts in casual conversation might notice Sellers starting to become them.

Multiple Talents, Multiple Characters

During his BBC radio comedy career of the 1950s and in audio recordings right up to his death, Sellers would play dozens of characters at a time, exchanging bits of dialogue with himself. For much of his career he claimed his talent for mimicry had the side effect of leaving him bereft, bland and uncompelling, a void where a true personality should have been. "There is no me," he would joke. "There used to be a me. But I had it surgically removed." Or was Sellers just impersonating someone who was an international man of mystery, even unto himself? He was born Richard Henry Sellers in 1925, to vaudeville parents whose only other child had died in infancy the previous year. That son was named Peter. (A case of imposture from the very start?) Moody, insecure, superstitious, and recklessly impulsive, Sellers would have been considered eccentric in any era. But the 1960s gave Peter Sellers's chameleon's skin an especially colorful backdrop, on camera and off.

He worked twice for director Stanley Kubrick, first in 1962 as the masquerade-happy villain Clare Quilty in the screen adaptation of Nabokov's *Lolita,* then in Kubrick's *Dr. Strangelove.* In that film he played three roles: a wimpy U.S. president, a British officer, and a German scientist; Sellers had dearly wanted to add a gung-ho Texas bombardier to that list, but the bit went to Slim Pickens instead.

Around the World with Peter

Onstage, Sellers portrayed an Arab potentate in a comic review called *Brouhaha* and the physician in one of the few public performances of the rock opera *Tommy.* He had no trouble being Spanish in *The Bobo,* Italian in *After the Fox,* and, of course, French in the *Pink Panther* comedies. In *The Millionairess* and *The Party* he impersonated Indians (the Asian variety) so persuasively that the subcontinent's greatest filmmaker, Satyajit Ray, vainly sought him for a lead.

Other never-to-be-realized offers included Captain Hook in a live-action *Peter Pan;* Sigmund Freud for a straight biopic, directed by John Huston (Montgomery Clift got that one instead); and the frustrated Vegas songwriter in Billy Wilder's *Kiss Me, Stupid.* On-set clashes and a near-fatal heart attack (brought on by Sellers's seesawing weight and drug use) led to Ray Walston taking over the latter part. The health crisis (and, perhaps, the fact that he never really enjoyed working in America much) disqualified Sellers from portraying seven different characters/species, from Merlin the Magician to the Abominable Snowman, in George Pal's fantasy *The 7 Faces of Dr. Lao.* Tony Randall substituted.

As the '60s got stranger, Sellers fit right in, memorably portraying a stolid Jewish American attorney who goes full hippie in *I Love You, Alice B. Toklas!* He did a surreal, tricksterish turn as the wealthiest man in the world (and adoptive father of Ringo Starr) in *The Magic Christian,* then turned 180 degrees for straight, stark dramas, in the rarely seen *Hoffman* and *The Blockhouse.* Off-screen, he delved into yoga, marijuana, spirit mediums, motorcars, and broken marriages (to actress Britt Ekland, among others).

Bonded Casino

Then there was Bond, James Bond. Sellers once said he wanted to play Ian Fleming's 007 as an overweight bungler. But when the opportunity came with 1967's *Casino Royale,* it was the bloated spy satire that fell flat instead. Any picture with a world-domination budget, five directors, and eight screenwriters was bound to be problematic, but Sellers, through habitual tardiness and petulantly refusing to be on the set at the same time as Orson Welles, helped force the rewrites, re-edits, and recastings that resulted in one of the '60s' strangest flicks. The psychedelic decade ended with a number of Peter Sellers films that were barely released. It seems the star had acquired a reputation of being difficult.

Thanks to his tilt toward crowd-pleasing comedy in the 1970s, as Clouseau in further *Pink Panther* installments—and an Oscar-nominated portrayal as a socially isolated gardener mistaken for a genius in *Being There*—Sellers's career was on an up note when his weakened heart failed for good in 1980. He had recently made the cover of *Time* magazine, and in a letter he thanked the magazine "for trying to figure out what the hell I am."

Posthumous biographers since then have disparaged Sellers as insane, callous, even evil. But in a 1962 interview for *Playboy* (only the second *Playboy* interview ever, right after Miles Davis), the protean performer explained himself as "someone who never grew up, a wild sentimentalist capable of great heights and black, black depths—a person who has no voice of his own. I'm like a mike. I have no set sound . . . I pick it up from my surroundings."

1970 (PG) 95m/C *UK* Peter Sellers, Ringo Starr, Isabel Jeans, Caroline Blakiston, Wilfrid Hyde-White, Spike Milligan, John Cleese, Laurence Harvey, Raquel Welch, Hattie Jacques, Christopher Lee, Graham Stark, Roman Polanski, Yul Brynner, Ferdy Mayne, Richard Attenborough. *D:* Joseph McGrath. *W:* Peter Sellers, Terry Southern, Graham Chapman, John Cleese, Joseph McGrath. *C:* Geoffrey Unsworth. *M:* Ken Thorne. *VHS, DVD*

—Charles A. Cassady Jr.

Morgan: A Suitable Case for Treatment ♫♫

Based on a British teleplay, this cult movie is a thoroughly uncomfortable screwball comedy. The classic premise has a nonconformist (David Warner) trying to win back his ex (Vanessa Redgrave). In a twist on that premise, however, the viewer begins sympathizing with the ex rather than with the nonconformist. Warner and Redgrave are terrific in the lead roles, but the willfully destructive behavior of Warner's character may grate on viewers' nerves.

Morgan Deft returns from a trip to Greece intent on regaining the affections of his ex-wife, Leonie. Leonie is engaged to art dealer Charles Napier (Robert Stephens) and is fed up with Morgan's bizarre actions—most of which have to do with his obsession with gorillas. Morgan repeatedly interferes in Leonie and Charles's relationship, to the extent of installing himself in her house and interrupting their private moments. After a number of his stunts misfire and Leonie's goodwill toward him starts to wither, he takes his boldest step: he kidnaps her, in the hope that their being together in an idyllic lakeside setting will change her mind.

Morgan stands in the great tradition of '60s and '70s movies featuring nonconformist characters who skillfully avoid employment (*A Thousand Clowns*), indulge in cinematic fantasies (*You're a Big Boy Now*), and generally have a saner approach to life than the conformists (*King of Hearts*). This film, however, has a political aspect that those other films (perhaps wisely) avoided. Morgan is a devoted Communist who continually debates Leninism/Stalinism with his working-class mum (Irene Handl). The fact that his political beliefs appear to be attributable to his mental instability is a matter best left to more politically minded critics to address; all that's certain is that the "this Commie's crazy!" oversimplification drags the film down at several points.

Director Karel Reisz excelled at spotlighting antiheroes, as demonstrated by his classic "angry young man" film *Saturday Night and Sunday Morning* (1960) and his character-driven action saga *Who'll Stop the Rain?* (1978). Here, however, he is fashioning a post–Richard Lester screwball comedy and thus indulges in the hallmarks of so many '60s features: accelerated action for comedy sequences, New Wave–style freeze-frames, jarring music, and the use of stock footage (Morgan views the world in terms of wildlife movies, Tarzan adventures, and *King Kong*).

Best known in recent years for playing villains and bureaucratic types, David Warner does a fine job depicting Morgan's jumbled mental state, particularly in the final sequences. The truth is, though, that Morgan's activities become so aggressive that it becomes harder and harder to sympathize with our "touched" antihero. Especially when he asks Leonie, in one cringe-worthy scene, "Did you know there's no such thing as rape between man and wife?"

That the viewer can consider Morgan worthy of redemption is entirely due to Redgrave's subtle brilliance. As written, Leonie clearly appears to approve of Morgan's outrageous behavior but is simply tired of having him complicate her existence. Redgrave's complicitous smiles and stern looks at her obviously demented ex betray her tangled emotions in gorgeous detail. Leonie playfully rebuffs Morgan but continues to sleep with him throughout the film—thus his stalker-like behavior seems curiously justified in this prefeminist comedy. Redgrave renders Leonie so sympathetic that when Morgan, clad in a gorilla suit, invades her wedding to Charles, the viewer can't help but feel that he needs to be locked up, if only to give his ex a moment's peace.

Redgrave won the Best Actress award at Cannes for her work here. Her status as one of swinging London's objects of desire was solidified in Antonioni's *Blow-Up,* while she gave what was arguably her best-ever film performance for Reisz in the biopic *Isadora* (1968). In *Morgan,* she shows the promise of things to come in two scenes: a scene of Morgan-less euphoria where she stands up and drunkenly sings while riding in Charles's convertible, and a pensive moment during the kidnapping sequence where she assumes a gloomy, forlorn look on a raft in the middle of the lake, as her "captor" imagines a mundane Tarzan fantasy.

1966 97m/B *UK* David Warner, Vanessa Redgrave, Robert Stephens, Irene Handl. *D:* Karel Reisz. *W:* David Mercer. *C:* Larry Pizer. *M:* John Dankworth. *VHS, DVD* *AKA:* *Morgan!*

—*Ed Grant*

> A love story about a girl, the man she is living for, and the man she is living with.
>
> —Tagline for *Poor Cow*

Poor Cow 🦴🦴

Set in the grim tenements a world away from swinging London, *Poor Cow* is a character study of an optimistic young woman, Joy (Carol White as the "poor cow" of the title), who yearns for a simple life of family and home but doesn't know how to go about achieving it. The first scene sets the blunt, documentary-like tone as Joy, foolishly married at seventeen, gives birth to her son, Jonny—an event of little interest to her husband, Tom (John Bindon), a small-time thief. Tom is focused on his next heist, but he gets "nicked" along with his gang before they can pull it off.

With Tom away in prison, most of the film concerns Joy's efforts to survive by working as a barmaid and a sometime model in a sleazy studio where leering men come to "pose" women and take cheesecake pictures. Mostly she gets by on favors from her male admirers, a situation that stops just short of prostitution.

Dave (Terence Stamp) brings a bit of light into the bleak life of Joy (Carol White) in *Poor Cow*.

VIC / FENCHURCH FILMS / THE KOBAL COLLECTION

The high point of her existence is a love affair with Dave (Terence Stamp), a pal of Tom's who also ends up in the slammer, but for a much longer twelve years. The movie ends ambiguously, with Joy seeking a divorce from just-released Tom (now belatedly trying to patch things up) and anticipating Dave's eventual return.

This early feature by Ken Loach (best known up to that time for TV work, and after *Poor Cow* as the director for such politically minded dramas as *Riff-Raff* and *Raining Stones*) reflects his social concerns about the plight of the urban poor and working class. His camera is magnetized by the pinched and worn faces of the downtrodden as they pass on the street. In his under-stated and glum style, which often reflects the naturalism of the French New Wave (as in the handheld shots of the arrest of Tom and his cronies), *Poor Cow* projects a pessimism that's at odds with the bubbly image of '60s British pop cinema, à la *Smashing Time* and *Georgy Girl*. Even the songs of Donovan on the soundtrack (including "Colors") are rather dirge-like and depressing.

The most enjoyable aspects are the performances of sunny Carol White as Joy and brooding Terence Stamp as Dave. Stamp, of course, went on to stardom, and bits of his scenes here as a young hood were revived to great effect as flashbacks in Steven Soderbergh's *The Limey*.

1967 **(R) 101m/C** *UK* Carol White, John Bindon, Kate Williams, Terence Stamp. *D:* Ken Loach. *W:* Nell Dunn, Ken Loach. *C:* Brian Probyn. *M:* Donovan. *VHS*

—*Andy Wickstrom*

VideoHound's Groovy Movies

Smashing Time ♫♫✔

Smashing Time has everything you could ask for in a "swinging London" movie: great shots of Carnaby Street and Piccadilly Circus, gaudy fashions, dated slang, and a mod party scene or two. Unfortunately, the movie also contains several ridiculously overdone slapstick sequences. The first few times a character steps in or is pelted with a viscous substance, it's mildly amusing, but eventually the emphasis on physical comedy detracts from the movie's klutzy charm.

Yvonne (Lynn Redgrave) and Brenda (Rita Tushingham) are North Country girls who make the big move to London. Know-it-all Yvonne has come to be a star; her mousy friend just wants to hold down a regular job. After a series of difficulties, the girls find an apartment together—sharing space with an exotic dancer—and eventually score jobs. Brenda gets works at a trendy boutique called Too Much, while Yvonne finds a waitressing gig at Sweeney Todd, a theme restaurant specializing in pies. Then, out of the blue, Yvonne receives a big check from a *Candid Camera*–like TV series and uses the money to buy herself into a singing career; within weeks she's a national sensation. In the meantime, Brenda has an affair with a photographer (Michael York) that results in her becoming a top model. The relationship between the two women is strained until odd incidents take place during a party Yvonne throws in an effort to maintain her hot-commodity image. Realizing their friendship is at stake, the women finally decide to do the right thing.

The teaming is perfect: the star of *Georgy Girl* playing the best mate of the confused young woman from *A Taste of Honey* (1961). The actresses had already played roommates in director Desmond Davis's 1964 film *The Girl with Green Eyes*, but here they are paired as a comedy team. Redgrave plays the "smarter" half of the duo (read: Oliver Hardy), with Tushingham as the resourceful, well-meaning innocent (read: Stan Laurel). Neither of the two is a singer, which makes the film's tongue-in-cheek musical "effect" (in which the songs are "thought" by the pair) seem even more extreme. They both have a deft touch for comedy, a fact that is easily forgotten as the film becomes a knockabout farce. Redgrave in particular walks a fine line, making Yvonne sympathetic while still affecting the very high pitch required for George Melly's archer-than-arch dialogue ("It can't be far . . . Carnaby Street, where it's all happening!"). Michael York has one of the only notable male roles, as he does a spoof on David Hemmings's character from *Blow-Up*. His character's secret: his mod hair and super-gear mustache are both removable.

So where does this charming concoction go wrong? Let's call it a case of "Blake Edwards-itis," in which a perfectly fine character comedy turns into a raucous Mack Sennett/Hal Roach slapstick orgy. The oddest thing about *Smashing Time* is that it switches tones not once, but several times—from endearing, small-town-girl fairy tale to pie-and-ooze fest, and then back to time-capsule-worthy '60s satire. One might've thought a single all-out slapstick sequence would have sufficed, but Davis and Melly include four: an aerosol spray battle; a self-destructing machine running amok in a gallery (a swipe at real-life Swiss "kinetic artist" Jean Tinguely, whose work was also

> ## Two Girls Go Stark Mod!
>
> —Tagline for *Smashing Time*

KEN RUSSELL'S ALTERED CINEMATIC STATES

For over four decades, Ken Russell has been known as cinema's madman, a director with more visual sense than common sense, delighting in his ability to deliver works that are both sensually appealing and somewhat appalling.

Russell came out of British TV, where he fashioned a series of attention-getting films on the lives of such musicians as Sergey Prokofiev and Claude Debussy and dancer Isadora Duncan. His first stab at feature filmmaking was 1967's *The Billion Dollar Brain,* the third in Michael Caine's Len Deighton–inspired Harry Palmer espionage efforts. Although *Brain* showed lots of power in terms of energetic style and plot complications, the film went bust at the box office, ending the series and sending Russell back to the tube for work.

Author Auteur

The director got another spot at feature filmmaking in 1969 when he adapted D. H. Lawrence's *Women in Love* to the big screen. The beautifully realized film clicked thanks to Glenda Jackson's Oscar-winning performance, its intelligent screenplay (penned by Larry Kramer), and the much-ballyhooed nude wrestling match between male leads Oliver Reed and Alan Bates.

Russell continued on a tear, tackling the classics and composers with distinctive devil-may-care brio. *The Music Lovers* (1971) focuses on Russian composer Peter Tchaikovsky's creative and carnal life, unveiling his bisexual lifestyle amidst the cannon fire of *The 1812 Overture.* Aldous Huxley's *The Devils of Loudon* got the Russell treatment as *The Devils,* earning an "X" rating and a whole lot of controversy and censorship problems due to its depiction of the horrors of witch hunting in seventeenth-century France. *Savage Messiah* looks at the artist Henri Gaudier-Brzeska, *Mahler* details the life of, you guessed it, Gustav Mahler, and *Lisztomania* draws parallels between Franz Liszt, Richard Wagner, Nazism, and rock music with a cast that boasts musicians Roger Daltrey, Rick Wakeman, and Ringo Starr. Additionally, Russell looked at the life of a silent-screen icon in *Valentino,* with dancer Mikhail Baryshnikov as a man tortured by the adoring women in his life.

mocked in Arthur Penn's *Mickey One*); a massive overflow of bubbles that engulf Yvonne, Brenda, and a creepy suitor; and a huge pie fight that has eerie similarities to the fracas that sinks Edwards's *The Great Race* (1965).

The high point of the film is the segment in which Yvonne attains pop stardom. The star-making machinery that produces a pop sensation is mercilessly spoofed, as is the lighter-sounding pop of the era. Capitalizing on the shamelessly off-key singing we've heard throughout the picture, Yvonne's breakthrough song is an appropriately appalling ditty called "I'm So Young." The recording session for the song features all the hallmarks of the period,

Mind-Expanding Exponent

The director's greatest across-the-board triumph (winning both popular and critical approval) came from his outrageous all-singing, all-star interpretation of the Who's rock opera *Tommy* in 1975. Band member Roger Daltrey played the titular deaf, dumb, and blind kid to Elton John's Pinball Wizard, Tina Turner's Acid Queen, and Keith Moon's pedophilic Uncle Ernie, while Jack Nicholson, Eric Clapton, Ann-Margret, and a geyser of baked beans loaned able support.

Russell found more box-office success with 1980's mind-bending *Altered States,* even though Paddy Chayefsky's bitter fight with him led the writer to pull his name off the finished project. Russell admits in his biography (entitled, appropriately, *Altered States*) that, in order to prepare for the story about a scientist who uses drugs and a sensory deprivation chamber to discover mankind's primordial essence (or something like that), he used mind-expanding peyote for research purposes. No wonder the film's hallucinogenic sequences are so . . . *intense!*

Since *Altered States,* Russell's output has been spotty. He faced problems from ratings boards around the world for two unflinching depictions of prostitution: 1984's *Crimes of Passion,* with Kathleen Turner's nasty tour de force turn as a hooker living a double life, and 1991's *Whore,* featuring Theresa Russell (no relation) as an L.A. streetwalker. The latter was actually retitled *If You're Afraid to Say It . . . Just See It* in edited U.S. video versions.

Russell did manage to win over a new generation of fans with 1988's *Lair of the White Worm,* a campy take on a Bram Stoker story about pagan rituals and vampirism with Hugh Grant and Amanda Donohue. The film was produced for Vestron Pictures, an offshoot of the independent Vestron Video, which also backed the director's *Gothic,* about the drug-filled night Mary Shelley created *Frankenstein;* the Oscar Wilde adaptation *Salome's Last Dance;* and D. H. Lawrence's *The Rainbow,* which reunited Russell with Glenda Jackson. "We're in trouble if Ken Russell is our star director," joked one Vestron production executive at the time of *The Rainbow*'s 1989 release. A few months later, the company went bankrupt.

Never one to be termed "bankable" by Hollywood standards due to his unpredictability, Russell has a batch of unrealized projects in his closet. Among them are a biography on jazz musician Charles Mingus, an all-star sagebrush epic called *How the West Was Lost,* and more biographies of composers and adaptations of classic books. Let's hope the trip continues.

---

from chirpy backup singers (seen here as old ladies with teenage voices) to a brass section and a sitar.

Smashing Time has two other major distinctions. Some credit it as one of the first modern female "buddy" movies—and it most certainly would have been, if it had possessed a tighter script. Perhaps its most important distinction, though, is that it spoofs '60s trends during the period itself. This makes it a fascinating little slice of history as well as a sporadically hysterical farce. Viewers with a high tolerance for physical comedy will be the ones most likely to have a smashing time.

1967 (R) 96m/C *UK* Lynn Redgrave, Rita Tushingham, Michael York, Anna Quayle, Irene Handl, Ian Carmichael, Jeremy Lloyd. *D:* Desmond Davis. *W:* George Melly. *C:* Manny Wynn. *M:* John Addison. *DVD*

—Ed Grant

To Sir, with Love ♪♪♪♪

It would be easy to dismiss *To Sir, with Love* as dated. And it is fair to acknowledge that the "bad" kids featured in the film are not wielding weapons, doing drugs, committing serious crimes, or even cutting class. These hoodlums even seem sensitive to the racism of the era and do their best to combat it. But while the issues it tackles may seem less serious than those of today, the movie was groundbreaking in its own way.

A tough school in a poor London neighborhood seems destined to employ teachers who do little more than go through the motions; they give minimal effort as they get through each day with the incorrigible, out-of-control students at North Quay Secondary School. Enter Mr. Mark Thackeray, played by Sidney Poitier. Born in British Guiana with time spent in California, Thackeray is an out-of-work engineer who takes on the teaching role of the senior class temporarily while actively pursuing a "real" job. He is the only black teacher in a predominantly white school.

With no experience as an educator, Thackeray meets his students and quickly realizes that, in addition to being ill-mannered, most of them are lacking basic reading, writing, and arithmetic skills. He is determined to command their respect and to make them use their textbooks.

Thackeray's pupils do not respond to his teaching methods and continue to exhibit an uninterested, disrespectful attitude toward him. He decides to treat them like adults and demand adult behavior in the classroom. He replaces the English and math textbooks with candid discussions on marriage, family, and hygiene. Initially, the students are intrigued by his unconventional style and begin to build a trust. But when Thackeray's moral demands strike an unpopular, unfair chord—to their immature minds—he is once again mistrusted. Soon more conflict arises, this time with strong racial overtones.

Interestingly enough, the students don't seem to have much of an issue with Thackeray's race, but they do harbor a general distrust of authority and a hopeless attitude. Nonetheless, race is an important element in the movie. A peer makes several references to things like "black magic" and "voodoo" when talking to Thackeray about his success with his students. Thackeray never verbally responds to these taunts but quietly goes about his business of trying to reach the children. The students, however, seem almost embarrassed by the community's racism.

One of the most realistic aspects of *To Sir, with Love* is that Thackeray isn't naive enough to aim at getting all of his students to rise above their economic situation. Instead, he wants to equip them with life skills that will serve them in any community—he teaches them manners and cooking skills. His goal is to keep them out of jail or out of early, unwise marriages. And while he doesn't have to deal with knives or guns in the classroom, he certainly encounters danger there. In addition to being the target of the racial barbs and gingerly sidestepping a young student's advances, he openly discusses marriage, poverty, sex, and family with his pupils.

Poitier is outstanding as Thackeray—or "Sir," as his students call him, first mockingly, then affectionately. You can feel the restraint Thackeray is employing while being goaded by the class wise guy (Christian Roberts). The rest of the cast is solid as well, with Judy Geeson delivering a particularly strong performance as a girl who develops a serious crush on Sir. She is being raised by her single mother, and Thackeray learns he's probably the first real man in her life. This situation requires Poitier to skillfully play both a firm educator and a gentle role model. His performance, subtle and dramatic, rises to the challenge.

Adapting E. R. Braithwaite's novel, writer and director James Clavell (author of *Tai-Pan* and director of *The Fly*) keeps things fairly straightforward and even a bit stagy throughout most of the proceedings. But his style proves a refreshing change of pace from some of the far-out, youth-oriented offerings coming out of England during the time.

Finally, you can't talk about *To Sir, with Love* without mentioning the title song performed by Lulu, who also plays a student in the movie. Some may call it sappy, but Lulu sings this sentimental tune with such a beautiful, soft voice that it seems to signal the end of innocence and the beginning of naiveté at the same time. It subtly reinforces the sad fact that these know-it-all tough kids are just realizing that they are entering the world armed with very little.

1967 105m/C *UK* Sidney Poitier, Christian Roberts, Judy Geeson, Suzy Kendell, Lulu, Faith Brook. *D:* James Clavell. *W:* James Clavell. *C:* Peter Beeson. *M:* Ron Grainer. *VHS, DVD*

—*Margaret Lloyd*

The Touchables 🎵🎵

The Touchables is a trippy, fluffy piece of mod-sploitation from England at the height of its swinging. Melanie (Ester Anderson), Sadie (Judy Huxtable), Busbee (*Benny Hill Show* regular Monika Ringwald), and Samson (Kathy Simmonds) are a quartet of groupies who are first seen stealing a figure of Michael Caine from a wax museum during a party. They're chastised for the abduction, which turns out to be practice for a much larger crime.

Disguised as nuns, the women kidnap pop star Christian (David Anthony) from backstage at a charity wrestling event. Their "appropriated" victim finds himself stripped and tied to a circular bed inside a gigantic transparent inflated dome somewhere in the countryside outside London. Either the dome is full of narcotic gas or their new boy-toy is even dumber than they are, because he goes along cheerfully with his captors' every whim. There's a bit of business about a mock trial, but most of his captivity is spent engaging in fun and games (such as watching the ladies jump on a trampoline and play Ping-Pong) in between sexual escapades. However, Christian's manager (John Ronane) has hired gangsters as "protection" for his celebrity client, and the Touchables soon find themselves up to their false eyelashes in trouble.

Director Richard Freeman was the Beatles' official photographer and the designer of the titles for *A Hard Day's Night* and *Help!,* so it's to be expected that his feature debut should attempt to imitate the style of Richard Lester. If *The Touchables* had been cast as a band, this movie would be much better known as a full-on Beatles knockoff. As it is, there's not much holding this concoction together as it meanders through random psychedelia and humor so low-key that it can't really be classified as comedy. *The Touchables* is pretentious and surprisingly poorly photographed given Freeman's background; it is tiresome fare to be endured only by the hardiest of mod fashion fans and camp followers. The one moment of fun comes in the sequence where David Anthony makes a weak escape attempt, which is foiled when Judy Huxtable shoots him in the face! International restaurateur Mr. (Michael) Chow puts in one of his many movie cameos.

1968 **(R) 88m/C** *UK* Monika Ringwald, Judy Huxtable, Ester Anderson, David Anthony, Harry Baird, Rick Starr, Michael Chow, John Ronane, Kathy Simmonds, James Villiers. *D:* Robert Freeman. *W:* Ian La Frenais. *C:* Alan Pudney. *M:* Ken Thorne. *VHS*

—Brian Thomas

Chapter 17

The Music
Connection

The music and movie connection began at the dawn of the movies, when musical accompaniment, usually by orchestra or organ, was added to enhance the experience of watching silent films. A huge step in cinematic evolution occurred with the first talkie, 1927's *The Jazz Singer,* when Al Jolson uttered the words, "Wait a minute, wait a minute, you ain't heard nothin' yet." This static landmark picture made a statement: yes, motion pictures can coexist with sound and music. And the film industry stuck by it.

Music found its place in movies from the late 1920s through the 1950s, whether the form was jazz, swing, boogie-woogie, gospel, or big band, and whether the music or its performers were part of the foreground or background. Then rock 'n' roll broke through in the 1950s, and since the kids constituted a solid portion of moviegoers, it was a natural to pair this new wild music with cinema. Rock acts like Bill Haley and the Comets, the Platters, Jerry Lee Lewis, Chuck Berry, Frankie Lymon and the Teenagers, and Chubby Checker checked into teenage-oriented movies, putting on their big shows in much the same manner as Judy Garland and Mickey Rooney did in MGM productions a decade earlier.

Elvis Presley proved that a rocker with charisma—or at least the name Elvis—could work as a lead performer, as he demonstrated in 1957's *Jailhouse Rock* and dozens of other entertaining, often innocuous, sometimes ridiculous films throughout the '60s. Later, Roy Orbison (in *The Fastest Guitar Alive*) and Sonny and Cher (in *Good Times*) tried to stretch their followings to film, but it just didn't work out.

Meanwhile, over in England, Tommy Steele and Cliff Richard were pop idols who also made their mark on the big screen. But the British Invasion really kicked into high gear when American-born TV director Richard Lester shot the Beatles just as they were becoming a phenomenon in 1964's *A Hard Day's Night.* The groundbreaking mix of fiction, performance, and documentary led the way for the next year's *Help!,* a less inventive but equally captivating musical farce. The men from Liverpool would also show the world their switched-on psychedelic side in 1967's *Magical Mystery Tour,* lend their images to the animated *Yellow Submarine,* and elicit bad vibrations as they bid adieu in 1970's *Let It Be.*

The invasion continued with English popsters Herman's Hermits (*Hold On!* and *Mrs. Brown, You've Got a Lovely Daughter*) and Gerry and the Pacemakers (*Ferry Cross the Mersey*) trying to emulate the success of the Beatles, but the groups remain best remembered for their infectious brand of pop music rather than their cinematic chops.

As in the 1950s, rock bands of the '60s began to make special musical appearances in "dramatic" movies. The Chocolate Watch Band played in *Riot on the Sunset Strip,* the Strawberry Alarm Clock clocked in for Russ Meyer's *Beyond the Valley of the Dolls,* the Yardbirds showed how swinging London really was in Antonioni's *Blow-Up,* and the Grateful Dead represented the San Francisco sound in *Petulia*—and Jerry Garcia even got to say a line!

At the same time, concert films clicked with the kids. *The TAMI Show* led the way, offering an awesome overview of musical talent from the mid-1960s, including the Beach Boys, James Brown, Marvin Gaye, Chuck Berry, the Rolling Stones, Jan and Dean, Lesley Gore, and the Supremes. *Monterey Pop* (1967) may not impress many in terms of cinematic style, but it boasts such an incredible cross-section of musicians, including Otis Redding, Jimi Hendrix, Janis Joplin, Jefferson Airplane, and the Who, who cares? Of course, it paved the way for 1970's *Woodstock,* the three-hour epic chronicle of the counterculture's dirtiest and greatest hit. The latter's success made "rockumentaries" a viable movie genre, leading to *Fillmore, Celebration at Big Sur, Mad Dogs and Englishmen, Wattstax,* and others.

Two of *Monterey Pop*'s filmmakers—D. A. Pennebaker and Albert Maysles—were also responsible for two of the most fascinating music-oriented films of the era. Pennebaker's 1967 *Dont Look Back* surveys Bob Dylan's 1965 British tour with rare intimacy, while Maysles's harrowing *Gimme Shelter* (1971) shows the Age of Aquarius at its ugliest with a fatal stabbing at the Rolling Stones' 1969 Altamont concert.

The Stones and their fearless leader would also play parts in two of the psychedelic '60s' oddest musical numbers. French auteur Jean-Luc Godard mixed rock and revolution in the innovative but often maddening *Sympathy for the Devil* (AKA *One Plus One*). And Mick Jagger took the lead in *Performance,* a hellish, hazy, horny descent into the decadent world of a pop idol. Critics may have read a lot into the film's identity- and personality-switching theme, but music fans went to see it for one reason. It was only rock 'n' roll, but they liked it.

Almost Famous Untitled: The Bootleg Cut (Director's Edition) ♪♪♪♪

Directors mining their own lives for film material have given us some brilliant international cinematic works like Fellini's *Amarcord,* Truffaut's *The 400 Blows,* and Louis Malle's *Au Revoir Les Enfants.* In the United States, Barry Levinson's four Baltimore-set films (*Diner, Tin Men, Avalon,* and the overlooked *Liberty Heights*), Woody Allen's *Annie Hall,* Oliver Stone's *Platoon,* and Martin Scorsese's *Mean Streets* have also been met with great acclaim.

So what exactly happened to *Almost Famous,* Cameron Crowe's autobiographical look at his life as a teenage rock 'n' roll writer for *Rolling Stone* magazine? Much talked about after Crowe's *Jerry Maguire* success, the film was poised to become *the* big movie of 2000. But despite lots of press and generally terrific reviews, *Almost Famous* turned out to be not so famous after all, and it unceremoniously disappeared within weeks from theaters.

The less-than-stellar reception is a real shame because *Almost Famous* was a very good movie, a fine story that was funny, well acted, sharply written, wonderfully directed, and compelling throughout.

But what would it require to take this movie beyond "very good" status? A funny thing happened to *Almost Famous* on the way to the theaters. Dreamworks, its studio, insisted Crowe trim the film by about fifteen minutes. What ended up on the screen sure looked good, but could those missing nine hundred seconds have elevated the film to classic status?

Thanks to the DVD format, we now can tell. In *Almost Famous Untitled: The Bootleg Cut (Director's Edition),* the version of the film that Crowe assembled for DVD, those fifteen minutes have been added back in, along with twenty-five minutes of additional footage that was scrapped earlier along the film-making trail. And good news: these additions move the film up a notch, from "very good" to "exceptional."

Perhaps *Almost Famous* is not for everyone, and it's certainly not for the teenage crowd that populates the fantasy and action-adventure flicks of summertime. An affection for classic rock, an interest in the machinations of

"And you can tell Rolling Stone magazine that my last words were ... I'm on drugs!"

—Russell Hammond (Billy Crudup), in *Almost Famous*

CAMERON CROWE: ROCKING AND REELING THROUGH THE YEARS by Amy Longsdorf

After the success of *Jerry Maguire,* studio execs stood in line to show writer/director Cameron Crowe the money. Luckily, he was ready for them. From the bottom of his drawer, he pulled the script for *Almost Famous,* his mash note to '70s rock 'n' roll. Starring Kate Hudson, Billy Crudup, Frances McDormand, Philip Seymour Hoffman, and newcomer Patrick Fugit, the movie tells the intensely personal story of Crowe's early days as a teenage rock journalist.

Q: How long has this film been gestating in your mind?

A: This is the film I wanted to make first. But then *Say Anything* took hold. And then after that, it felt like *Singles* was the right movie, and then *Jerry Maguire.* But given a few minutes to talk about it, I would always veer over into, "You know, there is this other thing that I really want to do . . . " and it would be this rock movie.

Q: Exactly how autobiographical is it?

A: I'd say it's 90 percent autobiographical.

Q: Even the stuff about your not being able to get backstage?

A: Especially that stuff. I still can't get backstage. When we came to the San Diego Sports Arena to shoot the movie, I went to the door, and it was like a Tuesday afternoon and the security guy said, "You can't come in." I couldn't come in to film a scene about not being able to come in.

the media, and the desire to see a touching coming-of-age tale certainly helps. Set in 1973, the story involves Cameron Crowe's alter ego, William Miller (newcomer Patrick Fugit), a wide-eyed fifteen-year-old with a love and talent for writing about rock 'n' roll. Miller gets to his idol, *Creem* magazine editor Lester Bangs (Philip Seymour Hoffman), who offers him advice in taking his writing career further. The disheveled but articulate Bangs tells him to be honest and to avoid making friends with the musicians he's covering. William takes the advice and, through some sharp maneuvers like disguising his voice to sound older when talking to a *Rolling Stone* editor, he gets a gig writing for the magazine, covering the band Stillwater (a fictional fusion of Led Zeppelin and the Allman Brothers) on tour.

After coercing his caring but overprotective teacher mother (Frances McDormand) into letting him take the assignment, William enters a world far from his own, a world he knew nothing of in his former life as part of the adoring crowd at rock shows. Backstage and in the hotels where Stillwater and

Q: When did you first become obsessed with rock 'n' roll?

A: I remember I got an assignment from a San Diego paper to cover a Yes and Black Sabbath concert. I went wild that night. I interviewed everyone. I went into every dressing room. And that was when the addiction began setting in.

Q: What was it like to go on the road with the Allman Brothers when you were fifteen?

A: It was an amazing experience. I had been skipped ahead grades in school. So I was always around people who were so much older than me and I was invisible to them, especially to girls. When I went on the road with these bands, some of whom were my idols, I was not invisible to them. So it was a dream come true, and then a dilemma.

Q: A dilemma in what sense?

A: I had to write about what I saw. I didn't want to squander the opportunity to write the truth for some reader out there like me. But, in the end, I wanted to write about why the music touched me. That's more important than writing about TVs going out the window.

Q: What did your mom say when you left to go on tour with Led Zepellin?

A: What she always said: "Call me every five minutes, and don't do drugs."

Q: Now you're married to Nancy Wilson of Heart. How does it feel to be the husband of a rock star?

A: Nancy is completely unaffected. No one ever said to her, "Hey, it's not cool to date a rock journalist." She didn't know until later, until we were already together. Then I had to say, "Honey, I've got to tell you this—you've crossed the line, and it's too late to turn back now."

their entourage stay, there is a plethora of drugs, drinking, and women. Some of the women are young groupies who call themselves "band aids," and one of them, Penny Lane (Kate Hudson), perks the virginal William's interest. At the same time, William is getting friendly with the group—a no-no according to guru Bangs—bonding in particular with guitar virtuoso Russell Hammond (Billy Crudup). Complicating matters even further is the fact that as William draws closer to Penny, he discovers that she and Russell have a history together.

How William deals with all of his predicaments, one of which is writing a truthful story about his experiences on tour with Stillwater, constitutes the emotional meat of *Almost Famous.* While that may seem like enough—and maybe even too much for a movie that originally clocks in at just over two hours—something seemed to be missing from *Almost Famous* in its original theatrical form. *The Bootleg Cut,* re-edited by Crowe several months after the film's debut, seamlessly adds several scenes. The sequences add more depth to William's background and allow us to see what drives the prodigy to become a writer. Also deepened are the relationships among William, his mother, and his stewardess sister (Zooey Deschanel), whose collection of albums originally got him interested in music. Further probed are the connections between William and the members of Stillwater, especially Russell, who is more of a surrogate father figure than in the original version.

Not surprisingly, Crowe proves meticulous in his period recreation of the early 1970s, and the clothing styles, production design, and witty, knowing dialogue are enhanced by the eclectic choice of songs on the soundtrack, songs that are often used to underscore the screen's action. The music is far-ranging, including everything from Neil Young to Yes to Elton John to Todd Rundgren to the Seeds to Iggy Pop and the Stooges—a wide sampling of rock music of the era.

It's not every day a filmmaker has the opportunity to step back, smell the roses (probably briefly, since Crowe was already in production on *Vanilla Sky* when *Almost Famous* was released), reconsider, and recut a film to his liking—especially if the film is a box-office disappointment. Crowe sensed that there was another version of the story aching to find its way to the public, and he acted upon his instincts. Although *Almost Famous* isn't perfect—it really could use a scene or two of the agony and ecstasy William gets out of writing—*The Bootleg Cut* is the next best thing: almost perfect.

2000 (R) 162m/C (original edition: 122m/C) Billy Crudup, Frances McDormand, Kate Hudson, Patrick Fugit, Philip Seymour Hoffman, Jason Lee, Fairuza Balk, Anna Paquin, Noah Taylor, Zooey Deschanel, Jimmy Fallon. *D:* Cameron Crowe. *W:* Cameron Crowe. *C:* John Toll. *M:* Cameron Crowe, Peter Frampton, Mike McCready, Ann Wilson, Nancy Wilson. *VHS, DVD*

Celebration at Big Sur ♫♫♫

Even with such noted names as Joni Mitchell, Joan Baez, the Edwin Hawkins Singers, Mimi Farina, John Sebastian, and Crosby, Stills, Nash & Young on the bill, the lead star of *Celebration at Big Sur* is still sideburns.

Big, hairy sideburns.

Everyone has them. OK, maybe not Joni or Joan or Mimi or some of the Edwin Hawkins Singers. But look at the monsters on Neil Young. They could be declared a peninsula in and of themselves. And Stephen Stills's mutton-chops? They make Martin Van Buren's facial mane look quaint. Of the lead male performers, only Graham Nash appears to have shunned the trend. Instead, he sports a tiny Fu Manchu goatee. Or was that just chocolate left over from when he had the munchies?

If you're looking for a drug-drenched post-*Woodstock* rockumentary, you may want to join this *Celebration*—if, that is, you can find it on TV or cable (it's never been offered by a video label). Not only should the hairstyles be placed in a time capsule, but the fashions (ponchos, fur parkas, leather vests with fringes) and visual effects (chroma-key, shots of waves hitting rocks, birds flying, butterflies) deserve preservation as well. Oh, there's even a group hot tub scene. And among those soaking up the suds is David Crosby. 'Nuff said.

The setting for *Celebration* is downright disconcerting. The performances emanate from the Esalen Institute, a popular spot for self-discovery therapy in the '60s—a place where the "in" crowd went to get in touch with themselves. Ken Kesey spent time there; Jack Keorouac wrote about it. The place looks like a suburban swim club, and the musicians perform in front of a swimming pool located near a cliff that overlooks the Pacific Ocean. People sit on chaise lounges and beach chairs or around the performers as they do their thing. Aerial shots show us thousands of other audience members huddled behind the poolside attendees, but all of the performance footage makes the Big Sur Folk Festival appear incredibly intimate. The location is high atop the mountains in Northern California, offering the filmmakers ample opportunity for impressive location photography.

Since *Woodstock* was still fresh in the minds of any filmgoer interested in such a project in the first place, it's no surprise that several 'Stock players are on view here. Joan Baez starts things off with a cover of Bob Dylan's "I Shall Be Released," then goes into "Song for David" (for her hubby, imprisoned at the time for draft evasion), and later sings "Sweet Sir Galahad." In the finale, she joins the Edwin Hawkins Singers and most of the fest's musical talent in the gospel hit "Oh, Happy Day." John Sebastian, another vet of *Woodstock,* duets with Stephen Stills and adds some of his own homespun numbers.

Of particular interest for rock fans are appearances by Joni Mitchell and Stills with Crosby, Nash, and Young. Mitchell, who was slated to play at Woodstock but didn't quite make it there (though she did get to *The Dick Cavett Show* the next day to discuss it), makes her first on-screen appearance, performing her song "Woodstock" to her own piano accompaniment. It's a lovely song, with her lilting voice in good shape, but in order to get that old, acid-laced *Woodstock* feeling, directors Baird Bryant and Johanna Demetrakas go wild with the hippie-dippy effects, chroma-keying Joni's face, fading from color to B&W to color again, placing swirling circles all over the screen, and throwing in an image of a butterfly or two for good measure. Way to ruin the mood of a sensitive ode to the three days of peace and music.

Events surrounding CSN&Y's performance provide the only tense moments in the film. After CSN&Y finish a set, a zonked-out audience member approaches the band, ranting and raving, looking to pick a fight. Stills takes things personally and approaches him. Somebody from the audience eggs Stills on, calling on him to punch the guy. The rock star approaches the verbal assailant. Pushing and shoving ensues. Onlookers and band members eventually intercede. Stills, the writer of the song "Love the One You're With," later says that the protestor's problem was with Stills's materialistic lifestyle. Luckily, Stills says, people "loved me out" in order to avoid a fight. Like, wow.

While it's not obvious, one can surmise there were some bad vibes among members of the short-lived (but eventually resurrected) CSN&Y supergroup. After all, they were on the verge of a split, with Young opting to go his own way, a path that would lead to great success for him. He appears in the background throughout most of the film, avoiding conversation with fellow musicians, just doing his own thing even while performing with the group. In spite of any tensions, the group is responsible for the film's musical highlights, with "4 + 20" and "Sea of Madness" and with Young taking charge on a blistering version of "Down by the River."

The producers of *Celebration at Big Sur* had hoped they'd catch lightning in a bottle with the *Woodstock* connection, but aside from some of the same talent and counterculture spirit, this outing falls short of rockumentary classic. Still, fans of classic rock curious to see their heroes in cozy surroundings may want to find a copy through a collector's website or eBay and bask in the glow of a post-*Woodstock* world of music.

1971 (PG) 82m/C Joan Baez, David Crosby, Stephen Stills, Graham Nash, Neil Young, Joni Mitchell, John Sebastian, Edwin Hawkins, Julie Payne, Mimi Farina. *D:* Baird Bryant, Johanna Demetrakas. *C:* Peter Smokler, Gary Weis, Joan Churchill, Bill Kaplan. *VHS*

Dont Look Back ♪♪♪♪

B ob Dylan is an enigmatic man. He's changed religions several times. He's altered his onstage persona from sensitive poet to homespun folkie to electrified rock star to Vegas showman to barnstorming troubador to born-again gospel belter. On the screen, Dylan has always been Mr. Mysterioso, whether it be in a supporting role as Alias in Sam Peckinpah's *Pat Garrett and Billy the Kid* or portraying a reclusive rock star in *Hearts of Fire* or playing pretty much himself in the "huh?"-inducing 2003 all-star weird-out *Masked and Anonymous.*

One gets the sense that Dylan enjoys all this mystery and the attention he gets from his unpredictable, inscrutable ways. And that's what makes the legendary chronicle of his 1965 British concert tour, *Dont Look Back* (spelled without the apostrophe, for some reason), so fascinating.

Given incredible access by Albert Grossman, Dylan's manager, filmmaker D. A. Pennebaker captures the twenty-five-year-old Dylan as few other rock stars have ever been captured by the camera. Dylan is seen being interviewed by members of the press, performing onstage and behind-the-scenes, and interacting with such fellow musicians as Joan Baez, Alan Price, and Donovan. One would assume, then, that the 16-millimeter camera, allowed to roam freely in and out of Dylan's life over a week-long period, would occasionally catch him with his guard down. But even after watching this feature-length documentary, we're quite sure he's been exposed. Are his nasty quips to journalists at a press conference really Bob, or is that just how he wants the public to perceive him? Is he really angry after somebody throws a glass out of a window onto the street below, or does he just want us to *think* he's upset? Does he really feel irritated by the attention he gets from everyone, including fellow musicians, or is he just getting off on looking resentful of his fame? While the answers to these questions that arise while watching *Dont Look Back* may never be answered, one thing seems certain: Bob Dylan, for

Bob Dylan holds up a cue card for "Subterranean Homesick Blues" in *Dont Look Back,* a film documenting his 1965 British concert tour.

all of his brilliance as a songwriter and, arguably, as a performer, is an incredibly uptight human being.

But what he lacks in looseness in regular life he seems to make up for while performing—at least as evidenced in the musical numbers in *Dont Look Back.* Onstage at Royal Albert Hall, Dylan offers passionate versions of such songs as "Don't Think Twice, It's All Right," "The Lonesome Death of Hattie Carroll," and "It's Alright, Ma (I'm Only Bleeding)." In hotel rooms, he's great with impromptu versions of "It's All Over Now, Baby Blue" and some Hank Williams tunes. Strap a guitar on the guy and self-assuredness pours out of him. Even in the legendary musical sequence for "Subterranean Homesick Blues" that opens *Dont Look Back,* with Dylan flashing cue cards with the song's key words, he appears at least comfortable about feeling uncomfortable.

Dont Look Back has been compared to the Beatles' *A Hard Day's Night.* For both Dylan and the Beatles, revolutionaries in the music world during the '60s, the films purportedly offer peeks of what goes on with the artists outside of the performance spotlight. Of course, Richard Lester's *A Hard Day's Night,* released the year before the Dylan documentary was filmed, presented a fictionalized account of a day in the life of the Beatles, an approximation of what their lives at least might be like sans audiences and fans. On the other hand, *Dont Look Back,* authenticated with its grainy, handheld camerawork, candid conversations, and exclusive backstage footage, offers the real deal: unexpurgated, 100 percent, maximum Bob Dylan. Or does it?

1967 96m/B Bob Dylan, Joan Baez, Donovan, Alan Price, Albert Grossman, Bob Neuwirth. **D:** D. A. Pennebaker. **C:** Howard Alk, Jones Alk, D. A. Pennebaker. **M:** Bob Dylan, Donovan. *VHS, DVD*
AKA: *Don't Look Back*

The Doors

D iscussion of the Doors begins and ends with Jim Morrison, lead singer, creative leader, poet, and notorious dead rock star. After he died in Paris in 1971, the remaining members of the band—Ray Manzarek, John Densmore, and Robby Kreiger—did put out other albums. But these were discovered in the $1.99 bins at department stores, while earlier works with Jim like *The Doors, Waiting for the Sun,* and *L.A. Woman* still commanded top prices.

It's no surprise, then, that when Oliver Stone finally got around to making *The Doors,* one of his many long-in-gestation dream projects, the focus of the film was Morrison. The problem is that Stone depicts him as a depressed, drunken, drug-taking, annoying, self-destructive creep. For this reason, it's tough to warm up to *The Doors* or to Jim Morrison.

Perhaps the problem is that Stone did his job too well in some ways. No stranger to capturing the turbulence of the 1960s and '70s with an idiosyncratic brand of hysteria (*Born on the Fourth of July, Platoon, JFK, Nixon*) and chronicling driven, near-psychopathic characters (*Salvador, Wall Street,* his screenplay for *Scarface*), Stone has a field day here. He gets to stage concerts, freak-outs, drunken binges, an obscenity trial, an orgy, a desert peyote excursion, and ritual sex sessions, all captured with handheld cameras, strobe lights, newsreel footage, Industrial Light and Magic–created visual effects, and flashy editing. To add even more authenticity to the proceedings, Stone hired Val Kilmer for the lead role. In what now appears to be a career-defining performance, Kilmer looks, sounds, sings, moves, and allegedly acts like Jim Morrison.

This means we're stuck with a very accurate depiction of that depressed, drunken, annoying, and self-destructive creep for almost every frame of the 138-minute picture. Give Stone credit, then, for not softening his version of the story and for making a film that's almost entirely unpleasant.

The framework of *The Doors* is fairly conventional. We first see a young Jim Morrison riding in the backseat of his family's car through New Mexico in 1949. The car slows down as it passes an accident on the side of the road. Jim looks out the window, witnessing the carnage of an accident victim. Thus does Stone foreshadow Morrison's fascination with death and his nihilistic view of the world.

In college, Jim's downer film project, which incorporates his poetry, assassination footage, and clips of Hitler from Leni Reifenstahl's Nazi propaganda film *Triumph of the Will,* is deemed "pretentious" by fellow students and by his professor (played by Stone). So he quits school, visits Haight-Ashbury during 1967's Summer of Love, and lives on the rooftops of houses around Venice Beach, California, then populated by body builders and hippies. Morrison spots cute, free-spirited redhead Pamela Courson (Meg Ryan) on the beach, then drops into her

"**Actually I don't remember being born. It must have happened during one of my blackouts.**"

—Val Kilmer as Jim Morrison, in *The Doors*

life, literally, plunging through her second-floor window, Tarzan-like. He begins writing and reciting poetry in local clubs. With film-school pal Ray Manzarek (Kyle MacLachlan) on keyboards, he forms a music group with guitrarist Robby Kreiger (Frank Whaley) and drummer John Densmore (Kevin Dillon).

The band takes off immediately, signing a record contract with Elektra and releasing their self-titled first album to instant success. Morrison adopts a bottle of alcohol as a constant traveling partner. Television comes calling. *The Ed Sullivan Show* books the group on the condition that Jim won't say the word "higher" when he performs "Light My Fire" live. He not only ignores the producer's instructions, he puts special emphasis on the word, singing, "Girl, you couldn't get much HIGHER." The *Sullivan* appearance turns out to be a really big show for the Doors, and Morrison goes from miserable, struggling, misunderstood poet to miserable, rich, misunderstood rock star almost overnight.

Morrison has trouble just saying "no" to sex, and, in addition to Pam and assorted groupie chicks, he takes on journalist Patricia Kennealy (Kathleen Quinlan) as a lover. Problems in bed inspire Kennealy to suggest weird, occult sex rituals. These must work because he later impregnates her.

As the Doors' success rolls on, Morrison becomes more and more wasted from drink and drugs. Tensions grow between Morrison and the band members and between Morrison and his romantic partners. Following an incident at a Miami concert where he exposes himself, Morrison's arrested, but he dodges jail time. Following the production of the album *L.A. Woman,* Jim and Pam move to Paris to get away from it all. The album is the group's last; Morrison dies in his bathtub at the age of twenty-eight from a heart attack that may have been caused by a drug overdose.

One can admire several aspects of Stone's take on Morrison and the Doors. There's no denying that the film captures that frenzied '60s feeling with a certain power and excitement. But this film is the Gospel According to Stone, and, despite its admirable technical prowess and Kilmer's electrifying performance, *The Doors* can be faulted for taking liberties with several incidents. (Many of the facts can be found in the numerous books on the market about the group.) With Stone's sledgehammer style, you're never sure where the excesses of Morrison's life end and the work of an excessive filmmaker begins. Viewers should take many of Oliver's twists with a grain of salt.

Drugs, sex, booze, wasted talent, antisocial behavior: they were a significant part of Morrison's sad slide, as was also the case with Jimi Hendrix and Janis Joplin. But where's the humanity in the man who was supposedly a brilliant poet, sensitive to the human condition? What fueled Morrison's recklessness, his desire to succeed and to destroy himself at the same time? Answers to these questions are only hinted at in the film. In lieu of insight, Stone tosses in Christ-like images of Morrison, nominating him for martyrdom in the process. Unfortunately, in this movie that has almost too much of everything, we are left with the feeling that so much more could have been shown of Morrison's tortured genius.

1991 (R) 138m/C Val Kilmer, Meg Ryan, Kyle MacLachlan, Frank Whaley, Kevin Dillon, Kathleen Quinlan, Michael Wincott, Crispin Glover, Bill Graham. **D:** Oliver Stone. **W:** Oliver Stone, Randall Johnson. **C:** Robert Richardson. **M:** The Doors. *VHS, DVD*

Fillmore 🎵🎵🎵

The hub of psychedelic rock in San Francisco was the Fillmore West, a club owned by Bill Graham. The feisty, finagling rock impresario became famous for the former dance hall and its New York City counterpart, the Fillmore East. But by 1971, Graham was burned out, dismayed by the demands of the groups he had mentored, and ready to shutter both auditoriums' doors. Graham went on to promote acts at San Francisco's Winterland venue, but for a going-away party at the Fillmore, he decided to give the natives a gift, booking, over a week-long period, popular local acts that had won national fame.

Fillmore looks at that finale, giving us behind-the-scenes access to Graham trying to set up the week's concerts and then capturing the various bands in concert. Most of the time, Graham—who died in a helicopter crash in 1991—is shown haggling on the phone, voraciously trying to iron out the kinks with managers and newly minted rock stars over such problems as billing, booking, and lighting preferences. One particularly ugly skirmish involves singer Boz Scaggs, who has changed his mind over whether he wants to headline his night at the Fillmore. The conversation turns into a pro-fanity-strewn shouting match, demonstrating why Graham is bidding adieu to running the place.

The rest of *Fillmore* is dedicated to the onstage activities, and much of it serves as a prime example of the San Fran sound. Scaggs does get to perform with his band, and he turns in a sultry version of "I'll Be Long Gone." It's a Beautiful Day, led by singer David LaFlamme and his electric violin, check in with their signature beauty, "White Bird." The forgotten Lamb turn out a few medley-propelled winners. And Hot Tuna, led by Jefferson Airplane members Jorma Kaukonen and Jack Casady, register a few bluesy numbers.

As for the leading psychedelic proponents, the Airplane, led by Grace Slick, Marty Balin, and Paul Kantner, are conspicuously short-shrifted here. In a scene that appears to have been shot elsewhere and dropped into the film, the Airplane perform "We Could Be Together," complete with its chorus of "tear down the wall motherfucker." The final two slots in *Fillmore* are reserved for the Grateful Dead and Santana. Led by the shockingly young tandem of Jerry Garcia and Bob Weir, the Dead delight the audience with "Casey Jones" and "Johnny B. Goode," while Santana deliver with two jam-packed Latin tribal jazz fusions.

Taking his cue from Michael Wadleigh's work in *Woodstock,* director Richard T. Heffron (*Futureworld*) uses split screens, but he also spikes the psy-chedelia quotient higher by superimposing images of the various group members during their performances. Much of *Fillmore* is shot in close-up with shaky camerawork. This approach gives the film a refreshingly raw edge, particularly to viewers accustomed to watching VH-1 or the slick concert DVDs of today.

1972 (R) 105m/C Bill Graham, Boz Scaggs, Carlos Santana, the Grateful Dead, Jefferson Airplane, Hot Tuna. ***D:*** Richard T. Heffron. ***C:*** Alan Capps, Albert Kihn, Eric Saarinen, Paul Lohmann. *VHS*
AKA: *Fillmore: The Final Days*

Gimme Shelter ♪♪♪♪

Members of the '60s generation never needed much assurance that they were somehow special, a hip breed apart. They exuded a cooler-than-thou attitude in every way imaginable—politics, fashion, sex, music, drugs. But the love-is-all-you-need spirit of the '60s smashed headlong into reality in the very last month of the flower-power decade. And the collision was caught on camera, at the feet of Mick Jagger. *Gimme Shelter* is the documentary record of that collision, and it retains the shocking power of a slap in the face, as if forcing a generation to snap out of its innocence.

Rock concerts can be dangerous for many reasons relating to the constant press of fevered flesh, but few have been the scene of a homicide. At the Altamont Speedway (located oddly enough near the hippie mecca of San Francisco), a free rock festival on December 6, 1969, featuring the Rolling Stones at the top of the bill, culminated in the stabbing and beating death of an eighteen-year-old spectator, Meredith Hunter. Hunter, seen on-camera wielding a gun, was overwhelmed and pummeled by a posse of Hell's Angels, who were acting as unofficial security for the Stones.

The facts of his death were well known by the time David and Albert Maysles released *Gimme Shelter* a year later, and audiences knew what the film's climax would be. Nonetheless, the impending sense of doom is magnificently manipulated by the Maysles and their codirector and editor, Charlotte Zwerin. Even ordinary images take on a dark foreboding—we see Mick and the Stones move from street to hotel room to car to recording studio in the way of any mundane rock doc, but we know the ultimate destination.

In fact, the Maysles play with our foreknowledge by making *Gimme Shelter* a movie within a movie: it is structured so that Mick himself (and sometimes Charlie Watts) is intermittently seen pensively watching the rough footage in an editing suite. The opening title comes up on the Moviola, not on the "real" screen. They are watching their own movie, and one of the film's final images is a freeze-frame of a haunted-looking Mick staring into the camera, having just witnessed the killing again.

Self-conscious about its disastrous denouement, *Gimme Shelter* is plainly structured as a journey, both physical (from East to West across the U.S.) and metaphorical (from an initial rousing concert to a pointless human tragedy). Thus each small moment seems infused with portent. But it's not all heavy premonition. Viewers who come to *Gimme Shelter* for simple rock 'n' roll pleasures will revel in the opening concert at Madison Square Garden, where the Stones unleash "Jumpin' Jack Flash" and "Satisfaction" in blistering full-length versions before an ecstatic crowd. This performance still gets the blood pumping, yet the Maysles technique here of focusing tightly on Mick even when he's not doing much, and sometimes nearly losing the shot, stands in raw cinema vérité contrast to today's frenetic MTV cross-cutting and godlike crane perspectives. The film seems to be saying, "You want Jagger? Well, take a good long look." In 1969 Mick and the boys were demonstrably in their glorious prime, and the New York concert is the sublime pinnacle before the devil demands his due.

One drawback for the uninitiated is the film's pointed lack of a narrator or explanatory subtitles. It's as if the Maysles purposefully shun the role of historian, and if you don't know who Melvin Belli is (the Stones' attorney who is seen arranging the Altamont venue via phone calls) or don't recognize Jerry Garcia in the crowd, then too bad. *Gimme Shelter* is not a VH1 special. It's a window on a brief era that was as fragile and beautiful and doomed as the huge soap bubble that the camera tracks over the blissed-out crowd.

1970 (R) 91m/C The Rolling Stones, Tina Turner, the Flying Burrito Brothers, Jefferson Airplane. **D:** David Maysles, Albert Maysles, Charlotte Zwerin. **C:** George Lucas, Albert Maysles, David Maysles, Ron Dorfman. **M:** Mick Jagger, Keith Richards. *VHS, DVD*

—*Andy Wickstrom*

> **The music that thrilled the world ... and the killing that stunned it!**
>
> —Tagline for
> *Gimme Shelter*

Godspell ♫♫

Hair ♫♫♫

If you're gonna put rock 'n' roll on the theatrical stage, then film versions of such shows can't be too far behind, can they? *Godspell* and *Hair,* 1960s-flavored musicals characterized by rock 'n' roll and by youthful vigor

Victor Garber (bottom right) leads the cast of *Godspell* through their song-and-dance numbers in the 1971 film adaptation of the successful stage show. COLUMBIA / THE KOBAL COLLECTION

rebelling against staid authority, presented challenges for directors David Greene and Milos Forman in their 1970s film versions of the shows. The trick was to keep those quintessential '60s attitudes fresh after the 1960s had passed. Only one of the films succeeded.

The two movies share many common features. Both shows produced hit songs, including "Day by Day" from *Godspell,* which was scored by Stephen Schwartz. The soundtrack from *Hair,* with songs by composer Galt MacDermot and lyricists Gerome Ragni and James Rado, produced several hits: the title track, "Aquarius," "Easy to Be Hard," and "Let the Sunshine In."

Each film pivots on its leaders. Berger (Treat Williams) is the free-wheeling hippie honcho in *Hair.* His mantra appears to be "have fun," while *Godspell*'s "teacher" (Victor Garber) only wants to follow the word of the Lord. Both men have followers, both have enormous vitality and energy, and both are sacrificed for the betterment of others.

Godspell director David Greene, who cowrote the screenplay with John-Michael Tebelak, the stage play's author, presents an energetic but lengthy film that wears the audience down. The stage show boasted an intimacy, a special connection to the audience members, who were even invited to share wine and cheese with the cast during intermission. The film version, however, loses that immediacy. It opens with its nine apostles stuck in dead-end jobs or fighting the rat race of the corporate ladder. Right off the bat, Greene, best known for such TV work as *Roots* and *Rich Man, Poor Man,* lets you know that this is essentially a '60s movie: the apostles toss away their work clothes and accoutrements to dress up like clowns, wear makeup, and cavort through the city. Greene falls into the trap of many directors adapting a stage show to the screen: he tries to "open up" the show from the smaller stage spaces by showing vistas of empty New York City streets and rooftop shots (some from the top of the World Trade Center towers). One of the show's best songs, "It's All for the Best," has Garber and David Haskell singing and dancing with canes in front of a giant neon sign while the camera pulls away. The charm of the scene is lost amid the vastness of the space. The scenes set in parks, junkyards, or abandoned buildings are actually stronger because of their limited space; in opening up the show the filmmakers lost the immediacy. And without that immediacy, the film's shortcomings become more apparent. This film has no plot, only parables; no character development, only stories and bromides.

While an attractive, energetic, talented cast is showcased in *Godspell,* only Garber, a busy character actor, and the late Lynne Thigpen, a regular on many TV shows and the voice of "Luna" on *The Bear in the Big Blue House,* achieved any measure of long-term fame. And having Haskell portray both John the Baptist and Judas Iscariot was a mistake. He just can't carry off the challenge of dual roles.

The final shot of *Godspell*—the cast "dissolving" into the mass of street people—doesn't work. In another parallel, Forman also ends *Hair* with a crowd shot, showing thousands of people protesting the Vietnam War, then freezing into a B&W still. It may be hokey, but it works.

As for Garber's "Christ," complete with painted tears on his face— what, foreshadowing?—he's tough to take seriously as a wise teacher bring-

ing the word of God. On the other hand, Williams brings an electric life force to Berger, a man who knows what he wants and gets it, and who also knows what he doesn't want, and avoids it (like the draft).

One of the obvious differences between the two films is budget: except for a few crowd scenes, *Godspell* primarily focuses on the core cast set in empty surroundings. Forman had money to work with, as evidenced by impressive aerial shots, several giant crowd scenes, a detailed boot camp. And he hired Twyla Tharp, who contributed the exuberant choreography.

This film was Oscar-winning Czech expatriate Forman's first (and only) attempt at a musical. In his desire to prevent the film from seeming "stage-bound," he presents the songs in constant motion. While characters are driving in a convertible on the open road, singing "Good Morning Starshine," Forman's helicopter-mounted camera swoops in front of, behind, and over the actors. For "Hare Krishna," presented as the visions of someone on LSD, people are seen flying across the sets.

Forman effectively uses cross-cutting in many musical numbers. When the group is imprisoned after attempting to crash a party and Berger is outside trying to raise bail money, the gang sings *Hair* behind bars, while Berger sings it from the outside, with the camera cutting back and forth. Forman also did this for "Black Boys" and "White Boys," sung by women in Central Park (look for Nell Carter) and officers at the induction center in front of naked soldiers. It's a riot.

Hud (Dorsey Wright), Jeannie (Annie Golden), and Woof (Don Dacus) support Berger (Treat Williams), the charismatic leader of a band of hippies in Milos Forman's *Hair.*

UNITED ARTISTS / THE KOBAL COLLECTION

THE SOUNDS OF SILENCE: HOLLYWOOD SAYS GOODBYE TO TRADITIONAL TUNES by Alan Cylinder

In the late 1960s, all of the major studios had in production a slate of very extensive, very expensive movie musicals. Many would go over budget, and none would show a profit. These musicals included *Star!*, a vehicle pitched to reunite the star and director of *The Sound of Music*, Julie Andrews and Robert Wise; *Darling Lili* (also with Julie Andrews); Bob Fosse's film-directing debut, *Sweet Charity*, with Shirley MacLaine; *Paint Your Wagon*, with those two great song-and-dance men, Lee Marvin and Clint Eastwood; and two Barbra Streisand films of Broadway stage hits, *Hello, Dolly!* and *On a Clear Day You Can See Forever*.

While the common wisdom is that Hollywood studios lost touch with their audience, little attention is paid to the hard fact that, amidst this glut of allegedly bad decision-making by the moguls, *Oliver!* won the Academy Award for Best Picture of 1968, and *Funny Girl* was one of 1968's biggest hits and a multiple Oscar winner, too. These, of course, were both musicals.

And the sad fact of the matter is that the aforementioned flops (along with *Dr. Dolittle, Camelot, Goodbye, Mr. Chips* and a handful of others) were all enjoyable movies—in a few cases, excellent ones.

Name Brands

Director Blake Edwards did some of his finest work to date on *Darling Lili,* a sumptuous valentine to his bride-to-be, Julie Andrews. Boasting a Henry Mancini score, a delightful star turn from leading man Rock Hudson, and an epic feel that encompassed at least three other film genres (romance, comedy, espionage), Edwards's ultraexpensive film tanked at the box office. Today it's well regarded, but in 1969 it seemed an anachronism. Even the director was prone to second-guess his own instincts, and two decades after the film's release, he recut it from 140 minutes down to a sleeker 114. In doing so, he mistakenly tried to modernize what was essentially (and gloriously) an old-fashioned movie.

Hair starts with Claude (John Savage), a visitor to New York City who hails from Oklahoma. Claude is about to join the army, but first he comes across the "army" of Berger and his friends in Central Park. A straight-arrow, clean-cut, all-American boy, Claude falls in love with Sheila (Beverly D'Angelo), the spoiled daughter of very rich and uptight parents. On the surface, Sheila is all debutante, but she has a rebellious side just aching to get out. And Berger and company are just the folks to help it break free. Forman lets the "outside" world of the '60s—parents, police, the court system, the draft board—peer into the story. In some respects, Forman leaves it to the viewer

The two wildly overbudget Streisand vehicles still look fresh today. *Hello, Dolly!*, though released by 20th Century Fox, has all the polish of an MGM production, due primarily to Roger Edens, a mainstay of MGM's Freed Unit, who brought his people to work on the movie, and to Gene Kelly, the MGM legend who directed the project.

The great Vincente Minnelli made his final masterpiece the next year with *On a Clear Day You Can See Forever*. Minnelli's visual flair is evident in each frame of this dark, thoughtful stage-to-film translation. With songs by Alan Jay Lerner (who also scripted) and Burton Lane, it reveals Streisand at her finest, supported by a very effective Yves Montand and a very young Jack Nicholson (Nicholson originally crooned a tune, but it was excised before the film's premiere). In a bow to the times, *On a Clear Day* even features psychedelic main and end titles. Minnelli, another veteran of MGM, made this film at Paramount, the studio most affected by the overspending (*Darling Lili, Paint Your Wagon,* and *Half a Sixpence* also got the green light from that studio).

Sour Notes

As panic due to bad audience calculations became the order of the day, many of the musicals were cut by the studios in an effort to achieve shorter running times and, hence, more shows per day in the theaters (this was long before the multiplexes made overlong movies fashionable). Warner Bros. hacked half an hour out of *Camelot,* MGM removed many of the songs from *Goodbye, Mr. Chips,* and Paramount's *Half a Sixpence* was destroyed beyond recognition.

Star!, 20th Century Fox's biopic of Broadway legend Gertrude Lawrence, had a full hour cut out. The resulting film, retitled *Those Were the Happy Times,* was an incoherent mess, becoming simply a bunch of Julie Andrews tunes with no discernible story.

The most desperate act of all was Universal's handling of *Sweet Charity.* Convinced no one wanted to see it, the studio quickly demoted its pedigree from reserved seat "roadshow" engagements to bleak neighborhood sub-runs, removing twenty minutes and a gigantic production number that featured Sammy Davis Jr. The executives further maligned it by disavowing its musical origins, creating an exploitation ad with the tagline "MEN called her SWEET CHARITY."

to decide whether the kids are irrepressible or irresponsible (one character left his wife and child behind to pursue his own thing).

Hair has held up far better than *Godspell* in part because nearly thirty years after its end, the Vietnam War remains a delicate subject for many Americans. Of the three major American movements of the 1960s—civil rights, women's rights, and antiwar—the feelings generated by the protests against Vietnam arguably remain the most volatile today. At least in can be said that the civil rights movement and the women's movement generated some positive outcomes, albeit through significant travails. *Hair* shows us that Vietnam was an open wound then and remains so today.

Godspell
1971 (PG) 103m/C Victor Garber, David Haskell, Lynne Thigpen, Jerry Sroka, Robin Lamont, Joanne Jonas. **D:** David Greene. **W:** David Greene, John-Michael Tebelak. **C:** Richard G. Heimann. **M:** Stephen Schwartz. *VHS, DVD*

Hair
1979 (PG) 121m/C John Savage, Treat Williams, Beverly D'Angelo, Annie Golden, Dorsey Wright, Don Dacus, Cheryl Barnes. **D:** Milos Forman. **W:** Michael Weller. **C:** Miroslav Ondrícek. **M:** Galt MacDermot, Gerome Ragni, James Rado. *VHS, DVD*

—Jon Caroulis

Groupies ♪

Plaster Caster ♪♪♪

Although female fans have been following around, and offering themselves to, musical performers since time immemorial, it was in the late '60s that the phrase "groupie" was coined to describe the phenomenon. Frank Zappa was one of the first to write songs about diehard groupies—they also figure in his first feature, *200 Motels.* It was the publication of Pamela Des Barres's *I'm with the Band,* however, that jump-started the chronicling of groupie "culture" as an important (or at least luridly interesting) part of rock history.

Groupies should therefore be an invaluable artifact of an era: the one true filmed record of the groupies' lifestyle—appearing around the same time as an interview LP and a pop paperback on the same subject—made while the phenomenon was still fresh. Unfortunately, filmmakers Ron Dorfman and Peter Nevard dropped the ball, as the film is a sadly amorphous creation. A few key figures—including Des Barres and the legendary Cynthia Plaster Caster—do speak on camera, but the bulk of the running time is taken up by prolonged "prep work" for a night on the town by one band of groupies, an endless scene of a very stoned male groupie, and concert clips that have no direct connection to the subject at hand.

Ten Years After, Spooky Tooth, and Joe Cocker are among the artists seen performing at various noted music venues of the time, including N.Y.C.'s Fillmore East and the Scene, and L.A.'s Whisky a Go-Go and Thee Experience. Unfortunately, Dorfman and Nevard felt no compunction to use identifying subtitles anywhere in the movie, so it's impossible to figure out where the artists are playing, or which groupie uses which name in the credits. A movie about groupies doesn't really revolve around music, though; it rises or falls based on the strength of its sleazy anecdotes. A few gems are included—the MC5 attending to two groupies, Jimmy Page whipping one worshipful fan—but the groupies we see the most seem to be girls who have partaken of stars whose reputations have been washed away by the sands of time; Mick Jagger is on one girl's wish list, but the names of their "conquests" do not include more recognizable monikers like Jimi, Jim, or Jeff. We can be certain of this because the one thing that Dorfman and Nevard impress upon us is that these girls *do* kiss and tell.

Aside from a fine version of "Delta Lady" by Joe Cocker and his Grease Band, only two scenes in *Groupies* are memorable: a fast-cut party scene dominated by the shrill-voiced but fun-to-watch "Andrea Whips" (Andrea Feldman, of *Andy Warhol's Trash* and *Heat*), and a brief discussion by Cynthia Plaster Caster about her method of making casts of rock stars' penises. Her explanation of the nuances of the casting process includes an interesting side note about the procedure's biggest dilemma: when the rock star's pubic hair got caught in the mold, and he had to be extricated in a genteel (and gentle) manner.

Cynthia P. C. has long been a subject of fascination among rock fans. She finally receives her due as one of the greatest characters in rock mythology in Jessica Villines's entertaining and amusing documentary, *Plaster Caster*. The shot-on-video feature focuses both on Cynthia's method of working and on other folks' opinions of her art—including a few musicians she has "immortalized" (Eric Burdon and Wayne Kramer of the MC5 note how their sessions went horribly wrong and the results were less than expected . . .). Speed-talking academic Camille Paglia proclaims that Cynthia isn't a pathetic worshiper of male rock stars but rather an empowered female who understood the phallic essence of rock 'n' roll. In the meantime, we watch as the master Caster sets her sights on two current musicians, 5ive Style guitarist Bill Dolan and Danny Doll Rod of the Demolition Doll Rods. She eventually gets them to visit her apartment and to allow her to reproduce their privates for posterity. (A few years ago, Cynthia picked up where she left off after a brief "retirement" from the casting business.)

Villines records the "final dimension" of groupie fame as she shows Plaster Caster assembling her first gallery show. Arranging her "babies" (her nickname for her casts) by the shapes of the penises and not the "star power" depicted (though Hendrix must forever remain her biggest conquest), the seasoned and still attractively bohemian fan girl proves she is egalitarian in her devotion to the male member.

Groupies
1970 (NC-17) 84 m/C Miss Pamela, Cynthia Plaster Caster, Miss Harlow, Goldie Glitters, Chaz, Iris, Andrew Whips, Patty Cakes, Ten Years After, Joe Cocker and the Grease Band, Terry Reid, Dry Creek Road, Spooky Tooth. **D:** Ron Dorfman, Peter Nevard. **C:** William Markle, Michael Becker, Peter Nevard, Joshua Wallace White, Phil Roberts. **M:** Joe Cocker, Ten Years After, Spooky Tooth. *VHS*

Plaster Caster
2001 97m/C Cynthia Plaster Caster, Camille Paglia, Bill Dolan, Danny Doll Rod, Eric Burdon, Wayne Kramer, Noel Redding, Jello Biafra, Pete Shelley, Momus. **D:** Jessica Villines. **C:** Jeff Economy, Ken Heinemann. *VHS, DVD*

—Ed Grant

Head 🎵🎵🎵

It's not uncommon to watch a rock band self-destruct in public, but it's entirely unique to see one deconstruct, dissect, and ridicule itself as thoroughly as the Monkees do in this, their only feature. By turns a mess and a masterpiece, it's always compulsively watchable as it qualifies as the cinematic missing link between the chipper optimism of *A Hard Day's Night* and the "We blew it, man" fatalism of *Easy Rider.* Screenwriter Jack Nicholson (yes, one and the same), director Bob Rafelson, and the four Monkees reportedly all developed the script during a drug-fueled weekend trip to Ojai, California—and it shows.

The movie places the group in a number of absurd situations: they travel through a movie-studio backlot, freefalling into numerous genre-movie sequences; wind up in some very non-Monkee-like Kafkaesque predicaments (the most extreme being a stint in a dark box without windows or doors); attend (natch) a groovy psychedelic party; and—in one of many moves calculated to alienate the teenybopper audience that had loved them on TV—bet on whether a bikini-clad girl on a ledge will jump or not.

> "I'd like a glass of cold gravy with a hair in it, please."
>
> —Davy Jones, in *Head*

No matter how you slice it, *Head* is a career killer, pure and simple. Although modern viewers can enjoy the movie as an offbeat artifact of another era, it was an unmitigated disaster when it came out, to the extent that it never even saw a general release. Monkees' fans were turned off by the strange (non)narrative and "meaningful" moments—as when the movie screen fragments into twenty small TV images, all showing footage of Vietnam atrocities, while our prefab heroes sing "Hey hey we're the Monkees / You know we love to please / A manufactured image / with no philosophies." The stoner audience, who came to embrace the film when it was rereleased in 1973 after scripter/producer Nicholson had achieved major stardom, would initially have nothing to do with a movie starring TV sitcom stars who, as the most common complaint went, "didn't even play their own instruments."

The band had, in fact, taken to playing their own instruments on live tours, as the film's killer version of Michael Nesmith's "Circle Sky" demonstrates quite nicely. But the TV series that had served as the catalyst for the group's formation had been canceled after two seasons, and it's clear watching the movie that the participants were all too eager to drive a stake into the heart of their wholesome, middle-of-the-road image. Davy Jones appears to be the only non-psychedelically inclined Monkee, but his solo song-and-dance turn indicates that he, too, wasn't averse to moving on.

The movie may have flopped miserably on its release, but several positive elements did emerge. Coproducers Rafelson and Nicholson forged a lasting connection and proceeded to collaborate on five movies as director and star. *Head* also provided the Monkees with a solid comedic showcase, allowing them to shed their "plastic Beatles" image and take part in a series of fourth-wall-bursting skits and quick parodies of war movies, westerns, boxing melodramas, and harem romances. The soundtrack produced no top-forty hits, but as had been the case with the Monkees' recordings up to that point,

it contains uncommonly catchy tunes by top-notch talents like Harry Nilsson as well as Carole King and Gerry Goffin.

The guest-star roster includes a host of '60s icons, including Frank Zappa, silicone-pioneer Carol Doda, and Sonny Liston, as well as appearances by a young Teri Garr, genre-movie stalwart Timothy Carey, Annette Funicello, and the man whose "head" the Monkees inhabit (don't ask), Victor Mature.

While *Head* does seem to have been intended as a massive kiss-off to the Monkees phenomenon, the quartet did work together on one final project, an even more absurd TV special entitled *33⅓ Revolutions per Monkee*. The boys oversee a '50s nostalgia jam that features good rockin' by Fats Domino, Jerry Lee Lewis, and Little Richard, but the special remains notable for being a further nail in the already well-weighted Monkee coffin. The special, which tanked in the ratings as it aired opposite the 1969 Academy Awards ceremony, features Micky, Davy, Mike, and Peter as robots, solo artists, and fur-suited simians. *Head*'s playful chaos continues to entertain successive generations of pop-culture addicts; *33⅓ Revolutions* is for Monkee fanatics only.

1968 (G) 110m/C Michael Nesmith, Micky Dolenz, Peter Tork, Davy Jones, Annette Funicello, Timothy Carey, Victor Mature, Frank Zappa. *D:* Bob Rafelson. *W:* Jack Nicholson, Bob Rafelson. *C:* Michael Hugo. *M:* Ken Thorne. *VHS, DVD*

The Monkees—Peter Tork, Micky Dolenz, Davy Jones, and Michael Nesmith— confounded fans' expectations in their 1968 film *Head*.

COLUMBIA / THE KOBAL COLLECTION

The Last Waltz ♪♪♪♪

There's little doubt that *This Is Spiñal Tap* would not have been made if it weren't for *The Last Waltz. Spiñal Tap* is, after all, a direct riff on the rockumentary, from the reminiscences by the hard-living members of the heavy metal group to the interview sessions conducted by director Rob Reiner himself, playing inquisitive filmmaker Marty De Bergi.

In *The Last Waltz,* the origin of the De Bergi character is Martin Scorsese and the inspiration for the *Spiñal Tap* band is the Band, veteran performers calling it quits after sixteen years on the road. But while the film offers a heartfelt look at the ravages of rock 'n' roll and the waning days of a group of tired veterans packing it in (at least as a group), it also works as a celebration of the Band's distinctive music and of the entire Woodstock generation.

The Last Waltz actually encompasses both the unofficial history of the Band and one party/show that began Thanksgiving night, 1976, marking the group's final gig. Staged at rock impresario Bill Graham's Winterland Theater in San Francisco, the event included a lavish dinner for 5,000 attendees and performances that lasted hours. Scorsese and a crack team of cinematographers captured the proceedings on an elegant stage with crystal chandeliers, later adding interviews and additional musical numbers to bridge some of the sequences for the film.

The Band, much admired for their musicianship and ability to blend blues, folk, country, traditional, and rock music in their repertoire, were joined by an impressive list of former collaborators and admiring fellow musicians who perform with the group and contribute some of their own music. What we get is an all-star jam session the likes of which has rarely been seen in the annals of rock-and-roll. First and foremost are the Band—Robbie Robertson, Garth Hudson, Richard Manuel, Levon Helm, and Rick Danko—playing such gems as the religious allegory "The Weight," with backing by the Staple Singers; the Civil War ballad "The Night They Drove Old Dixie Down"; "Stagefright," a telling show-biz confessional; and the celebratory "Life Is a Carnival."

Additionally, there are the diverse guests, a compendium not only of great musicians but of great rock 'n' roll characters, who chip in a slew of mostly memorable solo moments. Ronnie Hawkins, who once fronted the Band when they were starting out in Canada, growls "Who Do You Love?" with conviction. Bob Dylan, who used the group as backup musicians when he "went electric," performs "Forever Young" and leads a concert-ending jam-session version of "I Shall Be Released" in his trademark enigmatic style, wearing a feathered hat that makes him look like a countrified pimp. Van Morrison impersonates a possessed leprechaun, belting out a soulful "Caravan." Blues giant Muddy Waters offers a harmonica-laced, down-and-dirty version of "Mannish Boy." Joni Mitchell matter-of-factly delivers "Coyote." New Orleans hipster Dr. John croaks "Such a Night." And then there are the two Neils. Neil number one is Diamond, who might seem out of place here if not for his association with Robertson (an old pal who produced one of his albums). He does "Dry Your Eyes" in his glitzy, patented Neil Diamond style. And Neil number two is Young, who sings a show-stopping "Helpless" in trademark falsetto, with (notorious) help from some artificial substances uploaded in his nasal cavity.

Scorsese, who cut his choppers helping to edit *Woodstock,* avoids the audience shots and split screens so prevalent in that rock classic. Instead, he prefers to get up close and personal with the performers, a good move considering all of the colorful personalities onboard. Scorsese painstakingly storyboarded the show and the myriad complex camera movements, and while the finished product may have lost some of the spontaneity of other concert films in the process, his homework pays off in other ways. The musical numbers showcasing the complementary give-and-take between the members of the Band are among the film's highlights.

In the interview segments, the loquacious, ever-pensive Scorsese talks to the Band's members behind the scenes; not surprisingly, leader and guitarist Robertson, who once shared a home with the filmmaker, turns out to be the focus of the film. With his hound-dog eyes and brooding good looks, Robertson meaningfully expounds on the long-term effects rock 'n' roll has on its practitioners. He even mentions some victims of the process—Hank Williams, Otis Redding, Janis Joplin, Jimi Hendrix, and Elvis. After he has spoken for a few minutes, Robertson's charismatic world-weariness will have you think you've been on the road right alongside the Band for all those years. Robertson's words have proven to be remarkably prescient. He and Helm, who has throat cancer, have been involved in an ongoing feud over royalties. And a forty-two-year-old Manuel committed suicide in 1986, while Danko died in 1999 of natural causes at the age of fifty--seven. The site of Danko's death? Marbletown, New York, not far from Woodstock.

1978 (R) 120m/C The Band, Bob Dylan, Eric Clapton, Joni Mitchell, Neil Young, Dr. John, Ronnie Hawkins, Neil Diamond, Emmylou Harris, Muddy Waters, Van Morrison, the Staple Singers, Ringo Starr, Paul Butterfield. ***D:*** Martin Scorsese. ***C:*** Bobby Byrne, Michael Chapman, Laszlo Kovacs, Hiro Narita, David Myers, Michael Watkins, Vilmos Zsigmond. *VHS, DVD*

Magical Mystery Tour ♫♫

George Harrison's eyes are somewhere else, man. He's sitting cross-legged in a fog-enshrouded room—or is it a tarmac?—lip-synching "Blue Jay Way." The song states "There's a fog upon L.A.," but that ain't the only place a fog can be found in *Magical Mystery Tour.*

And Harrison isn't the only Beatle in a fog, either. Psychedelically speaking, the other three seem to be doing pretty well for themselves here.

Magical Mystery Tour offers a glimpse of the Fab Four at the height of their LSD experimentation period. This anecdotal, nonsensical outing—intended originally as a feature film, then clipped to a fifty-minute holiday special for British TV—would seem a great antidrug film if it weren't for the terrific music on the soundtrack.

JAZZ ON FILM: INTO THE GROOVY by Bruce Klauber

S ince the dawn of talking pictures, there have been films about jazz and jazz
musicians: a number of misguided biographies, short films featuring big-band
performances, "featurettes" with jazz-oriented performers involved in some type of
ridiculous story line, feature films with brief "guest spots" for name jazz performers,
and projects that have jazz as the basis for their soundtracks. And in one case, a
whole series of short movies were made about jazz that would not be shown in
movie theaters.

Boys in the Bands

As early as the late 1920s, bands and performers of the day, including Duke Ellington, Paul
Whiteman, Ben Bernie, and others were tapped to appear in short films, usually with some kind of
story, that would be shown in theaters before the feature. But when Benny Goodman broke
through nationally and made swing a household word around 1937, things changed. The Goodman
band, with stars like Gene Krupa and Harry James, appeared in its first feature film in 1937, entitled *The Big Broadcast of 1937*. Along with Goodman, moviegoers could also see all the radio stars
of the day in this film, including George Burns, Gracie Allen, and Jack Benny.

A year later, the Goodman crew had a more prominent role in an opus called *Hollywood
Hotel,* notable for introducing the original version of the song "Sing, Sing, Sing" to film audiences.
Drummer Gene Krupa became a star with the Goodman band, so much so that he was able to
leave Benny to form his own crew. Helped by his movie-star good looks, Gene costarred with Bob
Hope in *Some Like It Hot,* now retitled on video as *Rhythm Romance.* As a piece of cinema? Krupa
fans will love it. Bob Hope denies he ever made it, and it doesn't even appear on many of his "official" filmographies.

Short Riffs

The Vitaphone company joined the swing craze with a series of shorts in the late 1930s, the
most famous being Artie Shaw's *Symphony in Swing,* most notable for the first screen appearance
of a young Buddy Rich. Vitaphone did a number of these pieces over the years, but none is as well
known as this one.

In the meantime, virtually every swing band, from Krupa's to Harry James's to Woody Herman's to Lawrence Welk's, was signed to appear as guests in feature films and/or as subjects of
shorts. Among the best of these spots are Krupa's "Drum Boogie" number from Howard Hawks's
Ball of Fire (1941), starring Gary Cooper and Barbara Stanwyck; Harry James's appearance with
Esther Williams in *Bathing Beauty* of 1944; Goodman and a host of other jazz greats in 1942's *Syn-
copation;* Tommy Dorsey with Buddy Rich and Buddy DeFranco in 1942's *Ship Ahoy;* and the 1948
Howard Hawks remake of *Ball of Fire* called *A Song Is Born,* with Goodman, Louis Armstrong,
Lionel Hampton, and others sharing the screen with Danny Kaye.

The major black bands of the day—Count Basie's, Ellington's, Cab Calloway's, Louis Jordan's, and others—had screen time as well, with the best among them being Jordan's "western-

with-jazz" feature called *Look Out Sister.* And who can forget the infamous *New Orleans,* recently released to video more than fifty years after its 1947 release. This was the project that inspired Louis Armstrong to give up his tired big band and return to the small-group format he was noted for. Billie Holiday also scored her only featured film role in *New Orleans.* Her part? Sadly, she was relegated to playing a maid.

Jazz film shorts released over the years were usually "Soundies," which existed from 1940 to 1946 and were made to be shown on something that resembled a coin-operated film jukebox. The machines were located in many bars, restaurants, and hotels throughout the country, and if you put a dime in, you could watch Basie, Ellington, Nat King Cole, Stan Kenton, Krupa, Lionel Hampton, Calloway, and hundreds of others perform their latest hits. When the fad was over, the Soundies, which were produced at an incredible rate of about six per week, were sold off to television. With the rising popularity of television in the early 1950s, a company called Snader Telescriptions produced shorts similar to Soundies except that they were made expressly for televison. Among them are some great historical documents, one being footage of the legendary Count Basie small group of 1950, featuring saxophonist Wardell Gray and, as special guest star, Billie Holiday.

Big-Screen Beat

Outside of a pretty miserable attempt at a jazz-oriented film bio of Tommy and Jimmy Dorsey with 1947's *The Fabulous Dorseys* (miserable because the Dorseys played themselves and could get few of their former stars to appear in it), the major Hollywood studios pretty much had a hands-off policy when it came to jazz. But in 1954, they hit paydirt with *The Glenn Miller Story,* with Jimmy Stewart in the title role. Some jazz can be heard in this film, mainly via the Louis Armstrong jam-session sequence featuring Krupa and Cozy Cole. The music is good in 1956's *The Benny Goodman Story,* as it includes many of the original Goodman stars, but Steve Allen couldn't quite pull off the lead role, and the rest of the acting left much to be desired. *The Five Pennies,* a dramatic project from 1959 with Danny Kaye starring as famed trumpeter Red Nichols (and with Armstrong as guest star), has its moments. Meanwhile, 1959's *The Gene Krupa Story,* with Sal Mineo in the title role, was, as one critic said, "ludicrously inaccurate even by Hollywood standards." The drums, actually played by Krupa on the soundtrack, are the best thing in it.

Taking the realistic, low-budget, dramatic, B&W approach in the 1960s were two underappreciated films. *Sweet Love, Bitter* was a vehicle for comic Dick Gregory from 1966 that was based on the life of Charlie Parker. And in that same year, *A Man Called Adam,* a downer with Sammy Davis Jr., showed just how well Louis Armstrong could do in a dramatic role.

Flying High in the '80s and Beyond

The 1980s looked promising for jazz fans, with the release of Bertrand Tavernier's *'Round Midnight* in 1986 and Clint Eastwood's *Bird* two years later. *'Round Midnight* actually stars a legendary jazz musician, Dexter Gordon, in the lead, and he received an Oscar nomination for his performance. Loosely based on the lives and careers of the late geniuses Bud Powell and Lester Young, *Midnight* is a dark and depressing film featuring Gordon's tentative saxophone playing, filmed a few years before his death. Meanwhile, the well-intentioned but dreary *Bird* may have proved that Eastwood was a huge jazz fan (and he used Charlie Parker's sax on the sonically enhanced soundtrack), but Parker's life was a sad and tragic one.

Spike Lee did a few things with a jazz twist in the 1990s, *Mo' Better Blues* among them, but for the past several years there just hasn't been that much jazz on film. The Tinseltown track record for jazz is spotty at best. Now there's talk about a film bio of drummer Buddy Rich, to be produced by George Clooney and the Rich estate. But somebody, someday is going to produce a film about a happy, well-adjusted jazz musician who wasn't a drug addict or a drunk and who didn't die young. We'll have to wait patiently for *The Dizzy Gillespie Story* or *The Louis Armstrong Story* to hit screens. Or maybe just watch *The Eddie Duchin Story* for the twenty-fifth time.

The meandering storyline has Ringo and his cherubic Auntie riding a yellow bus on a "Magical Mystery Tour" through the English countryside, destination unknown. The other three Beatles are on board as well, along with a colorful crew of passengers—including a midget photographer, a guy with an annoying style of eating, and a few children—who play as Fellini Lite. With each stop comes another musical segment, featuring the Beatles.

The songs are wonderful, but their visual accompaniments are, for the most part, amateurishly executed or pointless. For "Fool on the Hill," Paul looks out the bus window and—voila!—he's a fool on a hill, seeing the world "spinning round." For the instrumental "Flying," the bus passengers look out their windows to find breathtaking aerial photography—of the Arctic! For "Your Mother Should Know," John, Paul, George, and Ringo don tuxedos and partake in a swanky ballroom party, complete with dancers and the rest of their bus daytrippers. Conspiracy theorists would later point to Paul's black carnation in the scene as an ominous foreshadowing of his imminent death.

It should come as no surprise that the film's most bizarre sequence should be tied to one of the band's oddest songs, "I Am the Walrus." The guys are in and out of animal costumes performing the song, but their instruments are not plugged in. The Beatles march behind a bus, followed by mental hospital patients. Goo goo g'joob, indeed.

Although it was filmed in color—and a grainy stock at that—*Magical Mystery Tour* was inexplicably shown in B&W when it debuted in England. Terrible word-of-mouth followed immediately. Audiences were worried about how far from reality the beloved Beatles had strayed. In making the film, each group member took turns at conceiving the various segments, which, in retrospect, come off as pre-MTV music videos. Filmed shortly after the death of manager Brian Epstein, the concept behind the project was for the Beatles to step away from the image of the band the public was used to seeing. Said McCartney around the time of its broadcast: "We could put on a moptop show, but we really didn't want that sort of entertainment anymore. We could

VideoHound's Groovy Movies

have sung carols and done a first-class Christmassy show starring the Beatles with lots of phony tinsel like everyone else. It would have been the easiest thing in the world, but we wanted to do something different."

Different, yes. But good? Not really. Even as an experimental TV show, shot on limited funds, *Tour* was a major mistake from a band that had never really made one before. What's ironic was that the film came out the same year as *Sergeant Pepper's Lonely Hearts Club Band,* one of the group's greatest triumphs. It wasn't until *Magical Mystery Tour* hit the States, playing at late-night showings on college campuses and in repertory cinemas in the mid-to-late 1970s, that the film picked up something of a cult following.

On the plus side, you have the aforementioned songs, as well as "Hello Goodbye." This *Tour* is also sergeant-peppered with some nifty musical in-jokes, with such classic Beatles tunes as "All My Loving" and "She Loves You" played in the most peculiar places in their most peculiar versions. There's a definite *Goon Show–Monty Python* brand of irreverence to the whole journey, too, notable because Harrison later produced several Monty Python projects with his Handmade Films enterprise.

As cinema, *Magical Mystery Tour* pales in comparison to *A Hard Day's Night, Help!* and even *Let It Be.* But this hallucinogenic doodle does offer an interesting state-of-the-band address, circa 1967.

1967 55 m/C *UK* Paul McCartney, John Lennon, George Harrison, Ringo Starr, Neil Innes, Vivian Stanshall, Victor Spinetti, Jessie Robbins. *D:* George Harrison, John Lennon, Paul McCartney, Ringo Starr. *C:* Daniel Lacambre. *M:* John Lennon, Paul McCartney, George Harrison, Ringo Starr. *VHS, DVD*

Monterey Pop ♪♪♪♫

Held over three days in June 1967—more than two years before Woodstock—the Monterey Pop Festival was the first important rock music festival. It's also considered to be *the* landmark musical event, along with the release of the Beatles' *Sgt. Pepper's Lonely Hearts Club Band* album, of the famed "Summer of Love."

Unlike the Beatles' masterpiece, however, director D. A. Pennebaker's documentary, *Monterey Pop,* is a mixed blessing. On the one hand, it contains fascinating concert footage. On the other, Pennebaker's lauded vérité style is often frustrating and occasionally inept. And the list of artists who aren't in the film but who performed at the festival is as long as that of those who appear on-screen.

Among those artists who did make the cut, the standouts are Janis Joplin, Otis Redding, and Jimi Hendrix. To the sturdy, if unexceptional, accompaniment of Big Brother and the Holding Company, the band she fronted at the time, the virtually unknown Joplin wows the audience—including Cass Elliot of the Mamas and the Papas—with her raw, apoplectic rendition of "Ball and Chain." Redding, a big bear of a man, tries a little tenderness that builds to a rousing climax on "I've Been Loving You Too Long." Hendrix pulls out all of the guitar voodoo that made him a star, playing his painted Fender Strato-caster with his teeth, behind his back, and between his legs before setting it on fire during his set-climaxing "Purple Haze."

The Who preceded Hendrix on stage by virtue of a coin toss, and it's easy to see why they wanted to go first. Their virtuosity isn't of the same caliber as Hendrix's. Nevertheless, their psychedelic puffy shirts and waistcoats are just as colorful, and the band's then-shocking "auto-destruction" of their instruments at the end of "My Generation" is still exciting to see.

It's also a thrill to watch some of the other artists, even if their onstage antics aren't as explosive. Best of the rest includes Eric Burdon, leading his New Animals through a cover of the Rolling Stones' "Paint It Black"; Simon & Garfunkel tenderly tripping their way across "The 59th Street Bridge Song (Feelin' Groovy)"; and the Mamas and the Papas re-creating some of their complex studio harmony parts on "California Dreamin'" and "Got a Feelin'." The film also contains decent footage of Canned Heat, Country Joe & the Fish, and jazz trumpeter Hugh Masekela, but a long instrumental by sitar virtuoso Ravi Shankar seems interminable.

Unfortunately, Pennebaker, who also chronicled Bob Dylan's 1965 tour of England in *Dont Look Back,* is so intent on documenting the whole Summer of Love hippie vibe that he wastes too much time on footage of the audience either camping, milling about the festival grounds, or gazing entranced at the performers. That may partially explain why only one or two songs by the selected artists are included in the film. And even when he's aiming his camera directly at the artists, Pennebaker sometimes gets it wrong, too often shooting them in close-up so you can't see them actually playing. His biggest blunder occurs during Jefferson Airplane's performance of Marty Balin's ballad "Today"—not once does the camera actually fall upon Balin, instead focusing exclusively on Grace Slick, who doesn't even sing the song.

Despite the movie's flaws, however, rock fans should be grateful for *Monterey Pop*—now more than ever, thanks to additional footage released well after the original film premiered. In 1986 Pennebaker released the forty-nine-minute *Jimi Plays Monterey* and nineteen-minute *Shake! Otis at Monterey,* which add (considerably, in the case of *Hendrix*) to what's in the mother film. These two short films are featured in a 2002 deluxe boxed DVD set by the Criterion Collection called *The Complete Monterey Pop Festival.* The set also includes *Monterey Pop—The Outtake Performances.* Put together in 1997, the latter program features the Association, Buffalo Springfield (without Neil Young but with David Crosby sitting in, an interesting preview for his partnership with band member Stephen Stills), the Paul Butterfield Blues Band, the Byrds, the Electric Flag, Al Kooper, Laura Nyro, Quicksilver Messenger Service, plus more by Joplin and Big Brother, Country Joe, Jefferson Airplane, the Who, and Simon & Garfunkel. But who invited Tiny Tim?

1968 78 m/C Jimi Hendrix, Janis Joplin, Otis Redding, Paul Simon, Art Garfunkel, Jefferson Airplane, the Who, the Mamas and the Papas, Eric Burdon, Ravi Shankar. *C:* Nick Dobb, Richard Leacock, D. A. Pennebaker, Barry Feinstein, Albert Maysles, Roger Murphy. *VHS, DVD*

—*Barry Gutman*

Performance ♪♪♪♪

Decadence, thy name is *Performance.*

Loathed and loved, *Performance* is one trip to Kinkville, a movie overloaded on sex, drugs, rock 'n' roll, and brutal violence. But then what would you expect from Rolling Stone Mick Jagger in his first screen role, directed by the delirious duo of Donald Cammell (*Demon Seed*) and Nicolas Roeg (*The Man Who Fell to Earth*)?

Inspired by tales of the ultraviolent exploits of the Krays and other gangsters who populated England in the 1960s, *Performance* is essentially an organized crime tale about a crook forced into entering a different environment while finding his way out of a tough spot. In this regard, it may remind some people of *Get Carter,* the Michael Caine classic. But all similarities end there.

The focus here is on Chas (James Fox), a dangerous, showboating strongarm for a London syndicate headed by Harry Flowers (Johnny Shannon). After he's taken to task for sticking his nose where it's not wanted, Chas kills a former enemy who has joined his own organization. This forces Chas to go into hiding as he becomes the underworld's most wanted.

But where can he go? He hears of a home in a trendy London neighborhood that's owned by Turner (Mick Jagger), a reclusive rock star. Posing ridiculously as a juggler, Chas is initially rejected by the rock star, but he eventually persuades Turner to take him in as a tenant in a basement apartment. Chas discovers that two free-spirited, bisexual women, Pherber (Anita Pallenberg, Keith Richards's wife) and Lucy (Michele Breton, a Jagger acquaintance), share Turner's home with him. Although Chas appears to have come from a different planet than the drug-taking, sexually uninhibited threesome, he insists he'll fit in with them—at least for a short time, until he hops a freighter and sneaks away to New York.

But fitting in soon takes on a new meaning as Chas begins to slowly change his own persona to that of Turner's. After dying his hair red, Chas starts living the rock star's lifestyle. He beds both Pherber and Lucy, whose questions about his masculinity make him uncomfortable. He also unknowingly ingests hallucinogen-spiked mushrooms and, after a trippy experience, begins questioning his own identity and his desire to be someone else. At the same time, Turner, who has lost his desire to perform, sees something in Chas that he needs and desires—a life force.

The metaphysical theme of switching identities can be found in both Ingmar Bergman's *Persona* (1966) and Robert Altman's *3 Women* (1977). Both of these thought-provoking films continue to intrigue audiences years after their release. *Performance* elicits impassioned reactions, either positive or negative, from all who see it, probably because the film basks in the immoral world in which it's set. Illicit substances and casual sex are accepted as commonplace in Turner's home, where Pherber matter-of-factly shoots up

> See them all in a film about fantasy. And reality. Vice. And versa.
>
> —Tagline for *Performance*

dope in the bathroom, drugs are gobbled up like cookies, and every night appears to be an orgy.

Upon its release, the film's brutality (seen mostly in the first half hour) and elliptical storytelling also drew strong reactions. Some saw the movie as innovative and daring. Others, however, denounced Cammell and Roeg's attention-getting style, which made use of such devices as fish-eye lenses, long camera zooms, staccato editing, handheld Super 8 footage, shifting from color to B&W, and an infamous shot that follows the trajectory of a bullet as it speeds through a man's skull. On top of these accoutrements, a funny, pre-MTV video of Jagger's "Memo to Turner" appears smack in the middle of the film. With all of these elements, it should come as no surprise that many top film critics really, really hated this movie. In fact, cranky, acerbic critic John Simon called *Performance* "the most loathsome film ever made."

What is inarguable is that Cammell, a former painter and Aleister Crowley enthusiast, and Roeg, a highly regarded cinematographer who shot *Petulia,* wanted to jolt filmgoers' senses—and perhaps draw attention to themselves at the same time. But *Performance* almost didn't see the light of day. It took Warner Bros. nearly two years after its completion to release it, and then only after severe cuts were made. The studio recognized that, whether well reviewed or not, any movie starring Mick Jagger should draw young audiences. While the film didn't fare well when it finally landed in the-aters, it played for years on the midnight circuit, gaining a devoted following. Have the uninitiated watch it today, step back, and watch the arguments begin.

1970 (R) 105m/C/B *UK* James Fox, Mick Jagger, Anita Pallenberg, Michele Breton, John Bindon, Johnny Shannon, Kenneth Colley. *D:* Donald Cammell, Nicolas Roeg. *W:* Donald Cammell. *C:* Nicolas Roeg. *M:* Jack Nitzsche. *VHS*

Privilege ♪♪♥

Sixties Britpop rules—literally, as the ultimate social control in this Orwellian parable concocted by Peter Watkins, a BBC-TV wunderkind who brought a mock-documentary approach to medieval history in *Culloden* (1964) and nuclear holocaust in *The War Game* (1965). *Privilege* is Watkins at his most overtly satirical—which is to say that its humor is drier than Carnaby Street after a draining by *Dracula A.D. 1972*. Really, ducks, while thought content is high here, you'll laugh harder at Kubrick's jokes in *A Clockwork Orange.*

The setting is a near-future England under a one-party government. Paul Jones (who had just quit as vocalist for the real-life band Manfred Mann to concentrate on acting), morosely portrays Steven Shorter, "the most desperately loved entertainer in the world." How trendy is Shorter? Whatever he says, does, eats, or wears affects the U.K. economy and political scene. Steven tunes play on all radio channels and Steven commercials promote consumption of apples. There are glittery discos cum shopping boutiques and a network of TV studios, all named after Steven Shorter. Female fans scream and riot as he sings in arena-rock shows. In reality, however, the pop messiah is a powerless prisoner, a fragile and withdrawn ex-con manufactured into a top-forty idol by handlers micromanaging his life to maintain the official U.K. status quo. Next up, Steven Shorter Enterprises and the Church of England unite to end Shorter's (oxymoronic) image as a carefully controlled rebel and remake him into a submissive, patriotic, and pious citizen. Shorter, after enduring police beatings onstage as part of his music act, is symbolically "freed" and sings rock arrangements of hymns as a clergyman leads concertgoers in a quasi-fascist mantra: "I will conform!"

Offstage, Shorter falls in love with Vanessa (Jean Shrimpton), an attractive artist painting his official portrait. But she won't accept the lonely megastar's marriage proposal, and her painting depicts a hollow shell of a man. Accepting an award on TV, Shorter breaks down and tells his fans he hates them. Okay, here's where the revolutionary mentalities behind *Easy Rider* and *If....* would've brought in federal storm troopers straight out of Kent State to assassinate the troublesome character. Watkins's wrap-up, however, is more disturbing: banned from the media, Steven Shorter is soon forgotten by the contented, conforming British public.

Watkins's documentary-style approach has a nameless, ironic narrator telling us the events of the film as they transpire rather than showing us. That can still be an effective gambit—ask anyone who's seen *The War Game,* which was censored by the BBC and had to play theaters instead. It also helps *Privilege* overcome a relatively small budget for a picture with such lofty intent. An even bigger drag than the film's lack of subtlety are perpetually pained performances by the principals. Jones's Shorter is a handsome but sullen International Man of Misery, an alienated bloke who only shows a spark of life during the few musical numbers. "That's the first time I've ever seen you smile," says Vanessa to Steve at one point, and she's in no position to criticize. Jean "The Shrimp" Shrimpton, a pouty beauty who was a fashion-model sensation on a par with Twiggy, seems equally tranquilized (Shrimpton later retired from show business in favor of domestic bliss and running an inn). A few precious bits of broad humor come from Victor Henry as Freddy K, a manically hip, motor-mouthed musical director and self-proclaimed anarchist in Shorter's retinue. Otherwise, when a marching band at a Nuremburg-style rally strikes up "The Washington Square March"—known to most bloody Yanks as the *Monty Python* theme—it unintentionally evokes just the playful irreverence this production sorely lacks. Not much of a hit despite (or because of) its timeliness, *Privilege* has never been legally issued on an American video label. So beware fuzzy import editions with muffled soundtracks.

1967 (PG) 103m/C *UK* Paul Jones, Jean Shrimpton, Mark Condon, Jeremy Child, Max Bacon, William Job, Victor Henry. *D:* Peter Watkins. *W:* Norman Bogner, Peter Watkins, Johnny Speight. *C:* Peter Suschitzky. *M:* Mike Leander. *VHS*

—Charles A. Cassady Jr.

Sympathy for the Devil ♫♫♪

Rolling Stones fans may disregard this complex and dated bit of agitprop, but its earnest, idealized political episodes and the fascinating, expertly shot footage of the Rolling Stones assembling a pop masterwork (the title song) make it a valuable, though often quaint, document of its time.

The film mixes two threads. In the first, we watch the Stones record their ode to the Horned One. Director Jean-Luc Godard captures their work in impressive long takes—no editing to the beat in this movie. The second thread shows a series of encounters with political radicals: a Black Panther–like group meets in an automobile junkyard near the Thames; lurid magazines are sold at a store run by fascist hippies; a pouty young woman (Godard's then-wife, Anne Wiazemsky) is interviewed about politics, answering only "yes" or "no" to the questions. Interspersed on the soundtrack are excerpts from a sleazy novel that finds public figures behaving in an Ian Fleming/Jacqueline Susann–like manner ("'You're my kind of girl, Pepita,' said Pope Paul, as she lay down in the grass . . . ").

Godard's influence on filmmaking in the 1960s was enormous. The irony was that as Hollywood directors started using his techniques, he abandoned storytelling altogether, in favor of creating overtly political filmed "essays." He later referred to *Sympathy* as his "last bourgeois film"—it was also his first in English, and the first to be significantly tampered with by a producer.

Producer Iain Quarrier okayed a change to the title from Godard's own *One Plus One* to the more Stones-centric *Sympathy.* And, looking for a decisive conclusion to the film (an odd move, given its lack of a clear beginning or middle), Quarrier also considered it essential to add in the finished version of the song, so the *Beggars Banquet* classic was thrown onto the soundtrack at the film's conclusion, over a freeze-frame of the final image (Wiazemsky, dead on a camera crane) rendered psychedelic with color filters. Godard reportedly was so incensed by the re-editing of the film that he punched Quarrier in the nose at an April 1968 screening at London's National Theater. New Line Cinema, the distributor of the film, decided the controversy could result in some solid box office, and so the studio made a move that was quite unusual for the time: alternate showings of the "producer's cut" and the "director's original" at a New York City art house. As the difference between the two versions amounts to a title, some color filters, and a six-minute song, not many film buffs were interested.

Godard's own response to the debacle was to leave mainstream filmmaking behind entirely—but not before he collaborated on another contentious project, an unfinished film made with D. A. Pennebaker and Richard Leacock that included guerrilla-theater sequences featuring Rip Torn, an interview with Eldridge Cleaver, and a pre-Beatles rooftop concert by Jefferson Airplane. Pennebaker later assembled the footage into a feature called *One P.M.*

In later interviews, the Stones dismissed Godard's movie. The truth is, however, that Godard offers the purest record of the band at the top of their form in a studio setting; all other Stones documentaries focus on their live shows (*Gimme Shelter, Let's Spend the Night Together*) or their offstage antics (the notoriously out-of-circulation *Cocksucker Blues*). Godard's fluid approach to filming their recording sessions definitely prefigures the smooth camerawork in Scorsese's *The Last Waltz* and Wim Wenders's *The Buena Vista Social Club,* and it also provides insight into the Stones' working relationships, as Brian Jones in his guitarist cubicle seems to be worlds away from "Glimmer Twins" Jagger and Richards.

The political vignettes are strictly a matter of taste. Students of the period will find them illuminating, while others will simply notice their "real duration" (underlined by Godard's long takes). One thing to keep in mind, though, is that while Godard was considered humorless in his Marxist phase, the ubiquitous voice-over narration is quite amusing, as is the absolute *slew* of lurid magazine covers that are shown in close-up during the bookshop sequence. He may have been adopting a dogmatic stance, but it appears he always recognized the role that hard-core kitsch could play in catching a viewer's attention.

1968 101m/CUK/FR The Rolling Stones, Anne Wiazemsky, Iain Quarrier, Frankie Dymon Jr. **D:** Jean-Luc Godard. **W:** Jean-Luc Godard. **C:** Tony Richmond. **M:** The Rolling Stones. *VHS, DVD*
AKA: *One Plus One*

—Ed Grant

Tommy ♫♫♫

Amazing U.K. rock fab fact: the Who performed their rock opera *Tommy* live, onstage in its entirety, on just two occasions, in 1969 and 1970. Until a rebirth as a 1990s Broadway stage musical, *Tommy* achieved renown largely as a concept album, a wellspring of hit singles, and this delirious 1975 movie version from the febrile lens of Ken Russell. Russell had, by that point, become a law unto himself—with bizarre and revisionist (not to mention visionary) biopics of classical composers; with *The Devils* in 1971; and with that same year's *The Boy Friend,* a retro '30s-style musical comedy (costarring Twiggy) that charmed even those critics appalled by his work and by his flamboyant reworking of historical facts.

Even in today's era of entire TV networks devoted to round-the-clock music videos of digitally edited eye candy, *Tommy* still knocks you over. The allegorical plot, a comment on child abuse, misplaced hero-worship, and religion, is overlong and hard to digest without liner notes, but it starts with the marriage of Nora (Ann-Margret) and the dashing Captain Walker (Robert Powell, who had just essayed the title role in Russell's *Mahler*), during the London Blitz. Walker's plane is shot down, leaving Nora pregnant with a boy born on V-Day, named Tommy. Mrs. Walker catches the eye of a seedy entrepreneur-showman, Frank Hobbs (Oliver Reed), and they fall in love and marry—but then Captain Walker shows up, unexpectedly alive, surprising them in bed. The married couple kill the intruder before Tommy's horrified gaze, then order the boy not to see, hear, or speak of the incident.

Thus does little Tommy lapse into a psychosomatic, catatonic state—blind, deaf, and dumb—that lasts into adulthood (whereupon Who member Roger Daltrey takes over from child actor Barry Winch). Smothering their guilt behind facades of wealth, religion, and opulence, Frank and Nora try to cure Tommy with myriad treatments, from faith-healing (a statue of Marilyn Monroe in her skirt-blowing *Seven Year Itch* pose stands in for the Virgin Mary) to sex and drugs (enter Tina Turner as the Acid Queen). But nothing works, and they give up hope. Then Tommy discovers a pinball machine. The deaf, dumb, and blind kid, miraculously, is able to play the game faultlessly, and he becomes a sensation, making Frank and Nora fabulously rich. But the mother continues to be obsessed by her son's impenetrable facade until a breakthrough that allows Daltrey to let loose with "I'm Free." Suddenly Tommy can see, hear, and speak, and in short order the youth is perceived as a messiah. But the attempt to build an organized religion around Tommy Walker fails even more dramatically than it began.

Russell's much-criticized style is not so much psychedelic as Warholean in its pop-arty visuals, from the recurring silver balls and circular patterns to the electrified silkscreen-print colors (not to mention, of course, that Tommy becomes world-famous for about fifteen minutes). The movie has held up well over the years, perhaps because, apart from the World War II trapppings near the beginning, nothing points to a specific time period or era, and the film's snazzy visual style and lyrical riddles mark it rather like *2001: A Space Odyssey*—as a '60s story the time of which, paradoxically, has not yet come.

Roger Daltrey (with Oliver Reed and Ann-Margret) stars as the title character in the Who's rock opera, *Tommy*.

Ann-Margret was nominated for an Academy Award for Best Supporting Actress for her strenuous performance (she dances, writhes, and vamps in a Mrs. Robinson–meets-Oedipus manner with her strapping, stricken son), but it's the blocky, bull-like Reed, part caring stepdad, part blustery (even murderous) opportunist, who seems to sum up creator Pete Townshend's wildly mixed worldview. In addition to Tina Turner's electrifying Acid Queen, Eric Clapton appears as a shamanic figure, Elton John sings his way into pop-culture immortality as the dethroned Pinball Wizard, and Jack Nicholson has a small part as a doctor (who flirts with Ann-Margret in an apparent wink to the previous steamy pairing of the two in *Carnal Knowledge*). Ken Russell's daughter Victoria has a bigger supporting part as Sally Simpson, an ill-fated worshiper of Tommy.

Aside from Daltrey, the member of the Who most visible is drummer Keith Moon as leering pervert Uncle Ernie, unwisely assigned to watch over Tommy. Moon died a few years later, in 1978, of a drug overdose, while Roger Daltrey, Ken Russell, and Paul Nicholas (who plays another of Tommy's sadistic sitters) reteamed straight after *Tommy* for another classical-music farrago, *Lisztomania,* which met with far less success.

1975 (PG) 111m/C *UK* Ann-Margret, Oliver Reed, Roger Daltrey, Keith Moon, Paul Nicholas, Robert Powell, Tina Turner, Victoria Russell, Eric Clapton, Elton John, Barry Winch, Jack Nicholson. *D:* Ken Russell. *W:* Ken Russell. *C:* Dick Bush, Ronnie Taylor, Robin Lehman. *M:* The Who. *VHS, DVD*

200 Motels 🦴🦴🦴

Although he became a rock star at the height of the psychedelic era, Frank Zappa was very forthright about the fact that he never did drugs. Well, maybe Frank didn't, but the members of his band, the Mothers of Invention, did, and so did his fans. And so this peculiar cult movie, which played the midnight circuit for years in the '70s, represents a challenge of sorts from Frank to his audience: Just try and wrap your mind around this.

There is no plot per se in *200 Motels,* only the idea that "touring can make you crazy." The Mothers are led around by two mystery figures: Rance Muhammitz (Theodore Bikel), a German-accented interrogator, and Larry the Dwarf (Ringo Starr), a stand-in for band leader Frank Zappa—who, as the Mothers state in the film, is perpetually using their experiences as fodder for his songs. The Mothers wind up in the sterile small town of Centerville, which is surrounded by a barbed-wire fence. As one member of the band, Jeff Simmons (a real-life person, played here by Ringo's real-life chauffeur, Martin Lickert), leaves the group because he feels their music has degenerated into "comedy," the rest of the Mothers devote themselves to scoring with local groupies, whose numbers include a curious figure in a nun habit (Keith Moon).

Zappa's *200 Motels* is a massively egotistical movie. He has his characters/bandmates engage in debates about his influence on the band, stops

LOST WOODSTOCK FOUND

For the twentieth anniversary of *Woodstock*'s 1970 theatrical release, Warner Bros. put together *Woodstock: The Lost Performances,* a collection of some of the material that was cut out of the original movie and the subsequent director's cut.

The Band, Bob Dylan's backup band at one time, conspicuously absent from the original film, start things off with a spirited version of "The Weight." Dylan, who didn't appear at the fest, is represented by his song "Walking Down the Line," interpreted in meandering style by Arlo Guthrie. Canned Heat, whose "Going Up the Country" is memorably used in the background during the beginning of *Woodstock,* are given the spotlight to perform it live here, and they don't disappoint—it remains one of the songs most closely associated with the film.

Others given a larger spotlight in which to shine this time out are Richie Havens, who performs the soulful program-ending cover of "Strawberry Fields Forever"; Joan Baez, good for a moving "Amazing Grace"; John Sebastian, playing "Darling Be Home Soon"; and grungy Joe Cocker, kicking out all the stops with an appropriate selection, "Let's Go Get Stoned." Best of all are Crosby, Stills & Nash, who chip in a lively "Marrakesh Express" and a treatment of Paul McCartney's "Blackbird," with Stills taking solo honors. In the singer-songwriter department, Melanie ("Birthdays of the Sun") and Tim Hardin (performing the definitive version of his own "If I Were a Carpenter") are welcome newcomers to the Woodstock vibe who were overlooked in the original film incarnations.

As for Jimi Hendrix, his set has been collected on the hour-long *Jimi Hendrix at Woodstock,* a separate entry released in 1992 that includes selections from the feature film like "The Star Spangled Banner," along with "Fire" and others.

Among those still missing in action from any Woodstock video release are Mountain, Blood, Sweat & Tears, Creedence Clearwater Revival, the Incredible String Band, and Crosby, Stills, Nash, *and* Young. We can only hope that we'll see and hear them on another anniversary date, when a definitive program is issued.

the action dead for musical interludes (including a lengthy mock-operatic suite), and indulges in in-jokes that presume the audience knows (or cares about) the Mothers' tangled history. Zappa receives directorial credit on-screen for "characterizations," while Tony Palmer (*Cream's Farewell Concert*) is credited with "visuals" for this pioneering attempt to shoot a feature film on video for later transfer to 35 millimeter. Zappa biographers note that Palmer merely introduced the equipment to the project and control-freak Frank was 100 percent responsible for the hallucinatory look of the film.

And why would a confirmed non-user of recreational chemicals make an extraordinarily druggy movie? Perhaps Zappa was merely extending his "control" of the proceedings to the other side of the screen—if his fans came to concerts stoned, it was likely they'd attend the movie in the same state and have a slightly *strange* reaction to the sight of synchronized dancers wearing fish-head masks or a man dressed up as a vacuum cleaner. Perhaps to ratchet up the mind games, *200 Motels* is one of the most claustrophobic "trip" movies of all time, as the whole thing was shot indoors at Pinewood Studios in England. The rapid video "flashes" and constant solarization of the images only add to the state of psychedelic paranoia the movie seems intended to produce.

The bum trip aside, *200 Motels* is worth catching for several reasons. First and foremost, Zappa assembles an impeccably talented ensemble cast. Loveable ol' Ringo gets to curse a bit as he laconically recites Zappa's off-beat dialogue (a speech on how orchestral musicians require "forced reorientation" to become rockers is by far the wildest). Mellow actor/folkie Theodore Bikel goes along with the joke, playing a friendly *Hogan's Heroes*–style Nazi, while Keith Moon looks right at home in his nun's habit—especially during the melodramatic sequence where the character talks about her broken heart to her fellow "road ladies."

The element that truly elevates the movie from being a mere surreal freakout, though, is the music. The Royal Symphony Orchestra put in time accompanying Zappa's musical flights of fancy, but it's his "vaudeville band" of regulars who actually deliver the goods. Mother emeritus Jimmy Carl Black gleefully enacts the role of über-redneck "Lonesome Cowboy Burt," while the movie's true stars, vocalists Howard Kaylan and Mark Volman (who later were renamed Flo and Eddie and were part of the pop group the Turtles), tear into Zappa's timeless meditation on well-equipped motel rooms, "Magic Fingers."

Three days of peace, music . . . and love

—Tagline for *Woodstock*

1971 (R) 100m/C Frank Zappa, the Mothers of Invention, Theodore Bikel, Ringo Starr, Keith Moon, Janet Ferguson, Lucy Offerall, Jimmy Carl Black, Martin Lickert. *D:* Frank Zappa, Tony Palmer. *W:* Frank Zappa, Tony Palmer. *C:* Tony Palmer. *M:* Frank Zappa and the Mothers of Invention. *VHS*

—*Ed Grant*

Woodstock ♪♪♪♪

You would think that Woodstock would get old after awhile. After all, here's a thirty-plus-year-old film that many of us have seen at least a few times. It runs well over three hours with an "interfuckingmission." It features lots of stoned people sloshing through the mud and skinny-dipping in dirty, mosquito-laden water. And the dialogue includes an overabundance of "man"s and "groovy"s. All this and Sha-Na-Na, too.

Yet viewed today, *Woodstock* remains surprisingly fresh and vital. One reason may be the care director Michael Wadleigh and his team (including a young editor named Martin Scorsese) put into it—care that is plainly evident on the screen. Concert films before and after Woodstock usually offered shaky camerawork, scratchy sound, and amateurish psychedelic imagery. Sure, you may think Wadleigh and team may have erred in their choice of the many performances available to them. But you can't deny that *Woodstock* is sophisticated and incredibly well done, especially in its use of split screens to capture the on- and offstage happenings. One senses that the ultimate goal of the film is to tell a story while presenting an official account of one of the 1960s' main social, political, and artistic events: "three days of love and music" that took place on Max Yasgur's Linden, New York, farm over three rainy mid-August days and nights in 1969.

While not everything is in exact chronological order, we're given a thread to follow through the movie, something rare among concert films. The background sounds of Crosby, Stills & Nash's "Long Time Gone" and Canned Heat's "Going Up the Country" set the proper mood as we witness the preparation for the event—clearing the farm, constructing a stage, putting up speaker towers. Then we're offered footage of attendees flocking en masse to the area. Most of the commentary is provided in "You Are There" fashion with an "Establishment" news reporter trying to act cool while interviewing some of the show's organizers, both cranky and understanding townspeople, and the freaky fans flocking to the festival. The cameras capture hippies, nuns, families, and a joint-rolling Jerry Garcia getting psyched.

Drama builds as the show approaches. Soon after the actual concert gets underway, the flimsy fence that surrounds the concert site is trampled by the overwhelming crowd. The music has barely started and already there are problems. We've been told millions of dollars are on the line. Rock impresario Bill Graham half-jokingly suggests building a moat with fire to alleviate the problem, but Woodstock's promoters determine nothing can be done, so their show becomes a freebie. A little later, a twenty-mile traffic jam wreaks havoc, closing the New York State Thruway. Over the loudspeakers, we hear that there's more than just a rock concert occurring among the 400,000 in attendance: bad acid, broken arms, a few births. It's a communal thing, and the film's audience becomes part of it.

It's the music that eventually brings everything and everyone together. Although the musical sequences play like one complete concert, they were heavily edited. Many of the acts played full sets, sometimes up to ten songs in one shot, but the film's editors selected a sampling of songs from a sampling of acts. (A handful of songs were restored in the late 1990s with a "director's cut" version of the film released on video.) Nevertheless, the film captures a cross-section of rock, folk, and blues at an important time, when themes of peace, love, and understanding permeate the music no matter what its style.

Folk music is well represented with Richie Havens, who starts the concert off with the compelling antiwar songs "Handsome Johnny" and "Freedom." Joan Baez offers the political ballad "Joe Hill" and also gets to discuss the travails of her husband, David Harris, in prison for draft evasion. In addition, Arlo Guthrie's "Coming into Los Angeles" provides appropriate backing for a pro-marijuana montage, and John Sebastian's "Younger Generation" is used to show us all the kids in the "house."

Surprisingly, two of the film's most talked-about spots come from the blues department, British division. Joe Cocker unchains his heart, spastic moves and all, with an unforgettable cover of the Beatles' "A Little Help from My Friends," while guitar virtuoso Alvin Lee leads Ten Years After in a show-stopping "Going Home."

The headliners score impressively as well. Crosby, Stills & Nash's performance of "Suite: Judy Blue Eyes" is an intricate beauty, performed with voices in top form, before drugs, booze, and age had taken their toll. (Neil Young also played with the trio at Woodstock, but his work is relegated to songs played over the closing credits.) And while the Who, led by fringe-vested, bare-chested lead singer Roger Daltrey, actually played *Tommy* almost in its entirety at Woodstock, only "See Me, Feel Me" makes the cut here, but it's bolstered with "Summertime Blues," accented by a Pete Townshend guitar-smashing demonstration in the finale.

Other big-name acts give their fans what they want. Carlos Santana's epic "Soul Sacrifice" has everybody up and dancing, Jefferson Airplane provide music to trip by with "Saturday Afternoon/Won't You Try" in an early morning slot, and Sly & the Family Stone surprise everyone, not so much with their overlong "I Want to Take You Higher," but by the fact that the unpredictable Sly actually showed up for the gig. Meanwhile, Country Joe & the Fish take novelty song selection honors with "The Fish Cheer" ("What's that spell? Fuck!") and the sing-songy Vietnam protest ditty "I-Feel-Like-I'm-Fixin'-to-Die Rag," complete with "follow the bouncing ball" lyrics on-screen.

In the soon-to-be-dead rock star category, Janis (Joplin) and Jimi (Hendrix) showed, but not Jim (Morrison). Janis's performance is "Want Me, Lord," a blues-injected screechfest that's all Joplin, love it or not. Hendrix, performing at the tail end of the festival to a sparse crowd, works his feedback-inflected guitar work through "The Star Spangled Banner," "Purple Haze," "Voodoo Child," and more.

Although some of their work has been collected on the 1990 VHS collection *Woodstock: The Lost Performances,* conspicuously absent from the original theatrical version of *Woodstock* and from the director's cut are the Grateful Dead, the Band, Creedence Clearwater Revival, Melanie, Mountain, and Blood, Sweat & Tears. Oh well. At least Sha-Na-Na's "At the Hop" has been preserved for posterity.

1969 (R) 228m/C Jimi Hendrix, Janis Joplin, Crosby, Stills & Nash, Sly & the Family Stone, Richie Havens, Joan Baez, Country Joe & the Fish, John Sebastian, the Who, Joe Cocker, Santana, Jefferson Airplane, Arlo Guthrie, Jerry Garcia, Alvin Lee, Bill Graham. **D:** Michael Wadleigh. **C:** Don Lenzer, Richard Pearce, David Myers, Michael Wadleigh, Al Wertheimer. *VHS, DVD*

Chapter 18

Not for Kids Only

J ust because a movie is animated, or has a man in a big, fluffy monster suit, or features comic-book superheroes wearing tights doesn't mean it can't appeal to clear-headed adults or people who want to tune in, turn on, and drop acid. In fact, many a movie designed first and foremost for kids caught fire with college students and repertory theater devotees in the 1960s and early 1970s and again finding new life years later when it appeared on home video.

Fantasia, Disney's expensive 1940 animated epic that meshed classical music with Mickey Mouse and mind-bending animation, never recouped its enormous budget even after years of rereleases. It was only when the film found favor with audiences who patronized such movies as *2001: A Space Odyssey* and *Barbarella* that Disney saw *Fantasia* move from the red into the black. Urban legends have swirled for years that Uncle Walt experimented with acid. He must have, *Fantasia* fans thought—and still think. How else do you explain the creepy weirdness of "A Night on Bald Mountain" and the hallucinogenic "Rite of Spring" sequence?

Anybody who watched Saturday-morning TV in the late 1960s and 1970s certainly can't forget the creations of Sid and Marty Krofft, two brothers specializing in bringing such weird fantasy worlds as *Lidsville,* *The Bugaloos,* and *Sigmund and the Sea Monsters* to life. The siblings, who scared a few kids and entranced a few stoners in their time, brought their colorful oversized puppet act to the big screen with the all-singing, all-oddball, all-creepy *Pufnstuf* (based on the TV show *H. R. Pufnstuf*) in 1970. The TV-to-screen transition was nothing new, as the hugely successful *Batman* series with Adam West had zoomed down a similar bat-route a few years earlier, in an adventure that pitted the Caped Crusader against an all-star lineup of villains.

Willy Wonka and the Chocolate Factory did solid business, mostly at kiddie matinees, when first released in 1971, but it wasn't until the kids who liked *Willy Wonka* grew up and turned their own kids on to the Roald Dahl adaptation that the movie became a bona fide cult hit. Seasoned fans looked beyond its upbeat hit theme song, "The Candy Man," and reveled in its darker elements. *Willy Wonka*'s fevered following, fermenting into the 1990s, warranted midnight showings, a theatrical rerelease, two special-edition DVDs, and a planned remake with Johnny Depp as the confectionery king and Tim Burton directing.

As Disney proved with *Fantasia* and George Dunning with *Yellow Submarine,* his mod, Peter Max–inspired feature-length film, animation didn't have to be kids' stuff anymore. Ralph Bakshi took it one step further, proving that the domain could also be strictly adult in nature. The former Terrytoons animator adapted cartoonist R. Crumb's *Fritz the Cat* to the big screen with much success, and the "'X'-rated and animated" feline paved the way for Bakshi's autobiographical *Heavy Traffic,* race-related *Coonskin,* and 1950s throwback *Hey, Good Lookin'* to follow down the animated alleyway. Other animated programs looking to go to the head of the midnight movie class included *Dirty Duck;* the French sci-fi tale *Fantastic Planet; The Fantastic Animation Show,* an anthology of sensory-expanding shorts; and the psychedelic, rock music–propelled *Heavy Metal.*

Ren and Stimpy, Spongebob Squarepants, Cartoon Network's Adult Swim lineup, and even *The Simpsons* are forever indebted to these animated pioneering efforts. *Ay caramba!*

Batman 🦴🦴🦴

T he Crest Movie Theater on Rising Sun Avenue was buzzing with anticipation. Every seat in the place was filled, and some of the crowd had
spilled over to the moldy maroon carpeting on the aisle floor. A few minutes after a Tom & Jerry cartoon and two coming attractions for horror
movies, over 350 kids, many wearing buttons and T-shirts emblazoned with
images of the Caped Crusader and the Boy Wonder, began to chant. "We want
Batman! We want Batman!"

The curtains suddenly closed, then opened again, the logo of 20th Century Fox now visible. The chants drowned out the familiar studio fanfare and
the dialogue of three salutes to real-life crime fighters that appeared on the
screen. Then, a searchlight in a dark alleyway, moving around, finding its subject, and . . . BAM! Adam West as Batman. The chants turned to deafening
cheers. Then, another searchlight, moving around and . . . KER-POW! Burt Ward
as Robin. More cheers. Searchlights on again, on the lookout for . . . CRASH!
The villains: the Joker (Cesar Romero). Hissss! The Penguin (Burgess Meredith). Boooo! The Riddler (Frank Gorshin). Hissss! Catwoman (Lee Meriwether).
Boooo! The level of electricity in the theater remained constant through all 105
minutes of *Batman.* It's likely the current was so strong the corn popped on
vibes. Sometimes the dialogue was drowned out by loud cheers or boos.

Batman, the movie (now known as *Batman: The Movie* on video), delivered everything the series had that made us go ga-ga and more. At times, too
much more. Sometimes, the TV shows were so ingenious and funny, Batman's rivals so neat, that you wished the superhero could go longer than the
allotted two weeks against the same villain. Here we have ninety minutes with
four all-star criminals; it's no wonder these bat finks seem to be jostling for
screen time. And you thought Tim Burton's *Batman Returns* with the Penguin
(Danny DeVito), Catwoman (Michelle Pfeiffer), Max Shreck (Christopher
Walken), and other criminal cronies was busy!

The storyline has the archfiends casting their collective noggins on
taking over the world. How will they achieve this bat-astrophe? With a device

Robin (Burt Ward) and Batman (Adam West) cruise onto the big screen for the first time in the 1966 movie *Batman.*

20TH CENTURY FOX / THE KOBAL COLLECTION

that dehydrates people, turning them into specks of colorful powder. The quartet of creeps uses the contraption to pulverize the entire U.N. Security Council. Then Catwoman will draw the attentions of millionaire Bruce Wayne to lure Batman and Robin into the villains' lair.

The plot, of course, takes a backseat to all of the Bat and bad-guy accoutrements. Nary a scene goes by without an introduction of some Bat product, from a Batboat to Bat shark repellent to the Bat-copter. If this film was made today, there would be so many toy tie-ins they'd have to open a store called Bats "R" Us. On the bad-guy side, the Penguin's submarine is filled with dials and buttons and nifty periscopes. It's enough to make you utter an approving "Wah-Wah," like the feathery fiend.

Batman doesn't stray far from the TV series, offering smartly choreographed action scenes (with all the comic-book exclamations intact), campy dialogue supplied by screenwriter Lorenzo Semple Jr., and amusing straight-faced acting by West and Ward, who supplies lots of "Holy" this-and-thats. In the villain department, all the actors ape their TV personas to a tee: Meredith cackles and waddles gloriously as the Penguin, Gorshin is a ball of delirious energy as the Riddler, and Romero captures the craziness of the clownish Joker. Only Meriwether, a former Miss America, wasn't on the TV show—she took the Catwoman part after Julie Newmar bowed out of the big-screen version. Meriwether does a solid job, though Newmar or Eartha Kitt, who played the part later in the TV series, would have been more arresting in the role.

VideoHound's Groovy Movies

SATURDAY MORNING SPY SHOWS: ANIMATED ADVENTURES FOR THE WHOLE FAMILY

by Gary Cahall

Just as a rash of prime-time TV imitators drew inspiration from the immensely popular James Bond films in the mid-1960s, so too did the makers of Saturday morning kids' shows jump at the chance to offer up their own take on the spy genre. In the great history of children's TV trends, spy shows really constituted little more than a blip between the cowboys and astronauts of the late '50s/early '60s and the superhero craze that followed the 1966 debut of *Batman,* but for that brief time, a fondly remembered array of secret agents—both human and animal—kept the world safe between sugar-drenched-cereal commercials.

The first of these trench-coated 'toons to make its way onto the tube was Hanna-Barbera's *Secret Squirrel* in 1965. The weaponry of the rodent of one thousand faces, as his theme song explained, included "a bulletproof coat, a cannon hat, [and] a machine gun cane with a rat-a-tat-tat-tat." Aided by Peter Lorre-esque sidekick Morocco Mole, Secret (voiced by Mel Blanc) traveled the world fighting an assortment of bad guys, most prominently the Goldfinger-like Yellow Pinky, whose voice recalled that of Sydney Greenstreet.

Debuting the next year was digit-sized detective *Tom of T.H.U.M.B.* Caught along with Asian aide Swinging Jack in an experimental shrinking ray, Tom became the top operative of the Tiny Human Underground Military Bureau and appeared on the *King Kong* show. Another 1966 cartoon crime fighter was actually created by Batman's papa, Bob Kane. *Cool McCool* was more *Get Smart* parody than Bond spoof, with his bumbling demeanor, "mustache-phone," and catchphrase of "Danger is my business." He also boasted a rogues' gallery to rival the Caped Crusader's, battling such oddball foes as the Rattler, Jack-in-the Box, Professor Madcap, and Hurricane Harry (who bore a striking resemblance to *Secret Squirrel*'s Yellow Pinky).

Not much came along in 1967 other than *Spy Shadow,* about a secret agent whose shadow could come to life and help him solve cases, and which ran as part of the classic, never-to-be-forgotten *Super President.* The following year's contribution to the genre was Filmation's *Fantastic Voyage,* loosely based on the 1966 20th Century Fox film and following the animated adventures of a quartet of miniaturized government operatives tracking down enemy spies and the like. The show was perhaps best known for the Marvel Comics–like bickering between two members of the squad, bespectacled scientist Busby Birdwell and an Indian mystic and guru known as, well, Guru.

The final 007-inspired children's series of the era, and the only live-action one, mixed one part *Dr. No* with one part *Planet of the Apes. Lancelot Link: Secret Chimp,* debuting in 1970, followed simian superspy Lance and gal pal Mata Hairi, top agents for A.P.E. (Agency to Prevent Evil), as they foiled the schemes of C.H.U.M.P. (Criminal Headquarters for Underworld Master Plan). There were no humans on the show, only voices that the creators attempted (and often failed) to match up to the chimps' mouth movements, à la *Mr. Ed.* The hirsute stars were seen driving cars, changing in and out of disguises, and even playing rock songs as the band the Evolution Revolution. One can only imagine what older folks, waking up after all-night Friday partying, must have thought when they turned on their sets and found this!

Batman may not have the dark edge, the elaborate special effects, Nicole Kidman and Kim Basinger, or even the prominent nipples of the later *Batman* films, directed by Burton or Joel Schumacher. But for any kid that was sitting at the Crest Theater on that Saturday afternoon in July 1966, it's the only *Batman* movie that really counts.

1966 (G) 105m/C Adam West, Burt Ward, Cesar Romero, Frank Gorshin, Burgess Meredith, Lee Meriwether, Alan Napier, Neil Hamilton, Stafford Repp, Madge Blake, Reginald Denny, Milton Frome. **D:** Leslie Martinson. **W:** Lorenzo Semple Jr. **C:** Howard Schwartz. **M:** Nelson Riddle. *VHS, DVD*
AKA: *Batman: The Movie*

Fantasia ♫♫♫♫

Poll critics and audiences of today, and you'll be told that Walt Disney's ambitious attempt to wed an octet of classical music opuses to animated imagery was the precursor of the music video phenomenon, and holds up as one of the greatest cartoon features ever crafted. Had you asked around in the wake of *Fantasia*'s disappointing opening run over sixty years earlier, you'd have been told that the Mouse Man's bid to bring high culture to the masses was a pretentious flop that pushed his studio into the red. What is now regarded as a capstone of the corporate creative portfolio spent years trying to reach the break-even mark, as a mortified Walt trotted ever-more-bowdlerized cuts into rerelease.

Something had to have happened between Point A and Point B, folks, and that would have been the advent of the psychedelic '60s, when a generation of youth craved eye candy for its chemically induced consciousness expansion. In 1969 Disney granted *Fantasia* its first theatrical run in six years, and Walt's Folly was pushed solidly into the black for the first time. Campus demand for rental prints of *Fantasia* subsequently exploded, and the family-oriented studio found itself in possession of America's hottest head movie. Blissfully blown-away college kids grooved to Mickey's battle with the animated brooms to the tune of Paul Dukas's "Sorceror's Apprentice," as well as to the hippo/crocodile ballet set to Ponchielli's "Dance of the Hours."

Not that the folks who were giving us *The Love Bug* and *The Boatniks* in that era would pander to such an unsavory market, of course, but their ad materials for *Fantasia*'s 1969 release rendered the film's trippiest images—the dancing mushrooms of "Nutcracker," the demon Chernobog from "Night on Bald Mountain"—in full Day-Glo head-shop-poster glory and proclaimed the feature as "The Ultimate Experience." The LSD generation performed similar magic with Disney's 1951 adaptation of *Alice in Wonderland,* which had also met with public indifference upon its initial release.

Recreational tastes have changed since then, but the '60s generation gained an appreciation of what Walt was shooting for and passed it along to the next generation. While the Stoned Age put *Fantasia* squarely into American iconography, those days have passed us by, and what do you know—you don't have to be wasted to enjoy the film after all.

1940 (G) 120m/C V: Leopold Stokowski. **N:** Deems Taylor. **D:** Ben Sharpsteen. **W:** Joe Grant, Dick Huemer, Lee Blair, Elmer Plummer, Phil Dike, Sylvia Moberly-Holland, Norman Wright, Albert Heath, Bianca Majolie, Graham Heid, Perce Pearce, Carl Fallberg, William Martin, Leo Thiele, Robert Sterner, John McLeish, Otto Englander, Webb Smith, Erdman Penner, Joseph Sabo, Bill Peet, Vernon Stallings, Campbell Grant, Arthur Heinemann. **C:** James Wong Howe, Maxwell Morgan. **M:** Johann Sebastian Bach, Paul Dukas, Modeste Mussorgsky, Amilcare Ponchielli, Franz Schubert, Igor Stravinsky, Pyotr Ilyich Tchaikovsky, Ludwig van Beethoven. *VHS, DVD*

—*Jay Steinberg*

Fritz the Cat ♫♫♫

Animator Ralph Bakshi managed to launch a number of feature projects throughout the 1970s on the strength of the acclaim, notoriety, and box-office reception granted to his adaptation of underground cartoonist Robert Crumb's creation *Fritz the Cat*. Time hasn't been very kind to Bakshi's oeuvre, which was regarded as revolutionary in its day. Likewise, much of what made *Fritz* outrageous back then now seems merely obvious, but the first animated feature ever to draw an "X" rating from the MPAA still retains a good chunk of the subversive charm that made the film a cause célèbre in the first place.

The Brooklyn-raised Bakshi, who spent the '60s rising to the top of the production chain for the old Terrytoons studio, was intrigued by Crumb's infusion of radical political, sexual, and scatological humor into familiar funny-animal comic forms, and Bakshi drew from several of Crumb's mid-'60s *Fritz* tales in crafting his screenplay. The film's pussycat protagonist, a cynical NYU collegian already weary of the world, spends the opening sequence in Washington Square trying to pass himself off as a sensitive artiste to a trio of young lovelies, in the hopes of getting some action. Once they start buying his line (to his own great surprise), he whisks them off to a crowded, hemp-clouded East Village crash pad, where his hoped-for intimate encounter in the bathtub turns into a risqué cartoon take on *A Night at the Opera*.

The party gets interrupted by a couple of bumbling cops (portrayed as—big surprise—pigs), and Fritz flees during a melee that spills into an Orthodox synagogue. The film goes from there into a comic odyssey reflective of the restless '60s, as Fritz unwittingly sets his dormitory ablaze, then tries to inconspicuously lay low in a Harlem populated by crows. After sparking a full-scale riot, he skips town, only to fall in with a radical cell that has targeted a power plant for destruction.

The visuals in *Fritz* are constantly compelling, with backgrounds that utilized watercolors made from photographs of the New York City locales. The score is likewise memorable, with its utilization of vintage performances from Billie Holiday and Bo Diddley and a now-recognizable vibes solo from Cal Tjader. Bakshi went with primarily nonprofessional voice talent, casting the roles by ear. Fritz was voiced by Skip Hinnant, an actor who owes his other claims

He's "X"-Rated and Animated!

—Tagline for *Fritz the Cat*

RALPH BAKSHI: ANIMATION ON THE FRITZ
by Charles A. Cassady Jr.

Considering that the cinematic era of the late '60s/early '70s experimented wildly with imagery and color, it's curious we don't associate many animators with the period. Animation, after all, knows no boundaries in line, shape, color, form, and logic. It can be as malleable as a lava lamp or as structured as a super-hero comic.

Edgy animation actually preceded the Aquarian Age. Purely abstract cartoon shorts, pioneered by Europeans in the 1920s, were done to the rhythm and melodies of classical music as part of Disney's *Fantasia,* a 1940 release from a notoriously conservative studio that, two decades later, would be embraced by hippies as a "head" film. Canada's Norman McLaren boldly experimented with drawing/scratching on celluloid in the 1940s. Way-cool visual jazz was being composed with brush and ink in San Francisco in the '50s by Hy Hirsch and other Beat movement filmmakers. And John and Faith Hubley had perfected their loose, informal style by the early 1960s with *Moonbird, The Hole,* and *Of Stars and Men.*

Perhaps if George Dunning, director of the amazing, Op-Art "modyssey" *Yellow Submarine,* had not died prematurely (leaving just a fragment of a follow-up project, Shakespeare's *The Tempest*), '60s 'toons would have looked even loonier. But it was in Ralph Bakshi that the cartoons and the counterculture collided.

Urban Cowboy

Bakshi was born in 1938 to a Russian-Jewish family in Haifa, in what is now Israel. The family emigrated to America, with Bakshi growing up in a squalid Brooklyn that would later be reflected vividly in his work—urban, gritty, and often violent, not green and pastoral with fluffy bunnies. Graduating from Manhattan's High School for the Industrial Arts, Bakshi got work with Terrytoons, the New Rochelle studio founded by Paul Terry, and worked on such characters as Mighty Mouse and Deputy Dawg, rising to prominence in the company. Yet there's a telling scene in his semi-autobiographical *Heavy Traffic* (1973), in which the filmmaker's stand-in, a boyish young animator, screens his blasphemous demo reel for a revered, decrepit, talking-animal cartoon mogul of yesteryear. The elder dies of shock.

For, even though he was once president of Paramount's New York cartoon division, Bakshi's sympathies were with the underground comix field, those outlaw scatological comic books (*Fabulous Furry Freak Bros., Little Annie Fanny*) that thrived in the '60s, celebrating their freedom from the censorship of the Comics Code Authority to flaunt anti-Establishment politics and outrageous humor. More closely allied with R. Crumb than with Toys "R" Us, Bakshi's adults-only stuff is replete with sex, drugs, gangs, ghettoes, ethnic slurs, and angry caricatures right out of Times Square at its seediest—*Who Framed Roger Rabbit* meets *Midnight Cowboy.*

An equal-opportunity offender, he turned an acid-dipped stylus on limp-wristed drag queens, black pimps, Italian American mafiosi, brute Irish cops, and Jewish mothers. Bakshi's 1971 *Fritz the Cat,* a Robert Crumb adaptation with anthropomorphized animals on the make for sex in the city, won a degree of public acceptance (in addition to the novelty of being the first "X"-rated cartoon feature). Bakshi's subsequent *Heavy Traffic* and *Coonskin* pushed the envelope further, so much so that Bakshi was assaulted by protestors during previews of *Coonskin*—a *Song of the South*–besmirching combo of live action and animation that brought the Uncle Remus fables into a lurid blaxploitation milieu, with Br'er Rabbit as a Harlem gangsta.

Paramount caved to the Congress of Racial Equality and pulled *Coonskin* out of theaters. Another Bakshi work-in-progress, *Hey Good Lookin'* (a cynical poke at *Grease* nostalgia, with leather-jacketed hoods and their debs on Coney Island in the 1950s), went into limbo. Bakshi spent the remainder of the '70s on thematically less inflammatory material, chiefly the heroic fantasies that had legions of college kids under their spell in the 1960s.

Flights of Fantasy

The antiwar, antitechnology *Wizards* (1977) is, according to Bakshi, an allegory of Jews seeking peace after the Holocaust, but it also owes a lot to the mushroomy *Cheech Wizard* panel strips of early-'70s comix illustrator Vaughn Bode. *Fire and Ice* (1983) was a collaboration with Frank Frazetta, popularizer of barbarian sword-and-sorcery imagery. J. R. R. Tolkien fans still debate the worth of Bakshi's 1978 *Lord of the Rings* feature, which faced impossible deadlines, finance problems, and studio meddling, and went out to theaters only half the hobbit saga Bakshi intended.

Bakshi continued making animation and live-action films into the 1990s (even reviving Mighty Mouse in a new TV series), but he grew disillusioned with "disgusting" Hollywood types. "I don't want to spend the rest of my life with those people," he told the *Onion.* "I'd rather spend my time with Rembrandt and Goya at home." Professing to find his early-'70s cartoon work too personal and disturbing to behold, Bakshi has turned to fine-art painting and prints, selling items via his website, www.ralphbakshi.com.

But the home viewer can discover Bakshi's portfolio on VHS or DVD; it's a Day-Glo snapshot of the psychedelic era, truer than *Sabrina and the Groovie Goolies.* Even *Coonskin* (also circulated under the title *Streetfight*) has escaped the briar patch of censure, while, ironically, Walt Disney's long-running *Song of the South* remains unreleased on video for its racist attitudes. *Fritz the Cat, Heavy Traffic, American Pop, Wizards, Fire and Ice, Hey Good Lookin',* the live-action/animated *Cool World,* and, of course, *Lord of the Rings* are all available. Some admirers also point to the *Spider-Man* TV cartoon Bakshi supervised for ABC-TV, a program that became increasingly wild and far out as it progressed from 1967 to 1969.

to fame to the comics as well, having been Schroeder in the original off-Broadway production of *You're a Good Man, Charlie Brown* and having provided the voice of Pogo in various TV specials.

Bakshi and producer Steve Krantz would ultimately split over the property, with Krantz ringing in Hinnant and other animators to deliver a barely watchable 1974 sequel, *The Nine Lives of Fritz the Cat*. Crumb's own support for this venture was never more than halfhearted at best, and he made an unsuccessful bid to have his name removed from the finished product. Soon after the film's release, the comix pioneer gave the film his final repudiation by killing Fritz off in print. In a story that also savagely jabbed Bakshi and Krantz, Fritz—depicted as a self-absorbed show-business sell-out—took an ice-pick in the base of the skull from an abused groupie.

1972 (NC-17) 78m/C *V:* Skip Hinnant, Rosetta LeNoire, John McCurry, Phil Seuling. *D:* Ralph Bakshi. *W:* Ralph Bakshi. *C:* Ted C. Bemiller, Gene Borghi. *M:* Ed Bogas, Ray Shanklin. *VHS, DVD*

—Jay Steinberg

Pufnstuf

During the 1970s, Canadian puppeteers Sid and Marty Krofft used their generations-old family craft to make themselves a remarkable niche in the annals of children's television. Their live-action, puppet-populated comedy and adventure series—amongst them *Sigmund and the Sea Monsters, The Bugaloos,* and *Land of the Lost*—were a desirable alternative to the bland animated weekend fare offered up by the networks, and they are fondly remembered by the late Boomers who grew up with them. The first such show that the Kroffts concocted—*H. R. Pufnstuf,* which debuted in 1969—drew such strong early buzz that Universal commissioned a feature film version for the following summer.

The premise of the series and the film centers around Jimmy (Jack Wild, the Artful Dodger of *Oliver!*), a British lad whose father's job transfer to America leaves him friendless and miserable, until he comes upon a jewel-encrusted talking flute answering to the name of Freddy. The new companions help themselves onto an inviting skiff resting seaside, and the boat spontaneously sets sail for Living Island, an amazing atoll where animals speak and rightfully inanimate objects speak *and* move. Jimmy's arrival is monitored by Witchiepoo (Billie Hayes), an overbearing crone riding a jet-powered "Vroom-Broom," who immediately covets Freddy for herself. Saving Jimmy and Freddy from her predations are the island's mayor, a genial, drawling, six-foot-long potbellied dragon known as Pufnstuf, and his sundry puppet populace.

Alas, the years have not been kind to *Pufnstuf*. The verbal gags, admittedly written down to kids, seem very creaky now, and the show tunes written for the production numbers have a closed-in-ten-days feel to

them. Then, as now, the series' greatest virtue was Hayes's batty, over-the-top villainy. The actress, whose prior career highpoint was her stint as Mammy Yokum in the Broadway run (and subsequent film) of *Li'l Abner,* would later work the good-guy shift as the genie in the Kroffts' *Lidsville.* Martha Raye and Mama Cass Elliott also offer fun turns in the film's climactic witches' convention.

In 1970 the gang from Sid and Marty Krofft's TV show *H. R. Pufnstuf* made the jump to the big screen in *Pufnstuf,* directed by Hollingsworth Morse.

For what it's worth, if you encounter the good folks of Living Island and find something familiar that you can't quite put your finger on, it's very understandable. At the height of *H.R. Pufnstuf'*s popularity, an ad agency approached the Kroffts about brokering a *Pufnstuf* tie-in for a major fast-food chain and then turned around and told the producers that the idea was dropped. Soon afterwards, the "McDonaldLand" ad campaign first surfaced, featuring characters that were designed and crafted by ex-Krofft employees. The puppeteers successfully sued the agency, as well as the Golden Arches, for having misappropriated the "look and feel" of their creations.

1970 (G) 98m/C Jack Wild, Billie Hayes, Martha Raye, Cass Elliot, Billy Barty, Sharon Baird, Joy Campbell. ***D:*** Hollingsworth Morse. ***W:*** John Fenton Murray, Si Rose. ***C:*** Kenneth Peach. ***M:*** Charles Fox. *VHS, DVD*

—*Jay Steinberg*

Willy Wonka and the Chocolate Factory 🦴🦴🦴

It's everybody's
non-pollutionary,
anti-
institutionary,
pro-confectionery
factory of fun!

—Tagline for *Willy
Wonka and the
Chocolate Factory*

One of the '70s' darkest and most off-the-wall family films had its genesis in the fondness that director Mel Stuart's daughter had for one of Roald Dahl's typically skewed children's tales, *Charlie and the Chocolate Factory*. Stuart successfully pitched the notion of adapting the story to film to his producer-friend David Wolper, who set out to round up financing. Proof positive that cross-marketing was alive and well even back then: the Quaker Oats Company was at that time desirous of launching a candy line, and they agreed to foot the production's considerable bill in anticipation of the promotional opportunities that would follow.

The narrative opens on Charlie Bucket (Peter Ostrum), a fatherless schoolboy who lives in caricatured squalor in a one-room shack shared by his mother and his four grandparents, who haven't moved in years from the bed they all share. Like everyone else in the world, Charlie has a pronounced sweet tooth for the amazing candies produced by Willy Wonka, a reclusive confectioner who keeps his factory secluded from all human eyes. Wonka then shocks the world with an announcement that five Wonka Bars have been shipped containing golden tickets to be redeemed for a personal tour of the facility guided by the Candy Man himself.

A hilarious global panic erupts as the lucky ducats are pursued. They ultimately fall to Charlie and a quartet of brats with diverse vices—the gluttonous Augustus Gloop (Michael Bollner); the spoiled, tantrum-tossing Veruca Salt (Julie Dawn Cole); the obnoxiously tube-fixated Mike Teevee (Paris Themmen); and the eternally gum-cracking Violet Beauregarde (Denise Nickerson). Each in the company of a parent figure (and each having been approached with an offer of a bribe by a Wonka competitor), they are greeted at the gate by Wonka (Gene Wilder), who leads them into a sugar paradise where lollipops sprout beside a chocolate stream. (The elaborate and bizarre factory sets evidence every dollar that was sunk into them.)

As they proceed through the facility manned by Wonka's dwarfish personnel, the orange-skinned, green-coiffed "Oompa-Loompas," the tone of *Willy Wonka* starts shifting from sweet to bitter. One by one, the kids each fall prey to industrial accidents that they're led into by their signature flaws, as a blasé Wonka makes passionless attempts to warn them off. Charlie is the only one who ultimately prevails, and whom Wonka deems worthy of his grand prize, a fulfillment of his agenda in offering the lottery in the first place.

Although promoted to the hilt at the time of its release, *Willy Wonka* performed only marginally, perhaps because of darker elements that generally weren't found in a family film of the era. "The Candy Man" became the only breakout song from the enjoyable Leslie Bricusse/Anthony Newley score, and Quaker Oats' "Wonka" candy line would never achieve more than moderate success. It took broadcast and home video to bring the film its richly deserved audience. Warner Home Video's thirtieth-anniversary edition of the DVD boasts one of the most enjoyable running commentaries ever captured, as the five Wonka kids were brought together in one room for the first time since the production wrapped and giddily shared their reminiscences of the set.

1971 (G) 98m/C Gene Wilder, Jack Albertson, Peter Ostrum, Roy Kinnear, Julie Dawn Cole, Leonard Stone, Denise Nickerson, Dodo Denney, Paris Themmen, Michael Bollner. *D:* Mel Stuart. *W:* Roald Dahl, David Seltzer. *C:* Arthur Ibbetson. *M:* Leslie Bricusse, Anthony Newley. *VHS, DVD*

—Jay Steinberg

Yellow Submarine ♫♫♫

Armed with arresting neon visuals, an insouciant verbal wit, and the audience-grabbing cachet that only the music of the Beatles could provide, the animated feature *Yellow Submarine* became a signature "head movie" for the tuned-in, turned-on, and dropped-out generation. Producer Al Brodax and director George Dunning, responsible for *The Beatles,* the mid-'60s Saturday morning cartoon based on the moptops, engaged German print graphics master Heinz Edelmann to establish the film's look, and the end result is a nonstop feast for the eyes that draws influence from Peter Max, M. C. Escher, and many others.

> **"It's all in the mind."**
>
> —George Harrison, in *Yellow Submarine*

The film's script, which had been doctored by a pre–*Love Story* Erich Segal, offered up a subsea utopia named Pepperland, where the content locals spend their days indulging their love of music. Their idyllic existence galls to no end the Blue Meanies, a diverse menagerie of azure-skinned brutes who launch a craven attack, pummeling the populace into suspended animation. The lone escapee, a dapper old salt answering to the name of Fred, makes a getaway in the eponymous craft, in search of allies who can restore song to the land.

His flight takes him to Liverpool, where he makes his entreaties to a skeptical John, Paul, George, and Ringo. The lads eventually pipe themselves aboard for an eye-popping quest that takes them through a series of surreal seas—a habitat for ever-more-absurd giant monsters; a vast nothingness solely inhabited by the "Nowhere Man," Jeremy Hillary Boob, Ph.D.; a field of dimension-hopping holes. The boys finally deploy in Pepperland for a climactic showdown with the malevolent Meanies.

The Fab Four in fact had minimal input into the film's creation, and that was precisely how they wanted it. They privately loathed the Brodax-helmed TV show and viewed the project as a convenient way to wrap up the three-picture deal with United Artists that kicked off with *A Hard Day's Night* (1964) and *Help!* (1965). Accordingly, the Beatles only delivered four original songs for the soundtrack. The end-product was enough of a pleasant surprise, however, that they acquiesced to appear in the film's live-action epilogue.

Aural attention must be paid to *Yellow Submarine* as well, since the script boasts an engaging stream of wordplay that's surprisingly evocative of

Lennon's written works. While a hit of its period, the film spent a surprising number of years languishing unnoticed. A major restoration of the film was embarked upon in the late '90s, culminating with a 1999 rerelease boasting a remixed soundtrack, enhanced visuals, and the inclusion of the sequence inspired by "Hey Bulldog," which made the original British cut but was trimmed for American release.

1968 (G) 90m/C V: Paul Angelis, Peter Batten, John Clive, Dick Emery, Geoff Hughes, Lance Percival, George Harrison, John Lennon, Paul McCartney, Ringo Starr. **D:** George Dunning. **W:** Al Brodax, Jack Mendelsohn, Lee Minoff, Erich Segal. **C:** John Williams. **M:** John Lennon, Paul McCartney, George Harrison, Ringo Starr, George Martin. *VHS, DVD*

—Jay Steinberg

Chapter 19

Something's Up—
Could Be a Heist

The formula is simple: get a group of eclectic, sometimes grizzled ex-cons together for one last haul. Add some spiffy technology, a nifty location where the jewels/cash/diamonds/artwork are held, unexpected law enforcement figures to turn up the suspense, and one unpredictable member of the band of thieves to almost screw things up. Voila! You have a heist film!

Of course, not every heist film fits that mold. But many of them do, albeit with some minor variations.

The granddaddy of all modern heist films is *The Asphalt Jungle*, John Huston's delicious 1950 caper with Sam Jaffe as the ex-con putting together a team of specialists for a jewelry robbery. Colorful sidemen played by the likes of Sterling Hayden, Louis Calhern, and James Whitmore, along with a very young Marilyn Monroe, added color to this B&W classic. The tall, gruff Hayden also starred in *The Killing* (1956), a gripping noir heist about a racetrack robbery, directed by an unknown twenty-eight-year-old director named Stanley Kubrick.

Rififi, a French film from 1955, directed by American expatriate Jules Dassin while he was blacklisted in the States, was so realistic in its silent thirty-minute depiction of a jewelry robbery that it was banned in some countries (almost in France, even). François Truffaut cited it in interviews and writings as the best film noir he had ever seen. Dassin, whose pre-HUAC American efforts include the tough crime dramas *Brute Force* and *Night and the City,* dipped back into the caper well successfully on a lighter note with 1964's *Topkapi,* featuring wife Melina Mercouri and Peter Ustinov, who won an Oscar for his colorful supporting effort.

France has been responsible for many classic caper excursions. The best of them came from Jean-Pierre Melville, whose atmospheric efforts often featured tough-talking crooks in trench coats and fedoras pulling off impossible thefts, then facing off against the no-nonsense detectives on their trail. In other words, they were homages to classic American film noirs of the 1940s and 1950s. *Bob Le Flambeur* (AKA *Bob the Gambler*), a 1956 tale of a gambling-addicted criminal plotting the robbery of a casino, was good enough to get two successful reissues in theaters and a 2003 remake—*The Good Thief,* with Nick Nolte—while 1961's *Le Doulos* and 1967's *Le Cercle Rouge* rank among the best crime thrillers ever.

The 1960s and 1970s were prime time for caper flicks in America and abroad. Anti-Establishment was in, and a number of unusual and colorful characters were willing and able to buck the system in order to cash out. The teams partaking in heist plots ranged from the Vegas cool of Sinatra and his Rat Pack robbing casinos in 1960's *Ocean's 11* to the Nick at Nite cool of 1967's *Who's Minding the Mint,* with its all-star cast of Jim Hutton, Dorothy Provine, Bob Denver, Milton Berle, and Joey Bishop (how did that Rat Packer get in there?). And in case of fears that too many crooks would spoil the dupe, there were always star pairings looking to get in the money, ranging from Warren Beatty and Goldie Hawn (*$*), to Audrey Hepburn and Peter O'Toole (*How to Steal a Million*), to Robert Redford and George Segal (*The Hot Rock*).

Over in England, the Brits were hot to get their hands on movies about hot rocks, hot pounds, hot anything. Heist films offered young, enterprising directors a chance to tighten the grip in the thriller department while strutting their stuff with flashy editing and camerawork, capturing the time's mod surroundings and saying "bollocks" to the royals and upper classes. Michael Winner, who scored big later with *Death Wish,* delivered *The Jokers* in 1966, a comedic caper in which Oliver Reed and Michael Crawford (yes, the Michael Crawford of *Phantom of the Opera* fame) team to attempt to steal the crown jewels from the Tower of London. Other U.K. offerings include *Perfect Friday,* Peter Hall's picture about a banker plotting to rob his own place of employment; *Robbery,* Peter Yates's take on *The Great Train Robbery;* and *The Italian Job,* the fanciful winner with Michael Caine, Noël Coward, Benny Hill, a fleet of Mini Coopers, and one of the oddest endings in movie history.

These days, Hollywood is good for about a heist film or two a year. Consider such recent releases as *The Score, Heist,* and the remake of *The Italian Job.* They all stick to the formula, but why shouldn't they? It works.

Grand Slam 🦴🦴🦴🦴

The heist movie goes international in *Grand Slam,* a crime caper that is much admired by those who recall viewing it in theaters in the late 1960s, but that had gone largely unseen until a release exclusively on DVD in 2003. The actors come from all over the world, the director is Italian, the production companies are West German, Spanish, and Italian, and the setting is primarily Rio de Janeiro. And while the story borrows heist film elements from such classics as *Rififi, The Asphalt Jungle,* and *Topkapi,* its international flavoring, high suspense quotient, and nifty plot surprises makes this goulash not only palatable but memorable.

In *Grand Slam,* Edward G. Robinson is James Anders, an American professor recently retired after teaching for thirty years in Rio. Anders has come up with a detailed plan to swipe $10 million in diamonds from a heavily secured Rio de Janeiro jewel company during Carnival. Anders seeks help from Mark Milford (Adolfo Celi), an old friend and crime honcho, who helps put together a team of experts needed for the robbery. The crew includes an electronics technician (Riccardo Cucciolla), a safecracker (Georges Rigaud), a strong-armed ex-military man (Klaus Kinski), and a playboy (Robert Hoffman).

As expected, there's no honor among thieves here. The wild card of the crew is Kinski, a former navy man whose skipper cap and tight, white uniform make him look like he just walked out of an Old Spice commercial directed by Rainer Werner Fassbinder. He makes no bones about detesting Hoffman, the French Lothario, but it isn't clear just why. Could it be jealousy, since Hoffman's primary role in the job is to get Janet Leigh, a diamond company worker, to go to bed with him? Or is Kinski angry that Hoffman is seducing Leigh and not him? We're never quite sure with the ever-menacing Kinski, who could exude pansexual creepiness if he were playing Santa Claus (now that could've been something!).

Nearly equaling Kinski's intensity is the heist sequence. Bearing some similarities to scenes in *Topkapi* and 2001's *The Score,* the ten-minute segment works wonderfully, sleekly cross-cutting between bikini-clad Carnival revelers on the street and crooks Cucciolla and Rigaud silently dismantling the jewels from a safe. Dressed in wet suits and wearing gloves, the crooks employ suction cups, shaving cream, and the '60s version of high-tech equipment. Of course, there are some monkey wrenches thrown into the proceedings, including an immoveable manhole cover that threatens the getaway and security guards who suddenly appear to investigate the premises.

Because of convoluted financing plans, 1960s-era international coproductions often had a slapdash feel to them. *Grand Slam* is no exception, but it's a level above the cut-and-paste European-made spaghetti westerns and Mafia massacres popular during the time. Robinson, in a truncated part that's almost a cameo, seems to have been recruited simply to add a legit American name to the proceedings, but he's engaging as the cagey perpetrator of the crime. Leigh, meanwhile, is introduced halfway through the effort and seems, at least at first, to be little more than American window dressing, too. In the end, however, her character provides the film's dandy surprise punch line.

Director Giuliano Montaldo (*Sacco & Vanzetti*) injects atmosphere into *Grand Slam* with nice touches of local color. He's adept both at capturing the sensuality of Rio's Carnival at night and at observing a group of local kids getting excited by a goal by Pelé in a soccer game broadcast on the radio. Ennio Morricone's idiosyncratic score, a mix of South American bossa-nova rhythms and bouncy *Casino Royale*–style pop, helps keep the action light on its feet.

Grand Slam may not be a grand slam in the annals of heist cinema, but it is an exhilarating triple, worth seeking if only to see if it lives up to its reputation. It does and then some.

1968 (NR) 121m/C Janet Leigh, Robert Hoffman, Edward G. Robinson, Klaus Kinski, Riccardo Cucciolla, Georges Rigaud, Adolfo Celi. **D:** Giuliano Montaldo. **W:** Augusto Caminito, Marcello Coscia, Marcello Fondato, Jose Antonio de la Loma, Mino Roli, Paulo Bianchini. **C:** Antonio Macasoli. **M:** Ennio Morricone. *DVD*
AKA: *Ad Ogni Costo; Top Job; Diamantes A Gogo*

The Italian Job (1969) 🦴🦴🦴🦴

The Italian Job (2003) 🦴🦴🦴

A quirky and flavorful caper flick, *The Italian Job* is a distinctly '60s British production that has gained a tremendous cult following over the years. Best known for its amazing car chase sequence that takes up at least twenty minutes of the last portion of the film, *The Italian Job* is an effortlessly breezy affair, featuring an eccentric cast led by Michael Caine at the height of his charming Cockney-bloke phase. That the film inspired a big-budget American remake in 2003 can be taken as either high praise or damnation, depending on your point of view of the 2003 model or big-budget

> **"It's a very difficult job and the only way to get through is we all work together as a team. And that means you do everything I say."**
>
> —Charlie Croker (Michael Caine), in *The Italian Job* (1969)

F. GARY GRAY: TAKING ON AN EXCITING JOB by Lou Gaul

When an offer came to direct the remake of *The Italian Job,* F. Gary Gray felt uninformed but interested.

The talented filmmaker had never seen the 1968 caper picture with Michael Caine, Noël Coward, Rossano Brazzi, and British comic Benny Hill, so he was in the dark in terms of the material's subject matter.

"The way this project came together for me is like a Hollywood love story," Gray said in a 2003 interview. "Sherry Lansing [the chair of Paramount Pictures] called my cell phone, told me the studio executives had a project they were very excited about, and said it could go right into preproduction if I agreed to direct it.

"Things never happen like this in Hollywood. It usually takes years to get a project going."

Gray asked Lansing for enough time to watch the first version before accepting the assignment and immediately rented *The Italian Job* from his favorite video store.

"As I watched the original, I recognized that it has the type of energy we associate with the 1960s," said Gray, whose directing credits include *A Man Apart,* with Vin Diesel and Larenz Tate; *The Negotiator,* with Samuel L. Jackson and Kevin Spacey; *Set It Off,* with Queen Latifah and Jada Pinkett Smith; and *Friday* with Ice Cube and Chris Tucker. "I knew an updated version could be fun, and then I read the script for the remake, which had different elements from the original but still contained the Mini Coopers, the gold heist, and the traffic jam."

The picture involves a complicated heist, and the main characters zoom through the streets in Mini Coopers and snarl traffic in Los Angeles to complete their crime. Gray had to shut down two blocks of Hollywood Boulevard near Grauman's Chinese Theatre and the Kodak Theater (the new home of the Oscar ceremony). He then used three hundred assorted automobiles, several armored trucks, a few motorcycles, and a handful of low-flying helicopters for the complicated sequence, which also includes the Mini Coopers being driven down the Hollywood Boulevard entrance to the Metro Rail Line.

Only three Mini Coopers—one red, one white, and one blue—are seen, but thirty-two different vehicles were actually used for the sequence that has the tiny cars crashing into things, flying through the air, and dodging obstacles.

According to Gray, the chase scenes proved a technical challenge, but the most important part of the process of *The Italian Job* was hiring the right actors, ensuring that people would care about what happened to the characters.

He called Mark Wahlberg to star as the gang leader due to the "commitment" the actor gave to his role as an ill-fated porn star in *Boogie Nights.* For the costarring role as a safecracker, Gray approached Charlize Theron, a model-turned-actress who intrigued him when he saw the "very human quality" she brought to her role as an ailing woman in *Sweet November.*

American remakes of well-regarded '60s British films in general (like *Get Carter* and *Payback*).

Michael Caine plays criminal mastermind Charlie Croker in the 1969 film *The Italian Job.*

In the original, Caine plays Charlie Croker, a criminal just out of the slammer. After Charlie receives word that an ally named Beckerman (Rossano Brazzi) has died in a mysterious car crash, he views a movie in which Beckerman explains a heist he was planning—an elaborate scheme in which $4 million in gold bullion would be swiped from a security truck in Turin, Italy. Charlie decides to carry out his departed associate's plan. Before he puts together a team of thieves, however, he needs the approval of Mr. Bridger (Noël Coward), an imprisoned crime lord who is treated like royalty while behind bars.

Like most heist films, *The Italian Job* spends substantial time on figuring out how to carry out the operation and recruiting the principals who are going to pull it off. This time, however, things are a little different. Director Peter Collinson (*The Penthouse*) and screenwriter Troy Kennedy-Martin (who penned the epic British miniseries *Edge of Darkness*) emphasize what has to be done to make the robbery succeed, teasing the audience with bits of information on how Charlie and a crew of goofballs (which includes comic Benny Hill as "The Professor") will go about the job.

We learn that surveillance cameras around the city of Turin will be shut down and a huge traffic jam will enable the crooks to escape with the stolen gold. But we're never quite sure how it will all play. Watching the precision of the thieves at work is part of the film's delight. Best of all are three cute Mini Coopers that dodge police cars and motorcycles, carrying the stolen goodies around the traffic jam, onto sidewalks, down stairs, and into alleyways.

The Minis are painted Union Jack red, white, and blue, a whimsical pro-British touch in a film filled with them. The score, credited to Quincy Jones, boasts satiric versions of "Rule Britannia" and "God Save the Queen," and a rousing football chant called "We're the Self-Preservation Society." A colorful van with pro-England statements plays a part in the heist. Meanwhile, a nasty ongoing rift develops between Charlie and Altabani (Raf Vallone), an Italian mobster, who sees Croker's heist plan as a slap to his Italian pride.

Along with the unforgettable Mini Coopers, *The Italian Job* is remembered for its bizarre, open-for-interpretation final shot. To give it away would not be fair. Let's just say it leaves audiences hanging, wondering what the fate of Charlie and his cronies will be. While not fulfilling, it is at least in tune with the rest of the refreshingly off-kilter criminal activities that preceded it.

The fanciful feel of the original is nowhere to be found in 2003's *The Italian Job*. Instead, we have a solid but predictable heist flick that reshuffles elements of the original with unspectacular but diverting results. Here, John Bridger (Donald Sutherland) is the leader of a gang of thieves who have recently taken $300 million (talk about inflation!) in gold bullion from a Venice safe. Gang member Steve Frezelli (Edward Norton) betrays the others, shooting Bridger and thinking he has left the rest of the crew at the bottom of a river in the Alps. He then takes off to Hollywood with the loot. The remaining gang members, led by Charlie Croker (Mark Wahlberg), actually survive the ordeal. A year later they reunite, and, with Bridger's safecracking daughter, Stella (Charlize Theron), joining them, contrive to take their cash back from Frezelli. To recapture the heavily guarded bullion, Croker must come up with an elaborate plan. And he does, devising a scheme involving Mini Coopers, Russian mobsters, and stalling traffic in Hollywood.

Give this version of *The Italian Job* points for sticking to a classic heist formula by peppering the proceedings with colorful side characters on the job. Among them are an explosives expert who is hearing impaired in one ear (played by Mos Def), an electronics wizard who claims he was the original inventor of the Internet music service Napster (Seth Green), and a devil-may-care British car expert (Jason Statham).

The problem here lies in the leads. Wahlberg displays little of Caine's charisma and annoyingly smiles at the camera a lot; Norton, who seems to be doing a Sean Penn impersonation (mustache and all), just seems dour and disinterested throughout; and Theron is sadly underused as the film's primary, potentially interesting female character. Thankfully, director F. Gary Gray does a solid job with the robbery and action stuff, especially the scenes in Venice early on and the Mini Cooper material late in the film. Those looking for something unique and lively should seek out the original, which will have you yearning for fish and chips and a spot of tea immediately after viewing.

The Italian Job (1969)
1969 (G) 96m/C Michael Caine, Noël Coward, Benny Hill, Raf Vallone, Tony Beckley, Rossano Brazzi, Maggie Bly, Irene Handl, John Le Mesurier. *D:* Peter Collinson. *W:* Troy Kennedy-Martin. *C:* Douglas Slocombe. *M:* Quincy Jones. *VHS, DVD*

The Italian Job (2003)
2003 (PG-13) 104m/C Mark Wahlberg, Charlize Theron, Edward Norton, Seth Green, Jason Statham, Mos Def, Donald Sutherland, Franky G., Christina Cabot. *D:* F. Gary Gray. *W:* Neal Purvis, Robert Wade, Donna Powers, Wayne Powers. *C:* Wally Pfister. *M:* John Powell. *VHS, DVD*

Ocean's 11 𝄞𝄞𝄞𝄞

Ocean's Eleven 𝄞𝄞𝄞

Ocean's 11 may not be the best damn heist flick ever, but it's certainly one of the coolest. Why expect anything different with the Rat Pack running rampant on the Vegas strip? See Frank and the boys smoke, drink, hang out, and make time with girls. The off-camera shenanigans are captured on camera—and there's a plot, too! For a movie that was made during the off hours while the Pack was playing two shows a night at the Sands, *Ocean's 11* looks a lot better these days than its reputation suggests. The "hey, guys, let's make a movie" battle plan brings a chummy ambience to the proceedings, helping this smooth entertainment go down easier than a bottle of Chivas.

Sinatra and his pals adapt cinematic versions of their real personas. Frank's Danny Ocean is the ringleader with an ex-wife (Angie Dickinson) and an addiction to gambling and trouble. He organizes a Las Vegas reunion with his former World War II paratrooper pals from the 82nd Airborne. There's laid-back Sam Harmon (Dean Martin), who likes crooning in casino lounges when time permits; Jimmy Foster (Peter Lawford), a spoiled rich kid with an air of sophistication; Josh Howard (Sammy Davis Jr.), a dancing and singing trash collector and explosives wizard; and Tony Bergdorf (Richard Conte), a stoic, tough-guy electrician just out of the slammer. Among the others in the troupe are ex-boxer Mushy O'Connors (Rat Pack regular Joey Bishop) and casino worker Peter Rheimes (Norman Fell).

At the suggestion of cantankerous mastermind Spyros (Akim Tamiroff), Ocean and company plan to rob the Sahara, the Riviera, the Flamingo, the Desert Inn, and the Sands, five of the biggest casinos on the Strip. They approach the job like one of their daring commando missions during the war. On New Year's Eve, Bergdorf makes the glitter disappear from Glitter Gulch while celebrants throughout the city are singing "Auld Lang Syne." Then Danny and his cronies enter the darkened rooms where the gambling money is counted, hold up the casino workers, and throw the loot into bags. Josh proceeds to heave the bags into his trash truck. When power is restored, everyone's rich.

It's simple, unspectacular stuff, but Sinatra and pals' casual anti-authority attitude goes a long way here. Veteran director Lewis Milestone may have been hired by studio chief Jack Warner to keep things in check, but the rascally Rat Packers knew they could get over on "Louie" because of his age. To his credit, Milestone, the then-sixty-five-year-old helmer of *All Quiet on the*

Western Front and *Of Mice and Men,* takes nearly an hour to introduce all of the main characters. Some have written off this approach as being slow and inconsequential in regard to the heist, but the camaraderie among the buddies, not the actual swindle, is the most important part of this film. The background also adds a human element to what could have been a Rat Pack cartoon. Danny's broken marriage, Bergdorf's relationship to his little son in military school, and Foster's uncomfortable reliance on his mother for financial support strike emotional chords.

Brad Pitt (Rusty Ryan) and George Clooney (Danny Ocean) survey the landscape during the 2001 version of *Ocean's Eleven.*

Ocean's 11 swings in a lot of other ways, too. Frequent Sinatra collaborator Nelson Riddle supplies a ring-a-ding score, accenting several variations on the film's catchy "E O-Eleven" theme. Cameos abound, from the billed (Red Skelton, spoofing himself as an obsessive gambler, and George Raft as a casino owner) to the unbilled (Shirley MacLaine, ad-libbing as a drunken floozy trying to put the moves on Martin, Milestone crony Richard Boone, musician Red Norvo, and several Sinatra pals). Dandy bits of dialogue are spread throughout, not all of it politically correct, of course, with some exchanges supplied by an uncredited Billy Wilder. The finale—set during a funeral, reportedly contrived at the last minute—is a genuine surprise, ingeniously realized.

Steven Soderbergh's 2001 reworking of the film, called *Ocean's Eleven* (notice the spelling out of the number for the remake), actually reverses the boilerplate of the original in several areas. For example, more time is spent on the planning of the heist and the heist itself—now staged with three casinos'

THE RAT PACK: SWINGING THROUGH THE '60S by Bruce Klauber

Lawford, Sinatra, Martin, and Davis, in *Sergeants Three*

Frank Sinatra couldn't stand the name "Rat Pack," and he disliked "the Clan" even more. He wouldn't be associated with anything that spoke of vermin, and he sure as hell wouldn't be associated with a "clan" of any kind. He preferred to call himself and his pals "the Summit," but the Rat Pack moniker has stayed with us long after Sinatra, Dean Martin, Sammy Davis Jr., and Peter Lawford have departed. Joey Bishop, the sole surviving member of the Pack—er, the Summit—doesn't have much to say about anything these days.

The guys started off the '60s with a bang, delivering a hit film with the caper enterprise *Ocean's 11* (1960). It was filmed on the fly, during the stars' spare time while Frank, Dean, and Sammy performed their nightclub act in Vegas. But how would Frank and the guys follow up this success? Now here's a great film idea: what about three saloon singers, a comic, and a Kennedy relative starring in a remake of *Gunga Din* to be called *Sergeants Three*? In 1962 it was actually done, with shooting on location in lovely Kanab, Utah. Sammy Davis played the role of Mr. Gunga himself, with an overweight Lawford and a bored Frank and Dean as the sergeants in question. Joey Bishop got in one scene as a drunk. Not only did the boys get action specialist John Sturges (*The Great Escape, The Magnificent Seven*) to direct it, but the western send-up actually made some money. One film critic described it as a "four-million-dollar home movie." For legal reasons, however, *Sergeants Three* is one of the few Sinatra projects that hasn't made it to video or DVD.

By 1963 Peter Lawford was out of the Pack and out of Sinatra's life for good. Lawford was given the unfortunate task of having to tell Sinatra that John F. Kennedy, Lawford's brother-in-law, would not be staying at the Sinatra compound in Palm Springs for vacation and would instead be staying at the Bing Crosby residence. Frank never spoke to Peter again. Lawford never did much of anything in the Pack anyway, so his absence wasn't terribly missed. Old Pete was still in there pushing to keep that Rat Pack affiliation intact, however, and in 1963, his production company produced an effort called *Johnny Cool,* with appearances by, believe it or not, Davis, Bishop, and Elizabeth (*Bewitched*) Montgomery. This Mafia/mobster opus, with Henry Silva in the title role as a vicious gangster, is deservedly forgotten today.

The same year, Frank and Dean teamed up in *Four for Texas,* a western comedy. A reviewer tagged it as "Sinatra and Martin basically playing themselves in the wild West." It is best remembered today for the off-camera antics of Frank and Dean, carrying on with hookers who had been imported to the set. The film's only true moment of hilarity, however, was a cameo appearance by the Three Stooges.

There was still some life, however little, remaining in what was left of the Rat Pack by 1964, when Frank, Dean, and Bing Crosby went before the cameras in a musical entitled *Robin and the Seven Hoods.* While the rumor still persists that Sinatra hired Crosby for a role originally written for

Peter Lawford, Crosby was a good choice and did bring some life to the proceedings. There are some good tunes, "My Kind of Town" and "Mister Booze" among them, but President John F. Kennedy was assassinated during the time when the boys were filming. According to Frank Sinatra Jr., that sad event took the life out of the whole project. Seen today, *Robin and the Seven Hoods* is, indeed, pretty lifeless.

One of the most underappreciated of the films with Rat Pack ties was an ahead-of-its-time project of 1966, *A Man Called Adam.* Very loosely based on the story of troubled jazz genius Charlie "Yardbird" Parker, the film stars Davis as a jazz trumpeter with plenty of problems. Peter Lawford plays a snake of a booking agent, Frank Sinatra Jr. is surprisingly effective as Davis's follower and fan, and a wonderful dramatic performance is turned in by none other than Louis Armstrong. Perhaps the picture, shot entirely on New York city locations, was too dark or disturbing for its time. Jazz fans liked it. The score was a good one, with Davis's trumpeting being done by Nat Adderley (Cannonball's brother).

Also in 1966, *Texas across the River,* another sagebrush spoof, was issued. It could be considered as some kind of Rat Pack movie, in that it had Martin and Bishop in the cast. It's still pretty funny today, with Bishop as a "deadpan Indian" who comments on the proceedings as they go along. Critical comment on *Texas across the River?* "Bishop is never really as funny as he probably thought he was at the time," wrote one reviewer.

By 1968 even Sammy was on the outs with Mr. S. and the gang. According to sources, Frank just didn't approve of Davis's reported drug use. In other words, booze and broads were okay, but Frankie drew the line when it came to other things. Still, a guy's got to work, and what better guy to team up with then the chronically unemployed Peter Lawford, also on Mr. S.'s "outs" list? In 1968 what remained of Lawford's production company "hired" Lawford and Sammy to appear in something called *Salt and Pepper,* directed by a young Richard Donner. Supposedly, the whole deal really appealed to the stars because the project would be filmed in London, where Sam and Uncle Pete could get into the whole "mod-and-free-love" movement. The story? Sam and Pete are co-owners of a discotheque who are later kidnapped and become involved in a plot by revolutionaries to overthrow Her Majesty's government. Some fun, eh? And somehow the film made enough money to inspire a sequel in 1970, entitled *One More Time,* directed by the one and only Jerry Lewis. Lawford hated what Lewis did to the film in the editing room; Sammy loved it. It didn't matter. The film was taken out of Lewis's hands and recut—butchered, some say—by a hired hand from the studio's editing department.

By 1981 it wasn't even cool to be cool anymore, but there were still some folks in Hollywood who dreamed of being the next Frank and Dean. Just two of them happened to be Burt Reynolds and Dom DeLuise. Producer Reynolds and sidekick DeLuise couldn't get Sinatra, but they did get Sammy and Dino to appear in *The Cannonball Run,* which they described as a "crazy, cross-country automobile race." Martin and Davis, who impersonate priests in this film, were sixth- and seventh-billed in the cast. And surprise of surprises, the darn thing was a mega-hit! The inevitable sequel, *The Cannonball Run 2,* came in 1984. When Sinatra heard that Dean and Sammy (Davis, by then, was again friends with Sinatra) and even former Rat Pack "mascot" Shirley MacLaine were all going to be in it, he sent word that he would agree to film a cameo appearance. Frankie spent only a few hours on the set, had a few martinis with his pals, and then went home. Some years later, MacLaine was asked about *Cannonball Run II.* She could only reply, "It was a disgrace."

cash in one vault during a heavyweight boxing match—than the swift introduction of the crew leader (George Clooney) and such accomplices as a card shark (Brad Pitt), pickpocket (Matt Damon), explosives wizard (an uncredited Don Cheadle), and a career criminal (Carl Reiner). Except for Clooney, Pitt, and a very funny Elliott Gould, the characters in the remake have no history together, so there's little at stake emotionally for them. In the 1960 outing, the job took precedence over Danny's marriage. In the 2001 edition, the victory for Danny would be winning back his former wife (Julia Roberts), now romantically involved with his archnemesis, a casino owner (Andy Garcia). And in the original, there's no doubt about whether the scheme succeeds or not, while in the update, there's a hint that something's going to happen after the film's fade-out. Obviously, there's more to the story: after a $180 million take at the U.S. box office, Danny and his juniors head to Europe for a 2004 sequel.

The 2001 film glides along smoothly on the good nature of Clooney and his spirited supporting cast, while Soderbergh, serving as his own cinematographer under the name Peter Andrews, hypnotically captures the gambling halls and high-tech private world of modern-day Vegas. Unfortunately, one of the film's major casting coups turns out to be its chief problem. Julia Roberts, taking a rare supporting part for her *Erin Brockovich* director, is simply miscast as the woman with whom both Clooney and Garcia are infatuated. Roberts looks and acts like Julia Roberts, but that's not enough to convince us that her character would send these two guys into a high-stakes battle over her.

Frank would have laid a couple of C-notes on the broad, bought her a bus ticket to Laughlin, and told her to "take a nap."

Ocean's 11
1960 (NR) 124m/C Frank Sinatra, Dean Martin, Sammy Davis Jr., Richard Conte, Peter Lawford, Angie Dickinson, Patrice Wymore, Joey Bishop, Akim Tamiroff, Henry Silva, Ilka Chase, Buddy Lester. *D:* Lewis Milestone. *W:* Harry Brown, Charles Lederer. *C:* William H. Daniels. *M:* Nelson Riddle. *VHS, DVD*

Ocean's Eleven
2001 (PG-13) 116m/C George Clooney, Brad Pitt, Julia Roberts, Matt Damon, Andy Garcia, Elliott Gould, Don Cheadle, Carl Reiner, Casey Affleck, Scott Caan, Bernie Mac, Jerry Weintraub *D:* Steven Soderbergh. *W:* Ted Griffin. *C:* Steven Soderbergh (here credited as Peter Andrews). *M:* Harold Arlen, James D'Angelo, Scott Davis, Claude Debussy, Duke Ellington, Percy Faith, Erroll Garner, Henry Mancini, Giorgio Moroder, Max Steiner, Billy Strange, Julius Wechter. *VHS, DVD*

He was young, handsome, a millionaire—and he'd just pulled off the perfect crime! She was young, beautiful, a super sleuth—sent to investigate it!

—Tagline for *The Thomas Crown Affair* (1968)

The Thomas Crown Affair (1968) 🦴🦴🦴

The Thomas Crown Affair (1999) 🦴🦴🦴

One of the signature romantic crime films of the 1960s, *The Thomas Crown Affair* was so self-consciously "now" when first released that it's blatantly "not now" today. Split-screens. Soft-focus photography. Weird

Steve McQueen is the title character—a wealthy businessman who pulls off intricate heists just for the fun of it—in the 1968 version of *The Thomas Crown Affair*. UNITED ARTISTS / THE KOBAL COLLECTION

angles. Abrupt editing. Schmaltzy, overdone score. Tons of eye makeup and mascara. Yep, definitely a film of its time.

Steve McQueen plays Thomas Crown, a nouveau riche bigwig from Boston who gets his kicks pulling off robberies when he's not brokering multi-million-dollar business deals. The latest illicit diversion has him anonymously recruiting seven men to pull off an elaborate bank job in broad daylight. The loot totals close to $3 million, but Crown is not in it for the cash. Thomas Crown would like nothing more than to get away from it all, settling down in Rio or somewhere else south of the border.

But this gambit has a hitch. After the heist, the bank wants the case looked at closely, and they hire glamorous, no-nonsense investigator Vicky Anderson (Faye Dunaway) to work with police detective Eddy Malone (Paul Burke) to find the culprit. Armed with a hunch and the knowledge of a Swiss bank account, Anderson suspects Crown is the mastermind and thinks she has to befriend him to find out more. Of course, the two soon fall in love, complicating Anderson's assignment.

From the opening credits alone, you can tell the glitz and gimmick quotient are going to be high in *The Thomas Crown Affair*. Noel Harrison, Rex's son and costar of *The Girl from U.N.C.L.E.*, recites the lyrics of Michel Legrand's catchy "The Windmills of Your Mind" as the screen divides into different sectors. Tinted B&W photos of cast members are unveiled as the credits appear. The split-screen technique, mastered by John Frankenheimer in such films as *Grand Prix* and *Seconds,* is used throughout by director Norman Jewison. Unfortunately, its use manages to detract from potentially suspenseful situations by getting in the way of the action unfolding.

McQueen was a surprising casting choice in the male lead. The rugged former marine can't quite seem to shake his inherent cragginess to make Thomas Crown a likable character, even after director Jewison reportedly told him to "act like Cary Grant" for the part. It should come as no surprise that McQueen was a racing addict in real life because he appears most comfortable in scenes zipping around on his dune buggy with Dunaway. Perhaps his uneasiness is because we're never quite sure why Crown is pulling off the heist in the first place. Is it simply because he's bored? For kicks? A desire to buck authority and/or the Establishment of which he has become a part?

Cast for the part before *Bonnie and Clyde* became a sensation, Dunaway brings the required toughness to Vicky, a character who appears appropriately wishy-washy throughout because she has to. Will she turn in Crown to Malone after she gets the goods on him? Or has the relationship tainted her judgment and desire to complete her assignment? Even when forced to wear ridiculously overstated eye makeup, floppy hats, and designer chiffon dresses, Dunaway makes Vicky a complex, emotionally torn figure.

At first, Jewison—they called him "Mr. Jewison" after *In the Heat of the Night* won the Best Picture Oscar the previous year—seems to be out to make a lark. But its fun factor often gets overwhelmed by its attention-getting stylistic flourishes. It screams, "Ain't we groovy."

This approach is apparent in the film's most famous scene, a six-and-a-half-minute sequence in which Crown and Anderson play a game of chess that turns into a shortcut to foreplay. Lips smack, fingers polish the bishops, hands rub against shoulders, nobody says much. Editor Hal Ashby goes nuts with the jump cuts like he's Jean-Luc Godard on amphetamines. It all ends with a long kiss and two figures embracing. Then the images blur into a colorful, distorted abstract image. Erotic? How about neurotic?

One of the film's more interesting elements is Jewison's decision to go against the grain of the classic heist films by making its principals ciphers to each other and even to Crown, the supervisor of the operation. Adding fun are some of the supporting players, such as Jack Weston as the one person in the robbery Crown meets, and the befuddled detective cartoonishly played by Burke, who exclaims to Dunaway, after learning how close she's getting to McQueen: "I'm running a sex orgy for a couple of freaks on government funds."

In the 1999 remake of *The Thomas Crown Affair,* director John McTiernan takes a similar angle to the story by focusing on the relationship between Crown (Pierce Brosnan) and the insurance investigator, now named Catherine Banning (Rene Russo), rather than on the heist. Here, however, the booty has been switched, from cash to classic paintings, while the ostentatious period style has been supplanted with a focus on the cat-and-mouse interplay of the two principals.

This emphasis makes for a movie that may not have the same kitschy kicks as the original but actually works better in several instances. Brosnan wears his slick wheeler-dealer with an affection for fine art and fine-tuned thievery comfortably, while Russo's insurance expert seems to genuinely enjoy the thrill of snagging her man, both for her job and in the bedroom. The latter is evidenced in a steamy dancing sequence that leads to a surprising nude lovemaking scene. The chemistry between Brosnan and Russo is really in full bloom in these scenes. And McTiernan (the *Die Hard* series) does well without the gimmicky split-screens in staging the pulse-pounding heist sequences.

Those enamored with the original version of the story will get a kick out of seeing Faye Dunaway in the update. Playing Crown's attentive psychiatrist, the actress seems to be enjoying herself immensely, saluting the original while listening to Brosnan's discursions about women, sex, and power, probing the windmills of his mind.

The Thomas Crown Affair (1968)
1968 (R) 102m/C Steve McQueen, Faye Dunaway, Paul Burke, Jack Weston, Biff McGuire, Addison Poe. *D:* Norman Jewison. *W:* Alan Trustman. *C:* Haskell Wexler. *M:* Michel Legrand. *VHS, DVD*
AKA: The Crown Caper; Thomas Crown and Associates

The Thomas Crown Affair (1999)
1999 (R) 113m/C Pierce Brosnan, Rene Russo, Denis Leary, Ben Gazzara, Frankie Faison, Charles Keating, Faye Dunaway. *D:* John McTiernan. *W:* Leslie Dixon, Kurt Wimmer. *C:* Tom Priestly Jr. *M:* Bill Conti. *VHS, DVD*

Topkapi 𝄞𝄞𝄞𝄞

Topkapi is a whirling dervish of a movie. Unpredictable and breezy, the film has many tricks up its sleeve. On the surface, it's an accomplished heist film, but it also serves as a travelogue of Athens and Istanbul and a showcase for director Jules Dassin's real-life lover and soon-to-be wife, Melina Mercouri. And that's not to mention the extended male oil-wrestling scene.

A New York–born director blacklisted in the 1950s after delivering such gritty film noirs as *Naked City* and *Brute Force,* Dassin found success in Europe with the 1953 heist classic *Rififi.* Like John Huston's *The Asphalt Jungle* and Stanley Kubrick's *The Killing* from the same era, *Rififi* serves as a primer for making a heist film that still stands today.

Topkapi follows the essentials, but it delights in taking little side trips along the way. Mercouri is Elizabeth Lipps, a professional thief with a fondness for expensive jewels. Dressed in white hat, white suit, and white gloves to give her the air of sophistication, she talks directly to the camera, pointing out several of the treasures displayed at the Topkapi Palace Museum in Istanbul. Diamonds may be a girl's best friend, but emeralds are what Lipps is hot for—specifically a sultan's dagger encrusted with emeralds that drives her into a tizzy.

Lipps contacts Swiss master criminal Walter Harper (Maximilian Schell) to come up with a plan and put together a crew to lift the prized artifact. Harper, an old pro who has worked with Lipps before, insists on hiring only amateurs because they have no criminal record. Soon on board for the job are a British mechanical expert (Robert Morley) out to beat the museum's elaborate alarm system; an acrobat (Gilles Segal) whose assignment entails swiping the dagger while being suspended in midair, then replacing it with a replica; and a circus strongman (Jess Hahn) assigned to anchor the acrobat. The wild card in this crooked soufflé is a shifty British tour guide (Peter Ustinov) elected to drive a car with hidden explosives from Greece to Germany.

Topkapi gets a lot of mileage out of the location's local color. Dassin and cinematographer Henri Aleken (*Roman Holiday*) seem to delight in showing us the visual splendors of Istanbul by framing several scenes against the city's breathtaking backdrop. The vibrant score by Manos Hadjidakis, who won an Academy Award for writing the bouncy theme to Dassin's *Never on Sunday,* helps propel the action even when stops are made for local belly dancers to gyrate, prostitutes to solicit business, and, in the aforementioned sequence, beefy men to grope each other.

Oh, about those beefy men. The heist is planned when the city's attention is diverted to an annual celebration that includes a parade, a carnival, and a marathon wrestling match. The wrestling is set in an area where shirtless participants douse each other with oil, then wrassle for hours. It's a spectacle that has Mercouri's Lipps literally licking her chops and two Greek secret service men (assigned to follow the crooks) fighting over who will get a better look at the event. This sequence is one of those episodes guaranteed to make you go "huh?" and then write it off as being a "'60s thing."

While Dassin's acclaimed work with *Rififi* may have had the public and critics proclaiming that he'd already "been there, done that" in regard to heist flicks, *Topkapi* shows Dassin could get more mileage from the same type of vehicle. The film is probably best known for its pressure-packed centerpiece sequence, copped practically shot-by-shot by Brian De Palma for Tom Cruise in *Mission: Impossible.* It's filled with tension and humor as the portly Ustinov, frightened by heights, is unexpectedly thrust into action, taking the injured strongman's role of steadying the rope from the museum's rooftop as the acrobat switches artifacts.

Ustinov won an Academy Award for Best Supporting Actor for his charismatic turn as the sweaty small-time tour guide and onetime college professor con who continually screws things up for himself. While the British actor steals the film, Schell's dashing ringmaster and Morley's eccentric electronics wizard score well, too. Unfortunately, the croaky-voiced Mercouri's overtly theatrical performance gets in the way of *Topkapi*'s lighter and more suspenseful moments, while her appearance—heavy eye makeup, dyed blonde hair, outré '60s fashions—screams, "Ain't I sexy!" She ain't. Mercouri would have been better off leaving the routine bottled up with her Oscar-nominated performance as an independently minded hooker four years earlier in Dassin's *Never on Sunday*. In the case of *Topkapi*, her character isn't appealing on Sunday, Monday, Tuesday. . . . You get the picture.

1964 (NR) 119m/C Melina Mercouri, Maximilian Schell, Peter Ustinov, Robert Morley, Jess Hahn, Gilles Segal, Akim Tamiroff, Titos Vandis. *D:* Jules Dassin. *W:* Monja Danischewsky. *C:* Henri Alekan. *M:* Manos Hadjidakis. *VHS, DVD*

Chapter 20

Criminal Elements

It used to be simple. The good guys wore the white hats; the bad guys wore the black hats. Moviegoers rooted for the white hats and hissed at the black hats. End of equation.

Not so, however, in the 1960s. That's when things reversed, or at least got a little muddier. People began rooting for crooks, bank robbers, hoods, swindlers. A term for these former creeps began cropping up again and again: they were antiheroes. They went up against the authorities, bank owners, corporations, businessmen. You know: the Establishment.

Director Arthur Penn had a lot to do with this trend. In 1967 he directed *Bonnie and Clyde,* about 1930s-era gangster lovers Bonnie Parker and Clyde Barrow. They were reckless young whippersnappers who went around robbing banks and killing people. Sure, they were a little screwed up and quite reckless in their approach to violence, but their rebelliousness was cool enough to click with young audiences, leading to lots of media attention and strong box office during an unusual second theatrical release after the film failed the first time out. When Faye Dunaway's Bonnie and Warren Beatty's Clyde took hundreds of rounds of ammo in slow motion in a memorable finale, audiences sat stunned. Some of them cried.

As "The Ballad of Bonnie and Clyde" by Georgie Fame blared out of the radio, and women wore berets and men snappy fedoras and all the latest in gangster chic, such followers as *Boxcar Bertha, Bloody Mama,* and *Dillinger* made their way onto movie screens over the next few years, supposedly offering new, more sympathetic, takes on the notorious.

The highly stylized, no-holds-barred violence of *Bonnie and Clyde* had great impact within the movie universe, especially in combination with the same-year release of *Point Blank,* John Boorman's brutal look at crime and punishment, contemporary style. In it, Lee Marvin's criminal resurrects himself miraculously after being shot by his partner and, against the backdrop of an eerily impersonal L.A., seeks retribution from those who done him in. "Go, Lee, go," we cheer, even though he's as cold-blooded as they come.

Equally merciless is Englishman Jack Carter, a strong-arm working for a crime syndicate who heads to his hometown to investigate his brother's shadowy death. As played by Michael Caine in Michael Hodges's

1971 *Get Carter,* Jack is a jacked-up timebomb whose seething anger fuels his dogged quest for the ugly truth. In a world of hit men, pornographers, and prostitutes, Jack Carter becomes a hero almost by default.

Not every crime-related effort took itself as seriously. For example, 1967's *The Happening* wasn't the psychedelic wavy crime gravy expected from its title—with a catchy hit song by Motown's Supremes, how could it be? Instead, we got old-school hood Anthony Quinn kidnapped and held for ransom by hipsters in an uneven satire of pretty much anything, everything, and ultimately, nothing. We root for the once-mighty Quinn because we feel sorry that none of his shady, wealthy associates or his spoiled wife wants to put up his ransom money.

We also cheer on a masked supervillain (John Phillip Law) who pulls off robberies ingeniously in 1968's *Danger: Diabolik,* a European production from Italy's Mario Bava that does have the happening accoutrements—such as way-out costumes and production design—that *The Happening* sorely lacks. Here, the lawmen are so baffled as to how to capture the mysterious thief that they enlist the dreaded mafioso to help them. The camoflagued crook may look like a Mexican wrestler after Atkins, but with a gorgeous accomplice (Marisa Mell) hanging around his secret domain to fondle his booty, how could you not want Diabolik to get out of danger?

And speaking of danger, audiences applauded how both Clint Eastwood's cop and Charles Bronson's grieving architect dealt with threats in 1971's *Dirty Harry* and 1974's *Death Wish,* respectively. Both characters pick up guns and take the law into their own hands with some vigilante violence. Who sent them over the edge? For Eastwood's Harry, it was a New Age sniper psycho named Scorpio from San Francisco, and for Bronson's Paul Kersey, it was a group of neo-hippie thugs who murder his wife and rape his daughter.

So, where have all the flowers gone, again?

The Big Bounce 🦴🦴

Can a strapping cucumber picker find love and happiness with the beautiful but psychotic secretary of a wealthy rancher affectionately known as "The Big Pickle"?

Believe it or not, that's the question probed in *The Big Bounce,* a confused adaptation of a book by Elmore Leonard, the celebrated western and crime author. Leonard has gone on record calling this film the worst adaptation of his work. Considering that *Stick,* starring and directed by Burt Reynolds, was based on another Leonard story, this statement speaks volumes.

As proof that Elizabeth Taylor and Richard Burton weren't the only power couple to make bad movies during the late 1960s, *Peyton Place* stars Ryan O'Neal and Leigh Taylor-Young are the leads in *The Big Bounce,* playing, respectively, the veggie plucker and shorthand specialist in miniskirts.

O'Neal is Jack Ryan, a hot-tempered Anglo migrant farm worker in California who gets his walking papers after a movie camera catches him smashing a Mexican worker in the face with a baseball bat during a baseball game. Ryan takes a job working as a handyman at a hotel for Sam (Van Heflin), where he meets an attractive, emotionally troubled single mother (Lee Grant). Ryan ignores her advances, preferring instead to get involved with Nancy (Taylor-Young), the stunning secretary for Ray "The Big Pickle" Ritchie (James Daly), his former employer. Ryan soon learns that Nancy is a manipulative vixen, out for kicks of both the sexual and violent variety.

The Big Bounce demonstrates that youthful recklessness shows no class distinction. Poor, bat-swinging drifters can be creeps, as can lithesome women with good jobs. But the film's depiction of aimlessness by director Alex March (*Paper Lion*) and screenwriter Robert Dozier is alternately meandering and soap-opera glossy. The result is a confused film that becomes more absurd, campy, and even borderline entertaining as it trudges along. Happily, when Ryan realizes Nancy is a total lunatic who will even kill to get her cookies off, the dialogue goes pleasantly purple. "Crime may turn me on, but it doesn't get me up there," Nancy confides to Ryan after she tries to mow down some innocent bystanders in her car.

ARTHUR PENN

Arthur Penn

THE KOBAL COLLECTION

Director Arthur Penn's career saw a meteoric rise in the 1960s, only to do a slow burnout in the mid-1970s, leading to his "whatever happened to . . . " status today.

A Philadelphia native, Penn got his start in theater while in the army in the 1950s. He then became a force in television drama, working as a writer and director on such landmark live shows as *Playhouse 90* and *Philco Playhouse.* With experience in Method acting and a stint studying at the Actors Studio, Penn made his film debut in 1958, directing fellow Method man Paul Newman in *The Left-Handed Gun,* a complex look at the outlaw Billy the Kid, based on Gore Vidal's book. The film's less-than-enthusiastic response steered Penn back to the stage, where he directed several theatrical hits, including *Two for the Seesaw.* He took *The Miracle Worker,* Helen Keller's award-winning autobiography, to the big screen in 1962. This striking film earned stars Patty Duke and Anne Bancroft Oscars and Penn an Oscar nomination as Best Director. In spite of that success, however, the filmmaker's next project was short-lived: producer-star Burt Lancaster had him bounced off of *The Train,* replaced by John Frankenheimer, another TV veteran.

Style Counselor

Penn followed up this firing with *Mickey One* in 1965, starring fellow Actors Studio alumni Warren Beatty as a nightclub comic in hot water with mobsters. The film features a number of unconventional stylistic devices—abrupt editing, shadowy B&W photography, and handheld camerawork—inspired by French filmmakers Jean-Luc Godard and François Truffaut. In fact, these two directors were being courted by Beatty to call the shots on *Bonnie and Clyde,* one of Beatty's upcoming projects. After they dropped out of the project, Beatty recruited Penn for the job.

Bonnie and Clyde focuses on 1930s gangster lovers Clyde Barrow (Beatty) and Bonnie Parker (newcomer Faye Dunaway) who "rob banks for a living." Clashing with the nostalgia of authentic costumes and precise period production detail was disturbing violence and heroes who were the type of brutal, psychologically and sexually confused hoods that Freud could write volumes about. *Bonnie and Clyde* opened to mostly negative reviews and lethargic business, but Beatty coerced Warner Bros. into repromoting it for a second release. With new attention devoted to the picture via major coverage in *Time* and *Newsweek,* critics reevaluated it, taking note of its sophisticated French New Wave–influenced techniques, brazen, attention-getting slow-mo and rat-tat-tat violence, and psychological complexity. At the same time, the youth audience, seeking antiheroes they could relate to, turned on to *Bonnie and Clyde* the second time it landed in theaters. Ten Oscar nominations, sizable box-office returns, copycat clothing lines, and a new vogue in period crime films all point to the movie's success.

Beyond Bonnie

Penn, then forty-seven years old, went whole hog into making movies for the kids who constituted the majority of the audience for *Bonnie and Clyde.* In 1969 he transformed Arlo Guthrie's epic antiwar story-song into the film *Alice's Restaurant,* with Guthrie pretty much playing himself, a folksinger who gets caught up in a Vietnam War protest situation in New England. The film captures the spirit of the counterculture, attracting mostly good notices and a decent but not sizable audience. Penn followed *Alice* with *Little Big Man,* a sprawling western featuring Dustin Hoffman as the only white survivor of Custer's Last Stand at Little Bighorn. Based on Thomas Berger's novel, the film offers a satirical view of American history, with its heroes and villains portrayed in strikingly different ways than what is shown in history books or in earlier Hollywood westerns. Penn's revisionist look at western archetypes and his humanist touch helped the film click on many levels, winning wide acceptance with audiences.

Night Moves (1975), his next effort, was an atmospheric thriller with Gene Hackman (who Penn helped make a star with his part as Buck Barrow in *Bonnie and Clyde*) as a detective hired to track down the runaway daughter (a teenage Melanie Griffith in her first featured role) of a wealthy family in Florida. While on the case, Hackman discovers there's more at stake than he first envisioned, and he eventually recognizes he may not be able to handle the ramifications of his investigative work. Now considered a classic of modern noir, the downbeat and disturbing *Night Moves* failed at the box office and was met with indifference by the critics.

Bad Breaks

Penn tried to rebound immediately from the film's less-than-enthusiastic reception with the most lavish project of his career. But 1976's *The Missouri Breaks,* an expensive, offbeat western hyped as a dream teaming of Marlon Brando and Jack Nicholson, tanked in theaters and with the press. More ink was allotted to Brando's freaky female wardrobe (in his role as an unpredictable regulator trying to snag cattle rustler Nicholson) than to anything else in the film. Today, *The Missouri Breaks* looks better than when first released and works as genuinely eccentric curio.

Unfortunately, Penn never seemed to rebound from *The Missouri Breaks*'s box-office flop. He took a five-year hiatus and then, in 1981, returned to the 1960s—the decade with which he's most closely associated—with *Four Friends,* an overlooked account of a quartet of pals coming of age during the '60s. "Uneven" would best describe Penn's output from the 1980s on: there's a formula action thriller (*Target,* again with Hackman), routine suspensers (*Dead of Winter*), and a truly enjoyable, oddball farce (*Penn & Teller Get Killed*) that barely played in theaters.

Like his contemporary, the late John Frankenheimer, who also came out of live television of the 1950s, Penn's best work was done in the 1960s and early 1970s. It was then, with *Mickey One, Bonnie and Clyde, Alice's Restaurant, Little Big Man,* and *Night Moves,* that "an Arthur Penn film" could be counted on to provide audiences with something daring that would entertain, enlighten, and provoke thoughts about the human condition.

A year before *Love Story* made him a major movie star, O'Neal swaggers and shows off his washboard stomach in many shirtless scenes. Taylor-Young often goes shirtless, too, displaying her body in nude swimming, bedroom, and—remember, she's a psycho!—cemetery scenes. Thankfully, Robert Webber has no nude scenes, but he's a hoot as the ex-supervisor of O'Neal and the other fieldhands. Sexually teased to the point of delirium by Taylor-Young and derisively called "the Little Pickle" by O'Neal, Webber finally snaps. Bodies fly and faces are smashed as Webber and O'Neal brawl on a lawn. But nobody seems to connect with any punches, sound effects notwithstanding. This scene could qualify as one of the lamest fight sequences ever staged in cinematic history.

The Big Bounce also delivers one of the worst and most annoying musical scores of its era. Credit goes to Mike Curb, the future lieutenant governor of California, for his miscalculated effort, mixing middle-of-the-road Ray Conniff–like choruses and flat, third-rate surf music. The sounds are memorably awful.

Although *The Big Bounce* is an utterly misguided movie, those seeking laughs may enjoy it as a guilty pleasure. The movie has the potential to become something entirely different, and we're not talking about the 2004 remake with Owen Wilson and Morgan Freeman. Let's see: kick the melodrama up a notch, go nuts with editing to accelerate the pace, and give Taylor-Young breast implants. Voila! *The Big Bounce* could be prime Russ Meyer stuff. At least the title is already there.

1969 (R) 102m/C Ryan O'Neal, Leigh Taylor-Young, Van Heflin, Lee Grant, James Daley, Robert Webber, Cindy Eilbacher. **D:** Alex March. **W:** Robert Dozier. **C:** Howard Schwartz. **M:** Mike Curb. *DVD*

ENJOY those "GOLDEN YEARS" with the most profitable pension plan any sweet little mother ever devised.

—Tagline for
Bunny O'Hare

Bunny O'Hare

Martin and Lewis. Hope and Crosby. Abbott and Costello. Davis and Borgnine.

OK—what's wrong with this picture? Yes, it's Bette Davis and Ernest Borgnine, and they're as wrong as wrong could be when mentioned in the context of great cinematic comedy teams.

That doesn't mean that they didn't give it shot. They did, in a 1971 wonder called *Bunny O'Hare.* Thankfully, the legendary actress and good ol' Quinton McHale weren't a romantic couple. But they were a comedy pair in this mismatched crime caper that tries really, really hard to spoof both the counterculture and the Establishment.

For a movie that purports to be a comedy, *Bunny O'Hare* is pretty sad. Davis, looking frail and disinterested, is the title character, an aging Albuquerque woman whose home is being repossessed. The reasons for this are never made clear in the film, but when the bulldozer actually arrives at her home she faces imminent homelessness. In near-hysterics, she phones her two kids to tell them of the dire situation. They ask her for money. Son Eb (John Astin) is a lecherous gambling addict in need of cash to pay off a bookie. Daughter Lulu (Reva Rose) seeks funding for her near-catatonic husband's therapy sessions. Did we mention that hubby was a butcher?

Bill Green (Borgnine) meets Bunny while repossessing her toilet. He feels bad for her, so he offers to take her away in his camper after her house is destroyed. Bunny learns that Bill is, in fact, a bank robber on the lam. Who knows how he got the toilet-repossessing job? Bunny decides that one way to seek revenge on the bank that repossessed her home is to rob that bank with Bill. But rather than keep the much-needed cash herself, Bunny decides to send it to her kids.

After a quick training session, Bunny and Bill pull off a series of bank robberies using Bill's motorcycle. While sizing up their first job, they see a group of hippies protesting in the street. A lightbulb goes off in Bunny's head: if we dress like hippies maybe we won't get caught because no one will recognize us as the most unlikely screen couple in history! Bill gets a phony beard, shades, a paisley shirt, a vest, and a cap. Bunny puts on a poncho and the type of floppy Boho hat Carly Simon wore on the cover of the *No Secrets* album. Soon, they're knocking off every bank in New Mexico.

The sight of matronly Davis and portly Borgnine in hippie garb on a cycle is supposed to be hilarious, but it's more surreal than anything else. When it comes time for the pair to peel out on their hog, it's so painfully obvious that stunt doubles are being employed that you wonder if the filmmakers just gave up on tricking the audience.

Other things are rotten in Albuquerque aside from the pairing of Borgnine and Davis. Jack Cassidy plays Horace Greeley, an overbearing, stock Establishment lawman. When he's not pontificating about capturing Bunny and Bill, whom he misperceives as antigovernment radicals, he's attempting to grope Miss Hart (*The President's Analyst*'s Joan Delaney), a hip new law lady in the department.

Bunny O'Hare is an odd picture in part because of its inconsistent tone. Bunny's gravely serious predicament is aggravated by the lack of compassion her children show her. At the same time, director Gerd Oswald (a British TV veteran of *The Outer Limits* and *Voyage to the Bottom of the Sea*) wants to be satiric, showing her children as needier than their recently homeless mother is. The result is uneasiness throughout. When the film spirals into broader directions with the motorcycle getaway sequences looking like outtakes from a geriatric *Easy Rider* but sounding like *Bonnie and Clyde* with bluegrass music in the background, it's really a ball of confusion.

The inconsistent tone could have something to do with the reported offscreen squabbling between the star actress, who wanted a harder edge to the proceedings, and the production company, American International Pictures, looking for a wackier comedy with chases that could appeal to their younger, drive-in audience. The film's final form irritated Bette so much she refused to help publicize it upon its release.

There's little doubt what diva Davis would say about *Bunny O'Hare* today if she were still alive: "What a dump!"

1971 (PG) 88m/C Bette Davis, Ernest Borgnine, Jack Cassidy, Joan Delaney, Jay Robinson, Reva Rose, John Astin, Robert Foulk. **D:** Gerd Oswald. **W:** Coslough Johnson. **C:** Loyal Griggs, John M. Stephens. **M:** Billy Strange. *VHS*

Danger: Diabolik 🦴🦴🦴

Mention the title *Danger: Diabolik* to some movie fans and you'll hear nothing but raves. "Visionary," "stylish," "thrilling" is what they might say of the Mario Bava effort. But others will not be so keen on the film, calling it "amateurish," "laughable," and "embarrassing enough to deserve its spot on *Mystery Science Theater 3000*." All of this, of course, makes *Danger: Diabolik* an immediate must-see.

The story is an odd combination of superhero adventure and crime caper. Diabolik (John Phillip Law), a creepy master criminal who is emotionless and ruthless, is feared by authorities throughout Europe for his daredevil robberies. Diabolik wears a mask and a tight wet suit–like uniform, looking like a well-toned version of El Santo, the famed Mexican wrestler. He lives in an elaborate underground lair that looks like the Batcave designed by Bob Guccione. It has cool showers, a revolving bed, and mod furnishings. There's ample room for Diabolik's gorgeous female assistant and lover Eva Kant (Marisa Mell) to stash her extensive collection of clothing and jewelry.

The crook's latest theft of $1 million took place in broad daylight, infuriating Diabolik's longtime nemesis, Inspector Ginko (Michel Piccoli), and the minister of finance (Terry-Thomas). The frazzled authorities call on an underworld figure to get the goods on Diabolik: Ralph Valmont (*Thunderball*'s Adolfo Celi), a brutish crime boss. A deal is struck. The cops will get off Ralph's back if he can snag the supercriminal. A series of traps are set for Diabolik. In one, a priceless emerald necklace is used to lure him out of hiding; in another, plans are hatched to have Eva kidnapped. But Diabolik's criminal prowess borders on the supernatural. He uses elaborate disguises and chemical expertise to stay ahead of the law. And when he gets really angry, he just blows things up real good. Give this masked malevolent marvel an "A" for anarchy.

Like *Barbarella,* which was shot around the same time but released a year later, *Danger: Diabolik* was made under the auspices of producer Dino De Laurentiis. Similarities to the Jane Fonda space flick abound. Both films are based on popular comic strips. And both are international productions, which, in *Diabolik*'s case, means a cast that includes Americans (pretty boy Law, also featured in *Barbarella*), Brits (Terry-Thomas), French (Piccoli), Italians (Celi), and Austrians (Mell). The uneven dubbing can be considered either a distraction (if you dig *Diabolik*) or just another facet of the production's overall incompetence (if you're a naysayer).

Fueled by an eerie acid jazz score by the great composer Ennio Morricone, the film also shows the distinctive touches of director Mario Bava, who employs odd camera angles, psychedelic colors, and mod backgrounds to give the film a hip feel. At times, *Danger: Diabolik* appears dream-like, mixing nostalgic, contemporary, and futuristic motifs in the same sequence. For example, take a look at the three factions represented in the movie. Valmont's hoods wear 1930s gangster-style pinstripe suits. Ginko dresses like a contemporary (circa 1968) police inspector would. And Diabolik, with his superhero threads, appears to have stepped out of the twenty-second century.

Bava, the Italian director behind horror classics *Black Sunday* and *Black Sabbath,* worked in every genre throughout his career. *Danger: Diabolik* seems to represent all of them in some way. It's a hodgepodge of comic book adventure, police procedural, caper flick, and "giallo" thriller with elements of westerns and gladiator sagas thrown in for good measure. The film remains clunky throughout, never settling on a steady tone, but that's part of its unique brand of delirium.

1968 (PG-13) 99m/C John Phillip Law, Marisa Mell, Michel Piccoli, Adolfo Celi, Claudio Gaura, Terry-Thomas, Mario Donen. *D:* Mario Bava. *W:* Adriano Baracco, Mario Bava, Brian Degas, Tudor Gates. *C:* Antonio Rinaldi. *M:* Ennio Morricone. *VHS* *AKA:* Diabolik

Get Carter

Abona fide classic from the British school of crime and grime, *Get Carter* is an in-your-face epic that is so tough it hurts.

Michael Caine is Jack Carter, an assassin with a powerful group of London mobsters, who is told that his brother has died in a car accident in Newcastle, England. Suspicious about the circumstances of the death, Carter heads to the northern working-class town where he grew up to prepare for the funeral. He becomes obsessed with finding out what really happened to his brother, particularly after the police label it a suicide, and he soon realizes that his brother was indeed murdered. In Newcastle, Carter meets some of his old associates, including a local crime boss (*Look Back in Anger* playwright John Osborne) and an enforcer-chauffeur (Ian Hendry), who try to persuade him to retreat to London. But the unrelenting Carter decides to dig deeper into the murder and soon finds some stunning revelations involving the local thugs, a relative, and his brother's secret, unsavory line of work.

In his debut effort, Mike Hodges (*Flash Gordon, Croupier*) shows an eye for capturing working-class grittiness and an intensity to match his protagonist's ticked-off demeanor. He refuses to pull punches and gets Caine to go for broke with Carter, delivering a performance of unmitigated brute force. He's the hero of the piece, but in how many movies do we find the protagonist stabbing people, tossing people off parking garages, smacking women around, and injecting hookers with hypodermic needles?

The violence reflects Carter's nature, but it remains pent up until he's provoked by the thugs around him and the secrets that they hide. Carter's return to his roots shows us some of the reasons he became the ruthless son-of-a-bitch he is.

Get Carter, adapted by Hodges from Ted Lewis's novel *Jack's Return Home,* is equally unflinching in the sex department. Carter is portrayed as a sexual animal as much as he is a creature of violence. A telephone sex scene with his mistress (played by Britt Ekland at the height of her beauty) sizzles. Carter also beds down his older Newcastle guesthouse owner, and he has a surprisingly explicit tussle with the local crime boss's moll. It's after that roundelay that Carter discovers the key to his brother's murder in the form of a porno movie. And it's here, near the film's finale, that Carter shows a sense of humanity for the first and only time in the film, as his eyes swell with tears when he learns a devastating secret.

It didn't take long for Hollywood to get *Carter.* A year later, Jack Carter was morphed into an African American named Tyrone Tackett when the film was remade with an all-black cast as *Hit Man.* The story was transposed to Los Angeles, with Bernie Casey as the man out to find the truth behind his brother's death and Pam Grier supplying able support. The locale shift worked decently, but the original's rougher edges were supplanted by an excess of bloody confrontations.

Of course, Carter was resurrected again, this time in the guise of Sylvester Stallone in the 2000 version of *Get Carter.* Shot primarily in Seattle, this effort boasted a fine supporting cast (Alan Cumming, Miranda Richardson, and Caine himself), but its irritatingly flashy camerawork and a mumbling, monosyllabic Sly made the dreary production rocky at best.

1971 (R) 112m/C Michael Caine, Ian Hendry, Britt Ekland, John Osborne, Tony Beckley, George Sewell, Geraldine Moffat, Dorothy White. *D:* Mike Hodges. *W:* Mike Hodges. *C:* Wolfgang Suschitzky. *M:* Roy Budd. *VHS, DVD*

The Happening 🦴🦴

Y ou'd think a 1967 movie with the title *The Happening* would have something to do with a drug-fueled, hippie-filled freak-out session. But this movie has nothing to do with this sort of activity. Like *Skidoo, The Happening* offers another example of mainstream Hollywood trying to hedge their bets by uneasily mixing the counterculture with characters the Establishment can relate to.

Anthony Quinn stars as Roc Delmonico, a successful Miami mobster who hides his shady business dealings through his ownership of a restaurant. One day, a quartet of drifters kidnaps Delmonico from his sizable suburban house, asking for $200,000 in ransom money. But his wife (Martha Hyer) of fifteen years doesn't want to part with the money and refuses to sell any of her jewelry or the family's artworks to meet the demands. The call for the cash also goes out to the hood's business associates, but none shows any interest in coming up with the dough. Angered by the lack of response, Delmonico decides to call the shots of his own kidnapping by threatening to tell the IRS of his pals' dirty dealings and upping his ransom to $3 million.

The Supremes' catchy title theme opens *The Happening,* but things go downhill after that. We meet the four kidnappers the morning after a big

Four Young Swingers Out for Kicks ... And Suddenly They've Got Terror on Their Tail!

—Tagline for
The Happening

Assassin Jack Carter (Michael Caine) applies pressure to Eric Paice (Ian Hendry) and others in an attempt to find out the truth about his brother's death in *Get Carter* (1971). MGM / THE KOBAL COLLECTION

PIPE DREAMS

For those who follow the ins and outs of the entertainment industry, news of filmmakers departing from film projects over "creative differences" or stories about long-in-gestation dream projects struggling to make it to the screen are commonplace. But such phenomena are not unique to contemporary Hollywood; for as long as films have been made, there have been such circumstances. Check out some of these groovy movies that coulda, shoulda, woulda happened, but didn't—at least not yet.

Dune: Alejandro Jodorowsky was the director attached to this one for a long time. Among his creative staff were *Alien* collaborators Dan O'Bannon, Moebius, and H. R. Giger, while Orson Welles, Gloria Swanson, and Salvador Dali were among its cast members, with Pink Floyd contributing the music. We'll never know if the Spanish surrealist would have given us a film as incomprehensible as David Lynch's effort, but weirdness was pretty much guaranteed.

Bikers' Heaven: The notion of this sequel to *Easy Rider* is still bandied about today, though long-running tensions between principals Peter Fonda and Dennis Hopper seem to have squelched it. The idea has Fonda's Wyatt and Hopper's Billy the Kid returning from the dead in the year 2068 and looking for revenge with legions of zombie bikers on their side. Word has also spread about *Easy Rider A.D.,* in which Fonda's Wyatt is accused of killing Jack Nicholson's lawyer character, George Hanson, and Wyatt's son has to clear his father's name. Talk about born to be wild.

On the Road: Reportedly, Francis Ford Coppola has been itching to make a cinematic version of Jack Kerouac's seminal Beat novel for a long time, but several false starts over the years seem to have derailed the attempt. Brad Pitt and Billy Crudup are the two stars most often linked to the project, as well as director Joel Schumacher; Coppola's involvement would be at the producing level.

booze-and-drug-fueled party in a Florida forest. Taurus (George Maharis), the leader, is a quick-talking creep whose followers include Sureshot (Michael Parks), a bleached-blond surfer dude; Harby (Robert Walker Jr.), a sidekick who doesn't do a whole lot; and Sandy (Faye Dunaway, in her debut), a spacey flower child. How these not-so-fab four got together is never clear, but they seem to represent some type of cross-section of the counterculture as imagined by screenwriter Frank R. Pierson and director Eliot Silverstein, who must have been given carte blanche after the success of *Cat Ballou,* their previous hit film. The dialogue is all over the place, punctuated by hippie lingo (lots of "groovy"s) and hipster terms like "splitsville." By film's end, you could be saying "oy vey."

Quinn is stuck in gregarious *Zorba the Greek* mode throughout. Sometimes this style works and he's good hammy fun, but when his portrayal reaches cartoon levels, the scenes with his abductors seem more culture crash than culture clash.

A Clockwork Orange: Depending on who you listen to and what you read, several alternative versions of Anthony Burgess's novel were in the works before Stanley Kubrick took the reins. Imagine how much satisfaction audiences would have gotten with Mick Jagger as Alex, the rest of the Stones as Droogs, and cinematic madman Ken Russell behind the camera.

Bonnie and Clyde: A number of directors were behind the wheels of this baby before Arthur Penn took it over. The most fascinating contender was French New Waver Jean-Luc Godard, no stranger to crooks and cars with the classic *Breathless* under his beret. How he would have handled Michael J. Pollard and "Foggy Mountain Breakdown" remains a mystery.

Spirits of the Dead: Fellini was always in; after all, his longtime producer Alberto Grimaldi also produced this Edgar Allan Poe–inspired three-part anthology film. But the other original directors were Ingmar Bergman and Orson Welles, who were replaced by Roger Vadim and Louis Malle, respectively. Fellini, whose "Toby Dammit" segment is considered the best of the trio, was so upset that Vadim was on board, he refused to acknowledge the French helmer's participation in the project.

The Other Side of the Wind: A legendary lost project from Orson Welles (who has many), the film focuses on an aging director (played by John Huston) trying to get financing for his last big film and dealing with young Hollywood executives in the process. Peter Bogdanovich, Susan Strasberg, and Dennis Hopper make appearances in the film, which was shot from 1970 to 1976. While the film has been worked on over the years by Welles's former technical associates, it remains tied up in legal entanglements with the government of Iran, which was involved in its funding. Footage that has been seen in the documentary *Orson Welles: The One-Man Band* and in 1975's *The American Film Institute Salute to Orson Welles* gives us a glimpse of the filmmaker's way-out visual style, highlighted by strange camera angles, expressive lighting, and bizarre editing.

The Happening intends to satirize the differences between the counterculture and the Establishment by showing us their similarities. While it misses its mark most of the time, some worthwhile things are happening in *The Happening.* For example, a mustachioed Milton Berle goes all out as a sleazeball Delmonico associate who shacks up with his friend's wife after the kidnapping. And a humorous sequence involves Delmonico's colorful mobster pals meeting in Miami to discuss how to handle the ransom demands. The closest thing to a real hippie freak-out happening in the film is when Delmonico joins his four kidnappers in ripping apart curtains, destroying artwork, and smashing flowerpots in Delmonico's tackily decorated house.

Far out. Too bad most of *The Happening* is far off the mark.

1967 101m/C Anthony Quinn, George Maharis, Michael Parks, Robert Walker Jr., Faye Dunaway, Oskar Homolka, Martha Hyer, Milton Berle, Jack Kruschen, Eugene Roche, Luke Askew. *D:* Eliot Silverstein. *W:* Frank Pierson. *C:* Philip H. Lathrop, Howard Winner. *M:* Frank De Vol. *VHS*

The Limey 𝄞𝄞𝄞

Using the classic modern film noirs of the 1960s like *Point Blank* and *Get Carter* as their reference point, Steven Soderbergh and screenwriter Lem Dobbs salute and slam the decade with *The Limey.*

Heading the cast are two icons of the era from different sides of the Atlantic: Terence Stamp, the English star of *The Collector* and *Far from the Madding Crowd,* and Peter Fonda, "Captain America" of *Easy Rider* fame. The director also conjures strong '60s vibes with such supporting performers as Lesley Ann Warren (TV's *Cinderella*), Barry Newman (*Vanishing Point*), and Joe Dallesandro, the Warhol star-boy of *Trash.*

Stamp plays Wilson, an ill-tempered Brit who learns that his daughter Jenny has been killed in a mysterious car crash in Los Angeles. Wilson, a career criminal who recently finished a nine-year stint in the slammer, travels to L.A. to investigate the death. He learns that Jenny was involved with Terry Valentine (Fonda), a successful middle-aged record producer.

After arriving in Los Angeles, Wilson gets help in his investigation from Elaine (Warren) and Ed (Luis Guzman), two of Jenny's friends from her days as an aspiring actress. Ed helps Wilson illegally purchase a gun—from a pair of high school students—and serves as his driver, while Elaine is around mainly for emotional support.

Jenny's death has Wilson in a violent rage, teetering on the edge of madness, as evidenced when, early in the film, he barges into a trucking company office, demanding to know of Valentine's whereabouts. After he's beaten to a pulp and thrown into the street by some of the company's brutish workers, Wilson heads back to the premises immediately with gun in hand. Without flinching, he blows some of his assailants away. But this is not just a few gunshots heard near the warehouse. They also serve as a warning shot to Valentine and his sleazebag legal and security adviser Avery (Newman) that Jenny's dad, the Limey, is in town.

On the surface, *The Limey* is solid but standard revenge stuff, akin in many ways to *Death Wish.* But it's hard to ignore its similarities to those seminal '60s films *Point Blank* and *Get Carter.* In the former, Lee Marvin is referred to as, simply, "Walker," close to Stamp's "Wilson" here. Initially, both Wilson and Walker believe their mission is against one man, but then they learn that others are involved as well. And the city of Los Angeles plays a major part in *Point Blank* as well as in *The Limey,* where Soderbergh contrasts such locations as the 'hood where Ed lives with his family and kids and the lavish Hollywood Hills home where Valentine shacks up with another pretty young thing. As for *Get Carter,* Michael Caine, like Stamp, is a criminal transformed into a human Terminator, unstoppable in a quest for truth and, ultimately, revenge.

While there are no stunning revelations at the end of *The Limey,* it is consistently intriguing, mostly because of Soderbergh's extreme stylization. The film most resembles the experimental work of French New Wavers Jean-Luc Godard and Alain Resnais when Soderbergh opens his bag of cinematic tricks, filling the film with jump cuts, recurring images of Wilson on an air-

Terence Stamp plays a hardened man seeking truth and revenge in Steven Soderbergh's 1999 film *The Limey*.

plane, disconcerting long shots during action sequences, and a soundtrack that mixes '60s-era songs such as the Who's "The Seeker" and Steppenwolf's "Magic Carpet Ride" with sitar and electronic incidental music. Soderbergh's boldest move, however, is using segments of *Poor Cow,* the 1967 film featuring a twenty-six-year-old Stamp, in flashbacks. In these fragmented yet heartbreaking images, we learn of Wilson's marriage, his neglect of Jenny, and his eventual road to crime. They give the Limey and *The Limey* a reason for being.

Stamp and Fonda are compelling presences throughout, each representing how things turned sour for two 1960s survivors. Stamp's Wilson, the working-class man whose life has been filled with wrongs, finally has a chance at redemption. Fonda's Valentine, on the other hand, has lived in the lap of luxury since the '60s and has allowed his hedonistic lifestyle to get the better part of him, leading him to lose whatever values he once held. The irony is that, for both men, murder is the only solution.

1999 (R) 89m/C Terence Stamp, Lesley Ann Warren, Luis Guzman, Peter Fonda, Barry Newman, Joe Dallesandro, Nicky Katt, Melissa George. *D:* Steven Soderbergh. *W:* Lem Dobbs. *C:* Edward Lachman Dobbs. *M:* Cliff Martinez. *VHS, DVD*

Point Blank 🦴🦴🦴🦴

Payback 🦴🦴🦴

R anking rght up there with *Get Carter* as one of the nastiest films of the 1960s, *Point Blank* is an art film disguised as an action thriller. Moody, disconcerting, and downright brutal, *Point Blank* salutes French New Wave directors Jean-Luc Godard and Alan Resnais and American primitives Don Siegel and Sam Fuller, yet it remains bracingly original in its execution and plotting.

Point Blank features Lee Marvin as Walker, a human time bomb on a mission. After being bilked of $93,000, shot twice, and left for dead in the abandoned Alcatraz penitentiary, Walker miraculously recovers. Several months later, he resurfaces in Los Angeles, out to find the culprits. That the guilty parties happen to be his cheating wife, Lynne (Sharon Acker), and his best friend, Reese (John Vernon), with whom Lynne is having an affair, offers enough reason why Walker will stop at nothing to get his cash and exact revenge. Walker's quest eventually takes him into contact with people in cahoots with Reese who have power and political clout and belong to a mysterious group called the Organization.

Based on "The Hunter," a story by Donald Westlake (writing as Richard Stark), *Point Blank* is propelled by Marvin's quietly menacing performance as Walker. He doesn't say a whole lot, and when he does say something it's usually, "Where's Reese?" He starts off mean and gets meaner as the film goes on. Walker's life is revealed in fragments through flashbacks during the first part of the film. He's a haunted character and a sad figure, but because of his brutal demeanor, it's difficult to have sympathy for him. At first, Walker's plight is personal—he is, after all, battling Reese, formerly his closest ally, and Lynne, his betraying wife. But as he gets closer to Reese, we learn that additional corrupt people were involved in Walker's attack, and that he's taking on what amounts to a war with a faceless but frightening corporation. Marvin is like a bowling ball searching for pins to knock down.

Point Blank is populated with a host of complex supporting characters, all of whom are either used or abused in some way by Walker while seeking vengeance. Angie Dickinson is his sexpot sister-in-law, whom he enlists to nail Reese in more ways than one. Carroll O'Connor's Brewster and Lloyd Bochner's Carter are two very different types of big men in the Organization, while Keenan Wynn is a mysterious acquaintance of Walker's who seems to show up at all the right times and who seems to have motives other than simply helping the film's troubled protagonist. And in one of his earliest roles is Vernon as Reese, the ultimate backstabber, a sex fiend with a violent streak and a well-protected penthouse bachelor pad. This role proved an appropriate tune-up for the future Dean Wormer of *Animal House* years later.

The second effort directed by Englishman John Boorman (*Zardoz, Deliverance*), *Point Blank* illustrates the fuzzy state of mind inhabited by Walker

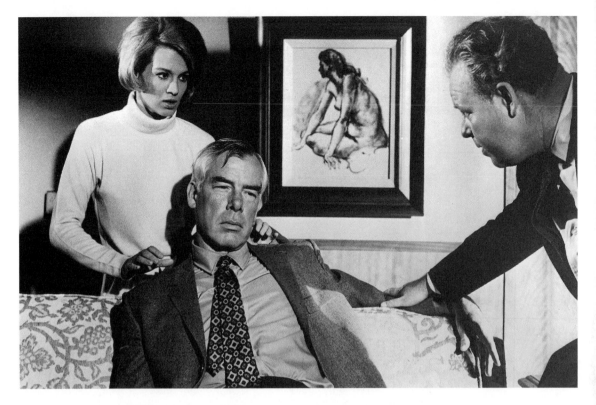

A woozy Walker (Lee
Marvin) contemplates
revenge against
Brewster (Carroll
O'Connor) and the
Organization, as sister-
in-law Chris (Angie
Dickinson) looks on in
John Boorman's *Point
Blank.*

MGM / THE KOBAL
COLLECTION

throughout the proceedings. The film employs bizarre camera angles, a jumpy, off-kilter editing style, an electronic jazz score, and lighting that seems either too dark or too bright. Except for a few sequences in dank Alcatraz, the movie is set and was shot in Los Angeles. But Boorman seems to have gone out of his way to film in the darkest nooks and crannies and in the coldest-looking office buildings in sunny Southern California. For the most part, Walker and members of the Organization wear suits and ties, forerunners to the hip Tarantino hoods to come decades later in *Reservoir Dogs* and *Pulp Fiction.* In stark contrast to the men around her, the red-headed Dickinson wears bright yellow outfits, sometimes with stripes. She's the sole ray of sunshine in the desolate, psychedelic, film-noir landscape that is *Point Blank.*

The 1999 film *Payback* is based on the same Evan Hunter source material as *Point Blank,* and even though Boorman's film is not mentioned in this film's credits, one can guess that star/producer Mel Gibson and director/coscripter Brian Helgeland have a fondness for their movie's predecessor.

The story follows the same path as *Point Blank,* as Gibson's one-named criminal (now "Porter") seeks revenge against a former friend who stole his share of robbery loot and shot him. The primary location has been moved from Los Angeles to Chicago in order to make the most of the urban grittiness in a film where the sleaze and bloodshed have been kicked up more than a notch. Now, Porter's two-timing wife (Deborah Unger) is a heroin addict, his former girlfriend (Maria Bello) is a hooker, and his ex-partner (Clark Henry) has a thing for violent sex with an Asian prostitute (Lucy Liu).

Gibson's Porter is probably the most unlikable character he's played on film. Porter's comfortable ripping rings out of drug dealers' noses and lifting cash from a homeless beggar's bowl. Helgeland, who won an Oscar for helping to adapt *L.A. Confidential* to the screen, seems to have his cameras set on making a genuine, nihilistic, modern film noir. He's also sprinkled in some sharp but quick references to the '60s with appearances by Kris Kristofferson and an unbilled James Coburn. Unfortunately, the second half of the film succumbs to Hollywood action-adventure formula and practically disregards the ominous mood and desolate characters established in the early going. Also, first-person narration by Porter seems to come and go intermittently. Perhaps these inconsistencies may have something to do with a well-publicized feud that occurred between Gibson and Helgeland during postproduction, leaving Gibson to oversee the film's final cut.

Still, *Payback* is tougher and meaner than most recent studio thrillers and at least seems comfortable delivering the goods as far as adult revenge movies go. It's a nice try, but it doesn't clobber its target like *Point Blank*.

Point Blank

1967 92m/C Lee Marvin, Angie Dickinson, Keenan Wynn, Carroll O'Connor, Lloyd Bochner, Michael Strong, John Vernon. *D:* John Boorman. *W:* Alexander Jacobs, David Newhouse, Rafe Newhouse. *C:* Philip H. Lathrop. *M:* Johnny Mandel. *VHS, DVD*

Payback

1999 (R) 100m/C Mel Gibson, Gregg Henry, Maria Bello, David Paymer, Bill Duke, Deborah Unger, John Glover, William Devane, Lucy Liu, Kris Kristofferson, James Coburn. *D:* Brian Helgeland. *W:* Brian Helgeland, Terry Hayes. *C:* Ericson Core. *M:* Chris Boardman. *VHS, DVD*

Alternate Title Index

The Alternate Title Index provides variant and foreign-language titles for movies released under more than one name. The alternate titles are listed here alphabetically, followed by the corresponding title under which the film is reviewed in this book. Please note that English-language initial articles ("a," "an," "the") are ignored in the alphabetical sort, while foreign-language articles (like "la" or "el" or "das") are *not* ignored. Bear in mind that the page number following the film title refers you to the location of the credits information for that film; in some cases you'll have to flip back a page or two to get to the beginning of the review.

Ad Ogni Costo
See Grand Slam *524*

Alligator Alley
See The Hooked Generation *208*

Alphaville, A Strange Case of Lemmy Caution
See Alphaville *172*

Alphaville, Une Étrange Aventure de Lemmy Caution
See Alphaville *172*

Barbarella: Queen of the Galaxy
See Barbarella *174*

Batman: The Movie
See Batman *510*

Before I Die
See Targets *163*

Black Evil
See Ganja & Hess *150*

Black Vampire
See Ganja & Hess *150*

Blackout: The Moment of Terror
See Ganja & Hess *150*

Blood Couple
See Ganja & Hess *150*

Blue Manhattan
See Hi, Mom! *293*

Chinchero
See The Last Movie *95*

Confessions of a Peeping John
See Hi, Mom! *293*

The Crown Caper
See The Thomas Crown Affair (1968) *535*

The Curse of Dr. Phibes
See The Abominable Dr. Phibes *143*

Dance of the Vampires
See The Fearless Vampire Killers *149*

The Degenerates
See Fellini Satyricon *322*

Demon Planet
See Planet of the Vampires *185*

Diabolik
See Danger: Diabolik *549*

Diamantes A Gogo
See Grand Slam *524*

Dr. Goldfoot and the Love Bombs
See Dr. Goldfoot and the Girl Bombs *41*

Dr. Goldfoot and the "S" Bomb
See Dr. Goldfoot and the Girl Bombs *41*

Dr. Goldfoot and the Sex Bombs
See Dr. Goldfoot and the Girl Bombs *41*

Dr. Phibes
See The Abominable Dr. Phibes *143*

Don't Look Back
See Dont Look Back *470*

Double Obsession
See Ganja & Hess *150*

Dracula Today
See Dracula A.D. 1972 *147*

Electric Shades of Grey
See The Psychedelic Priest *218*

Erotic Illusion
See Camille 2000 *407*

Erotic Instinct
See Camille 2000 *407*

Erotic Quartet
See Camille 2000 *407*

Fearless Vampire Killers, or: Pardon Me, but Your Teeth Are in My Neck
See The Fearless Vampire Killers *149*

52 Miles to Terror
See Hot Rods to Hell *264*

Fillmore: The Final Days
See Fillmore *472*

Free the Army
See F.T.A. *242*

Fuck the Army
See F.T.A. *242*

Future Woman
See Future Women *25*

Gas-s-s-s . . . or, It May Become Necessary to Destroy the World in Order to Save It
See Gas-s-s-s! *289*

The Gopher
See El Topo *320*

Gore Vidal's Myra Breckinridge
See Myra Breckinridge *426*

Grim Company
See Last House on the Left *156*

The Haunted Planet
See Planet of the Vampires *185*

Haunted World
See Planet of the Vampires *185*

Hell's Angels Unchained
See Angel Unchained *255*

Hide and Seek
See Camille 2000 *407*

Histoires Extraordinaires
See Spirits of the Dead *160*

Hollywood Vixens
See Beyond the Valley of the Dolls *399*

Hot City
See Original Gangstas *126*

Jag är nyfiken—en film i gult
See I Am Curious (Yellow) *324*

Cast Index

The Cast Index provides a listing for all actors cited in the credits of the movies reviewed in this book. The names of the actors are listed alphabetically by last name, as are their corresponding filmographies. (Note that only movies covered in this book are listed in the filmographies.) Following the movie titles, a (V) indicates voice work, and an (N), narration. Bear in mind that the page number following the film title refers you to the location of the credits information for that film; in some cases you'll have to flip back a page or two to get to the beginning of the review.

The Million Eyes of Su-Muru
25
Skidoo 227
Aykroyd, Dan
Spies Like Us 74
Ayres, Lew
The Man 123
Aznavour, Charles
Candy 411
Bacon, Max
Privilege 494
Badel, Alan
Arabesque 7
Baez, Joan
Celebration at Big Sur 468
Dont Look Back 470
Woodstock 502
Bailey, Pearl
The Landlord 371
Baird, Harry
The Touchables 458
Baird, Sharon
Pufnstuf 515
Baker, Lynn
Billy Jack 285
Balaban, Bob
The Strawberry Statement
309
Balin, Ina
The Projectionist 382
Balk, Fairuza
Almost Famous Untitled:
The Bootleg Cut
(Director's Edition) 466
Balsam, Martin
Little Big Man 98
The Man 123
Bancroft, Anne
The Graduate 364
The Band
The Last Waltz 485
Banderas, Antonio
Spy Kids 78
Spy Kids 2: The Island of
Lost Dreams 78
Spy Kids 3-D: Game Over
78
Bang, Joy
Cisco Pike 207
Maidstone 354
Banner, Jill
The President's Analyst 55
Bardot, Brigitte
Spirits of the Dead 160
Barlow, Ray
Faster, Pussycat! Kill! Kill!
262
Barnes, Cheryl
Hair 480
Barnes, Joanna
B.S. I Love You 360
Baron, Sandy
Targets 163
Barrault, Jean-Louis
Chappaqua 206

Barron, Baynes
Maryjane 216
Bartel, Paul
Hi, Mom! 293
Barty, Billy
Pufnstuf 515
Basie, Count
Blazing Saddles 89
Basil, Toni
Easy Rider 260
Greaser's Palace 340
Bass, Alfie
Alfie 437
The Fearless Vampire
Killers 149
Bates, Alan
Georgy Girl 445
King of Hearts 326
Bates, Michael
Bedazzled 440
Batten, Peter
Yellow Submarine (V) 518
Beacham, Stephanie
Dracula A.D. 1972 147
Beatty, Warren
McCabe and Mrs. Miller
100
Shampoo 384
Beck, John
Pat Garrett and Billy the Kid
101
Beck, Michael
Three in the Attic 427
Beckley, Tony
Get Carter 551
The Italian Job (1969) 527
Begley, Ed
Wild in the Streets 310
Bello, Maria
Payback 558
Belmondo, Jean-Paul
Casino Royale 38
Benedict, Paul
Taking Off 386
Bengell, Norma
Planet of the Vampires 185
Benjamin, Paul
Across 110th Street 115
Benson, Martin
Goldfinger 16
Bentley, Beverly
Beyond the Law 354
Maidstone 354
Wild 90 354
Bergen, Candice
Carnal Knowledge 415
The Day the Fish Came Out
177
Getting Straight 291
Soldier Blue 105
Berger, Senta
The Ambushers 59
The Quiller Memorandum
28

Berle, Milton
Can Heironymus Merkin
Ever Forget Mercy
Humppe and Find True
Happiness? 409
The Happening 553
Berlin, Jeannie
Getting Straight 291
Bernard, Ed
Across 110th Street 115
Bernard, Sue
Faster, Pussycat! Kill! Kill!
262
Bertoya, Paul
Hot Rods to Hell 264
Bey, Marki
The Landlord 371
Bhaskar
I Drink Your Blood 153
Biafra, Jello
Plaster Caster 481
Bianchi, Daniela
Operation Kid Brother 48
Bikel, Theodore
200 Motels 500
Bill, Tony
Shampoo 384
Bindon, John
Performance 493
Poor Cow 452
Bird, Laurie
Two-Lane Blacktop 273
Birkin, Jane
Blow-Up 443
Wonderwall 429
Bisacco, Roberto
Camille 2000 407
Bishop, Joey
Ocean's 11 532
Bishop, Larry
Angel Unchained 255
Wild in the Streets 310
Bissell, Whit
Soylent Green 191
Bisset, Jacqueline
Casino Royale 38
Black, Jimmy Carl
200 Motels 500
Black, Karen
Cisco Pike 207
Easy Rider 260
You're a Big Boy Now 390
Blackman, Honor
Goldfinger 16
Blake, Madge
Batman 510
Blakely, Colin
The Day the Fish Came Out
177
Blakiston, Caroline
The Magic Christian 450
Blanc, Mel
The Man Called Flintstone
(V) 45

Blodgett, Michael
Beyond the Valley of the
Dolls 399
Bloom, Claire
The Illustrated Man 181
Bloom, Verna
The Hired Hand 94
Medium Cool 307
Bluteau, Lothaire
I Shot Andy Warhol 345
Bly, Maggie
The Italian Job (1969) 527
Bochner, Lloyd
Point Blank 558
Bogarde, Dirk
Modesty Blaise 47
Bogdanovich, Peter
Targets 163
Bollner, Michael
Willy Wonka and the
Chocolate Factory 517
Bonerz, Peter
Medium Cool 307
Bonifassy, Luce
The Tenth Victim 193
Bonner, William
Satan's Sadists 269
Booth, Carol
The Love-Ins 213
Borden, Lynn
Dirty Mary Crazy Larry 258
Borgnine, Ernest
Bunny O'Hare 548
Born, Max
Fellini Satyricon 322
Bostwick, Barry
Spy Hard 75
Bottoms, Sam
Apocalypse Now Redux 238
Bouchez, Élodie
CQ 342
Boyd, Stephen
Fantastic Voyage 180
Boyer, Charles
Casino Royale 38
Boyle, Peter
Joe 299
Medium Cool 307
Brady, Scott
Satan's Sadists 269
Brando, Marlon
Apocalypse Now Redux 238
Candy 411
Brasseur, Pierre
King of Hearts 326
Brazzi, Rossano
The Italian Job (1969) 527
Breen, Mary
The Honeymoon Killers 152
Breton, Michele
Performance 493
Brialy, Jean-Claude
King of Hearts 326

Bridges, Beau
The Landlord 371

Briers, Richard
Fathom 41

Broadbent, Jim
The Avengers 73

Broderick, James
Alice's Restaurant 283

Brolin, James
Our Man Flint 52

Bron, Eleanor
Alfie 437
Bedazzled 440

Brook, Faith
To Sir, with Love 457

Brooke, Walter
The Landlord 371

Brooks, Iris
I Drink Your Blood 153

Brooks, Mel
Blazing Saddles 89
Putney Swope 340

Brosnan, Pierce
The Thomas Crown Affair
(1999) 535

Brown, Georg Stanford
The Man 123

Brown, Jim
Original Gangstas 126
Slaughter 130
Slaughter's Big Rip-Off 130

Browne, Roscoe Lee
Logan's Run 183

Brynner, Yul
The Magic Christian 450

Buckley, Hal
Kelly's Heroes 246

Buggy, Niall
Zardoz 197

Bujold, Geneviève
King of Hearts 326

Buono, Victor
The Silencers 59

Burden, Hugh
Funeral in Berlin 21

Burdon, Eric
Monterey Pop 490
Plaster Caster 481

Burghoff, Gary
B.S. I Love You 360

Burke, Patricia
The Day the Fish Came Out
177

Burke, Paul
The Thomas Crown Affair
(1968) 535

Burke, Walter
The President's Analyst 55

Burns, Catherine
Last Summer 302

Burns, David
Who Is Harry Kellerman and
Why Is He Saying Those
Terrible Things about Me?
389

Burroughs, William S.
Chappaqua 206

Burstyn, Ellen
Requiem for a Dream 224

Burton, Richard
Candy 411

Buscemi, Steve
Spy Kids 2: The Island of
Lost Dreams 78

Busch, Dennis
Faster, Pussycat! Kill! Kill!
262

Bush, Billy Green
The Jesus Trip 265

Busman, Gail
Taking Off 386

Butterfield, Paul
The Last Waltz 485

Caan, Scott
Ocean's Eleven 532

Cabot, Christina
The Italian Job (2003) 528

Caillou, Alan
The Losers 266

Caine, Michael
Alfie 437
The Billion Dollar Brain 21
Funeral in Berlin 21
Get Carter 551
The Ipcress File 20
The Italian Job (1969) 527

Cakes, Patty
Groupies 481

Calfa, Don
Greaser's Palace 340
Pound 340

Callan, K.
Joe 299

Cambridge, Godfrey
Come Back, Charleston
Blue 118
Cotton Comes to Harlem
118
The President's Analyst 55

Cameron, JoAnna
B.S. I Love You 360

Camp, Colleen
Apocalypse Now Redux 238

Campbell, Jean
Maidstone 354

Campbell, Joy
Pufnstuf 515

Candelli, Stelio
Planet of the Vampires 185

Cannon, Dyan
Bob & Carol & Ted & Alice
403

Cannon, J. D.
Cotton Comes to Harlem
118

Capucine
What's New, Pussycat? 387

Cardos, John "Bud"
Satan's Sadists 269

Carey, Timothy
Head 483

Carlin, Lynn
Taking Off 386

Carlson, Steve
Deadlier Than the Male 11

Carmel, Roger C.
Myra Breckinridge 426
The Silencers 59

Carmen
The Last of the Secret
Agents? 44

Carmichael, Ian
Smashing Time 456

Carr, Cynthia
Last House on the Left 156

Carr, Darleen
The Impossible Years 369

Carradine, John
Myra Breckinridge 426

Carradine, Keith
McCabe and Mrs. Miller
100

Carradine, Robert
Coming Home 241

Carrol, Regina
Satan's Sadists 269

Carson, L. M. Kit
David Holzman's Diary 342

Casey, Bernie
Spies Like Us 74

Cash, Rosalind
The Omega Man 185

Cassel, Sandra
Last House on the Left 156

Cassel, Seymour
The Revolutionary 308

Cassidy, Jack
Bunny O'Hare 548

Castelnuovo, Nino
Camille 2000 407

Castle, John
Blow-Up 443

Cavell, Marc
The Love-Ins 213

Celi, Adolfo
Danger: Diabolik 549
Grand Slam 524
King of Hearts 326
Operation Kid Brother 48

Cembrzynska, Iga
The Saragossa Manuscript
329

Chalet, Rich
The Impossible Years 369

Challee, William
Zachariah 107

Chamberlain, Richard
Petulia 377

Chambers, Marilyn
Behind the Green Door 397

Chambliss, Woody
Greaser's Palace 340

Champion, Marge
The Party 376

Chanderli, Michel
More 327

Chandler, John Davis
The Hooked Generation 208

Chandler, Len
F.T.A. 242

Chandler, Patti
The Million Eyes of Su-Muru
25

Channing, Carol
Skidoo 227

Charisse, Cyd
The Silencers 59

Chase, Chevy
Spies Like Us 74

Chase, Ilka
Ocean's 11 532

Chaz
Groupies 481

Cheadle, Don
Ocean's Eleven 532

Chen, Tina
Alice's Restaurant 283

Chi, Greta
Fathom 41

Child, Jeremy
Privilege 494

Chow, Michael
The Touchables 458

Chris, Marilyn
The Honeymoon Killers 152

Christie, Julie
McCabe and Mrs. Miller
100
Petulia 377
Shampoo 384

Chuckster, Simon
Sweet Sweetback's
Baadasssss Song 135

Cioffi, Charles
Shaft 127

Claire, Aubrey
Joe 299

Clapton, Eric
The Last Waltz 485
Tommy 497

Clarens, Carlos
Lion's Love 347

Clark, Bobby
Satan's Sadists 269

Clark, Fred
Dr. Goldfoot and the Bikini
Machine 40

Clark, Greydon
Satan's Sadists 269

Clark, Marlene
Ganja & Hess 150
Slaughter 130

Clark, Matt
Pat Garrett and Billy the Kid
101

Clarke, Shirley
Lion's Love 347

Terrible Things about Me?
389

Denney, Dodo
Willy Wonka and the
Chocolate Factory 517

Denny, Reginald
Batman 510

Depardieu, Gérard
CQ 342

Dern, Bruce
Coming Home 241
Psych-Out 221
Silent Running 190
The Trip 231

Deschanel, Zooey
Almost Famous Untitled:
The Bootleg Cut
(Director's Edition) 466

Devane, William
McCabe and Mrs. Miller
100
Payback 558

Devine, Andy
Myra Breckinridge 426

Devon, Richard
The Silencers 59

Diamond, Neil
The Last Waltz 485

Diaz, Vic
The Losers 266

Dickinson, Angie
Ocean's 11 532
Point Blank 558

Diesel, Vin
XXX 82

Dietz, Eileen
David Holzman's Diary 342

Dillon, Kevin
The Doors 471

Divine
Pink Flamingos 349

Dix, Robert
Satan's Sadists 269

Dixon, Donna
Spies Like Us 74

Dr. John
The Last Waltz 485

Dolan, Bill
Plaster Caster 481

Doleman, Guy
The Billion Dollar Brain 21
Funeral in Berlin 21
The Ipcress File 20

Dolenz, Micky
Head 483

Doll Rod, Danny
Plaster Caster 481

Donegan, Pamela
F.T.A. 242

Donen, Mario
Danger: Diabolik 549

Donovan
Dont Look Back 470

Doran, Ann
The Hired Hand 94

Dorff, Stephen
I Shot Andy Warhol 345

Dorléac, Françoise
The Billion Dollar Brain 21
Where the Spies Are 30

Downes, Terry
The Fearless Vampire
Killers 149

Downey, Elsie
Chafed Elbows 340
Greaser's Palace 340
Pound 340

Drago, Eleonora Rossi
Camille 2000 407

Drake, David
Two-Lane Blacktop 273

Dravic, Milena
W. R.: Mysteries of the
Organism 329

Drivas, Robert
The Illustrated Man 181

Dry Creek Road
Groupies 481

Dubbins, Don
The Illustrated Man 181

Duckworth, Dortha
The Honeymoon Killers 152

Duering, Carl
Arabesque 7

Duggan, Andrew
In Like Flint 52

Duke, Bill
Payback 558

Dullaghan, John
Sweet Sweetback's
Baadasssss Song 135

Dullea, Keir
2001: A Space Odyssey
196

Dunaway, Faye
The Happening 553
Little Big Man 98
The Thomas Crown Affair
(1968) 535
The Thomas Crown Affair
(1999) 535

Duncan, Andrew
The Hospital 368

Durning, Charles
Hi, Mom! 293
Spy Hard 75

Duvall, Robert
Apocalypse Now Redux 238
M*A*S*H 247
The Revolutionary 308

Duvall, Shelley
McCabe and Mrs. Miller
100

Dylan, Bob
Dont Look Back 470
The Last Waltz 485
Pat Garrett and Billy the Kid
101

Dymon, Frankie, Jr.
Sympathy for the Devil 495

Dysart, Richard A.
The Hospital 368

Eastham, Richard
Murderers' Row 59

Eastman, Marilyn
Night of the Living Dead
157

Eastwood, Clint
Kelly's Heroes 246

Eaton, Shirley
Future Women 25
Goldfinger 16
The Million Eyes of Su-Muru
25

Eccles, Aimée
Little Big Man 98

Edelman, Herb
I Love You, Alice B. Toklas!
210

Eikenberry, Jill
Between the Lines 284

Eilbacher, Cindy
The Big Bounce 546

Ekland, Britt
Get Carter 551

Elam, Jack
Pat Garrett and Billy the Kid
101

Elcar, Dana
Soldier Blue 105

Elliot, Cass
Pufnstuf 515

Elliott, Denholm
Alfie 437

Elliott, Stephen
The Hospital 368

Emery, Dick
Yellow Submarine (V) 518

Engel, Georgia
Taking Off 386

Engel, Mary
The Honeymoon Killers 152

Engelmann, Heinz
More 327

Evans, Michael
The Love-Ins 213

Everett, Chad
The Impossible Years 369

Evers, Jason
The Illustrated Man 181

Ewing, Bill
The Deathmaster 146

Fabian
Dr. Goldfoot and the Girl
Bombs 41
Maryjane 216

Faison, Frankie
The Thomas Crown Affair
(1999) 535

Faithfull, Marianne
The Girl on a Motorcycle
417
I'll Never Forget What's
'isname 446

Falk, Rossella
Modesty Blaise 47

Fallon, Jimmy
Almost Famous Untitled:
The Bootleg Cut
(Director's Edition) 466

Farbar, Buzz
Wild 90 354

Fargas, Antonio
Across 110th Street 115
Pound 340
Putney Swope 340

Farina, Mimi
Celebration at Big Sur 468

Farmer, Mimsy
Hot Rods to Hell 264
More 327

Fawcett, Farrah
Logan's Run 183
Myra Breckinridge 426

Feldman, Andrea
Trash 350

Ferguson, Janet
200 Motels 500

Fernandez, Emilio
Pat Garrett and Billy the Kid
101

Fernandez, José Luis
El Topo 320

Ferrare, Cristina
The Impossible Years 369

Ferrera, Juan
The Holy Mountain 321

Fiedler, John
The Deathmaster 146

Field, Shirley Anne
Alfie 437

Fiennes, Ralph
The Avengers 73

Finlay, Frank
I'll Never Forget What's
'isname 446

Finn, Michael
Faster, Pussycat! Kill! Kill!
262

Finocchio, Richard
A Safe Place 226

Fishburne, Laurence
Apocalypse Now Redux 238

Fisher, Carrie
Shampoo 384

Fix, Paul
Pat Garrett and Billy the Kid
101
Zabriskie Point 312

Fleming, Eric
The Glass Bottom Boat 43

Flemyng, Robert
The Quiller Memorandum
28

Flori, Agata
Operation Kid Brother 48

The Flying Burrito
Brothers
Gimme Shelter 474

Fonda, Jane
Barbarella 174
Coming Home 241
F.T.A. 242
Spirits of the Dead 160

Fonda, Peter
Dirty Mary Crazy Larry 258
Easy Rider 260
The Hired Hand 94
The Limey 555
Spirits of the Dead 160
The Trip 231

Fong, Benson
Our Man Flint 52

Foray, June
The Man Called Flintstone
(V) 45

Ford, Harrison
Apocalypse Now Redux 238
Getting Straight 291
Zabriskie Point 312

Forrest, Frederic
Apocalypse Now Redux 238

Forrest, Steve
Spies Like Us 74

Forster, Robert
Medium Cool 307

Forsyth, Bruce
Can Heironymus Merkin
Ever Forget Mercy
Humppe and Find True
Happiness? 409

Forth, Jane
Trash 350

Foster, Julia
Alfie 437

Foulk, Robert
Bunny O'Hare 548

Fox, James
Performance 493

Foxx, Redd
Cotton Comes to Harlem
118

Franchi, Franco
Dr. Goldfoot and the Girl
Bombs 41

Franciosa, Anthony
Across 110th Street 115
Fathom 41

Franken, Steve
The Party 376

Franz, Eduard
The President's Analyst 55

Fraser, Ronald
Fathom 41

Frazier, Sheila
Superfly 133

Frechette, Mark
Zabriskie Point 312

Frees, Paul
The Man Called Flintstone
(V) 45

Frey, Sami
Mister Freedom 374

Frobe, Gert
Goldfinger 16

Frome, Milton
Batman 510
Dr. Goldfoot and the Bikini
Machine 40

Frye, Virgil
The Jesus Trip 265

Fugit, Patrick
Almost Famous Untitled:
The Bootleg Cut
(Director's Edition) 466

Fuller, Samuel
The Last Movie 95

Fultz, Rhonda
I Drink Your Blood 153

Funicello, Annette
Head 483

Furth, George
Shampoo 384

G, Franky
The Italian Job (2003) 528

Gabriel, Roman
Skidoo 227

Gale, Edra
What's New, Pussycat? 387

Gale, West
Dolemite 121
Sweet Sweetback's
Baadasssss Song 135

Garber, Victor
Godspell 480

Garcia, Andy
Ocean's Eleven 532

Garcia, Jerry
Woodstock 502

Garcia, Stella
The Last Movie 95

Gardenia, Vincent
Little Murders 372

Garewal, Simi
Siddhartha 206

Garfield, Allen
Greetings 293
Hi, Mom! 293
Taking Off 386

Garfunkel, Art
Carnal Knowledge 415
Monterey Pop 490

Garr, Teri
Maryjane 216

Garwood, John
The Losers 266

Gaubert, Daniele
Camille 2000 407

Gaura, Claudio
Danger: Diabolik 549

Gavin, Erica
Beyond the Valley of the
Dolls 399

Gavin, James
Dirty Mary Crazy Larry 258

Gazzara, Ben
The Thomas Crown Affair
(1999) 535

Geary, Charles
Medium Cool 307

Geer, Will
The President's Analyst 55
Seconds 187

Geeson, Judy
To Sir, with Love 457

George, Chief Dan
Little Big Man 98

George, Melissa
The Limey 555

George, Susan
Dirty Mary Crazy Larry 258

Giallelis, Stathis
Blue 91

Giannini, Giancarlo
CQ 342

Gibbs, Alan
The Jesus Trip 265

Gibson, Mel
Payback 558

Giftos, Elaine
Gas-s-s-s! 289

Gillen, Linda
The Magic Garden of
Stanley Sweetheart 215

Ginsberg, Allen
Chappaqua 206

Ginty, Robert
Coming Home 241

Giraudy, Monique
La Vallée 327

Gleason, Jackie
Skidoo 227

Glitters, Goldie
Groupies 481

Glover, Crispin
The Doors 471

Glover, John
Payback 558

Goddard, Mark
Blue Sunshine 145
The Love-Ins 213

Godfrey, Arthur
The Glass Bottom Boat 43

Golan, Gila
Our Man Flint 52

Goldblum, Jeff
Between the Lines 284

Golden, Annie
Hair 480

Gonzalez, Ernesto
Last Summer 302

Göranzon, Marie
I Am Curious (Yellow) 324

Gordon, Don
The Last Movie 95
The Mack 122
Slaughter 130

Gordon, Ruth
Harold and Maude 366

Goring, Marius
The Girl on a Motorcycle 417

Gorshin, Frank
Batman 510
Skidoo 227

Gossett, Louis, Jr.
The Landlord 371

Gothard, Michael
La Vallée 327

Gottlieb, Louis
I Love You, Alice B. Toklas!
210

Gottlieb, Stan
Pound 340

Gough, Michael
Top Secret! 80

Gould, Elliott
Bob & Carol & Ted & Alice
403
Getting Straight 291
Little Murders 372
M*A*S*H 247
Ocean's Eleven 532

Graham, Bill
The Doors 471
Fillmore 472
Woodstock 502

Graham, Gerrit
Greetings 293
Hi, Mom! 293

Graham, Heather
Austin Powers: The Spy Who
Shagged Me 71

Grant, Lee
The Big Bounce 546
The Landlord 371
Shampoo 384

Grant, Shelby
Our Man Flint 52

Grantham, Lucy
Last House on the Left 156

The Grateful Dead
Fillmore 472

Green, Nigel
Deadlier Than the Male 11
The Ipcress File 20
The Wrecking Crew 59

Green, Seth
Austin Powers in
Goldmember 71
Austin Powers: International
Man of Mystery 71
Austin Powers: The Spy Who
Shagged Me 71
The Italian Job (2003) 528

Greer, Ellen
Harold and Maude 366

Greer, Michael
The Magic Garden of
Stanley Sweetheart 215

Gregorio, Rose
Who Is Harry Kellerman and
Why Is He Saying Those
Terrible Things about Me?
389

Gregory, James
The Ambushers 59
Murderers' Row 59
The Silencers 59

Gregory, Mary
Coming Home 241

Grier, Pam
Original Gangstas 126
Griffith, Andy
Spy Hard 75
Griffith, Hugh
The Abominable Dr. Phibes 143
Dr. Phibes Rises Again 143
Griffith, Kenneth
The Assassination Bureau 36
Grossman, Albert
Dont Look Back 470
Grünberg, Klaus
More 327
Gugino, Carla
Spy Kids 78
Spy Kids 2: The Island of Lost Dreams 78
Spy Kids 3-D: Game Over 78
Guinness, Alec
The Quiller Memorandum 28
Gunn, Bill
Ganja & Hess 150
Gunn, Moses
Shaft 127
Gurian, David
Beyond the Valley of the Dolls 399
Guthrie, Arlo
Alice's Restaurant 283
Woodstock 502
Gutteridge, Lucy
Top Secret! 80
Guzman, Luis
The Limey 555
Hackman, Gene
Cisco Pike 207
Hagen, Ross
The Mini-Skirt Mob 268
Hahn, Jess
Topkapi 537
Haji
Faster, Pussycat! Kill! Kill! 262
Hale, Jean
In Like Flint 52
Hall, Albert
Apocalypse Now Redux 238
Hall, Carolyn
The Psychedelic Priest 218
Hall, Grayson
End of the Road 288
Halprin, Daria
Zabriskie Point 312
Hama, Mie
What's Up, Tiger Lily? 62
Hamilton, Bernie
The Losers 266
Hamilton, Murray
The Graduate 364
Hamilton, Neil
Batman 510

Hamilton, Richard
Greetings 293
Hampton, James
Soldier Blue 105
Handl, Irene
The Italian Job (1969) 527
Morgan: A Suitable Case for Treatment 451
Smashing Time 456
Wonderwall 429
Harden, Marcia Gay
Spy Hard 75
Harding, John
The Impossible Years 369
Hardman, Karl
Night of the Living Dead 157
Harlow, Miss
Groupies 481
Harris, Ann
The Honeymoon Killers 152
Harris, Barbara
Who Is Harry Kellerman and Why Is He Saying Those Terrible Things about Me? 389
Harris, Emmylou
The Last Waltz 485
Harris, Jared
I Shot Andy Warhol 345
Harris, Julie
You're a Big Boy Now 390
Harris, Julius
Superfly 133
Harris, Richard
Caprice 43
Harrison, George
Magical Mystery Tour 489
Yellow Submarine (V) 518
Harrison, Noel
Where the Spies Are 30
Harrow, Richard
Ganja & Hess 150
Hart, Susan
Dr. Goldfoot and the Bikini Machine 40
Hartman, Elizabeth
You're a Big Boy Now 390
Harvey, Laurence
The Magic Christian 450
Harvey, Tony
Taking Off 386
Haskell, David
Godspell 480
Hatcher, Teri
Spy Kids 78
Hauser, Wings
Original Gangstas 126
Havens, Richie
Woodstock 502
Hawkins, Edwin
Celebration at Big Sur 468
Hawkins, Ronnie
The Last Waltz 485

Hawn, Goldie
Shampoo 384
Hay, Alexandra
Skidoo 227
Hayes, Billie
Pufnstuf 515
Heacock, Linnea
Taking Off 386
Heard, John
Between the Lines 284
Hedren, Tippi
The Harrad Experiment 418
Heflin, Van
The Big Bounce 546
Helpmann, Robert
The Quiller Memorandum 28
Hemmings, David
Blow-Up 443
Hendrix, Jimi
Monterey Pop 490
Woodstock 502
Hendry, Gloria
Slaughter's Big Rip-Off 130
Hendry, Ian
Get Carter 551
Henner, Marilu
Between the Lines 284
Henry, Buck
The Graduate 364
Taking Off 386
Henry, Gregg
Payback 558
Henry, Mike
Soylent Green 191
Henry, Victor
Privilege 494
Herren, Roger
Myra Breckinridge 426
Hershey, Barbara
Last Summer 302
Hess, David
Last House on the Left 156
Hesseman, Howard
Billy Jack 285
Heston, Charlton
The Omega Man 185
Soylent Green 191
Hewes, Arlington
The President's Analyst 55
Hewett, Christopher
The Producers 380
Hickey, William
The Producers 380
Hickman, Dwayne
Dr. Goldfoot and the Bikini Machine 40
Higby, Mary Jane
The Honeymoon Killers 152
Hill, Benny
The Italian Job (1969) 527
Hill, Marianna
Medium Cool 307

Hiller, Arthur
Petulia 377
Hills, Gillian
Blow-Up 443
Hinnant, Skip
Fritz the Cat (V) 514
Hoffman, Dustin
The Graduate 364
Little Big Man 98
Midnight Cowboy 423
Who Is Harry Kellerman and Why Is He Saying Those Terrible Things about Me? 389
Hoffman, Philip Seymour
Almost Famous Untitled: The Bootleg Cut (Director's Edition) 466
Hoffman, Robert
Grand Slam 524
Holbrook, Hal
Wild in the Streets 310
Holden, William
Casino Royale 38
Holoubek, Gustaw
The Saragossa Manuscript 329
Homolka, Oskar
The Billion Dollar Brain 21
Funeral in Berlin 21
The Happening 553
Hooper, Ewan
How I Won the War 243
Hopper, Dennis
Apocalypse Now Redux 238
Easy Rider 260
The Last Movie 95
The Trip 231
Hordern, Michael
How I Won the War 243
I'll Never Forget What's 'isname 446
Hot Tuna
Fillmore 472
Howard, Trevor
The Liquidator 23
Howard, Vanessa
Some Girls Do 12
Howat, Clark
Billy Jack 285
Hsueh, Nancy
Targets 163
Hubschmid, Paul
Funeral in Berlin 21
Huddleston, David
Blazing Saddles 89
Hudson, Kate
Almost Famous Untitled: The Bootleg Cut (Director's Edition) 466
Hudson, Rock
Seconds 187
Hughes, Barnard
The Hospital 368
Midnight Cowboy 423

Murphy, Michael
McCabe and Mrs. Miller
100

Mutton, Roger
The Girl on a Motorcycle
417

Myers, Cynthia
Beyond the Valley of the
Dolls *399*

Myers, Mike
Austin Powers in
Goldmember *71*
Austin Powers: International
Man of Mystery *71*
Austin Powers: The Spy Who
Shagged Me *71*

Nader, George
The Million Eyes of Su-Muru
25

Nakamaru, Tadao
What's Up, Tiger Lily? *62*

Napier, Alan
Batman *510*

Napier, Charles
Beyond the Valley of the
Dolls *399*
Original Gangstas *126*

Nash, Graham
Celebration at Big Sur *468*

Neame, Christopher
Dracula A.D. 1972 *147*

Near, Holly
F.T.A. *242*
The Magic Garden of
Stanley Sweetheart *215*

Nelson, Alberta
Dr. Goldfoot and the Bikini
Machine *40*

Nelson, Ozzie
The Impossible Years *369*

Nesmith, Michael
Head *483*

Neuwirth, Bob
Dont Look Back *470*

Newley, Anthony
Can Heironymus Merkin
Ever Forget Mercy
Humppe and Find True
Happiness? *409*

Newman, Barry
The Limey *555*
Vanishing Point *275*

Nicholas, Paul
Tommy *497*

Nicholson, Jack
Carnal Knowledge *415*
Easy Rider *260*
Psych-Out *221*
A Safe Place *226*
Tommy *497*

Nickerson, Denise
Willy Wonka and the
Chocolate Factory *517*

Nielsen, Leslie
Spy Hard *75*

Nilsson, Harry
Skidoo *227*

Niven, David
Casino Royale *38*
The Impossible Years *369*
Where the Spies Are *30*

Noble, Nancy Lee
She-Devils on Wheels *270*

Noel, Magali
Fellini Satyricon *322*

Noiret, Philippe
The Assassination Bureau
36
Mister Freedom *374*

Noonan, Christine
If. . . . *297*

North, Virginia
The Abominable Dr. Phibes
143
Deadlier Than the Male *11*

Norton, Edward
The Italian Job (2003) *528*

Nuckles, Paul
The Losers *266*

Nyman, Lena
I Am Curious (Yellow) *324*

Oates, Warren
The Hired Hand *94*
Two-Lane Blacktop *273*

O'Brien, Edmond
Fantastic Voyage *180*

O'Connell, Arthur
Fantastic Voyage *180*
The Silencers *59*

O'Connor, Carroll
Kelly's Heroes *246*
Point Blank *558*

O'Dea, Judith
Night of the Living Dead
157

Offerall, Lucy
200 Motels *500*

Ogier, Bulle
La Vallée *327*

Ogilvy, Ian
The Day the Fish Came Out
177

O'Horgan, Tom
Chafed Elbows *340*

O'Kelly, Tim
Targets *163*

O'Leary, Matthew
Spy Kids 2: The Island of
Lost Dreams *78*

Oliver, Susan
The Love-Ins *213*

O'Neal, Cynthia
Carnal Knowledge *415*

O'Neal, Ron
Original Gangstas *126*
Superfly *133*

O'Neal, Ryan
The Big Bounce *546*

Opalinski, Kazimierz
The Saragossa Manuscript
329

Osborne, John
Get Carter *551*

O'Shea, Milo
Barbarella *174*

Osment, Emily
Spy Kids 2: The Island of
Lost Dreams *78*

Ostrum, Peter
Willy Wonka and the
Chocolate Factory *517*

O'Toole, Peter
Casino Royale *38*
What's New, Pussycat? *387*

Outlaw, Geoff
Alice's Restaurant *283*

Owen, Bill
Georgy Girl *445*

Pace, Judy
Cotton Comes to Harlem
118
Three in the Attic *427*

Page, Geraldine
You're a Big Boy Now *390*

Page, Harrison
Beyond the Valley of the
Dolls *399*

Paglia, Camille
Plaster Caster *481*

Pallenberg, Anita
Barbarella *174*
Performance *493*

Palme, Olof
I Am Curious (Yellow) *324*

Pamela, Miss
Groupies *481*

Paquin, Anna
Almost Famous Untitled:
The Bootleg Cut
(Director's Edition) *466*

Paraluman
The Losers *266*

Parker, Lara
Hi, Mom! *293*

Parks, Michael
The Happening *553*

Pastrano, Willie
The Hooked Generation *208*

Patrick, Dennis
Joe *299*

Patrick, Robert
Spy Kids *78*

Patterson, George
I Drink Your Blood *153*

Patterson, Pat
Gas-s-s-s! *289*

Paymer, David
Payback *558*

Payne, Julie
Celebration at Big Sur *468*

Pearce, Mary Vivian
Pink Flamingos *349*

Pecheur, Bruce
Trash *350*

Peck, Gregory
Arabesque *7*

Percival, Lance
Yellow Submarine (V) *518*

Perkins, Millie
Wild in the Streets *310*

Peters, Brock
Slaughter's Big Rip-Off *130*
Soylent Green *191*

Peterson, Arthur
Targets *163*

Pettet, Joanna
Blue *91*
Casino Royale *38*

Piccoli, Michel
Danger: Diabolik *549*

Pickens, Slim
Blazing Saddles *89*
Pat Garrett and Billy the Kid
101
Skidoo *227*

Pickles, Vivian
Harold and Maude *366*

Pike, Hy
Dolemite *121*

Pitt, Brad
Ocean's Eleven *532*

Plaster Caster, Cynthia
Groupies *481*
Plaster Caster *481*

Pleasence, Donald
Fantastic Voyage *180*
Mister Freedom *374*
Soldier Blue *105*

Plimpton, George
Beyond the Law *354*

Plimpton, Martha
I Shot Andy Warhol *345*

Podel, Diane
Trash *350*

Poe, Addison
The Thomas Crown Affair
(1968) *535*

Pohlman, Eric
Where the Spies Are *30*

Poitier, Sidney
To Sir, with Love *457*

Polanski, Roman
The Fearless Vampire
Killers *149*
The Magic Christian *450*

Porter, Robert
The Jesus Trip *265*

Poston, Pat
She-Devils on Wheels *270*

Potter, Martin
Fellini Satyricon *322*

Potts, Cliff
Silent Running *190*

Powell, Robert
Tommy *497*

Pratt, Robert
The Hired Hand *94*

Prentiss, Paula
What's New, Pussycat? 387

Prévost, Françoise
Spirits of the Dead 160

Price, Alan
Dont Look Back 470

Price, Vincent
The Abominable Dr. Phibes 143
Dr. Goldfoot and the Bikini Machine 40
Dr. Goldfoot and the Girl Bombs 41
Dr. Phibes Rises Again 143

Proctor, Philip
A Safe Place 226

Pryor, Richard
The Mack 122
Wild in the Streets 310

Pyne, Joe
The Love-Ins 213

Quarrier, Iain
The Fearless Vampire Killers 149
Sympathy for the Devil 495
Wonderwall 429

Quarry, Robert
The Deathmaster 146
Dr. Phibes Rises Again 143

Quayle, Anna
Smashing Time 456

Quinlan, Kathleen
The Doors 471

Quinn, Anthony
Across 110th Street 115
The Happening 553

Quinn, Pat
Alice's Restaurant 283
Zachariah 107

Rado, James
Lion's Love 347

Raft, George
Casino Royale 38
Skidoo 227

Ragni, Gerome
Lion's Love 347

Rain, Jeramie
Last House on the Left 156

Rampling, Charlotte
Georgy Girl 445
Zardoz 197

Randolph, John
Seconds 187

Randone, Salvo
Fellini Satyricon 322
The Tenth Victim 193

Rassimov, Ivan
Planet of the Vampires 185

Ratliff, Frank
The Ipcress File 20

Ray, Aldo
Angel Unchained 255

Raye, Martha
Pufnstuf 515

Read, Dolly
Beyond the Valley of the Dolls 399

Redding, Noel
Plaster Caster 481

Redding, Otis
Monterey Pop 490

Redfield, William
Fantastic Voyage 180

Redgrave, Lynn
Georgy Girl 445
Smashing Time 456

Redgrave, Vanessa
Blow-Up 443
Morgan: A Suitable Case for Treatment 451

Reed, Alan
The Man Called Flintstone (V) 45

Reed, Lady
Dolemite 121

Reed, Oliver
The Assassination Bureau 36
I'll Never Forget What's 'isname 446
Tommy 497

Reed, Rex
Myra Breckinridge 426

Rees, Betty Anne
The Deathmaster 146

Reich, Wilhelm
W. R.: Mysteries of the Organism 329

Reid, Beryl
The Assassination Bureau 36

Reid, Frances
Seconds 187

Reid, Terry
Groupies 481

Reiner, Carl
Ocean's Eleven 532

Remberg, Erika
The Lickerish Quartet 407

Renzi, Eva
Funeral in Berlin 21

Repp, Stafford
Batman 510

Reves, Marta
Future Women 25

Revill, Clive
The Assassination Bureau 36
Fathom 41
Modesty Blaise 47

Rice, Stan
Billy Jack 285

Richards, Aubrey
The Ipcress File 20

Richter, Daniel
2001: A Space Odyssey 196

Rickles, Don
Kelly's Heroes 246

Ridley, Judith
Night of the Living Dead 157

Rifkin, Ron
Silent Running 190

Rigaud, Georges
Grand Slam 524

Rigg, Diana
The Assassination Bureau 36
The Hospital 368

Rilia, Walter
Future Women 25

Ringwald, Monika
The Touchables 458

Rivero, Jorge
Soldier Blue 105

Roarke, Adam
Dirty Mary Crazy Larry 258
The Losers 266
Psych-Out 221

Robards, Jason
Pat Garrett and Billy the Kid 101

Robbins, Jessie
Magical Mystery Tour 489

Roberts, Christian
To Sir, with Love 457

Roberts, Doris
The Honeymoon Killers 152

Roberts, Julia
Ocean's Eleven 532

Robertson-Justice, James
Spirits of the Dead 160

Robins, Jessie
The Fearless Vampire Killers 149

Robinson, Edward G.
Grand Slam 524
Soylent Green 191

Robinson, Jay
Bunny O'Hare 548

Roche, Eugene
The Happening 553

Rodd, Marcia
Little Murders 372

Rodrigues, Percy
Come Back, Charleston Blue 118

Roger, Rita
The Hired Hand 94

Rogers, Mimi
Austin Powers: International Man of Mystery 71

Rogers, Reg
I Shot Andy Warhol 345

Rohm, Maria
Future Women 25
The Million Eyes of Su-Muru 25

The Rolling Stones
Gimme Shelter 474
Sympathy for the Devil 495

Romanov, Stephanie
Spy Hard 75

Rome, Sydney
Some Girls Do 12

Romero, Cesar
Batman 510
Skidoo 227

Ronane, John
The Touchables 458

Rondell, Ronnie, Jr.
The Mini-Skirt Mob 268

Roof, Michael
XXX 82

Rooks, Conrad
Chappaqua 206

Rooney, Mickey
Skidoo 227

Rose, Reva
Bunny O'Hare 548

Ross, Elizabeth
The Man 123

Ross, Katharine
The Graduate 364

Rossi, Steve
The Last of the Secret Agents? 44

Roundtree, Richard
Shaft 127

Rouvel, Catherine
Mister Freedom 374

Rowland, Henry
Beyond the Valley of the Dolls 399

Roya, David
Billy Jack 285

Rubin, Ronald
Can Heironymus Merkin Ever Forget Mercy Humppe and Find True Happiness? 409

Rubinstein, John
Getting Straight 291
Zachariah 107

Rule, Janice
The Ambushers 59

Rush, Barbara
The Man 123

Russell, Victoria
Tommy 497

Russo, Rene
The Thomas Crown Affair (1999) 535

Ruth, Richard
Two-Lane Blacktop 273

Rutkowski, Richard
The Holy Mountain 321

Ryan, Meg
The Doors 471

Sabara, Daryl
Spy Kids 78
Spy Kids 2: The Island of Lost Dreams 78
Spy Kids 3-D: Game Over 78

Director Index

The Director Index lists all the directors cited in the credits of the movies reviewed in this book. The names of the directors are listed in alphabetical order, as are their corresponding filmographies. (Note that only movies covered in this book are listed in the filmographies.) Bear in mind that the page number following the film title refers you to the location of the credits information for that film; in some cases you'll have to flip back a page or two to get to the beginning of the review.

Abrahams, Jim
Top Secret! 80

Adamson, Al
Satan's Sadists 269

Allen, Woody
What's Up, Tiger Lily? 62

Altman, Robert
M*A*S*H 247
McCabe and Mrs. Miller 100

Anderson, Lindsay
If. . . . 297

Anderson, Michael
Logan's Run 183
The Quiller Memorandum 28

Antonioni, Michelangelo
Blow-Up 443
Zabriskie Point 312

Arkin, Alan
Little Murders 372

Aronofsky, Darren
Requiem for a Dream 224

Ashby, Hal
Coming Home 241
Harold and Maude 366
The Landlord 371
Shampoo 384

Avakian, Aram
End of the Road 288

Averback, Hy
I Love You, Alice B. Toklas! 210

Avildsen, John G.
Joe 299

Bakshi, Ralph
Fritz the Cat 514

Barbera, Joseph
The Man Called Flintstone 45

Bava, Mario
Danger: Diabolik 549
Dr. Goldfoot and the Girl Bombs 41
Planet of the Vampires 185

Bogdanovich, Peter
Targets 163

Boorman, John
Point Blank 558
Zardoz 197

Brahm, John
Hot Rods to Hell 264

Brooks, Mel
Blazing Saddles 89
The Producers 380

Bryant, Baird
Celebration at Big Sur 468

Cacoyannis, Michael
The Day the Fish Came Out 177

Cammell, Donald
Performance 493

Campus, Michael
The Mack 122

Cardiff, Jack
The Girl on a Motorcycle 417
The Liquidator 23

Chechik, Jeremiah
The Avengers 73

Clavell, James
To Sir, with Love 457

Cohen, Larry
Original Gangstas 126

Cohen, Rob
XXX 82

Collinson, Peter
The Italian Job (1969) 527

Coppola, Francis Ford
Apocalypse Now Redux 238
You're a Big Boy Now 390

Coppola, Roman
CQ 342

Corman, Roger
Gas-s-s-s! 289
The Trip 231

Craven, Wes
Last House on the Left 156

Crowe, Cameron
Almost Famous Untitled: The Bootleg Cut (Director's Edition) 466

Danton, Ray
The Deathmaster 146

Dassin, Jules
Topkapi 537

Davis, Desmond
Smashing Time 456

Davis, Ossie
Cotton Comes to Harlem 118

de Broca, Philippe
King of Hearts 326

De Martino, Alberto
Operation Kid Brother 48

De Palma, Brian
Greetings 293
Hi, Mom! 293

Dearden, Basil
The Assassination Bureau 36

Demetrakas, Johanna
Celebration at Big Sur 468

Dexter, Maury
Maryjane 216
The Mini-Skirt Mob 268

Donen, Stanley
Arabesque 7
Bedazzled 440

Donner, Clive
What's New, Pussycat? 387

Dorfman, Ron
Groupies 481

Douglas, Gordon
In Like Flint 52

Downey, Robert, Sr.
Chafed Elbows 340
Greaser's Palace 340
Pound 340

Putney Swope *340*

Dreifuss, Arthur
The Love-Ins *213*

Dunning, George
Yellow Submarine *518*

Durston, David E.
I Drink Your Blood *153*

Edwards, Blake
The Party *376*

Englund, George
Zachariah *107*

Fellini, Federico
Fellini Satyricon *322*
Spirits of the Dead *160*

Fleischer, Richard
Fantastic Voyage *180*
Soylent Green *191*

Fleming, Gordon
Slaughter's Big Rip-Off *130*

Flicker, Theodore J.
The President's Analyst *55*

Fonda, Peter
The Hired Hand *94*

Forman, Milos
Hair *480*
Taking Off *386*

Franco, Jesus
Future Women *25*

Frankenheimer, John
Seconds *187*

Freeman, Robert
The Touchables *458*

Friedberg, Rick
Spy Hard *75*

Fuest, Robert
The Abominable Dr. Phibes *143*
Dr. Phibes Rises Again *143*

Furie, Sidney J.
The Ipcress File *20*

Gibson, Alan
Dracula A.D. 1972 *147*

Gilbert, Lewis
Alfie *437*

Godard, Jean-Luc
Sympathy for the Devil *495*
Weekend *330*

Gordon, Michael
The Impossible Years *369*

Gray, F. Gary
The Italian Job (2003) *528*

Greene, David
Godspell *480*

Grefé, William
The Hooked Generation *208*
The Psychedelic Priest *218*

Grosbard, Ulu
Who Is Harry Kellerman and Why Is He Saying Those Terrible Things about Me? *389*

Guest, Val
Casino Royale *38*
Where the Spies Are *30*

Gunn, Bill
Ganja & Hess *150*

Hagmann, Stuart
The Strawberry Statement *309*

Hamilton, Guy
Funeral in Berlin *21*
Goldfinger *16*

Hanna, William
The Man Called Flintstone *45*

Harrison, George
Magical Mystery Tour *489*

Harron, Mary
I Shot Andy Warhol *345*

Has, Wojciech
The Saragossa Manuscript *329*

Havens, James Curtis
Hot Rods to Hell *264*

Heffron, Richard T.
Fillmore *472*

Helgeland, Brian
Payback *558*

Hiller, Arthur
The Hospital *368*

Hodges, Mike
Get Carter *551*

Hopper, Dennis
Easy Rider *261*
The Last Movie *95*

Horn, Leonard
The Magic Garden of Stanley Sweetheart *215*

Hough, John
Dirty Mary Crazy Larry *258*

Hughes, Ken
Casino Royale *38*

Hurwitz, Harry
The Projectionist *382*

Huston, John
Casino Royale *38*

Hutton, Brian G.
Kelly's Heroes *246*

Jaglom, Henry
A Safe Place *226*

Jewison, Norman
The Thomas Crown Affair (1968) *535*

Jodorowsky, Alejandro
El Topo *320*
The Holy Mountain *321*

Karlson, Phil
The Silencers *59*
The Wrecking Crew *59*

Kastle, Leonard
The Honeymoon Killers *152*

Klein, William
Mister Freedom *374*

Kubrick, Stanley
A Clockwork Orange *176*
2001: A Space Odyssey *196*

Landis, John
Spies Like Us *74*

Laughlin, Tom
Billy Jack *285*

Lennon, John
Magical Mystery Tour *489*

Lester, Richard
How I Won the War *243*
Petulia *377*

Levin, Henry
The Ambushers *59*
Murderers' Row *59*

Lewis, Herschell Gordon
She-Devils on Wheels *270*

Lieberman, Jeff
Blue Sunshine *145*

Loach, Ken
Poor Cow *452*

Losey, Joseph
Modesty Blaise *47*

Madden, Lee
Angel Unchained *255*

Mailer, Norman
Beyond the Law *354*
Maidstone *354*
Wild 90 *354*

Makavejev, Dusan
W. R.: Mysteries of the Organism *329*

Malle, Louis
Spirits of the Dead *160*

Mann, Daniel
Our Man Flint *52*

March, Alex
The Big Bounce *546*

Marquand, Christian
Candy *411*

Martin, D'Urville
Dolemite *121*

Martinson, Leslie
Batman *510*
Fathom *41*

Massot, Joe
Wonderwall *429*

Mayberry, Russ
The Jesus Trip *265*

Maysles, Albert
Gimme Shelter *474*

Maysles, David
Gimme Shelter *474*

Mazursky, Paul
Bob & Carol & Ted & Alice *403*

McBride, Jim
David Holzman's Diary *342*

McCartney, Paul
Magical Mystery Tour *489*

McGrath, Joseph
Casino Royale *38*
The Magic Christian *450*

McTiernan, John
The Thomas Crown Affair (1999) *535*

Merrill, Stewart
See Grefé, William

Metzger, Radley
Camille 2000 *407*

The Lickerish Quartet *407*

Meyer, Russ
Beyond the Valley of the Dolls *399*
Faster, Pussycat! Kill! Kill! *262*

Milestone, Lewis
Ocean's 11 *532*

Mitchell, Artie
Behind the Green Door *397*

Mitchell, Jim
Behind the Green Door *397*

Montaldo, Giuliano
Grand Slam *524*

Morrissey, Paul
Trash *350*

Morse, Hollingsworth
Pufnstuf *515*

Narizzano, Silvio
Blue *91*
Georgy Girl *445*

Nelson, Ralph
Deadlier Than the Male *11*
Soldier Blue *105*
Some Girls Do *12*

Nevard, Peter
Groupies *481*

Newley, Anthony
Can Heironymus Merkin Ever Forget Mercy Humppe and Find True Happiness? *409*

Nichols, Mike
Carnal Knowledge *415*
The Graduate *364*

Norton, Bill L.
Cisco Pike *207*

Oswald, Gerd
Bunny O'Hare *548*

Palmer, Tony
200 Motels *500*

Parker, Francine
F.T.A. *242*

Parks, Gordon
Shaft *127*

Parks, Gordon, Jr.
Superfly *133*

Parrish, Robert
Casino Royale *38*

Peckinpah, Sam
Pat Garrett and Billy the Kid *101*

Penn, Arthur
Alice's Restaurant *283*
Little Big Man *98*

Pennebaker, D. A.
Dont Look Back *470*

Perry, Frank
Last Summer *302*

Petri, Elio
The Tenth Victim *193*

Polanski, Roman
The Fearless Vampire Killers *149*

Writer Index

The Writer Index lists all screenwriters cited in the credits of the movies reviewed in this book. The names of the screenwriters are listed alphabetically, and their corresponding filmographies are also alphabetically arranged. (Note that only movies covered in this book are listed in the filmographies.) Bear in mind that the page number following the film title refers you to the location of the credits information for that film; in some cases you'll have to flip back a page or two to get to the beginning of the review.

Abbott, Norman
The Last of the Secret
   Agents? 44
Abrahams, Jim
Top Secret! 80
Adamson, Al
Satan's Sadists 269
Alaimo, Michael
F.T.A. 242
Allen, R. S.
The Man Called Flintstone
   45
Allen, Woody
What's New, Pussycat? 387
What's Up, Tiger Lily? 62
Altman, Robert
McCabe and Mrs. Miller
   100
Antonioni, Michelangelo
Blow-Up 443
Zabriskie Point 312
Armitage, George
Gas-s-s-s! 289
Aronofsky, Darren
Requiem for a Dream 224
Austin, Philip
Zachariah 107
Avakian, Aram
End of the Road 288
Aykroyd, Dan
Spies Like Us 74
Bachauer, Walter
Koyaanisqatsi 212

Baker, Herbert
The Ambushers 59
Murderers' Row 59
Bakshi, Ralph
Fritz the Cat 514
Baracco, Adriano
Danger: Diabolik 549
Barron, Fred
Between the Lines 284
Bava, Mario
Danger: Diabolik 549
Planet of the Vampires 185
Beatty, Warren
Shampoo 384
Benedictus, David
You're a Big Boy Now 390
Bennett, Julie
What's Up, Tiger Lily? 62
Bergman, Andrew
Blazing Saddles 89
Bergman, Peter
Zachariah 107
Bessy, Maurice
King of Hearts 326
Bevilacqua, Alberto
Planet of the Vampires 185
Bianchini, Paulo
Grand Slam 524
Black, John D. F.
Shaft 127
Blair, Lee
Fantasia 511

Blees, Robert
Dr. Phibes Rises Again 143
Bochco, Steven
Silent Running 190
Bogdanovich, Peter
Targets 163
Bogner, Norman
Privilege 494
Bonicelli, Vittorio
Barbarella 174
Boorman, John
Zardoz 197
Boulanger, Daniel
King of Hearts 326
Spirits of the Dead 160
Brach, Gerard
The Fearless Vampire
   Killers 149
Wonderwall 429
Brackett, Leigh
Dirty Mary Crazy Larry 258
Brodax, Al
Yellow Submarine 518
Brooks, Mel
Blazing Saddles 89
The Producers 380
Brown, Harry
Ocean's 11 532
Brule, Claude
Barbarella 174
Bullock, Harvey
The Man Called Flintstone
   45

Burke, Martyn
Top Secret! 80
Buxton, Fran
What's Up, Tiger Lily? 62
Cacoyannis, Michael
The Day the Fish Came Out
   177
Caillou, Alan
The Losers 266
Cain, Guillermo
Vanishing Point 275
Caminito, Augusto
Grand Slam 524
Cammell, Donald
Performance 493
Canaway, Bill
The Ipcress File 20
Cannon, Doran William
Skidoo 227
Canzio, Stefano
Operation Kid Brother 48
Cardiff, Jack
The Girl on a Motorcycle
   417
Carlino, Lewis John
Seconds 187
Carriere, Jean-Claude
Taking Off 386
Cassidy, Ted
The Harrad Experiment 418
Chapman, Graham
The Magic Christian 450

Hurwitz, Harry
The Projectionist 382

Infante, G. Cabrera
Wonderwall 429

Jacobs, Alexander
Point Blank 558

Jaglom, Henry
A Safe Place 226

Jayson, Jay
Caprice 43

Jodorowsky, Alejandro
El Topo 320
The Holy Mountain 321

Johnson, Charles
Slaughter's Big Rip-Off 130

Johnson, Coslough
Bunny O'Hare 548

Johnson, Randall
The Doors 471

Jones, Evan
Funeral in Berlin 21
Modesty Blaise 47

Jones, Jerry
Dolemite 121

Jones, Robert C.
Coming Home 241

Kastle, Leonard
The Honeymoon Killers 152

Kaufman, Robert
Dr. Goldfoot and the Bikini
  Machine 40
Dr. Goldfoot and the Girl
  Bombs 41
Getting Straight 291

Kavanaugh, Kevin
The Million Eyes of Su-Muru
  25

Kennedy-Martin, Troy
The Italian Job (1969) 527
Kelly's Heroes 246

Kent, Robert E.
Hot Rods to Hell 264

Klein, John
Taking Off 386

Klein, William
Mister Freedom 374

Kleiner, Harry
Fantastic Voyage 180

Koningsberg, Hans
The Revolutionary 308

Kreitsek, Howard B.
The Illustrated Man 181

Kubrick, Stanley
A Clockwork Orange 176
2001: A Space Odyssey
  196

Kwiatkowski, Tadeusz
The Saragossa Manuscript
  329

La Frenais, Ian
The Touchables 458

Lardner, Ring, Jr.
M*A*S*H 247

Lasser, Louise
What's Up, Tiger Lily? 62

Laughlin, Tom
Billy Jack 285

Law, John
Casino Royale 38

Leder, Karl
Future Women 25

Lederer, Charles
Ocean's 11 532

Levi, Paolo
Operation Kid Brother 48

Lieberman, Jeff
Blue Sunshine 145

Loach, Ken
Poor Cow 452

MacPherson, Don
The Avengers 73

Maibaum, Richard
Goldfinger 16

Mailer, Norman
Beyond the Law 354
Maidstone 354
Wild 90 354

Majolie, Bianca
Fantasia 511

Makavejev, Dusan
W. R.: Mysteries of the
  Organism 329

Malle, Louis
Spirits of the Dead 160

Mandel, Babaloo
Spies Like Us 74

Mankowitz, Wolf
Casino Royale 38
Where the Spies Are 30

Mannino, Vincenzo
Operation Kid Brother 48

Marcus, Lawrence B.
Petulia 377

Marshall, Peter
Maryjane 216

Martin, William
Fantasia 511

Massot, Joe
Zachariah 107

Maxwell, Len
What's Up, Tiger Lily? 62

Mayersberg, Paul
Siddhartha 206

Mazursky, Paul
Bob & Carol & Ted & Alice
  403
I Love You, Alice B. Toklas!
  210

McBride, Jim
David Holzman's Diary 342

McCullers, Michael
Austin Powers in
  Goldmember 71
Austin Powers: The Spy Who
  Shagged Me 71

McGivern, William P.
The Wrecking Crew 59

McGrath, John
The Billion Dollar Brain 21

McGrath, Joseph
The Magic Christian 450

McGuire, Dennis
End of the Road 288

McKay, Brian
McCabe and Mrs. Miller
  100

McLeish, John
Fantasia 511

Melly, George
Smashing Time 456

Mendelsohn, Jack
Yellow Submarine 518

Menken, Robin
F.T.A. 242

Mercer, David
Morgan: A Suitable Case for
  Treatment 451

Merrill, Terry
The Psychedelic Priest 218

Meyer, Russ
Beyond the Valley of the
  Dolls 399
Faster, Pussycat! Kill! Kill!
  262

Milius, John
Apocalypse Now Redux 238

Minahan, Dan
I Shot Andy Warhol 345

Minoff, Lee
Yellow Submarine 518

Mitchell, Jim
Behind the Green Door 397

Mitchell, Julian
Arabesque 7

Moberly-Holland, Sylvia
Fantasia 511

Moore, Dudley
Bedazzled 440

Moore, Rudy Ray
Dolemite 121

Moran, Jack
Faster, Pussycat! Kill! Kill!
  262

Morrison, Quinn
The Hooked Generation 208

Morrissey, Paul
Trash 350

Murray, John Fenton
Pufnstuf 515

Myers, Mike
Austin Powers in
  Goldmember 71
Austin Powers: International
  Man of Mystery 71
Austin Powers: The Spy Who
  Shagged Me 71

Naughton, Bill
Alfie 437

Near, Holly
F.T.A. 242

Newhouse, David
Point Blank 558

Newhouse, Rafe
Point Blank 558

Newley, Anthony
Can Heironymus Merkin
  Ever Forget Mercy
  Humppe and Find True
  Happiness? 409

Nichols, Peter
Georgy Girl 445

Nicholson, Jack
Head 483
The Trip 231

Norton, Bill L.
Cisco Pike 207

Osborn, David D.
Some Girls Do 12

Ossman, David
Zachariah 107

Palmer, Tony
200 Motels 500

Pearce, Perce
Fantasia 511

Peet, Bill
Fantasia 511

Penn, Arthur
Alice's Restaurant 283

Penner, Erdman
Fantasia 511

Peploe, Clare
Zabriskie Point 312

Perl, Arnold
Cotton Comes to Harlem
  118

Perry, Eleanor
Last Summer 302

Petri, Elio
The Tenth Victim 193

Pierson, Frank
The Happening 553

Pinter, Harold
The Quiller Memorandum
  28

Plummer, Elmer
Fantasia 511

Polanski, Roman
The Fearless Vampire
  Killers 149

Poole, Robert J.
The Mack 122

Poston, Don
The Jesus Trip 265

Powers, Donna
The Italian Job (2003) 528

Powers, Wayne
The Italian Job (2003) 528

Preston, Ray
The Hooked Generation 208

Price, Stanley
Arabesque 7

Proctor, Philip
Zachariah 107

Pryor, Richard
Blazing Saddles 89

Purvis, Neal
The Italian Job (2003) 528

Rafelson, Bob
Head 483

Rattan, Aubrey K.
Original Gangstas 126

Raucher, Herman
Can Heironymus Merkin
Ever Forget Mercy
Humppe and Find True
Happiness? 409

Reggio, Godfrey
Koyaanisqatsi 212
Naqoyqatsi 212
Powaqqatsi 212

Relph, Michael
The Assassination Bureau
36

Richards, Ken
Powaqqatsi 212

Roberts, Meade
Blue 91

Rodriguez, Robert
Spy Kids 78
Spy Kids 2: The Island of
Lost Dreams 78
Spy Kids 3-D: Game Over
78

Roli, Mino
Grand Slam 524

Roman, Antonio
Planet of the Vampires 185

Romero, George
Night of the Living Dead
157

Rondi, Brunello
Fellini Satyricon 322

Rooks, Conrad
Chappaqua 206
Siddhartha 206

Rose, Mickey
What's Up, Tiger Lily? 62

Rose, Si
Pufnstuf 515

Russell, Ken
Tommy 497

Russo, John
Night of the Living Dead
157

Sabo, Joseph
Fantasia 511

Salt, Waldo
Coming Home 241
Midnight Cowboy 423

Salvia, Rafael J.
Planet of the Vampires 185

Salvioni, Giorgio
The Tenth Victim 193

Sangster, Jimmy
Deadlier Than the Male 11

Santean, Antonio
Dirty Mary Crazy Larry 258

Sarne, Michael
Myra Breckinridge 426

Saul, Oscar
The Silencers 59

Sayers, Michael
Casino Royale 38

Schroeder, Barbet
La Vallée 327
More 327

Scott, Malcolm
Vanishing Point 275

Segal, Erich
Yellow Submarine 518

Selby, Hubert, Jr.
Requiem for a Dream 224

Sellers, Peter
The Magic Christian 450

Seltzer, Aaron
Spy Hard 75

Seltzer, David
Willy Wonka and the
Chocolate Factory 517

Semple, Lorenzo, Jr.
Batman 510
Fathom 41

Serling, Rod
The Man 123

Sharp, Alan
The Hired Hand 94

Shepard, Sam
Zabriskie Point 312

Sherwin, David
If. . . . 297

Sjöman, Vilgot
I Am Curious (Yellow) 324

Smith, Webb
Fantasia 511

Southern, Terry
Barbarella 174
Casino Royale 38
Easy Rider 261
End of the Road 288
The Magic Christian 450

Speight, Johnny
Privilege 494

Stallings, Vernon
Fantasia 511

Star, Harrison
Zabriskie Point 312

Starr, Ben
Our Man Flint 52

Steinberg, Norman
Blazing Saddles 89

Stern, Steven Hilliard
B.S. I Love You 360

Stern, Stewart
The Last Movie 95

Sterner, Robert
Fantasia 511

Stone, Oliver
The Doors 471

Stone, Peter
Arabesque 7

Tashlin, Frank
Caprice 43

Taylor, Delores
Billy Jack 285

Tebelak, John-Michael
Godspell 480

Thiele, Leo
Fantasia 511

Thom, Robert
Wild in the Streets 310

Thomas, Dave
Spies Like Us 74

Tidyman, Ernest
Shaft 127

Tolkin, Mel
The Last of the Secret
Agents? 44

Towers, Harry Alan
Future Women 25

Towne, Robert
Shampoo 384

Trumbo, Dalton
F.T.A. 242

Trustman, Alan
The Thomas Crown Affair
(1968) 535

Tucker, Larry
Bob & Carol & Ted & Alice
403
I Love You, Alice B. Toklas!
210

Ugar, Alan
Blazing Saddles 89

Ulius, Betty
Psych-Out 221

Ullman, Elwood
Dr. Goldfoot and the Bikini
Machine 40

Vadim, Roger
Spirits of the Dead 160

Van Peebles, Melvin
Sweet Sweetback's
Baadasssss Song 135

Varda, Agnès
Lion's Love 347

Wade, Robert
The Italian Job (2003) 528

Waldman, Frank
The Party 376

Waldman, Tony
The Party 376

Walker, Frank
Operation Kid Brother 48

Walpole, Alton
Koyaanisqatsi 212

Washburn, Deric
Silent Running 190

Waters, John
Pink Flamingos 349

Watkins, Peter
Privilege 494

Weller, Michael
Hair 480

Wells, George
The Impossible Years 369

Werner, Michael
The Harrad Experiment 418

Westbrook, Robert T.
The Magic Garden of
Stanley Sweetheart 215

Wexler, Haskell
Medium Cool 307

Wexler, Norman
Joe 299

White, James Gordon
The Mini-Skirt Mob 268

Whiton, James
The Abominable Dr. Phibes
143

Wilder, Billy
Casino Royale 38

Wilkes, Rich
XXX 82

Willett, E. Hunter
Psych-Out 221

Williams, Don
Slaughter 130

Willingham, Calder
The Graduate 364
Little Big Man 98

Wilson, Bryan
What's Up, Tiger Lily? 62

Wimmer, Kurt
The Thomas Crown Affair
(1999) 535

Wood, Charles
How I Won the War 243

Wood, Clement Biddle
Barbarella 174
Spirits of the Dead 160

Wright, Norman
Fantasia 511

Wright, Stanley
Operation Kid Brother 48

Wurlitzer, Rudy
Pat Garrett and Billy the Kid
101
Two-Lane Blacktop 273

Yafa, Stephen
Three in the Attic 427

Yeldham, Peter
The Liquidator 23

Zappa, Frank
200 Motels 500

Zapponi, Bernardino
Fellini Satyricon 322
Spirits of the Dead 160

Zucker, David
Top Secret! 80

Zucker, Jerry
Top Secret! 80

Cinematographer Index

The Cinematographer Index lists all cinematographers, or directors of photography (D.P.), credited in the movies reviewed in this book. The cinematographer listings are in alphabetical order, as are their corresponding filmographies. (Note that only movies covered in this book are listed in the filmographies.) Bear in mind that the page number following the film title refers you to the location of the credits information for that film; in some cases you'll have to flip back a page or two to get to the beginning of the review.

Composer Index

The Composer Index lists all composers, arrangers, lyricists, bands, and other musically inclined persons cited in the credits of the movies reviewed in this book as having contributed to the films' scores. Their names are listed alphabetically, as are their corresponding filmographies. (Note that only movies covered in this book are listed in the filmographies.) Bear in mind that the page number following the film title refers you to the location of the credits information for that film; in some cases you'll have to flip back a page or two to get to the beginning of the review.

Dankworth, John
Fathom *41*
Modesty Blaise *47*
Morgan: A Suitable Case for
 Treatment *451*

Darden, Severn
The Last Movie *95*

Davis, Scott
Ocean's Eleven *532*

De Jesus, Luchi
Slaughter *130*

De Vol, Frank
Caprice *43*
The Happening *553*
The Wrecking Crew *59*

Debney, John
Spy Kids 2: The Island of
 Lost Dreams *78*

Debussy, Claude
Ocean's Eleven *532*

Delerue, Georges
King of Hearts *326*

Dockstader, Tod
Fellini Satyricon *322*

Donovan
Dont Look Back *470*
Poor Cow *452*

The Doors
The Doors *471*

Duhamel, Antoine
Weekend *330*

Dukas, Paul
Fantasia *511*

Dylan, Bob
Dont Look Back *470*
Pat Garrett and Billy the Kid
 101

Earth, Wind & Fire
Sweet Sweetback's
 Baadasssss Song *135*

Edelman, Randy
XXX *82*

The Electric Flag
Easy Rider *261*

The Electric Prunes
Easy Rider *261*

Elfers, Konrad
Funeral in Berlin *21*

Elfman, Danny
Spy Kids *78*

Ellington, Duke
Ocean's Eleven *532*

Errnryd, Bengt
I Am Curious (Yellow) *324*

Faith, Percy
Ocean's Eleven *532*

Faris, Alexander
Georgy Girl *445*

Fox, Charles
Barbarella *174*
Pufnstuf *515*

Frampton, Peter
Almost Famous Untitled:
 The Bootleg Cut
 (Director's Edition) *466*

Frangipane, Roger
The Holy Mountain *321*

Franklin, Aretha
Coming Home *241*

The Fraternity of Man
Easy Rider *261*

Freebairn-Smith, Iain
The Strawberry Statement
 309

Gainsbourg, Serge
Mister Freedom *374*

Gale, John
Dr. Phibes Rises Again *143*

Garcia, Jerry
Zabriskie Point *312*

Garner, Erroll
Ocean's Eleven *532*

Glass, Philip
Koyaanisqatsi *212*
Naqoyqatsi *212*
Powaqqatsi *212*

Goldberg, Barry
The Trip *231*

Goldsmith, Jerry
The Illustrated Man *181*
In Like Flint *52*
Logan's Run *183*
The Man *123*
Our Man Flint *52*
Seconds *187*

Grainer, Ron
The Assassination Bureau
 36
The Omega Man *185*
To Sir, with Love *457*

Granda, Chabuca
The Last Movie *95*

The Grateful Dead
Zabriskie Point *312*

Gross, Charles
Blue Sunshine *145*

Grusin, Dave
Candy *411*

Guthrie, Arlo
Alice's Restaurant *283*

Hadjidakis, Manos
Blue *91*
Topkapi *537*

Hammond, John
Little Big Man *98*

Hancock, Herbie
Blow-Up *443*

Harrison, George
Magical Mystery Tour *489*
Wonderwall *429*
Yellow Submarine *518*

Hart, Mickey
Apocalypse Now Redux *238*

Haskell, Jimmie
Dirty Mary Crazy Larry *258*
Zachariah *107*

Hatcher, Harley
Satan's Sadists *269*

Hathaway, Donny
Come Back, Charleston
 Blue *118*

Havens, Richie
Coming Home *241*

Hayes, Isaac
Maidstone *354*

Hazlewood, Lee
The Last of the Secret
 Agents? *44*

Hefti, Neal
The Last of the Secret
 Agents? *44*

Hendrix, Jimi
Easy Rider *261*

Hess, David
Last House on the Left *156*

Holy Modal Rounders
Easy Rider *261*

Horunzhy, Vladimir
Original Gangstas *126*

Hutch, Willie
The Mack *122*

Jagger, Mick
Gimme Shelter *474*

James, Billy
Two-Lane Blacktop *273*

Jarre, Maurice
Top Secret! *80*

Jefferson Airplane
Coming Home *241*

Jodorowsky, Alejandro
El Topo *320*
The Holy Mountain *321*

Johnson, J. J.
Across 110th Street *115*

Jones, Quincy
Bob & Carol & Ted & Alice
 403
The Italian Job (1969) *527*

**Joplin, Janis, and Big
 Brother and the
 Holding Company**
Coming Home *241*

Kamen, Michael
Between the Lines *284*

Kantor, Igo
The Projectionist *382*

Karger, Fred
Hot Rods to Hell *264*
The Love-Ins *213*

Kaz, Eric
Greetings *293*
Hi, Mom! *293*

Kaz, Fred
Little Murders *372*

Khachaturyan, Aram
2001: A Space Odyssey
 196

King, Pete
The Last of the Secret
 Agents? *44*

Kirchin, Basil
The Abominable Dr. Phibes
 143

Komeda, Christopher
The Fearless Vampire
 Killers *149*

Kooper, Al
The Landlord *371*

Kristofferson, Kris
Cisco Pike *207*
The Last Movie *95*

Kumar, Hemant
Siddhartha *206*

Lai, Francis
I'll Never Forget What's
 'isname *446*

Langhorne, Bruce
The Hired Hand *94*

Le Blanc, Daniel
Behind the Green Door *397*

Leander, Mike
Privilege *494*

Legrand, Michel
The Thomas Crown Affair
 (1968) *535*

Lennon, John
Magical Mystery Tour *489*
Yellow Submarine *518*

Levin, Irma E.
The Projectionist *382*

Lewis, Herschell Gordon
She-Devils on Wheels *270*

Lewis, Jack
What's Up, Tiger Lily? *62*

Licina, Scott Vladimir
Night of the Living Dead *157*

Ligeti, György
2001: A Space Odyssey
 196

Little Eva
Easy Rider *261*

Lockyer, Malcolm
Deadlier Than the Male *11*

The Lovin' Spoonful
What's Up, Tiger Lily? *62*

Lowe, Mundell
Billy Jack *285*

MacDermot, Galt
Hair *480*

Macero, Teo
End of the Road *288*

Mahler, Gustav
The Honeymoon Killers *152*

Mancini, Henry
Arabesque *7*
Ocean's Eleven *532*
The Party *376*

Mandel, Johnny
M*A*S*H *247*
Point Blank *558*

Mansell, Clint
Requiem for a Dream *224*

Marijan, Bojana
W. R.: Mysteries of the
 Organism *329*

Marinuzzi, Gino, Jr.
Planet of the Vampires *185*

Composer Index